ALTERNATIVE ENERGY SYSTEMS IN BUILDING DESIGN

McGRAW-HILL'S GREENSOURCE SERIES

Gevorkian
Alternative Energy Systems in Building Design

Gevorkian
Solar Power in Building Design: The Engineer's Complete Design Resource

GreenSource: The Magazine of Sustainable Design
Emerald Architecture: Case Studies in Green Building

Haselbach
The Engineering Guide to LEED—New Construction: Sustainable Construction for Engineers

Luckett
Green Roof Construction and Maintenance

Melaver and Mueller (eds.)
The Green Building Bottom Line: The Real Cost of Sustainable Building

Nichols and Laros
Inside the Civano Project: A Case Study of Large-Scale Sustainable Neighborhood Development

Yudelson
Green Building Through Integrated Design

Yudelson
Greening Existing Buildings

About *GreenSource*

A mainstay in the green building market since 2006, *GreenSource* magazine and GreenSourceMag.com are produced by the editors of McGraw-Hill Construction, in partnership with editors at BuildingGreen, Inc., with support from the United States Green Building Council. *GreenSource* has received numerous awards, including American Business Media's 2008 Neal Award for Best Website and 2007 Neal Award for Best Start-up Publication, and FOLIO magazine's 2007 Ozzie Awards for "Best Design, New Magazine" and "Best Overall Design." Recognized for responding to the needs and demands of the profession, *GreenSource* is a leader in covering noteworthy trends in sustainable design and best practice case studies. Its award-winning content will continue to benefit key specifiers and buyers in the green design and construction industry through the books in the *GreenSource* Series.

About McGraw-Hill Construction

McGraw-Hill Construction, part of The McGraw-Hill Companies (NYSE: MHP), connects people, projects, and products across the design and construction industry. Backed by the power of Dodge, Sweets, *Engineering News-Record (ENR)*, *Architectural Record*, *GreenSource*, *Constructor*, and regional publications, the company provides information, intelligence, tools, applications, and resources to help customers grow their businesses. McGraw-Hill Construction serves more than 1,000,000 customers within the $4.6 trillion global construction community. For more information, visit www.construction.com.

ALTERNATIVE ENERGY SYSTEMS IN BUILDING DESIGN

PETER GEVORKIAN, Ph.D., P.E.

New York   Chicago   San Francisco   Lisbon   London   Madrid
Mexico City   Milan   New Delhi   San Juan   Seoul
Singapore   Sydney   Toronto

The McGraw·Hill *Companies*

Cataloging-in-Publication Data is on file with the Library of Congress.

1 2 3 4 5 6 7 8 9 0   DOC/DOC   0 1 5 4 3 2 1 0 9

ISBN 978-0-07-162147-2
MHID 0-07-162147-4

Sponsoring Editor: Joy Bramble Oehlkers
Editing Supervisor: Stephen M. Smith
Production Supervisor: Richard C. Ruzycka
Acquisitions Coordinator: Michael Mulcahy
Project Manager: Somya Rustagi, International Typesetting and Composition
Copy Editor: James K. Madru
Proofreader: Priyanka Sinha, International Typesetting and Composition
Indexer: Arc Films, Inc.
Art Director, Cover: Jeff Weeks
Composition: International Typesetting and Composition

Printed and bound by RR Donnelley.

McGraw-Hill books are available at special quantity discounts to use as premiums and sales promotions, or for use in corporate training programs. To contact a representative, please e-mail us at bulksales@mcgraw-hill.com.

 The pages within this book were printed on acid-free paper containing 100% postconsumer fiber.

About the Author

 **Peter Gevorkian, Ph.D., P.E.,** is President of Vector Delta Design Group, Inc., an electrical engineering and solar power design consulting firm, specializing in industrial, commercial, and residential projects. Since 1971, he has been an active member of the Canadian and California boards of professional engineers. Dr. Gevorkian is also the author of *Sustainable Energy Systems in Architectural Design,* *Sustainable Energy Systems Engineering,* and *Solar Power in Building Design,* all published by McGraw-Hill.

CONTENTS

Introduction *xiii*

Acknowledgments *xvii*

Disclaimer Note *xix*

Chapter 1 Global Warming: Climatic and Atmospheric Changes **1**
  Climate Change Factors   *1*
  Variations within the Earth's Climate   *1*
  Natural Factors Driving Climate Change   *2*
  The Memory of Climate   *6*
  Human Influences on Climate Change   *6*
  The Transition of Various Forms of Sequestered Solar Energy Use and
    Their Effect on Societies   *9*
  Industrial Sources of Atmospheric Pollution   *12*
  The Little Ice Age   *15*

Chapter 2 Energy Systems **19**
  Conservation of Energy   *19*
  The Concept of Energy in Various Scientific Fields   *19*

Chapter 3 Solar Power System Physics and Technologies **23**
  Brief History of the Photoelectric Phenomenon   *23*
  Solar Cell Physics   *26*
  Solar Cell Electronics   *30*
  Solar Cell Manufacturing and Packaging Technologies   *30*
  Dye-Sensitized Solar Cells   *34*
  Multijunction PV Cells   *40*
  Polymer Solar Cells   *42*
  Concentrators   *43*
  Solar Panel Arrays   *44*
  Solar Power System Components   *44*
  Crystalline, Amorphous, Thin-Film, and Sun-Tracker Technologies   *51*
  Solar Power System Design   *69*
  Storage Battery Technologies   *77*
  Solar Power System Configurations   *86*
  Ground-Mounted PV Module Installation and Support   *97*
  Roof-Mounted Installations   *98*
  Electrical Shock Hazard and Safety Considerations   *100*
  Solar Tracking Systems   *103*
  Field Safety Recommendations   *106*

Solar Power System Maintenance   *107*
Troubleshooting   *108*
Solar Power System Warning Signage   *109*
PV System Design Guidelines   *110*
Solar Power System Design Considerations   *111*
Solar Power Rebate Application Procedure   *124*
Solar Power System Deployment   *126*
Economics of Solar Power Systems   *139*
Special Note   *155*

Chapter 4   California Solar Initiative Program   **157**

CSI Fund Distribution   *158*
CSI Power-Generation Targets   *158*
Incentive Payment Structure   *159*
Expected Performance–Based Buydown (EPBB)   *160*
Performance-Based Incentive (PBI)   *161*
Host Customer   *161*
Solar Power Contractors and Equipment Sellers   *162*
PV System Sizing Requirements   *163*
Energy-Efficiency Audit   *163*
Warranty and Performance Permanency Requirements   *164*
Insurance   *164*
Grid Interconnection and Metering Requirements   *165*
Inspection   *165*
CSI Limitations   *165*
CSI Reservation Steps   *166*
Incentive Payments   *168*
Equipment Distributors   *168*
Special Funding for Affordable Housing Projects   *169*
Special Funding for Public and Charter Schools   *169*
Principal Types of Municipal Leases   *169*

Chapter 5   Energy Conservation   **173**

Energy-Saving Measures   *173*
Power-Factor Correction   *177*
Electric Power Generation and Distribution   *178*
Computerized Lighting Control   *180*
California Title 24 Electric Energy Compliance   *186*
Demand-Side Energy Management and Control   *195*
LEED—Leadership in Energy and Environmental Design   *203*
State of California Green Building Action Plan   *204*
LEED   *206*

Chapter 6   Passive Solar Heating Technologies   **223**

Passive Solar Water Heating   *223*
Concentrator Solar Technologies   *233*
Solar Cooling and Air-Conditioning   *236*
Direct Solar Power Generation   *240*
Innovations in Passive Solar Power Technology   *241*

Chapter 7 Fuel Cell Technology   **245**
 Fuel Cell Design   *245*
 Fuel Cell Application   *251*
 Fuel Cells as Alternatives to Internal Combustion Fuels   *259*
 Hydrogen Economy   *260*

Chapter 8 Wind Energy Technologies   **267**
 History of Wind Power   *267*
 Wind Power Generation   *268*
 Wind Power Management   *268*
 Betz' Law of Fluid Dynamics   *271*
 Structural Considerations   *274*
 Basics of Wind Turbine Operation   *276*
 Wind Turbine Energy Economics   *279*

Chapter 9   Ocean Energy Technologies   **287**
 Tidal Power   *287*
 Tidal Physics: Effects of the Terrestrial Centrifugal Force   *287*
 Tidal Power Generation   *288*
 Current Tidal Generation Technologies   *292*
 Marine-Current Turbine Technologies   *300*
 Some Interesting Oceanic Technologies   *303*

Chapter 10   Hydroelectric and Micro-Hydro Turbine Power   **307**
 Hydroelectric Power Plants   *307*
 Environmental Effects of Hydroelectric Power   *309*
 Hydroelectric Power Technology   *312*
 Classification of Hydropower Energy Facilities   *313*
 Hydroelectric Plant Equipment   *313*
 Case Studies of Hydroelectric Power Plants   *315*
 Micro-Hydropower Generation   *323*

Chapter 11   Geothermal Energy   **333**
 Thermal Power Extraction Potential   *334*
 Geothermal Technologies   *335*
 Geothermal Potential   *337*
 Cost of Geothermal Energy and Economics   *339*
 Geothermal Case Study in an Air-Conditioning Application   *341*
 Ocean Thermal Energy   *344*

**Chapter 12   Biofuel, Biogas, and Thermal Depolymerization
Technologies**   **345**
 History   *345*
 Chemical Composition   *346*
 Origins of Biomass   *346*
 Biomass Energy Potential   *347*
 Energy Value of Biomass   *348*
 Benefits of Biomass Energy   *348*
 Microturbine Generators   *350*
 Landfill, Wastewater Treatment, and Plant Biogas Generators   *353*

Hot Water and Generators   356
Economic Benefits of Using Landfill Gas   357
Environmental Benefits of Using Landfill Gas   357
Case Study of Successful Application of Microgenerator Technology   357
Cal Poly Biogas Case Study   360
Biomass Energy   362
Biofuels and Thermal Depolymerization   362
Biomass Energy Implementation   365
Carbon Black   366
Gasification Process   367
Biopower   368
Bioproducts   369
Some Interesting Facts about Bioenergy   370
Biodiesel   371

Chapter 13   Fission- and Fusion-Type Nuclear Power   **375**
Properties of Uranium   375
Nuclear Fission Power Plant   377
Construction of a Nuclear Power Plant   378
Subcriticality, Criticality, and Supercriticality   378
Advantages and Disadvantages of Fission Nuclear Reactors   378
Effects of Nuclear Radiation   379
Radioactive Decay   380
Radiation Danger   381
Nuclear Radiation Accidents   381
Case Study: San Onofre   383
Canadian CANDU Reactor   384
Pebble-Bed Reactor   387
Hyperion Nuclear Power Reactor   389
Fusion Reactors   394
Fusion as a Future Energy Source   401
Future Fusion-Reactor Research and Development   403

Chapter 14   Air Pollution Abatement   **405**
Effects of Pollution on Human and Animal Life   406
Pollution-Abatement Equipment   407
Emerging Future Technologies: Bioreactors   415
Groundwater Replenishment System   415

**Chapter 15   Carbon Dioxide Sequestration and Carbon
Trading Economics**   **421**
Chemical and Physical Properties of Carbon Dioxide   421
Carbon Dioxide Production   422
Industrial Production of Carbon Dioxide   423
Industrial Uses of Carbon Dioxide   423
Carbon Dioxide in Photosynthesis   423
Carbon Dioxide Sequestration in Ocean Waters and Aquatic Life   424
Pesticides and Plastics   424
Carbon Dioxide in the Oil and Chemical Industries   425
Role of Carbon Dioxide in Human Physiology   425
Carbon Dioxide Use in the Production of Ammonia and Fertilizer   425

Carbon Credits   *426*
Economics of Global Warming   *428*
Disagreement and Criticisms of the Kyoto Protocol   *430*

Appendix A   Unit Conversion and Design Reference Tables   *433*

Appendix B   Photo Gallery   *475*

Appendix C   Historical Time Line of Solar Energy   *485*

Appendix D   Glossary of Renewable Energy Power Systems   *493*

Bibliography   *503*

Index   *505*

INTRODUCTION

In the coming decades, the alternative energy technology industries will undergo unprecedented growth and will represent a significant component of the U.S. gross national product. The replacement of conventional fossil fuel and nuclear fission energy resources by renewable-energy sources will mandate that industries, academia, and research institutions provide immediate technological solutions to curb global environmental pollution. To mitigate global environmental and atmospheric pollution and to accelerate technological growth, it is imperative that international academia keep up with industry by educating carrier professionals to meet these imminent challenges.

In the very near future, global economies will face enormous challenges that they will need to resolve, increasing the ever-growing need for ecologically friendly renewable-energy resources. Despite its status as the economic bastion and technological leader of the free world and the largest atmospheric polluter of our planet, the United States has in the past few decades totally neglected the economic promotion of key alternative energy technologies such as solar and wind energy power generation. Even though both these technologies were invented in the United States, the nation has fallen far behind all developing countries, including Japan, Germany, and, soon, China.

Some of the most compelling factors supporting the promotion of alternative energy studies are discussed below. They indicate that alternative energy technologies will come to represent billions of dollars of new markets in the United States and around the world. A few highlights of the alternative energy industry, covered by the Renewable Energy Laboratories and the American Solar Electric Power Association, are as follows:

- By 2020, California's installed photovoltaic capacity is expected to increase 30- to 40-fold, at an average of 36 percent a year.
- Solar power generation, by 2020, is expected to provide approximately 10–17 percent of the electricity in California, as well as 3–6 percent of electricity in the United States.
- Over the next 3–7 years, California's unsubsidized solar energy cost to consumers is expected to compete with the cost of with grid power.
- Since 1970, the price of solar photovoltaic power has decreased 100-fold.
- Currently, the U.S. solar industry employs 3000 men and women. By 2020, this figure is estimated to exceed 150,000.
- By 2020, the solar photovoltaic industry is estimated to be worth close to $27 billion per year.
- The national goal of the United States is to meet 10 percent peak power by 2030, or the equivalent of 180 million barrels of oil per year.

■ State-by-state analysis shows that U.S. photovoltaic grid-connected potential in 2010 will be 2900 MW/year, and solar power will be reduced to $2.00–$2.50 per installed watt, representing a $6.6 billion business.

■ Residential rooftop space available could accommodate 710,000 MW of solar electric power.

■ The Pacific and Mid-Atlantic regions of the United States will account for 52 percent of solar power installation.

■ California has the potential to accommodate 40 percent of the total building rooftop solar power market in the United States.

■ Projections of global solar power demand for 2020 indicate that solar power energy will be in parity with grid energy.

■ By 2020, global solar power production is expected to increase from 10 to 300 GW, an investment that will represent approximately $500 billion.

■ Over the next decade, 20–40 GW of solar power installed globally would provide 15 percent of the annual power consumed.

■ Global polysilicon production capacity is estimated to triple within the next 5 years. The cost of silicon ingot production may drop by as much as 50–60 percent.

■ In California, principal electric service providers are undertaking measures to integrate substantial amounts of green energy into their grids.

All these indicators suggest that alternative energy technologies, particularly the solar photovoltaic industry, in the United States and the rest of the world will be expanding at an unprecedented rate that will result in the creation of thousands of job opportunities for trained scientists, engineers, and technologists.

Alternative Energy Systems in Building Design is intended primarily to be a design reference guide for engineers, architects, scientists, management personnel, and university students. This book also can be supplemented with a teacher's reference guide, which will allow it to be used in undergraduate and postgraduate courses.

The main objective of this book is to provide readers with a pragmatic design reference manual for the design and implementation of some of the most commercially viable alternative energy technologies. In view of the unprecedented worldwide demand for solar power cogeneration systems, this book has extensive coverage of solar physics, associated technologies, and pragmatic design guidelines for professionals who must assume responsibility for all aspects of a solar power project design. Design guidelines discussed in the book reflect my personal experiences as a consulting engineer and educator.

Material on fusion reactors is included. Although fission reactors are not considered an alternative energy technology, the coverage is intended to provide a comparative reference with the specifics of fusion reactors. In writing this book, I have attempted to incorporate all significant alternative energy technologies; in the process, I have made extensive use of material from my previous publications and published articles from the Department of Energy (DOE), National Renewable Energy Laboratories (NREL), Web resources such as Wikipedia, and many contributors (as cited and acknowledged throughout the book).

As part of solar power system design and implementation, this book also includes specific coverage of LEED design, energy conservation, and the unique economics of solar power financing and return on investment, which covers the details of personnel, material cost breakdowns, and energy cost analyses. In view of the recent developments of new financial strategies, this book includes a discussion about power purchase agreements (PPAs), brief coverage of the Kyoto Protocol, and a discussion of the national and international carbon cap and trade system, which would be of significant importance to program managers.

As custodians of our global village, we must urgently apply our collective human ingenuity and resources to stop and reverse global atmospheric and environmental pollution within the next generation. In the past couple of centuries, as engineers and scientists, we have advanced these technologies, elevated living standards, and, in the process, grossly neglected the need for harmony with Mother Nature. Even though the challenges ahead may seem difficult to overcome, historically, as a nation, we have overcome equally insurmountable challenges and succeeded in realizing the seemingly impossible.

Peter Gevorkian, Ph.D., P.E.

ACKNOWLEDGMENTS

I would like to thank my colleagues and other individuals who have encouraged and assisted me in writing this book. I am especially grateful to all agencies and organizations that provided photographs and allowed use of some textual material, and my colleagues who read the manuscript and provided valuable insight.

My thanks go to Ken Touryan, Ph.D.; Zareh Astourian, MMPE, Corporate President, TMAD TAYLOR & GAINES; Jorn Christensen, Ph.D., Aerospace Communication; Robert McConnell, Ph.D., Senior Vice President Business Development, and Vahan Garboushian, President, AMONIX; Mark Gangi, AIA; Mary Olson Kanian; Gene Beck, EnviroTech Financial, Inc.; William Nona, Architect, National Council of Architectural Registration Boards; Frank Pao, CEO, Atlantis Energy Systems; Deborah Blackwell, Vice President, Hyperion Power Generation, Inc.; Gustavo Fernandes; and Ricardo Abecassis. Special thanks go to Carla Gharibian for her meticulous editing of the manuscript.

Thanks also go to AMONIX, Torrance, CA; MARTIFER USA, Santa Monica, CA; A&M Energy Solutions, Santa Monica, CA; Atlantis Energy Systems, Inc., Sacramento, CA; California Energy Commission, Sacramento, CA; Fotoworks Studio, Los Angeles, CA; Museum of Water and Life, Hemet, CA, Center for Water Education; SolarWorld California, Camarillo, CA; SunPower Corporation, Oakland, CA; Solar Integrated Technologies, Los Angeles, CA; U.S. Green Building Council, Los Angeles Chapter; U.S. Department of Energy; National Renewable Energy Laboratories; Sandia National Laboratories; Hyperion Power Generation, Inc., Washington, DC; DWP Solar; Solectria Inverters; Solargenix Energy, Newport Beach, CA; TMAD TAYLOR & GAINES, Pasadena, CA; UMA/Heliocol, Clearwater, FL; and EnviroTech Financial, Inc., Orange, CA.

DISCLAIMER NOTE

This book examines solar power generation and renewable energy sources, with the sole intent to familiarize the reader with the existing technologies and to encourage policy makers, architects, and engineers to use available energy conservation options in their designs.

The principal objective of the book is to emphasis solar power cogeneration design, application, and economics.

Neither the author, individuals, organizations, or manufacturers referenced or credited in this book make any warranties, express or implied, or assume any legal liability or responsibility for the accuracy, completeness, or usefulness of any information, products, and processes disclosed or presented.

Reference to any specific commercial product, manufacturer, or organization does not constitute or imply endorsement or recommendation by the author.

ALTERNATIVE ENERGY SYSTEMS IN BUILDING DESIGN

GLOBAL WARMING: CLIMATIC AND ATMOSPHERIC CHANGES

Climate change refers to variation in global or regional climates over time. It describes variability in the average state of the atmosphere over time periods ranging from decades to millions of years. These changes can be caused by internal processes in the earth or by external forces such as variations in sunlight intensity and, more recently, human activity.

In the context of, the term *climate change* often refers to changes in modern climate that are likely caused in part by human, or anthropogenic, action. Climate change is frequently referred to as *global warming*. In some cases, this term is used with a presumption of human causation for variations that are in actuality not anthropogenic.

Climate Change Factors

Climate changes reflect variations within the earth's atmosphere, processes in parts of the earth such as the oceans, and and the effects of human activity. Other external factors that affect climate are referred to as *climate forcing factors,* which include variations in the earth's orbit and greenhouse gas concentrations.

Variations within the Earth's Climate

Weather change is a normal state of the atmosphere and appears to have unpredictable dynamics. However, from a climatic point of view, the average state of weather is relatively stable and predictable. Climate change is measured by the average temperature, amount of precipitation, days of sunlight, and other variables at a particular region of the globe. Earth's climate is also subject to change from within owing to glaciation, oceanic temperature variability, and myriad other factors.

Natural Factors Driving Climate Change

GREENHOUSE GASES

Recently, scientific studies conducted indicate that both natural or anthropogenic factors are the primary cause of global warming. Greenhouse gases are also important in understanding earth's climatic history. According to these studies, the *greenhouse effect,* the warming of the climate as a result of heat trapped by atmospheric gases, plays a significant role in regulating earth's temperature (Fig. 1.1).

Over the last 600 million years, concentrations of greenhouse gases have varied from 5000 parts per million (ppm) to less than 200 ppm owing primarily to the effects of geologic processes and biologic interventions. Studies also have shown that there is a direct correlation between carbon dioxide (CO_2) gas and global warming. Several historic examples of rapid change in greenhouse gas concentrations indicate a strong correlation with global warming during various geologic events, such as the end of the Varangian glaciation.

According to the Intergovernmental Panel on Climate Change (IPCC) in 2007, the atmospheric concentration of CO_2 in 2005 was 379 ppm[3], compared with preindustrial

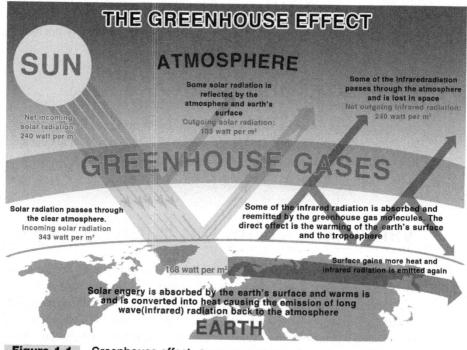

Figure 1.1   **Greenhouse effect.** *Courtesy of United Nations Environmental Program/GRID-Arendal.*

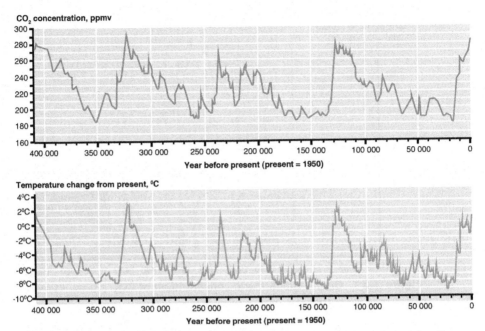

Figure 1.2   Temperature and CO_2 concentration in the atmosphere over the past 400,000 years (from the Vostok Ice Core). *Courtesy of United Nations Environmental Program/GRID-Arendal.*

levels of 280 ppm[3]. These measurements have been substantiated by verifying the dynamic equilibrium of vast amounts of CO_2 gas held in the world's oceans, which move into and return from the atmosphere (Figs. 1.2 and 1.3).

SOLAR VARIATION

Variations in sunspots and solar flare activity, which significantly affect the earth's temperature, also have been observed and studied for several centuries. As we know, the sun is the ultimate source of essentially all heat in the climate system. The energy output of the sun, which is converted to heat at the earth's surface, is the most signifi-cant factor controlling the earth's climate. Ever since the Big Bang, the sun, which is a nuclear fusion reactor furnace, has been burning by converting hydrogen into helium and is getting brighter by outputting higher amounts of energy. In its earlier days, the earth went through several extreme cold and hot periods when liquid water at its surface was completely frozen and liquefied several times, a phenomenon referred to as the *faint young sun paradox.*

Recent climatology studies have determined that the sun undergoes 11-year cyclic modulations. The 11-year sunspot cycle, however, has so far not been established as having a definitive effect on the global climate. Solar intensity variations, though, did have influence in triggering the global warming effect recorded from 1900 to 1950.

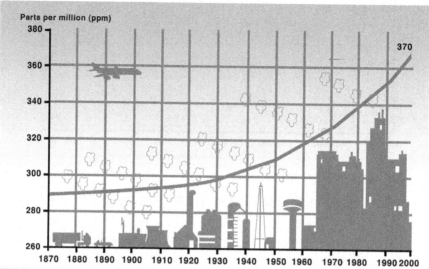

Figure 1.3   Global atmospheric concentration of CO$_2$. *Courtesy of United Nations Environmental Program/GRID-Arendal.*

ORBITAL VARIATIONS

Orbital variation patterns of the earth's movement around the sun result in solar energy absorption variability because small variations in the earth's orbit lead to much more considerable changes in the distribution and abundance of sunlight reaching the earth's surface. Such orbital variations are a consequence of basic physics owing to the mutual interactions of the earth, its moon, and the other planets. These variations are considered the driving factors underlying the glacial and interglacial cycles of the last ice age. Some of the most notable climatic variations observed, such as the repeated advance and retreat of the desert, have been the result of these orbital variations.

VOLCANISM

Large volcanic activities that occur several times per century also have had a significant effect on climate, causing cooling for periods of a few years. For instance, the 1991 eruption of the Mount Pinatubo in the Philippines affected the global climate substantially. The huge eruptions that have taken place a few times every hundred million years can be verified based on the magmatic variations in rocks and have reshaped the climate for millions of years. It has been speculated that the dust emitted into the atmosphere from large volcanic eruptions in the past has been responsible for cooling owing to the fact that the dust particles have partially blocked transmission of the sun's rays to the earth's surface. However, recent studies of and measurements taken from volcanic eruptions indicate that most of the dust thrown in the atmosphere returns to the earth's surface within 6 months.

Volcanoes also contribute to the extended atmospheric pollutants because over millennia of geologic time periods, they release carbon dioxide from the earth's interior, counteracting the uptake by sedimentary rocks and other geologic carbon sinks. However, CO_2 contribution resulting from volcanic eruptions is considered relatively insignificant compared with current anthropogenic emissions. Recent estimates indicate that anthropogenic activities generate more than 130 times the amount of carbon dioxide emitted by volcanoes.

GLACIATION

Glaciers are one of the most sensitive indicators of climate change. They advance substantially during climate cooling, as in ice ages, and retreat during climate warming on moderate time scales, a climatic cycle that has been repeating through the ages (Fig. 1.4). Glaciers are dynamic in nature; they grow in winter and collapse in summer, contributing to natural climatic variability. These are generally referred to as *externally forced changes*. However, in the last couple of centuries, glaciers have been unable to regenerate enough mass during the winter to make up for ice lost during summer months. The most significant climate processes that have taken place in the past several million years have been the glacial cycles that result from planetary gravitational forces and cause the formation of ice sheets.

OCEAN VARIABILITY

Climate changes also result from the interaction between the atmosphere and oceans. Many climatic fluctuations are a result of heat accumulation and storage in the oceans that cause water currents to move between different heat reservoirs. The movement process of oceanic water, *thermoline circulation,* plays a key role in redistributing and balancing heat and, consequently, climatic conditions throughout the globe.

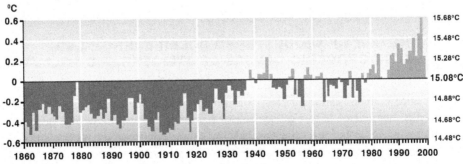

Figure 1.4   **Trend in global average surface temperature.** *Courtesy of United Nations Environmental Program/GRID-Arendal.*

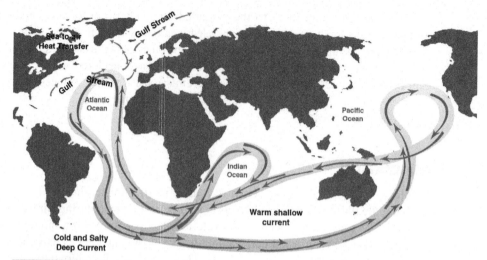

Figure 1.5   Great ocean conveyer belt. *Courtesy of United Nations Environmental Program/GRID-Arendal.*

The Memory of Climate

Most forms of internal variability in the climate system have not been created by humankind but have, through the ages, shown cyclic repeatability. This means that the current state of climate has a track record of how it behaves. For example, a decade of dry conditions may cause lakes to shrink, plains to dry up, and deserts to expand. In turn, these conditions may lead to less rainfall in the following years. In short, climate change can be a self-perpetuating process because different aspects of the environment respond in different ways to the fluctuations that inevitably occur. Figure 1.5 depicts graphic presentation of the great ocean conveyer belt.

Human Influences on Climate Change

THE USE OF SEQUESTERED SOLAR ENERGY AND ANTHROPOGENIC CAUSES OF ATMOSPHERIC POLLUTION

Anthropogenic factors are acts by humankind that affect the environment and influence climate. Various theories of human-induced climate change have been debated for many years. The biggest factor of present concern is the increase in CO_2 levels owing to emissions from combustion. Other concerns are particulate matter in the atmosphere that exerts a cooling effect. Other factors, such as land use, animal husbandry, agriculture, and deforestation, also affect climate.

FOSSIL FUELS

Carbon dioxide variations over the last 400,000 years have shown a rise since the industrial revolution. Beginning in the 1850s and accelerating ever since, the human consumption of fossil fuels has elevated CO_2 levels from a concentration of 280 ppm to more than 380 ppm today. These increases have been projected to reach more than 560 ppm before the end of the twenty-first century. It is known that CO_2 levels are substantially higher now than at any other time in the last 800,000 years. Along with rising levels of atmospheric pollutants, it is anticipated that there will be an increase in global temperature by 1.4–5.6°F between 1990 and 2100 (Fig. 1.6).

MILLENNIAL PERSPECTIVE OF CARBON DIOXIDE VARIATIONS

Organic materials such as plants (mainly formed from hydrocarbons and water molecules) under certain conditions, such as natural disasters, fires, volcanic activity, tectonic plate displacement, and extreme geoclimatic changes, lose significant amounts of their water content and are left with solely carbon and mineral materials. It is because of the sun's energy that organic life, in accordance with certain chemical processes, is transformed into various forms of hydrocarbon organic structures.

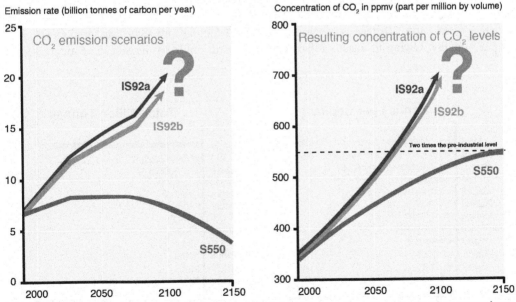

Figure 1.6   Projected changes in CO_2 and global temperature: summary of assumptions in the IPCC 1992 alternative scenarios. *Courtesy of United Nations Environmental Program/GRID-Arendal.*

Through the passage of millennia, these remains of organic carbonized material are manifested in the form of solid coal or liquid crude oils, referred to as *fossil fuels*. Fossil fuels, therefore, are considered to be sequestered forms of concentrated solar energy.

One of the most common sources of energy known to humans is the chemical combination of carbon molecules with oxygen. At a certain kindling point (elevated temperature), one atom of carbon (C) combines with two atoms of oxygen (O_2), giving rise to a carbon dioxide molecule ($C + O_2 = CO_2$). During this chemical combination, a certain amount of heat energy is released. We normally refer to this as a *burning process*.

Carbon dioxide, in its normal state, is a gas that is heavier than air. Under certain atmospheric pressures and temperatures, it liquefies. This liquid form of CO_2 is used in common fire extinguishers. Under normal temperature conditions, CO_2, when present in the air, displaces oxygen and ceases the spread of fire by preventing oxygen present in the air from reacting or combining with other forms of hydrocarbon-based material. This is referred to as *oxygen starvation*.

When heated, CO_2 molecules, owing to thermal agitation, distance themselves from each other, rendering the gas lighter than air. Large quantities of CO_2 result from burning fossil fuels. When heated by the sun's energy, CO_2 rises to higher elevations and surrounds the planet in a blanket of gas referred to as the *inversion layer* (Fig. 1.7).

When solar rays impinge on the earth, they are repelled from its surface and the north and south polar ice caps. The reflection of solar energy back into the earth's outer stratosphere moderates global temperature to levels that promote the existence of various life forms. Minor elevations in the earth's climatic conditions, in turn, affect the organic life and the reproductive cycles of all species.

As discussed earlier, global climatic temperature is moderated not only by the reflection of solar rays but also by the heat-absorption capability of the earth's oceans. Two-thirds of the earth's surface is covered by oceans, which absorb significant amounts of solar energy. Owing to earth's relative rotational tilt angle to the sun (23.5 degrees), the

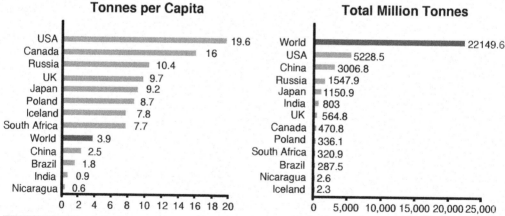

Figure 1.7   **CO_2 emissions of various countries in 1995.** *Courtesy of United Nations Environmental Program/GRID-Arendal.*

oceanic water at the equator and poles absorbs unequal amounts of solar energy, giving rise to a water temperature gradient differential that creates convective water circulation within the oceans. The movement or displacement of lighter warm waters from the equator to the north and cold water from the north pole to the south is referred to as the *gulf stream* or the *belt current* and regulates continental climatic conditions.

When fossil fuels are burned, the resulting blanket of CO_2 gas, referenced earlier, thickens, thus elevating the earth's temperature through energy entrapment. The entrapment of higher energy within this reflective blanket elevates the surface temperature of the oceans, thus increasing evaporation and water particulate release into the atmosphere. Water molecules, when released into the atmosphere, in turn, act as supplemental reflective shields, further reflecting the sun's rays and expanding the inversion layer, exacerbating global warming.

The Transition of Various Forms of Sequestered Solar Energy Use and Their Effect on Societies

WOOD BURNING

From the dawn of civilization until the mid-eighteenth century, humans used wood burning as their primary source of energy. It was used mainly for heating but also, to a lesser degree, for smelting and distillation. Owing to a smaller global population, the CO_2 gas generated did not saturate the absorption capacity of plants and the oceans. Consequently, it did not have a significant negative effect on the environment.

COAL BURNING

With the invention of the steam engine in 1750, historically cited as the dawn of industrial revolution, the use of coal as the primary source of energy turned the wheels of industries, shortened intercontinental travel time, enabled significant transcontinental transportation, displaced cultures, gave rise to significant advancements in farming automation, and increased farm production and manufactured goods.

The industrial revolution also resulted in a better standard of living for certain privileged populations in the Western world, improving levels of hygiene and life expectancy. As a result of the deployment of steam-driven farming equipment and the availability of larger amounts of food stock, population growth accelerated in an unprecedented manner.

Owing to greater energy demand and the global proliferation of the industrial revolution, the use of coal created significant atmospheric and environmental pollution in industrial centers such as London and Paris, causing major human health problems. Death from pulmonary and respiratory diseases, such as black lung and tuberculosis, were the norm of the times.

CRUDE OIL AND NATURAL GAS

At the beginning of the twentieth century, the advent of the internal combustion engine, the discovery of vast crude oil reservoirs in Texas, and the proliferation of electrical energy generation and distribution brought the industrial revolution into a new era of accelerated expansion.

Mass production of automobiles necessitated the construction of roadways (facilitating rapid land transportation), the creation of new suburban communities, unprecedented real estate development, and the production of new goods and services, all of which became possible owing to the abundance of fossil fuels. Advances in aviation technology furthered the demand for gasoline and created an acute increase in dependency on fossil fuels.

The rapid expansion of urban dwellings and technology created an ever-extensive demand for electrical energy and necessitated the massive construction of coal- and crude oil–fired steam turbines, which have contributed significantly to atmospheric pollution and deterioration of the global environment. In the past century, global dependency on crude oil has increased to such an extent that it has become the most significant commodity sustaining modern life. Without fossil fuel energy, hydroelectric and nuclear power plants would not have sufficient power production capacity to sustain the minimal energy requirements of 6.6 billion people globally.

FOSSIL FUEL DEPENDENCY

Dependency on fossil fuels over the last century has shaped our way of life, customs, moral standards, population distribution, demographics, hygiene, life expectancy, standard of living, global economies, security, and international politics. Control of global fossil fuel resources has caused political upheavals and international strife, defined international geographic boundaries, displaced multitudes of populations, caused wars, and resulted in the destruction of property and human life. However, the most significant effect has been the deterioration of the global habitat for all living species.

Control of fossil fuel resources, particularly crude oil and natural gas, has significantly shifted the international balance of trade and power, polarized ideologies, and created a divide between the resources of rich and poor countries.

IMPACT OF CLIMATE CHANGE ON HUMAN HEALTH

There is a close link between the increase in anthropogenic atmospheric pollution, increases in the size of the inversion layer, global temperature rise, and the occurrences of diseases related to elevated temperatures. It is well known that extreme global temperature rise can directly cause loss of life and promote environments for the growth of pathogens that cause serious diseases. Global temperature elevation, whether owing to natural or anthropogenic causes, increases air and water pollution, both of which harm human health.

The most significant effect of climate change is the increase in human causalities owing to dehydration and heat stroke. People with cardiovascular impairments become extremely vulnerable in hot weather because their cardiovascular systems overwork in order to regulate and maintain normal body temperature. In addition, higher temperatures exacerbate respiratory problems because increased temperature increases the concentration of ozone at ground level. The natural layer of ozone in the troposphere blocks harmful ultraviolet radiation from reaching the earth's surface. However, in the lower atmosphere, ozone becomes a significantly harmful pollutant that can damage lung tissue and cause pulmonary dysfunction and severe cases of asthma and other lung-related diseases. Even modest exposure to ozone can cause healthy individuals to experience chest pains, nausea, and pulmonary congestion.

A recent statistical analysis of mortality and hospital admissions showed that death rates in the United States increased during extreme temperatures, seriously endangering the old and very young urban populations. In July 1995, a heat wave in Chicago killed more than 700 people. Worse yet, a heat wave in 2005 killed 15,000 elderly in France, 7000 in Germany, 8000 in Spain and Italy, and 2000 in the United Kingdom. Recently, the BBC announced 25,000 deaths in England and Wales owing to cold weather, all of which went relatively unnoticed. It is also estimated that each year 200,000 people die from excess heat in Europe. However, an astonishing 1.5 million Europeans die annually from excess cold.

Global warming also increases the risk of some infectious diseases, particularly those that appear only in warm areas. Deadly diseases often associated with hot weather, such as West Nile viral infection, cholera, and Lyme disease, are spreading rapidly throughout North America and Europe because increased temperatures in these areas allow disease carriers such as mosquitoes, ticks, and mice to thrive. In the past decade, West Nile virus–carrying mosquitoes in the United States and Canada have increased significantly. It is a general consensus among scientists that global temperature rise will increase the frequency of disease outbreaks, particularly in areas with polluted waters.

Heat-related deaths can be prevented by emergency measures such as moving vulnerable people to air-conditioned buildings and by reducing the emissions of photochemical oxidants that cause ground-level ozone. Many of the impacts of climate change on health could be avoided through the maintenance of strong public health programs that monitor, quarantine, and treat the spread of infectious diseases and respond to other health emergencies as they occur.

IMPACT OF AIR POLLUTION AND ULTRAVIOLET RADIATION ON HUMAN HEALTH

It is estimated that air pollution, even with the U.S. Clean Air Act (among the most stringent air-quality laws in the world), causes as many as 50,000 Americans to die prematurely annually. Perhaps the leading cause of air pollution–related death in both industrialized and developing countries is particulate matter, such as soot and dirt particles, causing respiratory failure. Another significant health concern, aside from ground-level ozone, is lead emissions from gasoline, which cause neurologic damage and impairment to the intelligence of children. Sulfur dioxide emissions from coal-burning steam plants are a significant factor as well in respiratory diseases. Air pollution today poses a risk to millions worldwide, especially children in the world's urban areas.

Increased ultraviolet (UV) radiation, which results from depletion of the stratospheric ozone layer, has had numerous adverse effects on human health, including an increased risk of various forms of skin cancer, a weakening of the human immune system, and an increased risk for eye disorders such as cataracts.

CLIMATE PROTECTION POLICIES THAT COULD ENHANCE HUMAN HEALTH

Policies and measures that enforce the reduction of emissions of greenhouse gases are the only viable solutions to ameliorate human health problems. Measures that could improve air quality significantly include the extensive use of green energy and enhanced energy-efficiency movements that promote the use of noncarbon fuels. It is estimated that an international adoption of increased carbon emission control policies worldwide would reduce deaths from air pollution by about 8 million between 2000 and 2020.

AIR POLLUTION AND STRATOSPHERIC OZONE DEPLETION MITIGATION MEASURES

It is a well-established fact that human, industrial, and agricultural activity in the last century has been a significant factor in contributing to atmospheric pollution. Another family of human-made chemical compounds, chlorofluorocarbons (CFCs), which also are considered to be one of the leading causes of stratospheric ozone depletion and which result in the production of greenhouse gases, has been banned recently. This measure will help in climate protection as well as in preserving the stratospheric ozone layer.

It should be noted that the deployment of smoke stack scrubbers, used for reducing air pollution on coal-fired power plants, has resulted in more energy consumption and an increase in greenhouse emissions. Therefore, their use must be banned.

Industrial Sources of Atmospheric Pollution

CEMENT MANUFACTURE

Ever since the Roman discovery of concrete and the subsequent patenting of the cement manufacturing processes in the eighteenth century, concrete has become one of the most used building materials. Cement manufacturing, which involves the excessive burning of coal, is the third largest source of human-made CO_2 emissions. While fossil fuel combustion and deforestation each produce significantly more CO_2, cement making is responsible for approximately 2.5 percent of total worldwide emissions from industrial sources.

LAND USE

Prior to the widespread use of fossil fuels, humanity's largest effect on local climate likely resulted from changes to the environment. For example, human activities change the amount of water going into and out of a given location. They also change the local ecology by influencing ground cover and altering the amount of sunlight that is absorbed.

Historical evidence suggests that the climates of Greece and other Mediterranean countries were permanently changed between 700 BC and 1 AD because of widespread deforestation (the wood was used for shipbuilding and construction). This finding is supported by the archeologic discovery of a species of tree that was used for shipbuilding in the ancient world but which can no longer be found in the area.

There are also hypotheses that suggest that the rise of agriculture and the accompanying deforestation led to increases in CO_2 and methane gases during the period 5000–8000 years ago. The increases in CO_2 may have been responsible for delaying the onset of a more severe glacial period (Fig. 1.8).

In 2007 it was found that the average temperature has risen about 2°F over the past 50 years, with a much larger increase in urban areas. This change was attributed mainly to extensive human development of the landscape.

LIVESTOCK

According to a 2006 United Nations report, livestock is responsible for 18 percent of the world's greenhouse gas emissions, as measured in CO_2 equivalents. This includes land deforestation in order to create grazing land. In the Amazon Basin, 70 percent of deforestation has been to make way for grazing land. In addition to CO_2 emissions,

Greenhouse gases	Chemical formula	Preindustrial concentration	Concentration in 1994	Atmospheric lifetime (years)	Anthropogenic sources	Global warming potential (GWP)
Carbon dioxide	CO_2	278.00 ppbv	358.00 ppbv	Variable	Fossil fuel combustion Land use conversion Cement production	1
Methane	CH_4	700 ppbv	1721 ppbv	12.2±3	Fossil fuels Rice paddies Waste dumps Livestock	21
Nitrous oxide	N_2O	275 ppbv	311 ppbv	120	Fertilizer Industrial processes Combustion	310
CFC-12	CCl_2F_2	0	0.503 ppbv	102	Liquid coolants Foams	6200–7100
HCFC-22	$CHClF_2$	0	0.105 ppbv	12.1	Liquid coolants	1300–1400
Perfluoromethane	CF_4	0	0.070 ppbv	50,000	Production of aluminium	6500
Sulphur hexa-fluoride	SF_6	0	0.032 ppbv	3200	Dielectric fluid	23,900

Figure 1.8   **The main greenhouse gases.** *Courtesy of United Nations Environmental Program/GRID-Arendal.*

livestock produces 65 percent of human-induced nitrous oxide, which has 296 times the global-warming potential of CO_2, and 37 percent of human-induced methane, which has 23 times the global-warming potential of CO_2.

ARGUMENT ABOUT THE GLOBAL CLIMATIC TEMPERATURE BALANCE

As discussed earlier, the glacial and interglacial cycles of the last ice age provide important information. It is believed that orbital variations of the earth around the sun result in the growth and retreat of ice sheets. However, the ice sheets reflect sunlight back into space and therefore cool the climate, a phenomenon referred to as the *ice-albedo feedback*. Moreover, an increase in polar ice plates results in falling sea levels. It should be noted that the expansion of ice caps also indirectly diminishes the growth of plant life and therefore leads to reductions in CO_2 and methane. This causes further cooling of the atmosphere.

Using a similar argument, rising temperatures caused by anthropogenic emissions of greenhouse gases could lead to retreating snow lines, revealing darker ground underneath. Consequently, the result would be increased absorption of sunlight and thus excess water vapor, methane, and CO_2 generation. This eventually would act as significant positive feedback because increases in these levels would create an accelerated warming trend. Water vapor, unlike other major greenhouse gases, can act as a driving force, resulting in changing circulation patterns in the ocean or atmosphere. For instance, a significant melting of glacial ice from Greenland would interfere with sinking waters in the North Atlantic and inhibit the thermohaline circulation discussed earlier. This could significantly affect the distribution of heat to in the Atlantic Ocean (Fig. 1.9).

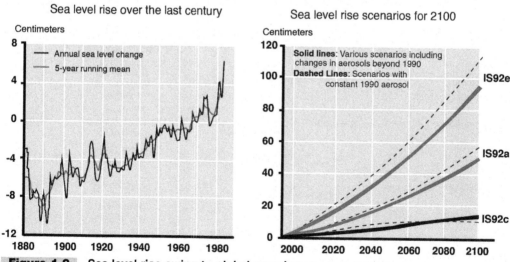

Figure 1.9   **Sea level rise owing to global warming.** *Courtesy of United Nations Environmental Program/GRID-Arendal.*

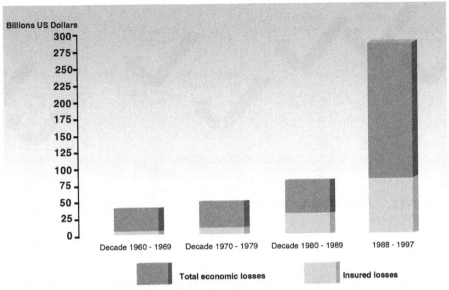

Figure 1.10   Great weather and flood and catastrophes over 40 years.
Courtesy of the United Nations Environmental Program/GRID-Arendal.

Other potential effects of global warming that have not yet been fully studied include the potential to either inhibit or promote certain natural processes. For instance, we do not know whether rising temperatures promote or inhibit vegetative growth, which, in turn, could either absorb more or have a saturation level that will decrease carbon dioxide levels. It should be noted that evidence for climate change in the past has been taken from a number of sources, allowing for the reconstruction of past climatic variations (Fig. 1.10). Most of the evidence gathered has been based on indirect climatic changes inferred from changes in indicators that reflect climate, such as pollens and fossilized remains of species.

The Little Ice Age

The following discussion outlines recorded historical global temperature variations and their resulting consequences, which affected population growth and survival, human health, nutrition, wars, and geopolitical events. Two principal climate changes, the *medieval climate optimum* and the *little ice age,* are the basis of this discussion. However, their existence is not entirely supported scientifically.

Medieval climate optimum refers to the global temperature elevation that resulted from heightened solar flare activity from the tenth until the mid-thirteenth century. During this time, most of the European continent experienced a period of elevated temperature, resulting in population migration toward northern countries. It is at this

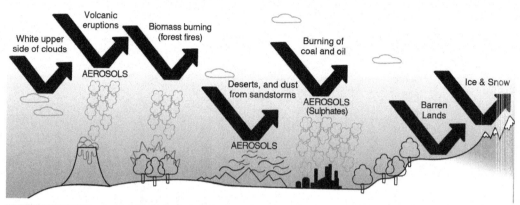

Figure 1.11   **Atmospheric cooling factors.** *Courtesy of United Nations Environmental Program/GRID-Arendal.*

period of time that the Vikings crossed the Atlantic Ocean, 500 years before Columbus, and settled in Greenland. On arrival, the Vikings found the land flourishing with vegetation, caribou, and myriad other flora and fauna. Historical evidence indicates that colonization and population of the new world continued to grow for nearly three centuries, after which a new era of climatic change, referred to as the *little ice age,* ushered in severe drops in global temperature. This resulted in a diminishment of nourishment, leading to the eventual demise of the entire Viking settlement in North America (Fig. 1.11).

Even though historical accounts and evidence substantiate global climate change, climatologists and historians find it difficult to agree on the start and end dates of these periods. All, however, concur that the little ice age began approximately around the sixteenth century and lasted until the mid-nineteenth century.

DATING OF THE LITTLE ICE AGE

As mentioned earlier, there is mixed concurrence by scientists about the beginning year of the little ice age. However, scientific discovery has shown that a series of events preceded the downward trend of climatic conditions. It has been established that in the thirteenth century, north polar ice and Greenland glaciers began advancing southward. It also has been recorded that from 1315 through 1318, torrential rains ushered in an era of extremely unstable weather conditions in northern Europe that lasted through the mid-nineteenth century. The following is a timeline of climatic change during the 400 years of the little ice age:

1250   Northern hemispheric pack begins to enlarge

1300   Northern Europe warm lasts a mere several years

1315   Profusion of annual rains devastates agriculture throughout Europe

1550   Beginning of worldwide glacial expansion

1650   Global temperatures drop to their lowest levels

It is believed that the little ice age lasted until the mid-nineteenth century.

NORTHERN HEMISPHERE

The following are anecdotal accounts of the effect of the little ice age on the northern hemisphere:

- Cold weather was experienced throughout many parts of the world.
- As a result of severe climatic conditions in the fourteenth century, most springs and summers were so cold and wet that common farming crops such as cereals could not yield sufficient sustenance.
- As a consequence, Europe experienced a severe famine from 1315 to 1317, resulting in new crops such as rye and barley that were better suited for shortened, less reliable growing seasons.
- The Thames River often froze over during the winter, and people skated and even held parties on the ice.
- In 1622, waters around the Potomac River froze in the winter.
- In the sixteenth century, vine growing completely disappeared from some northern regions of Europe, resulting in a severe reduction in wine production and increased use of beer as a substitute.
- In the early sixteenth century, violent storms caused massive flooding and loss of life. Some of these resulted in permanent losses of large tracts of land from the Danish, German, and Dutch coasts.
- In the mid-sixteenth century in southern Europe, warm weather crops, such as oranges, were abandoned in provinces where they had been grown for centuries.
- In the mid-seventeenth century, glaciers advanced, gradually engulfing farms and crushing entire villages.
- In 1758, General Washington's army marched across the Potomac River to invade the British garrison.
- In the winter of 1794–1795, the French army invaded Holland by marching over the frozen rivers of the Netherlands.
- The first Thames frost fair was recorded in 1607, and the tradition lasted through 1814.
- In the eighteenth century, owing to a lack of harvest, the population of Iceland fell by half.
- It has been said that the famous violin maker Stradivari produced his outstanding instruments during the little ice age, when the colder climate meant the wood used in his violins had denser growth rings (which are otherwise larger in warmer periods).
- It also has been speculated that severe mortality rates in Europe, East Asia, and the Middle East attributed to a decrease in agricultural output and deterioration of nutrition and immune systems were consequences of the little ice age. Ruddiman,

who first theorized the correlation, further suggests that massive depopulation in the New World during the 1500s was a result of the Americas being in contact with Europe.

PRINCIPAL CAUSES OF THE LITTLE ICE AGE

At present, scientists have identified two probable causes for the little ice age: a decrease or increase in volcanic eruptions. In essence, some researchers are of the opinion that anthropogenic atmospheric pollution that affects climate is extremely minor compared with natural events. As a matter of fact, some scientists consider glaciations to be normal cycles for earth, as in the medieval warm period and the inter-glacial glaciations period.

VOLCANIC ACTIVITY

Throughout the little ice age, the world also experienced severe volcanic eruptions, which spewed enormous amounts of ash that reached high into the atmosphere and covered the entire earth. In some instances, large amounts of volcanic ash can block out incoming solar radiation, leading to worldwide cooling that can last up to several years. Emitted volcanic ashes, in addition to large amounts of CO_2, contain significant amounts of sulfur dioxide (SO_2) gas. When the SO_2 gas reaches the upper atmosphere, it combines with water particulates and turns into sulfuric acid, which amplifies the reflection of the sun's rays, further reducing the amount of radiation reaching earth's surface.

OCEAN CONVEYOR SHUTDOWN

Another possible cause of the little ice age is related to the disruption or slowing of ocean conveyor, also known as the *gulf stream*. It could have been interrupted by the introduction of large amounts of freshwater in the North Atlantic, possibly caused by melting of glaciers during the medieval warming period. According to documented records, around 1850 the global climate began warming, and the little ice age ended. Notwithstanding, scientific opinion of the effects of the little ice age on climate change is that warming over the last 50 years has increased proportions of CO_2 in the atmosphere, stemming from human, or anthropogenic, activity.

2

ENERGY SYSTEMS

The following is a summarized narrative from Wikipedia, the Web encyclopedia. For broader details, refer to www.wikipedia.com. In order to differentiate alternative energy sources, it is important to understand the various definitions of energy. Energy in physics, chemistry, and nature occurs in numerous forms, all of which imply similar connotations as the ability to perform work. In physics and other sciences, energy is a scalar quantity that is a property of objects and systems and is conserved by nature. Several different forms of energy exist, including kinetic energy, potential energy, thermal energy, gravitational energy, electromagnetic radiation energy, chemical energy, and nuclear energy. These have been defined to explain all known natural phenomena.

Conservation of Energy

Energy is transformation from one form to another, but it is never created or destroyed. This principle, the *law of conservation of energy*, was first postulated in the early nineteenth century and applies to any isolated system. The total energy of a system does not change over time, but its value may depend on the frame of reference. For example, a seated passenger in a moving vehicle has zero kinetic energy relative to the vehicle but does indeed have kinetic energy relative to the earth.

The Concept of Energy in Various Scientific Fields

- In chemistry, the energy differences between chemical substances determine whether and to what extent they can be converted into or react with other substances.
- In biology, chemical bonds are often broken and made during metabolism. Energy is often stored by the body in the form of carbohydrates and lipids, both of which release energy when reacting with oxygen.

■ In earth sciences, continental drift, volcanic activity, and earthquakes are phenomena that can be explained in terms of energy transformation in the earth's interior. Meteorologic phenomena such as wind, rain, hail, snow, lightning, tornados, and hurricanes are all a result of energy transformations brought about by solar energy.

Energy transformations in the universe are characterized by various kinds of potential energy that have been available since the Big Bang and later "released" to be transformed into more active types of energy.

NUCLEAR DECAY

Examples of such processes include those in which energy that was originally "stored" in heavy isotopes such as uranium and thorium is released by nucleosynthesis. In this process, gravitational potential energy, released from the gravitational collapse of supernovae, is used to store energy in the creation of these heavy elements before their incorporation into the solar system and earth. This energy is triggered and released in nuclear fission bombs.

FUSION

In a similar chain of transformations at the dawn of the universe, the nuclear fusion of hydrogen in the sun released another store of potential energy that was created at the time of the Big Bang. Space expanded, and the universe cooled too rapidly for hydrogen to fuse completely into heavier elements. Hydrogen thus represents a store of potential energy that can be released by nuclease fusion.

SUNLIGHT ENERGY STORAGE

Solar power energy when converted to electricity can be used to pump water from lower body of water into a hydroelectric dam or reservoir stored again as gravitational potential energy. After being released at a hydroelectric dam, this water can be used to drive turbines and generators to produce electricity. Sunlight also drives all weather phenomena, including such events as hurricanes, in which large, unstable areas of warm ocean, heated over months, suddenly give up some of their thermal energy to power intense air movement.

KINETIC VERSUS POTENTIAL ENERGY

An important distinction should be made between kinetic and potential energy before continuing. *Potential energy* is the energy of matter owing to its position or arrangement. This stored energy can be found in any lifted objects, which have the force of gravity bringing them down to their original positions. *Kinetic energy* is the energy that an object possesses owing to its motion. A great example of this is seen with a ball that falls under the influence of gravity. As it accelerates downward, its potential energy is converted into kinetic energy. When it hits the ground and deforms, the kinetic energy converts into elastic potential energy. On bouncing back up, this potential energy once again becomes kinetic energy. The two forms, though seemingly very different, play important roles in complementing each other.

GRAVITATIONAL POTENTIAL ENERGY

The gravitational force near the earth's surface is equal to the mass m multiplied by the gravitational acceleration g and is 9.81 m/s^2.

TEMPERATURE

On the macroscopic scale, temperature is a unique physical property that determines the direction of heat flow between two objects placed in thermal contact. If no heat flow occurs, the two objects have the same temperature because heat flows from the hotter object to the colder object. These two basic principles are stated in the *zeroth law of thermodynamics* and the *second law of thermodynamics,* respectively. For a solid, these microscopic motions are principally the vibrations of its atoms about their sites in the solid.

In most of the world (except for the United States, Jamaica, and a few other countries), the degree Celsius scale is used for most temperature-measuring purposes. The global scientific community, with the United States included, measures temperature using the Celsius scale and thermodynamic temperature using the scale in Kelvin scale, in which 0 K $= -273.15$°C, or *absolute zero.*

SPECIFIC HEAT CAPACITY

Specific heat capacity, also known as *specific heat,* is a measure of the energy that is needed to raise the temperature of a quantity of a substance by a certain amount.

CHEMICAL ENERGY

Chemical energy is defined as the work done by electrical forces during the rearrangement of electric charges, electrons, and protons in the process of aggregation. If the chemical energy of a system decreases during a chemical reaction, it is transferred to the surroundings in some form of energy (often heat). On the other hand, if the chemical energy of a system increases as a result of a chemical reaction, it is from the conversion of another form of energy from its surroundings. Moles are the typical units used to describe change in chemical energy, and values can range from tens to hundreds of kilojoules per mole.

RADIANT ENERGY

Radiant energy is the energy of electromagnetic waves or sometimes of other forms of radiation. As with all forms of energy, its unit is the joule. The term *radiation* is used especially when radiation is emitted by a source into the surrounding environment.

Since electromagnetic (EM) radiation can be conceptualized as a stream of photons, radiant energy can be seen as the energy carried by these photons. EM radiation also can be seen as an electromagnetic wave that carries energy in its oscillating electric and magnetic fields. Quantum field theory reconciles these two views.

EM radiation can have a range of frequencies. From the viewpoint of photons, the energy carried by each photon is proportional to its frequency. From the viewpoint of waves, the energy of a monochromatic wave is proportional to its intensity. Thus it can be implied that if two EM waves have the same intensity but different frequencies, the wave with the higher frequency contains fewer photons.

When EM waves are absorbed by an object, their energy typically is converted to heat. This is an everyday phenomenon, seen, for example, when sunlight warms the surfaces it irradiates. This is often associated with infrared radiation, but any kind of EM radiation will warm an object that absorbs it. EM waves also can be reflected or scattered, causing their energy to be redirected or redistributed.

Energy can enter or leave an open system in the form of radiant energy. Such a system can be human-made, as with a solar energy collector, or natural, as with the earth's atmosphere. Greenhouse gases trap the sun's radiant energy at certain wavelengths, allowing it to penetrate deep into the atmosphere or all the way to the earth's surface, where it is reemitted as longer wavelengths. Radiant energy is produced in the sun owing to the phenomenon of nuclear fusion.

3

SOLAR POWER SYSTEM PHYSICS AND TECHNOLOGIES

Solar, or photovoltaic (PV), cells are electronic devices that essentially convert the solar energy of sunlight into electric energy or electricity. The physics of solar cells is based on the same semiconductor principles as diodes and transistors, which form the building blocks of the entire world of electronics.

Solar cells convert energy as long as there is sunlight. In the evenings and during cloudy conditions, the conversion process diminishes. It stops completely at dusk and resumes at dawn. Solar cells do not store electricity, but batteries can be used to store the energy.

One of the most fascinating aspects of solar cells is their ability to convert the most abundant and free forms of energy into electricity without moving parts or components and without producing any adverse forms of pollution that affect the ecosystem, as is associated with most known forms of nonrenewable energy production methods, such as fossil fuels, hydroelectric power, and nuclear energy plants.

In this chapter we will review the overall solar energy conversion process, system configurations, and economics associated with the technology. We also briefly look into the mechanism of hydrogen fuel cells. In addition, we will review the fundamentals of solar power cogeneration design and explore a number of applications, including an actual design of a 500-kW solar power installation project, which also includes a detailed analysis of all system design parameters.

Brief History of the Photoelectric Phenomenon

In the latter part of the nineteenth century, physicists discovered a new phenomenon. When light is incident on liquids or metal-cell surfaces, electrons are released. However, no one had an explanation for this bizarre occurrence. At the turn of the century, Albert

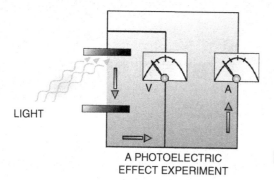

A PHOTOELECTRIC
EFFECT EXPERIMENT

Figure 3.1 The photoelectric effect experiment.

Einstein provided a theory for this that won him the Nobel Prize in Physics and laid the groundwork for the theory of the *photoelectric effect*. Figure 3.1 shows the photoelectric effect experiment. When light is shone on metal, electrons are released. These electrons are attracted toward a positively charged plate, thereby giving rise to a photoelectric current.

Einstein explained the observed phenomenon by a contemporary theory of quantized energy levels, which was developed previously by Max Planck. The theory described light as being made up of miniscule bundles of energy called *photons*. Photons impinging on metals or semiconductors knock electrons off atoms.

In the 1930s, these theorems led to a new discipline in physics called *quantum mechanics,* which consequently led to the discovery of transistors in the 1950s and to the development of semiconductor electronics.

HISTORICAL AC/DC DEBATE BETWEEN EDISON AND TESLA

The application of direct current (dc) electric power is a century-old technology that took a backseat to alternating current (ac) in the early 1900s when Edison and Tesla were having a feud over their energy transmission and distribution inventions. The following are some interesting historical notes that were communicated by two of the most brilliant inventors in the history of electrical engineering:

Nicola Tesla: "Alternating Current will allow the transmission of electrical power to any point on the planet, either through wires or through the air, as I have demonstrated."

Thomas Edison: "Transmission of ac over long distances requires lethally high voltages, and should be outlawed. To allow Tesla and Westinghouse to proceed with their proposals is to risk untold deaths by electricide."

Tesla: "How will the dc power a 1000 horsepower electric motor as well as a single light bulb? With AC, the largest as well as the smallest load may be driven from the same line."

Edison: "The most efficient and proper electrical supply for every type of device from the light bulb to the phonograph is Direct Current at low voltage."

Tesla: "A few large AC generating plants, such as my hydroelectric station at Niagara Falls, are all you need: from these, power can be distributed easily wherever it is required."

Edison: "Small DC generating plants, as many as are required, should be built according to local needs, after the model of my power station in New York City."

EARLY AC DOMINANCE

After Edison introduced his dc power stations, the first of their kind in the world, the demand for electricity became overwhelming. Soon, the need to send power over long distances in rural and suburban America was paramount. How did the two power systems compare in meeting this need? Alternating current could be carried over long distances, via a relatively small line given an extremely high transmission voltage of 50,000 V or above. The high voltage then could be transformed down to lower levels for residential, office, and industrial use.

While higher in quality and more efficient than alternating current, dc power could not be transformed or transmitted over distances via small cables without suffering significant losses through resistance. AC power became the standard of all public utilities, overshadowing issues of safety and efficiency and forcing manufacturers to produce appliances and motors compatible with the national grid.

THE 100-YEAR-OLD POWER SCHEME

With ac power the only option available from power utilities, the world came to rely almost exclusively on ac-based motors and other appliances, and the efficiencies and disadvantages of ac power became accepted as unavoidable. Nicola Tesla's development of the polyphase induction ac motor was a key step in the evolution of ac power applications. His discoveries contributed greatly to the development of dynamos, vacuum bulbs, and transformers, strengthening the existing ac power scheme 100 years ago. Compared with direct current and Edison's findings, ac power is inefficient because of the energy lost with the rapid reversals of the current's polarity. We often hear these reversals as the familiar 60 cycles per second (60 Hz) hum of an appliance. AC power is also prone to harmonic distortion, which occurs when there is a disruption in the ideal ac sinusoidal power wave shape. Since most of today's technologically advanced on-site power devices use direct current, there is a need to use inverters to produce alternating current through the system and then convert it back to direct current at the end source of power. These inverters are inefficient; energy is lost (up to 50 percent) when these devices are used. This characteristic is evident in many of today's electronic devices that have internal converters, such as fluorescent lighting.

ALTERNATING AND DIRECT CURRENT: 1950–2000

The discovery of semiconductors and the invention of the transistor, along with the growth of the American economy, triggered a quiet but profound revolution in how we use electricity. Changes over the last half-century have brought the world into the era of electronics, with more and more machines and appliances operating internally on dc

TABLE 3.1   AC AND DC DEVICE APPLICATIONS

AC DEVICES—1950	DC DEVICES—2000
Electric typewriters	Computers, printers, CRTs, scanners
Adding machines	CD-ROMs, photocopiers
Wired, rotary telephones	Wired, cordless, and touch-tone phones
Teletypes	Answering machines, modems, faxes
Early fluorescent lighting	Advanced fluorescent lighting with electronic ballasts
Radios, early TVs	Electronic ballast, gas-discharge lighting
Record players	HDTVs, CD players, videocassettes
Electric ranges	Microwave ovens
Fans, furnaces	Electronically controlled HVAC systems

power and requiring more and more expensive solutions for the conversion and regulation of incoming ac supply. Table 3.1 lists some ac and dc device applications of the mid-twentieth and twenty-first centuries.

As seen from this table, over the last 50 years we have moved steadily from an electromechanical to an electronic world, a world where most of our electric devices are driven by direct current and most of our non–fossil fuel energy sources (such as photovoltaic cells and batteries) deliver their power as a dc supply.

Despite these changes, the vast majority of today's electricity is still generated, transported, and delivered as alternating current. Converting alternating current to direct current and integrating alternative dc sources within the mainstream ac supply are inefficient and expensive activities that add significantly to capital costs and lock us all into archaic and uncompetitive utility pricing structures. With the advent of progress in solar power technology, the world that Thomas Edison envisioned (one with clean, efficient, and less costly power) is now, after a century of dismissal, becoming a reality. The following exemplify the significance of dc energy applications from solar photovoltaic systems: (1) on-site power using direct current to the end source is the most efficient use of power, and (2) there are no conversion losses resulting from the use of dc power, which allows maximum harvest of solar irradiance energy potential.

Solar Cell Physics

Most solar cells are constructed from semiconductor material, such as silicon (the fourteenth element in the Mendeleyev table of elements). Silicon is a semiconductor that has the combined properties of a conductor and an insulator.

Metals such as gold, copper, and iron are conductors; they have loosely bound electrons in the outer shell or orbit of their atomic configuration. These electrons can be detached when subjected to an electric voltage or current. On the contrary, atoms of insulators, such as glass, have very strongly bonded electrons in the atomic configuration and do not allow the flow of electrons even under the severest application of voltage or current. Semiconductor materials, on the other hand, bind electrons midway between that of metals and insulators.

Semiconductor elements used in electronics are constructed by fusing two adjacently doped silicon wafer elements. Doping implies impregnation of silicon by positive and negative agents, such as phosphor and boron. Phosphor creates a free electron that produces so-called N-type material. Boron creates a "hole," or a shortage of an electron, that produces so-called P-type material. Impregnation is accomplished by depositing the previously referenced dopants on the surface of silicon using a certain heating or chemical process. The N-type material has a propensity to lose electrons and gain holes, so it acquires a positive charge. The P-type material has a propensity to lose holes and gain electrons, so it acquires a negative charge.

When N- and P-type doped silicon wafers are fused together, they form a *PN junction*. The negative charge on the P-type material prevents electrons from crossing the junction, and the positive charge on the N-type material prevents holes from crossing the junction. A space created by the P and N, or PN, wafers creates a potential barrier across the junction. Figure 3.2 illustrates flow of electrons and holes in a semiconductor PN junction.

This PN junction, which forms the basic block of most electronic components, such as diodes and transistors, has the following specific operational uses when applied in electronics:

- In *diodes,* a PN device allows for the flow of electrons and, therefore, current in one direction. For example, a battery, with direct current, connected across a diode, allows the flow of current from positive to negative leads. When an alternating sinusoidal current is connected across the device, only the positive portion of the waveform is allowed to pass through. The negative portion of the waveform is blocked.
- In *transistors,* a wire secured in a sandwich of a PNP-junction device (formed by three doped junctions), when polarized or biased properly, controls the amount of direct current from the positive to the negative lead, thus forming the basis for current control, switching, and amplification, as shown in Fig. 3.3.
- In *light-emitting diodes* (LEDs), a controlled amount and type of doping material in a PN-type device, connected across a dc voltage source, converts the electric energy into visible light with differing frequencies and colors, such as white, red, blue, amber, and green.
- In *solar cells,* when a PN junction is exposed to sunshine, the device converts the stream of photons (packets of quanta) that form the visible light into electrons (the reverse of the LED function). This makes the device behave like a minute battery with a unique characteristic voltage and current depending on the material dopants and PN-junction physics.

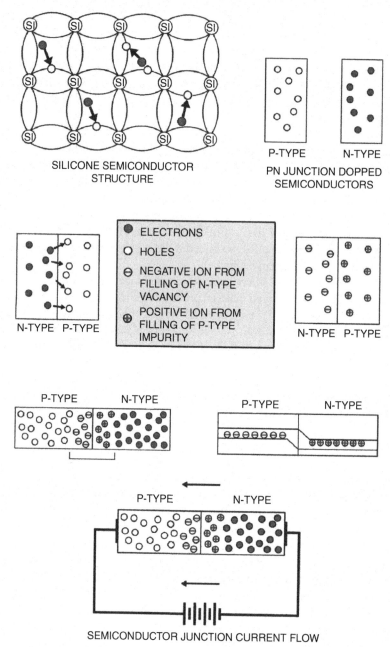

SILICONE SEMICONDUCTOR
STRUCTURE

PN JUNCTION DOPPED
SEMICONDUCTORS

P-TYPE   N-TYPE

ELECTRONS

HOLES

NEGATIVE ION FROM
FILLING OF N-TYPE
VACANCY

POSITIVE ION FROM
FILLING OF P-TYPE
IMPURITY

N-TYPE P-TYPE

N-TYPE P-TYPE

P-TYPE   N-TYPE

P-TYPE   N-TYPE

P-TYPE   N-TYPE

SEMICONDUCTOR JUNCTION CURRENT FLOW

Figure 3.2   Semiconductor depletion region formation.

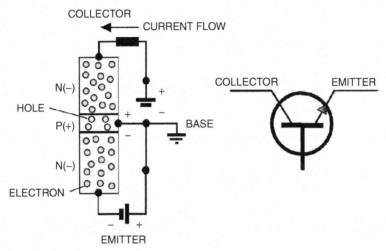

Figure 3.3   Junction showing holes and electron flow in an NPN transistor.

The bundles of photons that penetrate the PN junction randomly strike silicon atoms and give energy to the outer electrons. The acquired energy allows the outer electrons to break free from the atom. Thus, in the process, the photons are converted into electron movement or electric energy, as shown in Fig. 3.4.

It should be noted that the photovoltaic energy-conversion efficiency depends on the wavelength of the impinging light. Red light, which has a low frequency, produces insufficient energy, whereas blue light, which has more energy than needed to break the electrons, is wasted and dissipates as heat.

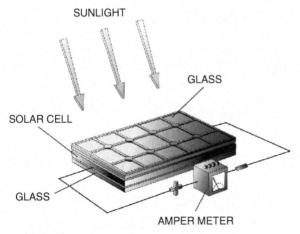

Figure 3.4   Photovoltaic module operational diagram.

Solar Cell Electronics

An electrostatic field is produced at a PN junction of a solar cell by impinging photons that create 0.5 V of potential energy, which is characteristic of most PN junctions and all solar cells. This miniscule potential resembles in function a small battery with positive and negative leads. These are then connected front to back in series to achieve higher voltages.

For example, 48 solar cell modules connected in series will result in 24 V of output. An increase in the number of solar cells within the solar cell bank will result in a higher voltage. This voltage is employed to operate inverters that convert the dc power into a more suitable ac form of electricity. In addition to the previously discussed PN-junction device, solar cells contain construction components, for mechanical assembly purposes, that are laid over a rigid or flexible holding platform or a substrate, such as a glass or a flexible film, and are interconnected by microthin, highly conductive metals. A typical solar panel used in photovoltaic power generation is constructed from a glass supportive plate that houses solar PV modules, each formed from several hundred interconnected PN devices. Depending on the requirements of a specific application, most solar panels manufactured today produce an output of 6, 12, 24, or 48 V dc. The amount of power produced by a solar panel, expressed in watts, represents an aggregate power output of all solar PN devices. For example, a manufacturer will express various panel characteristics by voltage, wattage, and surface area.

Solar Cell Manufacturing and Packaging Technologies

Solar cell technologies at present fall into three main categories: monocrystalline (single-crystal construction), polycrystalline (semicrystalline), and amorphous silicon thin film. A more recent undisclosed solar technology, known as *organic photovoltaics,* is also currently under commercial development. Each of these technologies has unique physical, chemical, manufacturing, and performance characteristics and is best suited for specialized applications. This section will discuss the basic manufacturing principles, and subsequent chapters will review the production and manufacturing process of several solar power cell technologies.

MONOCRYSTALLINE AND POLYCRYSTALLINE SILICON CELLS

The heart of most monocrystalline and polycrystalline PV solar cells is a crystalline silicon semiconductor. This semiconductor is manufactured by a silicon purification process, ingot fabrication, wafer slicing, etching, and doping, which finally forms a PNP junction that traps photons. This results in the release of electrons within the junction barrier, thereby creating a current flow.

The manufacture of a solar PV cell in itself is only one part of the process of manufacturing a whole solar panel product. To manufacture a functionally viable product that will last over 25 years requires that the materials be specially assembled, sealed, and packaged to protect the cells from natural climatic conditions and to provide proper conductivity, electrical insolation, and mechanical strength.

One of the most important materials used in sealing solar cells is the fluoropolymer Elvax manufactured by DuPont. This chemical compound is manufactured from ethylene vinyl acetate resin. It is then extruded into a film and used to encapsulate the silicon wafers that are sandwiched between tempered sheets of glass to form the solar panel. One special physical characteristic of the Elvax sealant is that it provides optical clarity while matching the refractive index of the glass and silicon, thereby reducing photon reflections. Figure 3.5 depicts various stages of the monocrystalline solar power manufacturing process.

Another chemical material manufactured by DuPont, Tedlar, is a polyvinyl fluoride film. It is extruded with polyester film and applied to the bottoms of silicon-based photovoltaic cells as a backplane that provides electrical insolation and protection against climatic and weathering conditions. Other manufacturing companies, such as Mitsui Chemical and Bridgestone, also manufacture comparable products to Tedlar that are used widely in the manufacture and assembly of photovoltaic panels.

Another important product manufactured by DuPont chemical is Solamet, a silver metallization paste used to conduct electric currents generated by individual solar silicon cells within each module. Solamet appears as micronwide conductors that are so thin that they do not block solar rays. A dielectric silicon-nitride product used in photovoltaic manufacturing creates a sputtering effect that enhances silicon, trapping sunlight more efficiently. Major fabricators of polycrystalline silicon are Dow Corning and General Electric in the United States and Shin-Etsu Handotai and Mitsubishi Material in Japan.

Because of the worldwide silicon shortage, the driving cost of solar cells has become a limiting factor for lowering the manufacturing costs. At present, silicon represents more than 50 percent of manufactured solar panels. To reduce silicon costs, at present, the industrial trend is to minimize the wafer thickness from 300 to 180 μm.

It should be noted that the process of ingot slicing results in 30 percent wasted material. To minimize this material waste, General Electric is currently developing a technology to cast wafers from silicon powder. Cast wafers thus far have proven to be somewhat thicker and less efficient than the conventional sliced silicon wafers. However, they can be manufactured faster and avoid the 30 percent waste produced by wafer sawing.

Thin-film solar cell technology   The core material of thin-film solar cell technology is amorphous silicon. This technology, instead of using solid polycrystalline silicon wafers, uses *silane gas,* which is a chemical compound that costs much less than crystalline silicon. Solar cell manufacturing involves a lithographic-like process in which the silane film is printed on flexible substrates such as stainless steel or Plexiglas material in a roll-to-roll process.

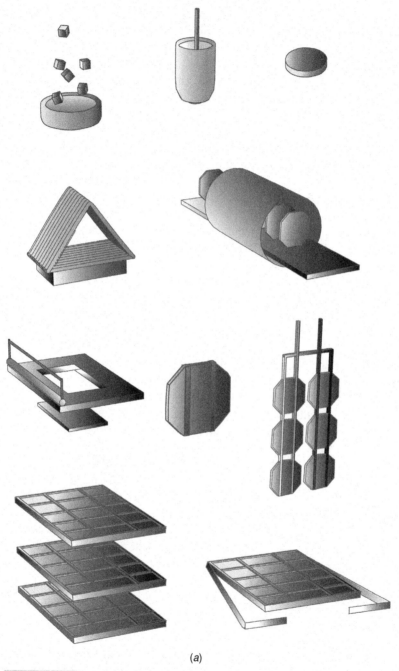

(a)

Figure 3.5   (a) Monocrystalline solar panel manufacturing process. (b) Solar panel frame assembly.

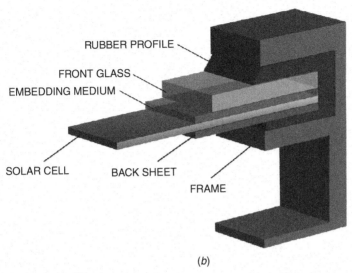

RUBBER PROFILE

FRONT GLASS
EMBEDDING MEDIUM

SOLAR CELL   BACK SHEET
                      FRAME

(b)

Figure 3.5   (*Continued*)

Silane (SiH$_4$) is also called *silicon tetrahydride, silicanel,* and *monosilane* and is a flammable gas with a repulsive odor. It does not occur in nature. Silane was first discovered in 1857 by F. Wohler and H. Buffy by reacting hydrochloric acid (HCl) with an aluminum-silicon alloy.

Silane is used principally in the industrial manufacture of semiconductor devices for the electronics industry. It is used for polycrystalline deposition, interconnection, masking, growth of epitaxial silicon, chemical vapor deposition of silicon diodes, and the production of amorphous silicon devices such as photosensitive films and solar cells.

Even though thin-film solar cells have only about 4 percent efficiency in converting sunlight to electricity when compared with the 15–20 percent efficiency of polysilicon products, they have an advantage in that they do not need direct sunlight to produce electricity, and as a result, they are capable of generating electric power over a longer period of time.

Polycrystalline PV solar cells   In the polycrystalline process, the silicon melt is cooled very slowly under controlled conditions. The silicon ingot produced in this process has crystalline regions that are separated by grain boundaries. After solar cell production, the gaps in the grain boundaries cause this type of cell to have a lower efficiency than the monocrystalline cells just described. Despite the efficiency disadvantage, a number of manufacturers favor polycrystalline PV cell production because of the lower manufacturing costs.

AMORPHOUS PV SOLAR CELLS

In the amorphous process, a thin wafer of silicon is deposited on a carrier material and doped in several process steps. An amorphous silicon film is produced by a method similar to the monocrystalline manufacturing process and is sandwiched between glass plates, which form the basic PV solar panel module.

Even though the process yields relatively inexpensive solar panel technology, it has the following disadvantages:

- Larger installation surface
- Lower conversion efficiency
- Inherent degradation during the initial months of operation, which continues over the lifespan of the PV panels

The main advantages of this technology are

- A relatively simple manufacturing process
- Lower manufacturing cost
- Lower production energy consumption

Thin-film cadmium telluride cell technology   In this process, thin crystalline layers of cadmium telluride (CdTe, of about 15 percent efficiency) or copper indium diselenide ($CuInSe_2$, of about 19 percent efficiency) are deposited on the surface of a carrier base. This process uses very little energy and is very economical. It has simple manufacturing processes and relatively high conversion efficiencies.

Gallium-arsenide cell technology   This manufacturing process yields a highly efficient PV cell, but as a result of the rarity of gallium deposits and the poisonous qualities of arsenic, the process is very expensive. The main feature of gallium-arsenide (GaAs) cells, in addition to their high efficiency, is that their output is relatively independent of the operating temperature, and thus these cells are used primarily in space programs.

Multijunction cell technology   This process employs two layers of solar cells, such as silicon (Si) and GaAs components, one on top of another to convert solar power with higher efficiency. The staggering of two layers allows the trapping of a wider bandwidth of solar rays, thus enhancing the solar cell solar energy-conversion efficiency.

Dye-Sensitized Solar Cells

Dye-sensitized solar cells (DSCs) are a class of solar cells that are formed by placing a semiconductor between a photo-sensitized anode and an electrolyte, which have photochemical properties that provide charge separation by absorbing solar energy. This class of cells is also referred to as *Grätzel cells,* the name of the inventor.

Even though these types of cells have lower conversion efficiency than the existing thin-film and solid-state semiconductor-based technologies, owing to the lower cost of materials and inexpensive production, in the near future they are expected to offer a price-performance ratio large enough to replace a significant amount of electricity generated by fossil fuels.

COMPARATIVE ANALYSIS

In order to compare differences between existing solid-state semiconductors and DSCs, it would be important to review the construction and operational characteristics of both technologies. As discussed earlier, conventional solid-state semiconductor solar cells are formed from two doped crystals, one doped with an impurity that forms a slightly negative bias (which is referred to as an N-type semiconductor and has a free electron) and the other doped with an impurity that provides a slight positive bias (which is referred to as a P-type semiconductor and lacks free electrons). When placed in contact to form a PN junction, some of the electrons in the N-type portion will flow into the P-type to fill in the gap, or electron hole.

Eventually, enough electrons flow across the boundary to equalize what is called the *Fermi levels* of the two materials. The resulting PN junction gives rise to the location where charge carriers are depleted or accumulated on each side of the interface. This transfer of electrons produces a potential barrier for electron flow that typically has a voltage of 0.6–0.7 V.

Under direct exposure to solar rays, photons in the sunlight strike the bound electrons in the P-type side of the semiconductor and elevate their energy, a process that is referred to as *photo-excitation*. Figure 3.6 shows a DSC epitaxial configuration.

HIGH-ENERGY CONDUCTION BAND

As a result of impact of photons, the electrons in the conduction band are prompted to move about the silicon, giving rise to electron flow, or electricity. When electrons flow

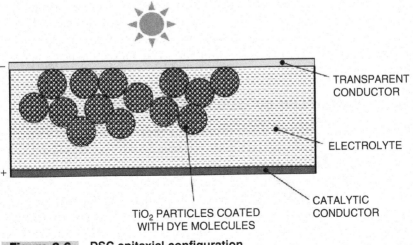

Figure 3.6   DSC epitaxial configuration.

out of the P-type and into the N-type material, they lose energy while moving or circling through an external circuit. Eventually, when they enter back into the P-type material, they recombine with the valence-band hole (at lower-energy potential) they left behind, therefore permitting sunlight energy to be converted into electric current.

Some of the disadvantages of the conventional solar power technology discussed earlier include a large bandgap difference in energy between the valence and conduction bands. The *bandgap* creates a situation in which only photons with that amount of energy can overcome the bandgap, the potential difference that contributed to producing a current.

Another shortcoming of conventional semiconductor-based solar power technology is that higher-energy photons, at the blue and violet ends of the solar spectrum, have more than enough energy to cross the bandgap. Even though a small fraction of this energy is transferred into the electrons, a much larger portion of it becomes wasted as heat, reducing cell efficiency owing to ohmic drop.

Another issue is that in order to have a reasonable chance of capturing a photon in the P-type layer, it has to be fairly thick, which, in turn, promotes the recombination of electrons and holes within the gap material before reaching the PN junction. These limitations result in an upper limit on the efficiency of silicon solar cells, which at present is about 12–15 percent for production-type solar cells and somewhat closer to 40 percent under ideal laboratory test conditions.

Besides these physical impediments, the most important disadvantage of semiconductor solar cells is their production cost because production requires a thick layer of silicon in order to have reasonable photon capture rates. The silicon necessary to accomplish this is becoming rare and thus is a very expensive commodity.

Some of the measures undertaken to reduce the use of semiconductor-based solar cells have resulted in the development of thin-film approaches, which, as discussed earlier, involve the use of P- and N-type semiconductor paste in a type of lithographic printing process. At present, owing to the loss of electrons and molecular decomposition, film-based solar cell technologies have had limited applications.

Another design approach that shows great promise for improvement in efficiency is the *multijunction* approach. This process involves stacking several layers of junctions of solar cells that capture a much wider spectrum of solar energy. However, at present, this type of cell is very expensive to produce and will be marketed mainly for large commercial applications.

BASIC PRINCIPLES OF DSCs

DSCs essentially separate the two functions provided by silicon in a conventional semiconductor type of solar cell. Under normal conditions, the silicon in a semiconductor cell both acts as the source of photoelectrons and also forms the potential barrier that allows for the separation of charges that creates current.

In contrast, in the DSC, the semiconductor is used for charge separation only; the photoelectrons are provided from a separate *photosensitive dye.* Furthermore, charge separation is not provided only by the semiconductor but also works in concert with a third element of the cell, an *electrolyte,* that is kept in contact with both the semiconductor and the dye.

Since the dye molecules are quite small in size, in order to capture a reasonable amount of incoming solar rays or sunlight effectively, the layer of dye molecules is made much thicker than the molecules themselves. To resolve this problem, a *nanomaterial* in the form of a scaffold is used to hold or bundle large numbers of dye molecules in a three-dimensional (3D) matrix. Bundles of large numbers of molecules thus provide a large cell surface area. At present, this scaffolding is fabricated from semiconductor material, which effectively serves double duty.

A DSC, as described earlier, has three primary parts. The top portion of the cell, termed the *anode,* is constructed from a glass coated with a layer of transparent material made of fluorine-doped tin oxide (SnO_2:F). On the back is a thin layer of *titanium dioxide* (TiO_2) that forms into a highly porous structure with an extremely large surface area. The TiO_2 plate, in turn, is immersed in a mixture of a photosensitive dye substance called *ruthenium-polypyridine* and a solvent. After immersing the film in the dye solution, a thin layer of the dye is covalently bonded to the surface of the TiO_2. Another layer of electrolyte, referred to as *iodide,* is spread thinly over the conductive sheets. Finally, a backing material, typically a thin layer of platinum metal, is placed as the lowest layer. On formation of these layers, the front and back parts then are joined and sealed together to prevent the electrolyte from leaking. Figure 3.7 illustrates the structural configuration of a DSC.

Although the preceding technology makes use of some costly materials, the amounts used are so small that they render the product quite inexpensive compared with the silicon needed for the fabrication of conventional semiconductor cells. For instance, TiO_2 is an inexpensive material used widely as a white paint base.

DSCs operate when sunlight enters the cell through the transparent SnO_2F, striking the dye on the surface of the TiO_2. Highly energized photons striking the dye are absorbed and create an excited state in the dye, which, in turn, injects electrons into the conduction band of the TiO_2 (the electrons are moved by a chemical diffusion gradient to the clear

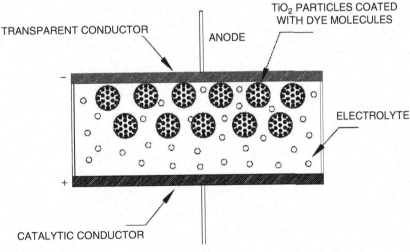

Figure 3.7   **A dye-sensitized solar cell.**

anode located on top). In the meantime, each dye molecule loses an electron, which could result in decomposition of the substance if another electron is not provided.

In the process, the dye strips one electron from iodide in the electrolyte below the TiO_2, oxidizing it into a substance called *triiodide*. This reaction takes place very quickly when compared with the time it takes for the injected electron to recombine with the oxidized dye molecule, thus preventing a recombination reaction that would cause the solar cell to short-circuit. The triiodide then recovers its missing electron by mechanically diffusing to the bottom of the cell, where the counterelectrode reintroduces the electrons after they flow through the external circuit load. Figure 3.8 shows a flexible nanotechnology solar PV module.

Power output measurement, is expressed as the product of short-circuit current I_{sc} and open voltage V_{oc}. Another solar cell efficiency measurement, defined as *quantum efficiency*, is used to compare the chance of one photon of impacted solar energy resulting in the creation of a single electron.

In quantum efficiency terms, DSCs are extremely efficient. Owing to their nanostructured configurations, there is a high chance that a photon will be absorbed. Therefore, they are considered highly effective in converting solar rays into electrons.

Most of the power conversion losses in DSC technology result from conduction losses in the TiO_2 and the clear electrode, as well as optical losses in the front electrode. Their overall quantum efficiency is estimated to be approximately 90 percent.

The maximum voltage generated by DSCs is simply the difference between the Fermi level of the TiO_2 and the potential of the dye electrolyte, which is about 0.7 V total (V_{oc}). This is slightly higher than semiconductor-based solar cells, which have a maximum voltage of about 0.6 V.

Even though DSCs are highly efficient in turning photons into electrons, it is only those electrons with enough energy to cross the TiO_2 bandgap that result in current

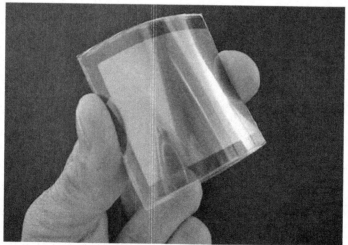

Figure 3.8   **A nanotechnology solar PV cell.** *Photo courtesy of Nano Solar.*

being produced. Also, since the DSC bandgap is slightly larger than it is in silicon, fewer photons in sunlight become usable for generating solar power.

Furthermore, the electrolyte in DSCs limits the speed at which the dye molecules can regain their electrons and become available for a renewed cycle of photo-excitation. As a result of these factors, the maximum current output limit for a DSC 20 mA/cm^2, compared with 35 mA/cm^2 generated by silicon-based solar cells. The preceding, in turn, is translated into a conversion efficiency of about 11 percent. Semiconductor-based solar cells, on the other hand, operate at between 12 and 15 percent efficiency. In comparison, flexible thin-film cells operate at a maximum of 8 percent efficiency.

Another approach used to enhance the efficiency of DSCs involves the process of injecting an electron directly into the TiO_2, where the electron is boosted within the original crystal. In comparison, the injection process used in the DSC does not introduce a hole into the TiO_2, only an extra electron. Although, in doing so, electrons have a better possibility of recombining when back in the dye, the probability that this will occur is so low that the rate of electron hole recombination efficiency becomes insignificant.

In view of low loss characteristics, DSCs can perform more efficiently under cloudy skies, whereas traditional designs would cut out power production at lower limits of illumination. This operational characteristic of DSCs renders them ideal for indoor applications.

A significant disadvantage of DSC technology is the use of a liquid electrolyte, which has stability problems relating to temperature. At low temperatures, the electrolyte can freeze, ending power production and potentially leading to physical damage. Higher temperatures cause the liquid to expand, making sealing of the panels very difficult.

FUTURE ADVANCEMENTS IN DSC TECHNOLOGY

The early, experimental versions of DSCs had a narrow bandwidth that functioned in the high-frequency ultraviolet (UV) and blue end of the solar spectrum. Subsequently, owing to the use of an improved dye electrolyte, a wider response to the low-frequency red and infrared range was achieved.

At present, with the use of a special dye with a deep brown-black color, referred to as *black dye,* the conversion rate of photons into electrons has improved significantly to almost 90 percent, with only a 10 percent loss, attributed to optics and the top electrode.

A critically significant characteristic of the black dye is that over millions of cycles of simulated exposure to solar irradiance, the output efficiency of DSCs is outstanding, with no discernible decrease. In recent tests using an improved electrolyte, the thermal performance of the solar cell has been pushed to 60°C with remarkable conversion efficiency. An experiment conducted recently in New Zealand used a wide variety of organic dyes, such as porphyrin, a natural hemoprotein present in hemoglobin, and chlorophyll, to achieve an efficiency of 7.1 percent.

At present, DSC technology is still in its infancy. It is expected that in the near future, with the use of newer dye electrolytes and quantum dots, there will be significant improvement in efficiency gains.

Multijunction PV Cells

Multijunction solar cells were first developed and deployed for satellite power applications, where the high cost was offset by the net savings offered by the higher efficiency. Multijunction PV cells are a special class of solar cells that are fabricated with multiple levels of stacked thin-film semiconductor PN junctions. Their production technique is referred to as *molecular-beam epitaxy* or the *metal-organic vapor-phase process*. Each type of semiconductor is designed with a characteristic valance bandgap that allows for the absorption of a certain bandwidth or spectrum of solar electromagnetic radiation.

In a single-layered or bandgap solar cell, valance-band efficiency is limited owing to the inability of the PN junction to absorb a broad range of electromagnetic rays or photons in the solar spectrum. Photons below the bandgap in the blue spectrum either pass through the cell or, owing to molecular agitation, are converted within the material into heat. Energy in photons above the bandgap in the red spectrum are also lost because only the energy necessary to generate the electron-hole pair is used. The remaining energy is converted into heat. Multijunction solar cells, which have multiple layers and therefore junctions with several bandgaps, allow different portions of the solar spectrum to be converted by each junction at greater efficiency. Figure 3.9 shows the epitaxial layers of a four-junction solar cell.

MULTIJUNCTION SOLAR CELL CONSTRUCTION

Multijunction PV cells use many layers of film deposition, or epitaxy. By using differing alloys within the eighth column of the periodic table, the semiconductors, the bandgap of each layer is tuned to absorb a specific band of solar electromagnetic radiation. The efficiency of multijunction solar cells is achieved by the precise alignment of respective superimposed bandgaps.

To achieve maximum output efficiency, all epitaxial layers that are in series are optically aligned from top to bottom such that the first junction receives the entire spectrum. Photons above the bandgap of the first junction are absorbed in the first layer (red-spectrum photons). Green and yellow photons below, which pass through the first layer, are absorbed by the second bandgap, and finally, the third bandgap absorbs the high-energy blue-spectrum photons.

Most commercial cells use a tandem P-N electrical connection, which allows series cumulative or composite current output through positive and negative terminals. An inherent design constraint of tandem-cell configuration is that in series connection, the current through each junction becomes limited by the ohmic resistance of the material, and since the point current of each junction is not the same, the efficiency of the cell is reduced.

MULTIJUNCTION SOLAR CELL MATERIALS

In general, most multijunction cells are categorized by the substrate used for cell manufacture. Depending on the bandgap characteristics, multijunction solar cell substrates are constructed from various epitaxial layers that make use of different combinations

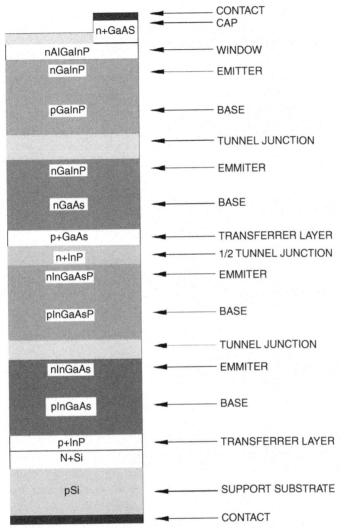

Figure 3.9 Multijunction solar cell epitaxial layers.

of semiconductors, metals, and rare earth metals alloys such as germanium, gallium-arsenide, and indium-phosphide.

Gallium arsenide substrate Twin-junction cells with indium-gallium-phosphide (InGsP) and gallium-arsenide (GaAs) are constructed on GaAs wafers. Alloys of $In_{0.5}Ga_{0.5}P$ through $In_{0.53}Ga_{0.47}P$ are used as high-bandgap alloys. This alloy range provides bandgaps with voltages ranging from 1.92 to 1.87 eV. GaAs, on the other hand, allows for the fabrication of junctions with a lower bandgap of 1.42 eV. Since the solar spectrum has a considerable quantity of photons in its lower regions than does the GaAs bandgap, a significant portion of the energy is lost as heat, limiting the efficiency of the GaAs substrate cells.

Germanium substrate Triple-junction cells consisting of indium-gallium-phosphide, gallium-arsenide or indium-gallium-arsenide, and germanium are fabricated on germanium wafers. Much like GaAs, owing to the large bandgap difference between GaAs (1.42 eV) and Ge (0.66 eV), the current match becomes very poor, and as a result, current throughput suffers limited output efficiency. At present, efficiencies for InGaP, GaAs, and Ge cells are within the 25–32 percent range. In a recent laboratory test of cells, using additional junctions between the GaAs and Ge junction produced efficiencies that exceeded 40 percent.

Indium-phosphide substrate Indium-phosphide is also used as a substrate to fabricate cells with bandgaps between 1.35 and 0.74 eV. Indium-phosphide has a bandgap of 1.35 eV. Indium-gallium-arsenide ($In_{0.53}Ga_{0.47}As$), lattice matched to indium-phosphide, has a bandgap of 0.74 eV. An alloy composed of four elements, indium, gallium-arsenide, and phosphide, has resulted in the fabrication of optically matched lattices that perform with greater efficiency.

Recently, multijunction cell efficiencies have been improved through the use of concentrator lenses. This has resulted in significant improvements in solar energy conversion and price reductions that have made the technology competitive with silicon flat-panel arrays.

Polymer Solar Cells

Polymer solar cells, also referred to as *plastic cells,* are a relatively new technology that coverts solar energy to electricity through the use of polymer materials. This class of solar cells, unlike conventional semiconductors, is based on PV system technologies (described earlier). Neither silicon nor any alloy material is used in their fabrication.

At present, polymer solar cells are being researched by a number of universities, national laboratories, and several companies around the world. Compared with silicon-based devices, polymer solar cells are lightweight, biodegradable, and inexpensive to fabricate. The use of polymer substances renders the cells flexible, facilitating greater design possibilities and diverse applications.

Because fullerene, a plastic-based material, is inexpensive and readily available, these solar cells are extremely easy to mass produce at a cost of approximately one-third that of traditional silicon solar cell technology. Some potential uses of polymer solar cells include applications in a wide variety of commercial products, including small televisions, cell phones, and toys.

BIONANOGENERATORS

Bionanogenerators are biologic cells that function like a fuel cell on a nanoscale, molecular level. Bionanocells are essentially electrochemical devices that function like galvanic cells. They use blood glucose, drawn from living cells, as a reactant or fuel. This is similar to how the body generates energy from food. The bionanogeneration

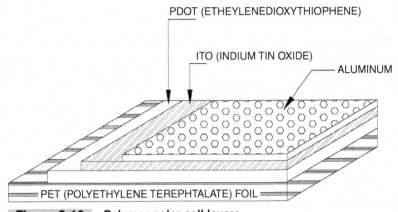

PDOT (ETHEYLENEDIOXYTHIOPHENE)

ITO (INDIUM TIN OXIDE)

ALUMINUM

PET (POLYETHYLENE TEREPHTALATE) FOIL

Figure 3.10   Polymer solar cell layers.

process is achieved by means of special enzymes that strip electrons from glucose, freeing them to generate electric current, much as in fuel cells.

It is estimated that the average person's body theoretically could generate 100 W of electricity using a bionanogenerator. The electricity generated by bionanoprocesses perhaps someday could power body-embedded devices such as pacemakers and blood circulation pumps. It is also suggested that the future development of bionanogenerator robots, fueled by glucose, could be embedded to perform various bodily functions. At present, research conducted on bionanogenerators is still experimental, but progress in the field holds significant prospects for advancing the technology. Figure 3.10 shows polymer solar cell layers.

Concentrators

Concentrators are lenses or reflectors that focus sunlight onto solar cell modules. Fresnel lenses, which have concentration ratios of 10–500×, are mostly made of inexpensive plastic materials and engineered with refracting features that direct sunlight onto the small, narrow PN-junction area of cells. Module efficiencies of most PV cells, discussed earlier, normally range from 10 to 18 percent, whereas concentrator-type solar cell technology efficiencies can exceed 30 percent.

In this technology, reflectors are used to increase power output by either increasing the intensity of light on the module or extending the length of time that sunlight falls on the module. The main disadvantage of concentrators is their inability to focus scattered light, which limits their use to areas such as deserts.

Depending on the size of the mounting surface, solar panels are secured on tilted structures called *stanchions*. Solar panels installed in the northern hemisphere are mounted facing south, with stanchions tilted to a specific angle. In the southern hemisphere, solar panels are installed facing north.

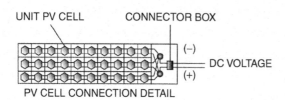

UNIT PV CELL   CONNECTOR BOX

PV CELL CONNECTION DETAIL

Figure 3.11   Internal wiring of a PV solar cell.

Solar Panel Arrays

Serial or parallel interconnections in solar panels are called *solar panel arrays* (SPAs). Generally, a series of SPAs is configured to produce a specific voltage potential and collective power production capacity to meet the demand requirements of a project.

SPAs feature a series of interconnected positive (+) and negative (−) outputs of solar panels in a serial or parallel arrangement, providing a required dc voltage to an inverter. Figure 3.11 shows the internal wiring of a solar power cell.

PV solar array installation in the vicinity of trees and elevated structures that may cast a shadow on the panels should be avoided. The geographic location of the project site and seasonal changes are also significant factors that must be taken into consideration.

In order to account for average daily solar exposure time, design engineers refer to world sunlight exposure maps. Each area is assigned an *area exposure-time factor,* which, depending on the location, may vary from 2 to 6 hours. A typical example for calculating daily watthours (Wh) for an SPA consisting of 10 modules with a power rating of 75 W in an area with a multiplier of 5 would be $(10 \times 75 \text{ W}) \times 5$ h, which equals 3750 Wh of average daily power.

Solar Power System Components

PV modules represent only the basic element of a solar power system. They work in conjunction with complementary components, such as batteries, inverters, and transformers. Power distribution panels and metering complete the energy-conversion process.

STORAGE BATTERIES

As mentioned previously, solar cells are devices that merely convert solar energy into a dc voltage. Solar cells do not store energy. To store energy beyond daylight, the dc voltage is used to charge an appropriate set of batteries.

The reserve capacity of batteries is referred to as the *system autonomy*. This varies according to the requirements of specific applications. Batteries in applications that require autonomy form a critical component of a solar power system. Battery banks in PV applications are designed to operate at deep-cycle discharge rates and generally are maintenance-free.

The amount of required autonomy time depends on the specific application. Circuit loads, such as telecommunications and remote telemetry stations, may require 2 weeks of autonomy, whereas a residential unit may require no more than 12 hours. Batteries must be selected properly to store sufficient energy for the daily demand. When calculating battery ampere-hours and storage capacity, additional derating factors, such as cloudy and sunless conditions, must be taken into consideration.

In solar power cogeneration systems, when using storage batteries for electrical energy storage, fluctuations in the dc power produced by PV systems caused by variations in solar irradiance are regulated by electronic devices referred to as *charge regulators*. Charge regulators are placed between the PV output and the battery banks to regulate the amount of electric charge current, which protects batteries from overcharging.

INVERTERS

As described earlier, PV solar panels generate direct current, which can be used by only a limited number of devices. Most residential, commercial, and industrial devices and appliances are designed to work with alternating current. Inverters are devices that convert direct current into alternating current. Although inverters usually are designed for specific applications, the basic conversion principles remain the same. Essentially, the inversion process consists of the following: In the *wave-formation process,* direct current characterized by a continuous potential of positive and negative references (bias) is essentially chopped into equidistant segments that are then processed through circuitry that alternately eliminates positive and negative portions of the chopped pattern, which results in a waveform pattern called a *squarewave*. Figure 3.12 shows a single-line diagram of an inverter.

Waveshaping or filtration process   A squarewave, when analyzed mathematically (by Fourier series analysis), consists of a combination of a very large number of sinusoidal (alternating) wave patterns called *harmonics*. Each wave harmonic has a distinct number of cycles (rise-and-fall patterns within a time period). An electronic device referred to as a *choke* (magnetic coils) filters or passes through 60-cycle harmonics, which form the basis of sinusoidal current. Solid-state inverters use a highly efficient conversion technique known as *envelope construction*. Direct current is sliced into fine sections, which are then converted into a progressive rising (positive) and falling (negative) sinusoidal 60-cycle waveform pattern. This chopped sinusoidal wave is passed through a series of electronic filters that produce an output current that has a smooth sinusoidal curvature.

Protective relaying systems   In general, most inverters used in PV applications are built from sensitive solid-state electronic devices that are very susceptible to external stray spikes, load short circuits, and overload voltage and currents. To protect the equipment from harm, inverters incorporate a number of electronic circuitry configurations:

- Synchronization relay
- Undervoltage relay

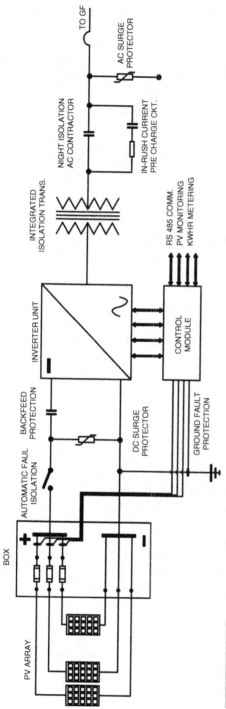

Figure 3.12 **Inverter single-line diagram.** *Courtesy of SatCon, Canada.*

■ Overcurrent relay
■ Ground trip or overcurrent relay
■ Overvoltage relay
■ Overfrequency relay
■ Underfrequency relay

Most inverters designed for PV applications are designed to allow simultaneous paralleling of multiple units. For instance, to support a 60-kW load, outputs of three 20-kW inverters may be connected in parallel. Depending on the power-system requirements, inverters can produce single- or three-phase power at any required voltage or current capacity. Standard outputs available are single-phase 120 V ac and three-phase 120/208 and 277/480 V ac. In some instances, step-up transformers are used to convert the output of 120/208-V ac inverters to higher voltages.

Input and output power distribution   To protect inverters from stray spikes resulting from lightning or other such high-energy events, dc inputs from PV arrays are protected by fuses housed in junction boxes located in close proximity to the inverters. Additionally, inverter dc input ports are protected by various types of semiconductor devices that clip excessively high-voltage spikes resulting from lightning activity.

To prevent damage resulting from voltage reversal, each positive (+) output lead within a PV cell is connected to a rectifier, a unidirectional (forward-biased) element. AC output power from inverters is connected to the loads by means of electronic or magnetic circuit breakers. These serve to protect the unit from external overcurrent and short circuits.

Grid-connected inverters   Earlier, I described the general function of inverters. Here, I will review their interconnection to the grid, which requires a thorough understanding of safety regulations that are mandated by various state agencies. Essentially, the goal of design safety standards for inverters used in grid-connected systems, whether they are deployed in PV, wind turbine, fuel cell, or any other type of power cogeneration system, is to have one unified set of guidelines and standards for the entire country. Standard regulations for manufacturing inverters address such issues as performance characteristics and grid-connectivity practices and are recommended by a number of national test laboratories and regulatory agencies.

Underwriters Laboratories Standards   For product safety, the industry in the United States has worked with Underwriters Laboratories (UL) to develop *UL1741, Standard for Static Inverter and Charge Controller for Use in Independent Power Systems,* which has become the safety standard for inverters used in the United States. Standard UL1741 covers many aspects of inverter design, including enclosures, printed circuit board configuration, interconnectivity requirements such as the amount of direct current the inverters can inject into the grid, total harmonic distortion (THD) of the output current, inverter reaction to utility voltage spikes and variations, reset and recovery from abnormal conditions, and reaction to islanding conditions when the utility power is disconnected.

Islanding is a condition that occurs when the inverter continues to produce power during a utility outage. Under such conditions, the power produced by a PV system becomes a safety hazard to utility workers, who could be exposed inadvertently to hazardous electric currents. Because of this, inverters are required to include anti-islanding control circuitry to cut the power to the inverter and disconnect it from the grid network.

Anti-islanding also prevents the inverter output power from getting out of phase with the grid when the automatic safety interrupter reconnects the inverter to the grid (which could result in high-voltage spikes that can cause damage to conversion and utility equipment). Figures 3.13 and 3.14 show the electronics of a Solectria Renewables inverter and a typical installation.

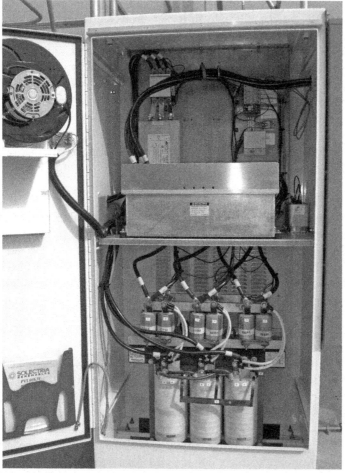

Figure 3.13   **Internal view of inverter electronics.** *Photo courtesy of Solectria Renewables.*

Figure 3.14   **External view of inverter electronics.** *Photo courtesy of Solectria Renewables.*

Institute of Electrical and Electronics Engineers   The Institute of Electrical and Electronics Engineers (IEEE) provides suggestions for customers and utilities alike regarding the control of harmonic power and voltage flicker, which occur frequently on utility buses, in its IEEE 929 guideline (not a standard), *Recommended Practice for Utility Interface of Photovoltaic (PV) Systems.* Excessive harmonic power flow and power fluctuation from utility buses can damage a customer's equipment. Therefore, a number of states, including California, Delaware, New York, and Ohio, specifically require that inverters be designed to operate under abnormal utility power conditions.

Power-limit conditions   The maximum size of a PV power cogeneration system is subject to limitations imposed by various states. Essentially, most utilities are concerned about large sources of private grid-connected power generation because most distribution systems are designed for unidirectional power flow. The addition of a large power cogeneration system, on the other hand, creates bidirectional current flow conditions on the grid, which in some instances can diminish utility network reliability. However, it is well known that, in practice, small amounts of cogenerated power do not usually create a grid disturbance significant enough to be a cause for concern. To regulate the maximum size of a cogeneration system, a number of states have set various limits and caps for systems that generate in excess of 100 kW of power.

UTILITY-SIDE DISCONNECTS AND ISOLATION TRANSFORMERS

In some states, such as California, Delaware, Florida, New Hampshire, Ohio, and Virginia, utility regulators require that visible and accessible disconnect switches be installed outside for grid service isolation. It should be noted that several states, including California, require that customers open the disconnect switches once every 4 years to check that the inverters are performing the required anti-islanding.

In other states, such as New Mexico and New York, grid-isolation transformers are required to reduce the noise created by private customers that could be superimposed on the grid. This requirement, however, is not a regulation that is mandated by the UL or the Federal Communication Commission (FCC).

PV power cogeneration capacity In order to protect utility companies' norms of operation, a number of states have imposed a cap on the maximum amount of power that can be generated by PV systems. For example, New Hampshire limits the maximum to 0.05 percent and Colorado to 1 percent of the monthly grid network peak demand.

Inverter capability to withstand surges In most instances, power distribution is undertaken through a network of overhead lines that are constantly exposed to climatic disturbances, such as lightning, that result in power surges. Additional power surges also could result from switching capacitor banks used for power factor correction, power conversion equipment, and during load shedding and switching. The resulting power surges, if not clamped, could seriously damage inverter equipment by breaking down conductor insulation and electronic devices.

To prevent damage caused by utility spikes, the IEEE has developed nationally recommended guidelines for inverter manufacturers to provide appropriate surge protection. A series of tests devised to verify IEEE recommendations for surge immunity are performed by the UL as part of equipment approval.

PV system testing and maintenance log Some states, including California, Vermont, and Texas, require that comprehensive commissioning testing be performed on PV system integrators to certify that the system is operating in accordance with expected design and performance conditions. It is interesting to note that for PV systems installed in the state of Texas, a log must be maintained of all maintenance performed.

Examples of UL1741 inverter specification The following is an example of a UL1741-approved inverter manufactured by SatCon, Canada. An optional combiner box, which includes a set of special ceramic overcurrent protection fuses, provides accumulated dc output to the inverter. At its dc input, the inverter is equipped with an automatic current fault isolation circuit, a dc surge protector, and a dc backfeed protection interrupter. In addition to the preceding, the inverter has special electronic circuitry that constantly monitors ground faults and provides instant fault isolation. On conversion of direct current to alternating current, the internal electronics of the inverter provide precise voltage and frequency synchronization with the grid.

An integrated isolation transformer within the inverter provides complete noise isolation and filtering of the ac output power. A night isolation ac contactor disconnects the inverter at night or during heavy cloud conditions. The output of the inverter also includes an ac surge isolator and a manual circuit breaker that can disconnect the equipment from the grid.

A microprocessor-based control system within the inverter includes, in addition to waveform envelope construction and filtering algorithms, a number of program subsets that perform anti-islanding, voltage, and frequency control.

As an optional feature, the inverter also can provide data communication by means of an RS 485 interface. This RS 485 interface can transmit equipment operational and PV measurement parameters such as PV output power, voltage, current, and totalized kilowatthour metering data for remote monitoring and display.

Crystalline, Amorphous, Thin-Film, and Sun-Tracker Technologies

This section is intended to familiarize readers with the four fundamental classes of solar power PV systems, namely, monosilicon wafer, amorphous silicon, thin-film, and concentrator-type technologies. The basic physical and functional properties, manufacturing processes, and specific performance parameters of these technologies will be reviewed. In addition, some unique case studies will provide a more profound understanding of the applications of these technologies.

Each of the technologies covered here has been developed and designed for a specific use and has unique applicative advantages and performance profiles. It should be noted that all the technologies presented here can be applied in a mixed-use fashion, each meeting special design criteria.

CRYSTALLINE PV SOLAR MODULE PRODUCTION

This section will review the production and manufacturing process cycle of a crystalline-type PV solar module. The product manufacturing process presented is specific to SolarWorld Industries. However, it is representative of the general manufacturing cycle for the monosilicon class of commercial solar power modules presently offered by a large majority of manufacturers.

The manufacture of monocrystalline PV cells starts with silicon crystals, which are found abundantly in nature in the form of flint stone. The word *silicon* is derived from the Latin *silex,* meaning "flint stone," which is an amorphous substance found in nature and consisting of one part silicon and two parts oxygen (SiO_2). Silicon (Si) was first produced in 1823 by Berzelius when he separated the naturally occurring ferrous silica (SiF_4) by heat exposure with potassium metal. Commercial production of silicon commenced in 1902 and resulted in an iron-silicon alloy with an approximate weight of 25 percent iron that was used in steel production as an effective deoxidant. At present, more than 1 million tons of metallurgical-grade 99 percent pure silicon is used by the

Figure 3.15   Silicon crystals.

steel industry. Approximately 60 percent of the referenced silicon is used in metallurgy, 35 percent in the production of silicones, and approximately 5 percent in the production of semiconductor-grade silicon.

In general, common impurities found in silicon are iron (Fe), aluminium (Al), magnesium (Mg), and calcium (Ca). The purest grade of silicon used in semiconductor applications contains about 1 ppb contamination. The purification of silicon involves several different types of complex refining technologies, such as chemical vapor deposition, isotopic enrichment, and a crystallization process. Figure 3.15 shows silicon crystals prior to the ingot manufacturing process.

Chemical vapor deposition   One of the early silicon-refining processes, known as *chemical vapor deposition,* produced a high grade of metallurgical silicon and consisted of a chemical reaction of silicon tetrachloride ($SiCl_4$) and zinc (Zn) under high-temperature vaporization conditions, yielding pure silicon through the following chemical reaction:

$$SiCl_4 + 2Zn \rightarrow Si + 2ZnCl_2$$

The main problem with this process was that $SiCl_4$ always contained boron chloride (BCl_3) when combined with zinc-produced boron, which is a serious contaminant. In 1943, a chemical vapor deposition was developed that involved replacement of the zinc with hydrogen (H), giving rise to pure silicon, because hydrogen, unlike zinc, does not reduce the boron chloride to boron. Further refinement involved replacement of silicon tetrachloride with trichlorosilane ($SiHCl_3$), which is readily reduced to silicon. Figure 3.16 shows a Czochralski silicon crystallization furnace.

Czochralski crystal growth   In 1916, a Polish metallurgist, Jan Czochralski, developed a technique to produce silicon crystals that bears his name. The crystallization

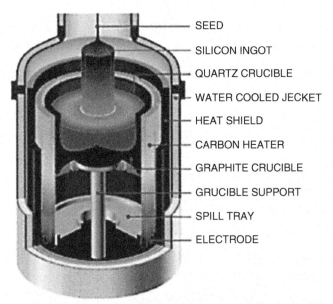

SEED

SILICON INGOT

QUARTZ CRUCIBLE

WATER COOLED JECKET

HEAT SHIELD

CARBON HEATER

GRAPHITE CRUCIBLE

GRUCIBLE SUPPORT

SPILL TRAY

ELECTRODE

Figure 3.16   **Czochralski crystallization furnace.**

process involves inserting a metal whisker into molten silicon and pulling it out with increasing velocity. This allows for the formation of a pure crystal around the wire and thus is a successful method of growing single crystals. The process was further enhanced by attaching a small silicon crystal seed to the wire rod. Further production efficiency was gained by attaching the seed to a rotatable and vertically movable spindle. Incidentally, the same crystallization apparatus is also equipped with special doping ports where P- or N-type dopants are introduced into the crystal for generation of PN- or NP-junction-type crystals used in the construction of NPN or PNP transistors, diodes, LEDs, solar cells, and virtually all large-scale, high-density integrated circuitry used in electronic technologies.

The chemical vaporization and crystallization process described here is energy-intensive and requires a considerable amount of electric power. To produce purified silicon ingots at a reasonable price, in general, silicon ingot production plants are located within the vicinity of major hydroelectric power plants, which produce an abundance of low-cost hydroelectric power. Ingots produced from this process are either circular or square in form and are cleaned, polished, and distributed to various semiconductor-manufacturing organizations. Figure 3.17 shows silicon ingot cylinders inspection.

Solar cell production   The first manufacturing step in the production of PV modules involves incoming ingot inspection, wafer cleaning, and quality control. On completion of the incoming process, in a clean-room environment, the ingots are sliced into 1-mm-thick wafers, and both surfaces are polished, etched, and diffused to form a PN junction. After being coated with antireflective film, the cells are printed with a metal-filled paste and fired at high temperature. Each individual cell is then tested for

Figure 3.17   A formed silicon ingot cylinder ready for inspection.

100 percent functionality and is made ready for module assembly. Figure 3.18 shows silicon ingot cylinders in a production chamber.

PV module production   The PV module production process involves robotics and automatic controls in which a series of robots assembles the solar cells step-by-step, laying the modules, soldering the cells in a predetermined pattern, and then laminating and framing the assembly as a finished product. On completion of framing, each PV module is tested under artificial insolation conditions, and the results are permanently logged and serialized. The last step of production involves a secondary module test, cleaning, packaging, and crating. In general, the efficiency of the PV modules produced by this technique ranges from 15 to 18 percent.

PV module life span and recycling   To extend the life span of PV solar modules, PV cell assemblies are laminated between two layers of protective covering. In general, the top protective cover is constructed from 1/4- to 5/8-in tempered glass, and the lower protective cover is constructed from either tempered glass or a hard plastic material. A polyurethane membrane is used as a gluing membrane that holds the sandwiched PV assembly together. In addition to acting as the adhesive agent, the membrane hermetically seals the upper and lower covers, preventing water penetration or oxidation. As a result of hermetic sealing, silicon-based PV modules are able to withstand exposure to harsh atmospheric and climatic conditions.

Even though the life span of silicon-based PV modules is guaranteed for a period of at least 20 years, in practice, it is expected that the natural life span of the modules will exceed 45 years without significant degradation.

Figure 3.18   Silicon ingot production chamber. *Photo courtesy of SolarWorld.*

In order to minimize environmental pollution, SolarWorld has adopted a material-recovery process whereby obsolete, damaged, or old PV modules (including the aluminium framing, tempered glass, and silicon wafers) are fully recycled and reused to produce new PV solar modules. Figure 3.19 shows a robotic arm used in the lamination of solar panels. Figure 3.20 shows a monosilicon solar cell inspection station.

Figure 3.19 A robotic solar power laminator. *Photo courtesy of MARTIFER.*

Figure 3.20 A solar panel inspection station. *Photo courtesy of MARTIFER.*

CONCENTRATOR TECHNOLOGIES

Concentrator-type solar technologies are a class of PV systems that deploy a number of lenses to concentrate and focus solar energy on semiconductor material used in the manufacture of conventional PV solar cells.

The advantage of these types of technologies is that for a comparable surface area of silicon wafer, it becomes possible to harvest considerably more solar energy. Since silicon wafers used in the manufacture of PV systems represent a substantial portion of the product cost, by using relatively inexpensive magnifying concentrator lenses, it is possible to achieve a higher-efficiency product at a lower cost than conventional PV power systems.

One of the most efficient solar power technologies available commercially for large-scale power production is a product manufactured by Amonix. This concentrator technology has been specifically developed for ground installation only and is suitable only for solar farm–type power cogeneration. The product efficiency of this unique PV solar power concentrator technology, under field test conditions in numerous applications in the United States (determined by over half a decade of testing by the Department of Energy, Arizona Public Service, Southern California Edison, and the University of Nevada, Las Vegas), has exceeded 26 percent, nearly twice that of comparable conventional solar power systems. At present, Amonix is in the process of developing a multijunction concentrating cell that will augment solar power energy production efficiency to 36 percent.

Why concentration?   Before PV systems can provide a substantial part of the world's need for electric energy, there needs to be a large reduction in their cost. Studies conducted by the Department of Energy (DOE), the Electrical Power Research Institute (EPRI), and others show that concentrating solar energy systems eventually can achieve lower costs than conventional PV power systems. The lower cost results from the following.

Less Expensive Material   Because the semiconductor material for solar cells is a major cost element of all PV systems, one approach to cost reduction is to reduce the required cell area by concentrating a relatively large area of solar insolation onto a relatively small solar cell. The solar power concentrator technology developed by Amonix deploys low-cost Fresnel lenses to focus sun power onto the cells, which reduces the required cell area and material by nearly 250 times. A 6-in wafer used in a flat-plate PV system will produce about 2.5 W, but will produce 1000 W in the Amonix system.

Higher Efficiency   Concentrating PV cells achieve higher efficiencies than do nonconcentrating PV cells. Flat-plate silicon cells have efficiencies in the range of 8–15 percent, whereas the Amonix concentrating silicon cell has an efficiency of 26 percent. Concentrating multijunction cells presently under development are expected to achieve efficiencies greater than 34 percent.

Further increased annual energy production is achieved by the incorporation of a two-axis sun-tracking system. All high-concentration system technologies require a sun-tracking control system. A computerized tracking system periodically adjusts the

Figure 3.21   A 54-kW MegaConcentrator two-axis hydraulic tracking system.
Photo courtesy of Amonix.

MegaConcentrator platform to optimize the insolation angle that results in additional annual energy generation. The average annual energy for 19 different fixed flat-plate installations under test conditions in Phoenix, Arizona, ranged from 1000 to 1500 kWh per rated kilowatt. An equivalent power-rated MegaConcentrator manufactured by Amonix generated in excess of 1900–2000 kWh per rated kilowatt. Figure 3.21 shows an Amonix 54-kW MegaConcentrator module two-axis solar tracking system.

System description   The solar PV concentrator technology described here is a proprietary product of the Amonix Corporation, located in Torrance, California. In essence, the solar power system referred to as a *MegaConcentrator* consists of six specific components that have resulted in a reduction in product cost. Figure 3.22 shows the Amonix MegaConcentrator hydraulic arm assembly.

MegaModule subsystem   The MegaModule concentrates the sun's energy on a solar cell that converts it into electric energy. It consists of Fresnel lenses, solar cells, and a support structure. Each system consists of five to seven MegaModules.

The drive subsystem rotates the MegaModules in azimuth and elevation to track the sun. The drive system consists of a foundation, pedestal, rotating bearing head, hydraulic actuators, and a torque tube.

Figure 3.22   Amonix MegaConcentrator hydraulic arm assembly. *Photo courtesy of Amonix.*

A hydraulic subsystem applies pressure to one side of the actuators to move the torque tube and MegaModules in elevation and azimuth to keep the system pointing at the sun. The hydraulic system consists of hydraulic valves, an accumulator, a pump, a reservoir, and pressure sensors. A tracking-control subsystem monitors sensors on the system, calculates the required movement for the operation selected, and applies signals to the hydraulic valves to move the system to the selected position. The selected position could be to track the sun, move to a night stow position, move to a wind stow position, or move to a maintenance position.

An ac/dc control subsystem combines the dc power, converts it to ac power, and interfaces with the ac grid. It consists of dc fuses, circuit breakers, and an inverter.

Control mechanism   Sun-tracking platforms (see below) result in additional annual energy generation per installed kilowatt. The average annual energy test of Mega-Concentrator installations in California and Arizona has indicated that 50 percent more power is produced than by comparable fixed flat-plate installations. Figure 3.23 shows a typical MARTIFER sun tracker.

Concentrator optics   Refractive optics is used to concentrate the sun's irradiance onto a solar cell. A square Fresnel lens incorporating circular facets is used to turn the

Figure 3.23   **A MARTIFER two-axis sun tracker.** *Photo courtesy of MARTIFER.*

sun's rays to a central focal point. A solar cell is mounted at this focal point and converts the sun power into electric power. A number of Fresnel lenses are manufactured as a single piece or parquet (Fig. 3.24).

The solar cells are mounted on a plate at locations corresponding to the focus of each Fresnel lens. A steel C-channel structure maintains the aligned positions of the lenses and cell plates. The lenses, cell plates, and steel structure are collectively referred to as an *Amonix MegaModule*. Each MegaModule is designed to produce 5 kW of dc power at 850 W/m^2 direct normal insolation and 20°C ambient temperature (IEEE standard). One to seven MegaModules are mounted on a sun-tracking structure to obtain 5 kW of dc power.

Recently Amonix announced the release of the series 7700 MegaConcentrator dual tracking system shown in Fig. 3.21. The company's seventh-generation field-proven solar power generator is capable of converting one-fourth of the sun's energy into usable power. At 53 kW, representing a 50 percent increase over the previous system, the 7700 MegaConcentrator is designed to be the world's most powerful and cost-effective PV system.

The 7700 is made up of seven of Amonix's proprietary MegaModules and uses multijunction solar cells. When mounted on the dual-axis tracker, it delivers an ac efficiency approaching 25 percent, resulting in 122,000 kWh of electricity generated annually. At present, the Amonix 7700 MegaConcentrator is the most efficient PV system in the world.

System operation The MegaConcentrator solar power systems are designed for unattended operation for either grid-connected or off-grid applications. As described previously, the system moves automatically from a night stow position to tracking the sun in the early morning. The system tracks the sun throughout the day, typically generating electric power whenever the direct normal irradiance (DNI) is above 400 W/m^2, until the sun sets in the evening. The controller monitors the sun's position with respect to the centerline of the unit and adjusts the tracking position if required to maintain the required pointing accuracy. If clouds occur during the day, sun-position mathematical algorithms are used to keep the unit pointing at the expected sun's position until the clouds dissipate

SUNRGI flat-panel solar power concentrator technology In SUNRGI solar flat-panel technology, solar rays are concentrated and magnified by means of staggered lenses. Each layer of lens has a specific magnification factor, which results in a 2000-fold amplification of the sunlight when it reaches the surface of the solar cell.

To increase power production, solar modules are secured on a heat sink that removes the heat from the PV cells. A central unattended remote monitoring system provides diagnostic information that can be retrieved from a central or distant location. In addition to providing system operational diagnostics, the monitoring system also indicates solar power output and such information as currents, voltages, and power data, which are stored in the central supervisory system memory. The cumulated data then are used to verify if there are any performance malfunctions in the inverter, fuses, or PV strings; tracking anomalies; or poor environmental conditions. The monitoring system is also used to determine when the lenses have become soiled and need to be washed.

The central supervisory system also provides diagnostic data acquisition from the hydraulic drive system operating parameters, such as fluid level, pump cycling frequency, and deviations from the normal operating range, which, in turn, are stored in the memory archives for monitoring and diagnostic purposes. These data are retrievable from a central operating facility and can be used to diagnose a current problem or to detect a potential future problem. The supervisory control program, in addition to the preceding, provides equipment parts replacement data for the site maintenance personnel. Figures 3.24 and 3.25 show the SUNRGI concentrator module and assembly.

FILM TECHNOLOGIES

Solar Integrated Technologies Solar Integrated Technologies has developed a flexible solar power technology specifically for use in roofing applications. The product meets the unique requirements of applications where the solar power cogeneration also serves as a roofing material. This particular product combines solar film technology with a durable single-ply polyvinyl chloride roofing material and offers an effective combined function as a roof covering and solar power cogeneration that can be readily installed on a variety of flat and curved roof surfaces. Even though the output efficiency of this particular technology is considerably lower than that of conventional glass-laminated mono- or polycrystalline silicon PV systems, its unique pliability and dual function, used

Figure 3.24   A SUNRGI solar power concentrator module.
Photo courtesy of SUNRGI.

as both a solar power cogenerator and a roof-covering system, make it indispensable in applications in which roof material replacement and coincidental renewable energy generation become the only viable options.

Over the years, Solar Integrated Technologies has evolved from a traditional industrial roofing company into the leading supplier of building-integrated photovoltaic (BIPV) roofing systems. The company's unique approach to the renewable energy market enables it to stand out from the competition by supplying a product that produces clean renewable energy while also offering a durable industrial-grade roof.

Solar Integrated Technologies has combined the world's first single-ply roofing membrane, under the Environmental Protection Agency's (EPA's) ENERGY STAR program, with the most advanced amorphous silicon PV cells. The result is an integrated, flexible

Figure 3.25   A SUNRGI solar power concentrator assembly. *Photo courtesy of SUNRGI.*

Figure 3.26   **A Manufacturing process for film technology.** *Photo courtesy of Integrated Solar Technologies.*

solar roofing panel that rolls onto flat surfaces. Figure 3.26 shows the manufacturing process for film technology and the single-ply PVC lamination process.

Until the introduction of this product, the installation of solar panels on large flat area or low-slope roofs was limited owing to the heavy weight of traditional rigid crystalline solar panels. This lightweight solar product overcomes this challenge and eliminates any related roof penetrations.

Solar Integrated Technologies BIPV roofing product is installed flat as an integral element of the roof and weighs only 12 oz/ft^2, allowing installation on existing and new facilities. Application of this technology offsets electric power requirements of buildings, and where permitted in net metering applications, excess electricity can be sold to the grid.

In addition to being lightweight, this product uses unique design features to increase the total amount of sunlight converted to electricity each day, including better performance in cloudy conditions (see Fig. 3.28). Both the single-ply PVC roofing material and the BIPV solar power system are backed by an extensive 20-year package operations and maintenance service warranty. Similar to all solar power cogeneration systems, this technology also offers a comprehensive real-time data acquisition and monitoring system whereby customers are able to monitor exactly the amount of solar power being generated with real-time metering for effective energy management and utility bill reconciliation.

Custom-fabricated BIPV solar cells   In essence, *BIPV* is a term used commonly to designate the custom-made assembly of solar panels specifically designed and manufactured to be used as an integral part of building architecture. These panels are used as architectural ornaments, such as window and building entrance canopies, solariums, curtain walls, and architectural monuments.

The basic fabrication of BIPV cells consists of the lamination of mono- or poly-crystalline silicon cells, which are sandwiched between two specially manufactured tempered-glass plates. This is referred to as a *glass-on-glass assembly*. A number of cells arranged in different patterns and spacings are sealed and packaged in the same process, as described previously. Prefabricated cell wafers used by BIPV fabricators generally are purchased from major solar power manufacturers.

The fabrication of BIPV cells involves complete automation, whereby the entire assembly is performed by special robotic equipment that can be programmed to implement solar cell configuration layout, lamination, sealing, and framing in a clean-room environmental without any manual labor intervention. Some solar power fabricators, such as Sharp Solar of Japan, offer a limited variety of colored and transparent PV cells for aesthetic purposes. Cell colors, which are produced in deep marine, sky blue, gold, and silverfish brown, usually are somewhat less efficient and are manufactured on an on-demand basis.

Because of their lower performance efficiency, BIPV panels are used primarily in applications where there is the presence of daylight, such as in solariums, rooms with skylights, or sunrooms. In these cases, the panels become an essential architectural requirement. Figures 3.27 through 3.29 show custom BIPV modules manufactured by Atlantis Energy Systems.

Figure 3.27   **BIPV modules in a window glazing.** *Photo courtesy of Atlantis Energy Systems.*

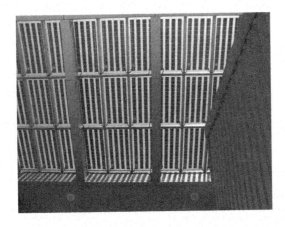

Figure 3.28 BIPV modules.
Photo courtesy of Atlantis Energy Systems.

Figure 3.29 An Atlantis Energy Systems custom-designed
BIPV. *Photo courtesy of Atlantis Energy Systems.*

SunSlate solar modules are PV products that serve two specific functions: They are constructed to be both a roof shingle and a solar power plant. This class of products is specifically well suited for residential and light-commercial applications where a large portion of a tiled roof structure could be fitted with relative ease. SunSlate tiles are secured to roof rafters and structures by means of storm anchor hooks and anchor nails that rest on 2 × 2-ft sleepers.

When the tiles are secured to the roof structure, they can withstand 120 mi/h winds. Adjacent SunSlate tiles interconnect with specially designed gas-tight male-female connectors, forming PV array strings that, in turn, are terminated in a splice box located under the roof. A grid-connected inverter located in the vicinity of the main service meter readily converts the direct current generated by the solar cells to alternating current. The entire wiring of such a system can be readily handled by one electrician in a matter of hours. Figure 3.30 shows a SunSlate solar power module manufactured by Atlantis Energy Systems.

Typically, 100 ft^2 of SunSlate roofing weighs about 750 lb, or 7.5 lb/ft, which is comparatively much lighter than a light-concrete roof, which can weigh nearly twice as much, and is slightly heavier than an equivalent composition shingle roofing tile, which can weigh about 300 lb. Figure 3.31 illustrates the application of SunSlate as roofing tile.

MegaSlate customized roof-mount PV system   MegaSlate is a BIPV roofing system. It consists of frameless individual modules that combine into an overall system that is adaptable to the dimensions of a roof.

Figure 3.30   A SunSlate solar power module. *Photo courtesy of Atlantis Energy Systems.*

Figure 3.31   **SunSlate solar power roofing.** *Photo courtesy of Atlantis Energy Systems.*

MegaSlate is an ideal, simple, and cost-effective solution for owners, architects, and planners who intend to implement functional yet also aesthetically appealing roofs. It provides simple and fast system assembly that can be installed very rapidly, saving a significant amount of time for owners and contractors alike.

Power production requirements   To obtain maximum output production efficiency, MegaSlate systems should conform to the following recommendations:

- The orientation of the roof preferably should be facing south (east over south to west).
- The PV-area exposure to sunlight always should remain unshaded.
- The PV-mounted area must be sufficiently large and unobstructed.
- For optimal efficiency, the PV support rafters or platform must have a 20-degree tilt.

Potential annual power production   Considering a system with optimal orientation and an installed power of 1 kWp (kilowatt peak), which corresponds to an area of 9 m^2, an average annual yield of around 980–1200 kWh or more can be anticipated in most parts of North America. Under adequate geoclimatic conditions, a PV system with this system configuration will have an annual power production capacity of about 120–128 kWh/m^2.

Custom solar solution   MegaSlate roof elements are manufactured at an optimal size specifically designed for use on a wide variety of roof surfaces. PV units are manufactured to be optimally appealing when homogeneously integrated as a component of the building architecture. In most instances, MegaSlate PV units are integrated in the construction of chimneys and skylights and for architectural effect whenever necessary. Dummy MegaSlate elements can be deployed to enhance aesthetic requirements. Figure 3.32 shows a solar window shading application.

PV support structure   The system-specific support structure consists of channel profiles that are mounted onto the roof substructure. These channels are fitted with specially designed rubber elements mounted on the sides, which serve to support MegaSlate elements and also to allow for rainwater drainage. Each MegaSlate element is secured within brackets specially coated to withstand long-term environmental exposure.

Field cabling   The MegaSlate PV modules deploy male-female plug-in connectors that interconnect strings of arrays in a daisy-chain fashion, which eventually terminate in a combiner box and, finally, connect to an inverter.

Figure 3.32   **Application of a solar PV system in window shading.** *Photo courtesy of AT&T Ballpark.*

Installation   In contrast to standard roof tiling, MegaSlate elements are preferably laid from top to bottom. Before being secured into the brackets, they are connected with touch-safe electrical connectors. An appropriate functioning check is required before operating the system.

After the cables are connected to the terminal box on the dc side and to the inverter on the ac side, electricity produced by the building can be fed into the grid.

In the event of malfunction, the MegaSlate PV elements are easy to replace or exchange. The MegaSlate roof-mount installations are also walkable. However, it is recommended that system maintenance be undertaken by qualified personnel.

Solar Power System Design

This section is intended to acquaint readers with the basic design concepts of solar power applications. The typical solar power applications that will be reviewed include stand-alone systems with battery backup, commonly used in remote telemetry; vehicle charging stations; communication repeater stations; and numerous installations where the installation cost of regular electrical service becomes prohibitive. An extended design application of stand-alone systems also includes the integration of an emergency power generation system.

Grid-connected solar power systems, which form a large majority of residential and industrial applications, are reviewed in detail. To familiarize readers with the prevailing state and federal assistance rebate programs, a special section is devoted to reviewing the salient aspects of existing rebates.

Solar power design essentially consists of electronics and power systems engineering, which requires a thorough understanding of the electrical engineering disciplines and the prevailing standards outlined in Article 690 of the *National Electrical Code* (*NEC*).

The solar power design presented, in addition to reviewing the various electrical design methodologies, provides detailed insights into PV modules, inverters, charge controllers, lightning protection, power storage, battery sizing, and critical wiring requirements. To assist readers with the economic issues of solar power cogeneration, a detailed analysis of a typical project, including system planning, PV power system cogeneration estimates, economic cost projections, and payback analysis, is presented later in this chapter.

SOLAR POWER SYSTEM COMPONENTS AND MATERIALS

As described below under "Ground-Mount PV Module Installation and Support Hardware," solar power PV modules are constructed from a series of cross-welded solar cells, each typically producing a specific wattage with an output of 0.5 V. Effectively, each solar cell could be considered as a 0.5-V battery that produces current under adequate solar ray conditions. To obtain a desired voltage output from a PV panel assembly, the cells, similar to batteries, are connected in series. For instance, to obtain a 12-V output, 24 cell modules in an assembly are connected in tandem. Likewise, for a 24-V output, 48 modules in an assembly are connected in series. To obtain a desired wattage, a group of several series-connected solar cells is connected in parallel.

The output power of a unit solar cell or its efficiency depends on a number of factors, such as crystalline silicon, polycrystalline silicon, and amorphous silicon materials, which have specific physical and chemical properties, details of which were discussed earlier. Commercially available solar panel assemblies mostly employ proprietary cell manufacturing technologies and lamination techniques, which include cell soldering. Soldered groups of solar cells are in general sandwiched between two tempered-glass panels, which are offered in framed or frameless assemblies.

SOLAR POWER SYSTEM CONFIGURATIONS AND CLASSIFICATIONS

Types of solar power systems include

1 Directly connected dc solar power systems
2 Stand-alone dc solar power systems with battery backup
3 Stand-alone hybrid solar power systems with generator and battery backup
4 Grid-connected solar power systems

Directly connected dc solar power   As shown in Fig. 3.33, this solar system configuration consists of a required number of solar PV cells, commonly referred to as *PV modules,* connected in series or in parallel to attain the required voltage output. The figure shows three PV modules that have been connected in parallel.

The positive output of each module is protected by an appropriate overcurrent device, such as a fuse. Paralleled output of the solar array, in turn, is connected to a dc motor via a two-pole single-throw switch. In some instances, each individual PV module is also

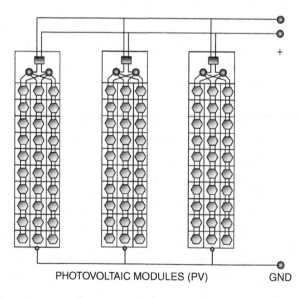

PHOTOVOLTAIC MODULES (PV)   GND

Figure 3.33   Diagram of a three-panel solar array.

protected with a forward-biased diode connected to the positive output of the panel (not shown in the figure).

An appropriate surge protector connected between the positive and negative supplies provides protection against lightning surges, which could damage system components. In order to provide equipment-grounding bias, the chassis or enclosures of all PV modules and the dc motor pump are tied together by means of grounding clamps. The system ground, in turn, is connected to an appropriate grounding rod. All PV interconnecting wires are sized, and the proper type is selected to prevent power losses caused by a number of factors, such as exposure to the sun, excessive wire resistance, and additional requirements that are mandated by the *NEC*.

This type of PV solar system is typically used in an agricultural application, where either regular electrical service is unavailable or the cost is prohibitive. A floating or submersible dc pump connected to a dc PV array can provide a constant stream of well water that can be accumulated in a reservoir for farm or agricultural use. Subsequent sections discuss the specifications and use of all system components employed in solar power cogeneration applications.

Stand-alone dc solar power system with battery backup   The solar power PV array configuration shown in Fig. 3.34, a dc system with battery backup, is essentially the same as the one without the battery except for a few additional components that are required to provide battery charge stability. Figure 3.34 presents a diagram of a directly connected solar power dc pump.

Stand-alone PV system arrays are connected in series to obtain the desired dc voltage, such as 12, 24, or 48 V, outputs of which, in turn, are connected to a dc collector panel equipped with specially rated overcurrent devices, such as ceramic-type fuses.

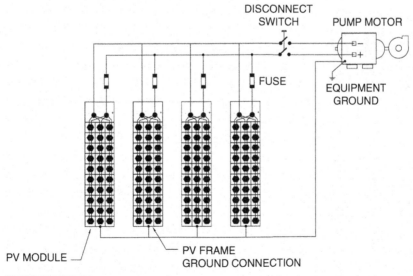

Figure 3.34   Diagram of a directly connected solar power dc pump.

The positive lead of each PV array conductor is connected to a dedicated fuse, and the negative lead is connected to a common neutral bus. All fuses are also connected to a common positive bus. The output of the dc collector bus, which represents the collective amperes and voltages of the overall array group, is connected to a dc charge controller, which regulates the current output and prevents the voltage level from exceeding the maximum needed for charging the batteries.

The output of the charge controller is connected to the battery bank by means of a dual dc cutoff disconnect. As shown in Fig. 3.35, the cutoff switch, when turned off for safety measures, disconnects the load and the PV arrays simultaneously.

Under normal operation, during the daytime when there is adequate solar insolation, the load is supplied with dc power while simultaneously charging the battery. When sizing the solar power system, take into account that the dc power output from the PV arrays should be adequate to sustain the connected load and the battery trickle-charge requirements.

Battery storage sizing depends on a number of factors, such as the duration of an uninterrupted power supply to the load when the solar power system is inoperative, which occurs at night or on cloudy days. It should be noted that battery banks, when in operation, inherently suffer a 20–30 percent power loss owing to heat, which also must be taken into consideration.

When designing a solar power system with a battery backup, the designer must determine the appropriate location for the battery racks and room ventilation to allow for dissipation of the hydrogen gas generated during the charging process. Sealed-type

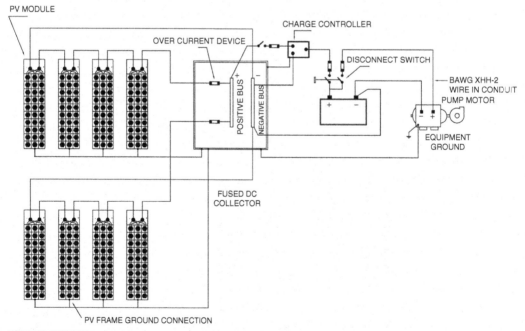

Figure 3.35   Diagram of a battery-backed solar power–driven dc pump.

batteries do not require special ventilation. All dc wiring calculations discussed take into consideration losses resulting from solar exposure, battery cable current derating, and equipment current resistance requirements, as stipulated in Article 690 in the *NEC*.

Stand-alone hybrid ac solar power system with a standby generator   The stand-alone hybrid ac solar power configuration is essentially identical to the dc solar power system just discussed, except that it incorporates two additional components, as shown in Fig. 3.36. The first component is an inverter. Inverters are designed to convert direct current into alternating current. The second component is a standby emergency dc generator, which will be discussed later.

AC Inverters   The principal mechanisms of dc-to-ac conversion consists of chopping or segmenting the dc current into specific portions, referred to as *squarewaves,* that are filtered and shaped into sinusoidal ac waveforms. Any power waveform, when analyzed from a mathematical point of view, consists of the superimposition of many sinusoidal waveforms, referred to as *harmonics.* The first harmonic represents a pure sinusoidal waveform, which has a unit base wavelength, amplitude, and frequency of repetition over a unit of time called a *cycle.* Additional waveforms with higher cycles, when superimposed on the base waveform, add or subtract from the amplitude of the base sinusoidal waveform.

The resulting combined base waveform and higher harmonics produce a distorted wave shape that resembles a distorted sinusoidal wave. The higher the harmonic content, the squarer the wave shape becomes.

Chopped dc output derived from the solar power is considered to be a numerous superimposition of odd and even numbers of harmonics. To obtain a relatively clean

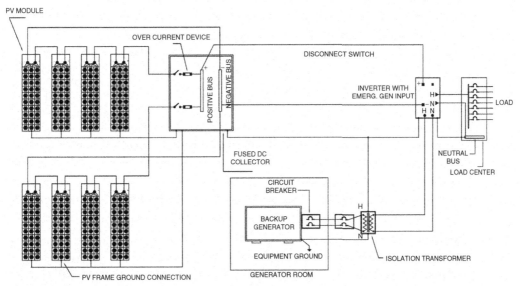

Figure 3.36   **Diagram of a stand-alone hybrid ac solar power system with a standby generator.**

sinusoidal output, most inverters employ electronic circuitry to filter a large number of harmonics. Filter circuits consist of specially designed inductive and capacitor circuits that trap or block certain unwanted harmonics, the energy of which is dissipated as heat. Some types of inverters, mainly of earlier design technology, make use of inductor coils to produce sinusoidal wave shapes.

In general, dc-to-ac inverters are intricate electronic power conversion equipment designed to convert dc to a single- or three-phase ac that replicates the regular electrical services provided by utilities. Special electronics within inverters, in addition to converting direct current to alternating current, are designed to regulate the output voltage, frequency, and current under specified load conditions. As discussed in the following sections, inverters also incorporate special electronics that allow them to automatically synchronize with other inverters when connected in parallel. Most inverters, in addition to PV module input power, accept auxiliary input power to from a standby generator, which is used to provide power when battery voltage has dropped to a minimum level.

A special type of inverter, referred to as a *grid-connected inverter,* incorporates synchronization circuitry that allows the production of sinusoidal waveforms in unison with the electric service grid. When the inverter is connected to the electric service grid, it can effectively act as an ac power-generation source. Grid-type inverters used in grid-connected solar power systems are strictly regulated by utility agencies that provide net metering.

Some inverters incorporate an internal ac transfer switch that is capable of accepting output from an ac-type standby generator. In such designs, the inverters include special electronics that transfer power from the generator to the load.

Standby Generators   A standby generator consists of an engine-driven generator that is used to provide auxiliary power during solar blackouts or when the battery power discharge reaches a minimum level. The output of the generator is connected to the auxiliary input of the inverter.

Engines that drive the motors operate with gasoline, diesel, natural gas, propane, or any type of fuel. Fuel-tank size varies with operational requirements. Most emergency generators incorporate under-chassis fuel tanks with sufficient storage capacity to operate the generator for up to 48 hours. Detached tanks also can be designed to hold much larger fuel reserves, which usually are located outside the engine room. In general, large fuel tanks include special fuel-level monitoring and filtration systems. As an option, the generators can be equipped with remote monitoring and annunciation panels that indicate power-generation data and log and monitor the functional and dynamic parameters of the engine, such as coolant temperature, oil pressure, and malfunctions. Engines also incorporate special electronic circuitry to regulate generator output frequency, voltage, and power under specified load conditions.

Hybrid System Operation   As discussed previously, the dc output generated from PV arrays and the output of the generator can be connected simultaneously to an inverter. The ac output of the inverter, in turn, is connected to an ac load-distribution panel, which provides power to various loads by means of ac-type overcurrent protection devices.

In all instances, solar power design engineers must ensure that all chassis of equipment and PV arrays, including stanchions and pedestals, are connected together via appropriate grounding conductors that are connected to a single-point service ground bus bar, usually located within the vicinity of the main electrical service switchgear. In grid-connected systems, switching of ac power from the standby generator and the inverter to the service bus or the connected load is accomplished by internal or external automatic transfer switches.

Standby power generators always must comply with the *NEC* requirements outlined in the following articles:

- Electrical Service Requirements, *NEC* 230
- General Grounding Requirements, *NEC* 250
- Generator Installation Requirements, *NEC* 445
- Emergency Power System Safety Installation and Maintenance Requirements, *NEC* 700

Grid-connected solar power cogeneration system   As shown in Fig. 3.37, the power cogeneration system configuration is similar to the hybrid system just described. The essence of a grid-connected system is *net metering*. Standard service meters are odometer-type counting wheels that record power consumption at a service point by means of a rotating disk that is connected to the counting mechanism. The rotating disk operates by an electrophysical principle called *eddy current,* which consists of voltage- and current-measurement sensing coils that generate a proportional power measurement.

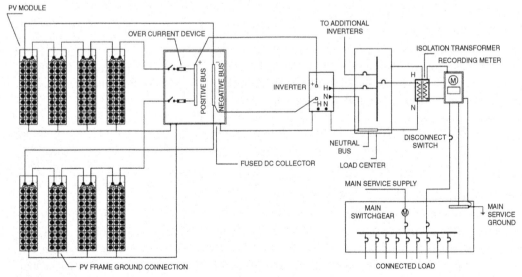

Figure 3.37   Diagram of a grid-connected hybrid solar ac power system with standby generator.

New electric meters make use of digital electronic technology that registers power measurement by solid-state current- and voltage-sensing devices that convert analog measured values into binary values that are displayed on the meter bezels by liquid-crystal display (LCD) readouts. In general, conventional meters only display power consumption; that is, the meter counting mechanism is unidirectional.

Net Metering   The essential difference between a grid-connected system and a stand-alone system is that inverters, which are connected to the main electrical service, must have an inherent line-frequency-synchronization capability to deliver the excess power to the grid.

Net meters, unlike conventional meters, have the ability to record consumed or generated power in an exclusive summation format; that is, the recorded power registration is the net amount of power consumed—the total power used minus the amount of power that is produced by the solar power cogeneration system. Net meters are supplied and installed by utility companies that provide grid-connection service systems. Net-metered solar power cogenerators are subject to specific contractual agreements and are subsidized by state and municipal governmental agencies. The major agencies that undertake distribution of the State of California's renewable energy rebate funds for various projects are the California Energy Commission (CEC), Southern California Edison, Southern California Gas (Sempra Power), and San Diego Gas and Electric (SG&E), as well as principal municipalities, such as the Los Angeles Department of Water and Power. When designing net-metering solar power cogeneration systems, designers and their clients must familiarize themselves with the CEC rebate fund requirements. Essential to any solar power implementation is the preliminary design and economic feasibility study needed for project cost justification and return-on-investment (ROI) analysis. The first step of the study usually entails close coordination with the architect in charge and the electrical engineering consultant. A preliminary PV array layout and a computer-aided shading study are essential for providing the required foundation for the design. Based on the shading study, the solar power engineer must undertake an econometrics study to verify the validity of and justification for the investment. On completion of the study, the solar engineer must assist the client in completing the required CEC rebate application forms and submit them to the service agency responsible for the energy cogeneration program.

Grid-Connection Isolation Transformer   To prevent spurious noise transfer from the grid to the solar power system electronics, a Δy isolation transformer is placed between the main service switchgear disconnects and the inverters. The delta winding of the isolation transformer, which is connected to the service bus, circulates noise harmonics in the winding and dissipates the energy as heat.

Isolation transformers are also used to convert or match the inverter output voltages to the grid. Most often, in commercial installations, inverter output voltages range from 208 to 230 V (three phase), which must be connected to an electric service grid that supplies 277/480-V power. Some inverter manufacturers incorporate output isolation transformers as an integral part of the inverter system, which eliminates the use of external transformation and ensures noise isolation.

Storage Battery Technologies

One of the most significant components of solar power systems is the battery backup system frequently used to store electric energy harvested from solar PV systems for use during the absence of sunlight, such as at night and during cloudy conditions. Because of the significance of storage battery systems and the fact that they represent a notable portion of the overall installation cost, it is important for design engineers to have a full understanding of the technology. More important, the designer must be mindful of the hazards associated with handling, installation, and maintenance. To provide an in-depth knowledge about the battery technology, this section covers the physical and chemical principles, manufacturing, design application, and maintenance procedures of the storage battery. This section also attempts to analyze and discuss the advantages and disadvantages of different types of commercially available solar power batteries and their specific performance characteristics.

HISTORY

In 1936, while excavating the ruins of a 2000-year-old village near Baghdad known as Khujut Rabu, workers discovered a mysterious small jar identified as a Sumerian artifact dated to 250 BC. This jar, which was identified as the earliest battery, was a 6-in-high pot of bright yellow clay that included a copper-enveloped iron rod capped with an asphalt-like stopper. The edge of the copper cylinder was soldered with a lead-tin alloy comparable with today's solder. The bottom of the cylinder was capped with a crimped-in copper disk and sealed with bitumen, or asphalt. Another insulating layer of asphalt sealed the top and also held in place the iron rod that was suspended into the center of the copper cylinder. The rod showed evidence of having been corroded with an agent. When the jar was filled with vinegar, it produced about 1.1 V of electric potential.

A German archaeologist, Wilhelm Konig, who examined the jar came to the surprising conclusion that it was nothing less than an ancient electric battery. It is stipulated that the Sumerians made use of the battery for electroplating inexpensive metals such as copper with silver or gold. Figure 3.38 shows the actual Baghdad battery, and Fig. 3.39 is an illustration of the elements of the Baghdad battery.

Subsequent to the discovery of this first battery, several other batteries were unearthed in Iraq, all of which dated from the Parthian occupation between 248 BCE and 226 CE. In the 1970s, German Egyptologist Arne Eggebrecht built a replica of the Baghdad battery and filled it with grape juice, which he deduced ancient Sumerians might have used as an electrolyte. The replica generated 0.87 V of electric potential. Current generated from the battery then was used to electroplate a silver statuette with gold.

However, the invention of batteries is associated with the Italian scientist Luigi Galvani, an anatomist who, in 1791, published works on animal electricity. In his experiments, Galvani noticed that the leg of a dead frog began to twitch when it came in contact with two different metals. From this phenomenon he concluded that there is a connection between electricity and muscle activity. Alessandro Conte Volta, an

Figure 3.38   The Baghdad battery.

Italian physicist, in 1800 reported the invention of his electric battery, or "pile." The battery was made by piling up layers of silver, paper or cloth soaked in salt, and zinc. Many triple layers were assembled into a tall pile, without paper or cloth between the zinc and silver, until the desired voltage was reached. Even today, the French word for *battery* is *pile,* pronounced "peel" in English. Volta also developed the concept of the

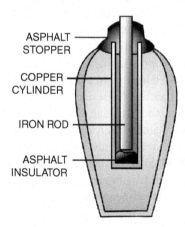

ASPHALT
STOPPER

COPPER
CYLINDER

IRON ROD

ASPHALT
INSULATOR

Figure 3.39   Elements of the Baghdad battery.

Figure 3.40   Alessandro Volta's pile.

electrochemical series, which ranks the potential produced when various metals come in contact with an electrolyte. Figure 3.40 presents an actual photograph of the Alessandro Volta's battery.

A battery is an electrical energy storage device that in physics terminology can be described as a device or mechanism that can hold kinetic or static energy for future use. For example, a rotating flywheel can store dynamic rotational energy in the wheel, which releases the energy when the primary mover such as a motor no longer engages the connecting rod. Similarly, a weight held at a high elevation stores static energy embodied in the mass of the object, which can release its static energy when it is dropped. Both these are examples of energy storage devices, or batteries.

Energy storage devices can take a wide variety of forms, such as chemical reactors and kinetic and thermal energy storage devices. It should be noted that each energy storage device is referred to by a specific name; the word *battery*, however, is used solely for electrochemical devices that convert chemical energy into electricity by a process referred to as *galvanic interaction.* A galvanic cell is a device that consists of two electrodes, referred to as the *anode* and the *cathode,* and an electrolyte solution. Batteries consist of one or more galvanic cells.

It should be noted that a battery is an electrical storage reservoir and not an electricity-generating device. Electric charge generation in a battery is a result of chemical interaction, a process that promotes electric charge flow between the anode and the cathode in the presence of an electrolyte. The electrogalvanic process that eventually results in depletion of the anode and cathode plates is resurrected by a recharging process that can be repeated numerous times. In general, when batteries deliver stored energy or during charging, they incur energy losses as heat.

The Danielle cell   The voltaic pile was not good for delivering currents over long periods of time. This restriction was overcome in 1820 with the Daniell cell. British researcher John Frederich Daniell developed an arrangement in which a copper plate was located at the bottom of a wide-mouthed jar. A cast-zinc piece commonly referred to as a *crowfoot* because of its shape was located at the top of the plate, hanging on the rim of the jar. Two electrolytes, or conducting liquids, were employed. A saturated copper sulfate solution covered the copper plate and extended halfway up the remaining distance toward the zinc piece. Then a zinc sulfate solution, which is a less dense liquid, was carefully poured over a structure that floated above the copper sulfate and immersed the zinc.

In a similar experiment, instead of zinc sulfate, magnesium sulfate or dilute sulfuric acid was used. The Daniell cell also was one of the first batteries that incorporated mercury, which was amalgamated with the zinc anode to reduce corrosion when the batteries were not in use. The Daniell battery, which produced about 1.1 V, was used extensively to power telegraphs, telephones, and even to ring doorbells in homes for over a century.

Plante's battery   In 1859, Raymond Plante invented a battery that used a cell by rolling up two strips of lead sheet separated by pieces of flannel material. The entire assembly, when immersed in dilute sulfuric acid, produced an increased current that was improved on subsequently by insertion of separators between the sheets.

The carbon-zinc battery   In 1866, Georges Leclanché developed the first cell battery in France. The battery, instead of using liquid electrolyte, was constructed from moist ammonium chloride paste and a carbon and zinc anode and cathode. It was sealed and sold as the first dry battery. The battery was rugged, easy to manufacture, and had a good shelf life. Carbon-zinc batteries were in use over the next century until they were replaced by alkaline-manganese batteries.

Lead-acid battery suitable for automobiles   In 1881, Camille Faure produced the first modern lead-acid battery, which he constructed from cast-lead grids that were packed with lead oxide paste instead of lead sheets. The battery had a larger current-producing capacity. Its performance was improved further by the insertion of separators between the positive and negative plates to prevent particles falling from these plates, which could short out the positive and negative plates from the conductive sediment.

The Edison battery   Between 1898 and 1908, Thomas Edison developed an alkaline cell with iron as the anode material (−) and nickel oxide as the cathode material (+). The electrolyte used was potassium hydroxide, the same as in modern nickel-cadmium and alkaline batteries. The cells were used extensively in industrial and railroad applications. Nickel-cadmium batteries are still being used and have remained unchanged ever since. Figure 3.41 is a diagram of current flow in a lead-acid battery.

In parallel with Edison's work, Jungner and Berg in Sweden were working on the development of a nickel-cadmium cell. In place of the iron used in the Edison cell, they used cadmium, with the result that the cell operated better at low temperatures and was capable of self-discharge to a lesser degree than the Edison cell. In addition, the cell could be trickle-charged at a reduced rate. In 1949, the alkaline-manganese battery, also referred to as the *alkaline battery,* was developed by Lew Urry at the Eveready Battery

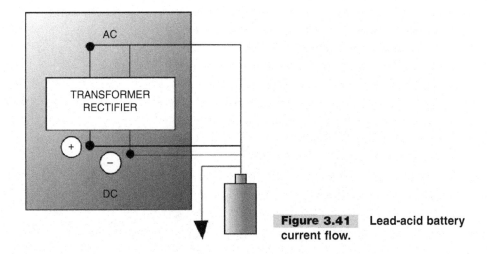

Figure 3.41 Lead-acid battery current flow.

Company laboratory in Parma, Ohio. Alkaline batteries are capable of storing higher energy within the same package size than comparable conventional dry batteries.

Zinc–mercuric oxide alkaline batteries In 1950, Samuel Ruben invented the zinc–mercuric oxide alkaline battery, which was licensed to the P. R. Mallory Company. The company later became Duracell, International. Mercury compounds have since been eliminated from batteries to protect the environment.

Deep-discharge batteries used in solar power backup applications in general have lower charging and discharging rate characteristics and are more efficient. A battery rated 4 Ah over 6 hours might be rated at 220 Ah at the 20-hour rate and 260 Ah at the 48-hour rate. The typical efficiency of a lead-acid battery is 85–95 percent, and that of alkaline and nickel-cadmium (NiCd) batteries is about 65 percent.

Practically all batteries used in PV systems and in all but the smallest backup systems are lead-acid batteries. Even after over a century of use, they still offer the best price-to-power ratio. Systems that use NiCd batteries are not recommended to use them in extremely cold temperatures below −50°F.

NiCd batteries are expensive to buy and very expensive to dispose of owing to the hazardous nature of cadmium. I have had almost no direct experience with these (alkaline) batteries, but from what I have learned from others, I do not recommend them—one major disadvantage is that there is a large voltage difference between the fully charged and discharged states. Another problem is that they are very inefficient— there is a 30–40 percent heat loss just during charging and discharging. Figure 3.42 shows various types of alkaline batteries.

It is important to note that all batteries commonly used in deep-cycle applications are lead-acid batteries. This includes the standard flooded (wet), gelled, and absorbed glass mat (AGM) batteries. They all use the same chemistry, although the actual construction of the plates and so forth can vary considerably. NiCd, nickel-iron, and other types of batteries are found in some systems but are not common owing to their expense and/or poor efficiency.

Figure 3.42   Various alkaline batteries.

MAJOR BATTERY TYPES

Solar power backup batteries are divided into two categories based on what they are used for and how they are constructed. The major applications where batteries are used as solar backup include automotive systems, marine systems, and deep-cycle discharge systems.

The major manufactured processes include flooded or wet construction, gelled, and absorbed glass mat (AGM) types. AGM batteries are also referred to as *starved-electrolyte* or *dry-type batteries* because instead of containing wet sulfuric acid solution, they contain a fiberglass mat saturated with sulfuric acid, which has no excess liquid.

Common flooded-type batteries are usually equipped with removable caps for maintenance-free operation. Gelled-type batteries are sealed and equipped with a small vent valve that maintains a minimal positive pressure. AGM batteries are also equipped with a sealed regulation-type valve that controls the chamber pressure within 4 lb/in^2.

As described earlier, common automobile batteries are built with electrodes that are grids of metallic lead containing lead oxides that change in composition during charging and discharging. The electrolyte is dilute sulfuric acid. Lead-acid batteries, even though invented nearly a century ago, are still the battery of choice for solar and backup power systems. With improvements in manufacturing, batteries can last as long as 20 years.

NiCd, or alkaline, storage batteries, in which the positive material is nickel oxide and the negative material contains cadmium, generally are considered very hazardous owing to the cadmium. The efficiency of alkaline batteries ranges from 65 to 80 percent compared with 85–90 percent for lead-acid batteries. The nonstandard voltage and charging current of alkaline batteries also make them very difficult to use.

Deep-discharge batteries used in solar power backup applications in general have lower charging and discharging rate characteristics and are more efficient. In general, all batteries used in PV systems are lead-acid batteries. Alkaline-type batteries are used only in exceptionally low-temperature conditions of below −50°F. Alkaline batteries are expensive to buy and, because of their hazardous contents, very expensive to dispose of.

BATTERY LIFE SPAN

The life span of a battery will vary considerably with how it is used, how it is maintained and charged, the temperature, and other factors. In extreme cases, it can be damaged within 10–12 months of use when overcharged. On the other hand, if the battery is maintained properly, the life span could be extended over 25 years. Another factor that can shorten the life expectancy by a significant amount is storage uncharged in a hot area. Even dry charged batteries have a maximum shelf life of about 18 months; as a result, most are shipped from the factory with damp plates. As a rule, deep-cycle batteries can be used to start and run marine engines. In general, when starting, engines require a very large inrush of current for a very short time. Regular automotive batteries have a large number of thin plates for maximum surface area. The plates, as described earlier, are constructed from impregnated lead-paste grids similar in appearance to a very fine foam sponge. This gives a very large surface area, and when deep-cycled, the grid plates quickly become consumed and fall to the bottom of the cells in the form of sediment. Automotive batteries generally will fail after 30–150 deep cycles if deep-cycled, whereas they may last for thousands of cycles in normal starting conditions. Deep-cycle batteries are designed to be discharged down time after time and are designed with thicker plates.

The major difference between a true deep-cycle battery and a regular battery is that the plates in a deep-cycle battery are made from solid lead and are not impregnated with lead oxide paste. Figure 3.43 shows a typical solar battery bank system.

Stored energy in batteries in general is discharged rapidly. For example, short bursts of power are needed when starting an automobile on a cold morning, which results in high amounts of current being rushed from the battery to the starter. The standard unit for energy or work is the joule (J), which is defined as 1 Ws of mechanical work performed by a force of 1 N or 0.227 lb pushing or moving a distance of 1 m. Since 1 hour has 3600 seconds, 1 Wh is equal to 3600 J. The stored energy in batteries is measured in either milliampere-hours (mAh) if small or ampere-hours (Ah) if large. Battery ratings are converted to energy if their average voltages are known during discharge. In other words, the average voltage of the battery is maintained relatively unchanged during the discharge cycle. The value in joules also can be converted into various other energy values as follows:

Joules divided by 3,600,000 yields kilowatthours.

Joules divided by 1.356 yields English units of energy foot pounds.

Joules divided by 1055 yields British thermal units.

Joules divided by 4184 yields calories.

Figure 3.43   **Deep-cycle battery packs.** *Photo courtesy of Solar Integrated Technologies.*

BATTERY POWER OUTPUT

In each instance when power is discharged from a battery, the battery's energy is drained. The total quantity of energy drained equals the amount of power multiplied by the time the power flows. Energy has units of power and time, such as kilowatthours or wattseconds. The stored battery energy is consumed until the available voltage and current levels of the battery are exhausted. On depletion of stored energy, batteries are recharged over and over again until they deteriorate to a level where they must be replaced by new units. High-performance batteries in general have the following notable characteristics: First, they must be capable of meeting the power-demand requirements of the connected loads by supplying the required current while maintaining a constant voltage, and second, they must have sufficient energy storage capacity to maintain the load power demand as long as required. In addition, they must be as inexpensive and economical as possible and be readily replaced and recharged.

BATTERY INSTALLATION AND MAINTENANCE

Unlike many electric apparatus, standby batteries have specific characteristics that require special installation and maintenance procedures, which, if not followed, can affect the quality of performance. As mentioned earlier, most of today's emergency power systems make use of two types of batteries, namely, lead-acid and NiCd. Within the lead-acid family, there are two distinct categories, namely, flooded or vented (filled with liquid acid) and valve-regulated lead acid (VRLA, immobilized acid). Lead-acid and NiCd batteries must be kept dry at all times and in cool locations, preferably below 70°F, and must not be stored for long in warm locations. Materials such as conduit, cable reels, and tools must be kept away from the battery cells.

Battery installation safety   What separates battery installers from laypeople is the level of awareness and respect for dc power. Energy stored in a battery cell is quite high, and sulfuric acid (lead-acid batteries) or potassium hydroxide (a base used in NiCd batteries) electrolytes can be very harmful if not handled professionally. Care always should be exercised when handling these cells. Use of chemical-resistant gloves, goggles, and a face shield, as well as protective sleeves, is highly recommended. The battery room must be equipped with an adequate shower or water sink to provide for rinsing of the hands and eyes in case of accidental contact with the electrolytes. Stored energy in a single NiCd cell of 100-Ah capacity can produce about 3000 A if short circuited between the terminal posts. Also, a fault across a lead-acid battery can send shrapnel and terminal post material flying in any direction, which can damage the cell and endanger workers.

Rack cabinet installation   Stationary batteries must be mounted on open racks of steel or fiberglass racks or in enclosures. The racks should be constructed and maintained in a level position and secured to the floor and must have a minimum of 3 ft of walking space for egress and maintenance.

Open racks are preferable to enclosures because they provide for better viewing of electrolyte levels and plate coloration, as well as easier access for maintenance. For multistep or bleacher-type racks, batteries always should be placed at the top or rear of the cabinet to avoid anyone having to reach over the cells. Always use the manufacturer-supplied connection diagram to ensure identification of the open positive and negative terminals when charging the cells. In the event of installation schedule delays, if possible, delay delivery.

Battery system cables   Appendix A provides code-rated dc cable tables for a variety of battery voltages and feed capacities. The tables provide American Wire Gauge (AWG) conductor gauges and voltage drops calculated for a maximum of a 2 percent drop. Whenever larger drops are permitted, the engineer must refer to *NEC* tables and perform specific voltage-drop calculations.

Battery charge controller   A charge controller is essentially a current-regulating device that is placed between the solar panel array output and the batteries. These devices are designed to keep batteries charged at peak power without overcharging. Most charge controllers incorporate special electronics that automatically equalize the charging process.

DC fuses   All fuses used as overcurrent devices, which provide a point of connection between PV arrays and collector boxes, must be dc rated. Fuse ratings for dc branch circuits, depending on wire ampacities, generally are rated from 15 to 100 A. The dc-rated fuses familiar to solar power contractors are manufactured by a number of companies, such as Bussman, Littlefuse, and Gould, and can be purchased from electrical suppliers. Various manufacturers identify fuse voltage by special capital-letter designations.

Photovoltaic output, as a rule, must be protected with extremely fast-acting fuses. The same fuses also can be used within solar power control equipment and collector boxes. Some of the fast-acting fuses used commonly are manufactured by the same companies just listed.

Junction boxes and equipment enclosures   All junction boxes used for interconnecting raceways and conduits must be of waterproof construction and be designed for outdoor installation. All equipment boxes, such as dc collectors, must either be classified as NEMA 3R or NEMA 4X.

Solar Power System Configurations

This section covers solar power wiring design and is intended to familiarize engineers and system integrators with some of the most important aspects related to personnel safety and hazards associated with solar power projects.

Residential and commercial solar power systems, until about a decade ago, because of a lack of technology maturity and higher production costs, were extremely expensive and did not have sufficient power output efficiency to justify a meaningful ROI. Significant advances in solar cell research and manufacturing technology recently have rendered solar power installation a viable means of electric power cogeneration in residential and commercial projects.

As a result of solar power rebate programs available throughout the United States, Europe, and most industrialized countries, solar power industries have flourished and expanded their production capacities in the past 10 years and are currently offering reasonably cost-effective products with augmented efficiencies. In view of constant and inevitable fossil fuel–based energy cost escalation and the availability of worldwide sustainable energy rebate programs, because of its inherent reliability and longevity, solar power has become an important contender as one of the most viable power cogeneration investments afforded in commercial and industrial installations.

In view of the newness of the technology and constant emergence of new products, installation and application guidelines controlled by national building and safety organizations such as the National Fire Protection Association, which establishes the guidelines for the *NEC,* have not been able to follow up with a number of significant matters related to hazards and safety prevention issues. In general, small-size solar power system wiring projects, such as residential installations commonly undertaken by licensed electricians and contractors who are trained in life safety installation procedures, do not represent a major concern. However, large installations in which solar power produced by PV arrays generates several hundred volts of dc power require exceptional design and installation measures. An improperly designed solar power system, in addition to being a fire hazard, can cause very serious burns and in some instances result in fatal injury. Additionally, an improperly designed solar power system can result in a significant degradation of power production efficiency and minimize the ROI.

Some significant issues relating to inadequate design and installation include improperly sized and selected conductors; unsafe wiring methods; inadequate overcurrent protection; unrated or underrated circuit breakers, disconnect switches, and system grounding; and numerous other issues that relate to safety and maintenance. At present, the *NEC* in general covers various aspects of PV power generation systems, but it does not cover special application and safety issues. For example, in a solar power system, a deep-cycle battery backup with a nominal 24 V and 500 Ah can discharge thousands of amperes of current if short circuited. The enormous energy generated in such a situation can readily cause serious burns and fatal injuries.

Unfortunately, most installers, contractors, electricians, and even inspectors who are familiar with the *NEC* often do not have sufficient experience and expertise with dc power system installation so the requirements of the *NEC* are seldom met. Another significant safety issue is related to the materials and components used, which are seldom rated for dc applications. Electrical engineers and solar power designers who undertake solar power system installation of 10 kWh or more (a nonpackaged system) are recommended to review 2005 *NEC* Section 690 and the suggested solar power design and installation practices report issued by Sandia National Laboratories.

To prevent the design and installation issues just discussed, system engineers must ensure that all materials and equipment used are approved by Underwriters Laboratories. All components, such as overcurrent devices, fuses, and disconnect switches, are dc-rated. On completion of installation, the design engineer should verify, independently of the inspector, whether the appropriate safety tags are permanently installed and attached to all disconnect devices, collector boxes, and junction boxes and verify if system wiring and conduit installation comply with *NEC* requirements.

The recognized materials- and equipment-testing organizations that are generally accredited in the United States and Canada are Underwriters Laboratories (UL), the Canadian Standards Association (CSA), and Testing Laboratories (ETL), all of which are registered trademarks that commonly provide equipment certification throughout the North America.

It should be noted that the *NEC*, with the exception of marine and railroad installations, covers all solar power installations, including stand-alone, grid-connected, and utility-interactive cogeneration systems. As a rule, the *NEC* covers all electrical system wiring and installations and in some instances has overlapping and conflicting directives that may not be suitable for solar power systems, in which case Article 690 of the *NEC* always takes precedence.

In general, solar power wiring is perhaps considered one of the most important aspects of the overall systems engineering effort; as such, it should be understood and applied with due diligence. As mentioned earlier, undersized wiring or a poor choice of material application not only can diminish system performance efficiency but also can create a serious safety hazard for maintenance personnel.

WIRING DESIGN

In essence, solar power installations include a hybrid of technologies consisting of basic ac and dc electric power and electronics—a mix of technologies, each requiring specific technical expertise. Systems engineering of a solar power system requires an intimate knowledge of all hardware and equipment performance and application requirements. In general, major system components such as inverters, batteries, and emergency power generators, which are available from a wide number of manufacturers, each have a unique performance specification specially designed for specific applications.

The location of a project, installation space considerations, environmental settings, choice of specific solar power module and application requirements, and numerous other parameters usually dictate specific system design criteria that eventually form the basis for the system design and materials and equipment selection.

Issues specific to solar power include the fact that all installations are outdoors, and as a result, all system components, including the PV panel, support structures, wiring, raceways, junction boxes, collector boxes, and inverters, must be selected and designed to withstand harsh atmospheric conditions and must operate under extreme temperatures, humidity, and wind turbulence and gust conditions. Specifically, the electrical wiring must withstand, in addition to the preceding environmental adversities, degradation under constant exposure to UV radiation and heat. Factors to be taken into consideration when designing solar power wiring include the PV module's short-circuit current (I_{sc}) value, which represents the maximum module output when output leads are shorted. The short-circuit current is significantly higher than the normal or nominal operating current. Because of the reflection of solar rays from snow, a nearby body of water or sandy terrain can produce unpredicted currents much in excess of the specified nominal or I_{sc} current. To compensate for this factor, interconnecting PV module wires are assigned a multiplier of 1.25 (25 percent) above the rated I_{sc}.

PV module wires, based on *NEC* requirements, are allowed to carry a maximum load or an ampacity of no more than 80 percent; therefore, the value of current-carrying capacity resulting from the previous calculation is multiplied by 1.25, which results in a combined multiplier of 1.56. The resulting current-carrying capacity of the wires, if placed in a raceway, must be further derated for specific temperature conditions, as specified in *NEC* wiring tables (Article 310, Tables 310.16 to 310.18).

All overcurrent devices also must be derated by 80 percent and have an appropriate temperature rating. It should be noted that the feeder-cable temperature rating must be the same as that for overcurrent devices. In other words, the current rating of the devices should be 25 percent larger than the total amount of current generated from a solar array. For overcurrent device sizing, *NEC* Table 240.6 outlines the standard ampere ratings. If the calculated value of a PV array somewhat exceeds one of the standard ratings of this table, the next higher rating should be chosen.

All feeder cables rated for a specific temperature should be derated by 80 percent or the ampacity multiplied by 1.25. Cable ratings for 60, 75, and 90°C are listed in *NEC* Tables 310.16 and 310.17. For derating purposes, it is recommended that cables rated for 75°C ampacity should use 90°C column values.

Various device terminals, such as terminal block overcurrent devices, also must have the same insulation rating as the cables. In other words, if the device is in a location that is exposed to higher temperatures than the rating of the feeder cable, the cable must be further derated to match the terminal connection device. The following example is used to illustrate these design parameter considerations.

A Wiring Design Example   Assuming that the short-circuit current I_{sc} from a PV array is determined to be 40 A; the calculation steps should be as follows:

1 PV array current derating: $40 \times 1.25 = 50$ A.
2 Overcurrent device fuse rating at 75°C: $50 \times 1.25 = 62.5$ A.
3 Cable derating at 75°C: $50 \times 1.25 = 62.5$. Using *NEC* Table 310.16, under the 75°C columns we find a cable AWG 6 conductor that is rated for 65-A capacity. Because of UV exposure, XHHW-2 or USE-2 type cable should be chosen, which has a 75-A capacity. Incidentally, the "-2" is used to designate UV exposure protection. If the conduit carrying the cable is populated or filled with four to six conductors, it is suggested, as noted previously, by referring to *NEC* Table 310.15(B)(2)(a), that the conductors be further derated by 80 percent. At an ambient temperature of 40–45°C, a derating multiplier of 0.87 is applied: $75 \text{ A} \times 0.87 = 52.2$ A. Since the AWG 6 conductor chosen with an ampacity of 60 A is capable of meeting the demand, it is found to be an appropriate choice.
4 By the same criteria, the closest overcurrent device, as shown in *NEC* Table 240.6, is 60 A; however, since in step 2 the overcurrent device required is 62.5 A, the AWG 6 cable cannot meet the rating requirement. As such, an AWG 4 conductor must be used. The chosen AWG 4 conductor under the 75°C column of *NEC* Table 310.16 shows an ampacity of 95 A. If we choose an AWG 4 conductor and apply conduit fill and temperature derating, then the resulting ampacity is $95 \times 0.8 \times 0.87 = 66$ A; therefore, the required fuse based on *NEC* Table 240.6 will be 70 A.

Conductors that are suitable for solar exposure are listed as THW-2, USE-2, and THWN-2 or XHHW-2. All outdoor installed conduits and wireways are considered to be operating in wet, damp, and UV-exposed conditions. As such, conduits should be capable of withstanding these environmental conditions and are required to be of a thick-wall type such as rigid galvanized (RGS), intermediate metal conduit (IMC), thin-wall electrical metallic (EMT), or Schedule 40 or 80 polyvinyl chloride (PVC) nonmetallic conduits.

For interior wiring, where the cables are not subjected to physical abuse, CNM-, NMB-, and UF-type cables are permitted. Care must be taken to avoid installation of underrated cables within interior locations such as attics where the ambient temperature can exceed the cable rating.

Conductors carrying direct current are required to the use color-coding recommendations stipulated in Article 690 of the *NEC*. Red wire or any other color other than green and white is used for positive conductors, white for negative, green for equipment grounding, and bare copper wire for grounding. The *NEC* allows nonwhite grounded wires, such as USE-2 and UF-2, that are sized No. 6 or above to be identified with a white tape or marker.

As mentioned earlier, all PV array frames, collector panels, disconnect switches, inverters, and metallic enclosures should be connected together and grounded at a single service grounding point.

PV system ground-fault protection   When a PV system is mounted on the roof of a residential dwelling, *NEC* requirements dictate the installation of ground-fault detection and interrupting devices (GFPD). However, ground-mounted systems are not required to have the same protection because most grid-connected system inverters incorporate the required GFPD devices.

Ground-fault detection and interruption circuitry performs ground-fault current detection, fault current isolation, and solar power load isolation by shutting down the inverter. Ground-fault isolation technology is currently going through a developmental process, and it is expected to become a mandatory requirement in future installations.

PV system grounding   PV systems that have an output of 50 V dc under open-circuit conditions are required to have one of the current-carrying conductors grounded. In electrical engineering, the terminologies used for grounding are somewhat convoluted and confusing. In order to differentiate various grounding appellations, it would be helpful to review the following terminologies, as defined in *NEC* Articles 100 and 250.

In the preceding paragraph, *grounded* means that a conductor connects to the metallic enclosure of an electrical device housing that serves as earth. A *grounded conductor* refers to a conductor that is intentionally grounded. In PV systems, it is usually the negative of the dc output for a two-wire system or the center-tapped conductor of an earlier bipolar solar power array technology.

Equipment-grounding conductor is a conductor that normally does not carry current and generally is a bare copper wires that also may have a green insulator cover. The conductor usually is connected to an equipment chassis or a metallic enclosure that provides a dc conduction path to a ground electrode when metal parts are accidentally energized.

Grounding electrode conductor connects the grounded conductors to a system grounding electrode, which usually is located at a single site within the project site and does not carry current. In the event of accidental shorting of equipment, the current is directed to the ground, which facilitates actuation of ground-fault devices. The grounding electrode is a grounding rod or a concrete-encased rebar (UFR) conductor, a grounding plate, or simply a structural steel member to which a grounding electrode conductor is connected. Based on the *NEC*, all PV systems, whether grid-connected or stand-alone, are required to be equipped with an adequate grounding system to reduce the effects of lightning and to provide a measure of personnel safety. Incidentally, grounding of PV systems substantially reduces radiofrequency noise generated by the inverter equipment.

In general, grounding conductors that connect PV module and enclosure frames to the ground electrode are required to carry full short-circuited current to the ground; as such, they should be sized adequately for this purpose. As a rule, grounding conductors larger than AWG 4 are permitted to be installed or attached without special protection measures against physical damage. However, smaller conductors are required to be installed within a protective conduit or raceway. As mentioned earlier, all ground elec-trode conductors are required to be connected to a single grounding electrode or a grounding bus.

Equipment grounding   Metallic enclosures, junction boxes, disconnect switches, and equipment used in the entire solar power system that could be accidentally ener-gized are required to be grounded. *NEC* Articles 690, 250, and 720 describe specific grounding requirements. *NEC* Table 25.11 provides equipment-grounding conductor sizes. Equipment-grounding conductors similar to regular wires are required to provide 25 percent extra ground current-carrying capacity and are sized by multiplying the calculated ground-current value by 125 percent. The conductors also must be oversized for voltage drops, as defined in *NEC* Article 250.122(B).

In some installations, bare copper grounding conductors are attached along the railings that support the PV modules. In installations where PV current-carrying conductors are routed through metallic conduits, separate grounding conductors could be eliminated because the metallic conduits are considered to provide proper grounding when coupled adequately. Nevertheless, it is important to test conduit conductivity to ensure that there are no conduction-path abnormalities or unacceptable resistance values.

ENTRANCE SERVICE POWER CONSIDERATIONS FOR GRID-CONNECTED SOLAR POWER SYSTEMS

When integrating a solar power cogeneration within existing or new switchgear, it is of the utmost importance to review *NEC* Article 690 related to switchgear bus capacity. As a rule, when calculating switchgear or any other power distribution system bus ampacity, the total current-bearing capacity of the bus bars is not allowed to be loaded more than 80 percent of the manufacturer's equipment nameplate rating. In other words, a bus rated at 600 A cannot be allowed to carry a current burden of more than 480 A.

When integrating a solar power system with the main service distribution switchgear, the total bus current-bearing capacity must be augmented by the same amount as the cur-rent output capacity of the solar system. For example, if we were to add a 200-A solar power cogeneration to the switchgear, the bus rating of the switchgear must, in fact, be augmented by an extra 250 A. The additional 50 A represents an 80 percent safety mar-gin for the solar power output current. Therefore, the service entrance switchgear bus must be changed from 600 to 1000 A or, at a minimum, to 800 A.

As suggested earlier, the design engineer must be fully familiar with the *NEC* Article 690 related to solar power design and ensure that solar power cogeneration system elec-trical design documents become an integral part of the electrical plan-check submittal documents. The integrated solar power cogeneration electrical documents must incor-porate the solar power system components, such as the PV array systems, solar collec-tor distribution panels, overcurrent protection devices, inverters, isolation transformers, fused service-disconnect switches, and net metering, within the plans and must be considered as part of the basic electrical system design.

Electrical plans should incorporate the solar power system configuration in the elec-trical single-line diagrams, panel schedule, and demand-load calculations. All exposed, concealed, and underground conduits also must be reflected on the plans with distinct design symbols and identification that segregate the regular and solar power system from the electrical systems.

It should be noted that solar power cogeneration and electrical grounding should be in a single location, preferably connected to a specially designed grounding bus, that must be sited within the vicinity of the main service switchgear.

LIGHTNING PROTECTION

In geographic locations such as Florida, where lightning is a common occurrence, the entire PV system and outdoor-mounted equipment must be protected with appropriate lightning-arrestor devices and special grounding that could provide a practical mitigation and a measure of protection from equipment damage and burnout.

LIGHTNING EFFECT ON OUTDOOR EQUIPMENT

Lighting surges consist of two elements, namely, voltage and the quantity of charge delivered by lightning. The high voltage delivered by lightning surges can cause serious damage to equipment because it can break down the insulation that isolates circuit elements and the equipment chassis. The nature and amount of damage are directly proportional to the amount of current resulting from the charge.

To protect equipment damage from lightning, devices know as *surge protectors* or *arrestors* are deployed. The main function of a surge arrestor is to provide a direct conduction path for lightning charges to divert them from the exposed equipment chassis to the ground. A good surge protector must be able to conduct a sufficient current charge from the stricken location and lower the surge voltage to a safe level quickly enough to prevent insulation breakdown or damage.

In most instances, all circuits have a capacity to withstand certain levels of high voltages for a short time; however, the thresholds are so narrow that if charges are not removed or isolated in time, the circuits will sustain an irreparable insulation breakdown.

The main purpose of a surge-arrestor device therefore is to conduct the maximum amount of charge and reduce the voltage in the shortest possible time. Reduction of a voltage surge is referred to as *voltage clamping* and in general depends on device characteristics, such as internal resistance and the response speed of the arrestor and the point in time at which the clamping voltage is measured. Figure 3.44 illustrates lighting surge-arrestor spikes.

When specifying a lightning arrestor, it is necessary to take into account the clamping voltage and the amount of current to be clamped. Figure 3.45 is a graphic diagram showing deployment of a lightning surge arrestor in a rectifier circuit.

CENTRAL MONITORING AND LOGGING SYSTEM REQUIREMENTS

In large commercial solar power cogeneration systems, power production from the PV arrays is monitored by a central monitoring system that provides a log of operation

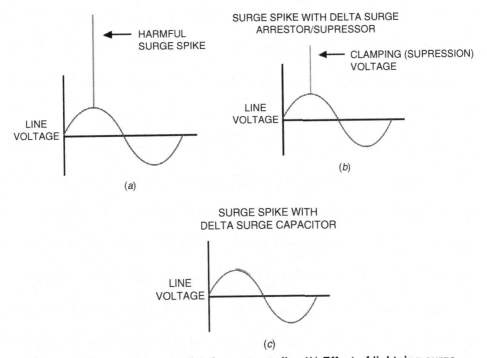

Figure 3.44   (*a*) Effect of a lighting surge spike. (*b*) Effect of lightning surge-spike clamping. (*c*) Effect of lightning surge-spike suppression.

performance parameters. The central monitoring station consists of a PC-type computer that retrieves operational parameters from a group of solar power inverters by means of an RS-232 interface, a power-line carrier, or wireless communication systems. On receipt of performance parameters, a supervisory software program processes the information and provides data in display or print format. Supervisory data obtained from the file also can be accessed from distant locations through Web networking.

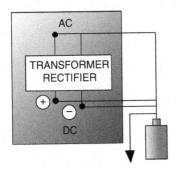

Figure 3.45   Diagram of a lightning surge arrestor in a rectifier circuit.

Some examples of monitored data include

- Weather-monitoring data
- Temperature
- Wind velocity and direction
- Solar power output
- Inverter output
- Total system performance and malfunction
- DC power production
- AC power production
- Accumulated, daily, monthly, and annual power production

Sun Viewer data-acquisition system   The solar power monitoring system by Heliotronics called the Sun Viewer is an example of an integrated data-acquisition system that has been designed to acquire and display real-time performance parameters measured by filed installed electrical power performance and atmospheric data. In addition to providing vital system performance data monitoring and measurement, the system provides the means to view instantaneous real-time and historical statistical energy measurement data essential for system performance evaluation, research, and education.

The system hardware configuration of the Sun Viewer consists of a desk to computer-based data-logging software that processes and displays measured parameters from the following sensors and equipment:

Anemometer (meteorologic data measurement)
- Ambient air temperature sensor
- Wind speed
- Outdoor air temperature sensor
- Pyrometer for measuring solar insolation

Photovoltaic power output performance measurement sensors
- AC current and voltage transducer
- DC current and voltage transducer
- Kilowatthour meter transducer
- Optically isolated RS-422 or RS-232C modem

Sun Viewer display and sun server monitoring software   The software provides acquisition and display of real-time data every second and displays the following on a variety of display monitors:

- DC current
- DC voltage
- AC current
- AC voltage
- AC kilowatthours

- Solar plane-of-array irradiance
- Ambient temperature
- Wind speed

Calculated parameters displayed include

- AC power output
- Sunlight conversion efficiency to ac power
- Sunlight conversion efficiency to dc power
- Inverter dc-to-ac power-conversion efficiency
- Avoided pollutant emissions of CO_2, SO_x, and NO_x gases

This information and calculated parameters are displayed on monitors and updated once every second. The data also are averaged every 15 minutes and stored in a locally accessible database. The software also includes a "Virtual Array Tour" that allows observers to analyze the components of the PV array and monitoring system. The software also provides an optional portal Web capability whereby the displayed data can be monitored from a remote distance over the Internet.

The monitoring and display software also can be customized to incorporate descriptive text, photographs, schematic diagrams, and user-specific data. Some of the graphing capabilities of the system include

- Average plots of irradiance, ambient temperature, and module temperature that are updated every 15 minutes and averaged over one day
- Daily values or totals of daily energy production, peak daily power, peak daily module temperature, and peak daily irradiance plotted over the specified month
- Monthly values of energy production, incident solar irradiance, and avoided emissions of CO_2, NO_x, and SO_x plotted over the specified year

General description of the monitoring system   The central monitoring system reflects the actual configuration of the Water and Life Museum Project located in Hemet, California, and designed by me. This state-of-the-art monitoring system provides a real-time interactive display for education and understanding of photovoltaic and the solar electric installation, as well as monitoring the solar electric system for maintenance and troubleshooting purposes.

The system is made up of wireless inverter data transmitters, a weather station, a data-storage computer, and a data-display computer with a 26-in LCD screen. In the Water and Life Museum Project configuration, the inverters, which are connected in parallel, output data to wireless transmitters located in close proximity. Wireless transmitters throughout the site transmit data to a single central receiver located in a central data-gathering and monitoring center.

The received data are stored and analyzed using the sophisticated software in computer-based supervisory systems that also serve as a data-maintenance interface for the solar power system. A weather station also transmits weather-related information to the central computer. The stored data are analyzed and forwarded to a display computer that is used for data presentation and also stores information, such as video, sound, pictures, and text file data.

Displayed information   A standard display usually incorporates a looping background of pictures from the site, graphic overlays of the power generation in watts and watthours for each building, and the environmental impact of the solar generating system. The display also shows current meteorologic conditions. Displayed data in general should include the following combination of items:

■ Project location (on globe coordinates—zoom in and out)
■ Current and historical weather conditions
■ Current positions of the sun and moon, with the date and time
■ Power generation from the total system and/or the individual solar power arrays
■ Historical power generation
■ Solar system environmental impact
■ Looping background solar system photos and video
■ Educational PowerPoint presentations
■ Installed solar electric power overview
■ Display of renewable-energy system environmental impact statistics

The display should also be programmed to periodically show additional information related to the building's energy management or the schedule of maintenance relevant to the project.

Transmitted data from the weather monitoring station should include air temperature, solar cell temperature, wind speed, wind direction, and sun intensity measured using a pyrometer. Inverter monitoring data must incorporate a watthour transducer that will measure voltage (dc and ac), current (dc and ac), power (dc and ac), ac frequency, watthour accumulation, and inverter error codes and operation.

The central supervising system must be configured with adequate CPU processing power and storage capacity to permit future software and hardware upgrading. The operating system preferably should be based on Windows XP or an equivalent system operating software platform.

Data communication system hardware must be such that it allows a switch-selectable RS-232/422/485 communication transmission protocol and has software-selectable data-transmission speeds. The system also must be capable of frequency hopping from 902 to 928 MHz on the FM bandwidth and be capable of providing transparent multi-point drops.

Animated video and interactive programming requirements   A graphic program builder must be capable of animated video and interactive programming and have an interactive animation display feature for customizing the measurements listed earlier. The system also must be capable of displaying various customizable chart attributes, such as labels, trace colors and thicknesses, axis scale, limits, and ticks. The interactive display monitor preferably should have a 30- to 42-in LCD or LED flat monitor and a 17- to 24-in touch-screen display system.

Ground-Mounted PV Module Installation and Support

Ground-mounted outdoor PV array installations can be configured in a wide variety of ways. The most important factor when installing solar power modules is the PV module orientation and panel incline. A ground-mounted solar power installation is shown in Fig. 3.46.

In general, maximum power from a PV module is obtained when the angle of solar rays impinge directly perpendicular (at a 90-degree angle) to the surface of the panels. Since solar ray angles vary seasonally throughout the year, the optimal average tilt angle for obtaining the maximum output power is approximately the local latitude minus 9 or 10 degrees (see App. B for typical PV support platforms and hardware and App. A for tilt-angle installations for Los Angeles, Daggett, Santa Monica, Fresno, and San Diego, California).

In the northern hemisphere, PV modules are mounted in a north-south tilt (high-end north), and in the southern hemisphere, in a south-north tilt. Appendix A also includes U.S. and world geographic location longitudes and latitudes. To attain the required angle, solar panels generally are secured on tilted prefabricated or field-constructed

Figure 3.46   **Typical ground-mounted solar power system installation.** *Photo courtesy of DPW Solar.*

frames that use rustproof railings, such as galvanized Unistrut or commercially available aluminum or stainless-steel angle channels, and fastening hardware, such as nuts, bolts, and washers. Prefabricated solar power support systems are also available from UniRac and several other manufacturers.

When installing solar support pedestals, also known as *stanchions,* attention must be paid to structural design requirements. Solar power stanchions and pedestals must be designed by a qualified registered professional engineer. Solar support structures must take into consideration prevailing geographic and atmospheric conditions, such as maximum wind gusts, flood conditions, and soil erosion.

Typical ground-mounted solar power installations include agricultural grounds, parks and outdoor recreational facilities, carports, and large commercial solar power-generating facilities, also known as *solar farms.* Most solar farms are owned and operated by electric energy-generating entities. Prior to the installation of a solar power system, structural and electrical plans must be reviewed by local electrical service authorities, such as building and safety departments.

Roof-Mounted Installations

Roof-mounted solar power installations are made of either tilted or flat-type roof support structures or a combination of both. Installation hardware and methodologies also differ depending on whether the building already exists or is a new construction. Roof attachment hardware material also varies for wood-based and concrete constructions. Figure 3.47 shows a prefabricated PV module support railing system used for roof-mounted installations.

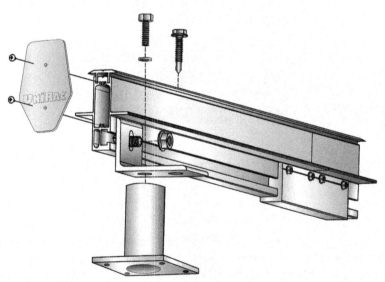

Figure 3.47   **Prefabricated PV module support railing for a roof-mounted system.** *Photo courtesy of UniRac.*

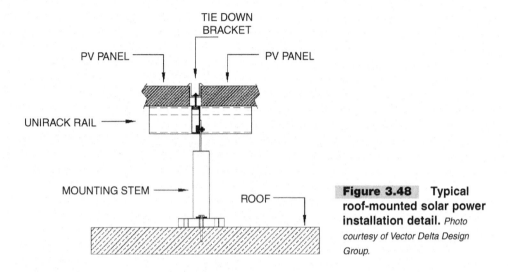

TIE DOWN
BRACKET

PV PANEL

PV PANEL

UNIRACK RAIL

MOUNTING STEM

ROOF

Figure 3.48   Typical roof-mounted solar power installation detail. *Photo courtesy of Vector Delta Design Group.*

WOOD-CONSTRUCTED ROOFING

In new constructions, PV module support system installation is relatively simple because locations of solar array frame pods, which are usually secured on roof rafters, can be readily identified. Prefabricated roof-mounted stands that support railings and associated hardware, such as fasteners, are available commercially from a number of manufacturers. Solar power support platforms are specifically designed to meet physical configuration requirements for various types of PV module manufacturers. Figure 3.48 is a diagram of a typical solar power support railing installation.

Some types of PV module installations, such as the one shown in Fig. 3.49, have been designed for direct mounting on roof framing rafters without the use of specialty railing or support hardware. As mentioned earlier, when installing roof-mounted solar panels, care must be taken to meet the proper directional tilt requirements. Another important factor to be considered is that solar power installations, whether ground- or roof-mounted, should be located in areas free of shade caused by adjacent buildings, trees, or air-conditioning equipment. In the event of unavoidable shading situations, PV module location, tilt angle, and stanchion separations should be analyzed to prevent cross-shading.

LIGHTWEIGHT CONCRETE ROOFING

Solar power PV module support systems for concrete roofs are configured from pre-fabricated support stands and railing systems similar to the ones used on wooden roof structures. Stanchions are anchored to the roof by means of rust-resistant expansion anchors and fasteners.

In order to prevent water leakage resulting from roof penetration, both wood and concrete standoff support pipe anchors are thoroughly sealed with waterproofing compounds. Each standoff support is fitted with thermoplastic boots that are, in turn, thermally welded to roof cover material, such as single-ply polyvinyl chloride (PVC). Figure 3.50 is a diagram of a wood-roof-mounted stand-off support post.

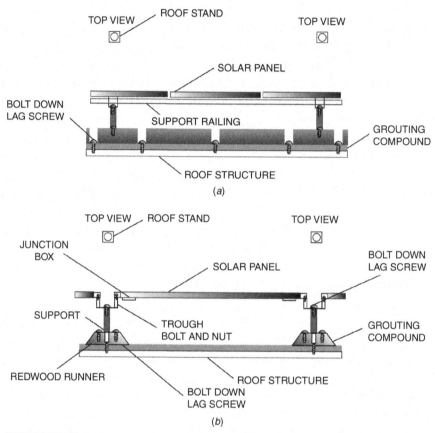

Figure 3.49   Solar panel attachment details. (*a*) Side view. (*b*) Front view.

PV STANCHION AND SUPPORT STRUCTURE TILT ANGLE

As discussed earlier, in order to obtain the maximum output from solar power systems, PV modules or arrays must have an optimal tilt angle that will ensure a perpendicular exposure to the sun's rays. When installing rows or solar arrays, spacing between stanchions must be such that no cross-shading occurs. In the design of a solar power system, the available roof area is divided into a template format that compartmentalizes rows or columns of PV arrays. Figure 3.51 shows of UNISTRUCT railing support system.

Electrical Shock Hazard and Safety Considerations

Power arrays, when exposed to the sun, can produce several hundred volts of dc power. Any contact with an exposed or uninsulated component of the PV array can produce serious burns and fatal electric shocks. As such, the electrical wiring design

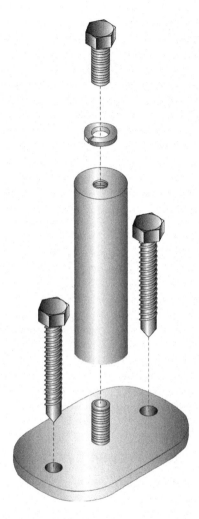

Figure 3.50   Wood-roof-mounted stand-off support railing system assembly detail. *Courtesy of UniRac.*

and installation methodology are subject to rigorous guidelines, which are outlined in *NEC* Article 690 (discussed later).

System components, such as overcurrent devices, breakers, disconnect switches, and enclosures, are specifically rated for the application. All equipments that are subject to maintenance and repair are marked with special caution and safety warning tags to prevent inadvertent exposure to hazards (see App. B for typical sign details).

SHOCK HAZARD TO FIREFIGHTERS

An important safety provision that has been overlooked in the past is collaborating with local fire departments when designing roof-mounted solar power systems on wood structures. In the event of a fire, the possibility of a serious shock hazard to firefighters will exist in instances when roof penetration becomes necessary.

Figure 3.51   Structural concrete roof-mounted solar support railing system assembly detail using double-sided UNISTRUCT railing. *Photo courtesy of Vector Delta Design Group, Inc.*

BUILDING-INTEGRATED PHOTOVOLTAIC (BIPV) SYSTEMS

As discussed in Chap. 1, custom-designed and manufactured PV modules are called *building-integrated photovoltaic* (BIPV) *modules*. These types of solar panels are constructed by laminating individual solar cells in a desired configuration, specifically designed to achieve some special visual effects. They are typically deployed in solarium or trellis-type of structures. Owing to the separation gap between the adjacent cells, BIPV modules, when compared with standard PV modules, produce less energy per square feet of area.

Under operating conditions, when solar power systems actively generate power, a line carrying current at several hundred volts could pose the threat of serious burns or bodily injury and electric shock if exposed during the roof demolition process. To prevent injury under fire hazard conditions, all roof-mounted equipment that can be accessed must be clearly identified with large red-on-white labels. Additionally, the input to the inverter from the PV collector boxes must be equipped with a crowbar disconnect switch that will short the output of all solar arrays simultaneously.

Another design consideration is that, whenever economically feasible, solar array groups should incorporate shorting contacts (normally closed) that can be activated from a multicontact relay that can by engaged during emergency conditions. Crowbar circuitry is not needed.

Solar Tracking Systems

Tracking systems are support platforms that orient solar PV module assemblies by keeping track of the sun's movement from down to dusk, thus maximizing solar energy power-generation efficiency. Trackers are classified as passive or active and may be constructed to track in single or dual axis. Single-axis trackers usually have a single-axis tilt movement, whereas dual-axis systems trackers also move in regular intervals, adjusting for an angular position.

In general, single-axis trackers, compared with fixed stationary tilted PV support systems, increase solar power capture by about 20–25 percent. Dual-axis trackers, on the other hand, can increase solar power production by 30–40 percent. Solar power concentrators that use Fresnel lenses to focus the sun's energy on a solar cell require a high degree of tracking accuracy to ensure that the concentrated sunlight is focused precisely on the PV cell.

Fixed-axis systems orient the PV modules to optimize power production for a limited time and generally have a relatively low annual power production. On the other hand, single-axis trackers, even though they are less accurate than dual-axis tracker applications, produce strong power in the afternoon hours and are deployed in applications such as grid-connected solar power farms that enhance power production in morning and afternoon hours.

Compared with the overall cost of PV systems, trackers are relatively inexpensive devices that increase power output performance efficiency significantly. Even though some tracker systems operate with good reliability, they usually require seasonal position adjustments, inspection, and periodic lubrication.

PHYSICS OF SOLAR INTENSITY

The degree of solar intensity of the light that impinges on the surface of solar PV panels is determined by an equation referred to as *Lambert's cosine law*, which is $I = k \times \cos A$, as depicted in Fig. 3.52. In words, the law states that the intensity of light falling on a plane is directly proportional to the cosine of the angle of light source to the normal of the plane. In other words, when in summer time the angle of the sun is

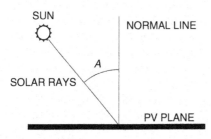

$I = k$ cosine A
I = SOLAR INTENSITY
k = LAMBERT'S CONSTANT
A = SOLAR ANGLE

Figure 3.52   Solar intensity equation diagram.

directly overhead, intensity is at its highest because the cosine of the angle is zero. Therefore, $\cos 0 = 1$, which implies that $I = k$ or equals Lambert's constant.

The main objective of all solar trackers is to minimize the value of the cosine of the angle and maximize the solar intensity on the PV planes.

POLAR TRACKERS

Polar trackers are designed to have one axis rotate in the same pattern as the earth. As such, they are referred to as *polar trackers*. In essence, polar trackers in general are aligned perpendicular to an imaginary ecliptic disk that represents the apparent mathematical path of the sun. To maintain relative accuracy, these types of trackers are adjusted manually to compensate for the seasonal ecliptic shifts that occur in autumn, winter, spring, and summer. Polar trackers frequently are used in astronomical telescope mounts, where high-accuracy solar tracking is an absolute requirement.

HORIZONTAL-AXLE TRACKERS

Horizontal trackers are designed to orient a horizontal axel by either passive or active mechanisms. A long tubular axle is supported by several bearings that are secured to some type of wooden, metallic, or concrete pylon structure. The tubular axes are installed in north-south orientation, whereas the PV panels are mounted on the tubular axel that rotates on an east-west axis and tracks the apparent motion of the sun throughout daylight hours. It should be noted that single-axis trackers do not tilt toward the equator, and as a result, their power-tracking efficiency is significantly reduced in midwinter. However, their productivity increases substantially during spring and summer seasons when the sun's path is directly above. Horizontal-axel single-axis trackers, because of the simplicity of their mechanism, are considered to be very reliable and easy to clean and maintain and are not subject to self-shading.

PASSIVE TRACKERS

The rotational mechanism of a passive tracker is based on use of low-boiling compressed gases that are moved or displaced from east to west side by solar heat, which converts liquid to gas, causing the tracker to tilt from one side to another. The imbalance created by movement of the liquid-gas material creates the fundamental principle of bidirectional movement. It should be noted that various climatic conditions such as temperature fluctuations, wind gusts, and clouding adversely affect performance of passive solar trackers. As a result, they are considered to have unreliable tracking efficiency. However, they do provide better solar output performance than fixed-angle solar support platforms. Figure 3.53 shows various tilt angles for a passive solar tracker.

One of the major passive solar tracker manufacturers is Zomeworks, which manufactures a series of tracking devices known as Track Rack. Tracking devices begin tracking the sun by facing the racks westward. As the sun rises in the east, it heats an unshielded west-side liquid-gas-filled canister, forcing the liquid into the shaded east-side canister. As the liquid moves through a copper tube to the east-side canister, the tracker rotates so that if faces east.

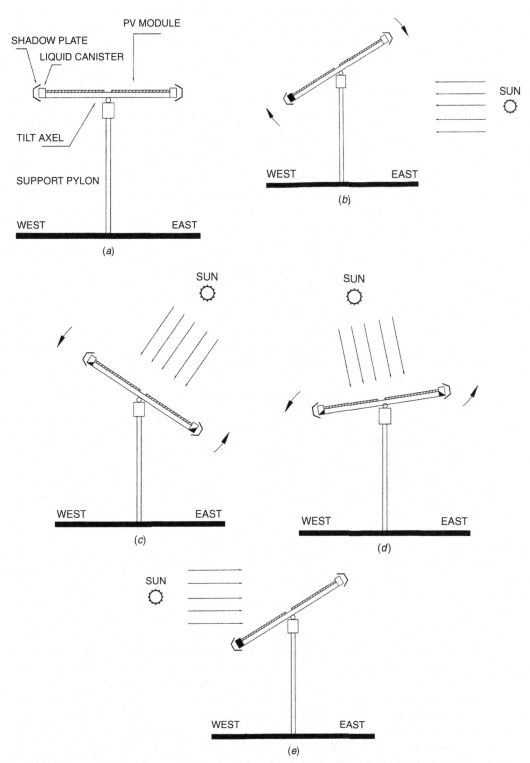

Figure 3.53 (*a*) Zomeworks passive solar tracker. (*b*) Solar tracker eastern sunrise position. (*c*) Sunrise shifting the position of the tracker. (*d*) Liquid movement shifting the position of the tracker. (*e*) Position of the tracker after completing the daily cycle.

The heating of the liquid is controlled by aluminium shadow plates. When one of the canisters is exposed to the sun more than the other, its vapor pressure is increased, forcing the liquid to the cooler, shaded side. The shifting weight of the liquid causes the rack to rotate until the canisters are equally shaded.

As the sun moves, the rack follows at approximately 15 degrees per hour, continually seeking equilibrium as the liquid moves from one side of the track to the other. The rack completes its daily cycle facing west. It remains in this position overnight until it is awakened by the rising sun the following morning.

ACTIVE TRACKERS

Active trackers use motors and gear trains to control axel movements by means programmable controlled timers, programmable logic controllers, and microprocessor-based controllers or global positioning–based control devices that provide precise power-drive data to a variety of electromechanical movement mechanisms. Programs within the control computational systems use a combination of solar movement algorithms that adjust rotational axis movement in orientations that constantly maintain minimal cosine angle throughout all seasons.

VERTICAL-AXLE TRACKERS

Vertical-axle trackers are constructed so as to allow pivotal movement of PV panels mounted about a vertical axis. These types of trackers have a limited use and usually are deployed in high latitudes, where the solar path travels in a long arc. PV panels mounted on a vertical-axis system are suitable for operation during long summer days in northern territories that have extended solar days. Figure 3.54 is a rendering of a dual-axis solar power tracker installation.

Field Safety Recommendations

- Do *not* attempt to service any portion of a PV system unless you understand the electrical operation and are fully qualified to do so.
- Use modules for their intended purpose only. Follow all module manufacturers' instructions. Do *not* disassemble modules or remove any part installed by the manufacturer.
- Do *not* attempt to open the diode housing or junction box located on the backside of any factory-wired modules.
- Do *not* use modules in systems that can exceed 600 V open circuit under any circumstance or combination of solar and ambient temperature.
- Do *not* connect or disconnect a module unless the array string is open or all the modules in the series string are covered with nontransparent material.
- Do *not* install during rainy or windy days.

Figure 3.54   **Self-contained dual-axis solar power–tracking system.** *Photo courtesy of MARTIFER.*

- Do *not* drop or allow objects to fall on the PV module.
- Do *not* stand or step on modules.
- Do *not* work on PV modules when they are wet. Keep in mind that wet modules, when cracked or broken, can expose maintenance personnel to very high voltages.
- Do *not* attempt to remove snow or ice from modules.
- Do *not* direct artificially concentrated sunlight on modules.
- Do *not* wear jewelry when working on modules.
- Avoid working alone while performing field inspection or repair.
- Wear suitable eye protection goggles and insulating gloves rated at 1000 V.
- Do *not* touch terminals while modules are exposed to light without wearing electrically insulated gloves.
- Always have a fire extinguisher, a first-aid kit, and a hook or cane available when performing work around energized equipment.
- Do *not* install modules where flammable gases or vapors are present.

Solar Power System Maintenance

In general, solar power system maintenance is minimal, and PV modules often only require a rinse and mopping with mild detergent once or twice a year. They should be visually inspected for cracks, glass damage, and wire or cable damage. A periodic

Figure 3.55   **SunPower T20 single-axis solar power–tracking system.** *Photo courtesy of SunPower.*

check of the array voltage by a voltmeter may reveal malfunctioning solar modules. Figure 3.55 shows a SunPower T20 single-axis tracker.

Troubleshooting

All PV modules become active and produce electricity when illuminated in the presence of natural solar or high ambient lighting. Solar power equipment should be treated with the same caution and care as regular electric power service. Unlicensed electricians or inexperienced maintenance personnel should not be allowed to work with solar power systems.

In order to determine the functional integrity of a PV module, the output of one module must be compared with that of another under the same field operating conditions. It should be noted that the output of a PV module is a function of sunlight and prevailing temperature conditions, and as such, electrical output can fluctuate from one extreme to another.

One of the best methods to check module output functionality is to compare the voltage of one module with that of another. A difference of greater than 20 percent or more will indicate a malfunctioning module.

When measuring electric current and voltage output values of a solar power module, short-circuit current (I_{sc}) and open-circuit voltage (V_{oc}) values must be compared with the manufacturer's product specifications.

To obtain the I_{sc} value, a multimeter amperemeter must be placed between the positive and negative output leads, shorting the module circuit. To obtain the V_{oc} reading, a multimeter voltmeter simply should be placed across the positive and negative leads of the PV module.

For larger current-carrying cables and wires, current measurements must be carried out with a clamping meter. Since current-clamping meters do not require circuit opening or line disconnection, different points of the solar arrays could be measured at the same time. An excessive differential reading will be an indication of a malfunctioning array.

It should be noted that when a PV system operates at the startup and commissioning, it is seldom that problems result from module malfunction or failure; rather, most malfunctions result from improper connections or loose or corroded terminals.

In the event of a damaged connector or wiring, a trained or certified technician should be called on to perform the repairs. Malfunctioning PV modules, which are usually guaranteed for an extended period of time, should be sent back to the manufacturer or installer for replacement.

Please be cautioned not to disconnect dc feed cables from the inverters unless the entire solar module is deactivated or covered with a canvas or nontransparent material. It is recommended that roof-mounted installations should have 3/4-in water hose bibs installed at appropriate distances to allow periodic washing and rinsing of the solar modules.

Solar Power System Warning Signage

For a solar installation system:

Electric shock hazard—Do not touch terminals—Terminals on both line and load sides may be energized in open position.

For switchgear and metering system:

Warning—Electric shock hazard—Do not touch terminals—Terminals on both the line and load side may be energized in the open position.

For pieces of solar power equipment:

Warning—Electric shock hazard—Dangerous voltages and currents—No user-serviceable parts inside—Contact qualified service personnel for assistance.

For battery rooms and containers:

Warning—Electric shock hazard—Dangerous voltages and currents—Explosive gas—No sparks or flames—No smoking—Acid burns—Wear protective clothing when servicing typical solar power system safety warning tags.

PV System Design Guidelines

When designing solar power-generation systems, the designer must pay specific attention to the selection of PV modules and inverters and installation material and labor expenses, as well as the financial costs of the overall project. The designer also must assume responsibility to assist the end user with the rebate-procurement documentation. The following are major highlights that must be taken into consideration:

PV MODULE DESIGN PARAMETERS

1 Panel rated power (185, 175, 750 W, and so on)
2 Unit voltage (6, 12, 24, 48 V, and so forth)
3 Rated amps
4 Rated voltage
5 Short-circuit amperes
6 Short-circuit current
7 Open-circuit volts
8 Panel width, length, and thickness
9 Panel weight
10 Ease of cell interconnection and wiring
11 Unit protection for polarity reversal
12 Years of warrant by the manufacturer
13 Reliability of technology
14 Efficiency of the cell per unit surface
15 Degradation rate during the expected life span (warranty period) of operation
16 Longevity of the product
17 Number of installations
18 Project references and contacts
19 Product manufacturer's financial viability

INVERTER AND AUTOMATIC TRANSFER SYSTEM

1 Unit conversion efficiency
2 Waveform harmonic distortion
3 Protective relaying features (as referenced earlier)
4 Input and output protection features
5 Service and maintenance availability and cost
6 Output waveform and percent harmonic content
7 Unit synchronization feature with utility power
8 Longevity of the product
9 Number of installations in similar types of applications
10 Project references and contacts
11 Product manufacturer's financial viability

It should be noted that solar power PV cells and inverters that are subject to the California Energy Commission's rebate must be listed in the commission's eligible list of equipment.

INSTALLATION CONTRACTOR QUALIFICATIONS

1 Experience and technical qualifications
2 Years of experience in solar panel installation and maintenance
3 Familiarity with system components
4 Amount of experience with the particular system product
5 Labor pool and number of full-time employees
6 Troubleshooting experience
6 Financial viability
7 Shop location
8 Union affiliation
9 Performance bond and liability insurance amount
10 Previous litigation history
11 Material, labor, overhead, and profit markups
12 Payment schedule
13 Installation warrantee for labor and material

Solar Power System Design Considerations

Essential steps for solar power systems engineering design include site evaluation, a feasibility study, site shading analysis, PV mapping or configuration analysis, dc-to-ac power-conversion calculations, PV module and inverter system selection, and total solar power array electrical power calculations. In order to have a holistic understanding of solar power cogeneration, system designers must have a basic appreciation of insolation concepts, shading analysis, and various design parameters that affect output performance and efficiency of the overall system. In view of the California Solar Initiative (CSI) and other state rebate programs (which will be discussed in later chapters), the importance of system performance and efficiency forms the foundation that will determine whether a project becomes financially viable or not.

BASICS OF SOLAR PHYSICS

Insolation   The amount of energy that is received from the sun's rays that strike the surface of our planet is referred to as *insolation I*. The amount of energy that reaches the surface of the earth is by in large subject to climatic conditions such as seasonal temperature changes, cloudy conditions, and the angle at which solar rays strike the ground.

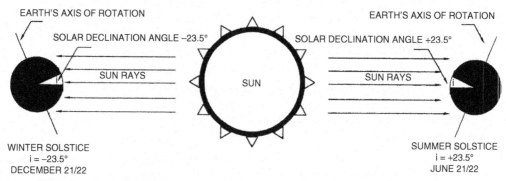

Figure 3.56   Solar declination angle in the northern hemisphere.

As our planet rotates around the sun on an axis tilted at approximately 23.5 degrees, the *solar declination angle I* (shown in Fig. 3.56), constantly varies throughout its revolution in oval-shaped orbit and changes from +23.5 degrees on June 21–22, when the earth's axis is tilted toward the sun, to −23.5 degrees by December 21–22, when the earth's axis is tilted away from the sun. The tilt of the earth's axis at these two seasonal changes, referred to as the *summer* and *winter equinoxes,* is 0 degrees.

The solar declinations (shown in Figs. 3.56 and 3.57) described below result in seasonal cyclic variations in solar insolation. For the sake of discussion, if we consider earth to be a sphere of 360 degrees, within a 24-hour period, it will have rotated 15 degrees around its axis each hour (commonly referred to as the *hour angle*). It is the daily rotation of the earth around its axis that gives the notions of sunrise and sunset.

The *hour angle H* (shown in Fig. 3.58) is the angle that the earth has rotated since midday or solar noon. At noon, when the sun is exactly above our heads and does not cast any shadow on vertical objects, the hour angle equals 0 degrees. By knowing the solar declination angle and the hour angle, we can apply geometry and find the angle of the observer's zenith point looking at the sun, which is referred to as the *zenith angle Z* (shown in Fig. 3.59).

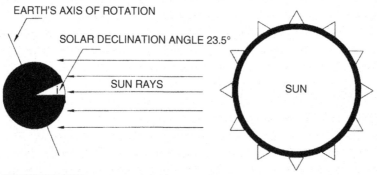

Figure 3.57   Solar declination angle.

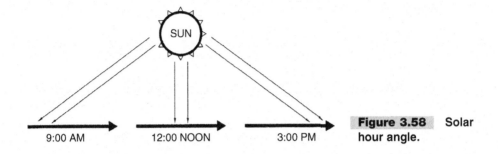

Figure 3.58 Solar hour angle.

The average amount of solar energy striking the surface of the earth is established by measuring the sun's energy rays that impact perpendicular to a square-meter area, referred to as the *solar constant S*. The amount of energy at the top of the earth's atmosphere, measured by satellite instrumentation, is 1366 W/m². Owing to the scattering and reflection of solar rays on entering the atmosphere, solar energy looses 30 percent of its power, and as a result, on a clear, sunny day, the energy received on the earth's surface is reduced to about 1000 W/m². The net solar energy received on the surface of the earth is also reduced by cloudy conditions and is also subject to the incoming angle of radiation.

Calculation of solar insolation is as follows:

$$I = S \times \cos Z$$

where $S = 1000$ W/m²
 $Z = (1/\cos) \times (\sin L \times \sin i + \cos L \times \cos I \times \cos H)$
 $L = $ latitude
 $H = $ hour angle = 15 degrees $\times$ (time $-$ 12)

Time in the preceding formula is the hour of the day from midnight.

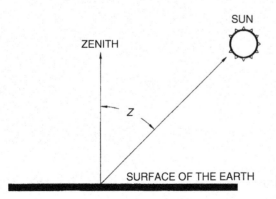

Figure 3.59 Solar zenith angle.

SHADING ANALYSIS AND SOLAR ENERGY PERFORMANCE MULTIPLIER

One of the most significant steps prior to designing a solar power system is investigating a location for the solar platform where the solar PV arrays will be located. In order to harvest the maximum amount of solar energy, theoretically, all panels, in addition to being mounted at the optimal tilt angle, must be totally exposed to the sun's rays without shading that may be cast by surrounding buildings, objects, trees, or vegetation.

To achieve this objective, the solar power mounting terrain or platform must be analyzed for year-round shading. It should be noted that the seasonal rise and fall of the solar angle has a significant effect on the direction and surface area of shadows cast. For instance, shadows cast by a building or tree will vary from month to month, changing in length, width, and the shape of the shade. In order to analyze yearly shading of a solar platform, solar power designers and integrators make use of a commercial shading-analysis instrument known as the Solar Pathfinder (shown in Fig. 3.60). This instrument

Figure 3.60   **Solar Pathfinder and shading graphs.** *Courtesy of Solar Pathfinder.*

Figure 3.61   Solar Pathfinder semispherical dome showing reflections of surrounding buildings. *Photo courtesy of Solar Pathfinder.*

is used for shade analysis in areas that are surrounded by trees, buildings, and other objects that could cast shadows on the solar platform.

The device consists of a semispherical plastic dome and latitude-specific disposable solar-shading graphic inserts (shown in Figs. 3.61 and 3.62). The disposable semicircular plates have 12-month imprinted curvatures that show the percentage of daily solar energy intensity from sunrise (around 5 a.m.) to sunset (around 7 p.m.). Each of the solar energy intensity curves, from January to December, is demarcated with vertical latitude lines that denote the separation of daily hours. A percentage number, ranging from 1 to 8 percent, is placed between adjacent hourly latitude lines. Percentage values progress upward from sunrise from a value of 1 percent to a maximum value of 8 percent during midday at 12:00 noon. They then drop back down to 1 percent at sunset.

Depending on the inclination angle of the sun, percentage solar energy values depicted on the monthly curves vary for each month. For instance, the maximum percent value for the months of November, December, and January is 8 percent at solar noon (12:00 noon). For the rest of the year, from February through October, the maximum percentage is 7 percent.

Figure 3.62   **Solar-shading graphic insert.** *Photo courtesy of Solar Pathfinder.*

The total sum of the percentage points shown on the monthly solar energy curves represents the maximum percent of solar insolation (100 percent) on the platform. The total energy percent shading multiplier for the month of December, January, or any other month is summed up to a total 100 percent multiplier. For example, according to charts 31 to 37 north latitude for the month of December, when summed up, yields the following:

$$\text{Efficiency multiplier } \% = 2 + 2 + 3 + 4 + 6 + 7 + 7 + 8 + 8 + 8 + 8 + 7 + 7 + 6 + 5 \\ + 4 + 3 + 2 + 2 + 1 = 100\%$$

The same summation for the month of June equals

$$\text{Efficiency multiplier } \% = 1 + 1 + 1 + 2 + 2 + 3 + 4 + 5 + 5 + 6 + 6 + 7 + 7 + 7 + 7 \\ + 7 + 6 + 6 + 5 + 5 + 4 + 3 + 2 + 2 + 1 + 1 + 1 = 100\%$$

It should be noted that the insolation angle of the sun increases and decreases for each different latitude; hence each plate is designed to cover specific bands of latitudes for the northern and southern hemispheres.

When placing the plastic dome on top of the platform that holds the curved solar energy pattern, surrounding trees, buildings, and objects that could cast shadows are reflected in the plastic dome, clearly showing shading patterns at the site, which are, in turn, cast on the pattern. The reflected shade on the solar pattern shows distinctly defined jagged patterns of shading that cover the plate throughout the 12 months of the year.

A 180-degree opening on the lower side of the dome allows the viewer to mark the shading on the solar pattern by means of an erasable pen. To determine the total yearly percentage shading multiplier, all the portions of the 12 monthly curves not exposed to shading are totaled. When taking the mean average percentage of all 12 months, a representative solar-shading multiplier is derived, which is applied in dc-to-ac conversion calculations, as discussed in the section on PV system power output rating.

It also should be noted that a number of rebate disbursement agencies, such as the Los Angeles Department of Water and Power, require the inclusion of solar performance multipliers in ac output power calculations.

The Solar Pathfinder dome and shading pattern assembly are mounted on a tripod, as shown in Fig. 3.60. For leveling purposes, the base of the assembly has a fixed leveling bubble at its center that serves to position the platform assembly on a horizontal level. At the lower part of the platform, which holds the pattern plate, a fixed compass indicates the geographic orientation of the unit (shown in Fig. 3.63). The pattern plate, in turn, is secured to the platform by a raised triangular notch.

Figure 3.63   **Solar Pathfinder platform showing the removable shading graph, the leveling bubble at the center, the triangular holder, and the compass.** *Photo courtesy of Solar Pathfinder.*

To record shading, the platform is placed on level ground, and the Pathfinder is adjusted for proper magnetic declination in order to orient the device toward the true magnetic pole. A small brass lever, when pulled downward, allows the center triangle to pivot or rotate the shading pattern toward the proper magnetic declination angle. *Magnetic declination* is the deviation angle of the compass needle from the true magnetic pole. Global magnetic declination angle charts are available through magnetic declination Web sites for all countries.

PHOTOVOLTAIC MAPPING AND CONFIGURATION ANALYSIS

On completion of the field evaluation and shading analysis, the solar power designer must construct the topologic configuration of the solar power arrays and subarrays in a fashion that allows for maximum harvest of solar energy. On choosing the most appropriate or suitable type of PV product, the solar platform footprint must be populated or mapped with the specific dimensional mosaic of the PV modules. It should be noted that the tilting angle of solar arrays must be weighed against the available solar platform footprint. In some instances, performance efficiency resulting from tilting PV support structures that cast shadows on adjacent arrays should be sacrificed for flat-mounting configurations in order to increase total output power-generation capacity of the overall solar system.

In certain other instances, climatic conditions may dictate specific PV array tilt-angle requirements. For example, in northern territories, to avoid the accumulation of snow and ice and to allow for natural self-cleaning, PV units must be mounted at the maximum latitude angle. However, in southern states, when summer electrical energy tariff charges are high, it may be advisable to install PV arrays in a flat configuration because in such a configuration, seasonal solar insolation will allow for harvest of the maximum amount of solar energy. In winter seasons, when electrical energy tariffs are low, lower solar power harvesting may be justified because in the winter there is much less use of air-conditioning systems, which in some instances represent 50–60 percent of electrical energy use. Even though optimal titling of PV arrays results in superior average yearly energy production for the same number of PV modules, lower efficiency resulting from flat-array installation may constitute a reasonable alternative.

DC-TO-AC POWER-CONVERSION CALCULATIONS

On completion of the preceding steps, the designer must evaluate the PV module electrical performance parameters and configure PV strings in a manner most appropriate for use with a dc-to-ac inverter system. It should be noted that on preliminary configuration of the PV arrays and subarrays, the design engineer must coordinate solar power dc and ac wiring details with the inverter manufacturer. In view of specific electrical design performance characteristics of PV modules, inverter manufacturers provide dc input boundary limitations for arrays in various types of configurations.

In general, the maximum allowable dc power voltages produced by a string of PV modules for a specific type of an inverter may be limited within a 300- to 600-V dc bandwidth, at which the inverter may perform power conversion within safe margins and yield the highest conversion efficiency. Excursion of output voltage produced by PV strings beyond the safe boundaries is determined by V_{mp} or combined series PV string maximum peak voltage when measured in open-circuit conditions. For instance, 11 SolarWorld PV module AG SW 175 monocrystalline cells, when connected in series at an average ambient temperature of 90°F ($V_{mp} = 35.7$ V), produce a swing voltage of 387 V, which will be within the input voltage boundaries of the inverter.

On determination of the allowed number of series PV strings, the designer will be in a position to configure the topology of the PV array and subarrays in a manner that will conform to inverter power input requirements.

In most instances, inverter manufacturers provide a Web-based solar array power calculator, and the designer may use it to choose the type of inverter, its power rating, the PV module manufacturer, and model number. By inserting these data, along with ambient operational temperature, tilt angle, and array derating coefficient figures (as outlined earlier), the calculations provide accurate inverter string connectivity and ac power output performance results.

The following is an example of a SatCon PV calculator used to determine the allowable string connectivity and power output performance for a 75-kW dc solar power system.

PV module specification

PV module	SolarWorld AG SW 175
STC W (standard test conditions)	175 W
CEC W (California Energy Commission Test)	162.7 W
V_{oc}	44.4 V
V_{mp}	35.7 V
I_{sc} (short-circuit current)	5.30 A
I_{mp} (max. peak current)	4.90 A
Max. system voltage (V dc)	600 V

Input assumptions

Inverter model	75 kW, 480 V ac
PV module	SolarWorld AG SW 175
Temperature scale	Fahrenheit
Min. ambient temperature	25
Max. ambient temperature	90

Mounting method	Ground-mounted/tilt
CEC or STC module power	STC (standard test condition)
Optimal array derating coefficient	0.8
Voltage drop in array wiring	1.5 V

Resulted design parameters

Ideal no. of modules (strings)	11
Nominal V_{mp} with 11 modules (V dc)	387
Min. no. of modules	11
Max. no. of modules	11
Max. allowed no. of modules	560
Max. no. of series of module strings	48
Inverter output	
Continuous ac power rating	75 kW
AC voltage (V ac line-line)	480 V, 3 phase
Nominal ac output current	91 A
Max. fault ac output current/phase	115 A
Min. dc input voltage	330 V dc
Max. dc input voltage	600 V dc
Peak efficiency	97%
CEC efficiency	96%
No. of subarrays	6

PV SYSTEM POWER OUTPUT RATING

In general, when designing a solar power cogeneration system, the designer must have a thorough understanding of PV system characteristics and associated losses when integrated in array configuration. In essence, the power output rating of a PV module is the dc rating that appears on the manufacturer's nameplate. For example, a SolarWorld SW175 monocrystalline cell is rated at 175 W dc. The dc power output of the PV usually is listed on the back of the unit in watts per square meter or kilowatts per square meter (watts divided by 1000). The rating of the module is established according to international testing criteria, referred to as the *standard test condition* (STC), defined as 1000 W/m² of solar irradiance at 25°C.

Another testing standard used in the United States is based on the dc rating of the nameplate, defined as 1000 W/m^2 of solar irradiance at $20°C$ ambient temperature and wind speeds of 1 m/s. This is referred to as *PVUSA test conditions,* or simply, *PTC.*

It should be noted that the difference between PTC and STC is that in the former, the ambient temperature and wind speed can result in PV module temperatures of about $50°C$ as opposed to $25°C$ for STC. As a result, under PTC test conditions, crystalline-based PV modules will show −0.5 percent degradation per each degree Celsius. Hence the power rating of silicon-type PV modules is reduced to 88 percent of the nameplate rating.

It also should be noted that energy calculations for PV systems evaluated by the CEC and the state of Nevada for rebate consideration take into consideration the PTC rating and not the dc power output. However, manufacturers always rate their PV products based on the dc output power.

PV SYSTEM LOSSES

When designing solar power cogeneration systems, the net energy output production must be calculated by taking into consideration losses associated with the totally integrated system. In general, losses occur owing to the following design elements and environmental conditions:

PV dc nameplate derating. Losses results from dc power output from modules that vary from 80 to 105 percent of the manufacturers nameplate rating. Such losses may result from solar cell physical dimensions, interconnecting cell solder path bridge resistance, and the likes. The default value applied for such losses is 95 percent of the dc nameplate value, which translates to a multiplier value of 0.95.

Inverter and matching transformer losses. This loss is a result of the conversion of dc to ac power. The efficiencies of inverters used in solar power cogeneration range from 88 to 96 percent. The mean value applied by STC power rating is 92 percent, which translates into a multiplier value of 0.92.

PV module array interconnection mismatch. As mentioned earlier, the dc output of manufactured PV modules does vary, and when such modules are connected in tandem, impedance mismatch results in power losses that may vary from 97 to 99 percent. Thus a median degradation multiplier of 0.98 is applied during solar array power output calculations.

Reverse diode losses. These losses are attributed to voltage drops across diodes, which are used in each PV module to prevent reverse current flow into the unit. Diodes are unidirectional electronic check valves that pass current only in one direction and have intrinsic resistive characteristics. As a result, they account for energy loss owing to heat dissipation.

DC wiring losses. Strings of electrical wires, which carry the dc output from PV to PV modules and to the inverters, are subject to ohmic resistive losses. Even though these losses could be reduced substantially by proper sizing of wires and conduits, nevertheless they account for 97–99 percent performance efficiency and therefore are assigned a multiplier value of 0.99.

AC wiring losses. Similar to dc wiring, ac wiring from inverters to the switchgear or service power-distribution hardware is also subject to voltage drop, conduit loss derating, and wire-way solar exposure. Theses losses likewise could be reduced substantially by proper engineering design. However, a median multiplier value of 0.99 generally is applied to the calculations.

PV module dirt and soling losses. When PV module surfaces are exposed to dirt, dust, and snow, the efficiency of their performance can drop by as much as 25 percent. Solar power installations in windy, desert, and high-vehicular-traffic areas should be cleaned periodically to maintain optimal levels of PV performance efficiency. PV modules supported by tilted platforms or inclined terrain, in addition to having higher performance efficiency, are less susceptible to dirt collection and are relatively easier to clean and maintain. Likewise, in northern locations in winter, accumulated snow blocks solar irradiance slides of the PV modules when PV arrays are tilted at an angle. It should be noted that snow accumulation in northern parts of the country can reduce solar power output performance by as much as 70–80 percent. Even though soiling is an empirical event, a derating factor of 0.95 is recommended.

System availability and mean time between failures (MTBF). It should be noted that solar power cogeneration configurations, whether grid-connected or otherwise, are extremely reliable systems because the most important active components, namely, PV modules manufactured as hermetically sealed solid-state electronic devices (with a life expectancy of over 40 years) and inverters, as well as solid-state power-conversion devices, are guaranteed to last at least 5 years by manufacturers.

Since solar power systems do not make use of any moving mechanical devices, they are not subject to wear and tear, like most energy-generating plants and equipment. The only downtime that may result from periodic equipment and module tests is essentially insignificant. However, a mean system availability multiplier of 0.98 is considered to be a safe derating factor. Other losses, such as shading and PV degradation owing to aging and sun tracking, are, in general, not taken into account.

With reference to the preceding, overall calculated dc-to-ac losses amount to 0.77, that is,

$$DC\text{-}AC \ loss = 0.95 \times 0.92 \times 0.98 \times 0.996 \times 0.98 \times 0.99 \times 0.95 \times 0.98 = 0.77$$

Array tilt-angle losses. The optimal tilt angle for PV module performance is the latitude angle of the particular terrain. As discussed earlier, irradiance at latitude is perpendicular to the solar PV module. At a latitude angle, annual solar power energy output from PV modules is at its optimum. An increased tilt angle above the latitude will increase power output production in the winter; however, it will decrease in summer. Likewise, decreasing the tilt angle from the latitude will increase power production in summer. The following table relates tilt angle and roof pitch, which is a measure of the ratio of the vertical rise of the roof to its horizontal run.

ROOF PITCH	TILT ANGLE, DEGREES
4/12	18.4
5/12	22.6
6/12	26.6
7/12	30.3
8/12	33.7
9/12	36.9
10/12	39.8
11/12	42.5
12/12	45.0

PV array azimuth angle (0–360 degrees). The azimuth angle is the angle measured clockwise from true north in the direction facing the PV array. For fixed PV arrays facing south, the azimuth angle is therefore 180 degrees clockwise from the north. PV arrays mounted on sun-tracking platforms can move in either one or two axes of rotation. In one-axis rotations, the azimuth angle is rotated clockwise from true north. In PV modules installed on platforms with two axes of rotation, the azimuth angle does not come into play.

As a rule, for optimal energy output, PV arrays in the northern hemisphere are mounted or secured in an azimuth angle of 180 degrees, or north facing south. In the southern hemisphere, the azimuth angle is reversed to south facing north. Figure 3.64 shows PV array fixed-tilt mounting positions.

The following table shows the relationship of azimuth angle and compass headings.

COMPASS HEADING	AZIMUTH ANGLE, DEGREES
N	0–360
NE	45
E	90
SE	135
S	180
SW	225
W	270
NW	315

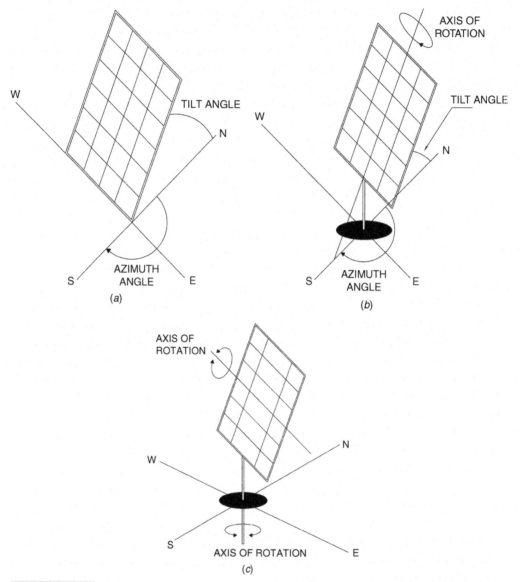

Figure 3.64   (*a*) PV array facing south at fixed tilt. (*b*) Single-axis PV array facing south. (*c*) Two-axis tracking PV array.

Solar Power Rebate Application Procedure

When applying for a solar power rebate, energy providers such as Nevada Power, the Los Angeles Department of Water and Power, Southern California Edison, and Southern California Gas Company, which disburse renewable energy rebate funds, have established special design documentation submittal requirements that are mandatory for rebate qualification and approval.

In essence, initial rebate application forms require minimal design justification for sizing the solar power cogeneration plant. Information on the application forms is limited to the following:

■ Name and address of the owner and the solar power contractor
■ PV module manufacturer and model number (must be listed in CEC-approved equipment)
■ PTC watts of the PV modules
■ Total number of PV modules
■ Total PV power output in PTC watts
■ The inverter manufacturer (must be listed in CEC-approved equipment)
■ Inverter model number and number of units (total output capacity)
■ Inverter efficiency in percent
■ The maximum site electrical demand load

On completion of the parameters, project incentive and cost calculations are calculated by the following formula:

Total eligible rebate watts (TERW) = total sum of PV PTC watts × inverter efficiency

Total rebate amount is calculated by multiplying the TERW by the rebate per watt amount.

The following example is used to demonstrate the eligible rebate amounts that can be expected from Southern California Gas Company.

Let's assume that the a solar power platform provides an unshaded area for a quantity of 530 SolarWorld model SW 175 monocrystalline modules, and a properly sized inverter is selected from a manufacturer that has been listed under CEC-approved solar power equipment. The rebate application calculation will be as follows:

■ PV module: SolarWorld Model SW 175 with dc rated output of 175 W
■ PV module PTC power output rating: 158.3 W
■ PV module area: 14 ft^2
■ Available unshaded platform space (approximately): 7500 ft^2
■ Total number of PV modules to be installed: 530 units
■ Total PTC output watts: 530 × 158.3 = 83,899 W
■ Inverter unit capacity chosen: 100 kW
■ Inverter efficiency: 94.5%
■ Total eligible rebate watts = 83,899 × 94.5% = 79,285 W
■ Adjusted incentive rebate per watt: $2.50
■ Total rebate eligibility: 79,285 × $2.50 = $198, 212.50

It should be noted that maximum allowable rentable solar energy is regulated and capped by various rebate administrative agencies. For instance, Nevada Power caps the small commercial rebate to 30 kW per user per meter, whereas the Los Angeles Department of Water and Power caps it at a maximum of 300 kW per user per meter, and Southern California Gas and Southern California Edison limit the cap to 1000 kW per user address or meter per year. It is suggested that solar power design engineers, before commencing their designs, should familiarize themselves with the specific requirements of energy service providers.

Additional documents that must be provided with the rebate application form are as follows:

- Electrical power system single line diagrams that show solar power PV arrays, dc combiner boxes, inverters, ac combiner boxes, conduit sizes, feeder cable sizes and associated voltage drops, solar power fused service disconnect switch, solar power meter, and the main service switchgear solar disconnect circuit breaker
- Total building or project electrical demand load calculations (TBDL)
- Calculated percentage ratio of the total eligible rebate watts: $(TERW/TBDL) \times 100$ (This figure is required to confirm that the overall capacity of the solar power cogeneration system does not exceed 125 percent of the total project or building electrical demand load.)

In order to protect the client and avoid design error and omission liabilities, it is suggested that all documents and calculations be prepared by an experienced, qualified, and registered electrical engineer.

Solar Power System Deployment

Previous sections covered the basic concepts of solar power system design, reviewed various system configurations, and outlined all major system equipment and materials required to implement a solar power design. This section discusses a number of solar power installations that have been implemented throughout the United States and abroad. The broad range of projects reviewed includes very small stand-alone pumping stations, residential installations, solar farm installations, large pumping stations, and a few significant commercial and institutional projects. Prior to reviewing these solar power projects, design engineers must keep in mind that each solar power system design presents unique challenges, requiring special integration and implementation, that may not have been encountered before and may recur in future designs.

DESIGNING RESIDENTIAL SOLAR POWER

A typical residential solar power system configuration consists of solar PV panels, a collector fuse box, a dc disconnect switch, some lightning-protection devices, a charge controller for a battery (if required), an appropriately sized inverter, the required number of PV system support structures, and miscellaneous components such as electrical conduits or wires and grounding hardware. Additional expenses associated with the solar power system will include installation labor and associated electrical installation permits.

Prior to designing the solar power system, the designer must calculate the residential power consumption demand load. Electrical power-consuming items in a household must be calculated according to the *NEC*-recommended procedure outlined in the following steps. The calculation is based on a 2000-ft^2 conventional single-residential unit:

Step 1: Lighting load. Multiply the living space square area by 3 W: $2000 \times 3 = 6000$ W.

Step 2: Laundry load. Multiply 1500 W for each set of laundry appliances, which consist of a clothes washer and a dryer: $1500 \times 1 = 1500$ W.

Step 3: Small-appliance load. Multiply kitchen appliance loads rated 1500 W by 2: $1500 \times 2 = \times 3000$ W.

Step 4: Total lighting load. Total the sum of the loads calculated in steps 1–3: $6000 + 1500 + 3000 = 10,500$ W.

Step 5: Lighting load derating. Use the first 3000 W of the summed-up load (step 4), and add 35 percent of the balance to it: $3000 + 2625 = 5625$ W.

Step 6: Appliance loads. Assign the following load values (in watts) to kitchen appliances:

■ Dishwasher	1200
■ Microwave oven	1200
■ Refrigerator	1000
■ Kitchen hood	400
■ Sink garbage disposer	800
■ Total kitchen appliance load	4600

If the number of appliances equals five or more, then the total load must be multiplied by 75 percent, which in this case is 3450 W.

Step 7: Miscellaneous loads. Loads that are not subject to power discounts include air-conditioning, Jacuzzi, pool, and sauna and must be totaled as per the equipment nameplate power ratings. In this example we will assume that the residence is equipped with a single five-tone packaged air-conditioning system rated at 17,000 W.

When totaling the highlighted load, the total energy consumption equals

17,000 (air conditioner) + 3450 (appliances) + 5625 (lighting power) = 26075 W

At a 240-V entrance service, this represents about 100 A of load. However, considering the average power usage, the realistic mean operating energy required discounts full-time power requirements by the air-conditioning, laundry equipment, and kitchen appliances; hence the norm used for sizing the power requirement for a residential unit boils down to a fraction of the previously calculated power. As a rule of thumb, an average power demand for a residential unit is established by equating 1000–1500 W/1000 ft^2 of living space. Of course, this figure must be augmented by considering the geographic location of the residence, the number of habitants, occupancy time of the population within the dwelling unit, and so forth. As a rule, residential dwellings in hot climates and desert locations must take the air-conditioning load into consideration.

As a side note when calculating power demand for large residential areas, major power distribution companies only estimate 1000–1500 W of power per household, and this is how they determine their mean bulk electric power purchase blocks.

When using a battery backup, a 30 percent derating must be applied to the overall solar power-generation output efficiency, which will augment the solar power system requirement by 2500 W.

In order to size the battery bank, one must decide how many hours the overall power demand must be sustained during the absence of sun or insulation. To figure out the ampere-hour capacity of the battery storage system, the aggregate wattage worked out earlier must be divided by the voltage and then multiplied by the backup supply hours. For example, at 120 V ac, the amperes produced by the solar system, which are stored in the battery bank, will be approximately 20 A. To maintain power backup for 6 hours, the battery system must be sized at about 160 Ah.

EXAMPLE OF TYPICAL SOLAR POWER SYSTEM DESIGN AND INSTALLATION PLANS FOR A SINGLE RESIDENTIAL UNIT

The following project represents a complete design and estimating procedure for a small single-family residential solar power system. In order to establish the requirements of a solar power system, the design engineer must establish the residential power demand based on *NEC* design guidelines, as shown in the following.

Project design criteria   The residential power demand for a single-family dwelling involves specific limits of energy-use allocations for area lighting, kitchen appliances, laundry, and air-conditioning systems. For example, the allowed maximum lighting power consumption is 3 W/ft^2 of habitable area. The laundry load allowed is 1500 W for the washer and dryer.

The first 3000 W of the total combined lighting and laundry loads are accounted at 100 percent, and the balance is applied at 35 percent. The total appliance loads, when there are more than five appliances, are also derated by 25 percent. Air-conditioning and other loads such as pools, saunas, and Jacuzzis are applied at their 100 percent value.

The demand load calculation for this 1400-ft^2 residential dwelling indicates a continuous demand load of about 3000 W/h. If it is assumed that the residence is fully occupied and is in use for 12 hours a day, the total daily demand load translates into 36,000 W/day.

Since the average daily insolation in southern California is about 5.5 hours, the approximate solar power system required to satisfy the daily demand load should be approximately 6000 W. Occupancies that are not fully inhabited throughout the day may require a somewhat smaller system.

In general, an average 8 hours of habitation time should be used for sizing the solar power system, which in this example would yield a total daily power demand of 24,000 Wh, which, in turn, translates into a 4000-W solar power system.

EXAMPLE OF A COMMERCIAL SOLAR POWER PROJECT

The following plan is provided for illustrative purposes only. The actual design criteria and calculations may vary depending on the geographic location of the project and the cost of labor and materials, which can vary significantly from one project to another. The following project is a collaboration among the identified organizations.

Project design criteria The project described here is a 70-kW roof-mounted solar power cogeneration system deployed on the rooftop of Arshag Dickranian School in Hollywood, California (Fig. 3.65). The design and estimating procedures of this project are similar to those of the residential project discussed earlier.

In order to establish the requirements of a solar power system, the design engineer must determine the commercial power-demand calculations based on the *NEC* design guidelines. Power-demand calculations for commercial systems depend on the project

Figure 3.65   Roof-mounted solar power system, Arshag Dickranian School, Hollywood, California. *Photo courtesy of Vector Delta Design Group, Inc.*

use, which is unique to each application. The solar power installed represents about 25 percent of the total demand load. Since the school is closed during the summer, energy credit cumulated for 3 months is expected to augment the overall solar power cogeneration contribution to about 70 percent of overall demand.

REMOTE SOLAR POWER FARM IN A DESERT SETTING

Project design criteria   The project described here is a 200-kW solar power farm cogeneration system installed in Boron, California, a desert setting. The design and estimating procedures of this project are similar to those of the two projects already described.

In view of the vast project terrain, this project was constructed by use of relatively inexpensive, lower-efficiency film-technology PV cells that have an estimated efficiency of about 8 percent. Frameless PV panels were secured on 2-in Unistrut channels, which were mounted on telephone poles that penetrated deep within the desert sand. The power produced from the solar farm is being used by the local Indian reservation. The project is shown in Fig. 3.66.

WATER AND LIFE MUSEUM, HEMET, CALIFORNIA

Project description   This project is located in Hemet, California, an hour-and-a-half drive from downtown Los Angeles. The project consists of a 150-acre campus with a Water Education Museum, sponsored by the Metropolitan Water District and the Water Education Board and Archaeology and Paleontology Museum sponsored by

Figure 3.66   Boron solar PV farm. *Photo courtesy of Grant Electric.*

the City of Hemet; several lecture halls, a bookstore, a cafeteria, and two auditoriums. In this installation, PV panels were assembled on specially prefabricated sled-type support structures that did not require roof penetration (Fig. 3.67). Roof-mounted PV arrays were strapped together with connective ties to create large island platforms that could withstand 120 mi/h winds. A group of three PV assemblies with an output power capacity of about 6 kW was connected to a dedicated inverter. Each inverter assembly on the support incorporated overcurrent protective circuitry, fusing, and power-collection bussing terminals.

The inverter chosen for this project includes all technology features, such as anti-islanding, ac power isolation, and voltage and frequency synchronization required for grid connectivity. In addition, the inverters are also equipped with a wireless monitoring transmitter that can relay various performance and fault-monitoring parameters to a centrally located data-acquisition system.

Strategically located ac subpanels installed on rooftops accumulate the aggregated ac power output from the inverter. Outputs of subpanels, in turn, are cumulated by a main ac collector panel, the output of which is connected to a central collector distribution panel located within the vicinity of the main service switchgear. Grid connection of the central ac collector panel to the main service bus is accomplished by means of a fused disconnect switch and a net meter. Figure 3.68 shows a nonpenetrating solar power system.

Figure 3.67   **Water and Life Museum rooftop solar power system.** *Photo courtesy of Vector Delta Design Group, Inc.*

Figure 3.68   Nonpenetrating roof-mounted solar power installation with adjustable tilt support platform. *Photo courtesy of DPW Solar.*

Data-acquisition system   The central supervisory system gathers and displays the following data:

- Project location (on globe coordinates, zoom in and out)
- Current and historical weather conditions
- Current positions of the sun and moon and the date and time (local and global)
- Power generation—total system or individual buildings and inverters
- Historical power generation
- Solar system environmental impact
- System graphic configuration data
- Educational PowerPoint presentations
- Temperature
- Wind velocity and direction
- Sun intensity
- Solar power output
- Inverter output
- Total system performance and malfunction
- DC power production

■ AC power production

■ Accumulated daily, monthly, and yearly power production

SOLAR POWER IN SMALL-SCALE WATER-PUMPING APPLICATIONS

The solar submersible pump is probably the most efficient, economical, and trouble-free water pump in existence. Figure 3.69 presents a diagram of a small submersed solar pumping system. In some installations, the procedure for installing a solar power pump simply involves fastening a pipe to a pump and placing the unit in a water pond, lake, well, or river. The output of the solar panel is connected to the pump, and the panel then is pointed toward the sun, and up comes the water. The pumps are generally lightweight and easily moved and are capable of yielding hundreds of gallons per day at distances of over 200 ft above the source. The pumps are of a rugged design and are capable of withstanding significant abuse without damage, even if they are run in dry conditions for a short time.

Pumping water with solar power is reliable and inexpensive and is accomplished with a combination of a submersible pump and a solar cell panel that can be procured inexpensively. Engineers have spent years developing a water-pumping system to meet the needs of ranchers, farmers, and homesteaders. These systems are reliable and affordable and can be set up by a person with no experience or very little mechanical or electrical know-how.

In some instances, the pumping system can be equipped with a battery bank to store energy, in which case water can be pumped at any time, morning, noon, or night, and on cloudy days. The system also can be equipped with a simple float-switch circuitry that will allow the pumps to operate on a demand basis. This type of solar pumping system requires very little maintenance.

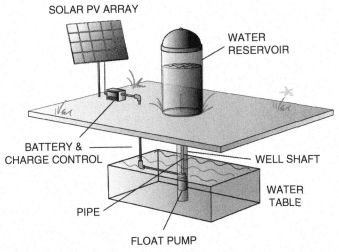

Figure 3.69 Diagram of a water well solar-powered pump.

The batteries used for most systems are slightly different from the ones used in cars. They are called *deep-cycle batteries* and are designed to be rechargeable and to provide a steady amount of power over a long period of time. In some farming operations, solar-powered water systems pump the water into large holding tanks that serve as reserve storage supplies during cloudy weather or at night.

SOLAR POWER IN A LARGE-SCALE IRRIGATION PUMPING APPLICATION

A typical large-scale solar power pumping system, presented in Fig. 3.70, is engineered and manufactured by WorldWater & Power Corporation, whose headquarters are located in New Jersey. WorldWater & Power is an international solar engineering and water-management company with a unique high-powered solar technology that provides solutions to water supply and energy problems. The company has developed patented AquaMax solar electric systems capable of operating pumps and motors up to 600 hp, which are used for irrigation, refrigeration and cooling, and water utilities, making it the first company in the world to deliver mainstream solar electric pumping capacity.

In large solar-powered irrigation projects, as a rule, grid power normally provides the power to the pumps. However, in the event of power loss, the system automatically and instantaneously switches power fully to the solar array. In keeping with the

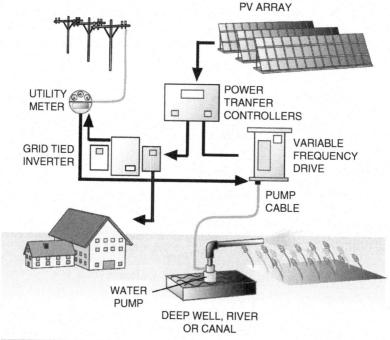

Figure 3.70 Grid-connected solar pumping system diagram.
Courtesy of WorldWater & Power Corporation.

islanding provisions of the interconnection rules, when the power to the grid is off, the pump or motor keeps operating from solar power alone without interruption. This solar pumping system is the only one of its kind; other grid-tied solar systems shut down when grid power is interrupted.

In an off-grid mode, the pump or motor can be run off-grid on solar power alone. This may be useful if there is a time of day when, for example, running the pump or motor would incur a large demand charge that the customer wishes to avoid. The system makes operation still possible while avoiding peak-demand charges imposed by the utility.

Pump performance characteristics The following discussion is presented to introduce design engineers to various issues related to pump and piping operational characteristics that affect power-demand requirements. In general, the pumping and piping design should be trusted to experienced and qualified mechanical engineers.

Every cooling tower requires at least one pump to deliver water. Pump selection is based on the flow rate, total head, and ancillary issues such as type, mounting, motor enclosure, voltage, and efficiency.

Pumping volume is dictated by the manufacturer of the equipment. The total head (in feet) is calculated for the unique characteristics of each project as follows:

Total head = net vertical lift + pressure drop at cooling-tower exit
+ pressure drop in piping to pump + pressure drop from pump to
destination storage compartment + pressure drop of storage + pressure
drop through the distribution system + velocity pressure necessary
to cause the water to attain the required velocity

The total head is usually tabulated as the height of a vertical water column. Values expressed in pounds per square inch (lb/in^2) are converted to feet by the following formula:

$$Head, ft = pounds\ per\ square\ inch \times 2.31$$

The vertical lift is the distance the water must be lifted before it is let to fall. Typically, it is the distance between the operating level and the water inlet. Pressure drop in the piping to the pump consists of friction losses as the water passes through the pipe, fittings, and valves. Fittings and valves are converted to equivalent lengths of straight pipe (from a piping manual) and added to the actual run to get the equivalent length of suction piping.

Then the tabulated pressure drop from the piping manual for a specific length of pipe is compared with the length and pressure drop calculated by proportion:

$$Pressure\ drop = pressure\ drop\ for\ specific\ length\ of\ pipe \\ \times equivalent\ pipe\ length/pipe$$

Typically, end-suction pumps are selected and are of the close-coupled type (where the pump impeller fastens directly to the shaft, and the pump housing bolts directly to the motor) for up to about 15 hp, and the base-mounted type (where the separate pump and motor fasten to a base and are connected by a coupling) is used for larger sizes.

The *static lift* is typically the distance between the operating level in the cold water basin and the reservoir inlet near the top of the towers. When selecting a pump, it is important to make sure the net available suction head exceeds the required net suction head. This ensures that the application will not cause water to vaporize inside the pump, resulting in a phenomenon called *cavitation.* Vaporization inside the pump occurs when small water particles essentially "boil" on the suction side of the pump. These "bubbles" collapse as they pass into the high-pressure side, producing the classic "marbles sound" in the pump. If operated under this condition, pumps can be damaged.

Pumps are also required to operate under conditions of net positive suction head (NPSH), which means that the pump lift must be able to cope with the local barometric pressure and handle the friction losses in the suction line and vapor pressure of the water being pumped.

SEMITROPIC OPEN-FIELD SINGLE-AXIS TRACKING SYSTEM PV ARRAY: TECHNICAL SPECIFICATIONS

The following project was designed and built by Shell Solar, which consists of a solar farm configured from 1152-kW solar array modules (Fig. 3.71). The project, referred to as the Semitropic Water District (SWD), is located in Wasco, California, approximately

Figure 3.71   A large-scale single-axis solar farming system, Semitropic Water District, Wasco, California. *Photo courtesy of SolarWorld.*

150 mi northeast of Los Angeles. The 550- × 380-ft land provided by the SWD is relatively flat, with no trees, which required minimal grading and brush clearing. As shown in the figure, PV arrays are mounted in a north-facing-south orientation.

Mechanical description PV array design for this single-axis tracking system was based on the use of 7200 Shell Solar Industries Model SQ-160 modules that were assembled into 1800 panels. The proposed configuration of the array provides 60 rows approximately 170 ft long and spaced at 21 ft on center. The proposed 21-ft row-to-row spacing extends the array's operational day and maximizes energy output by minimizing shadowing effects.

The north-south axis trackers use a 20-ton screw drive jack to provide 45 degree east to 45 degree west single-axis tracking to maximize the daily energy output from the array. The screw jacks are controlled by a square-D (or Allen Bradley) programmable logic controller (PLC). A clock-based controller provides ±2 percent tracking accuracy for the flat-plate PV arrays and allows backtracking to eliminate row-to-row shadowing.

The system was installed on top of 720 wooden utility-grade ground-embedded poles as foundation for the array structure. Each pole is 15 ft in length and is buried in the ground at a depth of approximately 7–8 ft. The panel support structure for the array uses square galvanized steel torque tubes that are free to rotate at ±45 degrees, which in turn are supported by galvanized steel bearing plates. The precise motion of this torque tube is provided by screw jacks that are regulated by the controller system. Prewired solar panels are clamped directly to the steel structure with two panel clamps per panel.

The steel subassemblies form 60 rows consisting of 30 rows of 2-pair matrices. These rows then are divided electrically to form five equal-sized subsystems consisting of 360 prewired panels. Each panel is factory prewired with four Shell Solar SQ160 modules and delivered to the site in reusable shipping racks. The panels are also equipped with factory quick disconnects to ease field wiring.

DC to ac power conversion is accomplished with five Xantrex Model PV-225208 inverters that are centrally located on a 12- × 74-ft concrete pad placed adjacent to five step-up transformers, collected output of which is connected to a low-voltage metering system. Centrally located power accumulation allows for shorter conductor runs to all five of the inverters.

Electrical description As described earlier, the array is electrically divided into five equal subsections consisting of 1440 SQ160 modules, dc circuit combiners, one 225-kW inverter, and a 225-kVA, 208 to 12.47-kV step-up transformer. Thirty panels each containing four modules are used on each of the 60 single-axis tracking rows.

The dc collectors feed underground current to each inverter's dc interface that incorporates prefabricated fusing and a manually operated disconnect switch. The ac output of the inverters also includes manually operated disconnect switches that feed the low-voltage section of the step-up transformer. The low-voltage winding of the transformer includes a metering section that is fitted with an energy-production meter. The meter includes a cellular modem so that it can be read remotely. The electronic meters are designed to store daily, weekly, and monthly energy-production parameters.

The transformers step up the 208 V ac to 12.47 kV ac. The high-voltage output of each transformer includes fusing and a "hot stick" disconnect. All five transformers are loop fed, and the final underground feed from the transformer pad extends 200 ft to the north section of the array, where it is terminated at a riser pole.

The Xantrex inverters used in this installation meet IEEE 929 and UL1741 standards, and as such, they do not require any anti-islanding hardware.

Energy performance Generally speaking, it is estimated that the annual energy production from a single-axis tracking system can be as much as 20 percent than that from a comparable fixed-tilt system. In general, single-axis tracking modeling software used in this project calculates energy production of a single north-south axis row of PV modules from sunrise to sunset (90 degrees east to 90 degrees west). The most popular software currently used for calculating solar array output performance such as PV Design Pro or PV Watts use a 90-degree east to 90-degree west algorithm to calculate the maximum available annual energy. As discussed earlier, when calculating energy output performance, shadowing effects must be accounted for in the annual energy production model.

When tracking multiple rows of solar panels, it should be noted that the higher the tracking limit angle (in this case 90 degrees), the larger will be the shadow cast in the morning and afternoon hours. This shadowing effectively will shut down energy production from all the rows located behind the eastern-most row in the morning and the western-most row in the evening. This effect can be reduced by limiting the tracking limit angle to 45 degrees. From a practical standpoint, the linear actuators used in the most popular systems easily accommodate a 45-degree limit angle and is the hardware used in the proposed system. To further improve the energy performance of the system, a backtracking scheme is used in the morning and evening hours of each day to eliminate the row-to-row shadowing.

Backtracking begins by adjusting the tilt angle of each row to 10 degrees east just before the sunrise in the morning. As the sun rises, each row begins tracking east just enough so that no row-to-row shading occurs. This backtracking continues until the tracker limit angle of 45 degrees is reached, at which time the tracker controller waits until the sun catches up with the 45-degree tilt angle and then begins to follow the sun throughout the day. In the afternoon, the controller will repeat the backtracking scheme until the sun sets.

Shell Solar Industries is including typical energy profiles for tracking arrays in December and June (the winter and summer solstices). These profiles illustrate the effects just described and the impact they have on the annual energy production of a multirow single-axis tracking system.

This project was constructed by Shell Solar Industries for customer Semitropic Water District and placed in service in April 2005. Owing to market conditions at the time, Shell SQ-85 modules were used in place of the SQ-160 modules. Owing to other project constraints (related to the California incentive funding program at the time), the project size ultimately was reduced to 979.2 kW (from 11,520 kW for the SQ-85 modules).

In July 2006, Shell Solar Industries and its projects and technology, including the Semitropic project and single-axis tracking technology, were purchased by SolarWorld Industries. Installation of a comparable system with SolarWorld's currently more efficient modules would require 6576 SW-175 modules = 1150.8 kW. The modules could be assembled into 1096 prewired panels. The basic elements of the single-axis tracking system design and array would remain the same, but owing to reduced solar module surface area, the system would require approximately 9 percent less space.

Economics of Solar Power Systems

Perhaps the most important task of a solar power engineer is to conduct preliminary engineering and financial feasibility studies, which are necessary for establishing an actual project design. The essence of the feasibility study is to evaluate and estimate the power generation and cost of installation for the life span of the project. The feasibility study is conducted as a first step in determining the limitations of the solar project's power production and ROI without expending a substantial amount of engineering and labor effort. The steps needed to conduct a preliminary engineering and financial study are presented in this section.

PRELIMINARY ENGINEERING DESIGN

Conduct a field survey of the existing roof or mounting area. For new projects, review the available roof-mount area and mounting landscape. Care must be taken to ensure that there are no mechanical, construction, or natural structures that could cast a shadow on the solar panels. Shade from trees and sap drops could create an unwanted loss of energy production. One of the solar PV modules in a chain, when shaded, could act as a resistive element that could alter the current and voltage output of the whole array.

Always consult with the architect to ensure that the installation of solar panels will not interfere with roof-mounted solar windows, vents, and air-conditioning unit ductwork. The architect also must take into consideration roof penetrations, installed weight, anchoring, and seismic requirements.

On establishment of solar power area clearances, the solar power designer must prepare a set of electronic templates representing standard array configurations. Solar array templates then can be used to establish a desirable output of dc power. It should be noted that when laying blocks of PV arrays, consideration must be given to the desirable tilt inclination to avoid cross-shadowing. In some instances, the designer also must consider trading solar power output efficiency to maximize the power output production. As mentioned earlier in this chapter, the most desirable mounting position for a PV module to realize maximum solar insolation is about latitude −10 degrees. For example, the optimal tilt angle in New York will be 39 degrees, whereas in Los Angeles, it will be about 25–27 degrees. To avoid cross-shading, the adjacent profiles of two solar rows of arrays could be determined by simple trigonometry. This could determine the geometry of the tilt by the angle of the associated sine (shading height) and cosine (tandem array separation space) of the support structure incline. It should be noted that flatly laid solar PV arrays may incur about a 9–11 percent power loss, but depending on the number of installed panels, it could exceed 30–40 percent on the same mounting space.

An important design criterion when laying out solar arrays is grouping the proper number of PV modules that would provide the series-connected voltages and current required by inverter specifications. Most inverters allow certain margins for dc inputs that are specific to the make and model of a manufactured unit. Inverter power capacities may vary from a few hundred to many thousands of watts. When designing a solar power system, the designer should make decisions about the use of specific PV and inverter makes and models in advance, thereby establishing the basis of the overall configuration.

It is not uncommon to have different sizes of solar power arrays and matching inverters on the same installation. In fact, in some instances, the designer may, for unavoidable occurrences of shading, decide to minimize the size of the array as much as possible, thus limiting the number of PV units in the array, which may require a small-power-capacity inverter. The most essential factor that must be taken into consideration is ensuring that all inverters used in the solar power system are completely compatible.

When laying out the PV arrays, care should be taken to allow sufficient access to array clusters for maintenance and cleaning purposes. In order to avoid deterioration of power output, solar arrays must be washed and rinsed periodically. Adequately spaced hose bibs should be installed on rooftops to facilitate flushing of the PV units in the evening only, when the power output is below the margin of shock hazard.

On completing the PV layout, the designer should count the total number of solar power system components and, by using a rule of thumb, must arrive at a unit-cost estimate, such as dollars per watt of power. This will make it possible to better approximate the total cost of the project. In general, net power output from PV arrays, when converted to ac power, is subjected to a number of factors that can degrade the output efficiency of the system.

The CEC rates each manufacturer-approved PV unit by a special power output performance factor, referred to as the *power test condition* (PTC). This figure of merit is derived for each manufacturer and PV unit model by extensive performance testing under various climatic conditions. These tests are performed in a specially certified laboratory environment. Design parameters that affect system efficiency are as follows:

- Latitude and longitude
- Climatic conditions (in cold weather, PV units work more efficiently)
- Associated yearly average insolation
- Temperature variations
- Building orientation (north, south, etc.)
- Roof or support structure tilt
- Inverter efficiency
- Isolation transformer efficiency
- DC and ac wiring losses resulting from the density of the wires in conduits
- Solar power exposure

- Long wire and cable runs
- Poor, loose, or corroded wire connections
- AC power transmission losses to the isolation transformers
- Poor maintenance and dust and grime collection on the PV modules

Meteorologic data   When the design is planned for floor-mounted solar power systems, designers must investigate natural calamities, such as extreme wind gusts, periodic or seasonal flooding, and snow precipitation. For meteorologic data, contact the NASA Surface Meteorology and Solar Energy Data Set Web site at www.eosweb.larc.nasa.gov/sse/.

To search for meteorologic information on this Web site, the inquirer must provide the latitude and longitude for each geographic location. For example, when obtaining data for Los Angeles, California, at latitude 34.09 and longitude 118.4, the statistical data provided will include the following recorded information for each month of the year for the past 10 years:

- Average daily radiation on horizontal surface in kilowatts per square meter per day
- Average temperature
- Average wind speed in meters per second

For complete listings of latitude and longitude data, please refer to App. A. The following are a few examples for North American metropolitan areas:

Los Angeles, California	34.09 N/118.40 W
Toronto, Canada	43.67 N/–79.38 W
Palm Springs, California	33.7 N/116.52 W
San Diego, California	32.82 N/117.10 W

To obtain ground surface-site insolation measurements, refer to the Web site *http://eosweb.lac.nasa.gov/sse.*

A certified, registered structural engineer must design all solar power installation platforms and footings. On completion and integration of the preliminary design parameters previously discussed, the design engineer must conduct a feasibility analysis of the solar power cogeneration project. Some of the essential cost components of a solar power system required for final analysis are

- Solar PV module (dollars per dc watts)
- Support structure hardware
- Electrical devices such as inverters, isolation transformers, and lightning protection devices and hardware such as electric conduits, cables, and grounding wire

Additional costs may include

- Material transport and storage
- Possible federal taxes and state sales taxes

■ Labor wages (prevailing or nonprevailing) and site supervision (project management)
■ Engineering design, which includes electrical, architectural, and structural disciplines
■ Construction drawings and reproduction
■ Permit fees
■ Maintenance training manuals and instructor time
■ Maintenance, casualty insurance, and warranties
■ Spare parts and components
■ Testing and commissioning
■ Overhead and profit
■ Construction bond and liability insurance
■ Mobilization cost, site office, and utility expenses
■ Liquidated damages

Energy cost factor   On completion of the preliminary engineering study and solar power-generation potential, the designer must evaluate the present costs and project the future costs of the electrical energy for the entire life span of the solar power system. To determine the present value of the electrical energy cost for an existing building, the designer must evaluate the actual electric bills for the past 2 years. It should be noted that the general cost per kilowatthour of energy provided by service distributors consists of numerous charges, such as commissioning, decommissioning, bulk purchase, and other miscellaneous cost items that generally appear on electric bills (and vary seasonally) but go unnoticed by consumers.

The most significant of these charges, which is in fact a penalty, is classified as *peak-hour energy*. This charge occurs when the consumer's power demand exceeds the established boundaries of energy consumption as stipulated in tariff agreements. In order to maintain a stable power supply and cost for a unit of energy (a kilowatthour), service distributors such as Southern California Electric (SCE) and other power-generating entities generally negotiate a long-term agreement whereby the providers guarantee distributors a set bulk of energy for a fixed sum. Since energy providers have limited power-generation capacity, limits are set as to the amount of power that is to be distributed for the duration of the contract. A service provider such as SCE uses statistics and demographics of the territories served to project power-consumption demands, which then form the baseline for the energy purchase agreement. When energy consumption exceeds the projected demand, it becomes subject to a much costlier tariff, which generally is referred to as the *peak bulk energy rate*.

PROJECT COST ANALYSIS

As indicated in the preliminary solar power cogeneration study, the average installed cost per watt of electric energy is approximately $8–$9, as shown in Fig. 3.72. The unit cost encompasses all turnkey cost components, such as engineering design documentation, solar power components, PV support structures, electric hardware, inverters, integration labor, and labor force training. Structures in that cost include roof-mount support frames and simple carport canopies only. Special architectural monuments, if

Economic Analysis:

INITIAL COSTS & CREDITS

		Hours	Rate		Total	%
Engineering Rate			$150.00 per hour			
Site Investigation		40 $	150.00	$	6,000.00	46.88%
Preliminary Design Coordination		24 $	150.00	$	3,600.00	28.13%
Report Preparation		8 $	150.00	$	1,200.00	9.38%
Travel & Accommodations		1 $	2,000.00	$	2,000.00	15.63%
Other				$	-	0.00%
	Sub Total			$	12,800.00	100.00%

DEVELOPMENT

Permits & Rebate Applications		8 $	150.00	$	1,200.00	5.41%
Project Management		120 $	150.00	$	18,000.00	81.08%
Travel Expenses		1 $	2,000.00	$	2,000.00	9.01%
Other		1 $	1,000.00	$	1,000.00	4.50%
	Sub Total			$	22,200.00	100.00%

ENGINEERING

PV Systems Design		90 $	150.00	$	13,500.00	10%
Architectural Design		90 $	150.00	$	13,500.00	10%
Structural Design		90 $	150.00	$	13,500.00	10%
Electrical Design		420 $	150.00	$	63,000.00	48%
Tenders & Contracting		48 $	150.00	$	7,200.00	5%
Construction Supervision		94 $	150.00	$	14,100.00	11%
Training Mauals		48 $	150.00	$	7,200.00	5%
	Sub Total			$	132,000.00	100%

RENEWABLE ENERGY EQUIPMENT

PV Modules (per kWh-DC)		255 $	3,900.00	$	994,500.00	92%
Transportation		1 $	5,000.00	$	5,000.00	0%
Other				$	-	0%
Tax (Equipment Only)		8.25%		$	82,046.25	8%
	Sub Total			$	1,081,546.25	100%

INSTALLATION EQUIPMENT

PV Module Support Structure (per kWh)		255 $	500.00	$	127,500.00	18%
Inverter (per kWh)		320 $	488.00	$	156,160.00	22%
Electrical Materials (per kW)		320 $	250.00	$	80,000.00	11%
System Installation Labor (per kWh)		320 $	1,000.00	$	320,000.00	45%
Transportaiton		1 $	3,000.00	$	3,000.00	0%
Other		0		$	-	0%
Tax (Equipment Only)		8.25%		$	30,001.95	4%
	Sub Total			$	716,661.95	100%

MISCELLANEOUS

Training		48 $	150.00	$	7,200.00	100%
Contingencies (If applicable)		0		$	-	0%
	Sub Total			$	7,200.00	100%

OVERHEAD & PROFIT   18% $ 355,033.48   100%

TOTAL PROJECT COST ESTIMATE: $ 2,327,441.68   100%

Figure 3.72   Material and equipment estimate for Water Education Museum.

Miscellaneous

	Hours	Rate		Total	
Training	48	$	150.00	$	7,200.00
Contingencies					
Total miscellaneous				$	**7,200.00**

Energy demand analysis

Ligthing kWh	413	
HVAC kWh	296	
Ave. hourly energy kWh	709	
Ave. cost of per kWh, current cost		$ 0.19
Ave. monthly energy expenditure		$ 48,495.60
Ave. yearly energy expenditure projection-kWh		$ 581,947.20

Projected energy cost

Projected cost escalation

		5 YEARS	10 YEARS
Energy cost escalation rate	6%	$ 34,916.83	$ 37,011.84
Inflation rate	3.0%	$ 17,458.42	$ 17,982.17
Total yearly cost escalation		$ 52,375.25	$ 54,994.01

Solar power energy generation

Energy generation capacity kWh-AC		212	212
Average daily solar irradiance-hrs		5.5	5.5
Yearly energy generation kWh		425037	425037
5-year inflation rate per kWh	15.0%	$ 0.19	$ 0.22
Yearly cost savings by PV modules		$ 80,757.01	$ 92,870.56
Yearly aggregate savings		$ 133,132	$ 147,865

Figure 3.72   Material and equipment estimate for Water Education Museum.
(*Continued*)

Projected cost escalation		15 YEARS		20 YEARS		25 YEARS
Energy cost escalation rate	$	39,232.55	$	41,586.51	$	44,081.70
Inflation rate	$	18,521.63	$	19,077.28	$	19,649.60
Total yearly cost escalation	$	57,754.19	$	60,663.79	$	63,731.30

Solar power energy generation

		15 YEARS		20 YEARS		25 YEARS
Energy generation capacity kWh-AC		212		212		212
Average daily solar irradiance-hrs		5.5		5.5		5.5
Yearly energy generation kWh		425037		425037		425037
5-year inflation rate per kWh	$	0.25	$	0.29	$	0.33
Yearly cost savings by PV modules	$	106,801.15	$	122,821.32	$	141,244.52
Yearly aggregate savings	$	164,555	$	183,485	$	204,976

Project Cost Summary				COST	%
Engineering	DC Kw		$/Watt	$	132,000	5.78%
Renewable energy equipment	255	$	3,900.00	$	994,850	43.54%
Renewable energy equipment tax	8.25%			$	82,075	3.59%
Trial transportation/crates	7	$	500.00	$	3,500.00	0.15%
Installation equipment				$	716,711	31.37%
Miscellaneous				$	7,200	0.32%
Total				$	1,936,336	
OH&P			18.0%	$	348,540	15.25%
Total initial cost				$	2,284,876	100.00%

Additional allowable expenses
Total allowable cost

Buy-back rebate Wh-SCE	$	4.50	Discount/W
Total DC Wh subject to rebate		255,090	DC- Watts
Maximum rebate			

Total rebate amount	50%	$	1,142,438

Net cost initial cost	$	1,142,438

Cost per DC watts	$	8.96

Figure 3.72   (*Continued*)

required, may necessitate some incremental cost adjustment. As per the CEC, all solar power cogeneration program rebate applications applied for before December of 2002 was subject to a 50 percent subsidy. At present, rebate allotments depend strictly on the amount of funding available at the time of application and are granted on a first-come, first-served basis.

Figure 3.72 offers detailed estimates, calculated by me, for a solar power project for the Water and Life Museum, located in Hemet, California. As discussed earlier in this chapter, the project consists of two museum campuses with a total of seven buildings, each constructed with roof-mounted solar power PV systems.

The cost estimate, as shown in Fig. 3.72, represents one of the main buildings, the actual Water Education Museum. This project is funded by the Los Angeles Metropolitan Water District (MWD). The solar power generation of the entire campus is 540 W dc. Net ac power output, including losses, is estimated to be approximately 480 kW. At present, the entire solar power-generation system is paid for by the MWD. As a result, all the power generated by the system will be used by the Water and Life Museum and represents approximately 70–75 percent of the overall electric demand load.

MAINTENANCE COSTS

As mentioned earlier, solar power systems have a near-zero maintenance requirement. This is due to solid-state technology, lamination techniques, and the total absence of mechanical or moving parts. However, to prevent marginal degradation in output performance from dust accumulation, solar arrays require biyearly rinsing with a water hose.

FEASIBILITY STUDY REPORT

As mentioned earlier in this chapter, the key to designing a viable solar power system begins with preparation of a feasibility report. A feasibility report is essentially a preliminary engineering design report that is intended to inform the end user about significant aspects of the project. The document therefore must include a thorough definition of the entire project from both material and financial perspectives.

A well-prepared report must inform and educate the client, as well as provide a realistic projection of all engineering and financial costs to enable the user to weigh all aspects of a project from start to finish. The report must include a comprehensive technical and financial analysis of all aspects of the project, including particulars of local climatic conditions, solar power system installation alternatives, grid-integration requirements, electric power demand, and economic cost projection analysis. The report also must incorporate photographs, charts, and statistical graphs to illustrate and inform the client about the benefits of the solar power or sustainable-energy system proposed.

POLLUTION ABATEMENT CONSIDERATIONS

According to a 1999 report by the U.S. Department of Energy, 1 kW of energy produced by a coal-fired electric power–generating plant requires about 5 lb of coal. Likewise, the generation of 1.5 kWh of electric energy per year requires about 7400 lb of coal, which, in turn, produces 10,000 lb of carbon dioxide (CO_2).

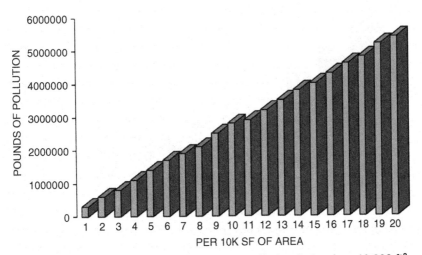

Figure 3.73   Commercial energy use pollution index (per 10,000 ft²
and pounds of pollution).

Roughly speaking, the calculated projections of the power demand for the project
totals about 2500–3000 kWh. This will require between 12 million and 15 million lb
of coal, thereby producing about 16–200 million lb of carbon dioxide and contributing to air pollution and global warming from greenhouse gases.

Solar power, in turn, if implemented as discussed here, will minimize the air pollution index substantially. In fact, the EPA soon will be instituting an air pollution index-
ing system that will be factored into all future construction permits. At that time, all
major industrial projects will be required to meet and adhere to the air pollution standards and offset excess energy consumption by means of solar or renewable-energy
resources. Figure 3.73 is a graph showing commercial energy pollution.

CO_2 EMISSIONS BY REGION

Owing to the comparatively large amount of power consumed in the United States,
which amounts to 25 percent of total global energy, Fig. 3.74 does not include U.S.
energy consumption so as to avoid dwarfing comparative values when comparing
industrial nations.

ENERGY COST ESCALATION

According to an Energy Information Administration data source published in 1999,
California is among the top 10 energy consumers in the world, and this state alone
consumes just as much energy as Brazil or the United Kingdom. Since all global crude
oil reserves are estimated to last about 30–80 years, and over 50 percent of the nation's
energy is imported from abroad, it is inevitable that in the near future, energy costs
will undoubtedly surpass historical cost-escalation averaging projections.

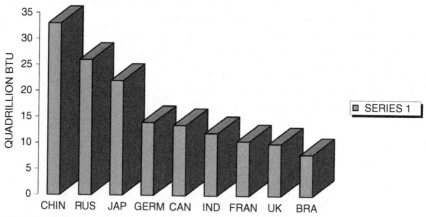

Figure 3.74   Top 10 energy consumers in the world by CO_2 emissions and region.

It is estimated that the cost of nonrenewable energy will, within the next decade, be increased by approximately 4–5 percent by producers. When compounded with a general inflation rate of 3 percent, average energy cost over the next decade could be expected to rise at a rate of about 7 percent per year. This cost increase does not take into account other inflation factors, such as regional conflicts, embargoes, and natural catastrophes.

In view of the fact that solar power cogeneration systems require nearly zero maintenance and are more reliable than any other human-made power-generation devices (the systems have an actual life span of 35–40 years and are guaranteed by the manufacturers for a period of 25 years), it is my opinion that in a near-perfect geographic setting such as Hemet, their integration into mainstream architectural design not only will enhance design aesthetics but also will generate considerable savings and mitigate adverse effects on ecology from global warming.

As indicated in the solar power cogeneration study, the average cost per installed watt of electric energy is approximately 40 percent of the total installed cost. The unit cost encompasses all turnkey cost components, such as engineering design documentation, solar power components, PV support structures, electrical hardware, inverters, integration labor, and labor training.

SYSTEM MAINTENANCE AND OPERATIONAL COSTS

As mentioned earlier, solar power systems have a near-zero maintenance requirement. However, to prevent marginal degradation in output performance from dust accumulation, solar arrays require a biyearly rinsing with a regular water hose. Since solar power arrays are completely modular, system expansion, module replacement, and troubleshooting are simple and require no special maintenance skills. All electronic dc-to-ac inverters are modular and can be replaced with minimum downtime.

An optional (and relatively inexpensive) computerized system-monitoring console can provide real-time performance status of the entire solar power cogeneration system. A software-based supervisory program featured in the monitoring system also can provide instantaneous indication of solar array performance and malfunction.

PROJECT FINANCING

The following financing discussion is specific to large alternative- and renewable-energy projects, such as solar, wind, and geothermal projects, that require extensive amounts of investment capital. Project financing of such large projects, similar to large industrial projects, involves long-term financing of capital-intensive material and equipment.

Since most alternative-energy projects in the United States are subject to state and federal tax incentives and rebates, project financing involves highly complex financial structures in which project debt and equity, rebate, federal and state tax incentives, and cash flow generated by grid-energy power are used to finance the project. In general, project lenders are given a lien on all the project assets, including property, which enables them to assume control of a project over the terms of the contract.

Since renewable-energy and large industrial projects involve different levels of transactions, such as equipment and material purchase, site installation, maintenance, and financing, a special-purpose entity is created for each project, thereby shielding other assets owned by a project sponsor from the detrimental effects of project failure.

As a special-purpose joint venture, these types of entities have no assets other than the project. In some instances, capital contribution commitments by the owners of the project company sometimes are necessary to ensure that the project is financially sound.

In particular, alternative-energy technology project financing is often more complicated than alternative financing methods commonly used in capital-intensive projects such as transportation, telecommunications, and public utility industries. Renewable-energy-type projects in particular are frequently subject to a number of technical, environmental, economic, and political risks. Therefore, financial institutions and project sponsors evaluate inherent risks associated with a particular project development and operation and determine whether projects are financeable.

To minimize risk, project sponsors create special entities, which consist of a number of specialist companies operating in a contractual network with each other and which allocate risk in a way that allows financing to take place. In general, a project financing scheme involves a number of equity investors known as *sponsors*, which include hedge funds as well as a syndicate of banks that provide loans for the project. The loans are most commonly nonrecourse loans, which are secured by the project itself and paid entirely from its cash flow, rebates, and tax incentives. Projects that involve large risks require limited-recourse financing secured by a surety from sponsors. A complex project finance scheme also may incorporate corporate finance, securitization, options, insurance provisions, and/or other measures to mitigate risk.

Power purchase agreements   Power purchase agreements (PPAs) for renewable-energy projects are a class of *lease-option-to-buy financing plans* that are specifically tailored to underwrite the heavy cost burden of the project. PPAs, which are also referred to as *third-party ownership contracts,* differ from conventional loans in that they require significant land or property equity that must be tied up for the duration of the lease. PPAs have the following significant features that make them unique as financial instruments:

- They take advantage of federal and state tax incentives, which otherwise may have no value for public agencies, municipalities, counties, nonprofit organizations, or businesses that do not have significant profit margins.
- Properties where renewable-energy systems equipment and materials such as solar PV power support structures are installed must be leased for the entire duration of the contract agreement, which may exceed 20 years.
- Solar power or the renewable-energy system must be connected to the electrical grid.
- Power generated by the renewable-energy system must be used primarily by the owner.
- Depending on the lease agreement, excess power produced from the power cogeneration system is accounted toward the third-party owner.
- Equity of the leased property must have liquidity value exceeding the value of the project.

Advantages of PPAs   In general, PPAs have the following significant advantages:

- Projects are financed on equity of properties, such as unused grounds or building rooftops, which otherwise have no value.
- Owners are not burdened with intensive project cost.
- PPAs guarantee owners a hedge against electrical energy escalation costs.
- Energy cost escalation associated with third-party PPAs have significantly less risk than grid-purchased electrical energy.
- The owners assume no responsibility for maintenance and upkeep of the leased equipment or grounds for the duration of the lease period.
- On completion of the lease agreement period, owners are offered flexible options for ownership.
- All PPAs intrinsically constitute turnkey *design-build contracts,* which somewhat relieve the owners from detail technical design.

Disadvantages of PPAs   Since PPAs essentially constitute a contractual rather than an engineering design and procurement agreement, they inherently include a number of undesirable features that in some instances can neutralize the associated benefits discussed earlier. Some of the undesirable features associated with PPAs are as follow:

- PPA contracts are extremely complex and convoluted. Contract agreements drafted include legal language and clauses that strongly favor the third-party provider.
- PPA contracts incorporate stiff penalties for premature contract terminations.

- PPA or third-party ownerships in general involve a finance company, an intermediary such as a sales and marketing organization, a design engineering organization, a general contractor, and in some instances a maintenance contractor. Considering the fragmented responsibilities and the complexities embodying the collaborative effort of all entities and the life cycle of the contract, the owners must exercise extreme diligence in executing PPA contracts.
- The owners have no control over the quality of design or materials provided; therefore, extra measures of caution should be exercised when evaluating final ownership of the equipment.
- In general, owners who elect to enter into a PPA, such as nonprofit organizations, municipalities, city governments, and/or large commercial industries, seldom have experienced engineering or legal staff that have had previous exposure to PPA-type contracts.
- The owners tie up the leased grounds or buildings for extended periods of time and assume responsibility for insuring the property against vandalism and damage owing to natural causes.
- In the event of power outages, third-party ownership agreement contracts penalize the owners for loss of power output generation.
- PPA contracts include yearly energy escalation costs, which represent a certain percentage of the installed cost and must be evaluated with extreme diligence and awareness because these seemingly small inflationary costs could neutralize the main benefit, which is the hedge against energy cost escalation.
- PPAs for large, renewable solar power cogeneration contracts are relatively new financial instruments. Therefore, their owners must be careful to take proper measures to avoid unexpected consequences.

Preparation for PPA proposal Unlike conventional capital-intensive projects, PPAs completely bypass proven engineering design measures, which involve project feasibility studies, preliminary design and econometric analysis, design documentation, construction documentation, design specification, and procurement evaluation, which are based on job-specific criteria. In order to ensure a measure of control and conformance to project needs, it is recommended that the owners refer to an experienced consulting engineer or legal consultant who is familiar with PPA projects.

To avoid or minimize unexpected negative consequences associated with PPAs, the owners are advised to incorporate the following documents, reports, and studies into their proposal request specification (RFP):

- For ground-mount installations, employ the services of qualified engineering consultants to prepare a negative environmental impact report, site grading, drainage, and soil study.
- Provide statistical power consumption and peak power analysis of present and future electrical demand loads.
- Provide a set of electrical plans, including single-line diagrams, main service switchgear, and power-demand calculations.

- Conduct an energy audit.
- Provide detailed data about site topology and present and future land use.
- Provide data regarding local climatic conditions such as wind, sand, or dust accumulation and cyclic flooding conditions, if applicable.
- For roof-mount systems, provide aerial photographs of roof plans that show mechanical equipment, air vents, and roof hatches. Drawings also must accompany architectural drawings that show parapet heights and objects that could cause shading.
- Specifications should outline current electrical tariff agreements.
- The document also should incorporate any and all special covenants, conditions, and restrictions associated with the leased property.
- To ensure system hardware reliability at the posterity of the contract, the RFP must include a generic outline of hardware and data-acquisition and monitoring software requirements.
- The specifications must request providers to disclose all issues that may cause noncompliance.
- Expected power output performance guarantees, as well as projected annual power generation requirements, must be delineated.

Owners are also advised to conduct preliminary renewable-energy production studies that would enable them to evaluate energy-production potential, as well as economic analysis of possible alternatives.

PPA contract structure for solar power systems   To prepare a PPA request for a proposal document, the owner's legal counsel and management personnel must familiarize themselves with various elements of the contract agreement. Agreements involving third-party ownership consist of two parts, namely, legal and technical. The following are some of the most significant points of PPA-type contracts that third-party purchase providers must respond to and evaluate accordingly:

Contractual matters of interest
- DC output size of the PV modules in kilowatthours
- AC or PTC output of the PV modules in kilowatthours
- Expected ac power output of the solar system in its first year of installation
- Expected life-cycle power output in kilowatthours dc
- Expected life-cycle power output in kilowatthours ac
- Guaranteed minimum annual power output performance in kilowatthours ac
- Terms of contractual agreement
- Penalty or compensation for performance failure
- Price structure at the end of the contract with client paying 0 percent of the cost
- Price structure at the end of the contract with client paying 50 percent of the cost
- Price structure at the end of the contract with client paying 100 percent of the cost
- Expected average yearly performance during life cycle of the contract
- Expected mean yearly performance degradation during life cycle of the contract
- Assumed PPA price per kilowatthour of electrical energy
- Initial cost of PPA

- PPA yearly escalation cost as a percentage of the initial energy rate
- Net present value over 25 years
- Proposed cost-reduction measures
- Net present value of reduction measures
- Annual inflation rate
- Projected annual electricity cost escalation
- First-year avoided energy cost savings
- Total life-cycle energy saved in kilowatthours
- Total life-cycle energy PPA payment
- Cost of PPA buyout at the end of life cycle
- PPA expenses
- Total life-cycle pretax savings
- Total project completion time in months
- Customer training
- Insurance rating

Technical matters of interest
- PV module manufacturer and type
- PV module technology
- PV module efficiency rating
- PV module dc watts
- PV module PTC watts as listed under CEC equipment and product qualification listing
- Total PV module count
- Percent yearly solar power output degradation
- PV module warrantee in years after formal test acceptance and commissioning
- Inverter make and model as listed under CEC equipment and product qualification
- Inverter kilowatt rating
- Number of inverters used
- Inverter performance efficiency
- Inverter basic and extended warrantees
- Solar power–tracking system (if used)
- Tracking-system tilt angle in degrees east and west
- Number of solar power–tracker assemblies
- Kilowatts of PV modules per tracker
- Ground or pedestal area requirement per 100 kW of tracker (For large solar-powered farms, tracker footprint must be accounted for in acres per megawatt of land required.)
- Tracker or support-pedestal ground-penetration requirements
- Tracker above-ground footing height
- Tracker below-ground footing height
- Wind shear withstand capability in miles per hour
- Environmental impact during and after system installation (if applicable)
- Lightning-protection scheme

- Electrical power conversion and transformation scheme and equipment platform requirements
- Equipment-mounting platforms
- Underground or above-ground dc or ac conduit installations
- PV module washing options, such as permanent water-pressure bibs, automatic sprinklers, or mobile pressure washers
- Service options and maintenance during life cycle of the PPA

Experience in large-scale installation
- Engineering staff's collective experience in PV design and power engineering
- In-house or subcontracted engineering
- In-house or subcontracted installation crew
- Years of experience in solar power–tracker system installations (if applicable)
- Years of collective experience in PPA contracting
- Location of management, engineering, installation, and maintenance depots
- Availability of PV modules and specific PPAs with major national and international manufacturers
- Name of the primary entity assuming full contractual responsibility and project bonding
- Names of each contractor or subcontractor taking part in the PPA
- Years of collaboration with outsourced entities

Data-acquisition and monitoring system
- Data-acquisition system certification by the rebate agency, such as the California Solar Initiative (CSI)
- Is data-acquisition system provided proprietary, or is it being provided by a third-party certified provider?
- Data-acquisition system power measurement and transmission intervals in minutes
- Monitored data, such as weather, wind speed, humidity, precipitation, and solar irradiance
- CSI-certified reporting scheme
- Customer Web access key
- On-site electrical display and printing capability and associated options
- On-site integration capability with customer's data-monitoring system
- Periodic data reporting format and frequency
- Presentation and visual aids, such as bar-chart displays of statistical solar power monitored information and solar power array configuration displays
- On-demand reporting
- Proactive solar power system diagnostic capability

Proposal evaluation   As mentioned earlier, long-term financing agreements such as PPAs are inherently complicated and demand extensive due diligence by the owner, legal counsel, and consulting engineers alike. In order to execute a PPA successfully, the owner must fully appreciate the importance of the collective effort of experts and the collaborative effort required in preparation of specifications and RFP documents. Prior knowledge of specification and evaluation points (outlined earlier) would prepare owners to evaluate comparative-value advantages among PPA providers.

CONCLUSION

Even though the initial investment in a solar power cogeneration system requires a large capital investment, the long-term financial and ecologic advantages are so significant that their deployment in the existing project should be given special consideration. A solar power cogeneration system, if applied based on the recommendations reviewed here, will provide considerable energy expenditure savings over the lifespan of the recreation facility and provide a hedge against unavoidable energy cost escalation.

Special Note

In view of the depletion of existing CEC rebate funds, it is recommended that applications for the rebate program be initiated at the earliest possible time. Furthermore, because of the design integration of the solar power system with the service grid, the decision to proceed with the program must be made at the commencement of the construction design document stage.

CALIFORNIA SOLAR INITIATIVE

PROGRAM

This chapter summarizes the California Energy Commission's (CEC's) California Solar Incentive (CSI) program, a detailed reversion of which is available at www .gosolarcalifornia.ca.gov/csi/index.html.

Beginning January 1, 2007, the state of California introduced solar rebate funding for the installation of photovoltaic (PV) power cogeneration that was authorized by the California Public Utilities Commission (CPUC) and the state senate. The bill, referenced as SB1, has allotted a budget of $2.167 billion to be used over a 10-year period.

The rebate funding program, known as the *California Solar Initiative* (CSI), awards an incentive plan on the basis of performance, unlike earlier programs that allotted rebates based on a calculated projection of system energy output. The new rebate award system categorizes solar power installations into two incentive groups. PV installations of 100 kW or larger receive a *performance-based incentive* (PBI), which provides rebate dollars based on the actual output over a 5-year period. Solar power systems with performance capacities of fewer than 30 kW receive an *expected performance–based buydown* (EPBB), which is a one-time lump-sum incentive payment based on the system's expected future performance.

The distribution and administration of CSI funds are delegated to three major utility providers that service various areas of the state. Three main service providers that administer the program are

- Pacific Gas and Electric (PG&E), which serves northern California
- Southern California Edison (SCE), which serves central California
- San Diego Regional Energy Office (SDREO)/San Diego Gas and Electric (SDG&E), which serves the greater San Diego area

It should be noted that municipal electric utility customers are not eligible to receive CSI funds from these three administrative agencies.

Each of the three service providers administering the CSI have Web pages that enable clients to access online registration databases, program handbooks, reservation forms,

TABLE 4.1 CSI BUDGET BY ADMINISTRATOR		
UTILITY	TOTAL BUDGET, %	DOLLAR VALUE, IN MILLIONS
PG&E	43.7	$946
SCE	46	$996
SDREO/SDG&E	10.3	$223

contract agreements, and all other forms required by the CSI. All CSI application and reservation forms are available at www.gosolarcalifornia.ca.gov/csi/index.html.

The principal objective of the CSI is to ensure that 3000 MW of new solar energy facilities are installed throughout California by 2017.

CSI Fund Distribution

The CSI fund distribution administered by the three agencies has a specific budget allotment that is proportioned according to the demographics of power demand and distribution. CSI budget allotment values are shown in Table 4.1.

The CSI budget shown in the table is divided into two customer segments, namely, residential and nonresidential. Table 4.2 shows relative allocations of CSI solar power generation by customer sector.

The CSI budget also has $216 million allocated to affordable or low-income housing projects.

CSI Power-Generation Targets

To offset the high costs associated with solar power installation and to promote PV industry development, the CSI has devised a plan that encourages customer sectors to take immediate advantage of rebate initiatives, which are intended to last for a limited duration of 10 years. The incentive program is currently designed to be reduced

TABLE 4.2 CSI POWER ALLOCATION BY CUSTOMER SECTOR		
CUSTOMER SECTOR	POWER, MW	PERCENT
Residential	557.50	33%
Nonresidential	1172.50	67%
Total	1750.00	100%

TABLE 4.3   CSI POWER-PRODUCTION TARGETS BY UTILITY AND CUSTOMER SECTOR

TRIGGER STEP	ALLOTTED	PG&E RES.	PG&E NONRES.	SCE RES.	SCE NONRES.	SDG&E RES.	SDG&E NONRES.
1	50 MW	—	—	—	—	—	—
2	70 MW	10.1	20.5	10.6	21.6	2.4	4.8
3	100 MW	14.4	29.3	15.2	30.8	3.4	6.9
4	130 MW	18.7	38.1	19.7	40.1	4.4	9.0
5	160 MW	23.1	46.8	24.3	49.3	5.4	11.1
6	190 MW	27.4	55.6	28.8	58.6	6.5	13.1
7	215 MW	31.0	62.9	32.6	66.3	7.3	14.8
8	250 MW	36.1	73.2	38.0	77.1	8.5	17.3
9	285 MW	41.1	83.4	43.3	87.8	9.7	19.7
10	350 MW	50.5	102.5	53.1	107.9	11.9	24.2
Total	1750 MW	764.8 MW		805.0 MW		180.3 MW	
Percent	100%	43.7%		46.0%		10.3%	

automatically over the duration of the 3000 MW of solar power reservation downtrigger levels that will distribute the power generation gradually over 10 allotted steps. CSI megawatt power-production targets are apportioned among the administrative agencies by residential and nonresidential customer sectors.

In each of the 10 steps, CSI applications are limited to the trigger levels. Table 4.3 shows set trigger stages for SCE and PG&E client sectors. Once the trigger-level allotments are complete, the reservation process is halted and restarted at the next trigger level. In the event of a trigger-level power surplus, the excess energy allotment is transferred forward to the next trigger level.

These power-production targets are based on the premise that solar power industry production output and client-sector awareness will be increased gradually within the next decade and that the incentive program eventually will promote a viable industry that will be capable of providing tangible sources of renewable energy in California.

Incentive Payment Structure

As mentioned earlier, the CSI offers PBI and EPBB programs, both of which are based on verifiable PV system output performance. EPBB output characteristics are basically determined by factors such as the location of solar platforms, system size, shading

TABLE 4.4 CSI PBI AND EPBB TARGETED ENERGY PAYMENT AMOUNTS

TRIGGER STEP	ALLOTTED	EPBB PAYMENT/W			PBI PAYMENT/W		
		RES.	COMM.	GOV.	RES.	COMM.	GOV.
1	50 MW	N/A	N/A	N/A	N/A	N/A	N/A
2	70 MW	$2.5	$2.5	$3.25	$0.39	$0.39	$0.50
3	100 MW	$2.2	$2.2	$2.95	$0.34	$0.34	$0.46
4	130 MW	$1.9	$1.9	$2.65	$0.26	$0.26	$0.37
5	160 MW	$1.55	$1.55	$2.30	$0.22	$0.22	$0.32
6	190 MW	$1.10	$1.10	$1.85	$0.15	$0.15	$0.26
7	215 MW	$0.65	$0.65	$1.40	$0.09	$0.09	$0.19
8	250 MW	$0.35	$0.65	$1.10	$0.05	$0.05	$0.15
9	285 MW	$0.25	$0.25	$0.9	$0.03	$0.03	$0.12
10	350 MW	$0.20	$0.20	$0.70	$0.03	$0.03	$0.10

conditions, tilt angle, and all the factors that were discussed in preceding chapters. On the other hand, PBIs are based strictly on predetermined flat-rate-per-kilowatthour output payments over a 5-year period. Incentive payment levels have been devised to be reduced automatically over the duration of the program in 10 steps that are directly proportional to the megawatt volume reservation (Table 4.4).

As seen from this incentive-distribution table, the rebate payments diminish as the targeted solar power program reaches its 3000-MW energy output. The main reasoning behind the downscaling of the incentive is the presumption that solar power manufacturers, within the next decade, will be in a position to produce larger quantities and more efficient, less expensive PV modules. As a result of the economies of scale, the state will no longer be required to extend special incentives to promote the PV industry with public funds.

Expected Performance–Based Buydown (EPBB)

As mentioned earlier, EPBB is a one-time upfront incentive that is based on the estimated or predicated future performance of PV-powered cogeneration. This program is targeted to minimize program administration costs for relatively small systems that do not exceed 100 kWh. As a rule, factors that affect the computation of estimated power performance are relatively simple and take into consideration such things as panel count,

PV module certified specifications, location of the solar platform, insolation, PV panel orientation, tilt angle, and shading losses. All these are entered into a predetermined equation that results in the buydown incentive rate.

The EPBB applies to all new projects other than systems that have building-integrated PVs (BIPVs). The EPBB one-time incentive payment calculation is based on the following formula:

$$\text{EPBB incentive payment} = \text{incentive rate} \times \text{system rating (kW)} \times \text{design factor}$$

$$\text{System rating (kW)} = \text{number of PV modules} \times \text{CEC photovoltaic module test}$$
$$\text{standard (PTC) value} \times \text{CEC inverter listed efficiency}$$
$$\text{(divided by 1000 for kilowatt conversion)}$$

Special design requirements are as follows:

- All PV modules must be oriented between 180 and 270 degrees.
- The optimal tilt for each compass direction should be in the range of 180 and 270 degrees for optimized summer power output efficiency.
- The system must take into account derating factors associated with weather and shading analysis.
- The system must be in an optimal reference and location.
- PV tilt must correspond to the local latitude.

Performance-Based Incentive (PBI)

As of January 1, 2007, this incentive applied to solar power system installations that delivered or exceeded 100 kW. As of January 1, 2008, the base power output reference was reduced to 50 kW, and by January 1, 2010, the incentive will be reduced to 30 kW. Each PBI payment is limited to a duration of 5 years following completion of the system acceptance test. Also included in the plan are custom-made BIPV systems.

Host Customer

All beneficiaries of the CSI are referred to as *host customers* and include not only the electric utility customers but also retail electric distribution organizations such as PG&E, SCE, and SDG&E. Under the rules of the CSI, all entities who apply for an incentive are referred to as *applicants, hosts,* or *system owners.*

In general, host customers must have an outstanding account with a utility provider at a location of solar power cogeneration. In other words, the project in California must be located within the service territory of one of the three listed program administrators.

On approval of reservation, the host customer is considered as the system owner and retains sole rights to the reservation. The reservation is a payment guarantee by CSI that cannot be transferred by the owner, although the system installer can be designated to act on behalf of the owner.

To proceed with the solar power program, the applicant or owner must receive a written confirmation letter from the administrating agency and then apply for authorization for grid connectivity. In the event of project delays beyond the permitted period of fund reservation, the customer must reapply for another rebate to obtain authorization.

According to CSI regulations, there are a several categories of customers who do not qualify to receive the incentive. Customers exempted from the program are organizations that are in the business of power generation and distribution, publicly owned gas and electricity distribution utilities, or any entity that purchases electricity or natural gas for wholesale or retail purposes. As a rule, the customer assumes full ownership on reception of the incentive payment and technically becomes responsible for the operation and maintenance of the overall solar power system.

It should be noted that a CSI applicant is recognized as the entity that completes and submits the reservation forms and becomes the main contact person to communicate with the program administrator throughout the duration of the project. However, the applicant also may designate an engineering organization, a system integrator, an equipment distributor, or even an equipment lessor to act as the designated applicant.

Solar Power Contractors and Equipment Sellers

State of California contractors who specialize in solar power installation must hold an appropriate California contractors' state license. In order to qualify as an installer by the CSI administrator, the solar power system integrator must provide the following information:

- Business name and address
- Principal name or contact
- Business registration or license number
- Contractor's license number
- Contractor's bond (if applicable) and corporate limited-liability entities
- Reseller's license number (if applicable)

All equipment, such as PV modules, inverters, and meters, sold by equipment sellers must be Underwriter's Laboratory (UL) approved and certified by the CEC. All equipment provided must be new and have been tested for at least a period of 1 year. Use of refurbished equipment is not permitted. It should be noted that experimental, field-demonstrated, or proof-of-concept operation-type equipment and materials are not approved and do not qualify for rebate incentives. All equipment used therefore must have UL certification and performance specifications that would allow program administrators to evaluate its performance.

According to CEC certification criteria, all grid-connected PV systems must carry a 10-year warranty and meet the following certification requirements:

- All PV modules must be certified to UL Standard 1703.
- All grid-connected solar watthour meters for systems under 10 kW must have an accuracy of ±5 percent. Watthour meters on systems generating more than 10 kW must have a measurement accuracy of ±2 percent.
- All inverters must be certified to UL Standard 1741.

PV System Sizing Requirements

It should be noted that the primary objective of solar power cogeneration is to produce a certain amount of electricity to offset a certain portion of the electrical demand load. Therefore, power production of PV systems is set in a manner so as not to exceed the actual energy consumption during the preceding 12 months. The formula applied for establishing the maximum system capacity is

$$\text{Maximum system power output (kW)} = \frac{12 \text{ months of previous energy used (kWh)}}{(0.18 \times 8760 \text{ h/year})}$$

The factor $0.18 \times 8760 = 1577$ h/year can be translated into an average of 4.32 h/day of solar power production, which essentially includes system performance and derating indexes applied in CEC PV system energy-output calculations.

The maximum for PV systems under the present CSI incentive program is limited to 1000 kW, or 1 MW. However, if the preceding calculation limits permit, customers are allowed to install grid-connected systems of up to 5 MW, for which only 1 MW will be considered for receiving the incentive.

For new construction, where the project has no history of previous energy consumption, an applicant must substantiate system power-demand requirements by engineering system demand-load calculations, which will include present and future load-growth projections. All calculations must be substantiated by corresponding equipment specifications, panel schedules, single-line diagrams, and building energy simulation programs, such as eQUEST, EnergyPro, or DOE-2.

Energy-Efficiency Audit

Recent rules enacted in January of 2007 require that all existing residential and commercial customers, when applying for CSI rebates, provide a certified energy-efficiency audit for their existing building. The audit certification, along with the solar PV rebate application forms, must be provided to the program administrator for evaluation purposes.

Energy-efficiency audits can be conducted either by calling an auditor or by accessing a special Web page provided by each administrative entity. In some instances, energy audits can be waived if the applicants can provide a copy of an audit conducted in the past 3 years or provide proof of a California Title 24 Energy Certificate of Compliance, which is usually calculated by mechanical engineers. Projects that have a national LEED certification are also exempt from energy audits.

Warranty and Performance Permanency Requirements

As mentioned earlier, all major system components are required to have a minimum of 10 years of warranty by manufacturers and installers alike. All equipment, including PV modules and inverters, in the event of malfunction, are required to be replaced at no cost to the client. System power-output performance, in addition to electrical equipment breakdown, must include 15 percent power-output degradation from the original rated projected performance for a period of 10 years.

To be eligible for the CSI, all solar power system installations must be permanently attached or secured to their platforms. PV modules supported by quick-disconnect means or installed on wheeled platforms or trailers are not considered legitimate stationary installations.

During the course of project installation, the owner or his or her designated representative must maintain continuous communication with the program administrator and provide all required information regarding equipment specifications, warranties, platform configuration, all design revisions and system modifications, updated construction schedules, and construction status on a regular basis.

In the event that the locations of PV panels are changed and panels are removed or relocated within the same project perimeters or service territory, then owner must inform the CSI administrator and establish a revised PBI payment period.

Insurance

At present, the owner or the host customer of all systems delivering 30 kW or more and receiving CSI payments is require to carry a minimum level of general liability insurance. Installers also must carry workers' compensation and business auto insurance coverage. Since U.S. government entities are self-insured, program administrators will only require proof of coverage.

Grid Interconnection and Metering Requirements

The main criteria for grid integration are that the solar power cogeneration system must be permanently connected to the main electrical service network. As such, portable power generators are not considered eligible. In order to receive the incentive payment, the administrator must receive proof of grid interconnection. To receive additional incentives, customers whose power demands coincide with California's peak electricity demand become eligible to apply for time-of-use (TOU) tariffs that could increase their energy payback. All installed meters must be physically located so as to allow the administrator's authorized agents to have easy access for tests or inspection.

Inspection

All systems rated from 30 to 100 kW that have not adopted a PBI will be inspected by specially designated inspectors. In order for the system to receive the incentive payment, the inspectors must verify system operational performance, installation conformance to application, eligibility criteria, and grid interconnection. System owners who have opted for EPBB incentives must install the PV panels in the proper orientation and produce power that is reflected in the incentive application.

In the event of inspection failure, the owner will be advised by the administrator about shortcomings regarding materials or compliance, and they must be mitigated within 60 days. Failure to correct the problem could result in cancellation of the application and a strike against the installer, applicant, seller, or any other party deemed responsible. Entities identified as responsible for mitigating the problem, if failed 3 times, will be disqualified from participating in CSI programs for a period of 1 year.

CSI Limitations

Prerequisites for processing in the CSI program are based on the premise that a project's total installed, out-of-pocket expenses by the owner do not exceed the eligible costs. For this reason, the owner or applicant must prepare a detailed project cost breakdown that will highlight only the relative embedded costs of the solar power system. A worksheet designed for this purpose is available on the CSI Web page.

It is important to note that clients are not permitted to receive incentives from other sources. In the event that a project may be qualified to receive an additional incentive from another source for the same power cogenerating system, the first incentive amount will be discounted by the amount of the second incentive received. In essence, the overall combined incentive amount must not exceed total eligibility costs.

At all times during project construction, administrators reserve the right to conduct periodic spot checks and random audits to make certain that all payments received were made in accordance with CSI rules and regulations.

CSI Reservation Steps

The following is a summary of steps for EPBB application:

1 The reservation form must be completed and submitted with the owner's or applicant's wet signature.
2 Proof of electric utility service or account number for the project site must be shown on the application. In the case of a new project, the owner must procure a tentative service account number.
3 The system description worksheet available on the CSI Web page must be completed.
4 Electrical system sizing documents, as discussed earlier, must be attached to the application form.
5 If the project is subject to tax-exemption Form AB1407, compliance for government and nonprofit organizations must be attached to the application.
6 For existing projects, energy-efficiency audits or Title 24 calculations must be submitted as well.
7 To calculate the EPBB, use the CSI Web-page calculator (www.csi-epbb.com).
8 Attach a copy of the executed purchase agreement from a solar system contractor or provider.
9 Attach a copy of the executed contract agreement if system ownership is given to another party.
10 Attach a copy of the grid-interconnection agreement, if available; otherwise, inform the administrator about steps taken to secure the agreement.

To submit a payment claim, provide the following documents to the administrator:

1 Submit a wet-signed claim form (available on the CSI Web page).
2 Submit proof of authorization for grid integration.
3 Submit a copy of the building permit and final inspection signoff.
4 Submit proof of warranty from the installer and equipment suppliers.
5 Submit the final project cost breakdown.
6 Submit a final project cost affidavit.

For projects categorized as PBI or nonresidential systems delivering 10 kW or larger, the owner must follow the following procedure:

1 The reservation form must be completed and submitted with owners or applicant's wet signature.

2 Proof of electric utility service or account number for the project site must be shown on the application. In case of a new project, the owner must procure a tentative service account number.

3 The system description worksheet available on the CSI Web page must be completed.

4 Electrical system sizing documents, as discussed earlier, must be attached to the application form.

5 Attach an application fee (1 percent of the requested CSI incentive amount).

6 If the project is subject to tax-exemption Form AB1407, compliance for government and nonprofit organizations must be attached to the application.

7 For existing projects, energy-efficiency audit or Title 24 calculations must be submitted as well.

8 Forward the printout of the calculated PBI. Use the CSI Web-page calculator.

9 Attach a copy of the executed purchase agreement from a solar system contractor or provider.

10 Attach a copy of the executed contract agreement if system ownership is given to another party.

11 Attach a copy of the grid-interconnection agreement if available; otherwise, inform the administrator about steps taken to secure the agreement.

12 Supply a completed proof-of-project milestone statement.

13 Supply a host customer certificate of insurance.

14 Supply a system owner's certificate of insurance (if different from the host).

15 Supply a copy of the project cost-breakdown worksheet.

16 Supply a copy of an alternative system ownership, such as a lease/buy agreement.

17 Supply a copy of a request for proposal (RFP) or solicitation document if the customer is a government, a nonprofit organization, or a public entity.

To submit the claim for the incentive to the administrator, the owner or the contractor must provide the following:

1 A wet-signed claim form (available on the CSI Web page)

2 Proof of authorization for grid integration

3 A copy of the building permit and final inspection signoff

4 Proof of warranty from the installer and equipment suppliers

5 Final project cost breakdown

6 Final project cost affidavit

In the event of incomplete document submittal, the administrators will allow the applicant to provide missing documentation or information within 20 days. Information provided must be in a written form mailed by the U.S. postal system. Faxed or hand-delivered documents are not allowed.

All changes to the reservation must be undertaken by a formal letter that justifies legitimate delay. Requests to extend the reservation expiration date are capped to a maximum of 180 calendar days. Written time-extension requests must explicitly highlight circumstances that were beyond the control of the reservation holder, such as the permitting process, manufacturing delays, extended delivery of PV modules or critical equipment, acts of nature, and so on. All correspondence associated with the delay must be transmitted by letter.

Incentive Payments

On completion of final field acceptance and submission of the above-referenced documents, for EPBB projects, the program administrator will within a period of 30 days issue a complete payment. For PBI programs, the first incentive payment is issued within 30 days of the first scheduled performance reading from the wattmeter. All payments are made to the host customer or the designated agent.

In some instances, a host could ask the administrator to assign the entire payment to a third party. For payment reassignment, the host must complete a special set of forms provided by the administrator.

The EPBB one-time lump-sum payment calculation is based on the following formula:

$$\text{EPBB incentive payment} = \text{final CSI system size} \times \text{reserved EPBB incentive rate}$$

PBI payments for PV systems delivering 100 kW or greater are made on a monthly basis over a period of 5 years. Payment is based on the actual electric energy output of the PV system. If chosen by the owner, systems delivering fewer than 100 kW also can be paid on the PBI basis.

The PBI payment calculation is based on the following formula:

$$\text{Monthly PBI incentive payment} = \text{reserved incentive rate} \times \text{measured kWh output}$$

In the event of PV system size change, the original reservation request forms must be updated and the incentive amount recalculated.

Equipment Distributors

Eligible enterprise resource planning (ERP) manufacturers and companies who sell system equipment must provide the CEC with the following information on the equipment seller information form (CEC-1038 R4).

- Business name, address, phone, fax, and e-mail address
- Owner or principal contact
- Business license number
- Contractor license number (if applicable)
- Proof of good standing in the records of the California Secretary of State, as required for corporate and limited-liability entities
- Reseller's license number

Special Funding for Affordable Housing Projects

California Assembly Bill 58 mandates the CEC to establish an additional rebate for systems installed on affordable housing projects. These projects are entitled to qualify for an extra 25 percent rebate above the standard rebate level, provided that the total amount rebated does not exceed 75 percent of the system cost. The eligibility criteria for qualifying are as follows:

- The affordable housing project must adhere to California health and safety codes.
- The property must expressly limit residency to extremely low, very-low, lower-, or moderate-income persons and must be regulated by the California Department of Housing and Community Development.
- Each residential unit (i.e., apartment, multifamily home) must have individual electric utility meters.
- The housing project must be 10 percent more energy efficient than current standards specify.

Special Funding for Public and Charter Schools

A special amendment to the CEC mandate enacted on February 4, 2004, established a solar schools program to provide a higher level of funding for public and charter schools to encourage the installation of PV generating systems at more school sites. At present, the California Department of Finance has allocated a total of $2.25 million for this purpose. To qualify for additional funds, the schools must meet the following criteria:

- Public or charter schools must provide instruction to kindergarten students or any students in grades 1 to 12.
- The schools must have installed high-efficiency fluorescent lighting in at least 80 percent of classrooms.
- The schools must agree to establish a curriculum tie-in plan to educate students about the benefits of solar energy and energy conservation.

Principal Types of Municipal Leases

There are two types of municipal bonds. One type is referred to as a *tax-exempt munic-ipal lease* and has been available for many years, being used primarily for the purchase of equipment and machinery that has a life expectancy of 7 years or less. The second type, generally known as an *energy-efficiency lease* or a *power-purchase agreement* is used most often on equipment being installed for energy-efficiency purposes that has a life expectancy of more than 7 years. Most often this type of lease applies to equipment classified for use as a renewable-energy cogenerator, such as solar PV and solar thermal systems. The other common type of application that can take advantage of municipal lease plans includes energy-efficiency improvement of devices such as lighting fixtures, insulation, variable-frequency motors, central plants, emergency backup systems, energy management systems, and structural building retrofits.

The leases can carry a purchase option at the end of the lease period for an amount ranging from $1 to fair market value and frequently have options to renew the lease at the end of the lease term for a lesser payment than the original payment.

TAX-EXEMPT MUNICIPAL LEASE

A tax-exempt municipal lease is a special kind of financial instrument that essentially allows government entities to acquire new equipment under extremely attractive terms with streamlined documentation. The lease term is usually for less than 7 years. Some of the most notable benefits are

- Lower rates than conventional loans or commercial leases
- Lease-to-own (there is no residual and no buyout)
- Easier application, such as same-day approvals
- No opinion of counsel required for amounts under $100,000
- No underwriting costs associated with the lease

ENTITIES THAT QUALIFY FOR A MUNICIPAL LEASE

Virtually any state, county, or city government and their agencies, such as law enforcement, public safety, fire, rescue, emergency medical services, water port authorities, school districts, community colleges, state universities, hospitals, and 501 organizations, qualify for municipal leases. Equipment that can be leased under a municipal lease includes essential-use equipment and remediation equipment, such as vehicles, land, or buildings. Some specific examples include

- Renewable-energy systems
- Cogeneration systems
- Emergency-backup systems
- Microcomputers and mainframe computers
- Police vehicles
- Networks and communications equipment
- Fire trucks
- Emergency-management service equipment
- Rescue construction equipment such as aircraft and helicopters
- Training simulators
- Asphalt paving equipment

- Jail and court computer-aided design (CAD) software
- All-terrain vehicles
- Energy-management and solid-waste-disposal equipment
- Turf-management and golf-course-maintenance equipment
- School buses
- Water-treatment systems
- Modular classrooms, portable building systems, and school furniture such as copiers, fax machines, and closed-circuit television surveillance equipment
- Snow- and ice-removal equipment
- Sewer-maintenance equipment

The transaction must be statutorily permissible under local, state, and federal laws and must involve something essential to the operation of the project.

DIFFERENCE BETWEEN A TAX-EXEMPT MUNICIPAL LEASE AND A COMMERCIAL LEASE

Municipal leases are special financial vehicles that provide the benefit of exempting banks and investors from federal income tax, allowing for interest rates that are generally far below conventional bank financing or commercial lease rates. Most commercial leases are structured as rental agreements with either nominal or fair-market-value purchase options.

Borrowing money or using state bonds is strictly prohibited in all states because county and municipal governments are not allowed to incur new debts that will obligate payments that extend over multiyear budget periods. As a rule, state and municipal government budgets are formally voted into law; as such, there is no legal authority to bind the government entities to make future payments.

As a result, most governmental entities are not allowed to sign municipal lease agreements without the inclusion of nonappropriation language. Most governments, when using municipal lease instruments, consider obligations as current expenses and do not characterize them as long-term debt obligations.

The only exceptions are bond issues or general obligations, which are the primary vehicles used to bind government entities to a stream of future payments. General-obligation bonds are contractual commitments to make repayments. The government bond issuer guarantees to make funds available for repayment, including raising taxes, if necessary. In the event that adequate sums are not available in the general fund, "revenue" bond repayments are tied directly to specific streams of tax revenue. Bond issues are very complicated legal documents that are expensive, time-consuming, and in general have a direct impact on the taxpayers and require voter approval. Hence bonds are used exclusively for very large building projects, such as creating infrastructure (e.g., sewers and roads).

Municipal leases automatically include a nonappropriation clause; as such, they are readily approved without counsel. Nonappropriation language effectively relieves the government entity of its obligation in the event that funds are not appropriated in any subsequent period for any legal reason.

Municipal leases can be prepaid at any time without a prepayment penalty. In general, a lease amortization table included with the lease contract shows the interest, principal, and payoff amount for each period of the lease. There is no contractual penalty, and a payoff schedule can be prepared in advance. It also should be noted that equipment and installation can be leased.

Lease payments are structured to provide a permanent reduction in utility costs when used for the acquisition of renewable-energy or cogeneration systems. A flexible leasing structure allows the municipal borrower to level out capital expenditures from year to year. Competitive leasing rates of up to 100 percent financing are available with structured payments to meet revenues that could allow the municipality to acquire the equipment without having current-fund appropriations.

The advantages of a municipal lease program include

- Enhanced cash-flow financing allows municipalities or districts to spread the cost of an acquisition over several fiscal periods, leaving more cash on hand.
- A lease program is a hedge against inflation because the cost of purchased equipment is figured at the time of the lease, and the equipment can be acquired at current prices.
- Flexible lease terms structured over the useful life span of the equipment can allow financing of as much as 100 percent of the acquisition.
- Low-rate interest on a municipal lease contract is exempt from federal taxation, has no fees, and has rates often comparable with bond rates.
- Full ownership at the end of the lease most often includes an optional purchase clause of $1 for complete ownership.

Because of budgetary shortfalls, leasing is becoming a standard way for cities, counties, states, schools, and other municipal entities to get the equipment they need today without spending their entire annual budget to acquire it. Municipal leases are different from standard commercial leases because of the mandatory nonappropriation clause, which states that the entity is only committing to funds through the end of the current fiscal year, even if it is signing a multiyear contract.

ENERGY CONSERVATION

Energy efficiency is an issue that affects all projects. Whether you are considering a renewable-energy system for supplying electricity to your home or business or just want to save money with your current electrical service supplier, the suggestions outlined in this chapter will help you to reduce the amount of energy that you use.

If your electricity is currently supplied by a local utility, increasing the energy efficiency of your project will help to conserve valuable nonrenewable resources. Investing in a renewable-energy system, such as solar or wind, and increasing the energy efficiency of your project will reduce the size and cost of the solar or wind energy system needed. There are many ways to incorporate energy efficiency into a design. Most aspects of energy consumption within a building have more efficient options than traditional methods.

This chapter will review the basic concepts of conventional electric power generation and distribution losses and provide some basic recommendations and suggestions about energy-conservation measures that could increase the efficiency of energy use significantly. In addition to providing energy-saving suggestions, we will review automated lighting design and California Energy Commission (CEC) Title 24 design compliance. In view of recent green building design measures and raised consciousness about energy conservation, we will review the U.S. Green Building Council's Leadership in Energy and Environmental Design (LEED).

Energy-Saving Measures

The recommendations herein involve simple yet very effective means of decreasing energy use. By following these recommendations, energy use can be minimized noticeably without resorting to major capital investments.

LIGHTING

Providing lighting within a building can account for up to 30 percent of the energy used. There are several options for reducing this energy usage. The easiest method for reducing the energy used to provide lighting is to invest in compact fluorescent lights, as opposed to traditional incandescent lights. Compact fluorescent lights use approximately 75 percent less energy than typical incandescent lights. A 15-W compact fluorescent light will supply the same amount of light as a 60-W incandescent light while using only 25 percent of the energy that a 60-W incandescent light would require. Compact fluorescent lights also last significantly longer than incandescent lights, with an expected lifetime of 10,000 hours on most models. Most compact fluorescent lights also come with a 1-year warranty.

Another option for saving money and energy related to lighting is to use torchieres. In recent years, halogen torchieres have become relatively popular. However, they create extremely high levels of heat; approximately 90 percent of the energy used by a halogen lamp is emitted as heat, not light. Some halogen lamps generate enough heat to fry an egg on the top of the lamp. These lamps create a fire hazard owing to the possibility of curtains touching the lamp and igniting or a lamp falling over and igniting carpet. Great alternatives to these types of lamps are compact fluorescent torchieres. Whereas a halogen torchiere used 4 hours per day will consume approximately 438 kWh in a year, a compact fluorescent torchiere used 4 hours per day will only consume 80 kWh in a year. If you currently pay $0.11 per kilowatthour, this would save you over $30 per year just by changing one lamp.

APPLIANCES

There are many appliances used in buildings that require a significant amount of energy to operate. However, most of these appliances are available in highly efficient models.

Refrigerators   Conventional refrigerators are a major consumer of energy. It is possible to make a refrigerator more effective and efficient by keeping it full. In the event a refrigerator is not fully stocked with food, one should consider keeping jugs of water in it. When a refrigerator is full, the contents will retain the cold. If a refrigerator is old, then consideration should be given to investing in a new, highly efficient star-rated model. There are refrigerators on the market that use less than 20 kWh per month. When you compare this with the 110 kWh used per month by conventional refrigerators, you can save over $90 per year (based on $0.11/kWh).

Clothes washers   Washing machines are a large consumer of not only electricity but also water. By using a horizontal-axis washing machine, also known as a *front loader* because the door is on the front of the machine, it is possible to save money by using less electricity, water, and detergent.

Front loaders have a more efficient spin cycle than top loaders, which further increases savings owing to clothes requiring less time in the dryer. These are the types of machines typically found in laundromats. The machines are more cost-effective than conventional top loaders. Another option is to use a natural gas or propane washer and dryer, which are currently more cost-effective than using electric models. If you are on a solar or wind energy system, gas and propane are options that will reduce the overall electricity usage of your home.

Water heaters   Water heaters can be an overwhelming load for any renewable-energy system, as well as a drain on the pocketbook for those using electricity from a local utility. The following are some suggestions to increase the efficiency of electric heaters:

- Lower the thermostat to 120–130°F.
- Fix any leaky faucets immediately.
- Wrap your water heater with insulation.
- Turn off the electricity to your indoor water heater if you will be out of town for 3 or more days.
- Use a timer to turn off the water heater during the hours of the day when no one is at home.

If you are looking for a higher-efficiency water heater, you may want to consider using a *flash* or *tankless* water heater, which heats water on demand. This method of heating water is very effective and does not require excessive electricity to keep a tank of water hot. It also saves water because you do not have to leave the water running out of the tap while you wait for it to get hot. Propane or natural gas water heaters are another option for those who want to minimize their electricity demand as much as possible.

INSULATION AND WEATHERIZATION

Inadequate insulation and air leakage are leading causes of energy waste in many homes. By providing adequate insulation in your home, walls, ceilings, and floors will be warmer in the winter and cooler in the summer. Insulation also can act as a sound absorber or barrier, keeping noise levels low within the home. The first step to improving the insulation of a building is to know the type of existing insulation.

To check the exterior insulation, simply switch off the circuit breaker to an outlet on the inside of an exterior wall. Then remove the electric outlet cover and check to see if there is insulation within the wall. If there is no insulation, it can be added by an insulation contractor who can blow cellulose into the wall through small holes, which are then plugged. The geometry of attics also will determine the ease with which additional insulation can be added. Insulating an attic will significantly increase the ability to keep heat in during winter and out during summer.

One of the easiest ways to reduce energy bills and contribute to the comfort of your home or office space is by sealing air leaks around windows and doors. Temporary or permanent weather stripping can be used around windows and doors. Use caulk to seal other gaps that are less than 1/4 in wide and expanding foam for larger gaps. Storm windows and insulating drapes or curtains also will help to improve the energy performance of existing windows.

HEATING AND COOLING

Every indoor space requires an adequate climate-control system to maintain a comfortable environment. Most people live or work in areas where the outdoor temperature fluctuates beyond ideal living conditions. A traditional air-conditioning or heating system can be a tremendous load on a solar or wind energy system, as well as a drain on the pocketbook for those connected to the utility grid. However, by following some of the insulation and weatherization tips mentioned previously, it is possible to reduce heating losses significantly and reduce the size of the heating system.

The following heating and cooling tips will help to reduce heating and cooling losses further and help your system work as efficiently as possible. These tips are designed to increase the efficiency of the heating and/or cooling system without necessitating drastic remodeling efforts. Table 5.1 shows energy distribution in residential and commercial projects.

TABLE 5.1 ENERGY DISTRIBUTION IN RESIDENTIAL AND COMMERCIAL BUILDINGS	
	PERCENT OF POWER USED
Apartment buildings	
Environmental control	70
Lighting, receptacles	15
Water heating	3
Laundry, elevator, miscellaneous	12
Single residential homes	
Environmental control	60
Lighting, receptacles	15
Water heating	3
Laundry, pool	22
Hotel and motels	
Space heating	60
Air-conditioning	10
Lighting	11
Refrigeration	4
Laundry, kitchen, restaurant, pool	15
Water heating	—
Retail stores	
Environmental control, HVAC	30
Lighting	60
Elevator, security, parking	10

Heating When considering the use of renewable-energy systems, electric space and water heaters are not considered viable options. Electric space and water heaters require a significant quantity of electricity to operate at a time of the year when the least amount of solar radiation is available.

Forced-air heating systems also use inefficient fans to blow heated air into rooms that may not even be used during the day. They also allow for considerable leakage through poorly sealed ductwork. Ideally, an energy-independent home or office space will not require heating or cooling owing to passive solar design and quality insulation. However, if the space requires a heating source, one should consider a heater that burns fuel to provide heat and does not require electricity. Some options to consider are woodstoves and gas or propane heaters.

Cooling A conventional air-conditioning unit is an enormous electrical load on a renewable-energy system and a costly appliance to use. As with heating, the ideal energy-independent home should be designed not to require an air-conditioning unit. However, since most homeowners considering renewable-energy systems are not going to redesign their home or office space, an air-conditioning unit may be necessary.

If you insulate your home or office space adequately and plug any drafts or air leaks, air-conditioning units will have to run less, which thus reduces energy expenditure. Air-conditioning units must be used only when it is absolutely necessary.

Another option is to use an evaporative cooling system. Evaporative cooling is an energy-efficient alternative to traditional air-conditioning units. Evaporative cooling works by evaporating water into the airstream. An example of evaporative cooling is the chill you get when stepping out of a swimming pool and feeling a breeze. The chill you get is caused by the evaporation of the water from your body. Evaporative cooling uses this evaporation process to cool the air passing through a wetted medium.

Early civilizations used this method by doing something as simple as hanging wet cloth in a window to cool the incoming air. Evaporative cooling is an economical and energy-efficient solution for your cooling needs. With an evaporative cooling unit, there is no compressor, condenser, chiller coils, or cooling towers. Therefore, the cost of acquiring and operating an evaporative cooling unit is considerably less than for a conventional air-conditioning unit, and maintenance costs are lower owing to the units requiring simpler procedures and lower-skilled maintenance workers. Also, unlike conventional air-conditioning units, evaporative cooling does not release chlorofluorocarbons (CFCs) into the atmosphere.

By following these recommendations, it is possible to turn a home or office space into an energy-efficient environment.

Power-Factor Correction

The intent of this discussion is to familiarize readers with the basic concepts of the power factor and its effect on energy-consumption efficiency. Readers interested in a further understanding of reactive power concepts should refer to electrical engineering textbooks.

In large commercial or industrial complexes where large amounts of electric power are used for fluorescent lighting or heavy machinery, the efficiency of incoming power, which depends on maintenance of the smallest possible phase angle between the current and the voltage, is usually lowered, thus resulting in a significant waste of energy. The cosine of the phase angle between the current and the voltage, referred to as the *power factor*, is the multiplier that determines whether the electric energy is used at its maximum to deliver lighting or mechanical energy or is wasted as heat. Power P in electrical engineering is defined as the product of the voltage V and current I times the cosine of the phase angle, or $P = V \times I \times$ cosine phase angle. When the phase angle between the current and the voltage is 0, the cosine equals 1, and therefore, $P = V \times I$, which represents the maximum power conversion or delivery.

The principal components of motors, transformers, and lighting ballasts are wound-copper coils referred to as *inductance elements*. A significant characteristic of inductors is that they have a tendency to shift the current and voltage phase angles, which results in power factors that are less than 1 and hence reduced power efficiency. The *power usage performance*, which is defined as the ratio of the output power to the maximum power, is therefore used as the figure of merit. The reduction in electric power efficiency resulting from reactive power is wasted energy that is lost as heat. In a reactive circuit, the phase angle between the current and the voltage shifts, thus giving rise to reactive power that is manifested as unused power, which dissipates as heat.

Mitigation measures that can be used to minimize inductive power loss include the installation of phase-shifting capacitor devices that negate the phase angle created by induction coils. As a rule, the maximum power affordable for efficient use of electric power should be above 93 percent. In situations where power-factor measurements indicate a value of less than 87 percent, power losses can be minimized by using capacitor reactance.

Electric Power Generation and Distribution

It is interesting to observe that most of us, when using electric energy, are oblivious to the fact that the electric energy provided to our household, office, or workplace is mostly generated by extremely low-efficiency conversion of fossil fuels such as coal, natural gas, and crude oils. In addition to producing substantial amounts of pollutants, electric plants operate with meager efficiency and deliver electricity to the end user with great loss. To illustrate this point, let us review the energy production and delivery of a typical electricity-generating station that uses fossil fuel.

By setting an arbitrary unit of 100 percent for the fossil-fuel energy input into the boilers, we see that owing to losses resulting from power-plant machinery such as turbines, generators, high-voltage transformers, transmission lines, and substations, the efficiency of delivered electric energy at the destination is no more than 20–25 percent. The efficiency of energy use is reduced further when the electric energy is used by motors,

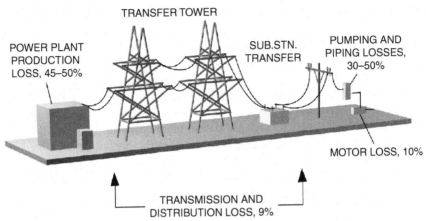

POWER PLANT
PRODUCTION
LOSS, 45–50%

TRANSFER TOWER

SUB.STN.
TRANSFER

PUMPING AND
PIPING LOSSES,
30–50%

MOTOR LOSS, 10%

TRANSMISSION AND
DISTRIBUTION LOSS, 9%

Figure 5.1   **Transmission and distribution losses associated with electric fossil-fuel power generation and delivery.**

pumps, and a variety of equipment and appliances that have their own specific performance losses. Figure 5.1 shows the transmission and distribution losses associated with electric fossil-fuel power-generation delivery. Table 5.2 lists the comparative losses between solar and fossil-fuel power-generation systems.

As seen in the preceding table, when comparing solar power generation with electric power generated by fossil fuels, the advantages of solar power generation in the long run become quite obvious.

A short-sighted assessment by various experts siding with conventional fossil-fuel power generation is that less burning of coal and crude oil to minimize or prevent

TABLE 5.2   SOLAR POWER AND FOSSIL-FUEL POWER-GENERATION COMPARISON

	SOLAR ELECTRIC POWER	FOSSIL-FUEL ELECTRIC POWER
Delivery efficiency	Above 90%	Less than 30%
Maintenance	Very minimal	Considerable
Transmission lines	None required	Very extensive
Equipment life span	25–45 years	Maximum of 25 years
Investment payback	8–14 years	20–25 years
Environmental impact	No pollution	Very high pollution index
Percent of total U.S. energy	Less than 1%	Over 75%
Reliability index	Very high	Good

global warming will increase the national expenditure to such a degree that governments will be prevented from meeting society's needs for transportation, irrigation, heating, and many other energy-dependent services. On the other hand, environmentalists argue that protection of nature and the prevention of global warming warrant the required expenditure to prevent inevitable climatic deterioration.

Advances in technology, the increased output efficiency of solar photovoltaic (PV) modules, and the reduction in cost of PV modules that would result from mass production will make solar power installation quite economical within the next decade. National policies should take into consideration that technologies aimed at reducing global warming indeed could be a major component of the gross national income and that savings from decreased fossil-fuel consumption could be much less than the expenditures for research and development of solar power and sustainable-energy technologies.

In the recent past, some industry leaders, such as DuPont, IBM, Alcan, NorskeCanada, and British Petroleum, have expended substantial capital toward the reduction of carbon dioxide and greenhouse gas emissions, which has resulted in billions of dollars of savings. For example, British Petroleum has reduced carbon dioxide emissions by 10 percent in the past 10 years and, as a result, has cut $650 million over 10 years of expenses. DuPont, by reducing 72 percent of its greenhouse gas emissions, has increased its production by 30 percent, which resulted in $2 billion per year of savings. The United States at present uses 47 percent fewer energy dollars than it did 30 years ago, which results in $1 billion per day of savings.

Computerized Lighting Control

In general, conventional interior lighting control is accomplished by means of hard-wired switches, dimmers, timers, lighting contactor relays, occupancy sensors, and photoelectric eyes that provide the means to turn various light fixtures on and off or to reduce luminescence by dimming. The degree of interior lighting control in most instances is addressed by the state of California Title 24 energy regulations, which dictate specific design measures required to meet energy-conservation strategies, including

- Interior room illumination switching
- Daylight illumination control or harvesting
- Duration of illumination control by means of a preset timing schedule
- Illumination level control specific to each space occupancy and task environment
- Lighting-zone system management
- Exterior lighting control

Figures 5.2 through 5.10 depict various wiring diagrams and lighting-control equipment used to increase illumination energy-consumption efficiency.

In limited spaces such as small offices and commercial retail and industrial environments (where floor spaces do not exceed 10,000 ft^2), lighting control is undertaken

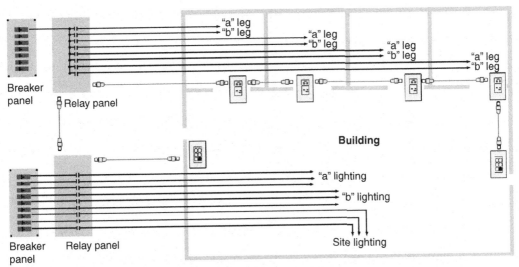

Figure 5.2   **A typical centralized lighting-control wiring plan.** *Photo courtesy of LCD.*

by hardwiring of various switches, dimmers, occupancy sensors, and timers. However, in large environments, such as high-rise buildings and large commercial and industrial environments, lighting control is accomplished by a computerized automation system that consists of a centralized control and display system that allows for total integration of all the preceding components (Fig. 5.2).

A central lighting-control system embeds specific software algorithms that allow for automated light-control operations to be tailored to meet specific energy and automation management requirements unique to a special environment. An automated lighting-control system, in addition to reducing energy waste to an absolute minimum, allows for total operator override and control from a central location.

Because of the inherent design of a centralized lighting system, the central monitoring system offers indispensable advantages that cannot be accomplished by hardwired systems. Some of the advantages of a centralized lighting-control system are as follows:

■ The unit allows remote manual or automatic on-off control of up to 2400 lighting groups within a predetermined zone.
■ The unit allows remote dimming of lighting within each zone.
■ The unit allows automatic sequencing control of individual groups of lights.
■ The unit allows sequencing and graded dimming or step activation of any group of lights.
■ The unit allows remote status monitoring of all lights within the overall complex.
■ The system controls inrush current for incandescent lights, which substantially prolongs the life expectancy of lamps.
■ The system provides visual display of the entire system illumination throughout the complex by means of graphic interfaces.

- The provider facilitates free-of-charge remote programming and maintenance of the central lighting and control from the equipment supplier's or manufacturer's headquarters.
- The system has optional remote radio communication interfaces that allow for control of devices at remote locations without the use of conduits and cables.

In some instances, radio control applications can eliminate trenching and cable installation, which can offset the entire cost of a central control system. Contrary to conventional wiring schemes, where all wires from fixtures merge into switches and lighting panels, an intelligent lighting-control system such as the one described here makes use of Type 5 cable (a bundle of four-pair twisted shielded wires), which can interconnect up to 2400 lighting-control elements. A central control and monitoring unit located in an office constantly communicates with a number of remotely located intelligent control boxes that perform the lighting-control measures required by Title 24 and beyond.

Since remote lighting, dimming, and occupancy sensing are actuated by means of electronically controlled relay contacts, any number of devices such as pumps, outdoor fixtures, and various numbers of devices with varying voltages could be readily controlled with the same master station. In addition to providing intelligent master control, remote station control devices and intelligent wall-mount switches specifically designed for interfacing with intelligent remote devices provide local lighting- and dimming-control override. Moreover, a centralized lighting-control system can readily provide required interlocks between heating, ventilating, and air-conditioning (HVAC) systems by means of intelligent thermostats.

Even though central intelligent lighting-control systems such as the one described here add an initial cost component to conventional wiring, in the long run, the extended expectancy of lamps, lower maintenance cost, added security, and considerable savings resulting from energy conservation undoubtedly justify the added initial investment. In fact, the most valuable feature of the system is flexibility of control and ease of system expansion and reconfiguration. Deployed in an application such as the Water and Life Museum project discussed in Chap. 3, such a system should be considered indispensable.

The major cost components of a centralized lighting-control system consist of the central and remote-controlled hardware and dimmable fluorescent T8 ballasts. It is a well-established fact that centralized lighting-control systems pay off in a matter of a few years and provide a substantial return on investment (ROI) by the sheer savings on energy consumption. Needless to say, no measure of security can be achieved without central lighting control.

The automated centralized lighting-control system manufactured by Lighting Control Design (LCD), and shown in Fig. 5.3, provides typical control components used to achieve the energy-conservation measures discussed earlier. It should be noted that the lighting-control components and systems presented in this chapter are also available from Lutron and several other companies.

Some of the major lighting-system components available for system design and integration include centralized microprocessor-based lighting-control relays that incorporate

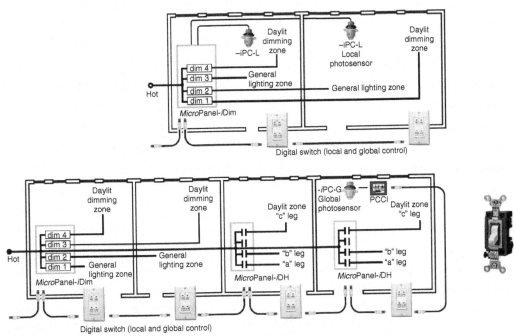

Figure 5.3   **Centralized dimming and lighting-control diagram.** *Courtesy of LCD.*

32 to 64 addressable relay channels, 365-day programmable astronomical timers, tele-communications modems, mixed-voltage output relays (120–277 V), manual override for each relay, and a linkup capability of more than 100 links to digital devices via Category 5 patch cables and RJ45 connectors. The preceding systems also include smart breaker panels that use solenoid-operated thermal magnetic breakers that effectively provide overcurrent protection as well as lighting control.

Overcurrent devices usually are available in single or three phases; a current rating of 15, 20, and 30 A; and an arc current interrupt capacity (AIC) of 14 kA at 120/208 V and 65 kA at 277/480 V. A microprocessor-based current-limiting sub-branch distribution panel provides lighting calculations for most energy-regulated codes. For example, California Title 24 energy compliance requirements dictate 45 W of linear power for track lighting, whereas the city of Seattle in the state of Washington requires 70 W/ft for the same track lighting system. The current-limiting subpanel effectively provides a programmable circuit current-limiting capability that lowers or raises the voltampere (VA) rating requirement for track lighting circuits. The current-limiting capacity for a typical panel is 20 circuits; with each capable of limiting current from 1 to 15 A. Figure 5.4 shows some of the lighting-control components.

Another useful lighting-control device is a programmable zone lighting-control panel, which is capable of the remote control of 512 uniquely addressable lighting-control relays. Groups of relays can be either controlled individually, referred to as

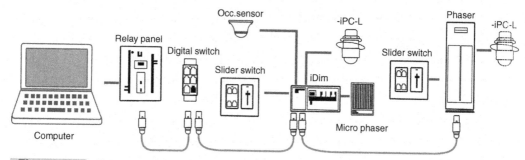

Figure 5.4   Remote lighting-control component configuration. *Courtesy of LCD.*

discrete mode, or controlled in groups, referred to as *zone mode.* Lighting relays in typical systems are extremely reliable and are designed to withstand 250,000 operations at full load capacity.

For limited area lighting control, a compact microprocessor-based device, referred to as a *microcontrol,* provides a limited capability for controlling two to four switches and dimmable outputs. All microcontrolled devices are daisy-chained and communicate with a central lighting command and control system.

A desktop personal computer with a monitor located in a central location (usually the security room) communicates with all the described lighting system panels and microcontrollers via twisted shielded Category 5 communication cables. Wireless modem devices are also available as an alternative hardwired system (Figs. 5.5 and 5.6).

Other optional equipment and devices available for lighting control include digital astronomical time clocks, prefabricated connector cables, dimmer switches, lock-type switches, indoor and outdoor photosensor devices, and modems for remote communication.

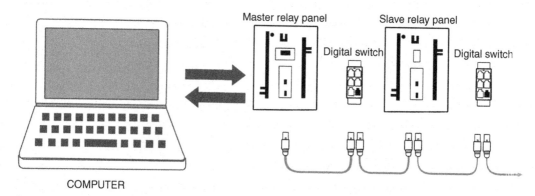

Figure 5.5   Centralized light monitoring and control system. *Courtesy of LCD.*

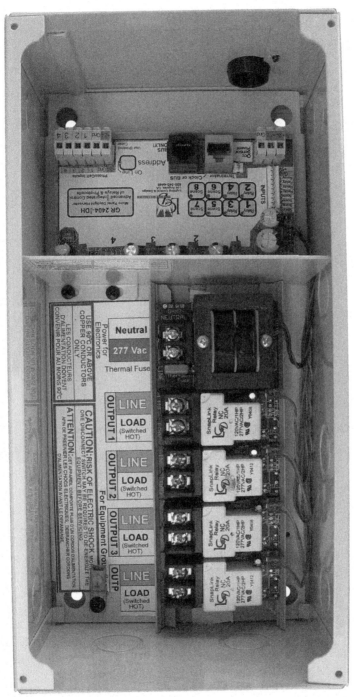

Figure 5.6   Local microprocessor-based control panel.

Photo courtesy of LCD.

California Title 24 Electric Energy Compliance

In response to the 2000 electricity crisis, the California legislature mandated the CEC to update existing indoor lighting energy-conservation standards and to develop outdoor lighting energy-efficiency-compliant cost-effective measures. The intent of the legislature was to develop energy-conservation standards that would reduce electricity system energy consumption.

Regulations for lighting have been enforced in California since 1977. However, the measures only addressed indoor lighting through control requirements and maximum allowable lighting power.

SCOPE AND APPLICATION

Earlier energy-regulation standards applied only to indoor and outdoor lighting of buildings that were air-conditioned, heated, or cooled. The updated standards, however, address lighting in non-air-conditioned buildings and also cover general site illumination and outdoor lighting. The standards include control requirements as well as limits on installed lighting power. The standards also apply to internally and externally illuminated signs. For detailed coverage of the energy-control measures and regulations, refer to CEC's standard publications.

INDOOR LIGHTING COMPLIANCE

This section will review the requirements for indoor lighting design and installation, including controls. It is addressed primarily to lighting designers, electrical engineers, and building department personnel responsible for lighting and electrical plan checking and inspection purposes.

Indoor lighting is perhaps the single largest consumer of energy (kilowatthours) in commercial buildings, which amounts to approximately one-third of overall electric energy use. The principal purpose of the standards is to mitigate excessive energy use and provide design guidelines for the effective reduction of energy use without compromising the quality of lighting.

The primary mechanism for regulating indoor lighting energy under the standards is to limit the allowable lighting power, in watts, installed in the buildings. Mandatory measures apply to the entire building's lighting systems, and equipment consists of the use of such items as manual switching, daylight area controls, and automatic shutoff controls. The mandatory requirements must be met either by prescriptive or performance approaches, as will be described here. Figures 5.7 and 5.8 depict electrical wiring and installation configurations.

As a rule, allowable lighting power for a building is determined by one of the following five methods:

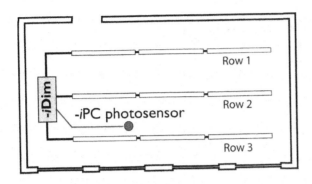

Figure 5.7 Photosensor-control wiring diagram.
Courtesy of LCD.

Complete-Building Method   This method applies to situations in which the entire building's lighting system is designed and permitted at one time. This means that at least 90 percent of the building has a single primary type of use, such as retail. In the case of wholesale stores, at least 70 percent of the building area must be used for merchandise sales functions. In some instances, this method may be used for an entire tenant space in a multitenant building where a single lighting power value governs the entire building.

Area-Category Method   This method is applicable for any permit situation, including tenant improvements. Lighting power values are assigned to each of the major function areas of a building, such as offices, lobbies, and corridors.

Tailored Method   This method is applicable when additional flexibility is needed to accommodate special task lighting needs in specific task areas. Lighting power allowances are determined room by room and task by task, with the area-category method used for other areas in the building.

Performance Approach   This method is applicable when the designer uses a CEC-certified computer program to demonstrate that the proposed building's energy consumption, including lighting power, meets the energy budget. This approach incorporates one of the three previous methods, which sets the appropriate allowable lighting power density used in calculating the building's custom energy budget. It may be used only to model the performance of lighting systems that are covered under the building permit application.

Actual Adjusted-Lighting-Power Method   This method is based on the total design wattage of lighting less adjustments for any qualifying automatic lighting controls, such as occupant-sensing devices or automatic daylight controls. The actual adjusted lighting power must not exceed the allowable lighting power for the lighting system to comply.

Lighting tradeoffs   The intent of energy-control measures is essentially to restrict the overall installed lighting power in the buildings regardless of the compliance

(a)

(b)

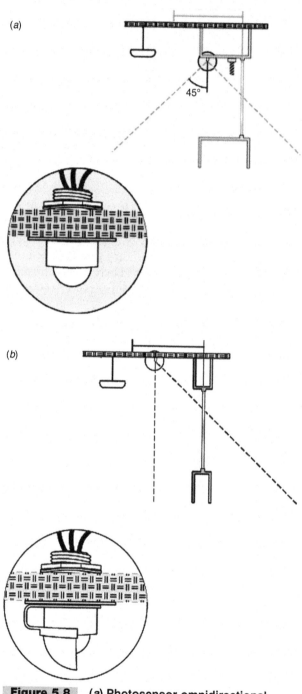

Figure 5.8   (a) Photosensor omnidirectional
control configuration scheme. *Courtesy of LCD.*
(b) Photosensor unidirectional control
configuration scheme. *Courtesy of LCD.*

approach. It should be noted that there is no general restriction regarding where or how general lighting power is used, which means that installed lighting could be greater in some areas and lower in others, provided that the total lighting energy wattage does not exceed the allowable lighting power.

A second type of lighting tradeoff, which is also permitted under the standards, is a tradeoff of performance between the lighting system and the envelope or mechanical systems. Such a tradeoff can be made only when permit applications are sought for those systems filed under performance compliance, where a building with an envelope or mechanical system has a more efficient performance than the prescriptive efficiency-energy budget, in which case more lighting power may be allowed. Figure 5.9 represents a typical energy distribution percentage in commercial buildings.

When a lighting power allowance is calculated using the previously referenced performance approach, the allowance is treated as if it is determined using one of the other compliance methods. It should be noted that no tradeoffs are allowed between indoor and outdoor lighting or lighting located in non-air-conditioned spaces.

Mandatory measures   Mandatory measures are compliance notes that must be included in the building design and on the engineering or Title 24 forms stating whether compliance is of the prescriptive or performance method building occupancy type. The main purpose of mandatory features is to set requirements for manufacturers of building products, who must certify the performance of their products to the CEC. However, it is the designer's responsibility to specify products that meet these requirements.

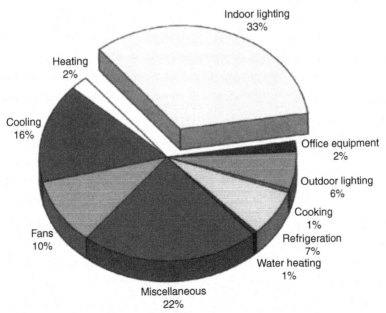

Figure 5.9   **Lighting energy-use distribution chart.** *Courtesy of CEC.*

Lighting equipment certification   The mandatory requirements for lighting-control devices include minimum specifications for features such as automatic time-control switches, occupancy-sensing devices, automatic daylighting controls, and indoor photo-sensor devices. Most of the requirements are currently part of standard design practice in California and are required for electrical plan checking and permitting.

Without exception all lighting-control devices required by mandatory measures must be certified by the manufacturer before they can be installed in a building. The manufacturer also must certify the devices to the CEC. On certification, the device is listed in the *Directory of Automatic Lighting-Control Devices.*

Automatic time switches   Automatic time switches, sometimes called *time clocks,* are programmable switches that are used to automatically shut off the lights according to preestablished schedules depending on the hours of operation of the building. The devices must be capable of storing weekday and weekend programs. In order to avoid the loss of programmed schedules, timers are required to incorporate backup power provision for at least 10 hours during power loss.

Occupancy-sensing devices   Occupancy-sensing devices provide the capability to automatically turn off all lights in an area for no more than 30 minutes after the area has been vacated. Sensor devices that use ultrasonic sensing must meet certain minimum health requirements and must have the built-in ability for sensitivity calibration to prevent false signals that may cause power to turn on and off unexpectedly. Devices that use microwave detection (rarely used) principles likewise must have emission controls and a built-in sensitivity adjustment.

Automatic daylight controls   Daylighting controls consist of photosensors that compare actual illumination levels with a reference illumination level and gradually reduce the electric lighting until the reference level has been reached. These controls are also deployed for power adjustment factor (PAF) lighting credits in the daylit areas adjacent to windows. It is also possible to reduce the general lighting power of the controlled area by separate control of multiple lamps or by step dimming. Stepped dimming with a time delay prevents cycling of the lights, which is typically implemented by a time delay of 3 minutes or less before electric lighting is reduced or is increased.

Light control in daylight is accomplished by use of photodiode sensors. It should be noted that this requirement cannot be met with devices that use photoconductive cells. In general, stepped switching-control devices are designed to indicate the status of lights in controlled zones by an indicator.

Interior photosensor devices   Daylight control systems in general use photo-sensor devices that measure the amount of light at a reference location. The photosensor provides light-level illumination information to the controller, which, in turn, enables it to increase or decrease the area electric light level.

A photosensor devices must, as stated previously, be certified by the CEC. Devices having mechanical slide covers or other means that allow for adjusting or disabling of the photosensor are not permitted or certified.

Multilevel astronomical time switches control areas with skylights that permit daylight into a building area and are required to be calculated by the prescriptive calculation method, as well as by the mandatory automatic controls that must be installed to reduce electric lighting when sufficient daylight is available. Multilevel astronomical time-switch controls or automatic multilevel daylight controls specially designed for general lighting control must meet the mandatory requirements for automatic controls when the particular zone has an area greater than 2500 ft^2.

The purpose of astronomical time-switch controls is to turn off lights where sufficient daylight is available. Astronomical timers accomplish this requirement by keeping track of the time since sunrise and the amount of time remaining before sunset. As a basic requirement, the control program must accommodate multilevel two-step control for each zone programmed to provide independently scheduled activation and deactivation of the lights at different times.

In the event of overly cloudy or overly bright days, the astronomical timers are required to have manual override capability. Usually, the override switches in a zone are configured so that lights will revert to the off position within 2 hours unless the time-switch schedule is programmed to keep the lights on.

To comply with power-consumption-regulation requirements, light control is not allowed to be greater than 35 percent at time of minimum light output. Device compliance also mandates that devices be designed to display the date and time, sunrise and sunset times, and switching times for each step of control. To prevent a loss of settings owing to a temporary loss of power, timers are required to have a 10-hour battery backup. Astronomical timers also are capable of storing the time of day and the longitude and latitude of a zone in nonvolatile memory.

Automatic multilevel daylight controls   Automatic multilevel daylight controls are used to comply with the mandatory requirements for automatic daylight controls when the daylight area under skylights is greater than 2500 ft^2. The controls must have a minimum of two control steps so that electric lighting can be reduced uniformly. One of the control steps is intended to reduce lighting power from 100 percent to 70 and 50 percent of full-rated power.

Multilevel daylight-control devices incorporate calibration and adjustment controls that are accessible to authorized personnel and are housed behind a switch-plate cover or touch-plate cover or in an electrical box with a lock. In circumstances where the control is used under skylight conditions and the daylight area is greater than 2500 ft^2, the power consumption must not be greater than 35 percent of the minimum electric light output. This is achieved when the timer control automatically turns all its lights off or reduces the power by 30 percent.

Fluorescent dimming controls, even though somewhat expensive, usually meet the minimum power requirements. Controls for high-intensity-discharge (HID) lamps do not meet the power requirements at minimum dimming levels, but a multistage HID lamp switching control can.

Outdoor astronomical time switches control outdoor lighting by means of astrological time switches, which are permitted if the device is designed to accommodate automatic multilevel switching of outdoor lighting. Such a control strategy allows all, half, or none of the outdoor lights to be controlled during different times of the day for different days of the week while ensuring that the lights are turned off during the daytime.

Incidentally, this feature is quite similar to the indoor multilevel astronomical control with the exception that this control scheme offers a less stringent offset requirement from sunrise or sunset. Mandatory certification for this device requires the controller to be capable of independently offsetting on-off settings for up to 120 minutes from sunrise or sunset.

Installation requirements   When using automatic time-switch control devices or occupant sensors for automatic daylight control, the device must be installed in accordance with the manufacturer's instructions. Devices also must be installed so that the device controls only luminaries within daylit areas, which means that photosensors must be either mounted on the ceiling or installed in locations that are accessible only to authorized personnel so that they can maintain adequate illumination in the area.

Certified ballasts and luminaries   All fluorescent lamp ballasts and luminaries are regulated by the Appliance Efficiency Regulations certified by the CEC and are listed in the efficiency database of these regulations.

Area controls   The best way to minimize energy waste and increase efficiency is to turn off the lights when they are not in use. All lights must have switching or controls to allow them to be turned off when not needed.

Room switching   It is mandatory to provide lighting controls for each area enclosed by ceiling-height partitions, which means that each room must have its own switches. Ganged switching of several rooms at once is not permitted. A switch may be operated manually or automatically or controlled by a central-zone lighting or occupant-sensing system that meets the mandatory measure requirements.

Accessibility   It is mandatory to locate all switching devices in locations where personnel can see them when entering or leaving an area. In situations when the switching device cannot be located within view of the lights or area, the switch position and states must be annunciated or indicated on a central lighting panel.

Security or Emergency Lights   Such lights within areas required to be lit continuously or for emergency egress are exempt from the switching requirements. However, the lighting level is limited to a maximum of 0.5 W/ft^2 along the path of egress. Security or emergency egress lights must be controlled by switches accessible only to authorized personnel.

Public areas   In public areas, such as building lobbies and concourses, switches are usually installed in areas accessible only to authorized personnel.

OUTDOOR LIGHTING AND SIGNS

In response to the electricity crisis in 2000, the California legislature mandated the CEC to develop outdoor lighting energy efficiency standards that are technologically feasible and cost-effective. The purpose of the legislation was to develop energy-efficiency standards that could provide comprehensive energy conservation.

Outdoor astronomical time-switch controls   As referenced briefly earlier, outdoor lighting control by means of astrological time switches is permitted if the device is designed to accommodate automatic multilevel switching of outdoor lighting. Basically, such a control allows all, half, or none of the outdoor lights to be controlled during different times of the day for different days of the week while ensuring that the lights are turned off during the daytime.

Outdoor lighting and sign energy-control measures are intended to conserve energy and reduce winter peak electric demand. The standards also set design directives for minimum and maximum allowable power levels when using large luminaries.

Permitted lighting power levels are based on Illuminating Engineering Society of North America (IESNA) recommendations, which are industry standard practices that have worldwide recognition. It should be noted that outdoor lighting standards do not allow tradeoffs between interior lighting, HVAC, building envelope, or water-heating energy-conformance requirements.

Outdoor lighting tradeoffs   Outdoor lighting tradeoffs are allowed only between the lighting applications with general site-lighting illumination, which includes hardscape areas, building entrances without canopies, and outdoor sales lots. The requirements do not permit any tradeoffs between outdoor lighting power allowances and interior lighting, HVAC, building envelope, or water heating. This includes decorative gas lighting; lighting for theatrical purposes, including stage, film, and video production; and emergency lighting powered by an emergency source as defined by the CEC.

Mandatory measures   The imposed mandatory measures on outdoor lighting include automatic controls that are designed to be turned off during daytime hours and during other times when it is not needed. The measures also require that all controls be certified by the manufacturer and listed in CEC directories. All luminaries with lamps larger than 175 W are required to have cutoff baffles so as to limit the light directed toward the ground. Luminaires with lamps larger than 60 W are also required to be high efficiency or controlled by a motion sensor.

The new CEC standards also limit the lighting power for general site illumination and for some specific outdoor lighting applications. General site illuminations specifically include parking lots, driveways, walkways, building entrances, sales lots, and other paved areas of a site. The measures also provide separate allowances for each of the previously referenced general site lighting applications and allow tradeoffs among these applications. In other words, a single aggregate outdoor lighting budget can be calculated for all the site applications together. Hardscape for automotive vehicular use, including parking lots; driveways and site roads; and pedestrian walkways, including plazas, sidewalks, and bikeways, are all considered part of general lighting.

General lighting includes building entrances and facades, such as outdoor sales lots, building facades, outdoor sales frontages, service-station canopies, vehicle service station hardscape, canopies, ornamental lightings, drive-up windows, guarded facilities, outdoor dining, and temporary outdoor lighting. Site lighting is also regulated by the Federal Aviation Regulation Standards.

General lighting also covers lighting standards used in sports and athletic fields, children's playgrounds, industrial sites, automated teller machines (ATMs), public monuments, and lights used around swimming pools or water features, tunnels, bridges, stairs, and ramps. Tradeoffs are not permitted for specific-application lighting.

Allowable lighting power for both general site illumination and specific applications are governed by four separate outdoor lighting zone requirements, as will be described later. The lighting zones in general characterize ambient lighting intensities in the surrounding areas. For example, sites that have high ambient lighting levels have a larger allowance than sites with lower ambient lighting levels. The following are Title 24 CEC zone classification:

Zone LZ1: Government-assigned area

Zone LZ2: Rural areas as defined by the U.S. 2000 Census

Zone LZ3: Urban area as defined by the U.S. 2000 Census

Zone LZ4: Currently not defined

Signs   Sign standards contain both prescriptive and performance approaches. Sign mandatory measures apply to both indoor and outdoor signs. Prescriptive requirements apply when the signs are illuminated with efficient lighting sources, such as electronic ballasts, whereas the performance requirement is applied when calculating the maximum power defined as a function of the sign surface area in watts per square foot.

Installed power   The installed power for outdoor lighting applications is determined in accordance with specific mandatory measure calculation guidelines. Luminaire power for pin-based and high-intensity discharge lighting fixtures may be used as an alternative to determine the wattage of outdoor luminaries. Luminaires with screw-base sockets and lighting systems that allow the addition or relocation of luminaries without modification to the wiring system must follow the required guidelines. In commercial lighting systems, no power credits are offered for automatic controls; however, the use of automatic lighting controls is mandatory.

Similar to indoor lighting, mandatory features and devices must be included in all outdoor lighting project documentation, whenever applicable. The mandatory measures also require the performance of equipment to be certified by the manufacturers and that fixtures rated 100 W or larger must have high efficiency; otherwise, they are required to be controlled by a motion sensor. Fixtures with lamps rated 175 W or more must incorporate directional baffles to direct the light toward the ground.

Fixture certification Manufacturers of lighting-control products are required to certify the performance of their products with the CEC. Lighting designers and engineers must assume responsibility to specify products that meet these requirements. As a rule, inspectors and code-enforcement officials are also required to verify that the lighting controls specified carry CEC certification. The certification requirement applies to all lighting-control equipment and devices such as photocontrols, astronomical time switches, and automatic controls.

Control devices are also required to have instructions for installation and startup calibration and must be installed in accordance with the manufacturer's directives. The control equipment and devices are required to have a visual or audio status signal that activates on malfunction or failure.

Minimum lamp efficiency All outdoor fixtures with lamps rated over 100 W must have either a lamp efficiency of at least 60 lm/W or be controlled by a motion sensor. Lamp efficiencies are rated by the initial lamp lumens divided by the rated lamp power (W) without including auxiliary devices such as ballasts.

Fixtures that operate by mercury-vapor principles and larger-wattage incandescent lamps do not meet these efficiency requirements. On the other hand, most linear fluorescent, metal halide, and high-pressure-sodium lamps have efficiencies greater than 60 lm/W and do comply with the requirements.

The minimum lamp efficiency does not apply to lighting regulated by a health or life-safety statute, ordinance, or regulation, which includes, but is not limited to, emergency lighting. Also excluded are fixtures used around swimming pools; water features; searchlights or theme lighting used in theme parks, film, or live performances; temporary outdoor lighting; light-emitting diodes (LEDs); and neon and cold-cathode lighting.

Cutoff luminaries Outdoor luminaries that use lamps rated greater than 175 W in parking lots, hardscapes, outdoor dining, and outdoor sales areas are required to be fitted with cutoff-type baffles or filters. The luminaries used must be rated specifically as "cutoff" in a photometric test report. A *cutoff-type luminaire* is defined as one in which no more than 2.5 percent of the light output extends above the horizon 90 degrees or above the nadir and no more than 10 percent of the light output is at or above a vertical angle of 80 degrees above the nadir. The nadir is a point in the direction straight down, as would be indicated by a plumb line. Ninety degrees above the nadir is horizontal. Eighty degrees above the nadir is 10 degrees below the horizontal.

Demand-Side Energy Management and Control

Given that climate control and water heating constitute approximately 50 percent of the overall energy-consumption bill, energy demand management and control must be given the most attention by the LEED design team. Some of the essential features of a centralized energy-management and supervisory system must include

- The ability to control of HVAC system components
- The ability to read and store data and display them on electric, gas, and water meters
- The ability to provide remote-control monitoring and programming using a variety of communication technologies
- The ability to provide local and remote alarm reporting
- The ability to manage and control local or remote demand-side loads

The system also must produce a high rate of internally verifiable energy savings in commercial and residential applications. In essence, the energy-management system must optimize HVAC energy efficiency by causing the equipment to operate in an energy-recovery mode for a significant portion of each cooling or heating cycle without affecting the comfort zone of the facility. The system also must be able to reduce energy consumption and demand by programming the HVAC equipment to cool or heat the facility on an optimal schedule. Typically, a well-designed centralized energy-management system also must incorporate software features to remotely program, control, and perform energy analyses of the utility demand-side loads. In essence, the significance of a centralized energy-management and control systems (CEMCS) is to enable cost savings through improved efficiency and operational and maintenance savings while allowing the utility to implement real-time demand-side management on a local or remote basis.

UTILITY DEMAND-SIDE MANAGEMENT

In centralized energy-management systems, utility demand-side management (DSM) is achieved by programmed efficient loading and operation of the HVAC equipment. Real-time DSM is achieved by allowing a utility to control the setpoint temperature used for either air-conditioning or heating on a local and remote basis through two-way modem communications or optionally with a radiofrequency paging system. The control setpoints also can be proportionally or continuously controlled and changed by the utility as the demand for electric power increases or decreases. The energy-management systems in general can be programmed to raise the cooling or heating setpoint temperature in small increments, cycle units on a timed operational basis, or shut units off while the system's data-acquisition aspect automatically provides display and reporting of changes and load-shedding capability to the utility via modem communications.

CONSUMER ELECTRICAL DEMAND SAVINGS

Consumers with single or multiple HVAC systems can achieve electrical demand savings by the programmed use of the centralized sequencing of the operation of multiple air-conditioning systems to limit the number of air-conditioner compressors operating at any one time. The utility/consumer also can place setpoint limits on the amount the room temperature can rise during DSM load-shedding control in cooling and establish priorities for unloading each HVAC system.

ENERGY CONSERVATION

Energy conservation is achieved by programming the centralized energy-management systems for more energy-efficient temperature settings for heating and cooling at all times and especially when a commercial building or residence is vacant. The systems also have the capability to control thermostats by programming holidays, vacations, and complex work schedules in commercial applications and produce significant energy savings. Additional capabilities also include use of programmable thermostats that conserve energy by operating the HVAC system in their most efficient mode by monitoring output or supply-air temperature, return-air temperature, room temperature, and outdoor temperature.

ALARMS AND PERFORMANCE MONITORING

Typical centralized energy-management systems monitor performance of the HVAC equipment and in some instances provide a routine maintenance schedule to ensure that the equipment continues to operate at their most efficient level. The data-acquisition system software accumulates performance records and stores the energy consumption and run times of each component of the HVAC system. Analysis of the data determines normal system efficiencies and identifies any degradation or deficiencies occurring in the system. The system software also generates alarms on a number of temperature and operational parameters for each HVAC unit. These alarms can be reported on a local and/or remote basis using modem communication back to a central monitoring computer.

HARDWARE SYSTEM CONFIGURATION

A centralized energy-management system consists of a master control unit, HVAC control module(s), and individual room-temperature sensor(s). The master control units most often are equipped with paging receiver and RS232 serial interface for local or remote operation with a personal computer.

Master control unit   The master control unit of an energy-management system is designed to replace conventional thermostats and can control from one to eight individual and different HVAC systems through an RS232 four-wire serial data line using existing thermostat wire. The keyboard and liquid crystal display (LCD) are used for entering control parameters, program data, and operating modes and is used to display the same data, as well as energy usage, demand, and energy efficiency of each system. An optional radiofrequency (RF) paging receiver allows the system to receive commands from a utility. An optional RS232 serial interface also allows communication with an on-site PC or a remote PC via a modem. All critical program and energy data are stored in nonvolatile memory within the unit, which ensures that the data are not lost in case of a power failure. Programming the master control unit is based on a tutorial process in which the unit displays information on the LCD, allowing the user only to answer yes or no or to increase or decrease a parameter by pressing a key.

HVAC control module   A control module (Fig. 5.10) is installed on each HVAC system. This module receives data from the master control unit via an RS232 data line by using existing thermostat wires and is updated continuously with temperature setpoints and operating instructions from the master control unit. The control module also informs the master control unit of the status of the systems so that it can monitor alarm conditions, energy usage, and energy efficiency. The control modules are designed to

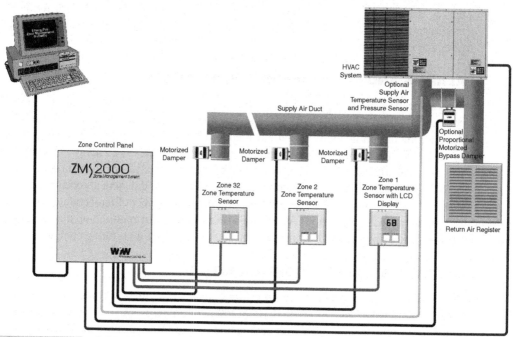

ZMS Control series

Zone management system

PC Controlled ZMS2000

Figure 5.10   **A EMS2000 control system.** *Photo courtesy of Winn Energy Controls.*

allow installation in a variety of configurations for different types of HVAC systems, such as condensing air conditioners, heat pumps, gas furnaces, and others. The control module in Winn Energy Control uses relay contacts rated at 10 A to control the 24-V ac controls within the HVAC system.

Room-temperature sensor   In multiple HVAC installations, a thermistor-type room-temperature sensor (see Fig. 5.11) is placed in each area where a thermostat was located previously and is connected to the HVAC control module using the existing thermostat wires in the walls. The sensor also has a WARMER and COOLER push-button switch that allow occupants at each remote location to adjust the room temperature setting over a preset limited range. If the system is in a night economy setting, pressing the WARMER or COOLER key returns the system to the comfort temperature for a 2-hour period. This provides a simple way of overriding the programmed temperature.

Figure 5.10 shows a EMS2000 control system diagram. Figure 5.11 shows EMS 2000 wall-mount controller module.

Utility demand-side energy management   The energy-management system just described allows a utility service provider to access any HVAC system to control

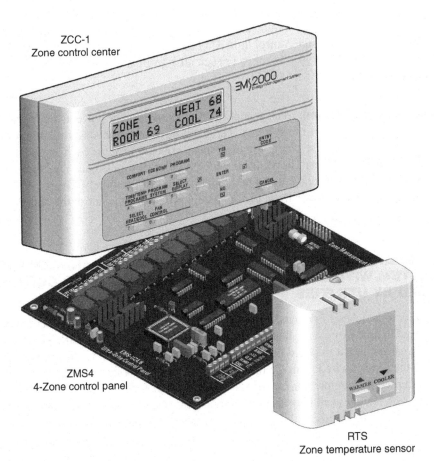

Figure 5.11   **A EMS2000 wall-mount controller module.** *Photo courtesy of Winn Energy Controls.*

raising and cooling setpoints so that electrical demand and energy consumption are reduced, as might be required during peak-demand periods. It has been widely accepted that raising the cooling setpoint by 5°F for a period of 8 hours would lower the average energy consumption by 15–30 percent depending on geographic location. The energy reduction during the period the setpoint temperature is setup is in addition to the energy savings produced by the system during normal system operation.

The electric utility service provider also can control any master control unit or group of master control units through the RF paging system and raise the cooling set-point or lower the heating setpoint by 1–15°F. This is accomplished by an optional RF paging receiver built into the master control unit. The new setpoint is activated by dialing the paging number corresponding to the master control group selected and entering a code in the same manner as entering a telephone number when paging someone. As an alternative, the paging also can be automated using a PC with the central software program. The number entered consists of a verification code, an area group number, a subgroup number, a unit number, and a command with both time and temperature instructions to the master control unit. This command structure allows up to 999 area groups with up to 99,999 subgroups in each area group and up to 9999 master control units in each subgroup.

Sender identification   The sender identification number prevents unauthorized or accidental accessing of the systems. There are three access codes available for entering commands into the energy-management control system, each associated with access restriction codes. The utility service provider using the code is allowed to have control of the heating and cooling setpoint temperatures remotely. The users also have an access code that allows them to completely program and control the master control unit remotely.

COMPARISON OF A CONVENTIONAL ENERGY-MANAGEMENT SYSTEM WITH DEMAND-SIDE MANAGEMENT (DSM) CONTROL USED BY UTILITIES

Earlier approaches to demand-side management by utilities used an external control, referred to as a *duty cycler,* that was installed at the HVAC system and was activated by an ac carrier signal imposed on the ac power lines. The control normally was wired to open the control wired from the thermostat to the contactor controlling the compressor. This turned the compressor off for varying periods of time to reduce energy consumption. Each facility would respond differently to the loss of compressor cooling, and there was no control over the indoor temperature. Typically, the user had no idea the utility had turned the air-conditioning off. This resulted in confusion and sometimes caused the user to call his or her HVAC service contractor because he or she believed that the HVAC system had failed or malfunctioned.

Advanced energy-management systems solve these problems by providing the service utility provider with proportional and continuous control over the cooling and heating setpoints. This allows the setpoints to be changed as demand arises. By using a smaller change in the setpoint over a larger number of customers, the impact on any one customer's comfort is minimized, and demand is still reduced. In addition, the customer can see from the LCD on the thermostat that the utility has modified the setpoint and is in control of the thermostat.

Consumer peak-power electrical demand savings   Consumer electrical demand savings are produced even without the intervention or control of the DMS system by a utility. This is accomplished by programming the energy-management system to sequence the different air-conditioning systems to minimize the number of compressors operating at any one time on a local basis. For example, each 5-ton air conditioner that can be kept offline can reduce demand by 6–7.5 kW. This is accomplished during the utility peak-demand period by programming a starting date, ending date, and the start and stop times each day.

Intelligent control   During the peak utility demand periods, the energy-management system periodically turns air-conditioning compressors off to control the number of compressors operating at any one time. Before turning a compressor off, the system looks at the setpoint temperature and the room temperature and selects the systems that have been running the longest and closest to the setpoint or satisfying the call for cooling. The software within the energy-management system also considers the priority of each system, the amount of temperature rise allowed for each system, and the number of systems that are allowed to operate at any one time.

Energy conservation   The energy-management systems conserve energy by minimizing the amount of time the HVAC systems operate and by monitoring the performance of the HVAC systems to ensure that all components are operating efficiently and together in the most efficient mode for the application.

Time/temperature programming   Energy-management systems in general can be programmed so that each day may have a different time and temperature schedule with up to four temperature changes per day for cooling and heating. Each program or schedule can use different temperatures for cooling and heating.

The energy savings achieved by raising the cooling setpoint 5°F for an 8-hour period are widely stated as 15–30 percent depending on the geographic location. Similarly, a 10°F setback in heating for an 8-hour period can reduce energy consumption by another 7–15 percent depending on geographic location.

Just-in-time temperature programming   The energy-management system monitors the outdoor temperatures and computes when it should turn on the heating or cooling to ensure that the temperature programmed will be reached at the proper time and not too early. Starting a heating or cooling call 30 minutes early can increase the energy consumption by 6 percent in 8 hours of call time.

Vacation/holiday programming   The energy-management system can be programmed at the beginning of the year for up to 12 vacation or holiday periods. These days are entered by date to program holiday temperature settings for both heating and cooling. In a commercial application, this results in significant energy savings.

Alarm reporting   The energy-management system can be programmed to report alarm conditions of peak demand or energy consumption. The alarms will be reported locally on the master control unit or PC and dialed out to report the alarms to an offsite PC for notification and action.

Energy conservation by improved system efficiency   The energy-management system conserve energy by operating the HVAC system in its most efficient mode by monitoring output or supply-air temperature, return-air temperature, room temperature, and outdoor temperature. This allows the energy-management system to make complex decisions about compressor, indoor fan, economizer, and gas valve/burner operation.

Energy recovery at the end of a cooling or heating call   Some new and more expensive heating and air-conditioning systems are furnished with a time-delay relay (TDR) that keeps the indoor fan operating 30–60 seconds at the end of a heating or cooling call to salvage the residual hot or cold energy stored in the mechanical system. The American Refrigeration Institute (ARI) has recognized this technique for improving energy efficiency, and it has reported an additional 15–25 percent improvement in the standard energy efficiency rating (SEER) of the equipment with this control.

The energy-management system performs this function for equipment that does not have a TDR and performs more than the simple TDR function. In air-conditioning, the system monitors the temperature of the supply air and keeps the indoor fan operating until the Btu output has dropped to 25 percent of normal. This is done by monitoring the temperature drop across the indoor coil (return-air temperature versus supply-air temperature). At the 25 percent level, the Btu output from the system is about equal to the power required to operate the indoor fan to recover the Btus.

Intelligent indoor fan operation   Many commercial users operate their indoor fan continuously without regard to the energy being consumed by the fan or the effect on cooling or heating call time. A fan that is operating continuously actually can be heating the indoor environment when the thermostat is in the cooling mode. This may be caused by high return-air temperatures, economizers stuck in the open position, poorly insulated return air ducts, or makeup air vents that are set improperly.

The energy-management system can reduce this wasted energy by operating the indoor fan in five different modes: continuously on, automatic, pulsed, timed, and continuous on/off controlled. The user can select one or more modes of operation that do not conflict.

Energy conservation by measured efficiency   Energy-management systems generally allow the consumer to measure both operating times and efficiency. This is accomplished by monitoring the amount of time the system operates in cooling or heating and monitoring the cooling- or heating-degree days for the period, which provides the consumer with a relative measure of system efficiency.

Energy conservation by monitoring efficiency and predictive maintenance
In most applications, a consumer does not repair or maintain an HVAC system until it has failed or its performance approaches failure, resulting in a severe negative impact on overall efficiency. The energy-management system continuously monitors HVAC system performance and will generate and report an alarm condition if minimum performance parameters are not maintained. The system also allows routine maintenance and repairs to be tracked over a 12-month period. After each service of the HVAC system, the repairs and service performed can be entered into the energy-management system and be displayed at any time. It should be noted that preventive maintenance is the best way to prevent degradation of system efficiency.

LEED—Leadership in Energy and Environmental Design

ENERGY USE AND THE ENVIRONMENT

Ever since the creation of tools, the formation of settlements, and the advent of progressive development technologies, humankind has consistently harvested the abundance of energy that has been accessible in various forms. Until the eighteenth-century industrial revolution, energy forms used by humans were limited to river or stream water currents, tides, solar, wind, and to a very small degree, geothermal energy, none of which had an adverse effect on the environment.

On discovery and harvesting of steam power and the development of steam-driven engines, humankind resorted to the use of fossil fuels and commenced the unnatural creation of air, soil, water, and atmospheric pollutants with increasing acceleration to a degree that fears about the sustenance of life on our planet under the prevailing pollution and waste-management control has come into focus.

Since global material production is made possible by the use of electric power generated from the conversion of fossil fuels, continued growth of the human population and the inevitable demand for materials within the next couple of centuries, if not mitigated, will tax global resources and this planet's capacity to sustain life as we know it. To appreciate the extent of energy use in human-made material production, we simply must observe that every object used in our lives, from a simple nail to a supercomputer, is made using pollutant energy resources. The conversion of raw materials to finished products usually involves a large number of energy-consuming processes, but products made using recycled materials, such as wood, plastics, water, paper, and metals, require fewer process steps and therefore less pollutant energy.

In order to mitigate energy waste and promote energy conservation, the U.S. Department of Energy, Office of Building Technology, founded the U.S. Green Building Council. The council was authorized to develop design standards that provide for improved environmental and economic performance in commercial buildings by the use of established or advanced industry standards, principles, practices, and materials. It should be noted that the United States, with 5 percent of the world population, presently consumes 25 percent of the global energy resources.

The U.S. Green Building Council introduced the Leadership in Energy and Environmental Design (LEED) rating system and checklist. This system establishes qualification and rating standards that categorize construction projects with certified designations such as silver, gold, and platinum. Depending on adherence to the number of points specified in the project checklist, a project may be bestowed recognition and potentially a set amount of financial contribution by state and federal agencies.

In essence, the LEED guidelines discussed in this chapter, in addition to providing design guidelines for energy conservation, are intended to safeguard the ecology and reduce environmental pollution resulting from construction projects. There are many ways to analyze the benefits of LEED building projects. In summary, green building design is about productivity. A number of studies, most notably a study by Greg Kats of Capital-E, have validated the productivity value.

There are also a number of factors that make up this analysis. The basic concept is that if employees are happy in their workspace, such as having an outside view and daylight in their office environment and a healthy environmental quality, they become more productive.

State of California Green Building Action Plan

The following is adapted from the detailed directions that accompany the California governor's executive order regarding the Green Building Action Plan, also referred to as Executive Order S-20-04. The original publication, which is a public-domain document, can be found on the CEC Web site.

PUBLIC BUILDINGS

State buildings   All employees and all state entities under the governor's jurisdiction must immediately and expeditiously take all practical and cost-effective measures to implement the following goals specific to facilities owned, funded, or leased by the state.

Green buildings   The U.S. Green Building Council (USGBC) has developed green building rating systems that advance energy and material efficiency and sustainability, known as the *Leadership in Energy and Environmental Design for New Construction and Major Renovations* (LEED-NC) and the *LEED Rating System for Existing Buildings* (LEED-EB).

All new state buildings and major renovations of 10,000 ft^2 and over and subject to Title 24 must be designed, constructed, and certified by LEED-NC silver or higher, as described below.

Life-cycle cost assessments, defined later in this section, must be used in determining cost-effective criteria. Building projects of less than 10,000 ft^2 must use the same design standard, but certification is not required.

The California Sustainable Building Task Force (SBTF) in consultation with the Department of General Services (DGS), Department of Finance (DoF), and the CEC is responsible for defining a life-cycle cost-assessment methodology that must be used to evaluate the cost-effectiveness of building design and construction decisions and their impact over a facility's life cycle.

Each new building or large renovation project initiated by the state is also subject to a clean on-site power-generation requirement. All existing state buildings over 50,000 ft^2

must meet LEED-EB standards by no later than 2015 to the maximum extent of cost-effectiveness.

Energy efficiency   All state-owned buildings must reduce the volume of energy purchased from the grid by at least 20 percent by 2015 as compared with a 2003 baseline. Alternatively, buildings that have already taken significant efficiency actions must achieve a minimum efficiency benchmark established by the CEC.

Consistent with the executive order, all state buildings are directed to investigate "demand response" programs administered by utilities, the California Power Authority, to take advantage of financial incentives in return for agreeing to reduce peak electrical loads when called on to the maximum extent cost-effective for each facility.

All occupied state-owned buildings, beginning no later than July 2005, must use the energy-efficiency guidelines established by the CEC. All state buildings over 50,000 ft^2 must be retrocommissioned and then recommissioned on a recurring 5-year cycle or whenever major energy-consuming systems or controls are replaced. This is to ensure that energy- and resource-consuming equipment are installed and operated at optimal efficiency. State facility leased spaces of 5000 ft^2 or more also must meet minimum U.S. Environmental Protection Agency (EPA) Energy Star guidelines.

Beginning in the year 2008, all electrical equipment, such as computers, printers, copiers, refrigerator units, and air-conditioning systems, that is purchased or operated by state buildings and state agencies must be Energy Star rated.

Financing and execution   Consultation with the CEC, the State Treasurer's Office, the DGS, and financial institutions will facilitate lending mechanisms for resource-efficiency projects. These mechanisms will include the use of the life-cycle cost methodology and will maximize the use of outside financing, loan programs, revenue bonds, municipal leases, and other financial instruments. Incentives for cost-effective projects will include cost sharing of at least 25 percent of the net savings with the operating department or agency.

SCHOOLS

New school construction   The Division of State Architect (DSA), in consultation with the Office of Public School Construction and the CEC in California, was mandated to develop technical resources to enable schools to be built with energy-sufficient resources. As a result of this effort, the state designated the Collaborative for High Performance Schools (CHPS) criteria as the recommended guideline. The CHPS is based on LEED and was developed specifically for kindergarten to grade 12 schools.

COMMERCIAL AND INSTITUTIONAL BUILDINGS

This section also includes private-sector buildings, state buildings, and schools. The California Public Utilities Commission (CPUC) is mandated to determine the level of ratepayer-supported energy efficiency and clean-energy generation so as to contribute to the 20 percent efficiency goal.

LEADERSHIP

Mission of Green Action Team   The state of California has established an interagency team knows as the *Green Action Team* that is composed of the director of the Department of Finance and the secretaries of business, transportation, and housing, with a mission to oversee and direct progress toward the goals of the green building order.

LEED

LEED project sustainable building credits and prerequisites are based on LEED-NC2.1 New Construction. There are additional versions of LEED that have been adopted or are currently in development that address core or shell, commercial interiors, existing buildings, homes, and neighborhood development.

SUSTAINABLE SITES

Sustainable site prerequisite: Construction activity pollution prevention
The intent of this prerequisite is to control and reduce top erosion and reduce the adverse impact on the surrounding water and air quality. Mitigation measures involve prevention of the loss of topsoil during construction by means of a storm-water-system runoff as well as the prevention of soil displacement by gusting wind. It also imposes measures to prevent sedimentation of storm-sewer systems by sand, dust, and particulate matter. Some suggested design measures to meet these requirements include deployment of strategies such as temporary or permanent seeding, silt fencing, sediment trapping, and sedimentation basins that could trap particulate material.

Site selection, credit no. 1   The intent of this credit is to prevent and avoid development of a site that could have an adverse environmental impact on the project location surroundings. Sites considered unsuitable for construction include prime farmlands; lands that are lower than 5 ft above the elevation of established 100-year flood areas, as defined by the Federal Emergency Management Agency (FEMA); lands that are designated habitats for endangered species; lands within 100 ft of any wetland; or a designated public parkland.

To meet site-selection requirements, it is recommended that the sustainable project buildings have a reasonably minimal footprint to avoid site disruption. Favorable design practices must involve underground parking and neighbor-shared facilities. The point weight granted for this measure is 1.

Development density and community connectivity, credit no. 2   The intent of this requirement is to preserve and protect green fields and animal habitats by means of increasing the urban density, which also may have a direct impact on reduction of urban traffic and pollution. A specific measure suggested includes project site selection within the vicinity of an urban area with high development density. The point weight granted for this measure is 1.

Brownfield redevelopment, credit no. 3 The main intent of this credit is the use and development of projects on lands that have environmental contamination. To undertake development under this category, the EPA must provide a sustainable redevelopment remediation requirement permit. Projects developed under brownfield redevelopment are usually offered state, local, and federal tax incentives for site remediation and cleanup. The point weight granted for each of the four measures is 1.

Alternative transportation, credit no. 4 The principal objective of this measure is to reduce traffic congestion and minimize air pollution. Measures recommended include locating the project site within 1/2 mile of a commuter train, subway, or bus station; construction of a bicycle stand and shower facilities for 5 percent of building habitants; and installation of alternative liquid and gas fueling stations on the premises. An additional requisite calls for a preferred parking facility for car pools and vans that serve 5 percent of the building occupants, which encourages transportation sharing. The point weight granted for this measure is 1.

Site development, credit no. 5 The intent of this measure is to conserve habitats and promote biodiversity. Under this prerequisite, 1 point is provided for limiting earthwork and the destruction of vegetation beyond the project or building perimeter, 5 ft beyond walkways and roadway curbs, 25 ft beyond previously developed sites, and restoration of 50 percent of open areas by planting of native trees and shrubs.

Another point under this section is awarded for 25 percent reduction of a building footprint by what is allowed by local zoning ordinances. Design mitigations for meeting the preceding goals involve underground parking facilities, ride-sharing among habitants, and restoring open spaces by landscape architecture planning that uses local trees and vegetation.

Storm-water management, credit no. 6 The objective of this measure involves preventing the disruption of natural water flows by reducing storm-water runoffs and promoting on-site water filtration that reduces contamination. In essence, these requirements are subdivided into two categories. The first one deals with the reduction of the net rate and quantity of storm-water runoff that is caused by the imperviousness of the ground, and the second relates to measures undertaken to remove up to 80 percent of the average annual suspended solids associated with the runoff.

Design-mitigation measures include maintenance of natural storm-water flows that include filtration to reduce sedimentation. Another technique used is construction of roof gardens that minimize surface imperviousness and allow for storage and reuse of storm water for no potable uses such as landscape irrigation and toilet and urinal flushing. The point weight granted for each of the two categories discussed here is 1.

Heat-island effect, credit no. 7 The intent of this requirement is to reduce the microclimatic thermal gradient difference between the project being developed and adjacent lands that have wildlife habitats. Design measures to be undertaken include shading provisions on site surfaces such as parking lots, plazas, and walkways. It is also recommended that site or building colors have a reflectance of at least 0.3 and that 50 percent of parking spaces be of the underground type.

Another design measure suggests use of Energy Star high-reflectance and high-emissivity roofing. To meet these requirements, the project site must feature extensive landscaping. In addition to minimizing building footprints, it is also suggested that building rooftops have vegetated surfaces and that gardens and paved surfaces be of light-colored materials to reduce heat absorption. The point weight granted for each of the two categories discussed here is 1.

Light-pollution reduction, credit no. 8   In essence, this requirement is intended to eliminate light trespass from the project site, minimize the so-called night-sky access, and reduce the impact on nocturnal environments. This requirement becomes mandatory for projects that are within the vicinity of observatories.

To comply with these requirements, site lighting design must adhere to Illumination Engineering Society of North America (IESNA) requirements. In California, indoor and outdoor lighting design should comply with CEC Title 24, 2005, requirements. Design measures to be undertaken involve the use of luminaries and lamp standards equipped with filtering baffles and low-angle spotlights that can prevent off-site horizontal and upward light spillage. The point weight granted for this measure is 1.

WATER EFFICIENCY MEASURES

Water-efficient landscaping, credit no. 1   This measure is intended to minimize the use of potable water for landscape irrigation purposes. One credit is awarded for the use of high-efficiency irrigation management-control technology. A second credit is awarded for the construction of special reservoirs for the storage and use of rainwater for irrigation purposes.

Innovative water technologies, credit no. 2   The main purpose of this measure is to reduce the potable-water demand by a minimum of 50 percent. Mitigation involves the use of gray water by construction of on-site natural or mechanical wastewater-treatment systems that could be used for irrigation and toilet or urinal flushing. Consideration is also given to the use of waterless urinals and storm-water usage. The point weight granted for this measure is 1.

Water-use reduction, credit no. 3   The intent of this measure is to reduce water usage within buildings and thereby minimize the burden of local municipal supply and water treatment. This measure provides 1 credit for design strategies that reduce building water usage by 20 percent and a second credit for a reducing water usage by 30 percent. Design measures to meet this requirement involve the use of waterless urinals, high-efficiency toilet and bathroom fixtures, and nonpotable water for flushing toilets.

ENERGY AND ATMOSPHERE

Fundamental commissioning of building energy systems, prerequisite no. 1
This requirement is a prerequisite intended to verify intended project design goals and involves design-review verification, commissioning, calibration, physical verification of

installation, and functional performance tests, all of which are to be presented in a final commissioning report. The point weight granted for this prerequisite is 1.

Minimum energy performance, prerequisite no. 2   The intent of this prerequisite is to establish a minimum energy-efficiency standard for a building. In essence, the basic building energy efficiency is principally controlled by mechanical engineering, heating, and air-conditioning design performance principles, which are outlined by American Society of Heating, Refrigeration, and Air-Conditioning Engineers (ASHRAE)/IESNA and local municipal or state codes. The engineering design procedure involves so-called building-envelop calculations that maximize energy performance. Building-envelop computations are achieved by computer simulation models that quantify energy performance as compared with a baseline building.

Fundamental refrigerant management, prerequisite no. 3   The intent of this measure is the reduction of ozone-depleting refrigerants used in HVAC systems. Mitigation involves replacement of old HVAC equipment with equipment that does not use CFC refrigerants.

Optimize energy performance, credit no. 1   The principal intent of this measure is to increase levels of energy performance above the prerequisite standard in order to reduce environmental impacts associated with excessive energy use. The various credit levels shown in Table 5.3 are intended to reduce the design-energy budget for the regulated energy components described in the requirements of the ASHRAE/IESNA standard. The energy components include building envelope, hot-water system, and other regulated systems defined by ASHRAE standards. Similarly to previous design measures, computer simulation and energy performance modeling software are used to quantify the energy performance compared with a baseline building system.

On-site renewable energy, credit no. 2   The intent of this measure is to encourage the use of sustainable- or renewable-energy technologies such as solar PV cogeneration, solar power heating and air-conditioning, fuel cells, wind energy, landfill

TABLE 5.3   NEW AND OLD BUILDING CREDIT POINTS

% INCREASE IN ENERGY PERFORMANCE		
NEW BUILDINGS	EXISTING BUILDINGS	CREDIT POINTS
14	7	2
21	14	4
28	21	6
35	28	8
42	35	10

TABLE 5.4 ENERGY-SAVING CREDIT POINTS	
% TOTAL ENERGY-SAVING	CREDIT POINTS
5	1
10	2
20	3

gases, and geothermal and other technologies discussed in various chapters of this book. The credit-award system under this measure is based on a percentage of the total energy demand of the building. See Table 5.4.

Additional commissioning, credit no. 3   This is an enforcement measure to verify whether the designed building is constructed and performs within the expected or intended parameters. The credit-verification stages include preliminary design documentation review, construction documentation review when construction is completed, selective submittal document review, establishment of commissioning documentation, and finally, postoccupancy review. It should be noted that all these reviews must be conducted by an independent commissioning agency. The point weight awarded for each of the four categories is 1.

Enhanced refrigerant management, credit no. 4   This measure involves installation of HVAC, refrigeration, and fire-suppression equipment that does not use hydrochlorofluorocarbon (HCFC) agents. The point weight awarded for this category is 1.

Measurement and verification, credit no. 5   This requirement is intended to optimize building energy consumption and provide a measure of accountability. The design measures implemented include the following:

■ Lighting system control, which may consist of occupancy sensors, photocells for control of daylight harvesting, and a wide variety of computerized systems that minimize the energy waste related to building illumination. A typical discussion of lighting control is covered under California Title 24 energy-conservation measures, with which all building lighting designs must comply within the state.
■ Compliance of constant and variable loads, which must comply with motor design efficiency regulations.
■ Motor size regulation that enforces the use of variable-speed drives (VFDs).
■ Chiller efficiency regulation measures that meet variable-load situations.
■ Cooling load regulations.
■ Air and water economizer and heat recovery and recycling.
■ Air circulation, volume distribution, and static pressure in HVAC applications.
■ Boiler efficiency.

- Building energy-efficiency management by means of centralized management and control equipment installation.
- Indoor and outdoor water consumption management.

The point weight awarded for each of the four categories is 1.

Green power, credit no. 6   This measure is intended to encourage the use and purchase of grid-connected renewable-energy cogenerated energy derived from sustainable energy such as solar, wind, geothermal, and other technologies described throughout this book. A purchase-and-use agreement of this so-called green power is usually limited to a minimum of a 2-year contract. The cost of green energy use is considerably higher than that of regular energy. Purchasers of green energy who participate in the program are awarded a Green-e products certification.

MATERIAL AND RESOURCES

Storage and collection of recyclables, prerequisite no. 1   This prerequisite is a measure to promote construction-material sorting and segregation for recycling and landfill deposition. Simply put, construction or demolition materials such as glass, iron, concrete, paper, aluminum, plastics, cardboard, and organic waste must be separated and stored in a dedicated location within the project for further recycling.

Building reuse, credit no. 1   The intent of this measure is to encourage the maximum use of structural components of an existing building that will serve to preserve and conserve a cultural identity, minimize waste, and reduce the environmental impact. It should be noted that another significant objective of this measure is to reduce the use of newly manufactured material and associated transportation that ultimately results into energy use and environmental pollution. Credit is given for implementation of the following measures:

- One credit for maintenance and reuse of 75 percent of the existing building.
- Two credits for maintenance of 100 percent of the existing building structure shell and the exterior skin (windows excluded).
- Three credits for 100 percent maintenance of the building shell and 50 percent of walls, floors, and ceiling.

This simply means that the only replacements will be of electrical, mechanical, plumbing, and door and window systems, which essentially boils down to a remodeling project.

Construction waste management, credit no. 2   The principal purpose of this measure is to recycle a significant portion of the demolition and land-clearing materials, which calls for implementation of an on-site waste-management plan. An interesting component of this measure is that the donation of materials to a charitable organization also constitutes waste management. The 3 credits awarded under this measure include 1 point for recycling or salvaging a minimum of 50 percent by weight of demolition materials and 2 points for salvage of 75 percent by weight of the construction and demolition debris and materials.

Material reuse, credit no. 3   This measure is intended to promote the use of recycled materials, thus reducing the adverse environmental impact caused by manufacturing and transporting new products. For using recycled materials in a construction, 1 credit is given to the first 5 percent and a second point for a 10 percent total use. Recycled materials used could include wall paneling, cabinetry, bricks, construction wood, and even furniture.

Recycled content, credit no. 4   The intent of this measure is to encourage the use of products that have been constructed from recycled materials. One credit is given if 25 percent of the building material contains some sort of recycled material or 40 percent of minimum by weight use of so-called postindustrial material content. A second point is awarded for an additional 25 percent recycled material use.

Regional materials, credit no. 5   The intent of this measure is to maximize the use of locally manufactured products, which minimizes transportation and thereby reduces environmental pollution. One point is awarded if 20 percent of the material is manufactured within 500 miles of the project, and another point is given if the total recycled material use reaches 50 percent. Materials used in addition to manufactured goods also include those that are harvested, such as rock and marble from quarries.

Rapidly renewable materials, credit no. 6   This is an interesting measure that encourages the use of rapidly renewable natural and manufactured building materials. Examples of natural materials include strawboards, woolen carpets, bamboo flooring, cotton-based insulation, and poplar wood. Manufactured products may consist of linoleum flooring, recycled glass, and concrete as an aggregate. The point weight awarded for this measure is 1.

Certified wood, credit no. 7   The intent of this measure is to encourage the use of wood-based materials. One point is credited for the use of wood-based materials such as structural beams and framing and flooring materials that are certified by Forest Council Guidelines (FSC).

INDOOR ENVIRONMENTAL QUALITY

Minimum indoor air quality (IAQ) performance, prerequisite no. 1   This prerequisite is established to ensure indoor air quality performance to maintain the health and wellness of the occupants. One credit is awarded for adherence to ASHRAE building ventilation guidelines such as placement of HVAC intakes away from contaminated air pollutant sources such as chimneys, smoke stacks, and exhaust vents. The point weight awarded for this measure is 1.

Environmental tobacco smoke (ETS) control, prerequisite no. 2   This is a prerequisite that mandates the provision of dedicated smoking areas within buildings that can effectively capture and remove tobacco and cigarette smoke from the building. To comply with this requirement, designated smoking rooms must be enclosed and designed with impermeable walls and have a negative pressure (air being sucked in rather than being pushed out) compared with the surrounding quarters. On completion of construction, designated smoking rooms are tested by the use of a tracer-gas method defined by ASHRAE standards that impose a maximum of 1 percent tracer-gas escape from the ETS area. This measure is readily achieved by installing a separate ventilation system that creates a slight negative room pressure. The point weight awarded for this measure is 1.

Outdoor air-delivery monitoring, credit no. 1   As the title implies, the intent of this measure is to provide an alarm monitoring and notification system for indoor and outdoor spaces. The maximum permitted carbon dioxide level is 530 ppm. To comply with the measure, HVAC systems are required to be equipped with a carbon dioxide monitoring and annunciation system, which is usually a component of building automation systems. The point weight awarded for this measure is 1.

Increased ventilation, credit no. 2   This measure is intended for HVAC designs to promote outdoor fresh-air circulation for building occupants' health and comfort. A credit of 1 point is awarded for adherence to the ASHRAE guideline for naturally ventilated spaces where air distribution is achieved in a laminar-flow pattern. Some HVAC design strategies used include displacement and low-velocity ventilation, plug-flow or under-floor air delivery, and operable windows that allow natural air circulation.

Construction (IAQ) air quality management plan, credit no. 3   This measure applies to air quality management during renovation processes to ensure that occupants are prevented from exposure to moisture and air contaminants. One credit is awarded for installation of absorptive materials that prevent moisture damage and filtration media to prevent space contamination by particulates and airborne materials. A second point is awarded for a minimum of flushing out of the entire space by displacement with outside air for a period of 2 weeks prior to occupancy. At the end of the filtration period, a series of tests is performed to measure the air contaminants.

Low-emitting materials, credit no. 4   This measure is intended to reduce indoor air contaminants resulting from airborne particulates such as paints and sealants. Four specific areas of concern include the following: (1) adhesives, fillers, and sealants, (2) primers and paints, (3) carpet, and (4) composite wood and agrifiber products that contain urea-formaldehyde resins. Each of these product applications is controlled by various agencies, such as the California Air Quality Management District, the Green Seal Council, and the Green Label Indoor Air Quality Test Program. The point weight awarded for each of the four measures is 1.

Indoor chemical and pollutant source control, credit no. 5 This is a measure to prevent air and water contamination by pollutants. Mitigation involves installation of air and water filtration systems that absorb chemical particulates entering a building. Rooms and areas such as document-reproduction rooms, copy rooms, and blueprint quarters that generate trace air pollutants are equipped with dedicated air exhaust and ventilation systems that create negative pressure. Likewise, water circulation, plumbing, and liquid waste disposal are collected in an isolated container for special disposal. This measure is credited a single point.

Controllability of systems, credit no. 6 The essence of this measure is to provide localized distributed control for ventilation, air-conditioning, and lighting. One point is awarded for autonomous control of lighting and control for each zone covering 200 ft^2 of area with a dedicated operable window within 15 ft of the perimeter wall. A second point is given for providing air and temperature control for 50 percent of the nonperimeter occupied area. Both these measures are accomplished by centralized or local-area lighting control and HVAC building-control systems. These measures are intended to control lighting and air circulation. Each of the two measures is awarded 1 point.

Thermal comfort, credit no. 7 The intent of this measure is to provide environmental comfort for building occupants. One credit is awarded for thermal and humidity control for specified climate zones and another for the installation of a permanent central temperature and humidity monitoring and control system.

Daylight and views, credit no. 8 Simply stated, this measure promotes architectural space design that allows for maximum outdoor views and interior sunlight exposure. One credit is awarded for spaces that harvest indirect daylight for 75 percent of spaces occupied for critical tasks. A second point is awarded for direct sight of vision glazing from 90 percent of normally occupied workspaces. It should be noted that copy rooms, storage rooms, mechanical equipment rooms, and low-occupancy rooms do not fall into these categories. In other words, 90 percent of the workspace is required to have direct sight of a glazing window. Some architectural design measures taken to meet these requirements include building orientation, widening of building perimeter, deployment of high-performance glazing windows, and use of solar tubes.

INNOVATION AND DESIGN PROCESS

Innovation in design, credit no. 1 This measure is in fact a merit award for an innovative design that is not covered by LEED measures and in fact exceeds the required energy-efficiency and environmental pollution performance milestone guidelines. The 4 credits awarded for innovation in design are (1) identification of the design intent, (2) meeting requirements for compliance, (3) proposed document submittals that demonstrate compliance, and (4) a description of the design approach used to meet the objective.

LEED-accredited professional, credit no. 2 One point is credited to the project for a design team that has a member who has successfully completed the LEED accreditation examination.

CREDIT SUMMARY

Sustainable sites	10 points
Water efficiency	3 points
Energy and atmosphere	8 points
Material and resources	9 points
Indoor environmental quality	10 points
Innovation in design	2 points

The grand total is 42 points.

OPTIMIZED ENERGY PERFORMANCE SCORING POINTS

Additional LEED points are awarded for building efficiency levels, as shown in Table 5.5.

Project certification is based on the cumulated points, as shown in Table 5.6.

TABLE 5.5 LEED CERTIFICATION CATEGORIES AND ASSOCIATED POINTS

% INCREASE IN ENERGY PERFORMANCE		
NEW BUILDINGS	EXISTING BUILDINGS	POINTS
15	5	1
20	10	2
25	15	3
30	20	4
35	25	5
40	30	6
45	35	7
50	40	8
55	45	9
60	50	10

TABLE 5.6 LEED BUILDING CERTIFICATION CATEGORIES AND ASSOCIATED POINTS

LEED certified	26–32 points
Silver level	33–38 points
Gold level	39–51 points
Platinum level	52–69 points

LEED DESIGN MEASURES

Solar power cogeneration   The following is a description the Center for Water Education's LEED solar system. The project is one of the largest private solar installations in the western United States. The system, composed of 2925 solar panels, also includes custom-designed BIPV panels manufactured by Atlantis Energy Systems that cover the loggia. Not only are these panels highly efficient, but they are also beautiful and add an architectural detail found nowhere else.

Part of the incentive to install such a large solar system was the generous rebate program provided by the CEC. At the time of purchase, the center invested $4 million on the design and installation of the solar power system.

Electrical engineering energy-conservation design measures   In process of designing an integrated electrical and solar power system, special design measures were undertaken to significantly minimize the long-term operational cost of energy consumption. Design measures undertaken consisted of significantly exceeding California Title 24 energy conformance minimum standards.

Lighting-control automation   In order to exceed the energy-economy standards, the electrical engineering design incorporated a wide variety of electronic sensing devices and timers to optimize daylight harvesting and zone-lighting controls. Specifically, lighting-control design measures incorporate the following:

■ All buildings over 5000 ft² are divided into lighting-control zones that are controlled by a central computerized programmable astrological timer. Each lighting zone is programmed to operate under varied timing cycles, which enables substantial reduction in lighting power consumption. Figure 5.12 is photograph of the BIPV solar power system in the Paleontology Museum in Hemet California.
■ All campus lighting fixtures used throughout the project are high-efficiency fluorescent fixtures.
■ All office lighting is controlled by occupancy sensors or photoelectric controls.
■ All lights adjacent to windows are controlled by dedicated switches or photocells.
■ Lighting levels in each room are kept below the minimum permitted levels of California Title 24 energy compliance levels.

Figure 5.12   Paleontology Museum building integrated photovoltaic (BIPV) solar power system. *Photo courtesy of Lehrer+Gangi architects.*

- Outdoor banner projectors use LED lamps that use minimal amount of electric power.
- All feeder conduits and branch-circuit wires, whenever warranted, have been oversized to minimize voltage-drop losses.

Solar power cogeneration design measures   One of the most significant energy-saving design features of the Water and Life Museum is integration of PV solar power as an integral component of the architecture. A 540 kW dc solar power system consists of 2955 highly efficient Sharp Electronic solar power panels that cover the entire rooftops of two museum campuses that make up the Water and Life Museum, the Anthropology and Paleontology Museum, a lecture hall, and cafeteria and gift shop.

At present, power-production capability of the aggregate solar power cogeneration system is designed to meet approximately 70 percent of the calculated demand load of the net meter, which is effectively 48 percent above the 20 percent maximum qualification requirement for USGBC 3-point credit. From the April 2006 commissioning date until December 2006, while the project was while under construction, solar power system generated over 550 MWh of electric power, which translates into approximately 8 percent of the net invested capital.

With 50 percent of the CEC solar power rebate received and projected escalation of electric energy cost, the solar power cogeneration system investment is expected to recover its cost in fewer than 5 years. In view of the 25-year guaranteed life span of the solar power panels and minimal maintenance cost of the system, the power cogeneration system, in addition to saving significant amounts of energy, will prevent atmospheric pollution by avoiding the dumping of millions of tons of carbon dioxide into the air.

ENGINEERED BY VECTOR DELTA DESIGN GROUP

Projected economic contribution   Considering maximum performance degradation over the life span of the solar power system, projected ac electrical output power throughout the system life span under worst-case performance conditions is expected to be as follows:

Energy Production

Daily energy production = 350 kWh (worst-case hourly energy output)
$\times$ 5.5 (hours of average daily insolation) = 1925 kWh

Yearly energy production = 1925 kWh $\times$ 365 days = 702,625 kWh

System lifetime (25 years) energy production = 702,625 kWh $\times$ 25 years
= 17,565,625 kWh or = 17.7 MWh

Assuming an optimistic rate of increase in electric energy cost escalation over 25 years of system life, at a mean value of $0.75/kWh, projected saving contributions by the solar power system could be approximately $13,174,218. If we assume a rate of 1 percent of the solar power system cost for general maintenance, the net energy savings over the life span of the system could be about $13 million.

Air pollution prevention   When generating electric power by burning fossil fuels, the carbon dioxide emitted into the atmosphere per kilowatt of electric energy ranges from 0.8 lb for natural gas to 2.2 lb for coal. The variation depends on the type of fossil fuel used, such as natural gas, crude oil, or coal. In view of this, pollution-abatement measures resulting from the use of the solar power at the Water and Life Museum over the life span of 25 years is estimated to be 28 million pounds of CO_2 that will be prevented from polluting the atmosphere.

As mentioned in Chap. 3, when generating electric energy by burning fossil fuels, power losses resulting from turbines and transformation and transmission losses, which in some instances can be as high as 70 percent, also contribute significantly to generating considerable amounts of air and water pollutants. Since solar power is produced on the site, there are no power-generation and distribution losses. Consequently, power-production efficiency compared with conventional electric power plants is significantly higher. In other words, the efficiency of solar power compared with conventional electric energy generated and transmitted hundreds or thousand miles is significantly greater, and it is cost-effective and less expensive when taking collateral expenses associated with state and federal pollution-mitigation expenses into consideration.

Solar power engineering design measures Special electrical engineering design measures undertaken to maximize the solar power production output include the following:

■ To maximize the available solar platform area, the PV modules were design to cover the rooftops in a flat-array formation. Losses resulting from the optimal tilt angle (about 11 percent) were significantly compensated by a gain of more than 40 percent in surface area, which resulted in deployment of a much larger number of PV modules and less expensive support-system platforms.
■ PV array-string grouping was modularized to within 6-kW blocks. Each block of the array has been assigned to a dedicated 6-kW highly efficient inverter. The distributed configuration of arrays was intended to minimize shading effect of a group PV system, which guarantees maximum independent performance by each array group.
■ The inverters used are classified as the most efficient by the CEC (CEC-approved component list) and are designed for direct connection to the electrical grid.
■ All ac solar power feeder conduits and cables were somewhat oversized to minimize voltage-drop losses.
■ In addition to direct power production, roof-mounted solar panels provide significant roof shading, which extends the roof covering life by approximately 25 percent; they also keep the roofs cool and therefore increase the R value of insulation, thus reducing the air-conditioning system operation, which accounts for a notable amount of energy reduction.
■ An advanced computerized telemetry and monitoring system is designed to monitor and display real-time power-output parameters from each building. Instantaneous display of power output in kilowatthours, system power efficiency, cumulated power-output statistics, barometric pressure, outdoor temperature, humidity, and many other vital operational parameters are displayed on a number of screens on the supervisory console.

A specially designed solar power display located in the Water and Life Museum provides an interactive display on a large flat plasma monitor whereby visitors to the museum are allowed to interact and request information regarding the solar power cogeneration system.

ADDITIONAL LEED CERTIFICATION DESIGN MEASURES

Half-flush/full-flush lavatories   All lavatories at the center have the option of a half flush or a full flush. This cuts back on water that is wasted when only a full flush is given as an option every time. Half flushes use half the amount of water a full flush uses.

Waterless urinals   The center's urinals are all waterless. This saves a significant amount of potable water.

Foam exterior   The center's foam insulation cuts back on heater and air-conditioner use and increases the R factor in the exterior walls, making it as energy efficient as possible.

Lithocrete   The center chose to use lithocrete rather than concrete because it is a superior paving process that blends both "old world" paving finishes such as granite and stone with innovative paving finishes incorporating select, surface-seeded aggregates.

Carpet from recycled materials   All the carpets at the center are made of recycled materials, making them environmentally safe.

Landscape, California-friendly plantings   The plants at the center are arranged such that they go from ice age native California plants on one side of the campus to modern-day native California plants on the other side of the campus. Native California plant species are an integral part of the design, allowing the ground cover to blend into the adjacent nature preserve. These drought-tolerant water-efficient plants are weaved in a unique and beautiful demonstration garden.

Smart controllers   Unlike most water-sprinkler systems, the Center for Water Education's landscape features smart controllers. Operated in conjunction with satellites, weather dictates the amount, and the system operates. Smart controllers are also available for residential installation.

Recycled water   State-of-the-art technology for irrigation and the use of reclaimed water is just a couple of the features incorporated into the irrigation plan. Not just any purple pipe, but a state-of-the-art coiled installation at the roots of the plants makes this more efficient than most systems.

Braided stream for storm water   This stream is the organizing element of the garden, and it doubles as a drainage channel. Exposing the structure is not only beautiful but also extremely useful in a natural setting.

Grounds   Rock and decomposed granite enrich the color and water efficiency, which allows the ground cover to blend into the adjacent nature preserve. These elements are also perfect for residential installations.

SUSTAINABLE SITES

Many of the points listed under "Sustainable Sites" were not applicable to the project, such as urban redevelopment or brownfield. The site selected was excess property from dam construction. The project is located on recreation ground covering 1200 acres and in the near future will become a recreation park that will include a golf course, a recreational lake, a swim and sports complex, and a series of bike trails, horse trails, and camp-grounds. The museum complex is the gateway to the recreational grounds and is intended to become the civic center of the area.

The Water and Life Museum building is designed to accommodate bicycle storage for 5 percent of building occupants and offers shower and locker facilities. This encourages alternative transportation to the site, which is intended to reduce negative environmental impacts from automobile use.

Owing to the expected volume of pedestrian and bicycle visitors, vehicle parking space was reduced to provide adequate space for bicycle stands that meet local zoning requirements. The architecture of the grounds blends magnificent building shapes and open spaces with interpretive gardens throughout the campus. The small footprints of the buildings occupying the open space qualify the project for LEED points because it resulted in reduced site disturbance.

Braided streams weaving throughout the site provide a thematic story of water in southern California. The streams also are designed to mitigate stormwater management for the site. The braided streams contain pervious surfaces conveying rainwater to the water table.

The parking grove consists of shade trees and dual-colored asphalt. The remainder of the paving is light-colored acid-washed concrete and light-color lithocrete. The roofs of the buildings are covered with single-ply white membrane, which are shaded by the solar panels. These light-shaded surfaces reduce heat-islanding effect.

The Water and Life Museum is located within the radius of the Palomar Observatory, which has mandatory light-pollution restrictions; as a result, all lamppost fixtures are equipped with full-cutoff fixtures and shut-off timing circuits.

WATER EFFICIENCY

The mission of the Center for Water Education is to transform its visitors into stewards of water. To this end, the campus is a showcase of water efficiency. The campus landscaping consists of native California plants. The irrigation systems deployed are state-of-the-art drip systems that use reclaimed water. Interpretive exhibits throughout the museum demonstrate irrigation technology from Native American to the satellite-controlled. Each building is equipped with waterless urinals and dual-flush toilets.

ENERGY AND ATMOSPHERE

Energy savings begins with the design of an efficient envelope and then employs sophisticated mechanical systems. The Water and Life Museum is located in a climate that has a design load of 105°F in summer. The structures provide shading of the building envelope. High-performance glass and a variety of insulation types create the most efficient building envelope possible. The building exterior skin is constructed from three layers of perforated metal strips. The roofs of all buildings within the campus are covered with high-efficiency PV solar power panels. The eastern elevations of the buildings have eight curtain walls that bridge the 10 towers. Each curtain wall is composed of 900 ft^2 of high-performance argon-filled glass. To compensate for heat radiation, a number of translucent megabanners are suspended in front of each curtain wall. The banners are located above the finish grade, which preserves the beautiful views of the San Jacinto Mountains.

MECHANICAL SYSTEM

The mechanical system employs a combination of radiant flooring, which is used for both heating and cooling, and forced-air units that run from the same chiller and boiler. The combination of an efficient envelope and a sophisticated mechanical system provides a project that is 38 percent more efficient than Title 24 requirements. This not only brings the project many LEED points in this category, but it also provides a significant cost savings in the operation of these facilities.

MATERIAL AND RESOURCES

The builder specified local and recycled materials wherever possible. During the construction phase, he kept a careful watch on how construction wastes were handled.

Materials were selected that were low emitters of VOCs. All contractors had restrictions regarding the types of materials they were allowed to use. The mechanical engineering design deployed a three-dimensional model for the project that tested the thermal comfort of the systems to comply with ASHRAE Standard 55 requirements. The architectural building design ensured that 90 percent of spaces view natural light.

INNOVATION AND DESIGN PROCESS

One of the significant points applied to the project design included use of the buildings as a learning center for teaching sustainability to visitors. Within the museums, exhibit spaces are uniquely devoted to solar cogeneration, which is presented by means of interactive displays where visitors can observe real-time solar and meteorologic statistical data on the display.

PASSIVE SOLAR HEATING

TECHNOLOGIES

This chapter will review the basic principles of passive solar energy and its applications. The term *passive* implies that solar power energy is harvested with the direct exposure of fluids, such as water or a fluid medium, that absorb the heat energy. Subsequently, the harvested energy is converted to steam or vapor, which, in turn, is used to drive turbines or provide evaporative energy in refrigerating and cooling equipment. Figure 6.1 shows the historical use of passive solar energy to power a printing press.

Solar power is the sun's energy, without which life as we know it on our planet would cease to exist. Solar energy has been known and used by humankind throughout the ages. As we all know, solar rays concentrated by a magnifying glass can provide intense heat energy that can burn wood or heat water to its boiling point. As discussed later, recent technological developments of this simple principle are currently being used to harness solar energy and provide an abundance of electric power. Historically, the principle of heating water to its boiling point was well known by the French, who in 1888 used solar power to drive printing machinery.

Appendix C provides a detailed solar power historical timeline.

Passive Solar Water Heating

The simplest method of harvesting energy is to expose fluid-filled pipes to the sun's rays. Modern passive solar panels, which heat water for pools and general household use, are constructed from a combination of magnifying glasses and fluid-filled pipes. Figure 6.2 illustrates the operation of a passive solar water-heating panel. In some instances, pipes carry special heat-absorbing fluids, such as a bromide solution, that heat up quite rapidly. In other instances, water is heated and circulated by small pumps. In most instances, pipes are painted black and are laid on a silver-colored reflective base that further concentrates the solar energy. Another purpose of silver backboards

Figure 6.1 Historical use of passive solar energy to power a printing press.

is to prevent heat transmission to the roofs or support structures. Figure 6.3 illustrates the operation of a residential passive solar water-heating system; Fig. 6.4 shows an industrial passive solar water-heating system.

POOL HEATING

Over the years, a wide variety of pool-heating panel types have been introduced. Each has its intrinsic advantages and disadvantages. At present, there are four primary types of solar pool collector designs:

1 Rigid black plastic panels (polypropylene)
2 Rubber mat or other plastic or rubber formulations
3 Tube-and-fin metal panels with a copper or aluminium fin attached to copper tubing
4 Plastic pipe systems

ENERGY FROM THE SUN

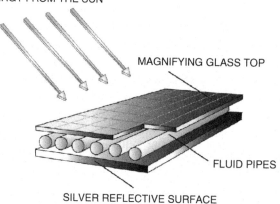

MAGNIFYING GLASS TOP

FLUID PIPES

SILVER REFLECTIVE SURFACE

Figure 6.2 Passive solar water-heating panel.

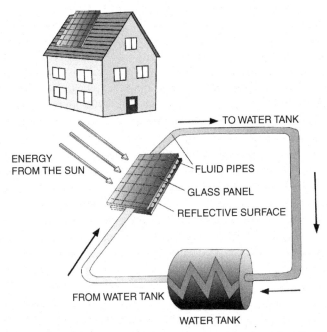

Figure 6.3 Residential passive solar water-heating system.

Plastic panels This technology makes use of modular panels with dimensions approximately 4 ft, 8 in wide by 10–12 in long. Individual panels are coupled together to achieve the desired surface area. The principal advantages of this type of technology are lightness of the product, chemical inertness, and high efficiency. The panels are

Figure 6.4 Industrial passive solar water-heating system.

also durable and can be mounted on racks. The panels are available in a glazed version to accommodate windy areas and colder climates. The disadvantage of this technology is its numerous system surface attachments, which can limit mounting locations.

Rubber mats   Rubber-mat systems are made up of parallel pipes, called *headers,* that are manufactured from extruded lengths of tubing that have stretching mats between the tubes. The length and width of the mat are adjustable and typically are custom-fit for each application.

The advantage of this technology is the great flexibility of the product, which allows it to be installed around roof obstructions such as vent pipes. Installations require few, if any, roof penetrations and are considered highly efficient. Because of the expand-ability of the product, the headers are less subject to freeze-expansion damage. The main disadvantage of the system is that the mats are glued to the roof and can be difficult to remove without damaging either the roof or the solar panels. The installa-tion also cannot be applied in rack-type installations. Figure 6.5 shows a residential roof-mounted rubber-mat solar pool heater.

Metal panels   Metal panels are constructed from copper waterways that are attached to either copper or aluminium fins. The fins collect the solar radiation and conduct

Figure 6.5   **Rubber-mat roof-mounted solar pool heater.** *Courtesy of UMA/Helicol.*

it into the waterways. The advantages of metal panels include their rigidity and their durability of construction. Like rubber mats, glazed versions of these panels are also available for application in windy areas and cold climates. A significant disadvantage of this type of technology is that these panels require significantly more surface area, have low efficiency, and have no manufacturer's warranty.

Plastic pipe systems   In this technology, plastic pipes are connected in parallel or are configured in a circular pattern. The main advantages of this system are that installation can be done inexpensively and the system easily can be used as an overhead "trellis" for above-deck installations. The main disadvantage of this type of installation is that it requires a significantly larger surface area than other systems, and like metal panels, it does not carry a manufacturer's warranty.

PANEL SELECTION

One of the most important considerations when selecting a pool-heating system is the amount of panel surface area that is required to heat the pool. The relationship of the solar collector area to swimming pool surface area must be adequate to ensure that your pool achieves the temperatures you expect, generally between 75 and 85°F, during the swimming season. The ratio of solar panel surface area to pool surface area varies with geographic location and is affected by factors such as local microclimates, solar collector orientation, pool shading, and desired heating season.

It is very important to keep in mind that solar energy is a very dilute energy source. Only a limited amount of useful heat falls on each square foot of panel. Consequently, whatever type of solar system is used, a large panel area is needed to collect adequate amounts of energy.

In southern California, Texas, and Arizona, where there is abundant sunshine and warm temperatures, the swimming season stretches from April or May to September or October. To heat a pool during this period, it is necessary to install enough solar collectors to equal a minimum of 70 percent of the surface area of the swimming pool (when the solar panels are facing south).

Generally, it is desirable to mount the panels on a southerly exposure. However, an orientation within 45 degrees of south will not decrease performance significantly as long as shading is avoided. A due-west exposure will work well if the square footage of the solar collector is increased to compensate. However, a due-east exposure generally should be avoided unless significantly more solar collectors are used. Figure 6.6 diagrams a roof-mounted solar power pool-heating system.

As the orientation moves away from the ideal, sizing should increase to 80–100 percent (or more for west or southeast orientations). If climatic conditions are less favorable, such as near the ocean, even more coverage may be required. In general, it is always recommended to exceed the minimum to offset changing weather patterns. However, there is a point of diminishing return, where more panels will not add significantly to the pool's heating function. Table 6.1 shows the economics for a typical pool-heating installation.

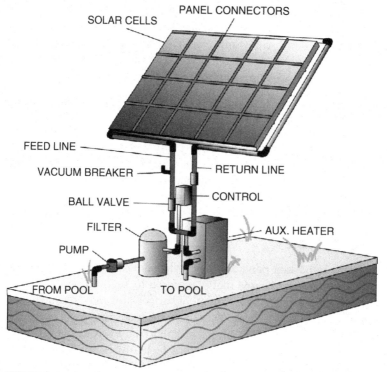

Figure 6.6 Diagram of a roof-mounted solar pool-heating system.

TABLE 6.1 ECONOMICS OF A TYPICAL POOL-HEATING INSTALLATION	
Pool size	7500 ft²
Pool depth	5 ft
Total purchase price	$18,000
First-year energy savings	$30,575 (fuel cost per therm = $1.00)
Ten-year energy savings	$38,505 (estimated)
Expected investment payback	5.3 years
Yearly average return	21%
Size of each panel	50 ft²
Number of panels	144
Total required area	7200 ft²
Panel tilt	2 degrees
Panel orientation	180 degrees
Total required area	7200 ft²

HELICOL SOLAR COLLECTOR SIZING

To determine the number of solar panels needed, divide the solar collector area needed by the total square footage of individual collectors. The following example demonstrates the use of an insolation chart.

Calculate the solar panel requirement for a 14 ft × 28 ft pool located in Las Vegas, Nevada.

Pool surface = 14 ft × 28 ft = 392 ft^2.

Las Vegas is located in zone 5, which has a multiplier of 0.52.

Collector area = 392 ft × 0.52 ft = 203.8 ft^2.

Approximate number of panels required using Heliocol HC-40 panels = 5.1, or 5 panels.

Sizing is an art as well as a science. There are so many factors that affect swimming pool heat loss that no one has yet come up with the "perfect" model or sizing calculation. Your company already may have a sizing guide or sizing method that works well for installations in your particular area, and you may not want to use the sizing method outlined in this chapter. Be sure to find out from your sales manager what sizing method or calculation you should use to determine the proper sizing for your systems.

This next section outlines a sizing method that can be applied to any geographic area. If you follow the guidelines detailed herein and have a thorough grasp of your geographic factors, you should be able to size all your solar system proposals properly with a reasonable degree of accuracy and confidence.

Average pool water temperatures, ranging from 75 to 85°F, are usually considered comfortable. In northern states, however, 72°F is considered warm, and in the south, swimmers usually want the temperature to be approximately 82°F.

SOLAR WATER-HEATING-SYSTEM SIZING GUIDE

The following guideline addresses all factors that must be taken into account when designing a solar water-heating system for a pool. It is assumed that the pool will be covered when nighttime temperatures drop below 60°F. If you heat a pool, you should use a solar blanket. Not to do so is much like heating a house without a roof; the heat just goes right out the top! A cover retains more than two-thirds of the collected heat needed to maintain a comfortable swimming temperature.

The key to sizing a system properly is taking into account all the environmental and physical factors that pertain to your area in general and the prospect's home in particular. There are 10 questions that you need to have answered to size a system. They are as follows:

1 How many months of the year do the owners swim in the pool?

2 How long can you reasonably extend their season, taking into account the geographic location?

3 Will there be a backup heating system? What kind?

4 Does the pool have a screen enclosure?

5 Will the owners use a blanket?

6 Do the owners have a solar window?

7 Is the wind going to be a problem?

8 Is shading going to be a problem? How many hours a day?

9 In what direction and at what angle will the collectors be mounted?

10 What is the surface area of the pool?

Some of these questions will be answered as part of your pool-heating survey. The rest will be determined by measurement and inspection.

The following guidelines will provide a factor that represents how many square feet of solar collector area is needed in relation to the pool's surface area. Once determined, this factor is multiplied by the pool's surface area. The resulting answer is divided by the selected collector area to determine the number of collectors required.

To begin, you will want to determine a sizing factor for optimal conditions in your geographic location. To obtain this information, you need to consult with a sales representative of a solar pool-heating system. You also can contact the local weather bureau and ask for the mean daily solar radiation (Langley's) for the coldest month of the desired swimming season. Using the following table, determine the starting sizing factor by the corresponding Langley reading:

LANGLEY READING	SIZING FACTOR
200	1.05
250	0.96
300	0.85
350	0.75
400	0.67
450	0.60
500	0.55
550	0.51
600	0.48

For optimal efficiency, solar collectors should face south. If you are unable to face your system south, multiply the sizing factor by the applicable following figure:

East facing   1.25

West facing   1.15

This figure should be increased if the roof pitches are equal to or greater than 6/12. Decrease this figure if you have a roof with a pitch equal to or less than 4/12.

If the pool is shaded, you need to multiply the sizing factor by the following figure:

25 percent shaded   1

50 percent shaded   1.25

75 percent shaded   1.50

100 percent shaded   1.75

As a general rule of thumb, if there is a screen enclosure, multiply the factor by 1.25. If the pool is indoors, multiply the sizing factor by 2.00.

In the northern states, the best collector angle is the latitude minus 10. This changes gradually as you move south, until it reaches the latitude plus 10 in south Florida. For each 10-degree variance from the optimal angle, multiply the sizing factor by the following figure:

DEVIATION	FIGURE
<10 degree	1.05
20 degree	1.10
30 degree	1.20

As a general rule of thumb, if collectors are laid flat, multiply the sizing factor by 1.10. For the collector area, use the following:

HC-50   50

HC-40   40

HC-30   30

Example This example illustrates sizing-factor determination and the number of collectors needed on a partially shaded flat roof for a 15 ft × 30 ft rectangular pool.

Langley's for coldest month of swimming is December: 0.55.

Collectors are going to face south.

Pool shaded 25 percent (multiply by): 1.1.

Collectors are going to go on a flat roof (multiply): 1.1.

Sizing factor: 0.67.

Surface area of the pool: 450 ft.^{2}

Multiply by sizing factor 0.67.

Collector area needed: 302 ft^2.

HC-40s collectors are going to be used on the project, so divide by 40 ft^2.

The number of HC-40 collectors needed: 8.

This guide is an approximation only. Wind speeds, humidity levels, desired pool temperature, and other factors can also affect proper solar pool system sizing. If the prospect does not want to use a cover, you may have to double or even triple the solar coverage to achieve the desired swimming temperature.

The choice of collector size and system configuration depends on the designer. What must be considered is the roof space as well as the associated cost. Installation of smaller collectors will be a great deal more difficult than larger ones. None of these rules is concrete, and a designer's best judgment should be followed. Figure 6.7 shows an industrial solar water heating panel installation.

SUGGESTED PRACTICES

The use of common sense when investing in solar pool heating is very important. First-time buyers should consider the following:

Figure 6.7   An industrial solar water-heating panel installation.

- Buy only from a licensed contractor, and check on his or her experience and reputation.
- Be aware that several factors should be considered when evaluating various system configurations. More solar panels generally means your pool will be warmer.
- Use a pool cover, if possible.
- Make sure that the system is sized properly. An inadequately sized system is guaranteed dissatisfaction.
- Beware of outrageous claims, such as "90°F pool temperatures in December with no backup heater." No solar heating system can achieve such performance.
- The contractor should produce evidence of adequate worker's compensation and liability insurance.
- Insurance certificates should be directly from the insurance company and not the contractor.
- Check the contractor's referrals before buying.
- Get a written description of the system, including the number of solar panels, the size of panels, and the make and model numbers.
- Get a complete operation and maintenance manual and startup demonstration.
- The price should not be the most important factor, but it also should not be dramatically different from prices of competing bidders for similar equipment.
- Be sure the contractor obtains a building permit, if required.

Concentrator Solar Technologies

Concentrating solar power (CSP) technologies concentrate solar energy to produce high-temperature heat that is then converted into electricity. The three most advanced CSP technologies currently in use are parabolic troughs (PTs), central receivers (CRs), and dish engines (DEs). CSP technologies are considered one of today's most efficient power plants; they can readily substitute solar heat for fossil fuels, fully or partially, to reduce emissions and provide additional power at peak times. DEs are better suited for distributed power, from 10 kW to 10 MW, whereas PTs and CRs are suited for larger central power plants, 30–200 MW and higher. Figure 6.8 illustrates a passive parabolic concentrator used in solar electric power–generating plants.

The solar resources for generating power from parabolic CSP systems are very plentiful and can provide sufficient electric power for the entire country if the systems could be arranged to cover only about 9 percent of the state of Nevada, which would amount to a 100-mi^2 plot of land. The amount of power generated by a CSP plant depends on the amount of direct sunlight. Like photovoltaic (PV) concentrators, these technologies use only direct beams of sunlight to concentrate the thermal energy of the sun.

The southwestern United States potentially offers an excellent opportunity for developing CSP technologies. As is well known, peak power demand generated as a result of air-conditioning systems can be offset by solar electric power–generating system (SEGS) resource plants that operate for nearly 100 percent of the on-peak hours.

CSP systems can be sized from 2 to 10 kW or could be large enough to supply grid-connected power of up to 200 MW. Some existing systems use thermal storage during

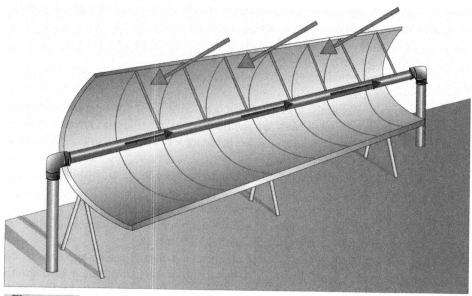

Figure 6.8   Passive parabolic concentrator used in solar electric power–generating plants.

cloudy periods and are combined with natural gas generation, resulting in hybrid power plants that provide grid-connected dispatchable power. Solar power–driven electric-generator conversion efficiencies make CSP technologies a viable renewable-energy resource in the Southwest. The U.S. Congress recently requested that the Department of Energy develop a plan for installing 1000 MW of concentrating solar power in the Southwest over the next 5 years. CSP technologies are also considered an excellent source for providing thermal energy for commercial and industrial processes.

ADVANTAGES

CSP technologies incorporating storage do not burn any fossil fuels and produce zero greenhouse gas, NO_x, and SO_x emissions. They are also proven and reliable. For the past decade, SEGS plants have operated successfully in the southern California desert, providing enough power for 100,000 homes. Plants with cost-effective storage or natural gas hybridization can deliver power to the utility grid whenever that power is needed, not just when the sun is shining. Existing CSP plants produce power now for approximately 11 cents/kWh (including both capital and operating costs), with projected costs dropping below 4 cents/kWh within the next 20 years as technology refinements and economies of scale are implemented. Because CSP plants use relatively conventional technologies and materials (e.g., glass, concrete, steel, and standard utility-scale turbines), production capacity can be scaled up to several hundred megawatts per year rapidly.

Emission reduction Emissions benefits of CSP technologies depend on many factors, including whether they have their own storage capacity or are hybridized with other electricity- or heat-producing technologies. CSP technologies with storage produce zero emissions, and hybrid technologies can reduce emissions by 50 percent or more.

PASSIVE PARABOLIC HEATING TECHNOLOGIES

In this technology, a large field of parabolic systems that are secured on a single-axis solar-tracking support is installed in a modular parallel-row configuration aligned in a north-south horizontal direction. Each of the solar parabolic collectors tracks the movement of the sun from east to west during daytime hours and focuses the sun's rays to linear receiver tubing that circulates a heat-transfer fluid (HTF). The HTF, in turn, passes through a series of heat-exchanger chambers where the heat is transferred as superheated vapor that drives steam turbines. After propelling the turbine, the spent steam is condensed and returned to the heat exchanger via condensate pumps. Figure 6.9 is a photograph of a parabolic heater installation.

At present, the technology has been applied successfully in thermal electric power–generation. A 354-MW solar electric power–generation plant installed in 1984 in the California Mojave Desert has been in operation with remarkable success.

SOLAR TOWER TECHNOLOGIES

Another use of CSP technology that generates electric power from the sun is a construction that focuses concentrated solar radiation on a tower-mounted heat exchanger. The system is basically configured from thousands of sun-tracking mirrors, commonly

Figure 6.9   **Passive parabolic concentrator installation.** *Courtesy of Solargenix.*

Figure 6.10   A passive solar tower concentrator. *Courtesy of Solar Reserve.*

referred to as *heliostats,* that reflect the sun's rays onto the tower. Figure 6.10 shows a passive solar tower concentrator.

The receiver contains a fluid that, once heated by a method similar to that of the parabolic system, transfers the absorbed heat in the heat exchanger to produce steam that then drives a turbine to produce electricity.

This technology produces up to 400 MW of electricity. The HTF, usually a molten liquid salt, can be raised to 550°F. The HTF is stored in an insulated storage tank and used in the absence of solar-ray harvesting.

Recently, a solar pilot plant located in southern California that uses nitrate salt technology, Solar Two, has been producing 10 MW of grid-connected electricity with a sufficient thermal storage tank to maintain power production for 3 hours. This has rendered the technology viable for commercial use.

Solar Cooling and Air-Conditioning

Most of us associate cooling, refrigeration, and air-conditioning with self-contained electromechanical devices connected to an electric power source. These provide conditioned air for the spaces in which we live as well as for refrigerating our food stuffs and groceries.

Technically speaking, the technology that makes refrigeration possible is based on a fundamental concept of physics: heat transfer. Cold is essentially the absence of heat. Likewise, darkness is the absence of light.

The branch of physics that deals with the mechanics of heat transfer is called *thermodynamics*. There are two principal universal laws of thermodynamics. The first law concerns the conservation of energy and states that energy can neither be created nor destroyed; however, it can be converted from one type to another. The second law deals with the equalization and transfer of energy from a higher state to a lower one. Simply stated, energy is always transferred from a higher potential or state to a lower one until the two energy sources achieve exact equilibrium. Heat is essentially defined as a form of energy created as a result of the transformation of another form of energy. A common example of this is when two solid bodies are rubbed together, resulting in friction heat. In general, heat is energy in a transfer state because it does not stay in any specific position and constantly moves from a warm object to a cooler one until such time that, as per the second law of thermodynamics, both bodies reach heat equilibrium.

It should be noted that the volume, size, and mass of the objects are completely irrelevant in the heat-transfer process. Only the heat energy levels are factors in the energy-balance equation. With this principle in mind, heat energy can flow from a small object, such as a hot cup of coffee, to one with much larger mass, such as your hand. The rate of travel of heat is directly proportional to the difference in temperature between the two objects; size plays no role in this matter.

Heat travels in three forms: radiation, conduction, and convection. As radiation, heat is transferred as a waveform similar to radio waves, microwaves, or light. For example, the sun transfers its energy to earth by rays, or radiation. In conduction, heat energy flows from one medium or substance to another by physical contact. Convection, on the other hand, is the flow of heat between air, gas, liquid, and a fluid medium. The basic principles of refrigeration are based on the second law of thermodynamics, that is, the transfer or removal of heat from a higher-energy medium to a lower one by means of convection. Figure 6.11 illustrates the evaporation and condensation cycle in refrigeration.

TEMPERATURE

Temperature is a scale for measuring heat intensity with a directional flow of energy. Water freezes at 0°C (32°F) and boils at 100°C (212°F). Temperature scales are simply temperature differences between freezing and boiling water temperatures measured at sea level. As mentioned earlier, based on the second law of thermodynamics, heat transfer or measurement of temperature does not depend on the quantity of heat.

MOLECULAR AGITATION

Depending on the state of heat energy, most substances in general can exist in vapor, liquid, and solid states. For example, depending on the heat-energy level, water can exist as solid ice when it is frozen, as a liquid at room temperature, and as a vapor when it is heated above its boiling temperature of 212°F (100°C). In each of the states, water is within or without the two boundary temperatures of 32°F (0°C) and 212°F (100°C).

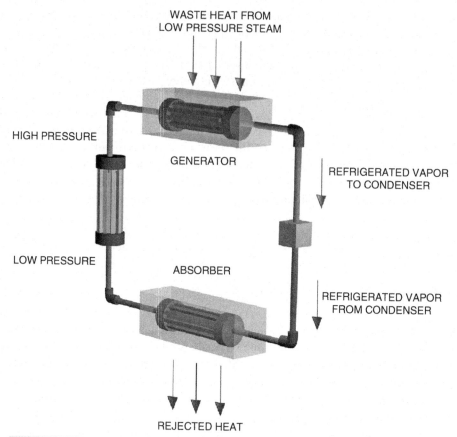

WASTE HEAT FROM
LOW PRESSURE STEAM

HIGH PRESSURE

GENERATOR

REFRIGERATED VAPOR
TO CONDENSER

LOW PRESSURE

ABSORBER

REFRIGERATED VAPOR
FROM CONDENSER

REJECTED HEAT

Figure 6.11 Evaporation and condensation cycle in refrigeration.

Steam will condense back to a liquid state if heat energy is removed from it. The liquid, in turn, will change into its solid state (ice) when sufficient heat energy is removed from it. The processes can be reversed when heat energy is introduced into the medium.

The state of change is related to the fact that in various substances, depending on the presence or absence of heat energy, a phenomenon referred to as *atomic thermal agitation* causes expansion and contraction of molecules. A close contraction of molecules forms solids, and a larger separation transforms matter into liquid and gaseous states. In border-state energy conditions, an excess lack (beyond the solid state) or excess surplus (beyond the gaseous state) of energy creates the states referred to as *supercooled* and *superheated,* respectively.

PRINCIPLES OF REFRIGERATION

Refrigeration is accomplished by two distinct processes (see Fig. 6.11). In one process, referred to as the *compression cycle,* a medium, such as Freon gas, is first given heat energy by compression, which turns the gas into a liquid. Then, in a

TABLE 6.2   TYPICAL BUILDING COOLING CAPACITIES

SPACE	SIZE	COOLING TONS
Medium office	50,000	100–150
Hospital	150,000	400–600
Hotel	250,000	400–500
High school	50,000	100–400
Retail store	160,000	170–400

subsequent cycle, energy is removed from the liquid in a form of evaporation or gas expansion that disperses the gas molecules and turns the surrounding chamber into a cold environment. Table 6.2 outlines air-conditioning cooling capacity requirement for various types of buildings.

A medium of energy-absorbing liquid, such as water or air, when circulated within the so-called evaporation chamber, gives up its heat energy to the expanded gas. The cold water or air, in turn, is circulated by means of pumps into environments that have higher ambient heat-energy levels. The circulated cold air, in turn, is passed into the ambient space through radiator tubes or fins, thus lowering the energy of the environment. Temperature control is realized by the opening and closing of cold medium circulating tube valves or air-duct control vanes, modulated by a local temperature-sensing device such as a thermostat or a setpoint-control mechanism.

COOLING TECHNOLOGIES

There are two types of refrigeration technologies currently in use, namely, electric vapor compression (Freon gas) and heat-driven absorption cooling. Absorption-cooling chillers are operated by steam, hot water, fossil-fuel burners, or combinations of these. There are two types of absorption chillers. One uses lithium bromide (LiBr) as an energy-conversion medium and water as a refrigerant. In this type of technology, the lowest temperature achieved is limited to 40°F. Another absorption-chiller technology uses ammonia as the energy-conversion medium and a mix of ammonia and water as the refrigerant. The lowest temperature limit for this technology is 20°F. Both these technologies have been around for about 100 years.

The basic principle of absorption chillers is gasification of LiBr or ammonia. Gasification takes place when either of the media is exposed to heat. Heat could be derived from fossil-fuel burners, hot water obtained from geothermal energy, passive solar water heaters, or microturbine generators, which use landfill gases to produce electricity and heat energy.

COEFFICIENT OF PERFORMANCE (COP)

The energy efficiency of an air-conditioning system is defined by a *coefficient of performance* (COP), which is the ratio of cooling energy to the energy supplied to the unit. A ton of cooling energy is 12,000 Btu/h, which, as defined in the past, is the energy required to remove heat from a space through melting a ton of ice. One ton, or 12,000 Btu, is equal to 3413 W of electric power.

Based on the preceding definitions, the COP of an air-conditioning unit that requires 1500 W of electric power per ton is equal to 12,000 Btu/h (1 kW = 3413 Btu). Therefore, 1.5 kW × 3414 = 5121 Btu of supplied energy, which means that COP = 12,000 Btu cooling energy/5121 Btu supplied energy = 2.343. A lower electric-energy requirement will increase the COP rating, which brings us to the conclusion that the lower the amount of energy input, the better is the efficiency.

HYBRID ABSORPTION CHILLERS

The combined use of passive solar and natural gas–fired media evaporation has given rise to a generation of hybrid absorption chillers that can produce a large tonnage of cooling energy by the use of solar- or geothermal-heated water. A class of absorption that commonly uses LiBr has been available commercially for some time, with solar power as the main source of energy. A 1000-ton absorption chiller can reduce electric energy consumption by an average of 1 MW, or 1 million W, which will have a very significant impact on reducing electric-power consumption and resulting environmental pollution, as described in earlier chapters.

DESICCANT EVAPORATORS

Another solar power cooling technology makes use of solar desiccant-evaporator air-conditioning, which reduces outside air humidity and passes it through an ultraefficient evaporative cooling system. This cooling process, which uses an indirect evaporative process, minimizes air humidity, making the use of this technology quite effective in coastal and humid areas.

Direct Solar Power Generation

This section discusses a project, undertaken by Solargenix Energy, that makes use of special parabolic reflectors that concentrate solar energy into circular pipes located at the focal center of the parabola. The concentrated reflection of energy elevates the temperature of the circulating liquid mineral oil within the pipes, raising the temperature to such levels that considerable steam generation via special heat exchangers drives power turbines. The following newspaper article discusses this viable electric-power generation in Arizona.

RED ROCK, ARIZ.—APS today broke ground on Arizona's first commercial solar trough power plant and the first such facility constructed in the United States since 1990.

Located at the company's Saguaro Power Plant in Red Rock, about 30 miles north of Tucson, the APS Saguaro Solar Trough Generating Station will have a one-megawatt (MW) generating capacity, enough to provide for the energy needs of approximately 200 average-size homes. APS has contracted with Solargenix Energy to construct and provide the solar thermal technology for the plant, which is expected to come online in April 2005. Solargenix, formerly Duke Solar, is based out of Raleigh, North Carolina. Solargenix has partnered with Ormat, who will provide the engine to convert the solar heat, collected by the Solargenix solar collectors, into electricity.

"The APS Saguaro Solar Trough Power Plant presents a unique opportunity to further expand our renewable energy portfolio," said Peter Johnston, manager of Technology Development for APS. "We are committed to developing clean renewable energy sources today that will fuel tomorrow's economy. We believe solar-trough technology can be part of a renewable solution."

The company's solar-trough technology uses parabolic-shaped reflectors (or mirrors) to concentrate the sun's rays to heat a mineral oil between 250 and 570 degrees. The fluid then enters the Ormat engine, passing first through a heat exchanger to vaporize a secondary working fluid. The vapor is used to spin a turbine, making electricity. It is then condensed back into a liquid before being vaporized once again.

Historically, solar-trough technology has required tens of megawatts of plant installation to produce steam from water to turn generation turbines. The significant first cost of multi-megawatt power plants had precluded their use in the APS solar portfolio. This solar trough system combines the relatively low cost of parabolic solar trough thermal technology with the commercially available smaller turbines usually associated with low-temperature geothermal generation plants, such as the Ormat unit being used for this project.

In addition to generating electricity for APS customers, the solar trough plant will help APS meet the goals of the Arizona Corporation Commission's Environmental Portfolio Standard, which requires APS to generate 1.1 percent of its energy through renewable sources—60 percent through solar—by 2007. APS owns and operates approximately 4.5 MW of photovoltaic solar generation around the state and has partnered on a 3-MW biomass plant in Eager, which came online in February, and a 15-megawatt wind farm to be constructed near St. Johns. APS, Arizona's largest and longest-serving electricity utility, serves about 902,000 customers in 11 of the state's counties.

Innovations in Passive Solar Power Technology

The following are a few innovations under development by Energy Innovations, a subsidiary of IdeaLab, located in Pasadena, California.

STIRLING ENGINE SUNFLOWER

The Stirling Engine Sunflower is a radical concept because it does not use stationary PV cell technology. Rather, it is constructed from lightweight, polished, and aluminized plastic reflector petals that are each adjusted by a microprocessor-based motor controller, enabling the petals to track the sun in an independent fashion. This heat engine is used to produce hot water by concentrating solar rays onto a low-profile water chamber.

At present, the technology is being refined to produce higher-efficiency and more cost-effective production models, and the company is working on bigger models for use in large-scale solar water-heating installations. Figure 6.12 shows a prototype Stirling Engine Sunflower.

Figure 6.12   A Stirling Engine Sunflower prototype. *Courtesy of IdeaLab eSolar.*

eSolar is utility-scale solar thermal concentrator power plant technology that consists of mass-manufactured solar sun-tracking heliostat reflection mirrors that focus the solar heat energy to a thermal receiver mounted atop a central power tower. The focused heat boils water within the thermal receiver tank and produces steam. The plant directs the steam from each thermal receiver through pipes and aggregates it at a power turbine, which powers an electric power generator. The cooled steam then reverts back to the tower and repeats the process. Figure 6.13 shows an eSolar power plant.

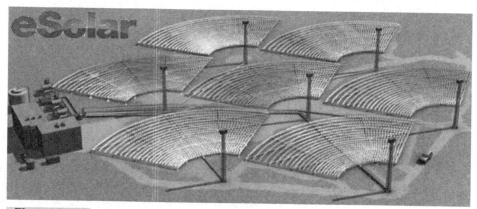

Figure 6.13   An eSolar power plant. *Courtesy of IdeaLab eSolar.*

Figure 6.14   Heliostat reflecting mirrors of an eSolar power plant. *Courtesy of IdeaLab.*

The plant is based on mass-manufactured components and is designed for rapid field installation in highly modular fashion and provides unlimited scalability. Solar power electric plant capacities range from 46 MW to more than 500 MW.

A small mass-manufactured heliostat is a patented dual-port solar thermal reflector that forms the building block of the eSolar system. The reflector referred to as a *heliostat stick* and is designed to be field installed with minimal skilled labor. The low wind profile of the design allows fields of heliostats to be installed rapidly. Each eSolar thermal unit mounted atop poles receives solar energy from field reflector mirrors through north- and south-facing dual ports.

A 46-MWt eSolar power unit consists of 16 towers, a turbine generator set, and a steam condenser. This 46-MW power unit occupies 160 acres of land. Figure 6.14 shows the heliostat reflecting mirrors of an eSolar power plant.

7

FUEL CELL TECHNOLOGY

Fuel cells are energy-conversion devices that produce electricity through the chemical oxidation of a reactant, or fuel, and an oxidant. The oxidation reaction takes place in the presence of electrolytes, which act as catalysts and strip electrons from atoms of the fuel, promoting the circulation of electrons, or electric current, through an external conduction path. In general, the fuel, or reactant, flows in, and reaction products flow out, whereas the electrolytes remain in the cell. Fuel cells can use numerous types of reactants and oxidants and can operate virtually continuously as long as the necessary flow is maintained.

A few examples of fuel cells include combinations of reactants and oxidants such as, hydrogen and oxygen, a hydrocarbon and alcohol, air and chlorine, and many more. Fuel cells differ from conventional batteries in that they consume the reactant, which must be replenished continuously, whereas batteries store electrical energy chemically in a closed system. Another difference is that the electrodes within a battery change and become depleted during the charging and discharging cycle, whereas fuel cell electrodes are catalytic and relatively stable.

Fuel Cell Design

As mentioned earlier, fuel cells operate by a catalytic process that involves the separation of the component electrons and protons from the reactant fuel, resulting in a flow of electrons that circulates through an electronic circuit that gives rise to electric power. Typical catalysts include platinum and a group of metal alloys. In some instances, the catalytic process involves the circulation and recombination of electrons with protons and produces waste products such as water and carbon dioxide.

In a typical hydrogen-oxygen proton-exchange-membrane fuel cell (PEMFC), a proton-conducting polymer membrane, or electrolyte, separates the anode and the cathode sides and produces water as a waste product. It should be noted that the PEMFC acronym applies equally to polymer-electrolyte-membrane and proton-exchange-membrane fuel cell.

In general in fuel cells, the reactant, or fuel, is introduced into a chamber that is exposed to an electrode referred to as the *anode*. For example, a reactant such as hydrogen, when placed in the intake chamber, diffuses to the anode catalyst, where it later dissociates into protons and electrons. The protons then react with oxidants such as oxygen. In the process, protons are conducted through the membrane to the cathode. However, electrons are forced to travel in an external circuit, supplying power to a load. On the cathode catalyst, oxygen molecules from air react with the hydrogen molecules that have been reconstructed by the recombination of electrons that have traveled through the external circuit with the protons. The chemical combination of oxygen and hydrogen results in the formation of water molecules in the form of water vapor as the waste product. In addition to electric power, the chemical reaction also produces a considerable amount of heat energy that can be used for steam cogeneration and many other industrial processes. In addition to hydrogen as a fuel, hydrocarbon fuels such as methanol and many other chemical hydrates are used in various types of fuel cells that produce electricity and different types of waste products.

CONSTRUCTION OF A LOW-TEMPERATURE POLYMER-ELECTROLYTE-MEMBRANE FUEL CELL

Polymer-electrolyte-membrane fuel cells (PEMFCs) are constructed from bipolar or dual electrode plates. These plates have an in-milled, or grooved, gas-channel structure fabricated from conductive plastic that use carbon nanotubes to enhance conductivity. A reactive layer constructed from porous carbon paper is adhered to a polymer membrane to promote conductivity. Small quantities of platinum in the membrane are also used as the catalytic component to promote electron and proton separation. Carbon paper is used to separate the electrodes from the electrolyte.

Materials used in the construction of bipolar electrode plates include various metals, such as nickel, and carbon, which are coated with a catalyst such as platinum or nano iron powder. Palladium electrolytes could also be used to construct ceramic artificial membranes. Gold wires embedded within the PEMFCs allow for electric current collection.

A typical PEMFC produces from 0.6 to 0.7 V at a full-rated load. Power output varies owing to voltage and current fluctuations. Power loss, or efficiency, in fuel cells is the result of several factors, including activation loss, ohmic loss owing to voltage drop in interconnecting conductive material, and mass-transport loss, which results from the depletion of reactants at catalyst sites under high current demand and causes rapid voltage drops.

To deliver the desired amount of energy, fuel cells, like conventional batteries, are combined in series and parallel circuits. Series design yield higher voltages, and parallel designs allow for a larger amount of electric current circulation. Parallel and series combinations of fuel cells are referred to as *fuel cell stacking*. Figure 7.1 is a diagram of a PEMFC, and Fig. 7.2 illustrates PEMFC condensed water extraction from an air channel.

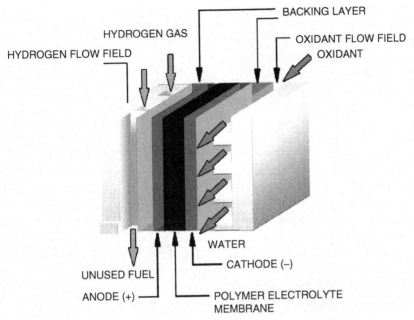

HYDROGEN FLOW FIELD
HYDROGEN GAS
BACKING LAYER
OXIDANT FLOW FIELD
OXIDANT
WATER
CATHODE (–)
UNUSED FUEL
ANODE (+)
POLYMER ELECTROLYTE
MEMBRANE

Figure 7.1   Diagram of a proton exchange membrane fuel cell.

FUEL CELL DESIGN ISSUES

One of the most important issues in fuel cell design is internal water and heat control. As mentioned earlier, the chemical reaction between the reactants and oxidants produces waste water and a significant amount of heat, both of which must be controlled and regulated. Otherwise, fuel cell operation cannot be sustained for extended periods of time. Figure 7.3 presents a cross section of a fuel cell.

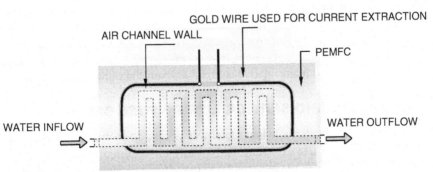

GOLD WIRE USED FOR CURRENT EXTRACTION
AIR CHANNEL WALL
PEMFC
WATER INFLOW
WATER OUTFLOW

Figure 7.2   Flow diagram of a fuel cell water-extraction channel.

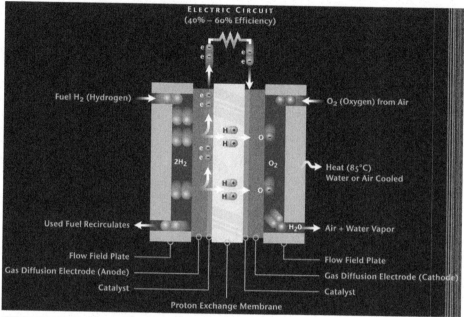

Figure 7.3   **Operational diagram of a fuel cell.** *Courtesy of Ballard Engineering.*

Water and air control   In hydrogen and hydrant-type fuel cells, owing to the production of water, the membrane must be dehydrated by means of precise evaporation at the same rate at which water is produced. If water evaporates too quickly, the membrane could dry and eventually crack, creating a gas "short circuit" where hydrogen and oxygen could combine directly, generating excessive heat that will damage the fuel cell.

If the water evaporates too slowly, the electrodes could flood, preventing the reactants from reaching catalytic reaction level. One methods used to control water in fuel cells involves an electroosmotic pump that maintains a steady ratio between the amount of reactants and the oxygen necessary to keep the fuel cell operating efficiently.

Temperature control   Another challenge posed in the design of fuel cells is the removal of large amounts of heat resulting from the exothermic reactions. If the combination of oxygen and hydrogen molecules ($2H_2 + O_2 \rightarrow 2H_2O$) is not controlled, destruction of the cell from thermal loading may occur. To prevent excessive thermal loading, the temperature must be maintained at acceptable levels throughout fuel cell operation.

DURABILITY AND SERVICE LIFE OF FUEL CELLS

In stationary applications, when the power generated by fuel cells ranges in the hundreds of kilowatts, life expectancies typically are required to exceed 40,000 hours of reliable operation at temperatures of –35 to 40°C. In the automotive industry, fuel cells are required to have a life span of 5000 hours, which is the equivalent of 150,000 miles under extreme temperatures. Automotive engines are also required to start reliably at –30°C. Table 7.1 outlines various types of fuel cell characteristics.

TABLE 7.1 TYPES OF FUEL CELLS AND THEIR CHARACTERISTICS

FUEL CELL NAME	ELECTROLYTE	QUALIFIED POWER	WORKING TEMPERATURE, °C	ELECTRICAL EFFICIENCY	STATUS
Metal hydride fuel cell	Aqueous alkaline solution (e.g., potassium hydroxide)	Unknown	Above −20 (50% P_{peak} at 0°C)	Unknown	Commercial/research
Electrogalvanic fuel cell	Aqueous alkaline solution (e.g., potassium hydroxide)	Unknown	Under 40	Unknown	Commercial/research
Direct formic acid fuel cell (DFAFC)	Polymer membrane (ionomer)	To 50 W	Under 40	Unknown	Commercial/research
Zinc-air battery	Aqueous alkaline solution (e.g., potassium hydroxide)	Unknown	Under 40	Unknown	Mass production
Microbial fuel cell	Polymer membrane or humic acid	Unknown	Under 40	Unknown	Research
Upflow microbial fuel cell (UMFC)	Unknown	Unknown	Under 40	Unknown	Research
Reversible fuel cell	Polymer membrane (ionomer)	Unknown	Under 50	Unknown	Commercial/research
Direct borohydride fuel cell	Aqueous alkaline solution (e.g., sodium hydroxide)	Unknown	70	Unknown	Commercial
Alkaline fuel cell	Aqueous alkaline solution (e.g., potassium hydroxide)	10–100 kW	Under 80	Cell: 60–70% System: 62%	Commercial/research
Direct methanol fuel cell	Polymer membrane (ionomer)	100 kW to 1 MW	90–120	Cell: 20–30% System: 10–20%	Commercial/research
Reformed methanol fuel cell	Polymer membrane (ionomer)	5 W to 100 kW	Reformer: 250–300 PBI: 125–200	Cell: 50–60% System: 25–40%	Commercial/research
Direct ethanol fuel cell	Polymer membrane (ionomer)	Up to 140 mW/cm²	Above 25 90–120	Unknown	Research
Direct formic acid fuel cell	Polymer membrane (ionomer)	Unknown	25+	Unknown	Research

(Continued)

TABLE 7.1 TYPES OF FUEL CELLS AND THEIR CHARACTERISTICS (CONTINUED)

FUEL CELL NAME	ELECTROLYTE	QUALIFIED POWER	WORKING TEMPERATURE, °C	ELECTRICAL EFFICIENCY	STATUS
Proton-exchange-membrane fuel cell	Polymer membrane (ionomer) (e.g., Nafion or Polybenzimidazole	100 W to 500 kW	Nafion: 50–120 PBI: 125–220	Cell: 50–70% System: 30–50%	Commercial/research
RFC redox	Liquid electrolytes with redox shuttle and polymer membrane (ionomer)	1 kW to 10 MW	Unknown	Unknown	Research
Phosphoric acid fuel cell	Molten phosphoric acid (H_3PO_4)	Up to 10 MW	150–200	Cell: 55% System: 40% Cogen: 90%	Commercial/research
Molten carbonate fuel cell	Molten alkaline carbonate (e.g., sodium bicarbonate, $NaHCO_3$)	100 MW	600–650	Cell: 55% System: 47%	Commercial/research
Tubular solid oxide fuel cell (TSOFC)	O^{2-}-conducting ceramic oxide (e.g., zirconium dioxide, ZrO_2)	Up to 100 MW	850–1100	Cell: 60–65% System: 55–60%	Commercial/research
Protonic ceramic fuel cell	H^+-conducting ceramic oxide	Unknown	700	Unknown	Research
Direct carbon fuel cell	Several different	Unknown	700–850	Cell: 80% System: 70%	Commercial/research
Planar solid oxide fuel cell	O^{2-}-conducting ceramic oxide (e.g., zirconium dioxide, ZrO_2, lanthanum nickel oxide, La_2XO_4, X = Ni, Co, Cu)	Up to 100 MW	850–1100	Cell: 60–65% System: 55–60%	Commercial/research

Source: Wikipedia.

FUEL CELL EFFICIENCY

The *efficiency* of a fuel cell is defined as the amount of power that can be delivered to a load. Larger loads require higher current, which increases the losses in the fuel cell. In other words, the more power desired, the more current is drawn, therefore giving rise to larger voltage drops and lowering efficiency.

As mentioned earlier, losses in fuel cells manifest as voltage drops in the cell, so the efficiency of a cell is directly proportional to its voltage. In general, a fuel cell running at 0.7 V will have an efficiency of about 50 percent, which means that 50 percent of the energy content of the hydrogen is converted into electrical energy. The balance will be converted into heat.

The efficiencies of typical hydrogen cells operating under standard conditions, based on the internal heating value, or enthalpy, are equal to the cell voltage divided by 1.48 V. Depending on the type of fuel and the internal exothermic temperature, cells may have efficiencies that are equal to cell voltage divided by 1.23 V.

Fuel Cell Application

Fuel cells that operate on air rather than bottled oxygen are less efficient. The loss of energy is the result of molecular density and the content of moisture in the air, which is much less than that of a pressurized bottle.

The efficiency of a fuel cell in automotive applications is referred to as the *tank-to-wheel efficiency* and is about 45 percent at low loads and 36 percent at larger loads. In comparison, diesel vehicles have an efficiency of 22 percent.

Fuel cell vehicles running with compressed hydrogen have a typical power-plant-to-wheel efficiency of 22 percent, and 17 percent of the fuel is used is in the form of liquid hydrogen.

STATIONARY FUEL CELL PLANTS

Fuel cells cannot store energy like batteries. However, there are stand-alone power-plant applications where hydrogen is produced by continuous sources, such as solar or wind energy. The overall efficiency of the cycle of electricity to hydrogen and back to electricity is referred to as the *round-trip efficiency*. Depending on various parameters and conditions, round-trip efficiencies may range from 30 to 50 percent. In comparison, lead-acid batteries have about 90 percent efficiency. Electrolyzer fuel cell systems could be designed to store large quantities of hydrogen and therefore could be used as a stationary power source that could provide electrical power for an extended period of time.

Another type of fuel cell technology, referred to as *solid-oxide fuel cells,* produces large amounts of exothermic heat from the recombination of oxygen and hydrogen. Ceramic-type catalytic membranes in this type of fuel cell can endure temperatures in excess of 800°C. Heat captured by means of heat-exchange units is used to heat water used for various applications, such as industrial and commercial processes. When fuel cells are used as heat-energy cogenerators, total efficiency can reach 80–90 percent.

System applications, referred to as *micro combined heat and power cogenerators,* are used extensively in residential buildings, office buildings, and commercial applications. These types of systems generate grid-connected electric power and produce hot air and water for heating pools and buildings. Since there is a certain amount of heat loss with the exhaust gas, the combined heat and power efficiency is typically around 80 percent.

Another fuel technology, which uses phosphoric acid fuel (PAFC), when used extensively, can provide combined efficiencies close to 90 percent. Some fuel cell applications include stationary base-load power plants, electric and hybrid vehicle auxiliary off-grid power supplies, notebook computers, portable charging docks, and small electronic appliances.

HISTORY

The principle of the fuel cell was discovered by German scientist Christian Friedrich Schönbein in 1838. Within 5 years of Schönbein's work, the first fuel cell was developed by Welsh scientist Sir William Robert Grove in 1843. The first fuel cell used phosphoric acid fuel. In 1955, W. Thomas Grubb, a chemist working for the General Electric Company (GE), enhanced the original fuel cell design by using a sulfonated polystyrene ion-exchange membrane as the electrolyte. Three years later, another GE chemist, Leonard Niedrach, found a way to deposit platinum onto a membrane, which served as the catalyst necessary for hydrogen-oxidation and oxygen-reduction reactions. This became known as the *Grubb-Niedrach fuel cell.* In subsequent years, GE, in joint collaboration with NASA and McDonnell Aircraft, produced a fuel cell that was used on the Project Gemini.

The commercialization of fuel cell technology came about when, in 1959, British engineer Francis Thomas Bacon successfully developed a 5-kW stationary fuel cell. Also in 1959, a team led by Harry Ihrig designed and built a 15-kW fuel cell that was used in a tractor manufactured by Allis-Chalmers. The fuel cell used potassium hydroxide as the electrolyte and compressed hydrogen and oxygen as the reactants. In the 1960s, Pratt and Whitney licensed Bacon's U.S. patents for use in the U.S. space program to supply electricity and drinking water from hydrogen and oxygen recombination (which was stored in the spacecraft's tanks).

Today, fuel cells continue to power space vehicles and are being used by the Space Shuttle program. They also have found extensive use in automobiles, buses, and cell phone towers.

HYDROGEN AS AN ENERGY CARRIER

It should be noted that industrial hydrogen gas production generally involves the artificial extraction of hydrogen molecules from hydrocarbon fuels or water by an oxidation process that releases significant amounts of carbon dioxide. Therefore, even though hydrogen fuel used in fuel cells produces clean water as a by-product, the extraction process remains inefficient and environmentally harmful.

In view of the fact that hydrogen energy production in fuel cells involves the separation and recombination of electrons and protons, unlike petroleum or fossil fuels, hydrogen is not considered an energy source but rather an energy carrier. In essence, commercial hydrogen is produced from the use of other energy sources, such as petroleum combustion and wind-powered solar photovoltaic (PV) energy in hydrolysis. Hydrogen is also produced from subsurface reservoirs of methane and natural gas by a combination of steam re-forming referred to as the *water-gas shift reaction* (from coal or shale-oil gasification).

HYDROGEN GAS PRODUCTION

Electrolysis requires electricity and high-temperature thermochemical production (ideal for nuclear reactors), two primary methods for the extraction of hydrogen from water.

STEAM RE-FORMING

Steam re-forming (also known as *hydrogen re-forming* or *catalytic oxidation*) is a process of producing hydrogen from hydrocarbons. The process, described below, is the dominant method for producing large amounts of commercial hydrogen gas.

INDUSTRIAL RE-FORMING

Steam re-forming of natural gas, referred to as *steam methane re-forming* (SMR), is the most prevalent method used in the production of commercial bulk hydrogen. This process, which involves the reaction of steam (H_2O) and methane (CH_4) at high temperatures (700–1100°C) in the presence of a metal-based catalyst such as nickel, is considered to be the least expensive method of hydrogen gas production.

In this process, steam reacts with methane to yield carbon monoxide and hydrogen:

$$CH_4 + H_2O \rightarrow CO + 3H_2$$

Additional hydrogen can be produced from this process by a lower-temperature gas-shift reaction with the production of carbon monoxide, which can yield carbon dioxide and hydrogen:

$$CO + H_2O \rightarrow CO_2 + H_2$$

This process is also used widely throughout the world in ammonia production, which requires large amounts of hydrogen gas. Hydrogen gas is also produced as a by-product of oil refining, which involves the catalytic re-forming of naphtha, also known as *high-octane gasoline.*

HYDROCARBON-BASED FUEL RE-FORMATION

In some fuel cell technologies, fuel in the form of liquid hydrocarbons is used. A process referred to as the *steam re-forming* of liquid hydrocarbons involves the steam re-formation of methanol, a process that separates hydrogen from hydrocarbon molecules.

Some of the challenges associated with this type of fuel cell technology include the control of high temperatures resulting from the reaction, slow startup, frequent replacement of catalysts owing to sulfur poisoning or contamination (which is present in most liquid fossil fuels), and carbon monoxide removal.

The chemical reactions that take place in the fuel re-formation process are expressed as follows:

$$C_nH_m + nH_2O \rightarrow nCO + (m/2 + n)H_2$$
$$CO + H_2O \rightarrow CO_2 + H_2$$

The thermodynamic efficiency of the hydrocarbon-based fuel cell process, depending on the purity of the hydrogen product, is between 70 and 85 percent.

One of the most difficult challenges associated with re-former-based systems remains the fuel cell's cost and durability. The polymer-electrolyte-membrane catalyst is quite readily poisoned by carbon monoxide, which cannot be removed during the re-formation process, resulting in rapid degradation of the catalytic membrane, perhaps one of the most expensive components of the fuel cell.

The re-former–fuel cell system currently in use commercially uses hydrocarbon fuels, such as natural gas, gasoline, or diesel fuel. However, owing to the production of residual pollutants, the use of re-former-type fuel cells in view of global warming has become a controversial issue.

ELECTROLYSIS

Electrolysis is a manufacturing process used to chemically separate bonded elements and compounds through the passage of dc current. Electrolysis involves the passage of an electric current through an ionic substance that is either molten or dissolved in an aqueous solution, resulting in chemical reactions at the positive and negative electrodes (referred to as the *anode* and *cathode,* respectively).

An ionic compound composed of covalently bonded substances or acids is dissolved with specific solvents or melted by heat in order to release ions in the liquid. On the application of an electrical current to the immersed anode and cathode, ions become attracted to electrodes of the opposite charge. As a result, positively charged ions, referred to as *cations* (pronounced "cat-ions"), move toward the cathode, whereas negatively charged ions, termed *anions* (pronounced "an-ions"), move toward the anode. At the anode and cathode probes, electrons are absorbed or released by the ions, forming a collection of the desired element or compound.

ELECTROLYSIS OF WATER

The electrolysis of water is an electrochemical ion-separation process that results in the separation of hydrogen and oxygen gases at anode and cathode probes:

$$2H_2O(l) \rightarrow 2H_2(g) + O_2(g)$$

The simplest form of the electrolysis of water is achieved by passing dc current from a battery or other dc power supply through a container of water and small amounts of salt, which increase the reaction's intensity. Using platinum electrodes, hydrogen gas cumulates and bubbles up at the cathode, as does oxygen at the anode. In general, various metals are used as anodes and cathodes, such as iron and platinum. In the case of iron, oxygen can react with the anode and prevent gas accumulation at the probe. For instance, if iron electrodes are used in a sodium chloride solution, iron oxide will be produced at the anode, which will react with iron to form hydroxide. It should be noted that one of the least expensive methods of water electrolysis is the use of electricity produced by wind and solar power.

During the electrolysis process, a significant portion of electrical energy is converted to heat, which is considered wasted energy and translates into the heating value of the hydrogen gas. In general, the energy-conversion efficiency of water electrolysis is at best 70 percent. The lower heating value of hydrogen is the thermal energy released when hydrogen is combusted.

It should be noted that only 4 percent of hydrogen gas produced worldwide is the result of water electrolysis. Aside from use in fuel cell applications, hydrogen is used extensively for the commercial production of ammonia for fertilizer and for the conversion of heavy-petroleum carbon chains into lighter products through a process called *hydrocracking.*

HYDROGEN ENERGY RESEARCH

Thermolysis *Water splitting* refers to a chemical reaction in which water is split into two separate molecules: hydrogen and oxygen. Unlike electrolysis, where the bonded elements are chemically separated by passing dc current in an electrolytic environment, this process deploys thermal decomposition, also called *thermolysis,* whereby chemical substances are broken down into two or more components under extreme temperatures that exceed 2000°C. The efficiency of water electrolysis is measured in terms of the percentage of electrical energy used.

An example of this is a process referred to as the *sulfur-iodine (S-I) cycle,* in which hydrogen is generated. The S-I cycle consists of three chemical reactions in which water is used as the reactant. Owing to the excessive amount of heat required in this process, it is not economical unless steam is harvested as a by-product from geothermal, steam-driven electrical, or nuclear power plants. Figure 7.4 is a diagram of a Hoffman voltmeter used in electrolyzing water.

COMMERCIAL USE OF HYDROGEN FOR ENERGY PRODUCTION

According to the U.S. Department of Energy (DOE), at present, electricity is produced in the United States from the following sources:

- 49.7 percent from coal
- 19.3 percent from nuclear

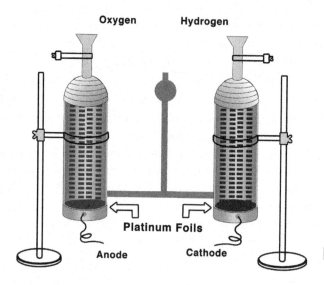

Figure 7.4 Hydrogen extraction by electrolysis.

- 18.7 percent from natural gas
- 6.5 percent hydroelectricity
- 3 percent from petroleum
- 2.8 percent from geothermal, solar, and biomass

As mentioned earlier, hydrogen production through electrolysis requires electrical power, most of which is derived from the energy sources listed above.

Even though hydrogen fuel cells, when operating, emit only heat and water as waste, significant pollution is caused when using electricity generated by fossil fuels during the hydrolysis process. The only way to reduce the carbon footprint of the electrolysis process is to use electricity produced by hydroelectric dams and geothermal, solar, wind, or other clean power sources. Therefore, hydrogen fuel is only as clean as the energy sources used to produce it.

In recent years, low-temperature fuel cells use specially designed proton-exchange membranes that allow them to use methanol as fuel. In order to reduce the cost of polymer electrolyte membranes, Brookhaven National Laboratory recently has developed a membrane coated with gold-palladium as a substitute for platinum, which is cheaper to manufacture and less susceptible to poisoning.

HYDROGEN PRODUCTION

Molecular hydrogen is not available in nature. Hydrogen is an atmospheric trace gas with a mixing ratio of 500 ppb by volume of air. In nature, hydrogen is produced and consumed by microbes and methanogen organisms, which constitute a rapid biologic hydrogen cycle. On earth, hydrogen is bonded to oxygen, forming bodies of water. At present, hydrogen is produced most economically through the use of fossil fuels such as methane. Hydrogen is also produced by a process referred to as *steam re-forming,* or the partial oxidation of coal. The production of hydrogen by hydrolysis, discussed previously, is more expensive because it involves the use of an excessive amount of electricity. For instance, the production of 1 kg of hydrogen requires about 50 kWh of electricity. In order to accelerate the hydrolysis process, platinum is used as a catalyst for the electrolytic separation of water into hydrogen and oxygen. As discussed previously, other means of hydrogen production through hydrolysis involve the use of other renewable-energy resources such as wind, solar, and geothermal energies.

While hydrogen as an element is abundant on earth and in the universe, in general, the manufacture of hydrogen does require the consumption of a hydrogen carrier, such as a fossil fuel or water. Fossil fuel resources, such as methane, produce CO_2, an air pollutant. However, when used as fuel, they produce only pure water as a by-product of oxidation.

BIOLOGIC PRODUCTION FROM ALGAE

Another hydrogen-production method, referred to as *biologic production,* involves the use of an algae bioreactor. The process, discovered in 1990, involves depriving the algae of sulfur, leading them to produce hydrogen (as opposed to the production of oxygen seen in normal photosynthesis). This process has been further refined to a level at which the commercial production of hydrogen is now economically viable. The conversion efficiency of the biohydrogen process generally ranges from about 7 to 10 percent.

In most instances, biohydrogen bioreactors, other than those with algae, also can use animal feedstock. In this process, bioreactors make use of special bacteria that feed on hydrocarbons and exhale hydrogen and CO_2. The CO_2 generally is sequestered by several methods, leaving hydrogen gas.

ELECTROLYSIS OF WATER AND ASSOCIATED CHALLENGES

Commercially, the predominant methods of hydrogen production are based on exothermic chemical reactions of fossil fuels, which provide the required energy for the chemical conversion of feedstock into hydrogen. In this process, which involves large-scale hydrolysis, most of the energy required is produced by hydropower or wind turbines. As mentioned earlier, 50 kWh of electricity is required to manufacture 1 kg of hydrogen, which translates into approximately 9 cents/kWh. Since this process makes use of literally nonpolluting electric power, despite the inefficiencies of electricity production and electrolysis, it is in fact the least expensive and safest way to produce hydrogen fuel.

HIGH-TEMPERATURE ELECTROLYSIS (HTE)

Hydrogen can be generated from energy supplied in the form of high heat, as a by-product of solar thermal concentrating, and from nuclear and electricity production technologies. In contrast with low-temperature electrolysis, discussed previously, the elevation of water to extreme temperatures allows water to convert the extreme heat energy into chemical energy (hydrogen), which results in 50 percent conversion efficiency. Since most of the energy in the HTE process is supplied in the form of heat, lesser amounts of energy are required to convert heat to electricity and then to a chemical reaction. At present, HTE has been demonstrated only in a laboratory environment.

HTE processes are ideally suited for deployment in nuclear power plants because a nuclear heat source is a nonchemical form of high-temperature heat and is much more consistent than heat produced by solar thermal concentrators. An added advantage of HTE and a nuclear reactor combination is that the process could produce both electricity and hydrogen simultaneously.

THERMOCHEMICAL PRODUCTION

Thermochemical hydrogen production is a process that makes use of the S-I cycle, which produces hydrogen, oxygen, and significant amounts of heat from water without the use of electrical energy. The thermochemical process is somewhat more efficient than HTE (discussed previously). Like HTE, the thermochemical hydrogen-production process has been demonstrated only in a laboratory environment.

REACTIVE PRODUCTION

Other chemical reactive processes that produce hydrogen involve a number of chemical reactions between metals, such as sodium, and water that results in sodium hydroxide and hydrogen. Similarly, aluminum-gallium alloy, when reacted with water, produces aluminum oxide and hydrogen.

HYDROGEN STORAGE CHALLENGES

Even though molecular hydrogen has a relatively high energy density on a mass basis, owing to its low molecular weight, as a gas at ambient temperatures it has a very low energy density by volume. In order for hydrogen to be used as a viable fuel for vehicles, the gas must be pressurized or liquefied so that it can provide sufficient driving range. To increase the energy density by volume, hydrogen must be liquefied under extremely low temperatures and pressure. Subjecting hydrogen gas to high pressures requires significant external energy. Liquid hydrogen is cryogenic, which means that it liquefies at extremely low temperatures and boils at 20.268 K (−252.882°C or −423.188°F). Low-temperature storage reduces hydrogen's mass, but the process of liquefaction requires substantial amounts of energy. The liquefaction process involves pressurizing and cooling steps, both of which are energy-intensive. Owing to the low density of liquefied hydrogen, it has a lower energy density by volume than gasoline by a factor of 4. Gasoline, which is a composition of hydrogen and carbon, effectively has 116 g of hydrogen in a liter, whereas a liter of pure liquid hydrogen has a mass of only 71 g.

METALLIC HYDROGEN COMPARTMENT

Specific chemical characteristics of hydrogen are such that, in its liquid form, it must have a storage compartment that is well insulated to prevent boiling. If poorly insulated, in freezing temperatures, ice accumulation around the tank can corrode the metal compartment. In order to withstand the intense pressure required to maintain liquefaction, the storage tank must have a significant mass, yet it must be light enough to reduce the vehicle's weight.

Owing to their small size and perpetual agitation, hydrogen molecules tend to diffuse through any liner material used in the construction of compartments, which may lead to hydrogen embitterment and weakening of the container.

CHEMICAL HYDRIDE STORAGE

Instead of using it in a liquefied form, hydrogen can be stored as a chemical hydride compound. In this type of process, hydrogen gas reacts with some other materials to produce the hydrogen storage or energy-carrier material, which can be transported relatively easily. At the point of use, the hydrogen storage material, under controlled conditions, decomposes, yielding hydrogen gas. In addition to the mass and volume density problems associated with molecular hydrogen storage, hydride storage schemes also require high-pressure and high-temperature conditions, also known as *external energy*. Another issue associated with the dehydration process is heat disposal and management, which has not yet been mitigated.

At present, the common method of onboard-type hydrogen storage used in vehicles is a compressed hydrogen gas maintained at a pressure of about 700 bars.

Present-day hydrogen fuel cells cost more by several orders of magnitude compared with the per-kilowatt output of conventional internal combustion engines. In view of the high cost associated with vehicular fuel cell technology, car manufacturers have been experimenting with Li-ion and Li-polymer batteries for onboard energy storage, which have proven to be more efficient and less expensive than hydrogen-fueled cars.

HYDROGEN FUEL EFFICIENCY FOR AUTOMOBILE USE

The economics of liquid hydrogen are definable in terms of energy that must be used to produce 1 kg of fuel and losses associated with transport and delivery to filling stations. As discussed earlier, well-to-tank energy loss is about 40 percent, whereas by comparison, regular gasoline requires less energy input per gallon at the refinery, and comparatively little energy is required for transport and storage. Therefore, well-to-tank gasoline supply-chain efficiency loss is about 20 percent. It is also noteworthy that the most efficient distribution is in electrical power, which has an efficiency loss of less than 5 percent. As a result, electric vehicles are three to four times as efficient as hydrogen-powered vehicles.

Fuel Cells as Alternatives to Internal Combustion Fuels

One of the most significant aspects of a hydrogen economy is that hydrogen fuel cells can replace internal combustion engines and turbines as the primary method of converting chemical energy into kinetic or electrical energy. The principal reason for such conversions is that fuel cells theoretically are assumed to be more efficient than internal combustion engines. At present, fuel cell technology is in a developmental stage and is significantly more expensive to manufacture than internal combustion engines. However, it is expected that recent advancements in new technologies will reduce the cost of fuel cell system production significantly.

In some fuel cell technologies, hydrocarbon fuels are used in their pure form, which makes the systems price-competitive with internal combustion engines. Significant advantages of fuel cell use in automotive applications include the facts that fuel cells have a superior power-to-weight ratio, are much more efficient than internal combustion engines, and produce no harmful emissions. In view of the depletion of natural hydrocarbon fossil fuels and the recent cost increase of gasoline, fuel cell technology will soon prove to be an economically viable alternative to conventional internal combustion engines and gas turbines used in electrical power generation.

SAFETY CONCERNS

Even though the autoignition temperature of hydrogen is somewhat higher than that of most hydrocarbons, hydrogen's lower ignition energy makes the ignition of a hydrogen-air mixtures more likely; therefore, air-hydrogen mixtures must be designed with extreme care. The condensed and solidified atmospheric air or trace air accumulated in manufacturing contaminates liquid hydrogen and may create a mixture that could detonate readily at the same explosive power as TNT.

Flames in and around a collection of pipes or structures also can create turbulence that causes detonation. In general, the containment of hydrogen owing to leakage, diffusion, and buoyancy is very hazardous; therefore, containment becomes quite difficult. Intrinsically, hydrogen diffuses extensively, and in the event of accidental spillage, liquid hydrogen becomes extremely combustible.

Hydrogen Economy

A *hydrogen economy* is defined as the energy needed for use as fuel in automobiles or electric power production by stationary-type fuel cells, which are primarily combustion processes derived from the reaction of hydrogen molecules (H_2) with oxygen. The main purpose of hydrogen is for use as a fuel to minimize the use of carbon-based fossil fuels and reduce carbon dioxide emissions. Another important principal goal of hydrogen fuel use is to replace dependency on petroleum.

HYDROGEN INFRASTRUCTURE

A hydrogen infrastructure essentially consists of an industrial hydrogen pipeline that can transport hydrogen to filling stations. A vehicular highway accommodated with hydrogen pipelines and filling stations will form a hydrogen highway. In such an infrastructure, filling stations located on peripheral roads will be supplied via hydrogen tanks, hydrogen tube trailers, liquid tankers, or onsite hydrogen-production facilities. Owing to hydrogen's embrittlement of steel, natural gas pipes must be coated from within with special carbon-fiber materials.

Considering that 70 percent of the U.S. population dwells in urban areas, the construction of hydrogen pipelines and local hydrogen-generating facilities becomes a daunting national task. It is estimated that the distribution of hydrogen fuel for vehicles in the United States would require numerous hydrogen filling stations that would cost several billion dollars.

The key to a successful hydrogen economy, as related to vehicular systems, is hydrogen fuel generation at the source. Such a scheme will allow combined solar, thermal, and PV technologies to produce the required electrical and thermal energy for high-temperature electrolysis that could provide liquid hydrogen at filling stations.

FOUNDATIONS OF THE HYDROGEN ECONOMY

A hydrogen economy is based on the premise of reducing dependency on petroleum fuel and reducing atmospheric pollution resulting from the use of hydrocarbon fuels in transportation. At present, a hydrocarbon economy is used for the production of petroleum-based fuels such as gasoline, diesel fuel, and natural gas. However, the combustion of hydrocarbon fuels causes the emission of greenhouse gases and other pollutants.

A significant characteristic of hydrogen fuel is that it has a high energy density by weight. When used in fuel cells, hydrogen produces more energy than internal combustion engines. Internal combustion engines, in general, operate at an efficiency of about 30 percent, whereas hydrogen fuel cell efficiency under ideal conditions is 35–45 percent.

The performance efficiency of hydrogen does not take into consideration losses in production, which would result in an overall efficiency reduction of about 15–25 percent. In fuel cell–based vehicles, when considering losses in the electric motor drives and associated controls, the engine-to-wheel efficiency is reduced to 24 percent.

For the past several decades, hydrogen production has represented a significant global segment of the petroleum fuel and fertilizer production industries. Worldwide production of hydrogen exceeds 50 million metric tons, which equals about 170 million tons of oil-equivalent fossil-fuel energy produced in 2006. Hydrogen energy production has experienced a consistent growth rate of about 10 percent per year. In the United States, annual hydrogen production is estimated to be about 12 million metric tons. The economic value of all the hydrogen produced worldwide is over $140 billion per year.

PRIMARY USES OF HYDROGEN

At present, there are two primary uses for hydrogen, namely, as petroleum fuel and for ammonia production. About half the hydrogen produced worldwide is used for ammonia (NH_3) via production or used directly or indirectly as fertilizer. In view of the world's rapid population growth and intensive use of fertilizer, ammonia demand has been growing at a rate of 12 percent per year. The balance of hydrogen produced is used to convert heavy petroleum sources into lighter fuels, such as gasoline and jet fuels. The process of hydrogen use in fuel refining is referred to as *hydrocracking*.

The scales of economies related to oil refining and fertilizer manufacture are classified into two categories, namely, *captive* for on-site production use and *merchant hydrogen* for smaller quantities of hydrogen production, which are manufactured and delivered to end users. According to the DOE, present U.S. use of hydrogen for hydro-cracking is roughly 4 million metric tons per year. It is also estimated that 38 million metric tons per year of hydrogen production would be sufficient to convert enough domestic coal to liquid fuels to significantly reduce U.S. dependence on foreign oil imports. However, it should be noted that the coal liquefaction process presents significantly more emissions of carbon dioxide than does the current system of burning petroleum.

Based on 2006 statistics, 48 percent of global hydrogen production was derived from natural gas, 30 percent from oil, and 18 percent from coal. Water electrolysis, as discussed earlier, accounted for only 4 percent of the total.

PHOSPHORIC ACID FUEL CELLS

This type of fuel cell uses phosphoric acid compounds as the catalytic conversion membrane. Phosphoric acid fuel cells generate electricity with a conversion efficiency of about 40 percent. The large amount of heat produced by the process (about 400°F) is used for steam production, which, through cogeneration, is used to produce additional electricity.

To date, hundreds of commercially available phosphoric acid fuel cells (PAFCs) have been installed throughout the world and are used by power utility companies, airport terminals, hotels, hospitals, municipal waste dumps, offices, and other such buildings. Recently, many automotive manufacturers, such as Toyota, DaimlerChrysler, and others, have used PEMFCs in their hybrid automobiles (using a combination of a fuel cell and an internal combustion engine) and are racing to produce more efficient production systems that ultimately will be used in transportation technology as the principal means of power generation.

MOLTEN CARBONATE FUEL CELLS

Fuel cells employing this electroconversion use molten carbonate as a catalyst to separate the hydrogen electrons from the molecule. The cells operate at a very high temperature (1200°F) and are considered to be very efficient. Heat generated as a by-product of fuel cell operation is recovered and used in heat exchangers that provide heated water for use in many commercial and industrial applications, substantially augmenting overall operational efficiency.

Molten carbonate fuel cells (MCFCs) operate on hydrogen, carbon monoxide, natural gas, propane, landfill gases, marine diesel fuels, and coal gasified products. In Italy and Japan, multimegawatt MCFCs have been installed successfully and tested as stationary stand-alone power-generation systems. At present, there are a number of stationary MCFCs in operation in California, used as base-load electricity and heat energy.

SOLID OXIDE FUEL CELLS

This technology uses a hard ceramic solid oxide material as an electrolytic conversion catalyst and operates at extremely high temperatures (1800°F). Solid oxide fuel cells (SOFCs) are cable of producing several hundred kilowatts of power at efficiency near or exceeding 60 percent. A special solid oxide fuel cell known as a *tubular solid oxide fuel cell* uses tubes of compressed solid oxide disks, resembling metal can tops, which are stacked up to 100 cm high.

Another experimental fuel cell technology, referred to as a *planar solid oxide fuel cell* (PSOFC), has promising potential for producing small-scale power generators at the 3- to 5-kW scale. They are intended for stationary power generation, for use as power supplies in remote areas, and as auxiliary power for use in vehicles. SOFC application at present is not considered to be suitable for use as a prime power source.

Recently, SOFC technologies have made significant progress in product development and are being manufactured commercially by a number of companies. At present, the main obstacle to the use of this technology is the high heat production resulting from the chemical reaction of hydrogen and oxygen, which must be mitigated. The fuel cell, owing to significant power-production capacity and high efficiency, will, in the near future, be used in motor vehicles and as a source for electric power generation.

ALKALINE FUEL CELLS

Alkaline fuel cells (AFCs) use potassium hydroxide in the electrochemical catalytic conversion process and have a conversion efficiency of about 70 percent. In the last few decades, NASA has used alkaline cells to power space missions.

Until recently, owing to the high cost of production, AFCs were not available commercially. However, improvements and cost reductions in fuel cell production have created a new opportunity for commercializing this technology.

DIRECT METHANOL FUEL CELLS

This type of fuel cell uses a proton-exchange electroconversion process similar to the one discussed earlier and uses a polymer membrane as the electrolyte. However, without a re-former mechanism, the anode acts as a catalyst that separates the hydrogen from the liquid. It should be noted that until recently, owing to the high cost of production, AFCs have not been available commercially. However, improvements and cost reduction in fuel cell production have created a new opportunity to commercialize this technology. Direct methanol fuel cells (DMFCs) operate at a relatively low temperature (120–200°F) and have about 40 percent efficiency. At more elevated temperatures, these fuel cells operate at higher conversion efficiency.

In the United States, the future commercialization of DMFC technology will depend on genetically modified corn, which can be fermented at low temperatures. Such a breakthrough could indeed make the technology a viable source of electrical energy production, which could contribute significantly to the reduction of air pollution and minimize the expensive import of crude oil.

REGENERATIVE FUEL CELLS

This technology, which is still at its early research and development stage, is a closed-loop electroconversion system that uses solar-powered electrolysis to separate hydrogen and oxygen molecules from water. Hydrogen and oxygen are fed into a fuel cell, which in addition to generating electricity produces heat and water. At present, NASA is researching the technology for space applications and for use as a stationary auxiliary power unit.

BENEFITS OF FUEL CELL TECHNOLOGY

It is estimated that the fuel cell market within the next decade could exceed $20 billion worldwide. In addition to expanding the market for alternative electrical energy, a significant percentage of the millions of vehicles produced annually throughout the world, which use internal combustion, will be converted through hybrid technology. It is also believed that the demand for fuel cells by the transportation industry within the next decade will increase annually by an additional $15 billion. In the United States, passenger vehicles alone consume over 6 million barrels of oil every day, which represents 85 percent of our oil imports.

If only 25 percent of vehicles could operate with fuel cells, oil imports could be reduced by 1.8 billion barrels a day, or about 650 billion barrels a year, eliminating an unfavorable balance of trade and considerable amounts of air pollution. Furthermore, if each vehicle produced in the future was designed to operate on fuel cells, the country's electric power-generation capacity would increase by 200 percent.

The DOE estimates that if only 10 percent of the nation's vehicles were powered by fuel cells, yearly imports of crude oil would be reduced by about 13 percent, or 800,000 barrels. The production of greenhouse gases, such as carbon dioxide, additionally would be reduced by 60 tons, and air pollution particulates would be reduced by 1 million tons.

IMPACT OF FUEL CELLS ON THE GLOBAL ECONOMY

In view of the wide-ranging applications of the technology in markets, including steel production, electric power generation, and the vehicle and transportation industries, fuel cells could have a significant impact on the global economy because they could provide employment for tens of thousands of people with high-quality jobs.

It is estimated that each 1000 mW of fuel cell energy production will create 5000 new jobs, and if only 25 percent of cars in the nation were to use the technology, jobs created would exceed 1 million, which will have a significantly positive impact on the U.S. gross national product.

CALIFORNIA FUEL CELL PARTNERSHIP

The California Fuel Cell Partnership (CaFCP) includes among its members the South Coast Air Quality Management District and a collaboration of auto manufacturers, fuel suppliers, fuel cell manufacturers, and state governments. Headquartered in Sacramento, the CaFC demonstrates and tests fuel cell vehicles under everyday conditions, investigates the viability of site-infrastructure technology, promotes public awareness of pre-membrane fuel cell–powered vehicles, and explores the path to commercialization through ideas for solutions to these problems.

VANCOUVER FUEL CELL VEHICLE PROGRAM

The Vancouver Fuel Cell Vehicle Program (VFCVP) is a 5-year, $9 million joint initiative between the government of Canada, Ford Motor Company, Technology Early Action Measures, and the government of British Columbia. This project will demonstrate five Ballard-powered fuel cell vehicles in real-world conditions on the British Colombian lower mainland, which will be the first fleet demonstration of fuel cell vehicles in Canada. Demonstrating third-generation Ford fuel cell vehicles will provide valuable information on performance and reliability, which can be applied to the evolution of fuel cell vehicles to the commercial marketplace in the transition to a hydrogen economy. Figure 7.5 shows a Ballard Engineering stationary fuel cell generator.

Ballard will have its own fuel cell for the duration of the program. Other vehicle users include the city of Vancouver, the government of British Columbia, Fuel Cells Canada, and the National Research Council (NRC).

SANTA CLARA VALLEY TRANSPORTATION AUTHORITY

The Santa Clara Valley Transportation Authority (VTA) has contracted with the Gillig Corporation and Ballard Power Systems of Burnaby, Canada, to build three

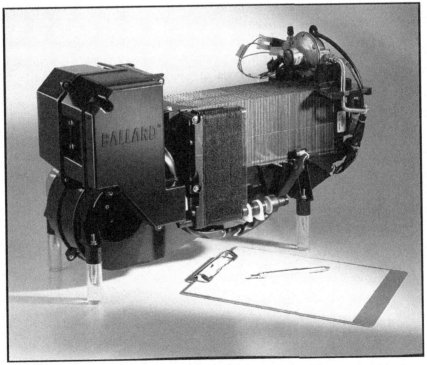

Figure 7.5 **A stationary fuel cell power generator.** *Courtesy of Ballard Engineering.*

hydrogen-powered, zero-emission fuel cell buses (ZEBs) for use in regular transit service. Air Products & Chemicals, Inc., will supply hydrogen, which is converted to hydrogen gas at VTA's fueling station at Cerone. Additional projects include Sunline Transit in Thousand Palms, California, a transit organization that has an extended history of use of alternative-fuel vehicles and buses. It is also a testing facility for many vehicle companies that conduct a variety of tests in the California desert.

EUROPEAN FUEL CELL BUS PROJECT

Ballard heavy-duty fuel cell engines are installed in 30 Mercedes buses running in revenue transit service in a dozen European cities, which include nine cities and the Ecological City Transport System in Reykjavik, Iceland, in yearly demonstration programs. The European Union has led the way for zero-emission fuel cell technology.

FUEL CELL APPLICATIONS IN THE U.S. SPACE PROGRAM

The fuel cell was first discovered in 1839 by Sir William Grove, a Welsh judge and a scientist. The discovery became dormant up until the 1960s, when practical applications of the electrochemical conversion in the U.S. space program paved the way for today's research and product development.

In the past, the U.S. space program chose fuel cells to power the Gemini and Apollo spacecrafts and still uses the technology to provide electricity and water for the Space Shuttle. Nowadays, most industrialized nations of the world, including the United States, Canada, Germany, Holland, Japan, and Italy, have extensive nationally sponsored research and development programs that promise to have a significant impact on the global economy and reduce global greenhouse gas production.

8

WIND ENERGY TECHNOLOGIES

This chapter describes the operation of wind turbine technology and provides an overview of its applications. Some of this material also can be found on the Web sites of the American Wind Energy Association, the U.S. Department of Renewable Energy Laboratories, and the Danish Wind Turbine Manufacturers Association.

History of Wind Power

VERTICAL-AXLE WINDMILLS

The earliest historical reference describes a windmill that was used to power an organ in the first AD, which is credited to Hero of Alexandria. Also, as early as the ninth century AD, vertical-axis windmills were used in Sistan, located in present-day eastern Iran. The ancient Iranian windmill designs consisted of 12 sails covered with reed matting or cloth material. The windmills were used to grind cereals and pump water. Similar types of vertical windmills, with rectangular blades, were used for irrigation in the thirteenth century AD in northern China during the Jurchen Jin Dynasty.

HORIZONTAL-AXLE WINDMILLS

Horizontal-shaft windmills were used extensively by the ancient Greeks for grinding flour. It has been recorded that on the island of Cyclades, millers received flour as payment for their services.

In the twelfth century AD, Flanders, France, and England used windmills extensively to grind flour. At present, there are many ancient Dutch windmills that are still operating.

With the advent of the industrial revolution, the use of windmills as primary industrial energy sources was replaced by steam and internal combustion engines. However, steam engines had a lesser effect on some of the remotely located mills in England, which were used as drainage pumps until the middle of the twentieth century.

In the United States, the use of water-pumping windmills contributed significantly to the development of farming and ranching in the vast expanses of the American and Canadian Midwest and West. In the early days of railroad transport, windmills were used throughout the world to pump water from wells to supply the water needs of steam locomotives. The modern wind turbines used today were developed as recently as the early 1980s.

Wind Power Generation

In essence, wind power generation results from the conversion of wind kinetic energy into electricity through the use of specially designed wind turbines. As mentioned earlier, wind power also can be used as to pump water or grind grain.

Wind circulation or convection results from an uneven distribution of solar heat. Owing to earth's 23.5-degree axial tilt, solar energy is absorbed unevenly at the poles and equator, which results in a heat differential that causes hot and cold air circulation, or convection, between the equator and the poles. Moreover, dry lands on the crust of the earth heat up and cool down more quickly than do the seas. This results in a differential heat distribution that causes a global atmospheric convection system within the earth's surface and spanning through its stratosphere.

A significant portion of wind dynamic energy occurs at high altitudes, where wind speeds exceed 100 mi/h. A large portion of the wind energy is converted into heat through friction with the earth's surface and particulates in the atmosphere. It is estimated that the stored power potential of wind energy exceeds 72,000 GW, which could be harvested for commercial use.

At the end of 2007, worldwide capacity for wind-powered generators was 94.1 GW. At present, wind produces about 1 percent of the world's electricity. According to the World Wind Energy Association's 2007 report, wind energy represents 19 percent of electricity production in Denmark, 9 percent in Spain and Portugal, and 6 percent in Germany and the Republic of Ireland.

Wind energy is one of the most abundant forms of renewable energy and could be harvested throughout the globe, reduce dependency on fossil fuels, and decrease greenhouse gas emissions. Owing to the intermittency of wind, power produced by wind turbines lacks stability and consistency. In order to stabilize and regulate electrical power production, wind power farms make use of special energy storage devices and supplemental power-cogeneration and energy-storage technology in order to harmonize power production.

Wind Power Management

In order to make wind energy a reliable source of electric power, a number of challenges, such as power-production intermittency, energy storage, and power-output regulation, must be overcome. The following are a number of measures used to regulate and stabilize wind energy production.

GRID COMPATIBILITY

In general, wind turbine generators designed for electrical power production require reactive power for excitation. However, the reactive power shifts current and voltage phase angles, which results in a loss of power production. The cosine of the shifted angle, which is referred to as the *power factor p,* is a multiplier that varies from 0 to 1. Electrical power output from generators is expressed as $E = V$ (voltage) $\times I$ (current) $\times \cos(p)$. It is at a maximum when $p = 0$ because $\cos(0) = 1$, which make $E = V \times I$. Thus, at the zero angle [$\cos(0)$], the *unity power factor* is achieved. In order to reach the unity power factor, the output of the generators is connected to large banks of capacitors that reduce the phase angle to achieve this goal. Since various types of wind turbine generators have unique power-output performance profiles, they could create transmission grid disturbances. In order to resolve this problem, manufacturers of wind turbines make use of extensive modeling of dynamic electromechanical characteristics with each wind farm. The modeling allows transmission-system operators to control the power output of the generators, ensuring predictable and stable power-output performance.

Unlike steam or hydroelectric power turbine-driven synchronous generators, wind turbines incorporate power-factor-correction capacitors along with electronic control of circuitry, which stabilizes power-output resonance. Wind turbines, referred to as *doubly fed machines,* deploy solid-state converters between the turbine generator and the collector system, making them suitable for grid interconnection. As a rule, grid transmission providers' supply wind farm developers with a specific *grid code* that specifies power factor, frequency stability, and dynamic characteristics of the wind farm turbines during a system fault.

CAPACITY FACTOR

In view of the fact that wind speed is never constant, a wind farm's annual energy production cannot match the generator's expected yearly nameplate ratings output. As a result, a multiplier known as the *capacity factor* is used to adjust the total annual hourly power production. The multiplier is the ratio of actual power productivity in a year and its theoretical maximum.

Typical capacity factors of wind turbines range from 20 to 40 percent. Upper values represent maximum power production for most favorable installation sites. As an example, a 2-MW turbine with a capacity factor of 30 percent will produce only $0.30 \times 2 \times 24 \times 365 = 5256$ MW per year as opposed to 17,520 MW.

The capacity factor essentially accounts for power-production limits that are inherent properties of wind. Capacity factors for other types of power plants, such as gas and hydroelectric power-generation systems, reflect the amount of downtime required for maintenance. For example, most nuclear plants that run full time at maximum output capacity have a capacity factor of 90–95 percent.

POWER-PRODUCTION INTERMITTENCY LIMITS

In general, electricity generated from wind power is quite intermittent, and power output differs from hour to hour and day to day and from one season to another. Since grid-connected power production and consumption must remain in balance and be stable at all times, this presents a substantial technical challenge for wind farm operators. To stabilize wind power production, wind electrical technologies resort to a number of energy-management strategies, including incremental operating reserves, energy demand management, load shedding, and storage solutions.

In the event of low levels of wind power production, commonly referred to as *penetration* (which may result from wind fluctuations or the partial failure of generating capacity), wind farms are required to provide a certain amount of reserve power-production capacity that can be used to regulate and stabilize the variability of wind generation. One such energy-management strategy is referred to as *pumped storage,* which is wind energy developed during high-wind periods that is stored and then released when needed. Energy storage is accomplished by pumping water uphill into reservoirs during peak power-production periods and making use of the stored potential energy of the water during peak demand periods. In some instances, in the absence of water-storage reservoirs, solar wind farms supplement additional stabilizing power by means of natural gas–fired electric generators.

In California and Texas, for example, during hot days in the summer, there is low wind speed at exactly the time when there is high electric demand. In contrast, in England during winter, the demand for electricity is higher than in summer, and so are the wind speeds. Since during most days of the year peak solar power tends to occur during the daytime in the absence of wind, it cannot be used as a complementary power production to wind.

PENETRATION

Wind energy *penetration* refers to the percentage of energy produced by wind turbines when compared with the total available wind kinetic energy potential. Factors affecting the penetration ratio are capacity for energy storage, cost of power production, and energy management.

In the event of equipment failure, all grid-connected wind energy farms, for power regulation purposes, are required to have a guaranteed energy storage capacity that will allow for consistent power transmission. Depending on the location and specifics of a wind farm, energy storage capacity may be as much as 20–25 percent of the overall power-generation capacity. This adds significant technical and economic challenges for operators.

WIND POWER FORECASTING

Owing to the intermittent nature of wind energy, in order to regulate power-plant production, operators are required to predict short-term hourly or daily plant output. As a result, as with all other grid-connected electricity sources, wind energy also must be scheduled. Wind power forecasting methods include sophisticated satellite data and ground-mounted wind-measurement instrumentation.

WIND FARM ECONOMICS

Critical factors associated with wind power generation economics are site location, land acquisition costs, land-use considerations, environmental-impact consideration, and most important, the availability of transmission lines. Even though the construction of wind farms in off-shore locations in general costs considerably more, owing to considerably consistent and stronger winds, the cost of energy production becomes much lower.

WIND POWER POTENTIAL

Presently, there are thousands of wind turbines operating throughout the world, producing a total of 73,904 MW of electric power; Europe alone accounts for 68 percent of this. Wind power is one of the fastest growing renewable-energy industries, and world wind generation capacity quadrupled between 2000 and 2006.

   World Wind Energy Association records indicate that worldwide wind energy production by 2010 is expected to increase from the present 80 GW to 160 GW, which represents a yearly growth rate of 20 percent. At present, Denmark generates one-fifth of its electricity with wind turbines. In recent years, Germany has become the leading producer of wind power, with a total output of 38.5 MWh, which represents 6.3 percent of the country's electric power production. By 2010, Germany's official target is to meet 12.5 percent of its electricity needs through the use of wind power. As of now, Germany has 18,600 wind turbines, mostly located in the north of the country. In 2005, the government of Spain also approved a new national goal for increasing wind power capacity to 20,000 MW by 2010. In the past decade, the United States has added significantly more wind energy to its grid than any other country in the world. U.S. wind power capacity in 2007 reached 16.8 GW.

Betz' Law of Fluid Dynamics

Betz' law of fluid dynamics formulates the maximum flow of possible energy that can be derived by means of an infinitely thin rotor, such as a wind mill, from a flowing fluid (in this case air) at a certain speed. To calculate the maximum theoretical efficiency of a windmill, we must pretend that the propeller of the wind turbine is constructed from a thin rotor made of a disk with surface area S that withdraws energy from the fluid or air passing. At a certain distance behind this disk, the fluid or the air flows with a reduced velocity (Fig. 8.1).

   If we designate v_1 as the speed of the fluid entering the tube in front of the disk and v_2 as the speed of the fluid downstream, then the average or mean flow velocity through the disk v_{avg} will be

$$v_{avg} = \frac{1}{2}(v_1 + v_2)$$

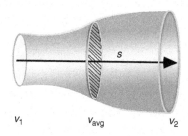

Figure 8.1   Schematic diagram of fluid flow through a constricted and expanded cylinder.

v_1 v_{avg} v_2

If we designate the disk area as being equal to S and have ρ be the fluid density, then the *mass flow rate,* or the mass of fluid flowing per unit time, could be represented by

$$\dot{m} = \rho S v_{avg} = \frac{\rho S(v_1 + v_2)}{2}$$

Since, by definition, kinetic energy or power equals mass multiplied by velocity, the power delivered is the difference between the kinetic energies of the fluid or airflow approaching and leaving the rotor in unit time (Fig. 8.2); that is,

$$\dot{E} = \frac{1}{2}\dot{m}(v_1^2 - v_2^2)$$

By substituting the mass from the previous equation and using the laws of geometry, we arrive at the following equation:

$$\dot{E} = \frac{1}{4}\rho S(v_1 + v_2)(v_1^2 - v_2^2)$$

$$= \frac{1}{4}\rho S v_1^3 \left[1 - \left(\frac{v_2}{v_1}\right)^2 + \left(\frac{v_2}{v_1}\right) - \left(\frac{v_2}{v_1}\right)^3\right]$$

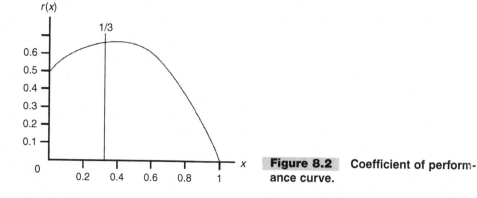

Figure 8.2   Coefficient of performance curve.

The graph in the figure represents the plot of the preceding equation, where the horizontal axis reflects the ratio v_2/v_1, and the vertical axis is the *coefficient of performance* C_p. By differentiating $\dot{E}$ with respect to v_2/v_2 for a given fluid speed, v_1, and a given area S, we can find the *maximum* or *minimum* value for $\dot{E}$. The result is that $\dot{E}$ reaches maximum value when $v_2/v_2 = 1/3$ or, simply stated, outgoing velocity equals one-third of the incoming liquid or air velocity.

Substituting the v_2/v_2 ratios in the preceding formula with 1/3 results in

$$P_{\text{max}} = \frac{16}{27} \times \frac{1}{2} \times \rho S v_1^3$$

Therefore, the work rate obtainable from fluid flow with area S and velocity v_1 is

$$P = \frac{1}{2} \rho S v_1^3$$

In electrical engineering, the *coefficient of performance* is defined as the ratio of the power output of a generator divided by the maximum power. In the case of wind turbines, the *coefficient of performance* C_p equals P/P_{max} and has a maximum value of

$$C_{p,\text{max}} = \frac{16}{27} = 0.593, \text{ or } 59.3\%$$

It should be noted that coefficients of performance in general are expressed as a decimal and not as a percentage.

Significant losses of power in wind energy turbines are attributed to a number of factors, such as rotor bearing friction, heat or copper loss, and air friction losses. In general, the C_p value of modern turbines used in windmills ranges from 0.4 to 0.5, which represents about 70–80 percent of the theoretically possible limit. Figure 8.3 illustrates the atmospheric air convection cycle.

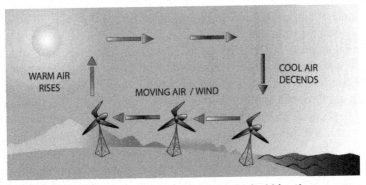

Figure 8.3 Graphic representation of wind kinetic energy at work.

The convection cycle causes portions of the atmosphere to warm differently. Hot air rises, reducing the atmospheric pressure at the earth's surface, and cooler air is drawn in to replace it. The result is wind. Air has mass, and when it is in motion, it contains the energy of that motion, or *kinetic energy*. Some portion of that energy can be converted into other forms, including mechanical force or electricity, that we can use to perform work.

Structural Considerations

Wind turbines typically are mounted on open, four-legged steel towers similar to supports for electric transmission lines or single circular steel columns similar to flag poles. Both support systems are mounted on concrete foundations at the ground level. The steel support column is connected to the concrete foundation with steel anchor bolts through a baseplate, which is welded to the column.

The vertical loads that the structural engineer must consider in the design include the weight of the turbine, the weight of the support column, and the weight of the foundation. There are also horizontal loads that are combined with the vertical load. The horizontal loads are induced either by earthquake or wind. In the case of wind towers, wind-induced horizontal loads typically govern the design. These wind loads include the horizontal thrust produced by the rotation of the turbine blades plus the wind load on the tower itself.

The horizontal forces resulting from the wind loads, which are applied at levels above the ground, produce a bending torque throughout the height of the structure. The stress induced by this bending effect is most critical at the welded interface between the column and the steel baseplate. There are two other critical elements that require structural engineering design expertise: the anchor bolts holding the column on the foundation and the concrete foundation that counteracts the wind loads and keeps the entire structure in place. Of course, the column itself also will be designed to resist both the vertical and horizontal loads.

For proper design of the foundation, the structural engineer will require that a geotechnical engineer investigate the soil's properties at the location where the wind tower will be constructed and make recommendations with regard to the soil's capacity to resist vertical and horizontal loads.

The structural engineer will design the foundation such that the entire structure will not slide, will not experience differential settlement along its base, and most important, will not overturn or be pulled out of the ground. It is important to point out that wind turbines are designed and installed with an internal feature that limits the speed of rotation of the blades. The structural engineer designs all aspects of the structure for maximum horizontal thrust, resulting from the maximum design speed of blade rotation. To limit the speed of rotation of the turbine blades, the turbine normally is designed in such a way that when the blades reach the maximum design rotation speed, the turbine yaws and changes its angle with respect to the direction of the blowing wind, thus controlling rotation speed. This yawing feature in the turbine is very critical. Should it fail, the entire structure could fall over.

Some locations where wind turbines are constructed may have unique site conditions that require special structural engineering considerations. Examples of such sites are offshore locations where the impacts of wave motion should be considered, as well as floodways, where the effects of soil erosion on the foundation should be taken into consideration (Fig. 8.4).

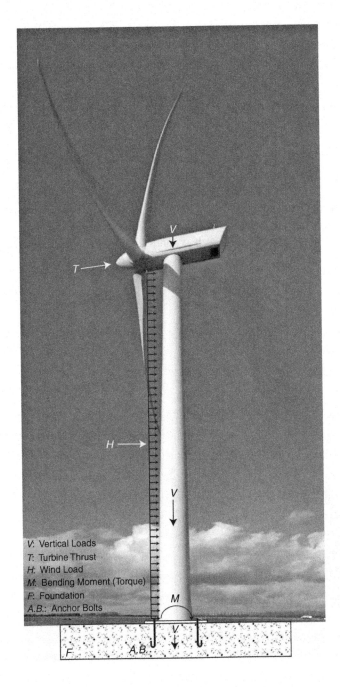

V: Vertical Loads
T: Turbine Thrust
H: Wind Load
M: Bending Moment (Torque)
F: Foundation
A.B.: Anchor Bolts

Figure 8.4   Wind turbine static and dynamic forces.

Basics of Wind Turbine Operation

A wind energy system transforms the kinetic energy of the wind into mechanical or electrical energy that can be harnessed for practical use. Mechanical energy is most commonly used for pumping water in rural or remote locations. The *farm windmill*, still seen in many rural areas of the United States, is a mechanical wind pump, but it also can be used for many other purposes (e.g., grinding grain, sawing). Wind electric turbines generate electricity for homes, businesses, and state utilities.

There are two basic designs in wind electric turbines: vertical-axis (11 eggbeater-style blades) and horizontal-axis (propeller-style blades) machines. Horizontal-axis wind turbines are most common today, constituting nearly all the utility-scale (100-kW capacity and larger) turbines in the global market. Turbine system components include the following (Fig. 8.5):

- A blade or a rotor that converts the wind energy into rotational shaft energy (which in some installations could span over 50 ft)
- An enclosure referred to as a *nacelle* that contains the drive mechanism, consisting of a gearbox and an electric generator
- A support structure, such as a tower, that supports the nacelle
- Electrical equipment and components, such as controls and interconnection equipment

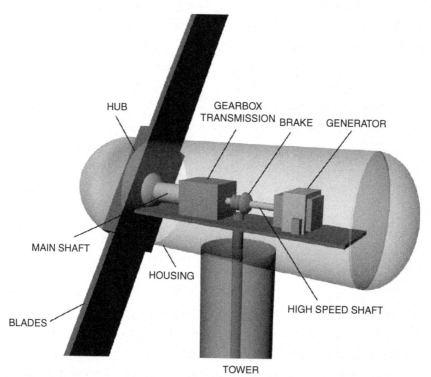

Figure 8.5   **Wind turbine mechanism.** *Courtesy of California Energy Commission.*

There are also types of turbines that directly drive the generator and do not require a gearbox. The amount of electricity that wind turbines generate depends on the turbine's capacity or power rating.

The electricity generated by a utility-scale wind turbine is normally collected and fed into utility power lines, where it is mixed with electricity from other power plants and delivered to utility customers.

ENERGY-GENERATION CAPACITY OF A WIND TURBINE

The ability to generate electricity is measured in watts. Watts are very small units, so the terms *kilowatt* (kW, 1000 W), *megawatt* (MW, 1 million W), and *gigawatt* (pronounced "gig-a-watt," GW, 1 billion W) are used most commonly to describe the capacity of generating units such as wind turbines and other power plants. Electricity production and consumption are measured most commonly in kilowatthours (kWh). A kilowatthour means 1 kW (1000 W) of electricity produced or consumed for 1 hour. One 50-W light bulb left on for 20 hours consumes 1 kWh of electricity (50 W × 20 hours = 1000 Wh = 1 kWh). The output of a wind turbine depends on the turbine's size and the wind's speed through the rotor. Currently manufactured wind turbines have power ratings ranging from 250 W to 1.8 MW.

For example, a 10-kW wind turbine, shown in Fig. 8.6, can generate about 10,000 kWh annually at a site with wind speeds averaging 12 mi/h, equivalent to about the amount

Figure 8.6   **Offshore wind turbine installation.** *Courtesy of AWEMA.*

needed to power a typical household. A 1.8-MW turbine can produce more than 5.2 million kWh in a year, enough to power more than 500 households. The average U.S. household consumes about 10,000 kWh of electricity each year.

A practical example of a project is a 250-kW turbine installed at the elementary school in Spirit Lake, Iowa, that provides an average of 350,000 kWh of electricity per year, more than is necessary for the 53,000-square-foot school. Excess electricity is fed into the local utility system, which earned the school $25,000 in the turbine's first 5 years of operation. The school uses electricity from the utility at times when the wind does not blow. This project has been so successful that the Spirit Lake School District has since installed a second turbine with a capacity of 750 kW.

Wind speed is a crucial element in projecting turbine performance, and a site's wind speed is measured through wind resource assessment prior to a wind system's construction. Generally, an annual average wind speed greater than 4 m/s, or 9 mi/h, is required for small wind electric turbines. Less wind is required for water-pumping operations.

Utility-scale wind power plants require minimum average wind speeds of 6 m/s (13 mi/h). The power available in the wind is proportional to the cube of its speed, which means that doubling the wind speed increases the available power by a factor of 8. Thus a turbine operating at a site with an average wind speed of 12 mi/h could, in theory, generate about 33 percent more electricity than one at an 11 mi/h site because the cube of 12 (i.e., 1768) is 33 percent larger than the cube of 11 (i.e., 1331). In the real world, the turbine will not produce quite that much more electricity, but it still will generate much more than the 9 percent difference in wind speed.

The important thing to understand is that what seems like a small difference in wind speed can mean a much larger difference in available energy and in electricity produced and therefore a larger difference in the cost of the electricity generated. Also, there is little energy to be harvested at very low wind speeds; 6 mi/h winds contain less than one-eighth the energy of 12 mi/h winds.

CONSTRUCTION OF WIND TURBINES

Utility-scale wind turbines for land-based wind farms come in various sizes, with rotor diameters ranging from about 50 m to about 90 m and with towers of roughly the same size. A 90-m machine, definitely at the large end of the scale, with a 90-m tower would have a total height, from the tower base to the tip of the rotor, of approximately 135 m (442 ft). Offshore turbine designs now under development have rotors that have a 110-m rotor diameter. It is easier to transport large rotor blades by ship than by land. Small wind turbines intended for residential or small-business use are much smaller. Most have rotor diameters of 8 m or less and would be mounted on towers of 40 m in height or less.

Most manufacturers of utility-scale turbines offer machines in the 700-kW to 1.8-MW range. Ten 700-kW units would make a 7-MW wind plant, whereas ten 1.8-MW machines would make an 18-MW facility. In the future, machines of larger size will be available, although they probably will be installed offshore, where larger transportation and construction equipment can be used. Units larger than 4 MW in capacity are now under development.

One megawatt of wind energy can generate between 2.4 and 3 million kWh annually. The towers are mostly tubular and made of steel. The blades are made of fiberglass-reinforced polyester or wood-epoxy.

Wind Turbine Energy Economics

The *energy payback time* is the term used to measure the net energy value of a wind turbine. In other words, it determines how long the plant has to operate to generate the amount of electricity that was required for its manufacture and construction.

Several studies have looked at this question over the years and have concluded that wind energy has one of the shortest energy payback times of any energy technology. A wind turbine typically takes only a few years (3–8 depending on the average wind speed at its site) to pay back the energy needed for its fabrication, installation, operation, and retirement.

Since you cannot count on the wind blowing, what does a utility gain by adding 100 MW of wind to its portfolio of generating plants? Does it gain anything? Or should it also add 100 MW of fueled generation capacity to allow for the times when the wind is calm?

First, it needs to be understood that the bulk of the value of any supply resource is in the energy that the resource produces, not the capacity it adds to a utility system. In general, utilities use fairly complicated computer models to determine the value in added capacity that each new generating plant adds to the system.

According to some models, the capacity value of a new wind plant is approximately equal to its capacity factor. Thus, adding a 100-MW wind plant with an average capacity factor of 35 percent to the system is approximately the same as adding 35 MW of conventional fueled generating capacity.

The exact answer depends on, among other factors, the correlation between the time that the wind blows and the time that the utility sees peak demand. Thus wind farms whose output is highest in the spring months or early morning hours generally will have a lower capacity value than wind farms whose output is high on hot summer evenings.

Since wind is a variable energy source, its growing use presents problems for utility system managers. At current levels of use, this issue is still some distance from being a problem for most utility systems.

A conventional utility power plant uses fuel, so it normally will run much of the time unless it is idled by equipment problems or for maintenance. A capacity factor of 40–80 percent is typical for conventional plants.

A wind plant is "fueled" by the wind, which blows steadily at times and not at all at other times. Although modern utility-scale wind turbines typically operate 65–80 percent of the time, they often run at less than full capacity. Therefore, a capacity factor of 25–40 percent is common, although they may achieve higher capacity factors during windy weeks or months.

The most electricity per dollar of investment is gained by using a larger generator and accepting the fact that the capacity factor will be lower as a result. Wind turbines are fundamentally different from fueled power plants in this respect.

If a wind turbine's capacity factor is 33 percent, this does not mean that it is running only one-third of the time. A wind turbine at a typical location in the midwestern United States runs about 65–80 percent of the time. Much of the time it will be generating at less than full capacity, though.

AVAILABILITY FACTOR

Availability factor, or just *availability,* is a measurement of the reliability of a wind turbine or other power plant. It refers to the percentage of time that a plant is ready to generate, that is, when it is not out of service or under maintenance or repairs. Modern wind turbines have an availability of more than 98 percent, higher than most other types of power plants. After two decades of constant engineering refinement, today's wind machines are highly reliable.

WIND TURBINE POWER-GENERATION CAPACITY

Utilities must maintain enough power plant capacity to meet expected customer electricity demand at all times plus an additional reserve margin. All other things being equal, utilities generally prefer plants that can generate as needed (i.e., conventional plants) to plants that cannot (i.e., wind plants).

However, despite the fact that the wind is variable and sometimes does not blow at all, wind plants do increase the overall statistical probability that a utility system will be able to meet demand requirements. A rough rule is that the capacity value of adding a wind plant to a utility system is about the same as the wind plant's capacity factor multiplied by its capacity, as shown in the preceding section. Thus a 100-MW wind plant with a capacity factor of 35 percent would be similar in capacity value to a 35-MW conventional generator. For example, in 2001, the Colorado Public Utility Commission found the capacity of a proposed 162-MW wind plant in eastern Colorado (with a 30 percent capacity factor) to be approximately 48 MW.

The exact amount of capacity value that a given wind project provides depends on a number of factors, including average wind speeds at the site and the match between wind patterns and utility-load (demand) requirements. It also depends on how dispersed geographically wind plants on a utility system are and how well connected the utility is with neighboring systems that also may have wind generators. The broader the wind plants are scattered geographically, the greater is the chance that some of them will be producing power at any given time. Figure 8.7 is a photograph of a land-based wind turbine.

WIND TURBINE ENERGY SUPPLY POTENTIAL FOR THE UNITED STATES

Wind energy could supply about 20 percent of the nation's electricity, according to Battelle Pacific Northwest Laboratory, a federal research laboratory. Wind energy resources used for generating electricity can be found in nearly every state.

Figure 8.7 **Wind turbine.** *Courtesy of MARTIFER.*

U.S. wind resources are even greater, however. North Dakota alone is theoretically capable of producing enough wind-generated power to meet more than one-third of U.S. electricity demand. The theoretical potentials of the windiest states are shown in Table 8.1.

Present projections show that wind power can provide at least up to a fifth of a system's electricity, and the figure probably could be higher. Wind power currently provides nearly 25 percent of electricity demand in the north German state of Schleswig Holstein. In western Denmark, wind supplies 100 percent of the electricity used during some hours on windy winter nights.

CONSISTENCY OF SUPPORT POLICY

Over the past 5 years, the federal production tax credit has been extended twice, but each time Congress allowed the credit to expire before acting and then only approved short durations. The credit expired again December 31, 2003 and as of March 2004 still had not been renewed. These expiration and extension cycles inflict a high cost on the industry, cause large layoffs, and hold up investments. Long-term, consistent policy support would help to unleash the industry's pent-up potential.

TRANSMISSION-LINE ACCESS

Transmission-line operators typically charge generators large penalty fees if they fail to deliver electricity when it is scheduled to be transmitted. The purpose of these

TABLE 8.1 TOP 20 WIND-ENERGY-PRODUCING STATES	
STATE	BILLIONS OF KILOWATTHOURS
North Dakota	1210
Texas	1190
Kansas	1070
South Dakota	1030
Montana	1020
Nebraska	868
Wyoming	747
Oklahoma	725
Minnesota	657
Colorado	481
New Mexico	435
Idaho	73
Michigan	65
New York	62
Illinois	61
California	59
Wisconsin	58
Maine	56
Missouri	52
Iowa	51

penalty fees is to punish generators and deter them from using transmission scheduling as a "gaming" technique to gain advantage over competitors. The fees therefore are not related to whether the system operator actually loses money as a result of the generator's action. But because the wind is variable, wind plant owners cannot guarantee the delivery of electricity for transmission at a scheduled time. Wind energy needs a new penalty system that recognizes the different nature of wind plants and allows them to compete on a fair basis.

The Great Plains, which cover the central third of the United States, need to be extensively redesigned and redeveloped. At present, systems on the plains consist mostly of small distribution lines. Instead, series of new high-voltage transmission lines are needed to transmit electricity from wind plants to population centers. Such a redevelopment will be expensive, but it also will benefit consumers and national security by making the electric transmission system more reliable and by reducing shortages and the price volatility of natural gas. Transmission will be a key issue for the wind industry's future development over the next two decades.

WORLD WIND POWER PRODUCTION CAPACITY

As of the end of 2003, there were over 39,000 MW of generating capacity operating worldwide, producing some 90 billion kWh each year—as much as 9 million average American households use or as much as a dozen large nuclear power plants could generate. However, this is but a tiny fraction of the potential of wind.

NEW TRANSMISSION LINES

According to the U.S. Department of Energy (DOE), the world's winds theoretically could supply the equivalent of 5800 quadrillion Btus (quads) of energy each year, more than 15 times the current world energy demand. (A *quad* is equal to about 172 million barrels of oil or 45 million tons of coal.) The potential of wind to improve the quality of life in the world's developing countries, where more than 2 billion people live with no electricity or prospect of utility service in the foreseeable future, is vast.

"Wind Force 12," a study performed by Denmark's BTM Consult for the European Wind Energy Association and Greenpeace, found that by the year 2020, wind could provide 12 percent of the world's electricity supplies, meeting the needs of 600 million average European households.

Denmark is revisiting and currently rewriting its wind policy. The degree to which this means that the United States should reexamine its own policy revolves around the degree to which our situation is similar to Denmark's. In fact, a brief analysis of some major differences suggests that there are strong reasons for continuing to support wind development in the United States rather than back away from it.

Wind supplies 20 percent of national electricity demand in Denmark. Although the United States has nearly twice as much installed wind equipment as Denmark, wind generates only 0.4 percent of our electricity, far below the 10 percent threshold identified by most analysts as the point at which wind's variability becomes a significant issue for utility system operators.

Denmark is also so small geographically (half the size of Indiana) that high winds can cause many of its wind plants to shut down almost at once. In the United States, wind plants are much more geographically dispersed (from California to New York to Texas) and do not all experience the same wind conditions at the same time.

Rapid development of wind and new small-scale power plants within the past 5 years has brought Denmark to the point where power produced by so-called nondispatchable resources in the country's west exceeds 100 percent of demand in the region. At many times, this excess generation leaves the country scrambling to increase electricity export capabilities to handle the surplus. This situation is essentially unimaginable in the United States.

Denmark's approach encourages community involvement but places particular stress on low-capacity distribution networks (at the "end of the line" on transmission systems).

In the United States, our larger wind plants require advance transmission planning but feed into main transmission lines and do not affect the customer distribution network.

GROWING USE OF WIND ENERGY FOR UTILITY SYSTEMS

Denmark's situation should not cause concern in the United States. Denmark's problem is that wind has been too successful too quickly in a small country, and it must now take steps to manage that success. It is unfortunate that the United States has not dealt with its energy problems so decisively. At current levels of use, this issue is still some distance from being a problem on most utility systems.

Up to the point where wind generates about 10 percent of the electricity that the system is delivering in a given hour of the day, there is not an issue. There is enough flexibility built into the system for reserve backup, varying loads, and so forth that there is effectively little difference between a 10 percent wind system and a system with 0 percent wind. Variations introduced by wind are much smaller than routine variations in load (customer demand).

At the point where wind is generating 10–20 percent of the electricity that the system is delivering in a given hour, wind variation becomes an issue that must be addressed, but that probably can be resolved with wind forecasting (which is fairly accurate in the time frame of interest to utility system operators), system software adjustments, and other changes.

Once wind is generating more than about 20 percent of the electricity that the system is delivering in a given hour, the system operator begins to incur significant additional expense because of the need to procure additional equipment that is solely related to the system's increased variability. These figures assume that the utility system has an "average" amount of resources that are complementary to the wind's variability (e.g., hydroelectric dams) and an "average" amount of load that can vary quickly (e.g., electric-arc-furnace steel mills). Actual utility systems can vary quite widely in their ability to handle as-available output resources such as wind farms. However, as wholesale electricity markets grow, fewer larger utility systems are emerging. Therefore, over time, more and more utility systems will look like an "average" system. Since wind is a variable energy source, doesn't it cost utilities extra to accommodate on a system that mostly uses fueled power plants with predictable outputs?

However, the added cost is modest. Three major studies of utility systems with less than 10 percent of their electricity supplied by wind have found the extra or "ancillary" costs of integrating it to be less than 0.2 cent/kWh. Two major studies of systems with wind at 20 percent or more have found the added cost to be 0.3–0.6 cent/kWh.

Advantage and disadvantages of wind power

Advantages

- Wind energy is available globally, the technology is mature, and energy production is relatively inexpensive.

■ After initial installation capital, wind turbines require relatively minimal maintenance and produce energy without producing any atmospheric pollution.
■ Even though wind turbines are very tall, they occupy a minimal footprint such that
the occupied land could be used for agricultural and cattle-rearing purposes.
■ Wind farms offer an economic alternative in rural locations, where grid utility service
installations are not readily available.
■ Wind turbines are one of the best means of providing electrical energy in third-
world countries.
■ In most installations, electric power produced by wind turbines is more competitive
than grid-supplied power.

Disadvantages

■ To produce power, wind turbines require minimum wind speeds of 7 mi/h, which
means that power produced by windmills must be supplemented with an alternative
source of electric power.
■ Owing to the possibility of accidental bird collision with wind turbine blades and
the disturbance of marine life in offshore installations, some animal protection
groups and environmentalists object to wind energy production.
■ Owing to the imposing structure heights of windmills, most people in urban areas
object to landscape disfigurement.
■ During the process of manufacturing, some pollution is produced.
■ To harvest dependable amounts of energy from wind, large numbers of turbines
must be installed in sufficient quantities in rural locations. These locations must
have appropriate atmospheric wind current conditions to ensure a higher probability
of power production. Wind turbine output production often must be supplemented
with auxiliary gas turbines or other energy-production means to provide some
degree of power-production stability.

9

OCEAN ENERGY TECHNOLOGIES

This chapter addresses a number of technologies that are used to harvest oceanic power, which is manifested in many different forms, including waves, tides, and ocean and undercurrents.

Tidal Power

Tidal movement occurs as a result of the twice-daily variations in sea level caused primarily by the moon and, to some extent, the sun. Tidal power has been in use in milling grain since the eleventh century in Britain and France.

Tidal Physics: Effects of the Terrestrial Centrifugal Force

The interaction of the moon and the earth results in bulging of the oceans facing the moon. In the mean time, on the opposite side of the globe, this gravitational effect is partly shielded by earth, which owing to the effect of the centrifugal force of earth's rotation, causes a small bulging out away from the moon. This is known as the *lunar tide*. This process is further complicated by the gravitational effects of the sun, which causes a similar bulging of waters on the facing and opposing sides of the earth. This is known as the *solar tide*.

Since the sun and moon are not in fixed positions in the celestial sphere but rather change positions with respect to each other, their influence on the tidal range, which is the difference between low and high tide, is also affected. For example, when the moon and the sun are in the same plane as the earth, the tidal range results from the superimposition of the ranges owing to the lunar and solar tides. This results in the maximum tidal range (also known as the *spring tides*). On the other hand, when the moon and the

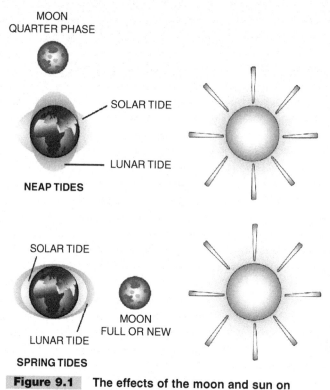

Figure 9.1   The effects of the moon and sun on ocean tides.

sun are at right angles to each other, lower tidal differences are experienced, which results in the *neap tides* (Fig. 9.1).

Tidal Power Generation

The generation of electricity from tides is similar to hydroelectric generation, with the exception that water flows in and out of the turbines in both directions. Therefore, generators are designed to produce power when the rotor is turned in either direction.

A tidal power station, known as an *ebb-generating system,* involves the construction of a dam, known as a *barrage,* across an estuary. A number of sluice gates on the barrage allow the tidal basin to fill with the incoming high tides and to exit through the turbine system on the outgoing tide, referred to as the *ebb tide.* As mentioned earlier, special generators used to produce electricity on both incoming and ebb tides are also possible.

Tidal power is a technology that makes use of captured energy contained in moving water mass owing to tides for conversion into electricity. Types of tidal energies extracted are kinetic energy, which results from currents arising between ebbing and surging tides, and potential energy, which results from the height or head differential between high and low tides.

Power generation from the kinetic energy of tidal currents has proven to be more pragmatic and much more feasible today than the building of ocean-based dams or barrages. At present, many coastal sites worldwide are being evaluated for their suitability for harvesting tidal current energy.

The technology for extracting tidal potential energy involves the construction of barrages and tidal lagoons. The barrage technology traps water at a certain level inside a basin, thus making use of created water differential heights that result when water level outside the basin or lagoon changes relative to the level inside. The differential head static energy is converted into dynamic energy when sluice gates open and a flow is used to drive turbines. Tidal power is considered a renewable resource because the tidal phenomenon is caused by the orbital mechanics of the solar system, which is inexhaustible for the foreseeable future.

The efficiency of tidal power generation largely depends on the amplitude of the tidal swell, which can rise up to 33 ft. These swells then are manifested as tidal waves, which are funneled into rivers, fjords, and estuaries. Amplitudes of up to 56 ft have been observed in the Bay of Fundy, Canada. Superimposition of tidal waves gives rise to tidal resonance, which amplifies tidal waves.

The energy potential contained in a volume of water is determined by the formula $E = xmg$, where x is the height of the tide, m is the mass of water, and g is the acceleration of gravitational energy.

Tidal energy generators are installed in locations where high-amplitude tides occur. Some of the most significant worldwide installation locations include Russia, the United States, Canada, Australia, Korea, and the United Kingdom, as discussed below. Smaller-scale tidal power plants are also in operation in Norway.

BARRAGES

Tidal barrages, as mentioned earlier, are used to trap water in basins by means of mechanical doors referred to as *sluice gates*. The basic elements of a barrage are caissons, embankments, sluice gates, turbines, and ship locks. Sluices, turbines, and ship locks are housed in the caisson, a large concrete-block compartment. Embankments are used to seal the basins where they are not sealed by caissons. Sluice-gate construction resembles a flap gate that is raised vertically.

INSTALLED CAPACITY

The total rated capacity of turbines is specially optimized to meet the performance requirements of each barrage construction. In small-capacity installations, where a barrage is capable of producing only small amounts of energy, the turbines will operate at low power-production capacity over a long period of time.

In large-capacity reservoirs, where the basins can be drained very quickly in every cycle, power generation is at a very high rate but lasts only for short periods of time. This makes it somewhat incompatible for grid interconnection. Fast pond water level drainage also can have negative effects on the environment.

MODES OF OPERATION

Ebb generation   In tidal ebbs, the basin is filled through the sluices when turbines are set in freewheeling mode until high tide. On filling the reservoir, the sluice gates and turbine gates are kept closed until the sea level falls to a low enough level to create sufficient head across the barrage. When the sluice gates are lifted, the turbines generate electric power until such time the head becomes low. This cycle is repeated over and over again. This process is known as *ebb generation* or *outflow generation* because power generation occurs as the tide ebbs.

Flood generation   In this power-generation process, the basin is emptied through the sluice gates, and turbines generate electricity at tide flood. This process is relatively less efficient than ebb generation because the volume contained in the upper half of the basin, where ebb-generation systems operate, is greater than the volume of the lower half, where flood generation occurs.

Another factor that contributes to the lower efficiency is based on the fact that main water flow to the basin is from a river and that as the tide rises, the difference between the basin and the sea side of the barrage becomes less than would be desirable.

Bidirectional-flow generation   Certain turbines, as discussed below, are designed in a manner that makes them capable of power generation at tide ebbs and floods.

Pumping   Turbines also can be powered in reverse by excess energy in the grid in order to increase the water level in the basin at high tide for ebb generation and two-way generation. The energy is returned to the grid during generation.

Two-basin schemes   In this type of construction, tidal power generating plants have two basins. One is filled at high tide, and the other is emptied at low tide. In this type of operation, turbines are placed between the two basins. In general, two-basin configurations have added advantages over the normal schemes just described because power-generation time can be adjusted with certain flexibility, allowing for continuous electric power production. Owing to larger construction and capital investment, two-basin schemes are more expensive to build. However, there are geographic locations for which this scheme would be well suited.

Bulb turbines   In general, tidal turbines are constructed to meet the specific requirements of a barrage design. One such turbine is seen at the La Rance tidal plant, near St. Malo on the Brittany coast in France, which uses a bulb turbine

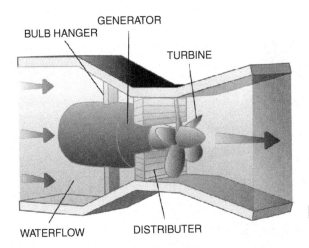

GENERATOR

BULB HANGER

TURBINE

WATERFLOW   DISTRIBUTER

Figure 9.2   Diagram of a bulb turbine.

(Fig. 9.2). In this type of system, water flows around the turbine, making access for maintenance difficult because the water must be prevented from flowing past the turbine.

Rim turbines   Another type of mechanism, referred to as a *rim turbine* (Fig. 9.3), can be seen at the Straflo turbine, in Annapolis Royal in Nova Scotia, Canada. The turbine overcomes maintenance access problem by mounting the generator in the barrage, at right angles to the turbine blades. However, this makes it difficult to regulate the performance of the turbine, and it is unsuitable for use in pumping applications. Another proposed turbine construction involves the use of a design where the blades are connected to a long shaft and are orientated at an angle so that the generator is mounted on top of the barrage. Figure 9.4 shows a tubular turbine diagram.

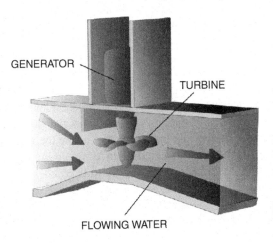

GENERATOR

TURBINE

FLOWING WATER

Figure 9.3   Diagram of a rim turbine.

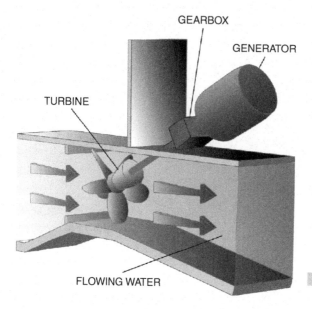

GEARBOX

GENERATOR

TURBINE

FLOWING WATER

Figure 9.4   Diagram of a tubular turbine.

Current Tidal Generation Technologies

The world's largest tidal power barrage station was constructed on the Rance estuary in France nearly 40 years ago. The project generates 240 MW of power. Annapolis Royal Barrage, located in Nova Scotia, Canada, was constructed in 1984. It produces 18 MW of power.

TIDAL FENCES

Tidal fences are composed of individual vertical-axis turbines that are mounted within the fence structure, known as the *caisson*. They can be thought of as giant styles completely blocking a channel and forcing water through them. Currently, there are two developing technologies for harvesting the oceans' energy, one from tidal barrages and the other from tidal streams.

TIDAL BARRAGE

A barrage, or dam, is built across an estuary or bay that has adequate tidal range, which is usually in excess of 5 m. The purpose of the barrage is to let water flow through it into the basin as the tide comes in. The barrage has gates that allow the water to pass through. The gates are closed when the tide stops coming in, trapping the water within the basin or estuary and creating a hydrostatic head. As the tide recedes, the barrage gates are opened, and the hydrostatic head causes the water to come through these gates, driving the turbines and generating power. Power can be generated in both directions through the turbine, although this usually affects efficiency and the economics of

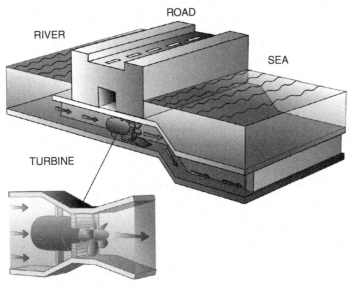

ROAD

RIVER

SEA

TURBINE

Figure 9.5   **La Rance tidal barrage.** *Courtesy of Popular Mechanics.*

the power plant. Turbine technology is inherently similar to hydropower turbines, and the construction of barrages in general requires extensive civil engineering design.

La Rance tidal barrage   The construction of the La Rance tidal barrage began in 1960 (Fig. 9.5). The system consists of a dam that is 330 m long and a basin with a tidal range of 8 m. It incorporates a lock to allow for the passage of small craft. During construction, two temporary dams were built on either side of the barrage to ensure that it would remain dry; this was for safety and convenience. The work was completed in 1967, when twenty-four 5.4-m turbines, rated at 10 MW, were connected to the 225-kV French transmission network.

This barrage uses bulb turbines, described earlier, that were developed by Electricite de France to allow for power generation on both ebbs of the tide.

Bulb-type turbines have been popular with hydropower systems and have been used on mainland Europe in dams on the Rhine and Rhone rivers. Estimates of power generated from the La Rance power station, which provides electricity to a large majority of homes in Brittany, is calculated as follows: The turbines are rated at 10 MW and therefore have a total capacity of 240 MW.

Maximum electricity generated per annum in kWh = 240,000 × 8760 (hours in a year)
= 2,102,400,000 kWh

Wave energy is like most other forms of renewable energy in that it cannot be relied upon 100 percent of the time. This means that the value just quoted almost certainly will never be generated in a year. A value called the *capacity factor* C_f is used to estimate the percentage of the maximum that actually will be generated in a year. A capacity factor of approximately 40 percent is assumed for Scottish waters. Thus

$$\text{Electricity generated per annum in kWh} = 2{,}102{,}400{,}000 \times 0.40$$
$$= 840{,}960{,}000 \text{ kWh}$$

To calculate the number of homes this quantity of electricity will provide for in a year, average annual household consumption is used. Average annual household consumption is assumed to be 4377 kWh/year. Thus

$$\text{Number of homes supplied} = 840{,}960{,}000/4377 = 192{,}131 \text{ homes}$$

Economics   The capital required to start the construction of a barrage is quite significant and has been the main obstacle in the deployment of the technology because it is associated with long payback periods. In general, the advancement of the technology always has been subsidized by government funding or by large organizations getting involved with tidal power. However, once the construction of the barrage is complete, there are few associated maintenance and operational costs. On average, the turbines need replacing only once every 30 years.

The key to the economic success of tidal barrages is an optimal design that can produce the most power with the smallest barrage possible.

Environmental concerns   When constructing tidal barrages, it is important to take into consideration environmental and ecologic effects on the local area, which may be different for each location. The change in water level and possible flooding could affect the vegetation around the coast, having an impact on the aquatic and shoreline ecosystems. The quality of the water in the basin or estuary also could be affected, and the sediment levels could change, affecting the turbidity of the water and thus the animals that live in and depend on it, such as fish and birds. Fish undoubtedly would be affected, unless provisions were made for them to pass through the barrages. Not all these changes adversely affect the environment, though, because some may result in the growth of different species of plants and animals, which may flourish in the area where they are not normally found.

Concerns over the environmental effects of barrage tidal plants present at the La Rance Tidal Power Station have been overcome recently by the development of technologies that have resulted in newly designed tidal turbines (known as *tidal mills*).

Social implications   The building of a tidal barrage can have many social consequences on the surrounding area. An example is seen at the world's largest tidal barrage, La Rance in France, which took over 5 years to construct. The barrage can be used as a road or rail link, providing a time-saving method of crossing the bay or estuary. The bays also could be used as recreation facilities or tourist attractions.

OTHER TIDAL TECHNOLOGIES

Stingray tidal energy   An alternate way of harnessing tidal energy is applied in Stingray. This technology consists of a parallel linkage that holds large hydroplanes to the flow of the tides. The angle of these hydroplanes to the flow of the tide is varied, causing them to move up and down. This motion is used to extend a cylinder that produces high-pressure oil that drives a hydraulic motor, which, in turn, drives an electric generator.

This concept has received recognition for its potential from the U.K. Department of Trade and Industry. Initially, the project was funded by the Department of Industrial Technology and the Water and Power Technologies Panel.

Annapolis Royal and Bay of Fundy, Canada   The following is a BBC news report covering the Bay of Fundy Tidal Power Plant in Canada, which is recognized as the world's most significant geographic location for heist tides:

The one thing that every schoolchild learns about the Bay of Fundy is that it has the highest tides in the world.

The North Atlantic waters are funneled up this deep inlet between the Canadian provinces of New Brunswick and Nova Scotia, swirling through the narrowest parts of the bay with impressive speed and power.

So when in the 1980s the Canadian government wanted to explore the feasibility of tidal power, this was a natural site for an experimental station.

The site chosen at Annapolis Royal had already been closed off by a causeway, built to control tidal flow further up the Annapolis River.

The idea was that water flowing through the sluices could also pass through a turbine and generate power on its way down the Bay of Fundy and out into the sea. Now there is a neat box-like structure in the middle of the causeway, one of only a handful of operational tidal power plants in the world.

PLANT ENGINEERING

Twice every day, as the tide rises, the sluice gates are opened to let water flow up into the lower part of the Annapolis River, which now serves as the headpond for the power station.

Just before high tide, the gates are closed, leaving only a narrow passage for fish to pass. Now all the operators have to do is wait for the tide to turn and the water level on the seaward side to drop.

When there is enough difference between the water levels on the two sides, they begin to let water flow through the giant turbine, slowly at first to get it turning, and then at full strength.

Once the huge 25-m-diameter wheel is up to its operating speed of 50 revolutions per minute, the station starts to generate. At peak power it supplies a very respectable 20 MW to the Canadian grid.

Once the tide has gone out and the water level is equalized, the turbine slows to a stop, before the whole cycle begins again.

Stuart MacDonald of Nova Scotia Power remembers the thrill of seeing the plant in action for the first time. He loves the elegant simplicity of its engineering and its reliability, but accepts that tidal power has its limitations.

BUILT FOR PURPOSE

It may be a predictable source of electricity, but only while the tide is going out. And it is not the sort of thing that can be bought off the shelf; machinery has to be purpose-built for the site, which makes it expensive for a power station which is always going to be idle for at least 12 hours a day.

But at least the fuel is free, and although the plant was designed for a 70-year lifespan, Stuart MacDonald believes that with proper maintenance it could last 200 years. The technology, though, has yet to take off in a significant way.

The biggest tidal station in world is in France, near St Malo, 12 times larger than Annapolis Royal. Russia has a much smaller plant, whereas China has constructed several small facilities.

With fossil fuels getting scarce and expensive and increasing concern about the damage they are causing to the atmosphere, interest in tidal power is growing because these plants produce no greenhouse gas emissions.

Other projects are planned, and designers are now working on plans involving individual turbines moored in the middle of the tidal flow, easier to build and less environmentally controversial than the fixed barrages used by the existing stations.

Islay LIMPET LIMPET stands for "Land-Installed Marine-Powered Energy Transformer," and Islay LIMPET is the world's first wave power device connected to a national grid. The project has been located on the Scottish island of Islay since 2000. The project was sponsored and developed by Wavegen, an investment-based company, in collaboration with Queen's University in Belfast. It is the result of research on the island, where the demonstration plant was capable of generating 75 kW of power (Fig. 9.6).

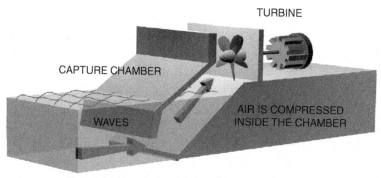

Figure 9.6   Diagram of the Islay LIMPET tidal turbine operation.

The concept involves a wave chamber that is constructed on the shore. The waves cause the air in the chamber to rise and decompress, resulting in a rush of air that drives a Wells' turbine that generates power. Therefore, the turbine has to be capable of turning regardless of the direction of airflow.

This device is currently generating 5 MW of power. This is an example of how the technology can be used to meet small-scale local needs. Wavegen has said that at present, the answer lies not in huge operating plants but rather in small ones such as these, which can concentrate on meeting local or regional needs.

The device, which is rated at 5005 kW according to the following calculations, provides power to 400 households.

$$\text{Maximum power generated per annum} = 500 \times 8760 \text{ (hours in a year)}$$
$$= 4{,}380{,}000 \text{ kWh}$$

Assuming a capacity factor of 40 percent,

$$\text{Annual electricity generated} = 4{,}380{,}000 \times 0.40 = 1{,}752{,}000 \text{ kWh}$$

Assuming a 4377-kWh power demand for each home every year,

$$\text{Number of homes receiving power} = 1{,}752{,}000/4377 = 400$$

Pumping   The turbines in a barrage also can be used to pump extra water into the basin at periods of low demand. This usually coincides with cheap electricity prices, generally at night, when demand is low. Establishments that provide tidal power generally buy inexpensive electrical energy from the grid during periods of low demand, such as night hours, to pump water in the basins and then generate power at times of high demand, when prices are high. This practice is commonly used by hydroelectric power providers and is known as *storage*.

TIDAL POWER SYSTEM OUTPUT

The tidal power schemes just described are not considered a constant source of energy because within a 24-hour period, power production is limited to a maximum of 6–12 hours. Since tidal cycles are based on the revolution of the moon, and electricity demand is based on the revolution of the sun, the energy-production cycle is not long enough to satisfy the power-demand cycle. As a result, grid connection becomes somewhat incompatible.

ENVIRONMENTAL CONSIDERATIONS

Impact on aquatic habitat   The construction of barrage systems in estuaries has a considerable negative impact on the aquatic life within the basin, such as shellfish. With proper ecologic design consideration, lagoons, however, could be used for fish or lobster farming, which could benefit local economies.

Turbidity   Turbidity is the amount of silt and sediment in water, which in time results in a smaller volume of water being exchanged between the basin and the sea. Suspended particulates in the water also prevent light from the sun from penetrating the water, which affects aquatic ecosystem conditions.

Salinity   Salinity, or the dissolved salt content in a body of water, is the result of less water exchange with the sea. The average salinity inside the basin decreases, which also affects the ecosystem. Lagoons, when designed properly, can remedy this problem.

Sediment Movement   In general, rivers flowing through estuaries provide a high volume of sedimentation, which eventually is moved to the sea. The introduction of a barrage into estuaries frequently results in sediment accumulation within the barrage, which negatively affects the ecosystem and creates a significant maintenance and drainage dilemma.

Pollutants   Biodegradable pollutants, such as sewage, increase in concentration and cause bacteria growth within the basin, which, in turn, results in negative human and ecosystem health consequences.

Fish Pass   In some instances, fish pass through these tidal power systems safely. However, when the gates are closed, fish get sucked through turbine fins. Mitigation measures, such as screens or fish-friendly turbine design, seldom prevent fish mortality. Recent research in sonic guidance hopes to provide a solution to this ongoing problem.

ECONOMIC CONSIDERATIONS

Tidal power is both labor- and material-intensive and requires very high capital expenditure. However, once implemented, these systems are relatively inexpensive to run. Most tidal power projects do not produce returns on investment for decades; as such, it is very difficult to attract investors. At present, worldwide projects have been supported by governments that have the required financial resources to support such undertakings.

TIDAL STREAMS

Tidal streams are fast-flowing volumes of water caused by the motion of the tide. These usually occur in the shallow depths of seas, where a natural construct forces the water to speed up. The technology involved is similar to wind energy, although there are differences.

Water is 800 times denser than air and has a much slower flow rate. This means that the turbine experiences much larger forces. This results in turbine designs that have much smaller diameters. The turbines are used to either generate power on both ebbs of the tide or to be able to withstand severe structural strain resulting from the currents. The technology is still in its developmental stage but has the potential to be a reliable and predictable renewable-energy source.

Tidal stream technology has the advantage over tidal barrages when comparing eco-logic issues. The technology is also less intrusive than offshore turbines or tidal bar-rages, which create hazards to navigation and shipping.

TIDAL TURBINES

Tidal turbines (Fig. 9.7) do not pose a problem for navigation and shipping and require the use of much less material in construction. They are also less harmful to the environment. They function best in areas where the water velocity is 2–2.5 m/s. Above this level, the turbine experiences heavy structural loads, and below this level, not enough generation takes place.

Economics   The tidal stream technologies (Fig. 9.8) have been in developmental stages for several years and thus far have been shown to have a significant potential to harvest renewable energy. The cost of using tidal streams is in general site-specific and depends on the type of technology used.

Once installed, electricity is produced with no fuel costs and with complete predictability. The only operational cost will be turbine maintenance, which will depend on the technology used.

There are only a few places on earth where this tide change occurs. Some power plants are already operating using this idea. One plant in France makes enough energy from tides to power 240,000 homes.

Figure 9.7   Stream-energy turbine test. *Courtesy of J. A. Consulting, UK.*

Figure 9.8   **Artist's rendering of a stream-energy turbine.** *Courtesy of J. A. Consulting, U.K.*

Marine-Current Turbine Technologies

Marine-current turbines are, in principle, like submerged windmills. They are installed in the sea at places with high tidal current velocities to take out energy from the huge volumes of flowing water, as shown in Fig. 9.9. These flows have the major advantage of being an energy resource as predictable as the tides that cause them. This is unlike wind or wave energy, which responds to the more random quirks of the weather system.

This technology, under development by Marine Current Turbines (MCT), consists of twin axial-flow rotors 15–20 m in diameter, each now driving a generator via a gearbox, much like a hydroelectric turbine or a wind turbine. The twin power units of each system are mounted on winglike extensions on either side of a tubular steel monopole some 3 m in diameter, which are set into a hole drilled into the seabed from a jack-up barge.

The technology for placing monopoles at sea is well developed by Seacore, Ltd., a specialist offshore engineering company, which is cooperating with MCT in this work. The patented design of the turbine is installed and maintained without the use of costly underwater operations. The diagram shows the turbines in place and one raised for maintenance from a small workboat. The turbine is connected to the shore by a marine cable lying on the seabed, which emerges from the base of the pile.

The submerged turbines generally will be rated at from 500 to 1000 kW each depending on the local flow pattern and peak velocity. They will be grouped in arrays

Figure 9.9   **Artist's rendering of a marine-current turbine.** *Courtesy of Marine Current Technologies, U.K.*

or "farms" under the sea, at places with high currents, in much the same way that wind turbines in a wind farm are set out in rows to catch the wind. The main difference is that marine current turbines of a given power rating are smaller because water is 800 times denser than air, and they can be packed closer together because tidal streams are normally bidirectional, whereas wind tends to be multidirectional. Also, the technology has a low profile and involves negligible environmental impact. Environmental impact analyses completed by independent consultants have confirmed that the technology does not offer any serious threat to fish or marine mammals.

The rotors turn slowly at 10–20 rpm. A ship propeller, by comparison, typically runs 10 times as fast. Moreover, the rotors stay in one place, whereas some ships move much faster than sea creatures can swim. There is no significant risk of leakage of noxious substances, and the risk of impact from the rotor blades is extremely small. This is so because the flow spirals in a helical path through the rotor, and nature has adapted marine creatures so that they do not collide with obstructions (marine mammals generally have sophisticated sonar vision). Another advantage of this technology is that it is modular, so small batches of machines can be installed with only a small period between investment in the technology and the time when revenue starts to flow. This is in contrast to large hydroelectric schemes, tidal barrages, nuclear power stations, or other projects involving major civil engineering, where the time between investment and gaining a return can be relatively large.

It is expected that turbines generally will be installed in batches of about 10–20 machines. Many of the potential sites investigated so far are large enough to accommodate many hundreds of turbines. As a site is developed, the marginal cost of adding more turbines and of maintaining them will decrease, as will the economy of scale as the project grows.

Marine Current Turbines, Ltd., is currently in the process of starting a program of tidal turbine development through research and development (R&D) and demonstration phases for use in commercial manufacture. An initial grant of 1 million euros has been received from the European Commission toward R&D costs, and this has been followed by a grant toward the cost of the first phase of work from the U.K. government worth 960,000 euros. The German partners also received a grant worth approximately 150,000 euros from the German government.

The company's plan is to complete the initial R&D phase by 2006 and to start commercial installations at that time. It is planned that some 300 MW of installations will be completed by 2010, and after that, there is a far larger growth potential from a market literally oceanic in size.

Phase 1 involved the installation of the first large monopole-mounted experimental 300-kW single 11-m diameter rotor system, off Lynmouth in Devon, U.K. (Fig. 9.10). The installation uses a dump load in lieu of a grid connection (to save cost) and generally will operate with the tide in only one direction. The cost is approximately 3.3 million euros.

Phase 2 involved the design, manufacture, installation, and testing of the first full-size twin-rotor system, to be rated at 750–1200 kW (each rotor being slightly larger than in the phase 1 system—the variation depends on the rated velocity for the site chosen). This will be grid connected and will function with the flow in both directions. It will, in fact, be the prototype and test bed for the commercial technology. This phase is expected to cost approximately 4.5 million euros, including grid connection.

Installation of the first small farm of tidal turbines, interconnected with the phase 2 system, probably will involve three to four extra units in order to give an aggregate power of about 4–5 MW for the system—the actual amount depends on how many units and the rated power for the site.

The project will be partly self-financing, through revenue generated from the sale of electricity. However, it still will very much be the final phases of the R&D program form, which means that much will need to be learned about operating several machines together in an array.

Figure 9.10   **Marine-current pile-mounted turbine installation.** *Courtesy of Marine Current Technology, U.K.*

Some Interesting Oceanic Technologies

OCEANIC WAVE POWER

These are technologies that harvest electric power from the dynamics of wave movements. The operationing principles of these technologies are based on an oscillating movement of water columns, as shown in Figs. 9.11 through 9.13. As waves enter the lower chamber, the pressure resulting from air compression forces the propeller to rotate, which, in turn, spins an electric generator shaft.

The impeller mechanism is avoids corrosion because the housing where the blades are mounted does not get in contact with seawater.

THE SLATER DUCK

This technology is quite recent and is similar in function and principle to the two generators just described. These devices harness ocean wave energy by a pendulum mechanism that resembles a floating duck. The mechanism bobs when moved up and down by waves and produces a pendulum movement that drives a turbine within each floating unit. It is anchored to the sea bed and arranged in special patterns that take maximum advantage of wave movements.

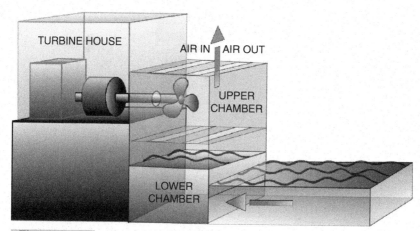

Figure 9.11   Diagram of an oceanic air column wave power.

POWER-GENERATING SEA BUOY

This U.S.-patented technology employs a pendulum-movement mechanism that is similar to preceding technologies. It develops power from the upward and downward movement of sea waves (Fig. 9.14).

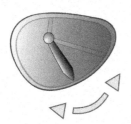

As the Salter Duck moves with the motion of the waves, the pendulum inside swings forward and backward generating electricity.

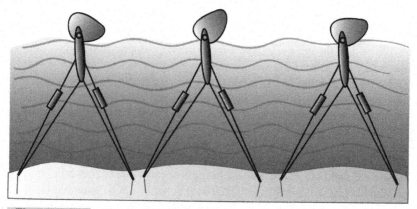

Figure 9.12   Diagram of an oceanic wave Slater Duck power generator.

Figure 9.13   Oceanic wave Slater Duck power generator
encasement. *Courtesy of MARTIFER.*

The system is used to provide power for buoys and monitoring devices that keep
track of oceanic parameters such as wave height, water temperature, and wave directional movement. The devices also do seismic monitoring of the ocean floor for tsunami
warnings. In most instances, the data are transmitted to a remote data-monitoring center
via satellite.

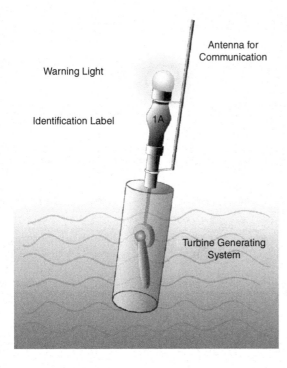

Antenna for
Communication

Warning Light

Identification Label

1A

Turbine Generating
System

Figure 9.14   Artist's rendering of oceanic buoy power
generator.

HYDROELECTRIC AND MICRO-HYDRO TURBINE POWER

As discussed in earlier chapters, the dynamics of water energy are a result of the constant movement and transformation of the global cycle, which results from the effects of solar energy. The cycle consists of the evaporation of oceans and seas, waters from which clouds and precipitation, as rain or snow, are formed. The cycle is completed after this water returns to the earth as precipitation and flows back to the oceans and seas. The energy of the water cycle is tapped by a wide variety of technologies, including hydropower stations.

Ancient civilizations used water wheels to relieve humans of some forms of manual labor. Water power was used by the Greeks around 4000 BC. The Greeks used hydropower to turn water wheels for grinding wheat into flour. With invention of the water turbine in the early 1800s, hydroelectric power technology soon was advanced to produce electricity.

The main advantage of hydroelectric power is that it is renewable and generates no atmospheric pollution during operation. It also has relatively low operational and maintenance costs. Another positive attribute of hydroelectric projects is that the dams that hold the water and the resulting reservoirs can be used as recreational facilities. Disadvantages associated with hydroelectric power generation include high initial capital cost and potential site-specific negative environmental and ecologic impacts, which will be discussed in detail below.

Hydroelectric Power Plants

Among the variety of renewable-energy resources, hydroelectric power is the most desirable for utility systems that have successful and proven track records. Power generated from hydroelectric plants can exceed 10 GW. On the European continent, Norway generates 98 percent of its electrical energy from hydroelectric power. It is estimated that at this time, only about 10 percent of the world's hydroelectric potential has been exploited. The remaining untapped potential is in Africa and Asia.

Presently, the world's total installed hydropower capacity is about 630,000 MW. Annual worldwide power production is estimated to be 2200 billion kWh, which means that power plants are running at 40 percent of their rated power-production capacity. The largest hydroelectric complex in the world, Itaipu, is located on the Parana River, which flows between Paraguay and Brazil. The Itaipu hydroelectric power-generation complex has 18 turbines, which collectively produce 12,600 MW of electricity.

Currently, a number of large hydroelectric power dams are being built throughout Asia. In 1999, China completed its 3300-MW Ertan hydroelectric power station, which has six turbines that generate a total of 550 MW. The Indian government similarly has approved the construction of 12 large-scale hydroelectric power station projects that would add 3700 MW to the country's electric power-generation capacity.

One of the world's largest hydroelectric projects is currently under construction in China. The project, with a capacity of 18.2 GW, has been named the *Three Gorges Dam* and has entered into the second phase of the three-phase construction. On completion of phase 3 in 2009, the power station will be providing full power generation. The estimated construction cost of the dam is projected to be about $25 billion (US). The Three Gorges Dam will extend 2 km across the Yangtze, will be 200 m tall, and will create a 550-km-long reservoir.

However, the construction of such a hydroelectric project comes with negative side effects. Construction of the dam has created serious environmental and social problems, including water pollution along the Yangtze River, with numerous pollutants from mining operations, factories, and human settlements that have been washed out to sea by the strong currents of the river.

In coming years, silt in the river is expected to be deposited at the upstream end of the dam, which inevitably will clog the major tributaries. According to recent reports, an estimated 2 million people have been resettled, and 1300 archaeological sites will be moved or flooded. Construction of the dam also has resulted in the destruction of the natural habitats of several endangered species and rare plants.

HYDROELECTRIC POWER POTENTIAL

Hydroelectric power plant potential consists of two parameters, namely, the amount of water flow per unit of time and the vertical height, or head, that water can be made to fall. In some instances, water head may be attributed to natural site topography, or it may be created artificially by constructing dams. Water accumulation in a dam depends on the intensity, distribution, and duration of rainfall, as well as direct evaporation, transpiration, ground infiltration, and the field moisture capacity of the basin or reservoir soil.

Potential power derived from waterfalls depends on their height and the rate of flow. The available hydropower is calculated from the following formula:

$$P = 9.8 \times q \times h$$

where P = acceleration of gravity in meters per second squared (m/s^2)
$\quad\quad q$ = water flow rate in cubic meters per second (m^3/s)
$\quad\quad h$ = water head in meters (m)

The calculated power derived by this formula does not include power losses resulting from friction and turbine efficiency. The overall power-generation efficiency of a hydropower generating plant could be as high as 90 percent or more.

The following example illustrates the power-production potential of a hydroelectric power-generation plant. It has a head of 300 m and an average flow of 1200 m^3/s, with the assumption that the dam dike covers an area of 2000 km^2.

Hydropower potential

$$P = 9.8 \times q \times h = 9.8 \times 1200 \times 300 = 3520 \text{ MW}$$

Since the flow is 1200 m^3/s, a drop of 1 m in water level corresponds to

$$2000 \times 1,000,000 = 2,000,000,000$$

The time taken for the volume of water to pass through the turbine is

$$t = 2,000,000,000/1200 = 463 \text{ hours} = 19.3 \text{ days}$$

Theoretically, an equivalent fossil fuel–powered generating operation, when compared with a hydroelectric plant with a power-generating capacity of 5000 kWh, would require approximately 20 million barrels of oil per day. A simple rule of thumb is this: If the amount of pollution by fossil fuels is conservatively estimated at 6 lb/kW, then the total generated hourly pollution created by the thermal power will be in the neighborhood of 30,000 lb. Figures 10.1 through 10.3 illustrate various aspects of a hydroelectric power-generating dam.

Environmental Effects of Hydroelectric Power

Some negative factors and setbacks associated with the construction of hydroelectric projects are related to the initial capital investment and irreversible ecologic and environmental damage associated with dam construction and operation. A watercourse is an ecologic system that can be seriously affected when disturbed by human intervention. For example, changes in water flow may affect the quality of the water and the reproduction of fish downstream. Dams and barriers are known to alter the ecologic

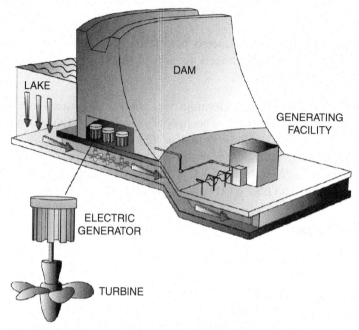

DAM

LAKE

GENERATING
FACILITY

ELECTRIC
GENERATOR

TURBINE

Figure 10.1   Diagram of a hydroelectric power-generating
system.

Figure 10.2   Diagram of a hydroelectric power dam.

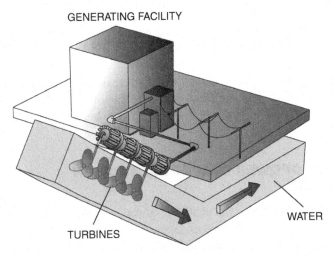

GENERATING FACILITY

WATER

TURBINES

Figure 10.3   Diagram of a hydroelectric generating facility.

conditions of aquatic life. The construction of artificial lakes and dam reservoirs often prevents the migration of downstream fish to upstream habitats.

Environmental changes resulting from the construction of dams affect aquatic ecology along entire stretches of rivers and streams, even affecting life at inlets to the sea. Changes in water flow resulting from the construction of dams also lead to changes in the transportation of sediment, which, in turn, reduces water nutrient quality, essential to the survival of aquatic life.

Dam reservoirs of hydropower plants affect the flow of watercourses and disturb natural groundwater levels in surrounding areas, which, in turn, influence the quality of water and sediment transport, often resulting in area runoff and ground erosion.

The entrapment of nutrients in reservoirs usually results in the excessive accumulation of ground-bed fertilization, often leading to an increased growth of algae. This, in turn, may cause anaerobic conditions, or a lack of oxygen, in the deep-water layers, which can destroy aquatic life.

Warm-weather conditions that cause water evaporation also may cause an increased concentration of nutrients, leading to excessive fertilization. As a result of changes in water quality, habitat reproduction for some species could be hindered or prevented during the spawning period. Submerged grounds and water-flow changes alter myriad habitats and can cause animal extinction.

EFFECTS OF DAM CONSTRUCTION ON LOCAL POPULATIONS

Large hydropower plants with dams require large reservoirs and discharge areas, which in some instances force inhabitants to evacuate the grounds. Adverse social consequences on local populations include the relocation and transfer of indigenous groups of people, which may endanger their entire cultural system. Evidence of such social disturbance has been associated with construction of the Three Gorges Dam in China, where thousands of villagers were forcefully displaced and relocated to newer grounds.

Similarly, construction of the Aswan Dam in Egypt resulted in the displacement of hundreds of villages and damaged and destroyed historical and cultural landscapes, including ancient monuments, holy places, and burial grounds of great importance.

IMPACT OF HYDROPOWER DAM CONSTRUCTION ON HUMAN HEALTH

Hydroelectric power plants increase the incidence of water-related diseases caused by pathogens such as typhus, cholera, dysentery, tapeworm, and roundworm. Some of the diseases that increased as a result of construction of the Aswan Dam include bilharzia, malaria, filariasis, sleeping sickness, and yellow fever.

Reservoirs with large, stagnant waters and slow water-level variations offer favorable growth conditions for a variety of pathogens. Excessive aquatic vegetation growth, resulting from increased fertilizer concentration, blocks ultraviolet rays and provides fertile ground for infection-carrying bacteria that otherwise would have been destroyed by sunlight. Vegetation also promotes the growth of mosquito species carrying malaria and filariasis. The seepage of contaminated water from reservoirs into groundwater wells increases the risk of infection that can spread by pathogens in the drinking water.

Hydroelectric Power Technology

As mentioned earlier, hydropower energy generation is achieved by turbines and generators that convert the dynamic or static energy of water into mechanical and then electrical energy. Turbines and generators are located either within the dam structure or in the vicinity of the dam and are driven by pressurized water, which is transported from the dam through penstocks or pipelines. Hydropower technology, when compared with conventional thermal power-generating plants, is much more efficient and can produce twice the amount of power. The efficiency of hydroelectric plants can be attributed to the fact that the kinetic energy of water that falls a vertical distance represents energy that gets converted into mechanical rotary power without efficiency loss. This is as opposed to the conversion of calorics of biomass into energy, which has a significant intrinsic loss of efficiency.

The turbines and generators associated with hydropower are based on well-established and well-developed technologies, are relatively simple to manufacture, are highly reliable, and have an extended lifespan of about 50 years. On the contrary, thermal combustion–based power-generation technology is relatively complicated, has a shorter life span, and has lower reliability.

Classification of Hydropower Energy Facilities

Hydropower technologies are classified into two types of operational categories: conventional and pumped-storage types. Power plants, in turn, are rated for power capacity. This includes large or small; low, medium, or high head of water; type of turbine used, such as Kaplan, Francis, or Pelton; and finally, the location and type of dam or reservoir.

CONVENTIONAL HYDROPOWER SYSTEMS

Conventional hydropower plants derive energy from rivers, streams, canal systems, and reservoirs. This category of power-generating station is further divided in two sub-categories: impoundment and diversion. Impoundment-type hydropower generating stations use dam structures to store water. Water from reservoirs is released, and flow is controlled by vanes that maintain a constant water level. In diversion-type hydropower technology, a portion of a river's water is diverted through a canal or penstock. Some installations require a dam.

PUMPED-STORAGE HYDROPOWER SYSTEMS

A pumped-storage hydropower plant is constructed from two reservoirs built at different altitudes. During periods of increased electric demand, water from the higher reservoir is released to the lower reservoir to generate electricity. Power generation results from the release of kinetic energy, which is created by discharge through high-pressure shafts that direct the water through turbines connected to generator motors. On completion of the power-generation period, which occurs during the daytime when the demand for and cost of energy are high, water is pumped back to the upper reservoir for storage, when the demand for and cost of energy are low. Even though pumped-storage facilities consume more energy than they generate, they are used by power utility companies to provide peak power production when needed. In some installations, pumped-storage plants operate on a full-cycle basis.

Hydroelectric Plant Equipment

Major components and machinery used in hydroelectric plants are dam water-flow controls, reservoir controls, turbine controls, electric generator controls, power-transformation equipment required for converting electricity from low to high voltages, transmission lines required to conduct electricity from the plant to the electric distribution system, and finally, penstock systems that carry water to the turbines. Turbines used in hydroelectric power systems are classified in several ways related to their method of functional operation, such as impulse and reaction turbines. Another classification is related to the way the turbine is constructed, such as shaft arrangement or feed-of-water arrangement. Turbines are also designed in a manner that allows them to operate as a pump or as a combination of mechanisms.

For example, impulse-turbine design employs a special nozzle that converts the water under pressure into a fast-moving jet. The jet of water then is directed at the turbine wheel, or runner, which converts the kinetic energy of the water into shaft rotational power. Another example is a Francis turbine, which uses the full head of water available to generate rotational power. Most hydraulic turbines consist of a shaft-mounted water wheel or runners that are located within a water passage that conducts water from higher elevations to lower ones below the dam. Without exception, all hydraulic turbine generators are designed to turn at a constant speed. Constant speed is achieved by a device called a *governor,* a rotating ball mechanism that is balanced by the rotational centrifugal force and keeps each generator operating at its proper speed through the operation of flow-control gates in water passage. Figure 10.4 is a graphic diagram of a pumped-storage hydroelectric power-generating system.

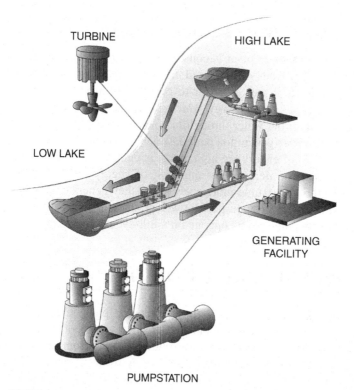

Figure 10.4   Diagram of a pumped-storage hydroelectric power-generating system.

PELTON TURBINE

A Pelton turbine is based on the same principals as a classic water wheel. This type of a turbine is used in applications where heads exceed 40 m. In some instances, the turbine is used for heads as high as 2000 m. In settings where the water head is lower than 250 m, Francis turbines are given preference.

FRANCIS TURBINE

The main difference between this technology and a Pelton turbine is that the runner is completely submerged in water, which results in decreased water pressure from the inlet to the outlet. Water flow in the turbine is directed radially toward the center. The guide vanes within the turbine are arranged so that the energy of the water is largely converted into rotary motion.

KAPLAN TURBINE

This type of turbine is designed for use in situations where the water head is low, but there are high flow rates. In the Kaplan turbine, the water flows through the propeller and sets it in rotation. The design of the turbine is such that the area through the water flow is as big as it can be to allow the entire blade area to be swept by water current, which makes the technology very suitable for large-volume flows where the head is only a few meters. Water enters the turbine laterally, is deflected by the guide vanes, and flows axially through the propeller, striking the blades during exit. The construction of this type of turbine is relatively simple. Its application is limited to heads that range from 1 to 30 m, and it also requires a relatively large flow of water. The engineering and construction of large hydroelectric power plants require extensive capital investment and involve very sophisticated manufacturing technology and electromechanical equipment and significant feasibility studies, environmental impact reports, and civil construction activities. Large-scale hydropower stations also require in-depth environmental investigation and social-impact considerations.

Case Studies of Hydroelectric Power Plants

HOOVER DAM

The following coverage of Hoover Dam was obtained from the U.S. Department of the Interior, Bureau of Reclamations Web site. The Web site provides the story of the dam's construction and development, which includes very interesting historical and engineering footnotes.

Hoover Dam is the highest and third-largest concrete dam in the United States. The dam, powerplant, and high-voltage switchyards are located in the Black Canyon of the

Colorado River on the Arizona-Nevada state line. Lake Mead, the reservoir behind the dam, holds an average 2-year flow of the Colorado River. Hoover Dam's authorized principal objective was to regulate river flow and improve navigation and flood control, the second objective was to deliver stored water for irrigation and other domestic uses, and the third objective was to harvest electrical energy. Lake Mead also provides outstanding outdoor water-based recreation opportunities and is home to a myriad of wildlife.

Project-development plan Water from the Colorado River is impounded by Hoover Dam. This water is released when needed to meet downstream demands for irrigation and domestic water or when the dam is being operated under flood-control criteria.

The water is released at a time and in a way so as to meet the water-delivery needs of the area and to maximize other benefits, including power generation. Irrigation water is provided to numerous projects in the lower Colorado River Basin, including the Imperial Irrigation District and the Coachella Valley Water District, through the All-American Canal System. The All-American Canal System includes the Gila Project, the Yuma Auxiliary Project, the Palo Verde Diversion Project near Blythe, California, the Colorado River Indian Reservation, and the Central Arizona Project. A dependable supply of water for domestic purposes is also provided to the semiarid southern California coastal region, central and southern Arizona, and southern Nevada. Water for southern California is diverted at Lake Havasu and transported through the Metropolitan Water District's Colorado River Aqueduct to the district's area of use. Water for Arizona is also diverted from Lake Havasu by the Central Arizona Project Aqueduct and transported into the state's interior. Southern Nevada withdraws its water from Lake Mead through the Robert B. Griffith Water Project, formerly called the Southern Nevada Water Project.

Lake Mead facilities Hoover Dam is located about 35 miles from Las Vegas, Nevada. It is constructed from very thick concrete and measures 726.4 ft high and 1244 ft long at the crest. The dam contains about 3,250,000 yd^3 of concrete. The total concrete in the dam and appurtenant works is 4,400,000 yd^3. The reservoir behind the dam, known as Lake Mead, has a total storage capacity of 32,471,000 acre-ft. Following completion of a sedimentation survey conducted in 1963–1964, it was calculated that the total storage capacity had been reduced to 27,377,000 acre-ft, which includes 1.5 million acre-ft of space reserved exclusively for flood control.

To bypass and control the river during construction, four 50-ft-diameter concrete-lined tunnels were constructed through the canyon walls, two on each side of the river. The tunnels averaged about 4000 ft in length. After completion of the dam, the upstream tunnel entrances were closed by huge steel gates, and concrete plugs were placed near the midpoint of each tunnel. The downstream sections were incorporated into the dam's spillway and outlet works. A total of 315,000 yd^3 of concrete was used to line the diversion tunnels. Figure 10.5 is a photograph of Hoover Dam and its hydroelectric power-generating station.

The dam complex includes two drum-gate controlled-channel spillways, one on each side of the canyon. Each spillway discharges through an inclined, concrete-lined

Figure 10.5 Hoover Dam and its hydroelectric power-generating station.
Courtesy of the U.S. Bureau of Reclamation.

tunnel that connects with the remaining portion of the original outer diversion tunnel downstream from the tunnel plug. The crest of each spillway is surmounted by three piers that divide the crest into four 100-ft sections. Each is equipped with a 16- by 100-ft drum gate. The spillway capacity at reservoir elevation is 1229 ft and has a discharge capacity of 64,800 ft^3/s. At a surface elevation of 1229 ft, with the gates lowered, the discharge capacity of the spillways is 400,000 ft^3/s.

The dam's design consists of a combination of four penstock and outlet units, each originating at one of the four intake towers located upstream from the dam. They are installed in a tunnel located at the back of the dam abutments. The penstock and outlet units originating at the upstream intake towers are installed in the inner pair of the four tunnels originally used for river diversion. The two penstock and outlet units originating at the downstream intake towers are installed in tunnels located about 170 ft above the lower units. Beyond the penstock outlets, each downstream unit branches into outlet pipes that terminate in the Arizona and Nevada canyon-wall valve houses.

The discharge capacity of the canyon-wall and tunnel-plug outlets at the reservoir's water surface, at an elevation of 1225 ft, is 52,600 ft^3/s. The total release capacity through the canyon-wall outlet works, which include the tunnel-plug outlet works and the generating units, is 100,600 ft^3/s.

Hydroelectric power plant   The hydroelectric power plant is located at the top of Hoover Dam and extends downstream 650 ft along each canyon wall. The turbines are designed to operate at heads ranging from 420 to 590 ft. The final generating unit, designated N-8, was installed at Hoover Dam in 1961, giving the dam a total of 17 commercial generating units. The installation of unit N-8 brought the power plant's rated capacity to 1,850,000 hp. Two station-service units, rated at 3500 hp each, increased the plant's total power output capacity to 1,857,000 hp. In terms of electrical energy, the total rated capacity for the plant was 1,344,800 kW. The dam complex also includes two transformer station-service units, each rated at 2400 kW. Between 1982 and 1993, the 17 commercial generating units were replaced with new turbines and transformers, which raised hydroelectric power capacity to its current level of 2,991,000 hp, or 2,074,000 kW.

The dam, power plant, and all its facilities are owned, operated, and maintained by the U.S. government. Prior to 1987, the power plant, transformer, and switching facilities were operated and maintained by the Los Angeles Department of Water and Power and the Southern California Edison Company.

Brief history   Through the conclusion of the Mexican-American War in 1848, the subsequent Treaty of Guadalupe Hidalgo, and the Gadsden Purchase of 1853, the United States acquired the territories of New Mexico, Arizona, and California. The discovery of gold in California in 1849 brought hordes of adventurers westward. They crossed the Colorado River near Yuma, Arizona, and at Needles, California. In 1857, Lieutenant J. C. Ives traveled 400 miles up the river by boat from the Gulf of California to the Black Canyon, the present site of the Hoover Dam. He reported the region to be valueless.

In 1869, Major J. W. Powell of the U.S. Geological Survey succeeded in leading a river expedition down the canyons of the Colorado River. The expedition went from the Green River in Utah to the Virgin River in Nevada through more than a thousand miles of unknown rapids and treacherous canyons.

In 1875, a route was mapped for a canal to irrigate southern California's rich but arid land. Construction of the canal began about 20 years later, and in 1901, the first water from the Colorado River flowed through the Imperial Canal into the Imperial Valley.

The river, annually fed by melting snows from the Rocky Mountains, typically swelled to a raging flood by spring. It then dried to a trickle in the late summer and fall so that crops frequently were destroyed. Farmers built levees to keep the river out, but even when the levees held, crops withered and died when the river ran too low to be diverted into the canals.

In 1905, a disastrous flood burst the banks of the river. It flowed for nearly 2 years into the Salton Sink in the Imperial Valley, creating what is now known as the Salton Sea. The river eventually was turned back into its original channel, but the continuing threats of floods remained.

Faced with constantly recurring cycles of flood and drought, residents of the Southwest appealed to the then U.S. Reclamation Service to solve the problem. Engineers began extensive studies of the river in search of a feasible plan for its control. In 1918, a plan was conceived for regulation of the river through the construction a single dam of unprecedented height in Boulder Canyon, about 8 miles upstream from the dam's eventual location. The Colorado River Compact, signed at Santa Fe, New Mexico, on November 24, 1922, cleared the way for construction of the dam by allocating most of the river's estimated flow between the upper and lower basins and providing for later division of what was thought to be excess water.

The project was authorized on December 21, 1928, and was subject to the terms of the Colorado River Compact. The act authorized the construction of a dam and power plant in either Boulder or Black Canyon. The Boulder Canyon Project Adjustment Act, dated July 19, 1940, provided for certain changes in the original plan.

On October 1, 1977, in accordance with the Department of Energy Organization Act of August 4, 1977, the power marketing function, which included transmission lines and attendant facilities of the U.S Bureau of Reclamation, was transferred to the Department of Energy. However, the operation and maintenance of federal hydroelectric generating plants along the Colorado River remained under the Bureau of Reclamation's jurisdiction. On October 9, 1977, the administrations of Hoover Dam and part of the Parker-Davis Dam Project were combined into one operational unit that was called the Lower Colorado Dams Project.

On August 17, 1984, Congress passed the Hoover Power Plant Act of 1984. This act authorized an increase in the capacity of existing generating equipment at Hoover Dam and included improvements in parking, visitor areas , roadways, and other facilities that would contribute to the safety and convenience of guests at Hoover Dam. A detailed timeline of the history of Hoover Dam can be found at the end of this section.

Benefits of the dam

Irrigation   The project ensures a dependable water supply for the irrigation of more than 1 million acres of land in southern California and southwestern Arizona and over 400,000 acres in Mexico. These irrigated lands supply enormous amounts of produce and other agricultural products for the nation's markets.

Municipal and Industrial   Hoover Dam helps to ensure a dependable water supply for municipal, industrial, and domestic use in southern Nevada, Arizona, and southern California. More than 16 million people and countless other industries in these three states receive Colorado River water that was stored by Hoover Dam.

Recreation and Fish and Wildlife   Surrounded by rugged mountains and canyon walls, Hoover Dam and Lake Mead are outstanding scenic and recreational attractions. More than 1 million people a year now take guided tours of Hoover Dam, and more than 9 million people visit the Lake Mead National Recreation Area annually. The Lake Mead National Recreation Area (LMNRA) is administered by the National Park Service. National Park Service concessionaires provide facilities such as lodge and trailer accommodations, boats for hire, and sightseeing boat trips on the lake, as well as through Black Canyon below the dam. Other popular activities are camping, picnicking, swimming, boating, water skiing, and year-round fishing for striped bass, large-mouth bass, and other game fish. A large part of the area is open to hunting.

Guided tours of the dam have been provided by the Bureau of Reclamation since 1936, with only a brief hiatus during World War II. Prior to 1995, physical limitations at the dam restricted the number of guided tours to about 750,000 people a year. New visitor facilities, opened at the dam in June 1995, made it possible for more people to take a guided tour of the dam and power plant. In the 1999 fiscal year (October 1, 1998 to September 30, 1999), nearly 1.2 million people took guided tours of the facility.

Hydroelectric Power   Hoover Dam is one of the world's largest producers of electric power, generating, on average, 4 billion kWh of firm hydroelectric energy annually. This energy played a vital role in the production of airplanes and other equipment during World War II. It also was instrumental in the development of industrial expansion in the Southwest.

Firm power generated at Hoover Dam is provided to 15 contractors in the states of California, Arizona, and Nevada under contracts that were signed in 1987 and that will expire in 2017. The approximate percentage of firm power delivered to each state is Nevada, 23.4 percent; Arizona, 19 percent; and California, 57.6 percent.

Flood Control   Hoover Dam has virtually ended the possibility of devastating floods striking the lower reaches of the Colorado River, as they did prior to project construction. About $25 million of the project cost was allocated by Congress to flood control. From 1950 to 1998, flood-control benefits provided by Hoover Dam and other structures on the mainstream Colorado River were approximated at nearly $1 billion dollars.

Chronology of Hoover Dam construction

- 1540: Alarcon discovers the Colorado River and explores its lower reaches. Cardenas discovers the Grand Canyon.
- 1776: Father Escalante explores the upper Colorado River and its tributaries.
- 1857: Lt. J. C. Ives navigates the Colorado River and with his steamboat, the *Explorer,* reaches the end of Black Canyon.
- 1869: Major John Wesley Powell makes the first recorded trip through the Grand Canyon.
- 1902: President Theodore Roosevelt signs the Reclamation Act. Reclamation engineers begin their long series of investigations and reports on the control and use of the Colorado River.
- 1905–1907: The Colorado River breaks into the Imperial Valley, causing extensive damage and creating the Salton Sea.
- 1916: An unprecedented flood pours down the Gila River into the Colorado River, and flood waters sweep into Yuma Valley.
- 1918: Arthur P. Davis, reclamation director and chief engineer, proposes control of the Colorado River by a dam of unprecedented height in Boulder Canyon on the Arizona-Nevada border.
- 1919: All-American Canal Board recommends the construction of the All-American Canal, and a bill is introduced to authorize its construction.

- 1920: Congress passes the Kinkaid Act, authorizing the Secretary of the Interior to investigate problems in the Imperial Valley.
- 1922: Fall-Davis report, entitled, "Problems of Imperial Valley and Vicinity," prepared under the Kinkaid Act and submitted to Congress on February 28, recommends construction of the All-American Canal and a high dam on the Colorado River at or near Boulder Canyon. Representatives of the seven Colorado River Basin states sign the Colorado River Compact in Santa Fe, New Mexico, on November 24. First of the Swing-Johnson bills to authorize a high dam and canal is introduced in Congress.
- 1924: Weymouth report expands Fall-Davis report and further recommends Boulder Canyon project construction.
- 1928: Colorado River Board of California reports favorably on the feasibility of the project. Boulder Canyon Project Act, introduced by Senator Johnson and Representative Swing, passes the Senate on December 14, the House on December 18, and is signed by President Calvin Coolidge on December 21.
- 1929: Six of the seven basin states approve the Colorado River Compact. Boulder Canyon Project Act declared effective on June 25.
- 1930: Contracts for the sale of electrical energy to cover dam and power-plant financing are completed.
- 1931: The Bureau of Reclamation opens bids for the construction of the Hoover Dam and Power Plant on March 4. It awards contracts to six companies on March 11 and gives contractors notice to proceed on April 20.
- 1932: Colorado River is diverted around the dam site on November 14. Repayment contract for construction of the All-American Canal is completed with the Imperial Irrigation District.
- 1933: First of the concrete is placed on June 6.
- 1934: All-American Canal construction begins in August. Repayment contract between the United States and the Coachella Valley Water District covering the cost of Coachella Main Canal is executed October 15.
- 1935: Dam starts impounding water in Lake Mead on February 1. Last of the concrete is placed in dam on May 29. President Franklin D. Roosevelt dedicates the dam on September 30.
- 1936: First generator, N-2, goes into full operation on October 26. Second generator, N-4, goes into operation on November 14. Third generator, N-1, starts production on December 28.
- 1937: Generators N-3 and A-8 begin operation on March 22 and August 16, respectively.
- 1938: Lake Mead storage reaches 24 million acre-ft, and lake extends 110 miles upstream. Generators N-5 and N-6 begin operation June 26 and August 31, respectively
- 1939: Storage in Lake Mead reaches 25 million acre-ft, more than 8 trillion gal. Generators A-7 and A-6 begin operation on June 19 and September 12, respectively. With an installed capacity of 704,800 kW, the Hoover Power Plant is the largest hydroelectric facility in the world, a distinction held until surpassed by Grand Coulee Dam in 1949.

- 1940: Power generation for the year totals 3 billion kWh. All-American Canal placed in operation. Metropolitan Water District of Southern California successfully tests its Colorado River Aqueduct.
- 1941: Lake Mead elevation reaches 1220.45 ft above sea level on July 30. The lake is 580 ft deep and 120 miles long. Spillways are tested on August 6, the first time they have ever been used. Generator A-1 is placed in service on October 9. Dam closes to public at 5:30 p.m. on December 7, the day of the attacks on Pearl Harbor, and traffic moves over the dam under convoy for duration of World War II.
- 1947: The Eightieth Congress passes legislation officially designating the Boulder Canyon Project's key structure *Hoover Dam* in honor of President Herbert Hoover.
- 1961: The power installation at Hoover Dam is complete when the final generating unit, N-8, goes online on December 1. The installed generating capacity of the Hoover Power Plant, including station-service units, reaches 1,334,800 kW.
- 1985: Hoover Dam celebrates its fiftieth anniversary. Most of the cost of the Boulder Canyon Project has now been repaid to the Federal Treasury.

ASWAN DAM

History The Aswan Dam was designed in 1899 by British engineer Sir William Willcocks. Construction was undertaken by two notable engineers, Sir Benjamin Baker and Sir John Aird, and the project was completed in 1902. The gravity dam measured 1900 m long and 54 m high. On completion of the project, it was found that the initial design was inadequate in curbing water spillage. Hence the design was modified, and the height of the dam was raised.

In 1946, the dam came close to a catastrophic overflow, at which time the Egyptian government decided to construct a new dam that would be built 4 miles up the Nile River. On completion of the initial investigation by Soviet engineers, project planning began in 1952, which coincided with the Nasser Revolution. Initially, the United States and Britain were to assist in financing the dam's construction through a loan of $270 million. This was in return for Nasser's leadership in a resolution to the Arab-Israeli conflict. However, owing to U.S. policy at the time, the offer was canceled in 1956. The dam would go on to be closed in April 1957 owing to bitter conflict surrounding its construction. Today, the dam is a major shipping route, averaging about 8 percent of the world's shipping traffic.

Dam construction and benefits The Aswan Dam measures 3600 m in length and 980 m in width at the base. It is 40 m wide and 111 m high at its crest. The dam reservoir holds 43 million m^3 of water and passes 11,000 m^3 of water through turbines every second. Emergency spillways also have a discharge capacity of 5000 m^3/s. The reservoir is named Lake Nasser, is 480 km wide, and has a surface area of 6000 ft^2. It holds 150,000–165,000 m^3 of water. The dam has twelve 175-MW generators and an aggregate power-generation capacity of 2.1 GW.

Environmental issues Construction of the dam has created many environmental difficulties and concerns, including the flooding of lower grounds, which forced the displacement of over 90,000 people in the Nubia Region. Lake Nasser has flooded valuable archeological sites, and silt deposits and yearly floods that provided nutrients to the Nile's fertile agricultural plains are held behind the dam.

Construction of the dam also has eroded topsoil in farmlands located down the Nile River. The Nile Delta's inundation has created a situation in which the land is now used for rice crops and brick-construction industries, causing delta mud to all but disappear. The growth of plants in the reservoir basin has given rise to snails that thrive in the lake.

Aswan Dam timeline

- 1902: Completion of the first Aswan Dam (6400 ft long, 176.5 ft high). Despite heightening efforts in 1912, 1929, and 1933, the dam was flooded by construction of the High Dam.
- 1953: A group of military officers overthrew the Egyptian monarchy and adopted the idea of a new dam along the Nile.
- 1954: Abdel Nasser becomes the president of Egypt and begins talks with the British, Germans, and French about construction of the dam.
- 1954: The United States and Great Britain offer loans of $270 million but back out as Nasser begins favoring the Soviet Union and other communist states.
- 1958: The Soviets agree to finance construction only if Soviet equipment and engineering methods are used.
- 1960: Construction begins on the High Dam after a power station is built upstream at the existing dam to provide needed energy for operations at the construction site.
- 1970: Construction is complete. The second dam is a rock-and-earth-filled dam acting as a ridge across the river.
- 1976: The High Dam Reservoir is filled.

Micro-Hydropower Generation

Microturbines, also referred to as *small hydroelectric turbines,* are similar in construction to the large hydroelectric turbines discussed in earlier. Micro-hydroelectric turbines operate on the same electromechanical principles as large power generators. That is, a moving stream of water turns turbine blades that are connected to a shaft that, in turn, spins a generator that produces electricity. Essential components of micro-hydroelectric turbines are a propeller, a connecting shaft, and an alternator.

Micro-hydroelectric turbines are designed for use in harvesting the kinetic energy of steaming waters that produce electrical energy on a small scale. They are made to serve small communities or industrial plants. In general, the power output of micro-hydroelectric turbines seldom exceeds 10 MW. In the United States and Canada, upper-limit microturbines are stretched to 25–30 MW.

Microturbines can produce power only in locations that are downstream of or have sufficient quantities of falling water. Therefore, their application is considered site-specific. The vertical distance that water falls is called *head* and is usually measured in feet, meters, or units of pressure. The quantity of water that spins the turbine is called *flow* and is measured in gallons per minute, cubic feet per second, or liters per second.

TYPES OF MICRO-HYDROELECTRIC TURBINES

Impulse-type turbines   Impulse-type turbines (Fig. 10.6) operate on the same principle used in water mills, which is that water strikes the turbine runner and pushes it to rotate in a circle. The water is delivered to the runner through a pipeline and is discharged from a small nozzle. This scheme maximizes the force available to operate the turbine. These types of water-propelled electrical generators work best in sites where the water source has a minimum header pressure of about 20 ft or more. Head is the vertical distance between where the water enters the turbine system through a pipeline and where it reaches the turbine runner or propeller.

Small impulse-type water turbines require minimal water flow volume, so they are ideal for sites where a relatively small amount of water runs down a fairly steep hill, as in a hillside stream or a small waterfall. The best known impulse-type micro-hydroelectric turbines use a type of propeller called a *Pelton propeller.* The wheel blades

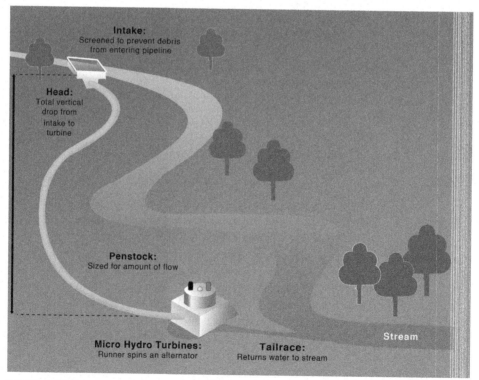

Figure 10.6   **Diagram of a downstream micro-hydroelectric turbine installation.**

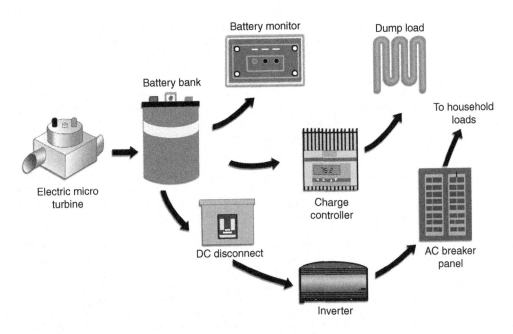

Figure 10.7   Diagram of typical micro-hydroelectric turbine components.

of such a propeller resemble an assembly of circular cups. Figure 10.7 shows typical micro-hydroelectric turbine components.

Reaction-type turbines   Reaction-type turbines require a much larger amount of water flow than impulse-type turbines. However, they can operate with much smaller head pressures (as little as 2 ft), which is ideal for the deployment in sites that have relatively shallow lands but a large amount of water flow.

The runner of these types of turbines is immersed in water, where the stream exits the housing through the turbine, turning the alternator as it drops through the runner blades. Reaction-type turbines have a specifically designed outlet tube that increases turbine power output by creating suction as water exits the system.

Submersible-propeller turbines   These turbines are perhaps the least efficient when compared with the preceding types of turbines. In this type of technology, the propeller is mounted in front of the turbine, which is attached to an alternator inside the main turbine housing. When submerged in a fast-moving water source, the propeller is rotated by the force of the passing water current.

The propellers of submersible turbines work well for locations with a fast-moving, relatively deep stream or river, where a water-diversion system is not possible. Propeller-type micro-hydroelectric turbines were designed originally for marine use but were deployed later in fast-moving rivers and large streams.

The amount of energy produced by hydroelectric generation depends on two factors, namely, header pressure and the amount of water flow.

WATER HEAD

Head is defined as the elevation difference between the source of the water and the turbine, or the total vertical drop, and typically is expressed in feet. Water head measurement is determined by transit, site-level topographic maps, and global positioning systems (GPS). In situations where water from a certain height is gravity-fed, water pressure is determined by the static head. A height of 2.3 ft of water produces 1 lb of pressure.

WATER FLOW

Flow is the volumetric measure of moving water, measured in gallons per minute or in cubic feet per minute. The common method for measuring water flow is the *container method,* in which water is collected in a bucket for a certain duration of time. In this type of measurement, the amount of accumulated water in the container is divided by the time in seconds it takes to fill the bucket and multiplied by 60. For example, a 5-gal bucket that fills in 3 seconds has a water flow of 100 gal/min (5 gal/ 3 s × 60 = 100 gal/min). To minimize the impact on stream ecology and aquatic life, the downstream flow design is limited to half the flow of the water in the stream.

PIPE LENGTH

In situations where the movement of water upstream of the turbine is by pipes, which are also referred to as *penstock,* the sizing of the pipe and its length must be such as to minimize the losses caused by friction. Manufacturers of turbines in general provide head-loss tables (per 100 ft of pipe) that are used to calculate these losses.

For example, at a static head of 100 ft, a 50-gal flow through a 3-in pipe may have a multiplier of 0.65. At a distance of 800 ft from the source, the head drop will be calculated as follows:

$$[0.65 \text{ (factor)} \times 50 \text{ (gal/min)}] \times 800 \text{ (ft)}/100 \text{ (per 100 m of pipe)} = 0.65 \times 50 \times 8$$
$$= 5.2 \text{ ft of head loss}$$

Therefore, the available head at the turbine will be equal to $100 - 5.2 = 94.8$ ft.

PHYSICAL PRINCIPLES OF MICRO-HYDROPOWER GENERATION

The energy released by a body of falling water is defined as the vertical distance of the fall times the weight or the downward force exerted. The force is a product of the water's mass m and gravitational acceleration g. The energy released therefore is the vertical distance h, or the head, multiplied by the force:

$$E \text{ (energy release in joules)} = mgh$$

If we define the specific mass m of the water as r times its volume v, when substituted, the energy release equals

$$E \text{ (joules)} = vrgh$$

Since power P is defined as energy per second (i.e., $P = E/s$), the energy of water entering the hydroelectric turbine at a certain volume flow rate Q in cubic feet or gallons per minute can be expressed by the following equation:

$$P \text{ (J/s)} = erQg \text{ W (J/s = W)}$$

In this equation, water density r is 1000 kg/m³. The gravitational constant $g = 9.8$ m/s². In view of the losses resulting from water friction within the pipe and heat losses within the generator, power produced at the turbine becomes much less than it would. In addition, the electrical power produced by the generator is also subjected to transformation and transmission losses. Therefore, the overall efficiency e of hydropower is factored into the equation. In general, efficiency values for micro-hydroelectric power generation vary between 40 and 60 percent. When adjusting the formula for efficiency, net power is given by

$$P_{net} = erQgh \text{ W} \quad \text{or} \quad P_{net} = e \times 1000 \times Q \times 9.8 \times h \text{ W} \quad \text{or} \quad P_{net} = eQ \times 9.8 \text{ kW}$$

For practical purposes, the formula applied becomes

$$P_{net} = 0.5 \times Q \times 10 \times h \text{ kW}$$

POWER OUTPUT

The power output of large or small turbines is directly proportional to the rate at which the power is delivered to the load (measured in watts). The power output of hydroelectric turbines is estimated by net head times the flow divided by an efficiency factor.

The efficiency factors for micro-hydroelectric turbines, depending on design, range from 9 to 14. For example, a factor of 10 corresponds to an efficiency of 53 percent, which is common in most micro-hydroelectric generation systems. Therefore, the power output of a microturbine is determined by the following formula:

$$\text{Estimated power (w)} = [\text{net head (ft)} \times \text{water flow (gal/min)}]/10$$

When the constant multiplier and efficiency (in hundredths) of a system are available, the power output can be calculated as follows:

$$\text{Estimated power (W)} = \text{net head (ft)} \times \text{water flow (gal/min)} \times \text{system efficiency (in hundredths)} \times \text{special multiplier } C$$

The following is an example of a power-output calculation:

Net head = 40 ft

Water flow = 1 ft^3/min

System efficiency = 0.53

Multiplier C = 85 (for watts) or 0.085 (for kilowatts)

Thus

$$\text{Estimated power (W)} = 40 \text{ ft} \times 1 \text{ ft}^3/\text{min} \times 0.53 \times 85 = 1802 \text{ W}$$

The following are some of the conversion factors used for power-output feasibility study analysis:

1 ft^3 = 7.48 gal

1 ft^3/s = 448.8 gal/min

1 in = 2.54 cm

1 ft = 0.3048 m

1 m = 3.28 ft

1 ft^3 = 0.028 m^3

1 cm = 35.3 ft^3

1 gal = 3.785 L

1 ft^3 = 28.31 L

1 ft^3/s = 1698.7 L/min

1 m^3/s = 15,842 gal/min

1 lb/in^2 of pressure = 2.31 ft (head) of water

1 lb = 0.454 kg

1 kg = 2.205 lb

1 kW = 1.34 hp

1 hp = 746 W

Examples   The following examples illustrate micro-hydroelectric turbine equations.

Example 10.1   Suppose that we are asked to design a small 100-kW hydroturbine project in a location that has a waterfall of 40 m. Determine the required flow.

Solution   Using the preceding equation,

$$Q = P_{net}/(h \times 10 \times e) = 100/(40 \times 10 \times 0.5) = 0.5 \ \text{m}^3/\text{s}$$

Example 10.2   Suppose that we have a stream with a water flow of 2 cm and a fall or head of 30 m. Calculate the net power output.

Solution

$$P_{net} = 30 \times 2 \times 10 \times 0.5 = 300 \ \text{kW}$$

SPECIAL DESIGN CONSIDERATIONS

Prior to designing a micro-hydroelectric power system, the installation site must be surveyed for a proper location for the turbine and a routing path for the stream-diversion pipe or penstock. Proper care must be taken to ensure that in the winter season the pipes are buried properly to avoid freezing. The pipes also must be protected against accidental damage, and the turbine or generator should be located above the stream's flood level.

Micro-hydroelectric systems with battery backup   In most instances, micro-hydroelectric generators are deployed in off-grid battery-based systems. Battery-based micro-hydroelectric systems have great flexibility and can be combined with other energy sources, such as wind generators and solar-electric arrays, which could minimize the stream's seasonal energy production. In high-water-flow streams, large micro-hydroelectric turbines are capable of producing constant power and can be connected directly to the grid.

Off-grid micro-hydroelectric systems without battery backup   In situations where the stream has enough potential, it is possible to generate ac electricity for direct consumption. In these types of installations, an ac turbine generator that produces 120 or 240 V output can be connected directly to a regular household panel. These systems include specially designed control electronic circuitry that diverts excess energy to various loads, such as water- or air-heating equipment. By using this technique, the total load on the generator is kept constant. The power production of these type of systems is limited in a sense because peak or surge loads cannot exceed the output of the generator. The peak power of micro-hydroelectric systems is determined by the stream's available head and flow.

Grid-connected micro-hydroelectric systems without battery backup   These types of installations generally use turbines and controls to produce electricity that can be connected directly into utility lines. The output of generators could be either ac or dc. AC-type systems use grid-compatible inverters, identical to the ones used in photovoltaic systems. As discussed in previous chapters, the islanding feature of grid-compatible inverters is such that when utility power is down, the electricity produced by the micro-hydroelectric generators will automatically shut down as well.

MICRO-HYDROELECTRIC COMPONENTS

The following are some of the essential components of micro-hydroelectric generating systems. Intake screens, also referred to as *impoundments,* are boxes submerged in the watercourse that divert debris from blocking the water intake into a pipeline.

One way of screening debris is by constructing a large pool of water at the intake of the turbine. Intakes are installed above the bottom of the pool but below the surface such that grit settles on the bottom of the stream and debris floats to the top. Another way to remove debris is to direct the water over a sloped screen.

Pipeline   In most instances, microhydroelectric turbines require a short run of pipe to bring the water to the generator propeller. The length of pipes varies depending on the distance between the source and the turbine. The pipe's diameter, which may range from 1 in to 1 ft, must be large enough to handle the design flow. As discussed earlier, losses owing to friction must be minimized to maximize the energy that is converted into electricity. To prevent damage caused by freezing temperatures, ultraviolet rays, and light degradation, pipes are buried underground.

Turbine   As a rule, the choice of turbine must match the site's conditions of head and flow. In impulse-type turbines, the water is routed through nozzles that directly turn some type of runner or propeller wheel. Reaction-type turbines, such as propeller machines and centrifugal pumps, use submerged propellers. In these types of turbines, the energy of the falling water is converted into rotary motion in the runner's shaft. This shaft, in turn, is coupled directly or belted to either a permanent-magnet alternator or a synchronous or ac induction generator.

Charge controllers and regulators   The function of a charge controller in a micro-hydroelectric system is to divert excess dc loads that otherwise could cause damage to the batteries. Controllers generally divert excess energy to a secondary load, such as an air or water heater. Unlike a solar-electric controller, micro-hydroelectric system battery-charge controllers do not disconnect the turbine from the batteries. Moreover, if not regulated, the excess power could create voltages that could cause the turbine to overwork, which could result in dangerous and damaging overvoltage.

Off-grid ac-direct micro-hydroelectric systems that operate without battery backup require controls as well. A load-control system governor connected to the output of the generator is used to monitor the voltage or frequency of the system. This maintains constant power output by diverting the excess load by connecting and disconnecting the dump-load capacity or by mechanically deflecting water away from the runner.

Diversion or shunted load   A diverted or dump load is an electrical resistance element of a heater and is sized exactly to handle the full generating capacity of the micro-hydroelectric turbine. Dump loads usually consist of nonessential loads, such as air or water heaters, regulated by the charge controllers. The battery charge controllers constantly monitor batteries and the grid capacities and divert or shunt excess energy that could damage the system to dump loads.

Storage batteries The types of batteries used in micro-hydroelectric system installations are deep-cycle lead-acid batteries, as discussed in Chap. 3. Deep-cycle batteries, unlike regular car batteries that are designed to store a fixed amount of energy, use reversible chemical reactions that allow surplus energy to be stored during peak power production. On an increase in the electric demand load, the batteries discharge energy to keep the loads operating.

A micro-hydroelectric system, unlike solar and wind renewable-energy systems, imposes the least amount of stress on batteries because they do not often remain in a discharged state, and as a result, battery-bank requirements are somewhat smaller than those used for a wind or photovoltaic system.

Energy-production and battery-monitoring system In order to monitor micro-hydroelectric power, a small data-acquisition system measures and displays several different parameters, such as watts, voltage, current, and battery charge status.

Power disconnect switches For protection purposes, all micro-hydroelectric systems with battery backup and inverters are required to have safety disconnect switches between the generator and the batteries and between the batteries and the inverter. The disconnect switch between the battery bank and the inverter is typically a large dc-rated breaker housed in a metal enclosure.

Inverter As discussed in Chap. 3, inverters transform dc electricity stored in battery banks into ac. Grid-tied inverters synchronize the system's output with the utility's ac electricity, which allows surplus power from micro-hydroelectric systems to be fed to the hydroelectricity utility grid. Battery-based inverters for off-grid or grid-tied systems often incorporate a battery charger, which charges the battery bank from either the grid or the generator.

Main entrance service ac breaker panel The main ac entrance breaker panel is the location where the main electric service from the grid is distributed to the loads. The panel contains a number of labeled circuit breakers that route electricity to the various rooms throughout a house. These breakers allow electricity to be disconnected for servicing and also protect the building's wiring from electrical fires. In micro-hydroelectric systems, much like solar or wind power systems, the ac output of the inverter is connected to an appropriately sized breaker that delivers synchronized ac power to the main entrance service bus.

Kilowatt-hour utility meter In grid-connected micro-hydroelectric systems, electric power enters and exits the grid in both directions. A dual-channel watthour meter with a reversible counter, referred to as a *net meter,* keeps track of how much grid electricity is used or provided to the grid. Grid connectivity is provided by utility companies at no charge.

Advantages of micro-hydroelectric turbines

■ Micro-hydroelectric turbines require as little as a few gallons per minute flow to harvest the kinetic energy of a flowing stream or the static energy of a column of water. Electrical power produced from a micro-hydroelectric generator can be transmitted to a load located several thousand feet away.

■ As opposed to other renewable energy sources, such as wind and solar power, micro-hydroelectric generators produce continuous amounts of electrical energy. A positive feature of the technology is that in rural farm and residential installations, the energy production of micro-hydroelectric generators peaks during the winter months, when large amounts of electricity are required for heating.

■ Micro-hydroelectric generator systems that operate as "run-of-river system," where the water passes through the generator and is directed back into the stream, have little or no impact on the surrounding ecology.

■ Building a small-scale hydroelectric power system can cost $1000–$20,000, depending on site electricity requirements and location. Maintenance fees are relatively small in comparison with those of other technologies.

■ Owing to simplicity of fabrication, low cost, versatility of deployment, and the reliability and longevity of the technology, developing countries can readily implement the technology and provide much-needed electricity in small communities and villages.

■ Excess power produced by micro-hydroelectric generators connected to the grid could be sold to electrical service providers.

Disadvantages of micro-hydroelectric generator systems

■ Micro-hydroelectric generator systems can be deployed only in locations that have sufficient streams for water flow.

■ The power-production potential of the technology is limited by the size and flow of the streams.

■ Stream flow and size usually fluctuate seasonally. In the summer months, stream flow is likely to be less, therefore producing less power output.

11

GEOTHERMAL ENERGY

The term *geothermal* is a composition of two Greek words: *geo*, meaning "earth," and *therm*, meaning "heat." Combined, *geothermal* means "heat generated from the earth."

The earth's center (Figs. 11.1 and 11.2) is made of molten iron, located about 4000 miles from its crust. The estimated temperature of the earth's core is about 5000°C, the heat from which conducts outward from the center and heats up the outer layers of rock, referred to as the *mantel*. When mantel melts and is spewed out of the crust, it is called *magma*.

Rain water seepage through geologic cracks and faults becomes superheated and emerges as geysers and hot springs. Sometimes water is trapped in underground voids, which become geothermal reservoirs. Geothermal energy as a technology involves the production of electrical energy by using the hot-water reservoirs just described. The process involves drilling wells as deep as 2 miles, which reach the geothermal reservoirs. The hot water is brought to surface as steam and is heated up to 250°F, if so required. The steam, in turn, is used to drive electric generator turbines.

In some areas, the water is not hot enough to become steam. This hot water thus is circulated through commercial, industrial, and residential projects for space-heating and drying processes. After such uses, the spent water is circulated back to the reservoir, and the process is repeated.

Geothermal resources, in general, are manifested in a wide variety of forms, some of which include hot-water reservoirs, which are exothermally heated underground water reservoirs, and natural steam reservoirs, which manifest as ground steam. They also include the following:

■ *Geopressurized reservoirs.* These consist of underground slated water (brine) that is extremely pressure saturated with natural gas, resulting from the weight of the overlaying land mass.
■ *Geothermal gradients.* These are drilled shafts that allow access to dry, hot rocks for heat-energy extraction. In general, the thermal gradient, or temperature rise, for every kilometer of drilled depth is 30°C. Holes drilled to 20,000 ft therefore can

THE EARTH

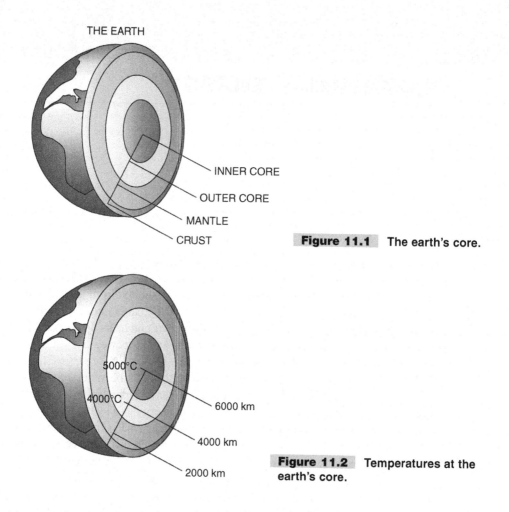

INNER CORE

OUTER CORE

MANTLE

CRUST

Figure 11.1   The earth's core.

5000°C

4000°C

6000 km

4000 km

2000 km

Figure 11.2   Temperatures at the earth's core.

reach a temperature of 190°C, which provides the potential for enormous commercial energy extraction.

■ *Molten magma.* This is produced as a result of volcanic activity and has a temperature of 2000°C, which is not suitable for thermal power extraction.

Thermal Power Extraction Potential

The following example is used to demonstrate the geothermal power potential calculation of a site that covers 50 km², with a thermal crust of 2 km, where the temperature gradient is 240°C. At this depth, the specific heat of rock is determined to be 2.5 J/cm³, and the mean surface temperature is measured at 15°C. Thermal heat generation is calculated as follows:

$$V = \text{volume of rock} = 50 \text{ km}^2 \times 2 \text{ km} = 100 \text{ km}^3$$

Heat content $Q_h = V \times$ specific heat $\times$ temperature difference between depth gradient and surface temperature ($240 - 15 = 225°C$)

Prior to completing the calculation, the volume of the bedrock must be converted from cubic kilometers to cubic centimeters, which is 10^{15}:

$$Q_h = 100 \text{ km}^2 \times 10^{15} \text{ cm}^3 \times 2.5 \text{ J/(cm}^3 \cdot °C) \times 225°C = 5.625 \times 10^{19} \text{ J}$$

Assuming that only 2 percent of the available thermal energy of the geothermal mass could be used to provide power for electricity generation, the question becomes, How many years would it take to produce 1000 MW/yr of power?

Taking the useful portion of the mass as being 2 percent, the overall power generated is calculated as follows:

$$\text{Total capacity to generate 1000 MW/yr} = 50,000 \text{ MW/yr}$$

$$1 \text{ J/s} = 1 \text{ W}$$

$$50,000 \text{ MW/yr} = 50,000 \text{ MW/yr} \times 1,000,000 \text{ W/MW}$$
$$\times (3150 \times 10^6 \text{ s/yr}) = 1.575 \times 10^{18} \text{ J/yr}$$

$$\text{Lifetime power production} = (5.625 \times 10^{19}) \div (1.575 \times 10^{18}) = 35 \text{ years}$$

Geothermal Technologies

DRY-STEAM PLANTS

This class of plants (Fig. 11.3) uses very hot water and steam that is heated to above 300°F and found in hot-water resources and geysers. The steam is either used directly or depressurized, or *flashed,* and purged to eliminate carbon dioxide, nitric oxide, and sulfur, which are usually associated with the process. The clean steam then is used to turn turbines, which drive generators. Pollution resulting from the removal of the toxic gases and elements is about 2 percent of what is generated by traditional fossil fuel–powered plants.

BINARY PLANTS

In this technology (Fig. 11.4), extracted geothermal steam from lower-temperature hot-water resources, with temperatures ranging from 100°F to superheated vapor at 300°F, is passed through heat exchangers, which produce a flow of secondary fluid (such as isobutene or isopentane) that has a lower boiling point.

The secondary fluid vaporizes and turns the turbines that generate electricity. Any remaining secondary fluid is then recycled through heat exchangers. On completion of the process, the geothermal fluid is condensed and returned to the reservoir.

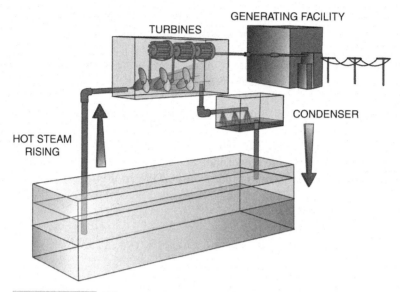

GENERATING FACILITY

TURBINES

CONDENSER

HOT STEAM
RISING

Figure 11.3   Diagram of a dry-steam geothermal plant.

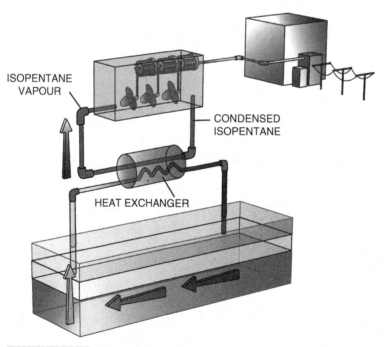

ISOPENTANE
VAPOUR

CONDENSED
ISOPENTANE

HEAT EXCHANGER

Figure 11.4   Diagram of a binary geothermal steam plant.

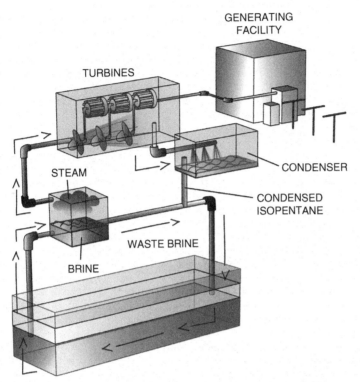

GENERATING
FACILITY

TURBINES

CONDENSER

STEAM

CONDENSED
ISOPENTANE

WASTE BRINE

BRINE

Figure 11.5 Diagram of a geothermal flash steam plant.

Because binary plants use a self-contained cycle, no pollutants are ever emitted or introduced into the atmosphere.

FLASH STEAM PLANT

In this geothermal technology (Fig. 11.5), hot water is pumped under extreme pressure to the earth's surface. On reaching the surface, the pressure is reduced, and as a result, the hot water is transformed into steam. This process is referred to as *steam blasting*. As mentioned earlier, the spent steam as water, in turn, is circulated back to the reservoir, and the cycle is repeated.

Geothermal Potential

In the United States, the Pacific Northwest has the potential to generate up to 11,000 MW of electricity from geothermal power. Although estimates of available resources are uncertain until exploratory work is done, the Northwest Power Planning Council has identified 11 specific areas where it expects that there are about 2000 MW to be developed, enough power to serve over 1.3 million homes. Figure 11.6 is a diagram of a geothermal power plant.

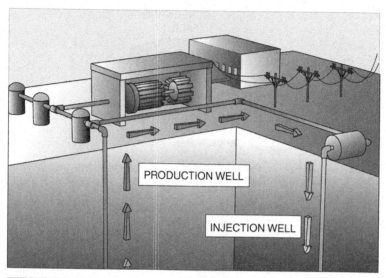

Figure 11.6 Diagram of a geothermal power plant.

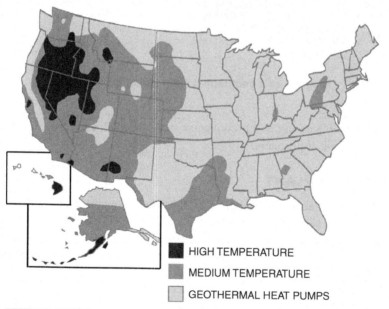

Figure 11.7 U.S. geothermal potential.

Figure 11.7 shows that geothermal areas in the western United States are usually found where there has been recent volcanic activity, such as the Northwest basins in Oregon, Washington, California, Nevada, and Utah. Low-temperature geothermal heating systems have been in operation for decades in Klamath Falls, Oregon, and Boise, Idaho and on the Big Island of Hawaii, which generates 25 percent of its power from geothermal sources. Geothermal power production between 1970 and 2000 is shown in Fig. 11.8.

MWe

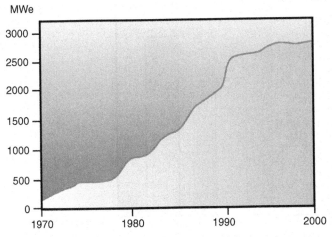

Figure 11.8   Graph showing growth in U.S. geothermal
power. *Courtesy of the Geothermal Education Office.*

Cost of Geothermal Energy and Economics

It is estimated that the average cost of geothermal electricity generation per kilowatthour is about 4.5–7 cents. This is comparable with some fossil fuel plants. However, power production does not produce any pollution, and when pollution-abatement costs are considered, the power produced is very competitive. Geothermal plants are built in modular system configurations. Each turbine is sized to deliver 25–50 MW of electric power. When burning fossil fuels such as coal to produce steam, plants generate substantial amounts of noxious gases and precipitants. In general, geothermal steam carries a lesser amount of contaminants. Geothermal plants are capital-intensive projects that require no fuel expenditure. Typical projects pay back their capital costs within 15 years.

ECONOMIC COST BENEFITS

Geothermal power, like other types of renewable-energy resources, maintains benefits in the geographic location of installation by providing local jobs and contributing royalties and taxes to the county.

ENVIRONMENTAL IMPACT

Although geothermal power is one of the less polluting power sources, it must be sited properly to prevent potential negative environmental impacts. New geothermal systems reinject water into the earth after its heat is used in order to preserve the resource and

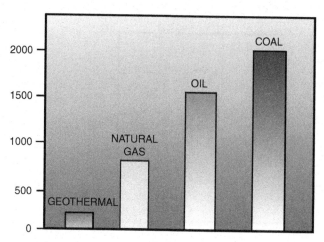

Figure 11.9 CO_2 **emissions comparison chart [in lb/(MW · h)].** *Courtesy of Geothermal Education Office.*

to contain gases and heavy metals sometimes found in geothermal fluids. Figure 11.9 presents a CO_2 emissions comparison bar chart.

Care must be taken in planning geothermal projects to ensure that they do not cool nearby hot springs or cause intermixing with groundwater. Geothermal projects can produce some carbon dioxide emissions, but these are 15–20 times lower than the cleanest fossil fuel power plants, as shown in Fig. 11.9.

Benefits of geothermal power

- Provides clean and safe energy using little land space.
- The energy produced is sustainable and renewable.
- Generates continuous, reliable power.
- Power produced is cost-competitive.
- Conserves use of fossil fuels.
- Reduces energy imports.
- Benefits local economies.
- Power plants are modular and can be increased in potential incrementally.

Direct uses

- Balneology—hot springs, baths, and bathing
- Agriculture—greenhouse and soil warming
- Aquaculture—fish, prawn, and alligator farms
- Industrial—product drying and warming
- Direct heating—residential and industrial

Worldwide, geothermal power is used in 40 countries and generates about 11,000 MW.

Geothermal Case Study in an Air-Conditioning Application

The operational principle of geothermal energy is based on the fundamental physical gradient differential between the earth's ground surface and subterranean temperature. When penetrating the ground, the temperature of a bore hole approaching the earth's mantle increases in a predictable manner. The differential temperature therefore depends on the depth of penetration.

When water is circulated through a ground-penetrating loop, the water temperature is elevated, carrying along energy extracted from the earth's mantle. The extracted energy then is used for thermal power cogeneration. At depths of several thousand feet, the temperature of a circulating liquid could rise to several hundred degrees centigrade, which converts water into steam that drives electricity-generating turbines. In shorter penetrations of several hundred feet, depending on the specific application, the water temperature differential can rise sufficiently above the earth's surface temperature, and the differential temperature gradient can be used by air-conditioning systems for temperature control during winter and summer seasons.

NORTH HIGH SCHOOL

The North High School ground-source heat-pump (GSHP) project is located in Riverside, California. In 2002, the existing high school underwent a major modernization. Before modernization, a central air-conditioning power plant served many of the core facilities and most of the outlying buildings by conventional packaged air-conditioning equipment.

Preliminary feasibility studies were undertaken to determine the conductivity of the soil in order to establish a geothermal underground heat-pump loop. A geothermal loop is a heat exchanger that operates as a cooling coil. The objective is to transfer the energy from the ground to the heat pump.

A 250-ft test bore was drilled to record the conductivity and diffusivity of the soil. The results of the test bore were used as the basis for configuring the geothermal loop.

The process of the geothermal heat-pump load calculations involves evaluation of various insulation thicknesses of the bore by use of insulating materials. On determination of the air-conditioning load, geothermal loops are calculated from the following basic equations:

$$Q_c = L(t_g - t_w)/R$$

where Q_c = the heat load
L = the pipe length
t_g = the ground temperature
t_w = the water temperature
R = the thermal resistance to heat transfer

Figure 11.10   A geothermal application in air-conditioning. *Courtesy of TMAD TAYLOR & GAINES.*

The results of the study show that the final loop arrangement should consist of eighteen 365-ft bores, with the original 250-ft bore used as the safety factor (Fig. 11.10).

The piping system will be constructed from high-density polyethylene (HDPE) below grade and copper piping above grade. A reserve return system will be implemented to ease in balancing of the system, and the loop field will be separated into two zones with balancing valves. The pumping arrangement will consist of a base-mount pump with a variable-speed drive controlled by a differential pressure sensor. This arrangement will allow control of the flow of water that will be delivered to the heat-pump units. The heat-pump units will be controlled by the campus's centralized direct digital control (DDC) system.

ADVANTAGES OF GEOTHERMAL POWER

Geothermal power, although it produces minute amounts of fumes during the well-drilling process, is environmentally friendly and does not produce harmful pollutants like those generated by fossil fuel power plants. Additional advantages include the following:

- Geothermal power production is reliable and can produce uninterrupted constant power.
- Geothermal energy is quite flexible. It can be used to produce electric power and hot water for heating or industrial drying processes.
- Geothermal power derived from natural steam is 97 percent efficient. A 3 percent loss of efficiency is attributed to turbine friction.

It should be noted that geothermal energy technology, which makes use of water recirculation as binary systems do, in fact withdraws the earth's thermal energy at a considerable rate and therefore cannot be considered an entirely renewable source of energy.

GEOTHERMAL ENERGY CHALLENGES

Geothermal energy is essentially best suited for a large, centralized chiller or boiler systems. Some of the challenges associated with this technology are as follow:

- Installation of a geothermal plant for a heat-cogeneration process entails significant expenditures associated the geologic study, environmental reports, multiple earth borings, and the cost of extensive mechanical components such as heat exchangers, circulating pumps, and associated maintenance.
- Deep penetration-type geothermal energy technologies typically are installed in special geographic locations; they do represent a significant engineering design and environmental challenge.
- In view of the fact that the school has many buildings and is undergoing significant expansion, installation of a geothermal energy could be a significant distraction, which could cause serious construction delays and, most of all, might not be viable financially.

As a result of these issues, geothermal energy is not considered a suitable alternative renewable-energy option for the school campus.

SOLAR PHOTOVOLTAIC ENERGY POWER COGENERATION

Solar power cogeneration, for numerous reasons, is considered to be the most viable renewable-energy alternative for the school campus. Some of the significant advantages of a solar photovoltaic system are as follows:

■ Solar power cogeneration, unlike conventional capital equipment investment, is not an asset that depreciates in a set number of predetermined years; rather, it is considered as electric power plant that has a lifespan of 40 years and can produce a predictable annual amount of energy without using any fuel and with zero emissions of environmental pollutants.

■ Power generation takes place at the source of consumption; therefore, it has no transmission or distribution losses, and it therefore operates at an efficiency near 100 percent.

■ The electric power produced minimizes time-of-use and peak-power penalties in an application where the electric power demand is inconsistent.

■ Cost of electrical energy produced is absolutely fixed and does not vary over the 30–40 years of projected lifespan of the solar power installation.

■ By reducing the electric power-generation demand from various forms of fossil fuels, millions of tons of CO_2 and NO_x gases are prevented from polluting the atmosphere and the environment.

■ The investment, after paying for itself in a relatively short time, will provide a steady savings and income for several decades after the payback period, which, in effect, is to be considered as an equity income.

■ With enforcement of California Assembly Bill 32 and conversion of electric power plants to natural gas and the future global economics of fossil fuel, it is rather obvious that the cost of electrical energy in the future will escalate far beyond the 7–8 percent annually, beyond the present 5 percent historical escalation recorded by the Department of Energy (DOE).

■ The increase in cost of electrical energy is also subject to geopolitical conditions and worldwide energy resources, supply, demand, and unpredictable risk factors that cannot be forecasted in advance nor be dismissed.

Ocean Thermal Energy

Ocean thermal energy principles employ temperature differences in the ocean. The difference in temperature between the ocean's surface and deeper water is quite significant, which allows power plants that make use of this difference in temperature to make energy. A difference of at least 38°F is needed between the warmer surface water and the colder deep ocean water.

The use of this energy source is called *ocean thermal energy conversion* (OTEC). Demonstration projects are currently operating in both Japan and Hawaii.

12

BIOFUEL, BIOGAS, AND THERMAL DEPOLYMERIZATION TECHNOLOGIES

Biomass is the stored energy in plant and animal tissues that can be used as fuel. It is considered to be among the most vital resources on the earth. Biomass, in addition to providing sustenance for plants and animals, is also used in the majority of human-made materials, including fabrics, medicines, chemicals, and construction materials. The use of biomass as a source of energy dates back to the discovery of fire, when wood was combusted for heat. This chapter will review biomass fuels and technologies that provide us with energy used in various forms, including for the fueling of cars, generating power, and constructing computer components.

History

Prior to invention of the diesel engine by Rudolf Diesel, the first transesterification process, glycerol removal from vegetable oil, was discovered in 1853 by Duffy and Patrick. Four decades later, the first diesel engine, which consisted of a single 10-ft iron cylinder and a flywheel, was demonstrated in Augsburg, Germany, on August 10, 1893. In remembrance of this event, August 10 has been declared International Biodiesel Day. Rudolf Diesel's engine, which won the grand prize at the World's Fair in Paris, France, in 1900, was powered by peanut oil, which is not as transesterified as biodiesel fuel. Diesel, in his 1912 speech, proclaimed that "the use of vegetable oils for engine fuels may seem insignificant today, but such oils may become, in the course of time, as important as petroleum and the coal-tar products of the present time."

In subsequent productions, manufacturers improved diesel engine design and made it operate with lower-viscosity fossil fuels rather than vegetable oil. In the mean time, the petroleum industries succeeded in producing diesel fuel, which was considerably less expensive than the biomass alternatives that quenched the development of biomass-fuel technology.

At present, in France, the production of biodiesel fuel, known as *diester,* is the result of the transesterification of sunflower and rapeseed oils. Diester, as a fuel additive, is mixed in proportions of 5 to 30 percent into regular diesel fuel and is used by some truck and bus fleets and for public transportation.

French car manufacturers Renault and Peugeot manufacture certified truck engines for use with mixed biodiesel fuel. Both car manufacturers currently have experimental engines that operate with a 50 percent mix of biodiesel fuel.

Mixed biodiesel-petroleum diesel fuel can be used in most modern engines at any concentration. Biodiesel fuel is a better solvent than regular petroleum diesel fuel. It is often added to fuels to break down deposits of residue in the lines of vehicles that usually run on petroleum. However, it has a major disadvantage in that it can gradually degrade rubber gaskets and hoses in older vehicles.

Chemical Composition

The chemical composition of biomass depends on the various types of tissues found among plant and animal species. In general, plant structure consists of about 25 percent lignin and 75 percent carbohydrates or sugars. The carbohydrates in plants consist of many sugar molecules that are linked together in long chains called *polymers*. Some of the carbohydrates contain significant amounts of cellulose and hemicellulose. Lignin is a nonsugar polymer that acts as the mortar in the building blocks of plants. It gives a plant its strength while acting as the "glue" that holds the cellulose fibers together.

Origins of Biomass

In essence, biomass in nature is formed when carbon dioxide from the atmosphere and water from the earth are combined in the photosynthetic process to produce carbohydrates and/or sugars, which are the building blocks of biomass. Solar energy, which promotes photosynthesis in plants through chlorophyll, leads to the sun's energy being stored in the chemical bonds of the structural components of biomass. When the temperature of biomass is elevated, the biomass burns, and the energy stored in the chemical bonds is extracted. In the process, oxygen from the atmosphere combines with the carbon in the plants to produce carbon dioxide and water. This is a cyclic process because the carbon dioxide is absorbed by other plants, which produce new biomass. As discussed in earlier chapters, for millennia, human beings have used biomass as fuel and have consumed plants as food for nutritional energy in the form of sugars and starches.

Fossilized biomass in the form of coal is essentially a compacted biomass resulting from very slow chemical transformations over millennia. Coal is a sugar polymer that has been transformed into a chemical composition, a concentrated source of energy. All fossil fuels, including coal, oil, and natural gas, are ancient biomass formed from plant and animal remains. Even though fossil fuels contain the same components as those found in living plants and animals, such as hydrogen and carbon, they are not considered renewable because nature has taken numerous years to create them.

Plants and animals, when they decay, release most of their chemical constituents back into the atmosphere. On the contrary, fossil fuels, when not burned or processed, do not affect the earth's atmosphere. Some well-known biomass residues used for generating energy include sugarcane, corn fiber, rice straw, hulls, nutshells, sawdust, timber slash, mill scrap, the paper trash and urban yard clippings in municipal waste, energy crops, fast-growing trees such as poplars and willows, grasses such as switchgrass and elephant grass, and the methane captured from landfills, municipal wastewater treatment facilities, and manure from cattle and poultry.

At present, in developed countries, biomass accounts for approximately 14 percent of the world's primary energy needs. However, populations living in developing countries use biomass as their most important source of energy. As mentioned in previous chapters, increases in the world's population and per capita demand for fuels, as well as depletion of fossil fuel resources, mean that the demand for biomass fuel is expected to increase very rapidly.

Biomass currently provides 40 to 90 percent of the energy used in developing countries and is expected to remain the major global source of energy for the foreseeable future. Owing to advances in biomass fuel production and use, energy-conversion technologies in some industrialized countries such as Sweden and Austria derive 15 percent of their primary energy production from biomass. At present, the United States derives only 4 percent, or 9000 MW, of electrical energy from biomass, equivalent to the amount of energy generated from its nuclear power plants. It is estimated that with further advancements in biomass technologies, the total power produced could supply 20 percent or more of U.S. energy consumption. In countries with significant agricultural infrastructures, biomass energy in such forms as ethanol, biogas, and/or biodiesel fuel could produce sufficient energy to offset the use of oil imports by as much as 50 percent.

The following is the global biomass energy distribution potential:

- Total mass of living matter including moisture = 2000 billion tons.
- Total mass in land plants = 1800 billion tons.
- Total mass in forests = 1600 billion tons (estimated).
- Per capita terrestrial biomass = 400 tons (estimated), and the net annual production of terrestrial biomass = 400,000 million tons.

Biomass Energy Potential

The potential for bioenergy extraction from biomass is enormous. With advances in applications of the technology, it is now possible to convert raw biomass into various forms of energy, including electricity, liquid or gaseous fuels, and processed solid fuels. This could result in significant social and economic benefits to the world. It is a well known that the quality of life for very large majorities of the world's population is directly related to the availability of one or another form of energy. It has been proven that improvements in infrastructure, health, social advancement, and jobs depend on the availability of dispersible energy.

Energy Value of Biomass

When referring to biomass energy, we consider the energy potential stored in plants, crops, forest residue, and animal wastes. The energy content of biomass, when used as a solid fuel, is usually comparable with that of coal. The stored heat-energy value of dry biomass composed of wheat, straw, and sugarcane is around 17.5 GJ/ton compared with about 20 GJ/ton for wood. Corresponding values for coal and lignite are 30 and 20 GJ/ton, respectively. Generally, freshly harvested biomass contains considerable amounts of moisture, which could represent 8 to 20 percent for wheat-straw mass, 30 to 60 percent for woods, and 75 to 90 percent for animal manure. On the other hand, the moisture content of most coal ranges from 2 to 12 percent. Therefore, the energy-content density for biomass is lower than that for coal. However, chemical attributes of biomass have many distinctive advantages, one of which is that the ash content of biomass is much lower than that of coals and is relatively free of toxic metals and other harmful contaminants.

Biomass fuels, when processed, offer a wide diversity of fuel supply. These fuels can be produced and used to generate electricity through direct combustion in modern devices or be processed to produce a wide variety of liquid fuels such as ethanol, biodiesel, and other alcohol-containing fuels used in motor vehicles. Biomass energy undoubtedly can increase global economic development without contributing to the greenhouse effect because biomass does not contribute to the inversion layer in global warming. This is so because the net amount of CO_2 produced from burning is recycled and absorbed by plants, therefore leading to biomass being considered a sustainable-energy resource. Table 12.1 represents energy content of various biomass fuels.

Benefits of Biomass Energy

No doubt the evolution of biomass technologies and the extended use of bioenergy-based fuels, which maximize the use of otherwise discarded agricultural and industrial methods, as well as plant and animal waste, can create an infrastructure that could have a major impact on industrial growth in rural areas. According to the U.S. Department of Agriculture, an estimated 17,000 jobs can be created per million gallons of ethanol produced. Likewise, the production of 5 quadrillion Btu of electricity on 50 million acres of land would increase overall farm income by $12 billion annually. It is important to note that the United States consumes about 90 quadrillion Btu of energy annually. Biomass energy generation, if promoted by state and federal governments, can provide farmers with stable incomes and higher standards of living. Rural industrial development and diversification can, in addition to strengthening local economies, contribute to the elevation of local community living standards.

TABLE 12.1 ENERGY CONTENT OF VARIOUS BIOMASS FUELS

FUEL	CONTENT OF WATER , %	MJ/kg	kW/kg
Oak tree	20	14.1	3.9
Pine tree	20	13.8	3.8
Straw	15	14.3	3.9
Grain	15	14.2	3.9
Rapeseed oil	—	37.1	10.3
Hard coal	4	30.0–35.0	8.3
Brown coal	20	10.0–20.0	5.5
Heating oil	—	42.7	11.9
Biomethanol	—	19.5	5.4
FUEL	**MJ/(N · m³)**		**kWh/(N · m³)**
Sewer gas	16.0		4.4
Wood gas	5.0		1.4
Biogas from cattle dung	22.0		6.1
Natural gas	31.7		8.8
Hydrogen	10.8		3.0

ENVIRONMENTAL BENEFITS

The extended use biomass technologies and bioenergy will provide a degree of ecologic balance and climate change, which will mitigate acid rain, minimize soil erosion, reduce water pollution, provide better sanctuaries and habitats for wildlife, and help to maintain forest health.

Impact of biomass energy on climatic conditions The extended use of fossil fuels over centuries as a primary energy resource has contributed to serious deterioration of the environment through the release of hundreds of millions of tons of greenhouse gases into the atmosphere. Greenhouse gasses, which include carbon dioxide (CO_2) and methane (CH_4), have altered the earth's climate, disrupting the entirety of the biosphere that currently supports life as we know it. Biomass energy technologies can help to minimize and perhaps even reverse the trend. Even though methane and carbon dioxide are the two most significant contributors to global warming, methane is short-lived in the atmosphere but has a significantly larger detrimental effect (20 times more potent) than carbon dioxide.

Trapping and harnessing methane gas from landfills, wastewater treatment plants, and manure lagoons, from which the gas otherwise would be vented into the atmosphere, could lead to its use in the generation of electricity, as well as for fuel in motor vehicles. Biomass energy crops, which have significant amounts of stored carbohydrates in their roots, stalks, and sinks, have roots that remain in the soil after harvest, which could regenerate carbon on a yearly basis.

Acid rain   Acid rain is a result of the combustion of fossil fuels, which release sulfur and nitrogen oxides into the atmosphere. Acid rain has been implicated in the killing of fish as well as the rendering of lakes as inhabitable for aquatic life. Since biomass contains no sulfur, when mixed with coal, it is referred to as *cofiring* and reduces sulfur emissions and prevents acid rain.

Soil erosion and water contamination   Biomass crops are considered excellent for reducing water pollution because they can be readily cultivated on more marginal lands, in floodplains, and as interseasonal crops between two adjacent harvest periods. Planted crops stabilize the soil, and by reducing soil erosion, they also play a significant role in reducing nutrient runoff, which can protect aquatic ecosystems. Shading from vegetation growth enhances the habitat for numerous aquatic creatures, such as fish, prawns, and shell fish. Since most bioenergy crops tend to be perennials, they do not have to be planted every year, which means a lesser use of farm machinery and soil deterioration.

Another property intrinsic of biomass energy is that it can reduce water pollution by capturing methane through anaerobic digestion from manure lagoons on cattle, hog, and poultry farms. As discussed below, by constructing and using large anaerobic digester lagoons, farmers can reduce odor, capture methane for energy production, and create either liquid or semisolid soil fertilizers.

Microturbine Generators

A microturbine, as shown in Fig. 12.1, is a compact turbine generator that delivers electricity close to the point where it is needed. It operates on a variety of gaseous and liquid fuels and is designed to operate with low-Btu landfill gases (LFGs). Microturbine technology use became commercialized in 1998.

Microturbines in general serve as primary power, emergency power, or standby power and add capacity and reduce grid-consumption bottlenecks for peak shaving purposes. The units deliver energy cost savings while supplying clean, reliable power with low maintenance needs. Microturbines are very compact and are packaged in compartments the size of a refrigerator, with power-generation capacities of 30 to 60 kW of electricity, enough to power a small business.

Microturbines are a third-generation technology that evolved from many years of research and development in civil, military aviation, and maritime technologies. The technology's principles are based on gas-turbine engine system engineering, which was developed in 1938 in England.

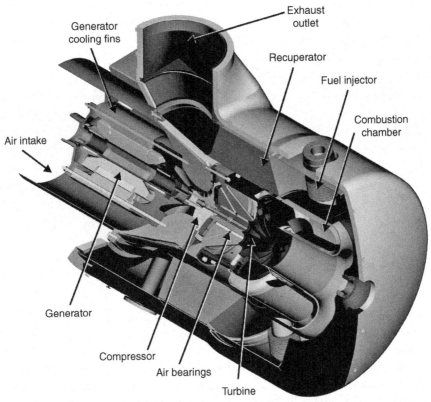

Figure 12.1 **Microturbine system components.** *Courtesy of Capstone Turbine.*

A microturbine's principal function is the use of very high internal-combustion pressures. The pressure develops in a chamber that provides rotational power output to a shaft, the torque of which is transferred to a microturbine generator that generates alternating current.

Typically, a microturbine is constructed from a few mechanical components, which include a recuperator chamber, where fuels such as methanol, ethanol, natural gas, petroleum distillates, liquid propane, and gasified coal are vaporized at very high temperatures. In a combustion chamber, the vaporized gases are combusted, resulting in an extremely high pressure and rotational torque produced by turbine blades. Frictional or rotational losses are minimized by an air-bearing mechanism that provides an air foil around the output shaft. The generator design also involves an intricate water or liquid cooling and filtration system that allows for operation at lower temperatures. Microturbine efficiency ranges from 21 to 31 percent. Higher system efficiencies are attained by using the waste heat generated from exhaust gases. Microturbines require natural gas at high pressures of at least 75 lb/in^2, which is achieved by the use of an onsite compressor. This somewhat reduces system efficiency and increases operational costs, though. Microturbine sizes range from 25 to 1000 kW.

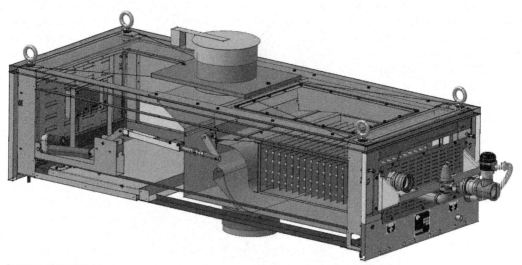

Figure 12.2   **Microturbine assembly diagram.** *Courtesy of Capstone Microturbine.*

They are designed as stand-alone modular power-generating units that are capable of tandem synchronized or combined operations, which can generate desired electrical power output.

Maximum thermal efficiencies of microturbines are achieved when the exhaust is used to recover generated heat, a process referred to as *cogeneration*. The generation capacity of the units is literally unlimited when running in parallel.

Like jet engines, microturbines mix fuel with air to create combustion, as shown in Fig. 12.2. This combustion turns a magnet generator, compressor, and turbine wheels on a revolutionary single-shaft air-bearing design at high speeds, with no need for additional lubricants, oils, or coolants. The result is a highly efficient, reliable, clean combustion generator with very low NO_x emissions. Unlike diesel generators, it can operate around the clock without restrictions. Unlike combined-cycle gas turbines, these power systems use no water.

Microturbines are low-emission generators that are used in applications where electricity and heat generation can be used simultaneously. For example, a typical microturbine manufactured by Capstone can provide up to 29 kW of power and 85 kW of heat for combined heat and power applications. The technology makes use of solid-state power electronics that allow for the tandem coupling of a 2- to 20-unit stand-alone (with no external hardware except computer cables).

The systems also incorporate circuits that allow for automatic grid and stand-alone switching, heat-recovery units, up to100-unit networking, remote monitoring and dispatch, and other such functionalities. Major functional units of a microturbine include the compressor, combustor, turbine, and permanent-magnet generator. The rotating components are mounted on a single shaft, supported by air bearings. Figure 12.3 illustrates a gas microturbine with regeneration, and Fig. 12.4 illustrates a microturbine with a grid connection.

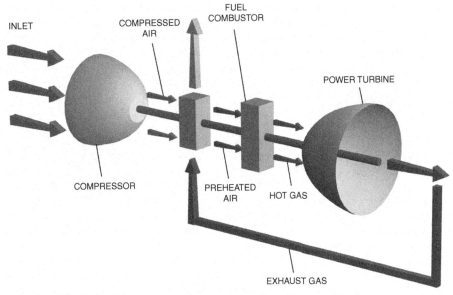

Figure 12.3   Diagram of a gas microturbine with regeneration.

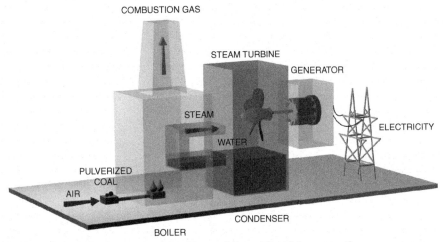

Figure 12.4   Diagram of a microturbine with grid connection.

Landfill, Wastewater Treatment, and Plant Biogas Generators

Methane gas is also commonly generated in very large volumes as a by-product of the biologic degradation of organic waste or as a result of numerous industrial processes. Although methane is an excellent waste-gas fuel for microturbines, such as, the one

Figure 12.5   **Microturbine system assembly.** *Courtesy of Capstone Microturbine.*

shown in Fig. 12.5, it is also an especially potent greenhouse gas. Landfill gases (LFGs) are created when organic waste in municipal solid-waste landfills decomposes. This gas consists of about 50 percent methane (CH_4), the primary component of natural gas, about 50 percent carbon dioxide (CO_2), and a small amount of nonmethane organic compounds.

Instead of allowing LFGs to escape into the air, they can be captured, converted, and used as an energy source, as shown in Fig. 12.6. The use of LFGs helps to reduce

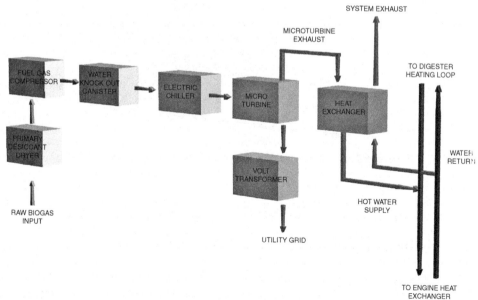

Figure 12.6   **Diagram of an LFG-recovery process.**

odors and other hazards associated with LFG emissions and also prevents methane from migrating into the atmosphere and contributing to local smog and global climate change.

LFG is a readily available, local, and renewable-energy source that offsets the need for nonrenewable resources such as coal and oil. In fact, LFG is the only renewable-energy source that, when used, directly prevents atmospheric pollution. LFG can be converted and used in many ways, generating electricity, heat, or steam. As an alternative-energy source, it can provide vehicle fuel for fleets such as school buses, taxis, and mail trucks. It also can be used in niche applications, such as with microturbines, fuel cells, and greenhouses.

Of the 6000 landfills across the United States, there are about 340 with energy projects currently in operation. However, the Environmental Protection Agency (EPA) estimates that as many as 500 additional landfills could have their methane turned into a cost-effective energy source, producing electricity to power 1 million homes across the United States. This is equivalent to removing the greenhouse gas emissions that would be generated in a year by 13 million cars. Figure 12.7 shows a Capstone microturbine assembly, and Fig. 12.8 shows a Capstone microturbine in a landfill installation.

Figure 12.7   **A microturbine assembly.** *Courtesy of Capstone Microturbine.*

Figure 12.8   **Microturbine in a landfill installation.** *Courtesy of Capstone Microturbine.*

Hot Water and Generators

With a hot-water heat exchanger fully integrated into its exhaust system, useful heat is easily extracted from microturbines. This built-in cogeneration allows overall system efficiencies to approach 80 percent, depending on the temperature of the inlet water.

Facilities can use this heat in a variety of ways. In suitable climates, the hot water can reduce the amount of building-heating fuel used by providing space heating. Since the hot-water heat exchanger is rated for potable water use, the system can supply domestic hot water directly.

The hot water also can be used in conjunction with other heat-driven devices, such as absorption chillers or desiccant wheels for dehumidification. In the latter case, the heat provided by the microturbine helps to regenerate the desiccant wheel by driving out the captured moisture. Of course, the 400°F (204.4°C) exhaust from the microturbine also can be used directly in some applications. Since gas turbine engine emissions are low, the exhaust is relatively clean. Owing to the design of the engine, the exhaust still contains plenty of oxygen and can support follow-up burners to further raise the temperature.

Economic Benefits of Using Landfill Gas

LFG projects are a win-win opportunity for all parties involved, whether they are the landfill owners or operators, the local utility, the area government, or the surrounding community. Even before LFG projects produce profits from the sale or use of electricity, they produce a related benefit for communities. LFG projects involve engineers, construction firms, equipment vendors, utilities, and end users of the power produced. Much of this cost is spent locally for drilling, piping, construction, and operational personnel, providing additional economic benefits to the community through increased employment and local sales. Once the LFG system is installed, the captured gas can be sold for use as heat or fuel or be converted and sold on the energy market as renewable "green" power. In doing so, the community can turn a financial liability into an asset.

Environmental Benefits of Using Landfill Gas

Converting LFG to energy offsets the need for nonrenewable resources, such as coal and oil, and reduces emissions of air pollutants that contribute to local smog and acid rain. In addition, LFG can improve on the global climate changes discussed earlier.

Case Study of Successful Application of Microgenerator Technology

This application reflects the use of a Capstone microturbine in an LFG-recovery project. The HOD Landfill, located within the village of Antioch in Lake County, northeastern Illinois, is a Superfund site consisting of approximately 51 acres of landfill area. On September 28, 1998, the EPA issued a record of decision (ROD) for the site requiring that specific landfill closure activities take place. Remedial action in response to the ROD, which was completed in January 2001, included the installation of a landfill gas-collection system with 35 dual gas and leachate extraction wells. This system collects about 300 ft^3/min of LFG. In 2001, RMT, Inc., an environmental engineering contractor who undertook project installation, in concordance with the Antioch Community School District (ACSD), began exploring the option of using this LFG to generate electricity and heat for the local high school. In April 2002, the ACSD applied for and received a $550,000 grant from the Illinois Department of Commerce and Community Affairs' (DECCA's) Renewable Energy Resources Program (RERP) to construct a cogeneration system to use the LFG to produce electricity and heat for the high school. Shortly after this, RMT and the ACSD entered into an agreement to turn the LFG into the primary energy source for the high school. The overall cost of this project, including design, permits, and construction, was approximately $1.9 million. On December 24, 2002, construction of the system began.

The work presented many challenges, including resolving easement issues, meeting local utility requirements, connecting to the existing heating system, crossing railroads, cleaning the LFG, and meeting the EPA's operational requirements to control LFG migration. RMT staff worked with the local government, school officials, and the EPA, in addition to leading the design efforts and managing the construction activities throughout the project. RMT also provided public-relations assistance to the ACSD by attending Antioch village board meetings to describe the project and to answer any questions from concerned citizens and village board members. Potential options evaluated included using the LFG to produce electricity for use in the school's existing boilers and for use in a combined heat and power system through these evaluations. It was determined that the only economically viable option was to produce electricity and heat for the school through the use of microturbines.

The design of the energy system included tying it into the existing gas-collection system at the landfill, installing a gas conditioning and compression system, and transferring the gas a half mile to the school grounds, where combustion in the microturbines generates electricity and heat for the school.

One-half mile of piping was installed to transfer approximately 200 ft^3/min of cleaned and compressed LFG to the school grounds, where 12 Capstone microturbines are located in a separate building. The 12 microturbines produce 360 kW of electricity and, together with the recovered heat, meet the majority of the energy requirements for the 262,000-ft^2 school. The system began operating in September 2003.

This use of LFG has proved beneficial to all parties involved. It provides energy at a low cost for the high school; clean, complete combustion of waste gas; decreased emissions to the environment by reducing the need for traditional electrical generation sources; public-relations opportunities for the school and community for being the first school district in the United States to get electricity and heat from LFG; and educational opportunities in physics, chemistry, economics, and environmental management for the Antioch Community High School (ACHS) students as a result of this state-of-the-art gas-to-energy system being located at the school.

RMT was the designer and general contractor on the project. The team was responsible for designing the system, administering contracts, coordinating access rights (e.g., with railroad access), obtaining all appropriate permits, creating a health and safety plan, managing construction, and coordinating utility connections. Figure 12.9 is a diagram of the LFG-recovery and electricity- and heat-generating process.

PROJECT DESIGN

This project included 12 Capstone microturbines used to turn LFG into the primary energy source for the 262,000-ft^2 Antioch Community High School. This is the first LFG project in the United States, which in addition to being owned by a school provides heat and power requirements for the institution.

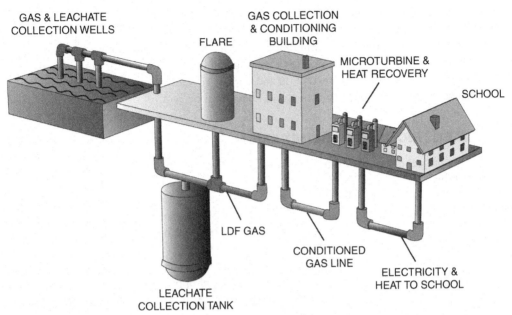

Figure 12.9   **Diagram of the Antioch Community High School gas-to-energy system.**
Courtesy of Capstone Microturbine.

The collection system at the HOD Landfill, which includes 35 LFG-extraction wells, a blower, and a flare, must remain operational to control LFG migration. Therefore, construction of the new cogeneration system required connection to the existing system to allow for excess LFG to be used.

High-density polyethylene (HDPE SDR 9) pipe 4 in in diameter and one-half mile long was installed 4 to 12 ft below the ground, running from the HOD Landfill to the microturbines at the school. The use of horizontal drilling techniques allowed the pipe to cross beneath a stream, a road, public utilities, athletic fields, and a railroad with minimal disturbance of the ground surface. This was extremely important for the community and the school's athletic programs.

Twelve Capstone microturbines are located at the school to provide the electricity and heat from the LFG. Each Capstone microturbine fueled by the LFG produces up to 30 kW of three-phase electricity at 480 V using 12 to 16 ft^3/min of LFG, for a total of 360 kW of electricity—enough to power the equivalent of approximately 120 homes. The microturbine system incorporates a combustor, a turbine, and a generator. The rotating components are mounted on a single shaft, supported by air bearings that rotate at up to 96,000 rev/min (rpm). The generator is cooled by airflow into the gas turbine. Built-in relay protection (over/undervoltage and over/underfrequency) automatically trips off the microturbines in the event of a utility system outage or a power quality disturbance. Excess electricity not used by the Antioch Community High School is sold to Commonwealth Edison. A 12-turbine system was selected to provide power and will remain functional as LFG production from the HOD Landfill decreases.

The project's design and construction can be a model for other communities that are interested in the beneficial reuse of nearby LFG resources. It is an example of how to deal with the numerous community concerns related to developing an alternative-energy system based on LFG. Determining suitable equipment for system design, as well as the specifics of construction and operation, while considering local community needs and requirements is critical to a successful project.

ELECTRIC POWER GENERATION

This project is a prime example of how innovative partnerships and programs can take a liability and turn it into an asset. The solution created a win-win situation for all involved, including HOD Landfill, the ACSD, the village of Antioch, the state of Illinois, Commonwealth Edison, and the EPA. Each key player is seeing significant benefits from the energy system: low energy costs and the use of waste heat for internal use in the high school; the clean and complete combustion of waste gas and decreased emissions to the environment through the reduced need for traditional electricity-generation sources; reduction in greenhouse gas emissions; educational opportunities in physics, chemistry, economics, and environmental management as a result of this on-campus project; and a state-of-the art gas-to-energy system.

Cal Poly Biogas Case Study

This is an interesting case study that demonstrates the application of a microturbine in farming. The study was conducted by Cal Poly University, San Luis Obispo, California. The study was conducted to convert animal waste to electricity and heat through the use of microturbine technology. The project site was a dairy farm that was populated by 300 cows and other such animals. The animals were kept in a covered barn, where a large percentage of their manure was deposited initially on the concrete floor. The manure was flushed out by water periodically and collected in a lagoon, which had a volume of 19,000 m³. A small percentage of the manure was deposited on corrals and was collected seasonally.

Methane energy–production technologies that use gases generated from covered lagoons with anaerobic digesters had shown a certain degree of success previously. Essentially, the choice of digester technology depends on the specific characteristics of the animal waste. One type of technology makes use of a packed-bed upflow anaerobic sludge blanket digester for soluble organic waste. Waste is collected in a lagoon covered with 1-mm-thick reinforced polypropylene that is sealed and tied down by weights. Digested gas is allowed to exit through a manifold. Figure 12.10 is a diagram of the project.

Based on this model, the Cal Poly project employed a microturbine that used the digested gases generated by the 19,000-m³ (4 million gal) earthen lagoon. With the simple use of pumps and piping, diluted dairy manure wastewater was transferred to the lagoon.

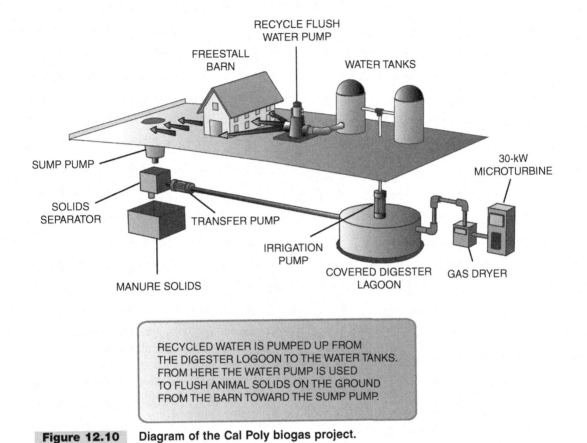

RECYCLE FLUSH
WATER PUMP

FREESTALL
BARN

WATER TANKS

SUMP PUMP

30-kW
MICROTURBINE

SOLIDS
SEPARATOR

TRANSFER PUMP

IRRIGATION
PUMP

COVERED DIGESTER   GAS DRYER
LAGOON

MANURE SOLIDS

RECYCLED WATER IS PUMPED UP FROM
THE DIGESTER LOGOON TO THE WATER TANKS.
FROM HERE THE WATER PUMP IS USED
TO FLUSH ANIMAL SOLIDS ON THE GROUND
FROM THE BARN TOWARD THE SUMP PUMP.

Figure 12.10   Diagram of the Cal Poly biogas project.

Digested biogas from the lagoon is compressed and dried in a desiccant tank and is then used by a Capstone Model 30-kW, 440-V microturbine that generates grid-connected electricity. The system also used a Unifin heat-recovery system from the microturbine generator exhaust that recovers heat for space and water heating.

CAPITAL COST AND ELECTRICITY BENEFITS

The costs of this methane-recovery system, the lagoon construction, the flexible cover, piping, gas handling, the microturbine system, and associated labor and engineering was approximately $225,000. Based on the measured biogas production and rated efficiency of the completed methane-recovery system, it is estimated that it will produce about 170,000 kWh of electricity and 77,000 kJ of hot water annually, which is estimated to be worth approximately $16,000.

In this case study, it was found that the 30-kW turbine, with an input of 13 m^3/h of biogas, produces 28 kW of electricity, which translates into 27 percent efficiency.

The project was supported in part by the California State University Agricultural Research Initiative and also was funded by the Western Regional Biomass Energy Program, whose contribution was matched in part by contributions from Capstone Microturbine.

Biomass Energy

For thousands of years, human beings have used biomass energy in the form of burning wood for heat and cooking food, which generated relatively small amounts of carbon dioxide. Since trees and plants, in order to grow, removed carbon dioxide from the atmosphere, the net effect of excess gas production on the environment was kept in balance.

With the advancement of societies and the growing sophistication of lifestyles, the use of diverse nonrenewable forms of biomass, such as coal and fossil fuels, shifted the balance of carbon dioxide generation and absorption. The net effect, as discussed earlier, was the greenhouse effect and other such air pollution and contaminants, all of which now challenge our very existence.

Fortunately, human intelligence has opened a window of opportunity that allows for the use of various forms of biomass, which include plants; agricultural waste; forestry and lumber residue; organic components of residential, commercial, and industrial waste; and even landfill fumes, that can be used as bioenergy sources not only to reduce atmospheric pollution but also to enable the creation of biodegradable products, biofuels, and biopower. These substantially reduce the need for nonrenewable fossil fuels.

Biofuels and Thermal Depolymerization

PYROLYSIS

Pyrolysis is the chemical decomposition of materials and polymers that occurs when they are heated in the absence of (and in some instances in the presence of) other reagents. The process is also referred to as *thermal depolymerization.*

In essence, the process involves the breakdown of complex matter into simpler molecules. It is also used for molecular identification in gas chromatography and mass spectrometry. Figure 12.11 presents a block diagram of biomass liquefaction via pyrolysis.

In industrial applications, pyrolysis is used to convert a single chemical substance such as enthylene dichloride into polyvinyl chloride. The process is also used extensively in the conversion of complex materials into useful products and gases.

Under extreme heat, pyrolysis is known as *thermolysis* or *carbonization.* In this process, substances are simply converted into their most basic elements as residue.

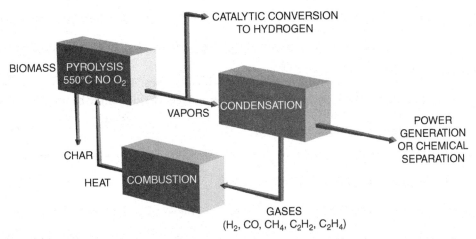

Figure 12.11   **Diagram of biomass liquefaction via pyrolysis.** *Courtesy of DOE/NERL.*

ANHYDROUS PYROLYSIS

Classes of pyrolysis processes that operate without water. These processes occur when-ever solid organic materials are heated at high temperatures in the absence of oxygen. This process usually is carried out under normal atmospheric conditions or in open air, which allows the exterior layers of the material to be burned or oxidized. However, the burned exterior shields the interior material and prevents exposure to atmospheric oxygen.

The process also occurs when compact solid fuels, such as wood, are burned. In fact, the visible flames of a wood fire are due to the combustion of gases released by pyrolysis, not due to the fact that the wood is being burned.

Anhydrous pyrolysis is also used to produce liquid fuels from solid biomass and plastic products that have properties similar to fuel. A process called *fast* or *flash pyrolysis* involves exposure of materials to extreme temperatures ranging between 350 and 500°C for less than 2 seconds.

BIOMASS PYROLYSIS

Biomass pyrolysis involves a procedure characterized by the rapid heating of biomass particles, which results in high yields of liquid hydrocarbons. The residency time to yield vapor products ranges from 0.5 to 2 seconds. To facilitate the process, biomass materials are ground into very fine particles. To insulate the interior particles from exposure to oxygen, the charred exterior layer at the surface of the reacting particles is continuously removed.

Since pyrolysis is a chemical process that requires heat absorption, making it an endothermic process, various methods have been devised to provide the required heat and to promote the chemical reaction. Some of the methods used involve the following:

■ Partial combustion of the biomass products through air injection. This results in poor-quality products, though.
■ Direct heat transfer with a hot gas. The problem is providing enough heat with reasonable gas flow rates.
■ Indirect heat transfer with surface walls or tubes. This technique has not yet been proven to be capable of transferring heat on both sides of the heat-exchange surface.
■ Direct heat transfer with circulating solids. This technique is quite effective, but it involves complex technology.

STACKING

This is a traditional process that involves the stacking of biomass materials such as wood in fixed beds and is used in the traditional production of charcoal. Owing to low heat transfer, this process does not yield liquid hydrocarbon materials.

EXPERIMENTAL PYROLYSIS TECHNOLOGIES

The following are some experimental pyrolysis technologies that are also used in biomass pyrolysis. Most of them have not been used in large-scale industrial applications.

This technology is adapted from the coal gasification process. It involves a mixture of sand and biomass particles that are fed into a screw conveyor. At the screw uptake, the screw mixes heated sand and biomass, which provides a good control of the biomass heat and residence time. This process is advantageous in that it does not dilute the pyrolysis products with the fluidizing gas.

Ablation processes   In this technology, the biomass particles are moved at high speeds, rubbing against a hot-metal surface. The process, which is referred to as *ablation,* allows biomass particles to char rapidly by maintaining a high rate of heat transfer. Another version of the process involves biomass particles that are suspended in a carrier gas that travels through a heated cyclone at very high speeds. In such a process, hydrocarbon particles are diluted within the carrier gas. A problem associated with all ablative processes is control of the ratio of the wall's surface to the reactor's volume, which decreases as the reactor size is increased.

Rotating cone   Preheated hot sand and biomass particles are introduced into a rotating cone in this process. Owing to the rotation of the cone, the mixture of sand and biomass is transported across the cone's surface by centrifugal force.

Much like the rotating cone, in this process, biomass particles are introduced into a bed of hot sand fluidized by a carrier gas, which provides circulation. High heat-transfer rates from fluidized sand result in the rapid heating of biomass particles.

Circulating fluidized beds   In this process, biomass particles are introduced into a circulating fluidized bed of hot sand. A separator separates the product gases and vapors from the sand and char particles. The sand particles are reheated in a fluidized burner vessel and recycled into the reactor.

Refuse pyrolysis   This is a process specifically developed to pyrolize domestic waste. Advanced forms of this technology, in addition to extracting various hydrocarbon-based gases, produce additional by-products, such as pressed charcoal and glass, that are reclaimed as usable material. Other pyrolysis processes convert waste film plastic into synthetic diesel fuel and agricultural waste and sawdust from wood into methane.

Biomass Energy Implementation

The following is an example of a biomass energy implementation. TMAD TAYLOR & GAINES have been working with Envirepel Energy, Inc., based in Vista, California, in the design and construction of the first of five biomass energy plants. Currently, they are working on modifications of their steam system for code and standards compliance, designing their cooling loop system, reviewing the design of the entire plant, and leading the effort in obtaining plan check approval for the entire installation. The facility that they are presently working on is known as Kittyhawk. The next four projects are known as Vista 2, Los Coyotes, Fallbrook Renewable Energy Facility, and the Ramona Landfill Facility.

The company was founded to solve multiple local environmental and energy problems by capturing waste streams at the source and converting them into "clean" forms of energy. The business model is intended to create tailored solutions to local energy and environmental challenges through a fully integrated system that is compliant with today's environmental laws. These systems convert solid fuels into usable thermal energy at 96 percent conversion efficiency from almost any biomass source, including green waste, sludge, plastics, municipal solid waste (MSW), wood, and other organics.

The company currently has 115 MW of projects in construction or in various stages of development in San Diego County. These project sites include business parks, rural agricultural areas, and metropolitan landfill sites. The company has developed a proprietary gasification and emissions-control system that produces inexpensive thermal and electrical energy. The gasification process takes place in a series of ceramic-lined units specifically designed to provide for the gasification/combustion of biomass materials and is suited to accommodate biomass materials of varying sizes and moisture contents. Highlights of the biomass process include

- Diversion of waste streams from landfills
- Gasification of waste streams to produce thermal energy
- Thermal-energy conversion into electricity
- Air pollution offset credits not required because of low-level exhaust emissions

The equipment installed at each facility (Fig. 12.12) includes a series of material grinders used to reduce the size of the waste to approximately 1 in. Ground materials

Figure 12.12   Photograph of Envirepel biomass energy plant.

are fed into a proprietary gasification/combustion system in which the prepared green waste is reduced to its mineral components at an approximate temperature of 600°F. The mineral components recovered are used as concrete filler material. As a by-product of this process, considerable amounts of thermal energy, in the form of hot gases, will be released. The hot gases are cleaned by several pieces of equipment, including a cyclone dust collector, a selective catalytic reactor, a scrubber, and a wet electrostatic precipitator, and will be cooled to less than 120°F before being released into the atmosphere. During the cooling process, a portion of the energy is recovered to heat water to produce steam, which then is used to drive turbines to convert further thermal energy into electrical energy. A portion of the steam energy and electrical energy is used to operate each facility.

Carbon Black

Carbon black, a hard-wearing black tread used in the production of tires, is also used as a premium fertilizer product called *biochar* and is produced from the pyrolysis of heavy-oil fractions. Biochar is somewhat different from conventional chemical fertilizers in that it contains *oligoelements* such as selenium that help to achieve higher crop yields. Biochar, when compared with other "natural" fertilizers, is safer because during the high heat of the pyrolysis process, it is totally disinfected.

Gasification Process

The gasification process is based on the extraction of a flammable gas mixture of hydrogen, carbon monoxide, methane, and other nonflammable by-products from coal and wood. The process involves partially burning and partially heating the biomass in the presence of charcoal. Gases, when they are produced, are compressed, liquefied, and used as a substitute for gasoline. Such fuels generally reduce the power output of a car by 40 percent.

SYNTHETIC FUELS

In the fabrication of synthetic fuels, the gasification process uses oxygen rather than air, which produces a gas consisting mainly of H_2, CO, and CO_2. When the CO_2 is removed, the mixture left is called *synthetic gas.*

The most significant property of synthetic gas is that almost any hydrocarbon compound may be synthesized from its molecules. The reaction of H_2 and CO, with the use of a catalyst, is another method for producing methane gas. Another possible product from the gasification process is methanol (CH_3OH), a liquid hydrocarbon that has an energy caloric value of 23 GJ/ton.

Methanol production consists of highly sophisticated chemical processes under very high temperature and pressure conditions. The use of methanol as a substitute for gasoline in recent years has made the fuel a significant commodity.

ETHANOL

Ethanol is a very high-energy liquid fuel that is used as a direct substitute for gasoline in cars. The fuel, which is produced from the fermentation of sugar solution leftovers from sugarcane or sugar beet harvest, has been produced successfully in large quantities in Brazil.

As mentioned earlier, feedstock used in fermentation includes crushed sugar beets and fruit. Sugars also can be manufactured from vegetable starches and cellulose by a pulping and cooking process or can be derived by a process that involves milling and the treatment of cellulose with hot acids.

After approximately 30 hours of fermentation, the brew, which contains 6–10 percent alcohol, is removed from the liquid by distillation. Fermentation is an anaerobic biologic process in which sugars are converted into alcohol by the action of microorganisms, usually yeast. The resulting alcohol is ethanol (C_2H_5OH), which is used in internal combustion engines either directly in specially modified engine carburetors or is mixed with gasoline, which then is referred to as *gasohol.*

The fermentation process of a biomass as media depends on the ease with which it can be converted into sugars. The best-known source of ethanol is sugarcane or the molasses remaining after the cane juice has been extracted. Other plants that can be readily fermented and have a high content of starch include potatoes, corn, and other grains that can be converted from starch to sugar. Biomass carbohydrates, such as cellulose, that do not readily ferment are pulverized into a fine dust and broken down into sugars by acid or enzymes.

The energy content of the final products produced from these processes is about 30 GJ/ton. The fermentation process requires an enormous amount of heat, which is usually derived by burning crop residue leftovers from sugarcane bagasse or from maize stalks and cobs.

Biofuels are renewable-energy sources derived from biomass, such as ethanol or wood alcohol, by a fermentation process. All plant and vegetation material carbohydrates, in the form of starch, sugar, and cellulose, are, much like beer and wine, fermented and converted into ethanol under proper conditions.

Another process for producing ethanol is gasification, which involves vaporizing the biomass at very high-temperature conditions. On vaporization, biomass gases are purged of impurities by the use of special catalytic media. Ethanol is commonly mixed with gasoline and diesel fuel to reduce vehicular smog emissions. Vehicles designed with flexible fuel–type engines not only can use ethanol as additives but also are capable of using animal fat, vegetable oil, or recycled cooking greases. Biomass-based alcohols used as pollution-reducing additives are sold commercially as methyl tertiary-butyl ether (MTBE) and ethyl tertiary-butyl ether (ETBE). Each year in the United States we blend 1.5 billion gal of ethanol with gasoline to reduce air pollution and improve vehicle performance. Most mixed fuels use 10 percent ethanol and 90 percent gasoline, which works best in trucks and cars. A mixed gasoline and ethanol fuel is referred to as an *E85 grade fuel.*

Biopower

Biopower or biomass power comes from the direct fire or burning of biomass residue, including feedstock and forestry residue, to produce steam. The generated steam from the boilers then is used to turn steam turbines that convert rotational mechanical energy into electricity. Steam generation is also used to heat buildings, such as industrial and commercial facilities. Figure 12.13 depicts MARTIFER's biofuel-production plant in Portugal.

GASIFICATION SYSTEM

In this process, the biomass is exposed to extremely high temperatures, which cause the hydrocarbon chains to break apart in an oxygen-starved environment. Under such conditions, biomass is converted and broken into a mixture of carbon monoxide, hydrogen, and methane. The gas fuels generated are used to run a jet engine–like gas turbine that is coupled with an electric generator.

BIOMASS DECAY

Biomass, when decayed, produces methane gas that can be used as an energy source. The decaying organic matter in landfills releases considerable amounts of methane

Figure 12.13   **A biofuel-production plant.** *Courtesy of MARTIFER.*

gas, which is harvested by drilling wells. Partially perforated pipes are strategically placed in a number of locations throughout the landfill and are connected to a common header pipe that feeds the collected gas to a chamber. The gas collected is compressed and cleansed by a purging process, which uses water steam to capture corrosive gases such as hydrogen sulfides. Compressed methane is used either as a direct-burning fuel or for microturbines and fuel cells in order to generate electricity and cogenerate heat.

Bioproducts

Interesting uses of biomass are in processes that convert them into any product that is presently made from petroleum-based nonrenewable fossil fuel. When converting biomass into biofuels, scientists have developed a technique for releasing sugars, starches, and cellulose that make up the basic structure of plants and other such vegetation.

Biomasses that have carbon monoxide and hydrogen as their building blocks are used to produce a large variety of products, such as plastics, antifreeze, glues, food sweeteners, food coloring, toothpaste, gelatin, photographic film, synthetic fabrics, textiles, and hundreds of other products that are completely biodegradable and recyclable.

Figure 12.14   Biofuel filling station. *Courtesy of MARTIFER.*

Chemicals used to produce various renewable materials derived from biomass are referred to as *green chemicals*. Figure 12.14 is a MARTIFER biofuel filling station in Portugal.

Some Interesting Facts about Bioenergy

According to the California Energy Commission (CEC), California produces over 60 million dry tons of biomass each year, only 5 percent of which is burned to generate electricity. If all the biomass generated were used, the state could generate 2000 MW of electricity, which would be sufficient to supply electricity for about 2 million homes.

Today, biomass energy provides about 3 to 4 percent of the energy in the United States. Hundreds of U.S. power plants use biomass resources to generate about 56 billion kWh of electricity each year.

Combined biopower plants in the United States generate a combined capacity of 10.3 GW of power, which is equal to 1.4 percent of the nation's total electricity-generating capacity. With improvements in biopower technology, by the year 2020, power capacity could increase by about 7 percent, or 55 GW. It should be noted that biomass fuel, like hydroelectric power, is available on a continuous basis.

Biodiesel

Biodiesel is now considered one of the most promising alternatives to petroleum-based diesel fuel. Biodiesel, which has the appearance of a yellowish cooking oil, is made from renewable vegetable oils or animal fats. Its chemical composition consists of a combination of long chains of fatty acids known as *monoalkyl esters*. The process of producing biodiesel is called *transesterification* and involves the removal of esters or fatty acids from the base oil. On completion of the process, biodiesel becomes combustible with properties similar to those of petroleum diesel fuel and can replace it in most applications. At present, biodiesel is used as an additive to diesel fuel, which improves the lubricity of pure-petroleum diesel fuel. With the inevitable cost escalation of crude oil, the use of biodiesel has proven to be a viable candidate in partially mitigating the shortage of fossil fuels, which at present are the world's primary transport energy source. Since biodiesel is a renewable-fuel resource, it can replace petroleum diesel in current engines, be produced in large quantities, and be transported and sold using today's commercial infrastructure. Biodiesel production and use have increased rapidly in recent years, and biodiesel is currently being used in Europe. In some provinces of France, farmers extract biodiesel from sunflower seed oil and can use it to fuel tractors and agricultural combines. In the United States and Asia, biodiesel sales and use gradually are growing, and a number of fuel stations are making biodiesel available to consumers. Recently, a growing number of large transport fleets have started to use biodiesel as an additive to diesel fuel.

Biodiesel has a flash point of 150°C and is not as readily ignited as petroleum diesel, which has a flash point of 64°C. Biodiesel is also much less combustible than gasoline, which has a flash point of −45°C. Biodiesel is in fact considered a nonflammable liquid by the Occupational Safety and Health Administration (OSHA). However, it burns if heated to a high enough temperature, which makes it a much safer fuel in the presence of vehicular accidents.

One significant property of biodiesel fuel is that it gels and solidifies at much lower temperatures than petroleum diesel. The gelling characteristic depends greatly on the property of the base feedstock of which the biodiesel is made. To overcome this problem, fuel-holding reservoirs are equipped with thermostatically controlled thermal elements that maintain the biodiesel at an appropriate temperature level.

One of the most significant properties of biodiesel is that unlike petroleum diesel, it is completely biodegradable and nontoxic, which can significantly reduce toxic gas emissions when it is burned.

At present, owing to the economic scale of production, biodiesel is somewhat more expensive to produce than petroleum diesel, which is one of the main reasons why the fuel has not found widespread use. However, as the cost of crude oil escalates and pollution abatement and the emission of exhaust from automobiles become more stringent, biodiesel could become a viable substitute for petroleum-based diesel fuel. Presently, worldwide production of vegetable oil and animal fat is not sufficient to produce large amounts of biodiesel to replace liquid fossil fuel use. Another issue related to the worldwide large-scale production of biodiesel is that it will require vast increases in farming the feedstock, which will result in overfertilization, pesticide use, and land-use conversion that would be needed to produce the additional vegetable oil.

ADVANTAGES OF PYROLYSIS

One of the most notable advantages of pyrolysis is that during the thermal molecular decomposition of chemical bonds, organic poisons, bacteria, and pathogens are destroyed completely. Another advantage of the process is that heavy metals can be separated from materials by the ionization of oxides. They also can be readily separated from the other products as well.

DISADVANTAGES OF PYROLYSIS

Agricultural and animal wastes that contain considerable amounts of methane are not suitable for pyrolysis, nor should they be used as boiler fuel. Table 12.2 represents a sample of residual components extracted from the thermal depolymerization process.

ENVIRONMENTAL EFFECTS

The environmental benefits of biodiesel include the reduction of carbon monoxide (CO) emissions by approximately 50 percent and carbon dioxide (CO_2) emissions by 78.45 percent on a net life cycle basis because the carbon in biodiesel emissions is produced by vegetation and is reabsorbed by plants. Biodiesel use also eliminates sulfur emissions present in conventional diesel fuels because biodiesel extracted from animal

TABLE 12.2 SAMPLE OF RESIDUAL COMPONENTS EXTRACTED FROM THE THERMAL DEPOLYMERIZATION PROCESS

FEEDSTOCK	OUTPUT		FEEDSTOCK	OUTPUT		FEEDSTOCK	OUTPUT	
Plastic bottles	Oil	70%	Turkey offal	Oil	39%	Paper (cellulose)	Oil	8%
	Gas	16%		Gas	6%		Gas	48%
	Carbon solids	6%		Carbon solids	5%		Carbon solids	24%
	Water	8%		Water	50%		Water	20%
Sewage sludge	Oil	26%	Medical waste	Oil	65%	Tires	Oil	44%
	Gas	9%		Gas	10%		Gas	10%
	Carbon solids	8%		Carbon solids	5%		Carbon and metal solids	42%
	Water	57%		Water	20%		Water	4%

and vegetable fats does not include sulfur. Biodiesel fuel use does produce emissions, but the emissions can be reduced through the use of catalytic converters.

BIODIESEL POTENTIAL ENERGY REQUIREMENT

According to U.S. Department of Energy figures for the year 2004, annual transportation fuel and home-heating oil use in the United States was estimated to be about 230,000 million gal. The amount of biodiesel needed to meet this demand cannot be met with waste vegetable oil and animal fat. At present, in the United States, the estimated production capacity of vegetable oil is approximately 23,600 million lb, or 3000 million gal. The estimated production of animal fat is 11,638 million lb.

Currently, U.S. projections of plant production required to produce biodiesel include the following:

- Soybeans—40 to 50 U.S. gallons per acre
- Rapeseeds—110 to 145 U.S. gallons per acre
- Mustard seeds—140 U.S. gallons per acre
- Jatropha—175 U.S. gallons per acre
- Palm oil—650 U.S. gallons per acre
- Algae—10,000 to 20,000 U.S. gallons per acre

The reason for such low soybean production is related to the fact that soybeans are not an efficient crop that could be used for the production of biodiesel. However, they are used extensively in food products.

In Europe, rapeseed oil is the preferred feedstock in biodiesel production. In India and Southeast Asia, the Jatropha tree is considered the most efficient fuel source and is also grown for watershed protection. Another plant specially bred for biodiesel fuel production is the mustard plant, which can produce a high yield of oil.

Production technology for algae harvest and oil-production technology for biodiesel has not yet been commercialized.

WORLD PRODUCTION OF BIODIESEL

United States　Even though biodiesel is somewhat more expensive than conventional diesel fuel, it is available commercially in most oilseed-producing states in the United States. To promote the use of biodiesel, as of 2003, tax credits have been made available in the United States. It is estimated that in 2004, 30 million gal of biodiesel were sold in the United Statement. As environmental pollution measures become more stringent, the U.S. biodiesel market, by the year 2010, is estimated to grow to 1 to 2 billion gal. At present, the cost of biodiesel fuel in the United States is about $1.85 per U.S. gallon, which has made it competitive with diesel fuel.

A pilot project in Harbor, Alaska, is currently producing biodiesel from fish oil derived from local fish-processing plants. The project is being developed in joint collaboration with the University of Alaska in Fairbanks.

Brazil   In the past decade, Brazil has commercialized ethanol use in automobiles and has recently completed construction of a commercial biodiesel refinery that was inaugurated in March 2005. The refinery is capable of producing 3.2 million gal of biodiesel fuel per year. The feedstocks used consist of a variety of sunflower seeds, soybeans, and castor beans.

Canada   Ocean Nutrition, Mulgrave, Nova Scotia, produces 6 million gal of fatty acid ethyl esters annually as a by-product of its omega-3 fatty-acid processing. The by-product is used by Halifax-based Wilson Fuels as fuel blended for use in transportation and heating.

13

FISSION- AND FUSION-TYPE

NUCLEAR POWER

This chapter will review nuclear fission and nuclear fusion reactor power technologies. Even though power generated from nuclear fission is not a sustainable source of energy, understanding the basic concepts of the technology will enable readers to appreciate essential differences between it and a fusion nuclear reactor system, which will provide the ultimate source of sustained energy in the future.

Another important consideration given to fission reactor technology is its present-day importance as a significant source of energy, providing about 17 percent of the world's electricity. In some countries, such as France, 75 percent of electric power is generated by nuclear power. In the United States, 100 nuclear power plants provide about 15 percent of the nation's electricity. According to the International Atomic Energy Agency, presently there are more than 400 nuclear power plant installations around the world. To understand nuclear power generation, we will first review the physics of atomic fission.

Properties of Uranium

Uranium is one of the most abundant elements on the earth, created during the Big Bang. When old stars exploded, the scattered dust aggregated and fused together to form new planets. Uranium-238, designated as U-238 (as discussed later in this chapter), has a half-life that is greater that 4.5 billion years, the same age as earth. The *half-life* of a radioactive substance is the time required for half its atoms to disintegrate; therefore, uranium is still present in very large quantities. U-238 makes up about 99 percent of the uranium found on our planet. U-235 makes up about 0.7 percent of the remaining uranium that is found naturally. Another form of the element uranium, U-234, is even scarcer and is formed by the decay of U-238. When U-238 decays, it goes through stages referred to as alpha and beta decay. It eventually becomes stable when it reaches

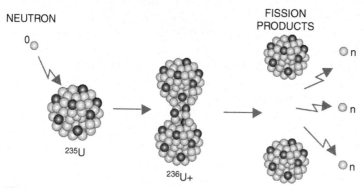

NEUTRON

0

^{235}U

$^{236}U+$

FISSION
PRODUCTS

n

n

n

Figure 13.1   **Fission-reaction process.**

its last chain of reaction and becomes U-234. Figure 13.1 shows a fission-reaction process.

U-235 has a unique property that makes it the main candidate for bomb and nuclear power production. U-235, much like U-238, decays naturally, and in the process, it generates radiation called *alpha rays*. It also undergoes spontaneous fission before stabilization. U-235 also has another unique property: it can undergo induced fission. This phenomenon occurs when a free neutron is impacted into the nucleus of a U-235 atom, which readily becomes unstable and splits into two lighter sub-component elements. In the process, the newly created elements emit gamma radiation as they settle into a stable state. In general, the ejection of neutrons depends how the U-235 atoms are split.

In atomic reactors, multiple collisions of neutrons with U-235 reach a boundary limit, referred to as the *critical state,* when one neutron ejected from each collision causes multiple fissions to occur. The splitting process occurs extremely quickly, in a matter of picoseconds (1×10^{-12} s). The multiplicity of collisions results in an enormous energy release, in the form of heat and gamma radiation. On the splitting of the first atom, the two atoms that result release beta and gamma radiation.

Heat energy released from the fission process is due to the fact that the resulting subelements, plus the neutrons, weigh less than the original U-235 atom. The difference in weight is converted directly to energy at a rate governed by Einstein's famous $E = mc^2$ equation.

When U-235 decays, the energy released in electronvolts amounts to 200 MeV. One electronvolt translates into 1.602×10^{-12} erg, each 1×10^7 erg being equal to 1 J or 1 Ws. The commutation of small energy release from one atomic collision, when translated into 1 lb of uranium, is equivalent to the energy generated by burning 1 million gallons of gasoline. It should be noted that uranium is one of the heaviest elements and therefore is far denser than many others. A single pound of uranium is about the size of a small orange, whereas a holding tank for a million gallons of gasoline would be the size of a five-story building with a footing that measures 2500 ft^2.

To increase the efficiency of fission reactions for commercial power production, uranium is concentrated in a process referred to as *enrichment,* where the total fuel mass is purified to elevate the U-235 concentration by 2 to 3 percent or more.

Nuclear Fission Power Plant

Nuclear reactors are constructed from several process chambers that typically consist of a nuclear-reaction chamber, a heat-transfer or heat-exchanger compartment, and an electric power steam turbine section (Fig. 13.2). Heat generation within the reactor takes place according to the nuclear fission processes just described.

The main nuclear chamber is constructed from a honeycomb of metallic tubes that resembles a Gatling gun chamber. A robotic fuel rod insertion mechanism holds numerous tubular fuel rods, each containing enriched uranium pellets that measure approximately the size of a dime in diameter and have a length of about an inch. Fuel rods are collected together into bundles and are kept cool while submerged in a pressurized water vessel. In the holding compartment, the rods naturally reach a slight supercritical state. This process is timed because if the rods were left in a supercritical state, the uranium eventually would overheat and melt.

To prevent such melting, moderator rods, constructed from materials such as carbon or heavy water that absorbs neutrons, are inserted into the bundle using a robotic mechanism that raises or lowers them into the reactor chamber. Raising and lowering the moderators allows control of the reaction rate in the nuclear-reaction chamber. To lower heat-energy generation, the rods are pushed into the chamber. In the event of an accident or fuel replacement, the moderators are immersed completely in the reaction chamber, thus shutting the reactor down.

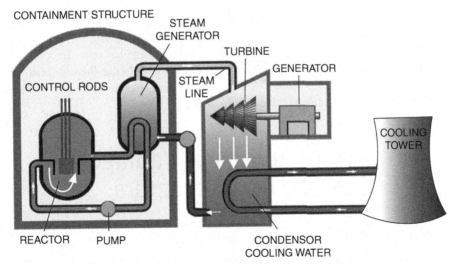

Figure 13.2   Components of a nuclear fission reactor plant. *Courtesy of AECL.*

Construction of a Nuclear Power Plant

The exterior a nuclear power plant resembles that of a conventional fossil fuel–fired plant, with the exception that the reactor's pressure vessel typically is housed inside a thick-liner dome that is intended to shield radiation. The liner, in turn, is housed within a much larger steel containment vessel, which houses the reactor core as well as fuel-handling cranes. The containment vessel is also protected by an outer concrete building, a dome referred to as *secondary containment,* that is designed to withstand severe earthquakes or accidental collisions with large jetliners. Secondary containment structures are also specially engineered to prevent the escape of radiation in the event of accidents or meltdowns, such as the infamous one at the Three Mile Island.

The lack of a proper secondary containment structure at Chernobyl, in the former Soviet Union, created a major disaster in Ukraine, causing large amounts of radioactive radiation to affect all of Europe. Plutonium-239, a by-product of the fission process, is an extremely dangerous cancer-causing agent.

Extreme temperatures generated within the reaction chamber liquefy carbon dioxide or metals such as sodium or potassium salt solution, which are then directed to a heat-exchange chamber as a result of heat transfer. Water is converted into steam, which drives steam turbines that produce electric power. The principal role of the heat exchanger is to isolate the radioactive superheated reactor liquid from passing radioactive isotopes on the way to the turbines.

Subcriticality, Criticality, and Supercriticality

As described earlier, when a U-235 atom splits, it gives off two or three neutrons. In turn, these free neutrons hit another U-235 nucleus and create a chain reaction, until such time that the entire mass of uranium reaches a critical state. In order to operate, nuclear reactors must be maintained in a critical state. In the event of insufficient free neutron collisions with other U-235 atoms, the fuel mass is said to be in a *subcritical state.* A subcritical state is ended with induced fission.

Advantages and Disadvantages of Fission Nuclear Reactors

Unlike fossil fuel power plants, in general, nuclear power plants, when designed properly, produce electrical energy without atmospheric contamination. From an environmental standpoint, a coal-fired power plant, in addition to contaminants such as carbon dioxide, sulfurs, and countless others, also releases some radioactivity into the atmosphere, far more than that of any nuclear power plant. However, nuclear power generation is also associated with some significant problems, including contamination associated with the uranium mining and purification process.

The malfunction of nuclear power plants, which can be a major source of public hazard, such as with the Chernobyl and Three Mile Island disasters, and containment of spent fuel, which is extremely toxic, can have repercussions that last for thousands of years. Another critical issue concerning spent fuel is its storage and transportation between plants, which poses a very serious risk for accidents and terrorism.

Effects of Nuclear Radiation

In elementary physics, we learn that atoms consist of three subatomic particles: protons, neutrons, and electrons. Protons and neutrons bind together to form the nucleus of the atom, whereas the electrons surround and orbit the nucleus. Protons and electrons have opposite charges: electrons are negatively charged, and protons are positively charged. Electrons and protons, having an opposite charge, attract and react with each other. Neutrons are neutral, chargeless particles, and their main purpose in the nucleus is to bind protons together. Since all protons have the same positive charge, they tend to repel each other. However, the neutrons act as the "glue" that hold the protons tightly together in the nucleus.

The number of protons in the nucleus, or the atomic number, determines the characteristic behavior of each atom. For example, the combination of an atom that consists of 13 protons with an atom consisting of 14 neutrons results in an element with a combined atomic weight of 27, which in Mendeleev's periodic table is called *aluminum-27*. In essence, a large majority of naturally occurring elements are a combination of different atoms that were fused together in the process of star creation.

In some instances, an element in nature could appear in a different atomic structure, where one element could have some extra neutrons. In this case, the elements would be referred to as *isotopes* of each other. For example, 70 percent of copper has an atomic mass of 63.55, whereas its isotope has an approximate atomic mass of 65. In the preceding example, the former copper element has 29 protons and 34 neutrons. The latter has 29 protons and 33 neutrons. Both isotopes of this element have the same physical characteristics and are quite stable. Figure 13.3 illustrates isotopes of hydrogen and helium.

In some instances, various isotopes of some elements are radioactive, and others are not. For example, hydrogen in nature appears in several types of isotopes, some of which are radioactive. The most common isotope of hydrogen has one proton and no neutrons and is designated ^1H. A second form of the hydrogen isotope, which is found in very small quantities in nature, is designated ^2H and is also called *deuterium*; it has one proton and one neutron. The deuterium isotope, which is 0.15 percent of the total hydrogen found in nature, is also very stable. Both ^1H and ^2H have identical physical appearances. Another hydrogen isotope, referred to as *tritium* (^3H), is composed of one proton and two neutrons. However, unlike the two previous elements, this isotope is

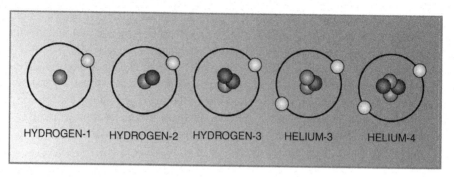

○ ORBITAL ELECTRONS

● PROTONS

● NEUTRONS

Figure 13.3   Isotopes of hydrogen and helium.

unstable such that in time, owing to radioactive decay, it is converted into helium-3, which has two protons and one neutron.

In other instances, some elements, such as uranium isotopes, appear in nature only in radioactive form. Other radioactive elements that appear in nature are polonium, astatine, radon, francium, radium, actinium, thorium, and protactinium.

Radioactive Decay

Radioactive decay is a natural process that occurs when an atom of a radioactive isotope decays spontaneously into another element by three types of processes: alpha decay, beta decay, and spontaneous fission.

Americium, which has an atomic mass of 241, is a radioactive element used frequently in smoke detectors and constantly emanates alpha particles. Alpha particles, which are composed of two protons and two neutrons, have the mass as a helium-4 nucleus. In the process of emitting alpha particles, the americium-241 atom loses mass and becomes a neptunium-237 atom. Americium-241 is known to lose half its atoms in 458 years. As such, 458 years is the half-life of americium-241.

All radioactive elements appearing in nature, depending on the type of isotope, have different half-lives, which can range from fractions of a second to millions of years. For example, another isotope of the same element, americium-243, has a half-life of 7370 years.

Tritium, or ^{3}H, is an isotope that undergoes beta decay, during which a neutron in the nucleus spontaneously turns into a proton, an electron, and a third particle called an *antineutrino*. In beta decay, the nucleus ejects the electron and antineutrino, whereas the proton remains in the nucleus. The ejected electron is referred to as a *beta particle* and becomes an ^{3}H atom.

In spontaneous fission, however, instead of throwing off an electron, an atom splits into two subparticles and throws off an alpha or beta particle.

Radiation Danger

Radioactive radiation, which results from the natural decay of elements, is without exception extremely dangerous to all organisms. The emission of electrons is the principal cause of cell death and genetic mutation, which it causes in humans and animals.

Alpha particles, as relatively large as they are, do not penetrate very far into matter, so they do not cause any harm. On the contrary, beta particles, which are somewhat smaller, can penetrate matter, but their harm is limited to ingestion and respiration. Beta particles are not capable of penetrating some materials, such as aluminum foil or Plexiglas. Gamma rays, like x-rays, can only be stopped by lead.

Owing to a lack of electric charge, neutrons can readily penetrate through very deep layers of matter. They can only be blocked by extremely thick layers of concrete or by liquids such as water.

Gamma rays and neutrons have an extreme potential for penetrating all sorts of matter and can readily destroy animal cells. In fact, the principle of the neutron bomb is based on the dispersion of gamma rays, which can affect living creatures without damaging material goods and buildings.

Nuclear Radiation Accidents

The following is a report on major accidents that have occurred in the history of civil nuclear power generation. Entitled "The Nuclear Safety Report," it was posted on January 6, 2006 by Uranium Information Centre, Ltd., Australia.

Three Mile Island (USA 1979): where the reactor was severely damaged but radiation was contained and there were no adverse health or environmental consequences.

Chernobyl (Ukraine 1986): where the destruction of the reactor by explosion and fire killed 31 people and had significant health and environmental consequences. These two significant accidents occurred during some 12,000 reactor-years of civil operation. Only the Chernobyl accident resulted in radiation doses to the public greater than those resulting from the exposure to natural sources. Other incidents (and one "accident") have been completely confined to the plant. Apart from Chernobyl, no nuclear workers or members of the public have ever died as a result of exposure to radiation due to a commercial nuclear reactor incident. Most of the serious radiological injuries and deaths that occur each year (2–4 deaths and many more exposures above regulatory limits) are the result of large, uncontrolled radiation sources, such as abandoned medical or industrial equipment. (There also have been a number of accidents in experimental reactors and in one military plutonium-producing pile—at Windscale, UK, in 1957—but none of these resulted in loss of life outside the actual plant or long-term environmental contamination.) It should be emphasized that a commercial-type power reactor simply cannot under any circumstances explode like a nuclear bomb.

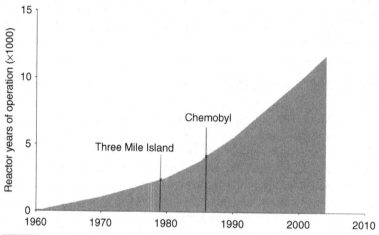

Figure 13.4   Diagram of a reactor lifespan operation.

The International Atomic Energy Agency (IAEA) was set up by the United Nations in 1957. One of its functions is to act as an auditor of world nuclear safety. It prescribes safety procedures and the reporting of even minor incidents. Its role has been strengthened in the last decade. Every country that operates nuclear power plants has a nuclear safety inspectorate that works closely with the IAEA. Figure 13.4 shows cumulative years of reactor operation.

Safety is also a prime concern for those working in nuclear plants. Radiation doses are controlled by the use of remote handling equipment for many operations in the core of the reactor. Other controls include physical shielding and limiting the time workers spend in areas with significant radiation levels. These measures are supported by the continuous monitoring of individual doses and the work environment to ensure very low radiation exposure than with other industries.

One mandated safety indicator is the core damage frequency. The U.S. Nuclear Regulatory Commission (NRC) specifies that reactor designs must meet a core damage frequency of 1 in 10,000 per plant per year, but modern designs exceed this. U.S. utility requirements are 1 in 100,000. Currently, the best operating plants are about 1 in 1 million, and those likely to be built in the next decade are almost 1 in 10 million. The Three Mile Island reactor, conforming to NRC safety criteria, was contained as designed, without radiologic harm to anyone.

Regulatory requirements today specify that any core-melt accident must be confined to the plant itself, without the need to evacuate nearby residents. The main safety concern always has been the possibility of an uncontrolled release of radioactive material, leading to contamination and consequent radiation exposure offsite. At Chernobyl, this tragically happened with severe consequences, once and for all vindicating the extra expense involved in designing to high safety standards.

The use of nuclear energy for electricity generation can be considered to be extremely safe. In comparison, every year, over 1000 people die in coal mines in order to provide this widely used fuel for electricity. There are also significant health and environmental effects arising from fossil fuel use.

Case Study: San Onofre

The San Onofre Nuclear Generating Station (SONGS) is located approximately 70 mile south of Los Angeles, California. The power plant incorporates two nuclear reactors, each powering three generators. Southern California Edison, the plant's majority owner, has recently signed an agreement with Mitsubishi Heavy Industries to manufacture replacements for existing 40-year-old generators. If approved, this would be the largest capital project in the plant's history. The current power-generation capacity of the plant is 2200 MW.

San Diego Gas & Electric, which has a 20 percent stake in San Onofre, has decided not to help pay for the improvements because the steam-generator replacement project is too expensive and would cost its 1.2 million customers approximately $163 million to pay its share. Figure 13.5 is a photograph of San Onofre Nuclear Generating Station in California.

Figure 13.5 San Onofre Nuclear Generating Station. *Courtesy of SCE.*

Canadian CANDU Reactor

The Canadian Deuterium (CANDU) reactor was designed by Atomic Energy of Canada, Ltd., as an alternative to reactors that use enriched uranium U-235 at concentrations of 2–5 percent. The reactor's fuel comes from pellets of uranium dioxide with a 0.7 percent concentration of U-235, which appears in nature. This renders power production considerably cheaper and theoretically can extend the life of the reactor.

Most underdeveloped countries find unprocessed fuel attractive because it does not require costly enrichment facilities. The Nuclear Non-Proliferation Treaty (NPT), which safeguards regimes under the auspices of the IAEA, regulates access to nuclear materials such as enriched uranium.

The moderators in the reactor (used to control the rate of fission reaction) are held in large tanks and are pushed into the core of the reactor by several horizontal pressure tubes. Channels for the fuel are cooled by a flow of water under high pressure in the primary cooling circuit, and such flows can reach 290°C. The high pressure within the tank prevents heavy water from boiling. As in the pressurized water reactor, the primary coolant generates steam in a secondary circuit to drive the turbines. The pressure-tube design means that the reactor can be refueled continuously because the channels can be accessed individually. Figure 13.6 shows a reactor heat-exchange diagram.

The CANDU reactor was designed without large pressure vessels. Large pressure vessels commonly used in light-water reactors are expensive and require heavy industry that is lacking in many countries. Instead, the reactor pressurizes only small tubes that actually contain the fuel. The tubes are constructed of a special alloy (Zircaloy) that is relatively transparent to neutrons.

A CANDU fuel assembly consists of a bundle of 37 half-meter-long fuel rods (ceramic fuel pellets in tubes) plus a support structure, with 12 bundles lying end to

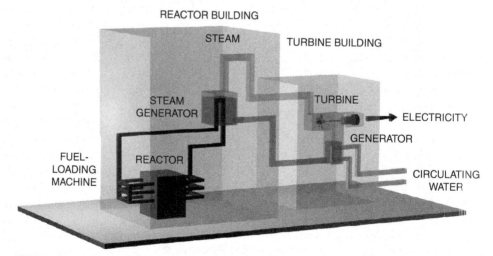

Figure 13.6   A reactor heat-exchange diagram.

Figure 13.7   A CANDU reactor fuel rod.

end in a channel. Control rods penetrate the calandria (a CANDU reactor's core) vertically, and a secondary shutdown involves injecting gadolinium nitrate solution into the moderator. The heavy-water moderator circulating throughout the body of the calandria vessel also yields some waste heat. Figure 13.7 shows a CANDU reactor fuel rod.

Since the bulk of the reactor is maintained at relatively low pressures, the equipment that monitors and acts on the core is quite a bit less complex. It only has to cope with high radiation and high neutron flux. In particular, the control rods and emergency equipment are simpler and more reliable than in other reactor types.

The reactor has the least accidents of any known type. This is partly because so much of the reactor operates at low pressure. This is also caused by the unique fuel-handling system. The pressure tubes containing the fuel rods can be opened individually, and the fuel rods can be changed without shutting the reactor off. The use of heavy-water moderators increases efficiency of operation because refueling the fuel assemblies is considered to be the most efficient feature of the reactor core while it is in operation, allowing control of reactivity. On the other hand, most other reactor designs require the insertion of degradable poisons to lower the high reactivity when refueling.

Another advantage of the fuel-management system is that the reactors potentially can be operated as low-temperature breeder reactors, a type of nuclear reactor that uses a mixture of plutonium and uranium or thorium and U-233 as fuel. These reactors consist of essentially bred isotopes of plutonium in the core, with a blanket of depleted or natural uranium. Breeder reactors use liquid sodium as the main heat-transfer agent, and because sodium has a very high boiling point, reactor coolant operates at high temperatures, under atmospheric pressure, without boiling. The high temperature, in turn, produces high-pressure steam, which contributes to high-efficiency power-plant operation. Unlike water, sodium is not a corrosive agent and in its molten form can be circulated in heat-transfer loops for long periods of time without any damage to its holding chamber or piping.

Heavy water, as described previously, slows down the neutrons that create nuclear fission. Heavy water consists of a higher proportion of deuterium, which, as discussed earlier, is a nonradioactive isotope of hydrogen with one proton and one neutron. Deuterium atoms, which represent about 1.5 percent of hydrogen found in nature, are much more efficient in retarding or blocking neutron activity resulting from fission. Deuterium, which appears in very low concentrations in lakes, is separated through a relatively complex process, which is added to the initial capital cost.

In a CANDU reactor, heat generated by the fission process is absorbed by water, which is circulated within an isolated, pressurized vessel. The primary superheated heavy water is pumped into a heat exchanger, where it transfers its heat energy to normal water that is vaporized to run turbines and generate electricity. The heavy water has a separate heat exchanger and circulation system for cooling the moderator.

A CANDU reactor's cooling-water tubes are pressurized to 1525 lb/in², which is lower than pressurized water-reactor system designs. The heavy water in the moderator system is not pressurized.

A CANDU reactor incorporates considerable control-system redundancy, which allows equipment to operate at extended cycles. In 1994, reactor operation cycle time for CANDU reactor number 7 reached 894 days. Fuel consumption, or burn-up, in a CANDU reactor is 6500 to 7500 MW per metric ton uranium (MTU), which compares favorably with the 33,000 to 50,000 MW per MTU obtained by many equivalent reactors.

The reactor power stations are designed to house multiple generator turbines, which are enclosed in a vacuum building for containment protection. The vacuum building is constructed as a large cylindrical building that houses eight reactors. In general, CANDU reactor power stations have between one and eight reactors per site. The Pickering Nuclear Generating Station, east of Toronto on Lake Ontario, has eight reactors per site. Nominal electrical energy output from the plant is 600 MW per unit. CANDU reactors, in addition to the 15 installations in Canadian provinces, have been providing power in Argentina, South Korea, Pakistan, and Romania.

USED-UP FUEL

Used nuclear fuel is both hot and radioactive. It is stored underwater in large cooling pools for up to 2 years after use (Fig. 13.8), until it cools. Some of the used fuel will remain radioactive for up to several thousand years. The storage of used fuel is a major concern for environmentalists. At present, there is no ideal solution for the disposal of wasted fuel. Currently, the storage of waste in underground salt mines is the only partially acceptable solution. Decommissioning nuclear reactors, once they have completed their useful service, is another issue that raises serious concern.

One waste material from a nuclear reactor is plutonium, which is known to cause cancer in even extremely small exposure doses. Plutonium is also the principal fission material used in nuclear weapons. For example, even though India's purchase of a CANDU reactor was based on the premise that it would be used for peaceful purposes, the reactor's waste was used to develop a nuclear bomb.

Figure 13.8   **CANDU reactor used-fuel container.** *Courtesy of CAEL.*

Pebble-Bed Reactor

The pebble-bed reactor was invented by Professor Rudolf Schulten in the 1950s. The basic concept was to make a very simple, very safe reactor with the idea of combining fuel, structure, containment, and neutron moderator in a small, strong sphere. To realize the concept, the fissile fuel was engineered from a silicon carbide and pyrolytic carbon that could withstand temperatures as high as 2000°C (3632°F).

The pebble-bed reactor (PBR) is nuclear reactor that uses a graphite moderator and is cooled by an inert gas. The reactor, when active, operates at very high temperatures and is categorized as a very high-temperature reactor (VHTR) that includes six classes of nuclear reactors. All six categories of high-temperature reactors use unique spherical fuel elements called *pebbles* (Fig. 13.9).

The pebbles, which are the size of a tennis ball, are constructed from pyrolytic graphite shells that contain microminiature fissile material particles such as U-235

Figure 13.9   A pebble of fuel for a pebble-bed reactor.

called *TRISO fuel.* The TRISO fuels are coated with a ceramic layer of SiC that provides a strong structural shell.

Each PBR contains approximately 360,000 pebbles that are compiled to form the reactor. The reactor, when operational, is cooled by inert gases such as carbon dioxide, helium, and nitrogen.

A unique characteristic of a PBR is that the reactor is cooled by natural convection or circulation of the inert gases, which maintains the reactor temperature under the safe temperature of 1600°C. A significant feature of the design is that the gases do not dissolve contaminants or absorb neutrons like water, which generally is used to cool conventional fission reactors. As a result, in the event of malfunction, PBRs are not subject to meltdown and contamination and are power limited or inherently self-controlling. In other words, the design of PBRs is that the core generates less power as its temperature rises, and therefore, the reactor cannot have an uncontrolled temperature rise when the machinery fails.

Modern PBR power plants combine a gas-cooled core with special stacking of the fuel that dramatically reduces the complexity while improving safety. A PBR power plant consists of a container that holds the fuel. Inert gases, mentioned earlier, circulate through the spaces between the fuel pebbles and carry heat away from the reactor. The heated gas is run directly through a turbine heat exchanger, where it heats another gas or produces steam. The exhaust of the turbine generally is very warm, and in some application, the exhaust steam is used to warm buildings or industrial plants.

It should be noted that much of the cost of conventional fission reactors is the result of the complexity of the cooling system. Water-cooled reactors have extensive and complex cooling systems, and the cooling water, when circulated through the core, is irradiated with neutrons. Therefore, the water, as well as impurities dissolved in it, become radioactive. Furthermore, owing to the extremely high pressure, the primary piping system becomes brittle and requires frequent replacement.

On the other hand, PBRs are gas-cooled and operate at lower pressures. Since the spaces between the pebbles form the "piping" in the core, there is no need for additional piping in the core, and the coolant gases do not contain hydrogen or cause embrittlement or failure. In most PBRs, the coolant gas is helium because it does not absorb neutrons or impurities, and hence, unlike water-cooled reactors, PBRs are more efficient and less likely to become radioactive. Another significant technical advantage of PBRs is that owing to simplicity of the design, the temperature of the reactor is not controlled by moderator control rods but rather coolant-gas circulation.

Hyperion Nuclear Power Reactor

The Hyperion nuclear power reactor (Fig. 13.10) is an innovative highly compact reactor that features a self-regulating power module that complements existing nuclear reactors by filling a niche for moderately sized distributed-power applications. The nuclear power module has been specifically designed to avoid the high construction costs and safety-related uncertainties associated with traditional reactor technology. Each unit has an electric power output capacity of approximately 27 MW. The reactor core measures $1\frac{1}{2}$ m in diameter and is factory-sealed, which prevents any external intrusion. The factory-assembled unit is designed to be sited underground, and on consumption of the nuclear fuel, it is returned to the factory for fuel recycling and refueling. The average useful life of the reactor is estimated to be 5 to 7 years. The Hyperion reactor has the following attributes:

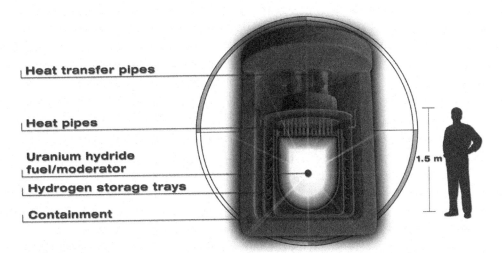

Heat transfer pipes

Heat pipes

Uranium hydride fuel/moderator

Hydrogen storage trays

Containment

1.5 m

Figure 13.10   **Hyperion nuclear reactor.** *Courtesy of Hyperion Power Generation.*

- Single-unit, sealed construction, and dispersed underground sitting that provides antitampering and antiterrorist protection
- Inherent simplicity and compactness of the design enabling mass production of Hyperion modules as turnkey devices
- Compact size that greatly reduces the financial investment risk in both the development and eventual deployment of the reactors
- Mass production potential that is very economical and competitive with conventional fission reactor technologies, which could substantially improve national energy independence

The reactor is small enough to be transported on a ship, truck, or train. Hyperion power modules are about the size of a hot tub—approximately 1.5 m wide. Out of sight and safe from nefarious threats, Hyperion power modules are buried far underground and are guarded by a security detail. Like a battery, Hyperion modules have no moving parts to wear down and are delivered factory-sealed. They are never opened on site. Even if one were compromised, the material inside would not be appropriate for proliferation purposes. Further, owing to the unique, yet proven science on which this new technology is based, it is impossible for the module to go supercritical, "melt down," or create any type of emergency situation. If opened, the very small amount of fuel that is enclosed would cool immediately. The waste produced after 5 years of operation is approximately the size of a softball and is a good candidate for fuel recycling.

Generating nearly 70 MW of thermal energy and from 25 to 30 MW of electrical energy, the Hyperion power module is the world's first small mobile reactor, taking advantage of the natural laws of chemistry and physics and leveraging all the engineering and technology advancements made over the last 50 years.

The reactor was invented at Los Alamos National Laboratory. Through the U.S. government's technology-transfer initiative, the exclusive license to develop and commercialize the invention has been granted to Santa Fe, New Mexico–based Hyperion Power Generation, Inc. (HPG). At present, HPG retains the proprietary nuclear power design and engineering for the reactor. Specific application that would be well suited for the Hyperion reactor include military bases, oil and gas recovery and refining, remote communities lacking accessibility to a source of electricity generation, and anyplace needing quickly installed backup and emergency power, such as disaster areas. Figure 13.11 shows the Hyperion reactor in an oil field deployment.

Significantly, deployment of this technology may help in reducing dependence on foreign oil, enable military installations to operate independent of local electric grids, and prevent pollution and greenhouse gases emitted by fossil fuel's electric power plants. Hyperion reactors provide a safe, nonpolluting method in which to provide electric power to remote regions for pumping and cleaning water. The lack of clean water frequently is at the root of poverty and societal instability.

HYDRIDE MATERIALS

Hydride materials (Table 13.1) have long been recognized as possible controls for self-regulating nuclear reactors. In addition, uranium hydrides were found to be a successful

Figure 13.11 **Hyperion nuclear reactor in an oil field deployment.** *Courtesy of Hyperion Power Generation.*

TABLE 13.1 COMMON HYDRIDE MATERIALS		
ATOMIC NO.	NAME	SYMBOL
89	Actinium	Ac
90	Thorium	Th
91	Protactinium	Pa
92	Uranium	U
93	Neptunium	Np
94	Plutonium	Pu
95	Americium	Am
96	Curium	Cm
97	Berkelium	Bk
98	Californium	Cf
99	Einsteinium	Es
100	Fermium	Fm
101	Mendelevium	Md
102	Nobelium	No
103	Lawrencium	Lr

reactor fuel very early in the nuclear era. They were cast into blocks using a polymeric binder to prevent the hydrogen from escaping. This binding of the fuel precluded any observation of the self-regulation characteristics inherent to the material. Hydride materials are chemical compositions of actinide (Greek for "ray emitting") elements.

ACTINIDE ELEMENTS

Even though the Hyperion reactor has been around for a long period, because of the requirement for a self-regulating condition, until recently, it was not deployed to determine the limits of the performance.

REACTOR SAFETY FEATURE

Uranium hydride (UH_3) stores vast quantities of hydrogen, equivalent to the density of hydrogen in water or in liquid hydrogen. This hydrogen, however, is volatile and is easily driven out of the hydride by any increase in temperature over the operating point of 550°C. The resulting decrease in moderator density drives the core reactivity negative. This drop in moderation occurs with very little change in core temperature because the excess power goes into the dissociation of the hydride. Potential overexcursions in temperature are limited by this chemical conversion in a manner similar to other phase changes, such as the boiling of water. A decrease in core temperature reverses the process by causing hydrogen absorption, which increases the moderator density and thereby increases core reactivity. Figure 13.12 shows the Hyperion reactor in a military base deployment.

The customary control of nuclear power devices by the mechanical insertion and removal of control rods has been replaced by the self-regulating, temperature-driven desorption/absorption of the moderating hydrogen. The complex arrays of detectors, analyzers, and control systems responsible for the safety and stability of conventional nuclear reactors have been superseded by the fundamental science and properties of the active materials.

System safety requires high-volume gas transport between the core and a hydrogen-storage medium. This dictates that both media be contained in a common chamber with substantial open space for this gas flow. The gas storage medium must have

Figure 13.12 **Hyperion nuclear reactor in military base deployment.** *Courtesy of Hyperion Power Generation.*

substantial storage capacity, suggesting another metal hydride, such as depleted uranium, with excessive surface area to absorb the escaping gas. As a final safety measure, an overpressure relief valve is included in the gas container to release the hydrogen if it ever exceeds a preset value, thereby eliminating any possibility of a catastrophic temperature increase. While the volume of gaseous hydrogen stored in the hydride is very large, the controlled combustion of that gas will produce a water volume approximately equivalent to the volume of uranium hydride in the core. Finally, in the event of an inadvertent increase in temperature owing to the inherent properties of the hydride moderator/fuels, the reactor activity will safely shut off.

REACTOR STARTUP AND SHUTDOWN

Under normal operating conditions, the Hyperion power module is started up from standby or low-power operation by raising the temperature of the hydrogen storage trays to drive stored hydrogen over to the core. Similarly, the system is shut down or put into standby by cooling these trays so that they will absorb hydrogen, extracting it from the core. Under equilibrium operation, the core temperature is saved to the storage-tray temperature. When the module is producing significant power, the storage-tray temperature is raised sufficiently to keep hydrogen in the hydride volumes affected by the temperature gradients that extract power from the fuel. This characteristic generates an additional safety feature. As a rule, the storage tray is maintained at a temperature above the average temperature of the fuel. This prevents the core from inadvertently heating the storage volume.

The modules are started initially after installation at their operating site by the carefully monitored addition of hydrogen into the sealed chamber. Making the storage-tray temperatures higher than the core ensures that the hydrogen fills the core first. At the first indication of fission, the hydrogen transfer is terminated. Stable and safe operation of the reactor requires that the chamber contain only enough hydrogen to bring the core up to criticality, leaving the storage medium almost empty of hydrogen. The storage material is kept at a level to absorb massive volumes of hydrogen in the event of any overtemperature excursions of the core.

Permanent shutdown and safety from any further fission activity would reverse this process. Initial shutdown would be accomplished by cooling the storage medium. This would be made permanent by evacuating the hydrogen from the gas-confining chamber. Residual radioactivity stored in the core normally keeps the core temperature elevated, ensuring that the core would be emptied first of most of its hydrogen. The reactor is permanently safe from any possible fission activity as soon as enough hydrogen is extracted that what remains cannot moderate the core up to criticality. Hydrogen extraction is accomplished at pressures above ambient by ensuring that the uranium powders are above 430°C during the extraction procedure.

EXPENDED FUEL

The hydride reactor can maintain control of the fission activity for a large excess of reactivity and fuel, which permits extended operational life and significant burn-up of the fuel. A reactor designed to burn a significant fraction of the fuel must be large enough to still reach nuclear criticality at the terminal enrichment design point.

FUEL REPROCESSING

One of the remarkable advantages of the Hyperion power reactor is the novelty of the fuel form. The hydride chemistry greatly simplifies the problems normally associated with nuclear fuel reprocessing. At the end of the useful life of the original fuel, the module is returned to the factory.

Adding heat to the fuel drives any remaining hydrogen off, leaving uranium metal. This metal is stripped of its fission product contaminants by simple zone refining. The small fraction of the processed fuel that contains the concentrated waste may require further processing to extract residual actinides to be blended back into the fuel fraction. Such extraction and recycling of the actinides would remove the long-lived radioactive components from the waste and reduce concerns over its long-term management. Reuse of the fuel would require blending in an admixture of enriched or otherwise fissile material to bring the fissile component up to the original 5 percent reactor-grade design level. This reprocessing requires only the addition of power to process the fuel, thereby adding no new material to the waste stream. The fission fragments can be further concentrated if it is economically useful or can be further processed to extract economically valuable radiation sources.

The simplicity of the process and the zone refining equipment make reprocessing this fuel economically viable. This permits the contaminated but unburned fuel to be recycled, greatly reducing the waste stream and dramatically improving the economics of future nuclear power production. Only the fission fragments mixed with some residual uranium requires permanent disposal.

Fusion Reactors

The following discussion of the physics and research development of fusion-reactor technology is based on articles published by the European Fusion Development Agreement (EFDA), whose Close Support Unit coordinates the Joint European Torus (JET), the largest nuclear fusion experimental reactor built. For more detailed coverage of fusion power research and development, interested readers should look to the Web pages of the preceding organizations.

PRINCIPLES OF FUSION REACTORS

Fusion power principles are based on fusing light-nuclei isotopes of hydrogen, which results in the release of significant amounts of energy. The process of energy release by fusion reaction is identical to that which occurs in the sun and other stars. In essence, energy release in fusion-reaction processes occurs when a combination of the hydrogen isotopes deuterium and tritium are heated at high temperatures, up to 100 million degree Centigrade, in a magnetically confined environment that lasts a few seconds.

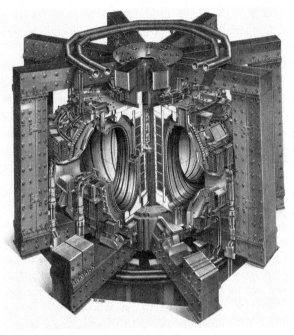

Figure 13.13 Diagram of
the Tokomak fusion reactor.
Courtesy of EFDA-JET.

At present, the most promising fusion-reactor configuration is based on early Russian experimental work on fusion. It is referred to as the *Tokomak*, which denotes a toroidal magnetic chamber.

The original large-scale fusion research device, which British scientists experimented on during the 1940s and 1950s, was housed in an aviation hangar located in Harwell in Oxfordshire. The device, which was called the *Zero Energy Toroidal Assembly* (ZETA), was at first a highly classified secret project, declassified only in the late 1950s when Khrushchev and Bulganin visited England. Accompanying this entourage was the renowned Russian fusion physicist Igor Kurchatov, who gave a lecture entitled, "The Possibility of Producing Thermonuclear Reactions in a Gas Discharge." The lecture disclosed the Soviet Union's research activity in the field, which eventually led to joint international cooperation. On declassification of the project, the United Kingdom undertook the construction of the first fusion-reactor research laboratory at Culham. At present, nations participating in this research include the European Union, the United States, Russia, Japan, China, Brazil, Canada, and Korea. Figure 13.13 is a diagram of the Tokomak fusion reactor.

One Russian scientist is believed to have prophetically expressed an opinion about the development of fusion reactor technology when he said, "We will not harness the potential of fusion until it becomes a necessity."

FUSION-REACTION PROCESS

As mentioned earlier, fusion occurs only at the extremely high temperature of about 100 million degree Centigrade. At this extreme temperature, the deuterium (D) and tritium (T) gas mixture becomes plasma, a hot, ionized gas. In plasma, the electrons are stripped from the atomic nuclei, which leads to ionization. In order for the positively charged ions to fuse, their temperature or energy must be adequate to overcome their natural charge repulsion.

To harness fusion energy, scientists and engineers are currently performing experiments to control very high-temperature plasmas. Much lower-temperature plasmas are now used widely in industry, especially for semiconductor manufacture. However, the control of high-temperature fusion plasma presents several major scientific and engineering challenges. These include heating plasma in excess of 100 million degree Centigrade and finding methods for containing the high-temperature plasma by sustaining it in a magnetically confined environment so as to allow the fusion reaction to become established.

CONDITIONS FOR A FUSION REACTION

In order to achieve sustained fusion parameters, the necessary plasma temperature, density, and confinement time must be achieved. The simultaneous occurrence of these three conditions is referred to as the *triple product*. In order to fuse deuterium and tritium, the triple product must exceed a certain mass, as recognized in the Lawson criterion. This criterion is named after British scientist John Lawson, who in 1955 formulated the fundamental theory. Attaining the conditions needed to satisfy the Lawson criterion ensures that the plasma can *exceed* the breakeven point, meaning that the fusion power generated exceeds the energy-input power required to heat and sustain the plasma.

Density   The density of fuel ions must be sufficiently large for fusion reactions to take place at the required rate. Reduced density or dilution of fuel, which usually results from gas impurities such as the accumulation of helium ions produced during the fusion process, can reduce performance efficiency. In the event of dilution, the fuel must be replaced, and helium products, referred to as the *ash,* must be removed. Figure 13.14 is a photograph of the plasma within the Tokomak reactor.

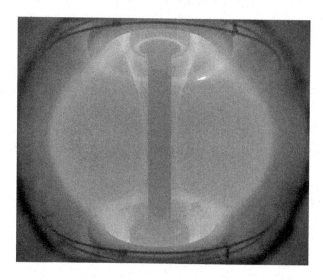

Figure 13.14   Plasma within the Tokomak reactor. *Courtesy of EFDA-JET.*

Energy confinement Energy confinement time is a measure of how long the energy in plasma is retained before being lost. The *confinement time* is defined as the ratio of the thermal energy contained in the plasma and the power input required to maintain these conditions. The JET, in order to retain energy for the minimum amount of time, uses magnetic fields to isolate the hot plasmas from the cold vessel walls for as long as possible. Plasma lost while magnetically confined is due mainly to radiation. Confinement time increases dramatically with plasma size because large volumes retain heat much better than small volumes.

In order for sustained fusion to occur, plasma temperature must be maintained at 100–200 million degree Centigrade. The energy confinement time must be at least 1–2 seconds, and the core density of the plasma must be at least $2-3 \times 10^{20}$ particles/m^{-3}, which is approximately 1/1000 g/m^{-3}.

Magnetic plasma confinement Plasma is comprised of positively charged ion particles and negative electrons. In fusion reactors, extremely powerful magnetic fields are used to isolate the plasma from the walls of the containment vessel, enabling the plasma to be heated to temperatures in excess of 100 million degree Centigrade. Isolation of the plasma from the magnetic field containment chamber reduces the conductive heat loss through the vessel wall. It also minimizes the release of impurities from the vessel walls into the plasma, which cause contamination and cooling of the plasma by radiation.

In a magnetic field, the charged plasma particles are forced to spiral along the magnetic field lines. The most promising magnetic confinement systems are the toroidal, doughnut-shaped rings used in the most advanced experimental fusion reactor, the Tokomak, which is currently being used by the JET research team. In the future, a much larger toroidal fusion reactor, sponsored by an international research effort named the *International Thermonuclear Experimental Reactor* (ITER), will be constructed in Europe.

Other nonmagnetic plasma–confinement methods, such as inertial confinement and cold fusion laser-induced systems, are also being investigated. Figure 13.15 shows photograph of interior magnetic plasma–confinement chamber of EFDA-JET reactor.

THE TOKOMAK

In a Tokomak toroidal fusion reactor, magnetic confinement is produced and maintained by a large number of magnetic field coils that surround the vacuum vessel. The toroidal field around the plasma cross section pushes the plasma away from the walls of the confinement vessel and maintains the plasma's shape and stability. The poloidal field is induced by an internal current, which is driven in the plasma and is also one of the plasma-heating mechanisms and by external coils that are positioned around the perimeter of the vessel.

The main plasma current is induced by a large transformer that changes current in the primary winding, a solenoid constructed of a multiturn coil wound onto a large iron core. It induces a powerful current of up to 5 million A in the plasma, which acts as the transformer's secondary circuit.

Figure 13.15 Interior magnetic plasma confinement chamber.
Courtesy of EFDA-JET.

NUCLEAR FUSION HEATING OF THE PLASMA

As mentioned earlier, one of the main requirements for fusion is that the plasma particles are heated to very high temperatures or energies. The heating process deployed in the Tokomak fusion reactor is shown in Fig. 13.16.

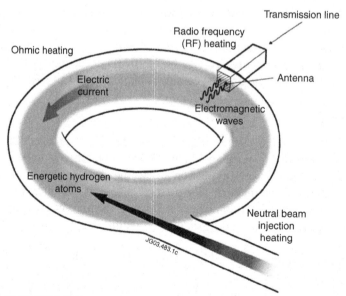

Figure 13.16 Plasma heating diagram for JET's
Tokomak fusion reactor. *Courtesy of EFDA-JET.*

Ohmic heating and current drive   The main-core transformer, discussed earlier, in addition to inducing currents of up to 5 million A, also isolates the plasma from the magnetic containment vessel walls. The current inherently heats the plasma by energizing electrons and ions within a perpendicular direction to the toroid, which results in many megawatts of heating power.

Neutral-beam heating   In addition to ohmic heating, beams of high-energy neutral deuterium or tritium atoms are injected into the plasma, transferring their energy to the plasma via collisions with the plasma ions. The neutral beams are first injected into the plasma by applying an accelerating voltage of up to 140,000 V. Since a beam of charged ions cannot penetrate the confining magnetic field, the beams are neutralized by turning the ions into neutral atoms before injection into the plasma. The beam-neutralization process, which requires additional energy, is derived from special heating systems.

Radio frequency heating   Through the use of electromagnetic wave frequency resonance, which matches ion frequency, plasma confined within the vessel is rotated around the toroid. Electromagnetic wave resonance provides a means by which to accelerate or slow the rotation of the plasma particles, allowing for the transfer of energy to the plasma at the precise location where the radio waves resonate. This allows localized heating at a particular location in the plasma. In the JET Tokomak, eight antennas in the vacuum vessel propagate waves in the frequency range of 25–55 MHz into the core of the plasma. These waves are tuned to resonate with particular ions in the plasma, thus heating them up.

Waves are also used to drive current in the plasma and can push electrons to travel in a specific direction. The electron direction control in the JET Tokomak is achieved by a lower hybrid microwave accelerator (at 3.7 GHz), which generates a plasma current of up to 3 million A.

Self-heating of plasma   Helium ions, or so-called alpha particles, are produced when deuterium and tritium fuse and remain trapped within the plasma and are, in turn, pumped away through the diverter. The neutrons, which are neutral, escape the magnetic field. Future fusion reactors currently under consideration will capture neutrons and use them as a source of fusion power to produce electricity.

The fusion energy contained within the helium ions heats the deuterium and tritium fuel ions by collisions and continues the fusion reaction. When this self-heating mechanism becomes sufficient to maintain the required plasma temperature for fusion, the reaction becomes self-sustaining, which means that there is no more energy input requirement to heat the plasma externally. This condition is referred to as *ignition*.

PLASMA MONITORING AND MEASUREMENT

Measuring key plasma properties, such as temperature, density, and radiation loss, is extremely important in understanding plasma behavior. However, since the plasma is contained in a vacuum vessel, its properties, which are characterized by extremely low density and high temperature, cannot be measured by conventional methods. Therefore, plasma parametric diagnostics require an innovative process of physical information detection and analysis.

Measurement techniques are categorized as active or passive. In active plasma diagnostics, the plasma is probed by laser beams, microwaves, and other probes to verify how the plasma responds to externally induced control. For instance, by use of interferometers, a microwave beam passing through the plasma slows down, especially when compared with its passage through a vacuum. This allows for measurement of the refractive index of the plasma, from which the density of plasma ions and electrons can be interpreted. The use of such real-time diagnostics is undertaken in a manner so as to ensure that the probing mechanism does not significantly affect the behavior of the plasma.

Passive measurement in plasma diagnostics, as with radiation and particle movement in the plasma, allows scientists to deduce how the plasma behaves under certain conditions. For instance, during deuterium-to-tritium fusion, neutron detectors measure the flux of neutrons emitted from the plasma. All wavelengths of radiation, including visible, ultraviolet, and x-rays, are also measured, which provides a detailed knowledge of fusion. Figure 13.17 is a graphic diagram of measuring devices used to verify properties of plasmas.

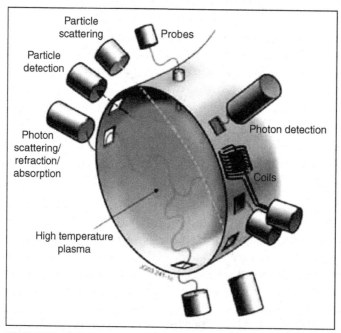

Figure 13.17   Techniques used for measuring the properties of plasmas. *Courtesy of EFDA-JET.*

Fusion as a Future Energy Source

As discussed in earlier chapters, the emission of CO_2 from burning fossil fuels is producing climatic changes. As global demand for energy continues to increase year by year, and as the world's population grows ever so rapidly, humankind becomes more and more dependent on energy supplies. Our obligation to mitigating environmental pollution and maintaining the survival of life as we know it depends on developing new sources of sustainable and renewable energy.

The future energy supply was discussed in a 2000 EU green paper that provides a European strategy for securing the energy supply. The main concern of the European Union was the dependency of Europe, which imports 50 percent of its energy from outside sources. If not mitigated, in 2030, the percentage of imported energy in Europe is projected to be 70 percent. In view of a long-term energy policy, the report highlighted the importance of fusion-reactor research and development. At the national and international levels, the future energy supply is becoming one of the key issues. As such, fusion offers a viable alternative to fossil fuels.

In the past, the JET has provided valuable research data in optimizing plasma stability and confinement. This has provided the basis for design of the next generation of fusion reactor device, referred to as ITER. This is an international collaboration with seven partners, which include the European Union, Japan, the United States, South Korea, Russia, China, and India. The research project will be a more advanced and larger version of the JET Tokomak. ITER will be capable of producing 500 MW of fusion power, which is 10 times that needed to heat plasma. In comparison, JET presently produces fusion power that is 70 percent of the power required to heat plasma. The ITER research center is currently located in Cadarache, France. The ITER reactor is scheduled to operate by the year 2015. During operation of ITER, a parallel materials testing program will be undertaken to develop and evaluate materials needed for the construction of commercial power plants. The experience gained from both these facilities is expected to be operational within 30 years.

ADVANTAGES OF FUSION ENERGY

Fuels Deuterium is extremely abundant because it can be extracted from all forms of water. If the entirety of the world's electricity were to be provided by fusion power stations, present deuterium supplies from water would last for millions of years.

Tritium occurs naturally when cosmic rays interact with atmospheric gases. Tritium also can be produced in heavy-water-moderated reactors. This occurs when deuterium captures a neutron in the reactor. When ^6Li and ^7Li are bombarded with neutrons, tritium is also produced.

Lithium is the lightest metallic element and is plentiful in the earth's crust. If all the world's electricity were to be provided by fusion, known lithium reserves would last for at least 1000 years.

The energy gained from a fusion reaction is so enormous that 10 g of deuterium, which can be extracted from 500 L of water and 15 g of tritium (which is produced

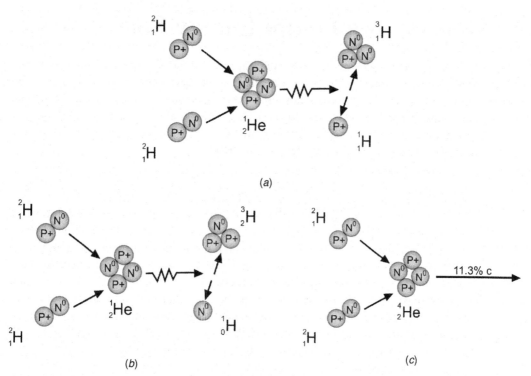

Figure 13.18   Fusion fuel production process. *Courtesy of EFDA-JET.*

from 30 g of lithium reacting in a fusion power plant), would produce enough energy for the lifetime electricity needs of an average person. Figure 13.18*a*, 13.18*b*, and 13.18*c* show the fusion fuel production process.

Environmental advantages

Inherent Safety   The fusion process is inherently safe because the amount of deuterium and tritium in the plasma at any one time is very small, usually just a few grams. The conditions required for fusion to occur, including the correct plasma temperature and confinement, are difficult to attain. Any deviation from these conditions will result in a rapid cooling of the plasma and its termination. Therefore, there are no circumstances in which the plasma fusion reaction can lose control and reach a critical condition, such as with a meltdown in a fission reactor.

Unlike conventional fission nuclear power plants, fusion power stations will not produce any pollution or greenhouse gases and will not contribute to global warming. Since fusion is a nuclear process, power plant operations owing to the energetic action of neutrons will cause radioactivity. However, the resulting radioactivity will cease to exist within 50 years. In addition, unlike fission reactors, there will be no radioactive waste produced from fusion reactors because the only by-product is inert helium gas.

INTERNATIONAL RESEARCH AND TECHNOLOGY DEVELOPMENT

The United Kingdom has contributed significantly to the research of fusion reactors, and in the past several decades, it has been a focal research center for the JET project. Key research programs in the United Kingdom are as follows:

- *Mega Ampere Spherical Tokomak,* which has been in operation since 1999. This program is the successor to the Small Tight Aspect Ratio Tokomak, which was put into operation at Culham from 1991 until 1998 and was the first high-temperature spherical Tokomak in the world.
- The United Kingdom Atomic Energy Authority (UKAEA) operates the JET facilities on behalf of Europe. The experimental program is coordinated by a European unit at Culham and involves scientists from all over Europe.

Future Fusion-Reactor Research and Development

The International Thermonuclear Experimental Reactor (ITER), which was referenced earlier, is located in France. It will have the same, but much larger, magnetic geometry as JET and will have several additional key technologies essential for the development of future power stations. ITER's design will allow the fusion reactor to be able to operate for much longer periods and will help to demonstrate the scientific and technological feasibility of fusion power. It is hoped that ITER will be the first fusion device designed to achieve a sustained burn, at which point the reactor will become self-sustaining. ITER, which is currently being built in Cadarache, France, is an international project that involves the collaboration of the European Union, the United States, Japan, the Russian Federation, China, South Korea, and India.

14

AIR POLLUTION ABATEMENT

Air pollution is a major global problem that has created numerous health problems that did not exist in past generations. It has resulted in an unprecedented number of illnesses, including asthma and cancer, that cause thousands of deaths each year. Air pollution is responsible for a wide variety of environmental problems, such as damage to forests, crops, and natural earth and aquatic habitats, all of which have had significant impacts on global economics. As environmental deterioration becomes more severe, the costs of rehabilitation and pollution abatement become increasingly important. Presently, there are numerous pollution-abatement techniques available for mitigating the problem.

It should be noted that air pollution is not a recent phenomenon. Ever since the outset of industrial revolution, environmental contamination and atmospheric pollution have been on the rise. The severity of air pollution and the public's awareness of it, however, are relatively recent. Ever since World War II, the pace of industrialization has significantly increased anthropogenic, or human-made, air pollution, contaminating the atmosphere with numerous toxic gases, such as sulfurous oxides (SO_x), nitrous oxides (NO_x), ozone, hydrocarbons, chlorofluorcarbons (CFCs), and heavy metals. Air pollution concentration and the composition of pollutants are directly attributable to the specific geographic locations of industrialized countries. Naturally occurring pollution, such as those resulting from forest fires and volcanic eruptions, also can cause significant deterioration in air quality but cannot be controlled or mitigated by policy action.

Atmospheric pollution released from identifiable sources, such as with volcanic eruption or chemicals released from a factory, is referred to as *primary pollution*. Pollutants that occur as a result of the chemical interaction of primary pollutants within the atmosphere are referred to as *secondary pollutants*. In turn, categories of primary pollution sources are subdivided into various classes, including mobile or stationary, combustion or noncombustion, area or point source, and direct or indirect. Mobile sources of pollution include automobiles, trains, and airplanes. Stationary sources include fossil fuel power-generation plants, whose emissions have a significant impact on air quality. An area source is one that is not a significant polluter, although it contributes to air pollution as part of a group of relatively small polluters.

Another class of "nontraditional" air pollution sources includes noise, odor, heat, ionizing radiation, and electromagnetic fields, which are associated with the function of various types of equipment, such as internal combustion engines, sewage treatment plants, metal smelters, jet aircraft, etc.

Effects of Pollution on Human and Animal Life

Air pollution has been linked to countless human and environmental health problems. In 1952, an incident known as the London "black fog" killed thousands of people and ever since has been an ongoing general health concern. Pollution also has been identified as the main factor in building deterioration, global warming, and widespread damage to the rain forests. If gone unchecked, it will bear serious economic consequences and alter the human way of life as we know it.

The costs of not solving the global pollution dilemma, regardless of the burden of capital investment required, is simply unthinkable, and the resulting consequences are difficult to predict or calculate.

The following are some of the effects of air pollution episodes in recent memory, which caused significant loss of life. In 1930, severe air pollution in Belgium's Meuse Valley caused the death of 60 citizens. In 1948, as a result of air pollution, nearly 7000 individuals lost their lives in Donora, Pennsylvania. In 1952, the infamous London "black fog" claimed the lives of approximately 4000 people. Similarly, air pollution in 1873, referred to as the "fogs," killed thousands of Londoners. At present, high levels of air pollution generated in England are attributed to the residential and industrial use of coal-fired furnaces.

Athens has recently experienced a sixfold increase in the number of deaths resulting from air pollution. Similarly, Hungary and India have recently reported that air pollution in metropolitan areas is the equivalent of smoking 10 cigarettes a day. Some researchers are convinced that the combination of sulfur dioxide and water in the air has created a situation in which people breathe toxic metals and gases deep into their lungs. This has caused as many as 50,000 deaths in the Untied States. Some of the diseases directly related to air pollution include

- Chronic respiratory and cardiovascular disease
- Alterations in body functions, such as lung ventilation and oxygen transport
- Reduced work and athletic performance
- Sensory irritation of the eyes, nose, and throat
- Aggravation of existing disease, such as asthma
- Storage of harmful substances in the body

In a recent study in the United States, it was determined that every ton of sulfur dioxide emitted into the atmosphere causes over 3000 pollution-related illnesses. In affected communities, this translates into $25 billion of medical expenses resulting from emissions from midwestern coal-fired power plants alone. Atmospheric pollutants also produce indirect effects on human health. Aside from acid rain, emissions of toxic and carcinogenic metals, such as aluminum, cadmium, lead, and mercury, are soluble in water and the surrounding area when they are leached from soil and lake sediments into aquatic environments. Here, they can contaminate water supplies. Acidic water also dissolves toxic metals from municipal and home water systems, thereby poisoning and contaminating drinking water.

Pollution-Abatement Equipment

A group of air pollution–abatement technologies, referred to as *selective catalytic reduction* (SCR), has been designed to reduce emitted gases such as NO_x, N_2O, CO, and volatile organic compounds (VOCs) through the use of catalysis processes. One such technology by Ducon uses ceramic honeycomb-shaped or plate-type catalysts constructed from titanium dioxide as a base material, with active coatings of vanadium pentoxide and tungsten trioxide that have been arranged at different levels. The working temperature of the catalyst ranges from 600 to 800°F. For NO_x pollutants, Ducon uses ammonia injection systems kept in storage tanks, which are vaporized and injected into the ceramic grids. These units are capable of trapping about 90 percent of NO_x, N_2O, CO, and high VOC gases.

BAGHOUSE FILTERS

Baghouse filters are pulse-air and reverse-air filters designed for industrial and utility applications. These filters trap industrial and mining residues as well as particulates such as coal, cement, and steel. Baghouse filters are state-of-the-art high-efficiency modular filters designed to handle gas volumes from several hundred to several thousand cubic feet per minute. These filters are custom-designed for efficient particulate removal. In large applications, such as with power plants, the air bags can measure up to 35 ft long and are constructed from a wide choice of materials, such as polyester, NOMAX, acrylic, Teflon, glass, Ryton, and fiberglass. These bags provide 90 percent particulate removal, including the removal of mercury that is released from coal-fired boiler exhaust gases.

DRY FLUE-GAS DESULFURIZATION SYSTEM

Flue-gas removal is accomplished by the use of several filtration technologies that use semidry removal processes (SDRs) or dry flue-gas desulfurization (FGD) systems, as well as dry injection–type systems. The semidry removal filters are custom-designed to absorb gaseous pollutants through the use of a spray dryer and a baghouse filter. Specially designed air-atomizing nozzles provide the liquid-reagent slurry in the spray dryer for the high-efficiency removal of SO_2, HCl, mercury, and other toxic components of flue gases.

Dry injection systems use lime, Trona, activated carbon, and other dry reagents to remove sulfur dioxide, dioxins, mercury, hydrogen chloride, and fumes. For higher absorption, the reagents are added in a recirculating-type reactor and then are injected into the filter. The particulates then are recovered downstream using a baghouse filter. Dry injection systems remove over 90 percent of SO_2.

Dry-type scrubbers used with the preceding desulfurization process generate a dry waste product that is disposed of by conventional fly ash–handling equipment.

MULTITUBE CYCLONES

Another product manufactured for trapping pollution particulates is referred to as the *multitube cyclone*. These filters are constructed from long tubes that trap particulates by creating a cyclone through an air-suction process. This type of equipment has no moving parts, has a sturdy construction, and is designed to trap a wide range of gases at various inlet loadings. This technology has served the industry successfully for over 50 years. Cyclones are capable of removing up to 99.9 percent of particles of 7 μm and larger in size.

WET AND DRY PRECIPITATORS

Wet electrostatic precipitators This technology uses a wet electrostatic precipitator process that traps particulates and gases by bombarding the medium with electrons. Polarized plates, electronically controlled, create polarization and achieve over 99.9 percent precipitation and removal of particles measuring from 0.01 to 0.05 μm in size. A condensing-type precipitator is used to trap metal oxides. Notable advantages of this technology are that it is nonclogging owing to widely spaced electrodes, has a simple construction, is heavy-duty and maintenance-free, and is also resistive to corrosion.

Dry electrostatic precipitators This type of precipitator uses dry electrostatic precipitation principles for trapping particulates. The precipitators use high-voltage power for particulate polarization and sometimes use 100 kVA of electrical energy in a single precipitator. The units, which can be used in modular fashion, each measure from 10 to 30 ft in height. Standard modules are installed in parallel or series arrangements so as to fulfill a wide range of collection-surface requirements.

ACTIVATED-CARBON FILTER

Carbon absorbers are custom filters designed to remove odor-causing components, such as hydrogen sulfide, mercaptans, organic acids, aldehydes, and ketones, in various industrial and municipal applications. These units are constructed in single-bed forms and are available in capacities of up to 10,000 ft³/min. Dual-bed units are also used for higher capacities.

W-3 DYNAMIC SCRUBBERS

These compact modular scrubbers have self-cleaning wet-fan features that provide high dust-collection efficiency in minimum spaces. They also have low water requirements.

Multivane centrifugal scrubber Centrifugal scrubbers use a multivane centrifugal design and are particularly well suited for applications involving heavy dust loads and large particulates. Their operation is based on the principle of centrifugal action that takes place between gas streams and liquid, and they are designed with either spin vanes or spray manifolds for liquid distribution. These types of scrubbers are capable of removing particles in the 1- to 8-μm range.

Wet-approach Venturi scrubbers These scrubbers feature a wetted wall inlet that eliminates wet-dry line buildup and permits the direct recycling of solids and liquids. The scrubbing liquid is distributed by spray nozzles in the Venturi tube and creates a mist that results in the efficient scrubbing of particulates. These scrubbers are capable of removing 99.9 percent of particulates in the submicron range.

CHEMICAL ABSORPTION TOWERS

Chemical absorption towers (CATs) are designed to absorb and remove SO_2, HCl, H_2S, TRS, organics matter, odors, fumes, and other toxic components. A proprietary technology by Ducon provides spray towers that use special nozzles that entrap up to 99.9 percent particulate-removal efficiency.

FLUE GAS DESULFURIZATION

A class of filtration system known as *flue gas desulfurization* is designed to remove sulfur dioxide from flue gases using a variety of reagents, such as limestone, ammonia, fly ash, magnesium oxide, soda ash, seawater, and double alkali. The efficiency of removal with these technologies can exceed 99 percent.

CHEMICAL STRIPPERS

Chemical stripers are engineered units that remove benzene, VOCs, and other inorganic chemicals and gases from groundwater and wastewater streams. Strippers are capable of removing benzene and chlorinated hydrocarbons at flow rates ranging from 1 to 100,000 gal/min.

SEWAGE TREATMENT

Sewage treatment is the process of removing the majority of contaminants from wastewater or sewage. The process produces a liquid sludge suitable for disposal in the environment. In general, sewage produced from residential and industrial buildings is channeled into treatment plants by pipes and underground canals. The most primitive type of treatment of sewage and most wastewaters is the separation of solids and liquids by use of a settlement process.

Sewage is the liquid waste from toilets, bath tubs, showers, and kitchens and also may contain some liquid waste from industry and commerce. Sometimes sewage also may include surface and storm water resulting from rain drained from roofs. In the

United States and Canada, sewage has a separate conduit from surface and storm water systems. However, European countries transport liquid discharges and storm water together to a common treatment facility in integrated sewer systems.

The site where the water is processed is called the *sewage treatment plant.* Sewage treatment plants use biologic processes to purify water. The process of treatment consists of the following:

- *Mechanical treatment process:* Consists of removal of large objects, sand, and precipitants.
- *Biologic treatment process:* Consists of oxidation or an oxidizing bed and is also referred to as an *aerated system* or *postprecipitation.* It involves the removal of solids by filtration.
- *Chemical treatment process:* This is usually combined with the settlement process, which removes solids during filtration. The combined process is referred to as *physical-chemical treatment.*

Primary treatment process   The main purpose of primary treatment is to reduce the amount of oils, grease, fats, sand, grit, and coarse solids. This step is accomplished by special machinery; hence it is known as *mechanical treatment.*

The removal of large objects from the effluent is achieved by straining and removal of all rags, sticks, condoms, sanitary napkins or tampons, cans, fruit, etc. that are deposited in the sewer system. This process involves a manual or automated mechanically raked screen. In some instances, manual intervention is required to avoid damage to sensitive equipment, which can be caused by such large objects.

Sand and sedimentation removal   Sand and grit removal is accomplished by the use of grit channels, in which the velocity of the incoming wastewater is carefully controlled to allow grit and stones to settle but still maintain the majority of the organic material within the flow. Such machinery is comparable to a sand catcher. Sand and stones are removed at the primary stages of the process to avoid damage to pumps and other equipment in subsequent treatment stages. The treatment process includes a sand washer, also called a *grit classifier,* followed by a conveyor that transports the sand to a container for disposal. The contents of the sand catcher are also fed into an incinerator along with the sludge, although in some instances the sand and grit are sent to a landfill.

Effluent screening   Screening, or maceration, is a process that removes large floating objects such as rugs and cardboard from the effluent by means of fixed or rotating screens. Materials collected through the screening process are returned to the sludge or sent to a landfill or incinerator. Solid objects collected by maceration are also shredded into pieces by rotating knifes.

Primary sedimentation   On completion of large-object removal, the sewage is passed through large circular or rectangular tanks called *sedimentation basins.* The tanks are large enough to allow human waste and solids to settle. Floating material, such as grease and plastics, can rise to the surface, where they are skimmed off. The main purpose of the primary stage is to produce a homogeneous liquid capable of being treated biologically and a sludge or scum that can be processed or treated separately. Primary settlement tanks usually are equipped with mechanically driven sludge and scum scrapers and pumps that automatically dump the material into hoppers that are transported to sludge treatment equipment.

Secondary treatment   Secondary treatment is a process designed to alter the biologic content of sewage, such as that derived from human waste, food waste, soaps, and detergents. The biologic breakdown is accomplished by oxygen, which destroys bacteria living within the effluent. In general, bacteria and protozoa consume biodegradable and organic substances such as sugars, fats, etc. Arid, less soluble matter in the secondary treatment system is classified into two categories: fixed and suspended. In fixed-film systems, the biomass grows on a medium, and the sewage passes over its surface. In suspended systems, such as in activated sludge, the biomass is well mixed with the sewage. In essence, film-process systems require a smaller space than equivalent suspended-growth systems. However, suspended-growth systems are more efficient in removing suspended solids. Figures 14.1 and 14.2 shows a filtration and a sedimentation system at the Hyperion Sewage Treatment Plant in Los Angeles, California.

Roughing   Roughing filters are constructed from synthetic media that treat and trap industrial organic waste. Theses filters have a tall cylindrical shape and are designed to allow large amounts of hydraulic liquid and a flow of air to pass through. In some installations, the air is forced through the medium by blowers.

Figure 14.1   View of sedimentation tanks at the Hyperion Sewage Treatment Plant, Los Angeles, California. *Courtesy of Hyperion.*

Figure 14.2   View of sedimentation basins at the Hyperion Sewage Treatment Plant, Los Angeles, California.
Courtesy of Hyperion.

Activated sludge   Activated sludge plants use a variety of mechanisms and processes that dissolve oxygen within the clarified effluent to substantially remove organic material. They also trap particulate material and convert ammonia into nitrite, which is eventually transformed into nitrogen gas.

Oxidizing filter beds   In this stage, a trickling filter bed constructed of plastic spreads sewage onto a large, deep basin made up of coke, carbonized coal, chips, or a specially perforated synthetic or plastic medium that has a large surface area to provide support for a thin film referred to as the *sewage liquor.* The liquor is distributed by means of large paddle arms that rotate at a central pivot. The drained water collected within the basin is then exposed to a source of forced air that percolates up through the bottom of the bed, keeping it aerated. Biologic films of bacteria, such as protozoa, collected on the surface of the filter medium digest and reduce the organic content. In some plants, slowly rotating paddles submerged in the liquor are used to enhance aeration.

Secondary sedimentation   Secondary sedimentation is the last stage of treatment in which low-level suspended biologic and organic materials are filtered.

Tertiary treatment   Tertiary treatment is the final stage of the filtration process, in which the quality of the effluent is raised to required local standards before it is discharged into the sea, river, lake, ground, or natural environment. Depending on local sewage treatment regulations, tertiary treatment also can be followed by disinfection.

Effluent polishing   Effluent polishing is a stage in which the processed sewage is passed through sand filters that remove much of the suspended residual matter. An activated carbon filter also removes residual toxins.

Lagooning   Lagooning is a filtration stage that provides additional settlement and improved biologic properties for the treated water. The process involves storage of the treated sewage in large human-made ponds or lagoons. These lagoons have very large surface areas, which provide natural aerobic conditions that encourage myriad invertebrates and macrophyte reeds to filter and digest fine particulates. In some instances, human-engineered wetlands are designed to provide the natural settings provided by lagoons.

Nutrient removal   In general, residential and industrial sewage contains high levels of nutrients such as nitrogen, ammonia, and phosphorus that in certain forms may be toxic to fish and aquatic invertebrates. Nutrients also encourage the growth of unwanted weeds or algae, which produce toxins, promote bacterial growth, and eventually deplete oxygen in the water and suffocate desirable fish. The transport of nutrients by streams and rivers to lakes or shallow seas also can cause severe oxygen starvation or eutrophication, which kills sweet-water fish. The removal of nitrogen and phosphorus from wastewater is done either biologically or by chemical precipitation.

Nitrogen removal is accomplished by the biologic conversion or reduction of nitrogen from ammonia to nitrate in a process called *nitrification.* Nitrate is converted to nitrogen gas in a process called *denitrification* and then is released into the atmosphere.

Phosphorus removal is also achieved by a process in which biologically enhanced phosphorus that contains specific bacteria is introduced into the treated sewage water in large quantities. Phosphorus removal also can occur through chemical precipitation by the use of ferric chloride or an aluminum salt called *alum.*

Disinfection   The purpose of disinfection is to destroy and reduce the number of microorganisms and pathogens. The effectiveness of disinfection is subject to properties of the water, such as turbidity, pH level, type of disinfection agent used and its dosage, water temperature, and other environmental variables. Elevated water turbidity diminishes disinfection because solid matter can shield organisms from exposure. Longer periods of exposure to disinfection increase bacterial reduction. Common methods of disinfection include exposure to ozone, chlorine, or ultraviolet (UV) light. Disinfection is not generally used in European wastewater treatment, but owing to the low cost of the process, it is the most common wastewater treatment method in North America.

A major disadvantage of disinfection by the chlorination process is that residual organic matter can generate chlorinated organic matter, which is considered carcinogenic and toxic to the environment and aquatic species. UV light is considered the safest method because it destroys pathogens without affecting the quality of the wastewater. UV radiation damages the genetic structure of viruses and other pathogens, making them incapable of reproduction. The main disadvantage of UV disinfection is that the process requires frequent lamp replacement and maintenance, and its effectiveness diminishes with the presence of floating particulates that block the UV rays.

Ozone exposure is another way of destroying bacteria. Ozone is produced by passing regular oxygen through a voltage arc in which it joins with a third oxygen atom, forming ozone. Ozone is an exceedingly powerful oxidizing agent that reacts with and oxidizes most organic material, thereby destroying any microorganisms that come into contact with it. Ozone use in disinfection is much safer than chlorine because it destroys bacteria without introducing additional chemicals into the water. The disadvantage of ozone is its production, which requires sophisticated equipment and maintenance personnel.

BATCH REACTORS

Batch reactors are compact, simplified plants that occupy little space and treat wastewater to meet required environmental standards. Batch reactors essentially combine several processes of treatment into a single stage and provide an alternative to the construction of large treatment facilities.

An example of a combined process is secondary treatment and settlement, where activated sludge is mixed with raw incoming sewage and aerated. The resulting mixture is then allowed to settle, which produces a high-quality effluent. This type of treatment technology is deployed in many parts of the world.

The main disadvantage of a batch reactor is that the filtration process requires precise control and timing, which can be achieved only by means of computerized automation, necessitating a sophisticated level of operation and maintenance.

SLUDGE TREATMENT

The coarse solids and secondary biosolids accumulated in the wastewater treatment process consist of toxic organic and inorganic compounds and metals such as lead and chromium. A process referred to as *digestion* is implemented to reduce the amount of organic matter and disease-causing microorganisms present in the solids. The digestion process consists of anaerobic digestion, aerobic digestion, and composting.

Anaerobic digestion   Anaerobic digestion is either a thermophilic ("heat loving") process in which sludge is fermented in special tanks that are heated to about 38°C or a mesophilic ("moderate temperature loving") process in which sludge is kept in large tanks for weeks. Thermophilic digestion generates a large amount of methane, which is filtered, dehumidified, compressed, and used to heat the tanks and run microturbines, as described earlier in large treatment plants, where considerable quantities of methane are harvested, sufficient energy can be generated to produce electricity that can run the digestion facility machinery. Methane digestion by the anaerobic process requires about 30 days for gas production.

Aerobic digestion   Aerobic digestion is a bacterial process in which digestion occurs in the presence of oxygen. These are referred to as *aerobic conditions,* where special bacteria convert organic matter into carbon dioxide. On the depletion of organic matter, bacteria die and are in turn consumed by other bacteria. This process is called *endogenous respiration,* in which solids within the water are reduced. The aerobic digestion process is significantly faster than the anaerobic digestion process described earlier. In addition, capital-cost requirements for the process are much lower. However, owing to the higher energy requirements, the operating costs are greater.

Composting   Composting is essentially an aerobic process that involves mixing wastewater solids with other sources of hydrocarbon by-products such as sawdust, straw, and wood chips. In the presence of oxygen, bacteria digest the wastewater solids and the mixed carbon source. In the process, they produce a large amount of heat, which destroys bacterial pathogens and microorganisms and produces solid fertilizers that are used as soil builders in agriculture.

SLUDGE DISPOSAL

Remnant sludge, after treatment, is a thickened cake that is produced by dewatering the settlement tank and lagoon sludge using centrifugal spinning machinery. The thickened cake is disposed of by injection on land, a dangerous practice that can produce leachates, which can be mixed and deposited in landfills or incinerated. In some instances, liquid sludge also can penetrate groundwater.

Emerging Future Technologies: Bioreactors

A new technology that is expected to emerge within the next few years is based on the use of natural photosynthesis by plants that absorb carbon to grow while producing oxygen. Experiments conducted at numerous laboratories indicate that a special species of algae, in addition to absorbing carbon dioxide, also absorbs sulfur dioxide and nitrogen oxides, major contributors to acid rain. An experimental vessel, called a *bioreactor,* intakes flue gas emissions at 55°C and mixes them with water, which embeds a recently discovered cyanobacteria called *Chroogloeocystis siderophila,* found in the hot springs of Yellowstone National Park. By spreading inside the bioreactor by means of parabolic mirror reflectors and plastic fiberoptic cables, it was found that the algae devoured the toxic gases and thrived in the process. Presently, an issue that concerns scientists is that if released outside the bioreactor, the cyanobacteria might constitute an invasive species with unknown consequences.

Groundwater Replenishment System

This section describes a groundwater replenishment system deployed at the Orange County Water District, in Orange County, California.

DESCRIPTION

The Orange County Water District Groundwater Replenishment (GWR) System is the largest water-purification and reuse project of its kind in the world. The new system increases Orange County's water independence by providing a locally controlled, drought-proof supply of safe, high-quality water. At full capacity, it will generate enough pure water to meet the needs of 500,000 people. The purified water exceeds all state and federal drinking water standards and has water quality similar to that of distilled water.

The GWR system takes highly treated wastewater that is currently going to the ocean and purifies and reclaims it to produce 72,000 acre-ft of purified water each year. It produces water using half the energy required to pump water to southern California from northern California—saving enough energy to power 21,000 homes each year.

This project was more than a decade in development, and the elected leaders of the Orange County Water District (OCWD) and the Orange County Sanitation District (OCSD) were visionary in their pursuit of the GWR system and their understanding of water reuse and its potential as a new water resource. The partnership between the two agencies to develop the GWR system is groundbreaking and has already significantly assisted in the advancement of water reuse throughout the world. The GWR system is being replicated in Australia and other locations in the United States facing water-supply challenges, such as Florida and Colorado. Additionally, the GWR system's water-quality research and data aided Singapore in pursuing its world-renowned "New Water" project.

AGENCY DESCRIPTIONS

The OCWD was formed in 1933 as a California special district to manage the large groundwater basin that underlies north and central Orange County. The groundwater basin supplies more than half the water needs of 2.3 million residents in the cities of Anaheim, Buena Park, Cypress, Costa Mesa, Fountain Valley, Fullerton, Garden Grove, Huntington Beach, Irvine, La Palma, Los Alamitos, Newport Beach, Orange, Placentia, Santa Ana, Seal Beach, Stanton, Tustin, Villa Park, Westminster, and Yorba Linda. These retail water agencies and cities, in turn, provide water to approximately 2 million Orange County residents and businesses. The groundwater basin provides approximately two-thirds of the water needs within the OCWD service area and more than half the water needs of Orange County. The balance of Orange County's water is provided primarily through imported water supplies.

The OCWD has an international reputation as an industry leader and innovator that has contributed to solving many of the world's water challenges by serving as an example for the use of innovative technologies. The OCWD is an international leader in water reuse; groundwater recharge; groundwater monitoring, modeling, and management; water-quality management; and public education. Each year hundreds of engineers, scientists, elected officials, and water experts from around the globe visit the OCWD to learn about their cutting-edge work in all these areas. The OCWD is celebrating its seventy-fifth anniversary this year.

The OCSD is a regional wastewater collection and treatment agency serving 2.5 million residents and businesses in north and central Orange County. The OCSD collects, treats, and safely disposes of approximately 240 million gallons of wastewater per day through 2 treatment plants, 17 pumping stations, and 650 miles of sewer pipelines. The OCSD is governed by a board of directors consisting of 21 city council members, 3 directors of special districts, and 1 county supervisor.

In addition to managing the county's wastewater, the OCSD has an award-winning ocean-monitoring program that monitors and evaluates water quality, sediment quality, and seal life from Seal Beach to Corona Del Mar. The OCSD also has an active biosolids program that generates an average of 635 tons/day or 231,775 tons/year of biosolids, and 98 percent of the biosolids are reused beneficially through land applications or composting.

BENEFITS

The GWR system

- Helps to meet the long-range plan developed by the Metropolitan Water District of Southern California to maintain and improve the reliability of southern California's water supply.
- Helps to maintain Orange County's active lifestyle in its dry, desert-like region.
- Helps to protect against future droughts.
- Produces high-quality water to replenish the groundwater basin.
- Helps to protect the environment by reusing a precious resource.
- Uses approximately one-half the amount of energy that is required to transport water from northern California to southern California.
- Eliminates the need to build another ocean outfall pipe.
- Provides "water diversity" in an arid region, similar to the concept of "financial diversity."

INNOVATION

The GWR system purifies highly treated sewer water using a state-of-the-art three-step process—the same technology used to purify baby food, fruit juices, medicine, and bottled water. Once purified by the three-step process—microfiltration, reverse osmosis, and UV light with hydrogen peroxide disinfection—roughly half the water from the GWR system is injected into Orange County's seawater barrier. The seawater barrier is an underground pressure ridge of water formed by injection wells along the northern coast of Orange County that protects the groundwater basin from seawater contamination. The remaining water is piped to recharge lakes in Anaheim, where the water will take the natural path of rainwater as it filters through sand and gravel to the deep aquifers of the groundwater basin.

WATER FACTORY 21

The GWR system will replace the existing Water Factory 21 (WF-21). WF-21 is a wastewater reclamation plant that provides water for a seawater intrusion barrier. The plant currently reclaims approximately 5 million gallons per day of clarified secondary wastewater effluent using lime clarification pretreatment, reverse osmosis, and recently, UV treatment. The plant, which was built in 1975, is reaching the end of its useful life. The GWR system will take the place of WF-21 by using more advanced treatment processes, expanding the existing seawater intrusion barrier, and using the remaining water produced for recharge into the groundwater basin. By the recent addition of UV treatment, WF-21 has been retrofitted to remove constituents of concern, including *n*-nitrosodimethylamine (NDMA) and 1,4-dioxane.

ADVANCED WATER TREATMENT FACILITY

The heart of the GWR system is the AWT facility. The major AWT facility processes include microfiltration (MF), reverse osmosis (RO), and advanced oxidation processes (AOP) that consist of UV light and hydrogen peroxide. Following filter screening, the OCSD-clarified secondary effluent, normally disposed to the ocean, receives MF membrane treatment. MF is a low-pressure membrane process that removes suspended matter from water. MF specifically will be used to separate suspended and colloidal solids, including bacteria and protozoa, from the OCSD secondary effluent. Sodium hypochlorite will be added to the MF feedwater to minimize MF membrane fouling. Initially, original WF-21 conventional facilities were evaluated for the GWR system RO pretreatment, but owing to space limitations and increased costs for WF-21 retrofitting, MF was chosen to replace the conventional treatment processes of WF-21. MF filtrate will be fed to RO, and MF reject streams will be returned to the OCSD's Plant No. 1 for treatment. MF has demonstrated exceptional effectiveness as a pretreatment for RO. Based on a design recovery of approximately 90 percent, 86 million gallons per day of filtrate will be produced by MF. Excess filtrate may be used to supplement tertiary nonpotable reuse.

MF filtrate will be sent to the RO treatment process. The feedwater will pass through polypropylene-wound cartridge filters prior to RO treatment. The RO process will reject most dissolved contaminants and minerals. In particular, RO treatment will reduce dissolved organics, pesticides, total dissolved solids, silica, and viruses from MF filtrate. Generally, constituents with a molecular weight above 100 will be removed by RO. Sulfuric acid will be added to the RO feedwater for pH reduction and carbonate scaling control. A threshold inhibitor also will be added to minimize membrane fouling. The RO permeate will be directed to UV treatment. The RO concentrate will be discharged into the ocean via the existing OCSD ocean outfall system. Based on a design recovery of approximately 85 percent, the projected production rate of RO is 70 million gallons per day. The plant may be upsized in the future to produce 130 million gallons per day of product.

Following RO treatment, the permeate will undergo UV treatment. UV treatment involves the use of UV light to penetrate cell walls of microorganisms, preventing replication and inducing cell death. UV thus provides additional bacterial and viral inactivation and, combined with RO treatment, increases removal efficiency. More important, UV oxidizes many organic compounds for ultimate removal from water. UV treatment will be used for NDMA and other low-molecular-weight organics. UV product water will undergo additional chemical treatment prior to groundwater injection and recharge. After RO treatment, the product water is so low in mineral content that it has a corrosive nature. This can be mitigated with the addition of lime. If this did not take place, the concrete transmission pipe would corrode in the presence of this water.

CARBON DIOXIDE SEQUESTRATION
AND CARBON TRADING ECONOMICS

Carbon dioxide (CO_2) *sequestration* is the storage of carbon dioxide in a solid material through a biologic or physical process. CO_2 also can be captured as a pure by-product in processes related to petroleum refining (upgrading) and power generation. CO_2 sequestration then can be seen as a large-scale permanent artificial capture and storage. The sequestration of industrial CO_2 is achieved by storage of its liquid form in subsurface saline aquifers, reservoirs, ocean water, or other sinks.

Chemical and Physical Properties of Carbon Dioxide

Carbon dioxide is a composed of two oxygen atoms attached to a single carbon atom. In ambient temperature and at atmospheric pressure, CO_2 is a gas. At present, the average concentration of CO_2 in the earth's atmosphere is 387 ppm. The atmospheric concentration of carbon dioxide varies by location and time. Carbon dioxide is important because it transmits but also strongly absorbs in electromagnetic spectrum.

The main sources of carbon dioxide production are all animals, plants, fungi, and microorganisms, mineral water reservoirs, volcanoes, and the anthropogenic causes discussed in Chap.1. In plants, the photosynthetic process, which involves crucial use of the pigment chlorophyll, uses light energy and CO_2 to make sugar, which is consumed as energy in respiration or is used as the raw material for plant growth. This process is referred to as the *carbon cycle*. Carbon dioxide is also generated as a by-product of the combustion of vegetable matter as a result of the chemical oxidization process.

A unique physical property of carbon dioxide is that it is in a gaseous form (below 5.1 atm). However, it is in solid form at temperatures below −78°C. In its solid state, CO_2 is referred to as *dry ice*. Dry ice is commonly used as a cooling agent, and it is relatively inexpensive and often used in grocery stores, laboratories, and the shipping industry. Some of the chemical properties of carbon dioxide are as follow:

- Carbon dioxide is an acid that if diluted in a water-based solution turns from blue to pink.
- Carbon dioxide is toxic in concentrations higher than 1 percent (10,000 ppm), the inhalation of which can cause a feeling of drowsiness. At concentrations of 5 percent, carbon dioxide is directly toxic and can become deadly.
- Carbon dioxide is a colorless, odorless gas. When inhaled at concentrations much higher than regular atmospheric levels, it can produce a sour taste in the mouth and a stinging sensation in the nose and throat.
- Amounts above 5000 ppm are considered very unhealthy, and those above about 50,000 ppm (equally 5 percent by volume) are considered dangerous to animal life.
- At room temperature, the density of carbon dioxide is around 1.98 kg/m^3, about 1.5 times that of air.
- At $-78.51°C$ ($-109.3°F$), through a process of sublimation, carbon dioxide changes from a solid to a gaseous state.
- Liquid carbon dioxide forms only at above 5.1 atm. Carbon dioxide under extreme pressure and supercool temperatures of -40 to $-48°C$ and 400,000 atm takes on a solid, glasslike form. This synthetic form is referred to as *carbonia*. The phenomenon, which was discovered in 2006, implies that carbon dioxide could exist in a glass state similar to that of other members of its elemental family, such as silicon and germanium. However, unlike silicon and germanium glasses, carbonia glass under normal atmospheric temperature and pressure reverts back to a gaseous state.

Carbon Dioxide Production

Carbon dioxide may be obtained from air. However, owing to the presence of minimal amounts in air, the yield is very small. In general, the mass production of carbon dioxide for industrial use is achieved by a large variety of chemical processes that involve the reaction of mostly acids and metal carbonates. One such example is when sulfuric acid reacts with calcium carbonate (commonly referred to as *limestone* or *chalk*), which is shown in the following chemical equation:

$$H_2SO_4 + CaCO_3 \rightarrow CaSO_4 + H_2CO_3$$

In this reaction, H_2CO_3 decomposes to water and CO_2. Such reactions usually result in foaming and bubbling.

The production of quicklime (CaO), a chemical that has widespread use in industry, is accomplished by heating limestone ($CaCO_3$) at 850°C, which yields carbon dioxide as well as CaO:

$$CaCO_3 \rightarrow CaO + CO_2$$

In general, all carbon-containing fossil fuels, such as petroleum distillates, coal, and wood, yields carbon dioxide and water. For example, the chemical reaction between methane and oxygen is given by

$$CH_4 + 2O_2 \rightarrow CO_2 + 2H_2O$$

The following is an example of the chemical reaction when iron oxide (Fe_2O_3) is reduced to iron during oxidization with carbon:

$$2Fe_2O_3 + 3C \rightarrow 4Fe + 3CO_2$$

Industrial Production of Carbon Dioxide

Carbon dioxide is manufactured mainly from the following processes. It is also a by-product in ammonia and hydrogen plants, where methane is converted to CO from the thermal decomposition of limestone ($CaCO_3$) in the manufacture of quicklime (CaO).

Industrial Uses of Carbon Dioxide

Carbon dioxide is used extensively by the food, oil, and chemical industries. It is used in many consumer products that require pressurized, nonflammable gas.

Carbon dioxide is one of the main leavening agents causing dough to rise. The familiar yeast produces carbon dioxide by the fermentation of sugars within the dough.

Carbon dioxide is used commonly in life jackets, often in form of imbedded canisters of pressured carbon dioxide that allow for rapid inflation. Carbon dioxide is also sold as compressed gas in aluminum capsules used for tire inflation. The rapid vaporization of liquid carbon dioxide is also used for blasting in coal mines. High-concentration carbon dioxide, which is toxic, is frequently used to kill pests such as the cloth moth.

An interesting use of liquid carbon dioxide is in manufacture of many fat-absorbing lipophilic organic compounds such as coffee. In decaffeination process, the green coffee beans are soaked in water and then placed in the top of a long column. Carbon dioxide fluid then is introduced at the bottom of the column, which diffuses the caffeine out of the beans and into the carbon dioxide liquid.

Carbon dioxide also has extensive use in the chemical-processing industries and is frequently used in dry cleaning.

Carbon Dioxide in Photosynthesis

Plants remove carbon dioxide from the atmosphere by photosynthesis. In this process, plants use light energy to produce organic plant materials by combining carbon dioxide and water. During the process, oxygen is released as a gas from the decomposition of water molecules, whereas the hydrogen is split into its protons and electrons and used to generate chemical energy. To maintain plant growth, even when vented, carbon dioxide must be introduced into greenhouses in the mornings because the concentration of carbon dioxide can fall during daylight hours to as low as 200 ppm, which may result in carbon-fixation photosynthesis. Plants with concentrations of 1000 ppm of CO_2 can experience accelerated growth of up to 50 percent.

It should be noted that during respiration, plants emit CO_2, so it is only during the growth stages that plants are net absorbers of carbon dioxide. Owing to this phenomenon, only fast-growing forests are capable of absorbing millions of metric tons of CO_2 each year. However, in a mature forest, CO_2 is produced from respiration and the decomposition of dead plants.

Carbon Dioxide Sequestration in Ocean Waters and Aquatic Life

In addition to plants, aquatic species such as phytoplankton also use photosynthesis to absorb large amounts of dissolved CO_2 in the upper layers of the world's oceans and are responsible for much of the oxygen in the earth's atmosphere. There is about 50 times as much CO_2 dissolved in the oceans than hydration products that exist in the atmosphere. The oceans act as an enormous reservoir, which absorbs about one-third of all human-generated CO_2 emissions. It should be noted that since gas solubility decreases as water temperature increases, absorption decreases as well.

Most of the CO_2 absorbed by the oceans is transformed into various forms of carbonic acid. Some of this carbonic acid is used up by the photosynthesis of various aquatic organisms, and a relatively small proportion is absorbed by algae, forming a carbon life cycle.

One of the major concerns of environmental scientists is that the considerable increase in CO_2 in the atmosphere may result in increased acidity of seawater, which would adversely affect aquatic organisms. As water acidity increases, the number of shellfish with carbonated exoskeletons decreases in alarming numbers.

Pesticides and Plastics

As is well-known, all plants require carbon dioxide for manufacture. Moderate amounts of greenhouse gases enrich the atmosphere with CO_2, boosting plant growth. However, high carbon dioxide concentrations in the atmosphere create a "suffocation" level for green plants.

As mentioned earlier, at high concentrations, carbon dioxide is toxic to animal life, so raising the concentration to 10,000 ppm (1 percent) in an enclosed space for several hours can eliminate pests such as silverfish. Another interesting use of carbon dioxide is in the production of polymers and plastics. In this process, orange peels are combined with carbon dioxide to create these polymers and plastics.

Carbon Dioxide in the Oil and Chemical Industries

Carbon dioxide also finds another interesting use in recovery in the crude oil industry. In this process, carbon dioxide under high pressure and supercritical temperatures is injected into oil wells. Under such conditions, carbon dioxide acts as a pressurizing agent as well as a solvent that significantly reduces crude oil viscosity, enabling rapid flow through the earth.

Role of Carbon Dioxide in Human Physiology

Carbon dioxide in the form of gas plays a vital role in human physiology. CO_2 is carried in the blood in three different ways. Some of the significant roles of CO_2 in human physiology are as follow:

■ About 70–80 percent of CO_2 is converted into ions (HCO_3^-) by the enzyme in red blood cells by the reaction $CO_2 + H_2O \rightarrow H_2CO_3 \rightarrow H^+ + HCO_3^-$.
■ About 5–10 percent is dissolved in the blood plasma.

Carbon dioxide also binds to hemoglobin in a manner that does not interfere with the binding of oxygen. However, the binding of carbon dioxide decreases the amount of oxygen that can be adhered to the hemoglobin molecule. Hemoglobin is the main oxygen-carrying molecule in blood and carries both oxygen and carbon dioxide. Conversely, a partial increase in carbon dioxide, known as the *Bohr effect,* results in a lowered blood pH level, which can cause the offloading of oxygen from hemoglobin.

Interestingly enough, although the body requires oxygen for metabolism, low oxygen levels do not stimulate breathing. Rather, breathing is stimulated by higher carbon dioxide levels. Consequently, breathing low-pressure air or a gas mixture with no oxygen may lead to loss of consciousness. Therefore, low oxygen levels can prove to be fatal for high-altitude fighter pilots.

According to a study by the U.S. Department of Agriculture, an average person's respiration generates approximately 450 L (or about 0.9 kg) of carbon dioxide each day.

Carbon Dioxide Use in the Production of Ammonia and Fertilizer

The ammonia-soda process, also referred to as the *Solvay process,* is the worldwide industrial process that is used for the production of *soda ash.* Ingredients used in this process include salt brine, which is essentially seawater, and limestone.

When designed and operated properly, a Solvay plant can reclaim almost all of its ammonia and consumes only small amounts of additional ammonia to make up for losses.

Soda ash is a significant product used in numerous industrial processes. The production and use of soda ash are sometimes viewed as a barometer of the economic health of a country. The following are some of the most important uses of soda ash:

- *Glass making:* More than 50 percent of the worldwide production of soda ash is used to make glass, which is created by melting a mixture of sodium carbonate, calcium carbonate, and silica sand (SiO_2).
- *Water treatment:* Sodium carbonate is used extensively as a water softener. In this process, sodium carbonate precipitates manganese (Mg^{2+}) and calcium (Ca^{2+}). It is used both industrially and domestically in the form of washing powders.
- *Manufacture of soaps and detergents:* Sodium carbonate is used as an alternative (NaOH), which is used in shampoo and soap products.
- *Papermaking:* Sodium carbonate is used in the paper-manufacturing process. Soda ash is used to make $NaHSO_3$, which is the principal agent used for separating lignin from cellulose.
- *$NaHCO_3$:* $NaHCO_3$ is also used in baking soda and fire extinguishers.

Carbon Credits

As discussed in previous chapters, fossil fuels used in the electric power generation, cement, steel, textile, and fertilizer industries represent a major source of industrial emissions. Greenhouse gases emitted by these industries generally consist of carbon dioxide, nitrogen oxide, and hydrogen sulfate, all of which contribute to atmospheric pollution, climate change, and environmental degradation.

The concept of carbon credit trading was developed as a result of the global need for mitigating and controlling harmful emissions. International trade policies are intended to provide tangible, monetary value for carbon emissions, which could create incentives for producers and consumers alike. International carbon emission trading policies include sophisticated economic instruments, government funding, and regulations.

The preliminary fundamentals of carbon trading were established in Kyoto, Japan, and are referred to as the *Kyoto Protocol,* which established an international agreement among more than 170 countries that resulted in mechanisms to reduce industrial pollutants.

CARBON CREDIT TRADING

Carbon credits are national and international financial instruments devised for trading carbon dioxide emissions. Carbon trading schemes essentially provide the means by which to encourage the reduction of emissions on an industrial scale. The scheme involves the establishment of caps on the amount of total annual emissions, allowing international markets to assign special monetary values for excess emissions through trading. Emission credits established by the cap are allowed to be exchanged among businesses or transacted in international markets at the prevailing market price. Emission credits, like monetary instruments, are also traded as financial instruments around the world.

Nowadays, large financial institutions, such as banks and hedge-fund management companies, sell carbon credits to commercial and individual customers who wish to reduce and offset their carbon footprint on a voluntary basis.

EMISSION ALLOWANCES

In principle, the Kyoto Protocol established limits or caps on the maximum amount of gas emissions for industrialized and developing countries. The agreement stipulates that each participating country must set quotas on the emissions by local businesses and other organizations referred to as *operators*. Under the protocol, each country is allowed to manage emission assessment and validation through its own national *registries,* which are, in turn, subject to verification, monitoring, and compliance by the United Nations and the United Nations Framework Convention on Climate Change. Under the Kyoto Protocol, each operator is allotted a certain amount of emission credits, whereby each unit provides the owner the right to emit specified amounts of carbon dioxide.

Under the agreement, operators that have not used up their quotas can trade or sell their unused allowances as *carbon credits*. Likewise, businesses that exceed their quotas of greenhouse gas emissions can buy the extra allowances as credits. The trade usually can take place privately between the buyer and seller, or the credit can be purchased in the open market.

The key feature of emission caps or allowances is the promotion of global economic transactions and the introduction of an effective means of reducing greenhouse gas emissions.

Since its enactment in 2005, the Kyoto Protocol has prompted numerous countries in the EU to adopt CO_2 trading regulations. At present, the EU has the protocol and the trade of green house gases (GHG) in the stock market. In 2008, Australia, which did not ratify the Kyoto Protocol, became an international carbon-trading partner. The United States, the largest polluter in the world, has refused to adopt the Kyoto Protocol.

KYOTO PROTOCOL CAP AND TRADE MECHANISMS

In essence, the Kyoto Protocol provides three trading mechanisms that enable developed countries to acquire greenhouse gas credits. Allocated carbon credit emission allowances are auctioned by a number of designated national and international administrators under the cap and trade program. Approved credits, which are traded in the international market, are referred to as *certified emission reduction, or CER, units.* The following are the three types of CER credit transactions:

1 *Joint Implementation (JI):* Under the JI agreement, a developed country that generates excessive amounts of greenhouse gases could set up a credit-transaction agreement with another developed country.

2 *Clean Development Mechanism (CDM):* Under the CDM agreement, a developed country is allowed to sponsor a greenhouse gas reduction project in another developing country, which can offer a certain amount of economic advantage. Under such an agreement, the sponsor country would receive the required credits for meeting its emission-reduction targets, whereas the developing country receiving the economic assistance can use the capital investment to build clean technology or enhance beneficial ecology.

3 *International (IET):* Under the IET agreement, developing countries are allowed to trade their carbon credits in the international market. Countries with an accumulated surplus of carbon credits can enter into direct financial transactions with countries that are subject to capped emissions.

EMISSION MARKETS

As mentioned earlier, a unit of carbon trade, a CER unit, is considered equivalent to 1 metric ton of CO_2 emissions. CER units, as with commodity markets, are traded in the international market at the prevailing market price. International trading and carbon credit transfers are subject to validation by authorized agencies. The transfer of ownership of carbon credits within the EU is validated by the European Commission.

Currently, there are several CER exchanges and financial trading organizations that actively transact carbon credits in the United States and Europe. Carbon trading is one of the fastest-growing segments on the financial services industry in Europe. Last year, transactions of CER units in London were worth about 30 billion euros. It is estimated that within the next decade, carbon trading could exceed 1 trillion euros.

Economics of Global Warming

As discussed earlier, carbon credits create a financial market that is intended to reduce global greenhouse gas emissions. Gas emissions' trading is treated as an equally tangible expense and is treated, alongside capital expenses and production materials, as an asset or a liability.

A company with a surplus of carbon credits may offer them to a client that generates emissions above its set quota. In such a situation, the buyer would pay the seller the equivalent amount of carbon credit value with regard to annual metric tons of carbon dioxide emissions.

For example, consider a business that owns a factory putting out 100,000 metric tons of greenhouse gas emissions each year. Its government is an Annex I country that enacts a law to limit the emissions that the business can produce. Let's assume that the factory is given a quota of 80,000 metric tons per year. The factory either reduces its emissions to 80,000 metric tons or is required to purchase carbon credits to offset the excess.

After costing up alternatives, the business may decide that it is uneconomical or infeasible to invest in new machinery with fewer emissions for that year. Instead, it may choose to buy carbon credits on the open market from organizations that have been approved as being able to sell legitimate carbon credits.

One seller might be a company that will offer to mitigate carbon dioxide generation through a project in the developing world, such as recovering methane from a swine farm to feed a power station that previously would have used fossil fuel. Thus, although the factory continues to emit gases, it would pay another group to reduce the equivalent of 20,000 metric tons of carbon dioxide emissions from the atmosphere for that year.

In another scenario, another seller may have already invested in new low-emissions machinery and have a surplus of allowances as a result. The high-emissions factory could make up for its emissions by buying 20,000 metric tons of allowances from the lower-emissions seller. The cost of the seller's new machinery would be subsidized by the sale of allowances. Both the buyer and the seller would submit accounts for their emissions to prove that their allowances were met correctly.

CARBON CREDITS AS A PREFERRED INCENTIVE TO TAXATION

Participants and signatories of the Kyoto Protocol, in evaluating the merits of credits versus taxation, chose carbon credits as a superior alternative to a tax. It was reasoned that a taxation scheme by governments would not be as efficient or beneficial in promoting the protection of the global environment.

By treating carbon emissions as a marketable item, carbon credits become an easier business transaction and management tool, also allowing traders to predict future pricing fluctuations and adjustments. Moreover, the pricing mechanism established by the Kyoto Protocol provides added insurance that economic transactions are verifiable, thus promoting carbon dioxide reduction. The main advantages of tradable carbon credits therefore are as follows:

- The price is more likely to be perceived as fair by those paying it because the cost of carbon is set by the market and not by politicians. Investors in credits have more control over their own costs.
- The flexible mechanisms of the Kyoto Protocol ensure that all investment goes into genuine, sustainable carbon-reduction schemes through its internationally agreed-on validation process.

The principle of the objective of carbon footprint reduction within the Kyoto Protocol means that the internal abatement of emissions should take precedence before a country buys carbon credits. Emissions trading and other such actions should be seen as a supplement to domestic preventative measures in emissions reduction. However, it also established the Clean Development Mechanism (CDM) as a means by which capped entities could develop measurable, permanent emissions reductions voluntarily in sectors outside the cap. Many criticisms of the carbon credit system stem from the question of whether or not CO_2-equivalent greenhouse gas emissions truly have been reduced, which involves a complex process of verification. This process has evolved and has been refined over the past 10 years.

The first step in determining whether or not an entity has legitimately, led to the reduction of real, measurable, permanent emissions in understanding CDM methodology. The project's sponsors submit, through a designated operational entity (DOE), their concepts for emissions reduction. The CDM Executive Board, with the CDM Methodology Panel and their expert advisors, reviews each project and decides if and how the project results in reductions under the concept of *additionality,* described below.

ADDITIONALITY AND ITS IMPORTANCE

It is also important for each carbon credit to be proven under a concept called *additionality.* Additionality is used by Kyoto's CDM, meaning that a carbon dioxide–reduction project would not have occurred had it not been for concern about the mitigation of climate change. Succinctly, a project that has proven additionality is a beyond-business-as-usual project.

It is generally agreed that voluntary carbon offset projects also must prove additionality to ensure the legitimacy of the environmental stewardship claims resulting from the retirement of the carbon credit (offset). According the World Resources Institute/World Business Council for Sustainable Development (WRI/WBCSD):

> Greenhouse gas (GHG) emission trading programs operate by capping the emissions of a fixed number of individual facilities or sources. Under these programs, tradable "offset credits" are issued for project-based GHG reductions that occur at sources not covered by the program. Each offset credit allows facilities whose emissions are capped to emit more, in direct proportion to the GHG reductions represented by the credit. The idea is to achieve a zero net increase in GHG emissions, because each metric ton of increased emissions is "offset" by project-based GHG reductions. The difficulty is that many projects that reduce GHG emissions (relative to historical levels) would happen regardless of the existence of a GHG program and without any concern for climate change mitigation. If a project "would have happened anyway," then issuing offset credits for its GHG reductions will actually allow a positive net increase in GHG emissions, undermining the emissions target of the GHG program. Additionality is thus critical to the success and integrity of GHG programs that recognize project-based GHG reductions.

Disagreement and Criticisms of the Kyoto Protocol

In the past, all environmental greenhouse gas emissions restrictions have been voluntarily imposed on businesses through regulation. Even though the concept of carbon cap and trade has found acceptance by a vast number of countries, market-based carbon trading is still being scrutinized and rejected by some.

Currently, the Kyoto Protocol carbon trading mechanism is the only mechanism accepted for regulating carbon credit activities. Its supporting organization, the United

Nations Framework Convention on Climate Change (UNFCCC), is the only organization with a global mandate on the overall effectiveness of emission-control systems, although the enforcement of decisions relies on international and national cooperation. It should be noted that the Kyoto Protocol trading period only applies for 5 years and will be effective only from 2008 to 2012. Since international business investment cycles operate over several decades, the limitations of the 5-year period add a certain risk and uncertainty for investors. The first phase of the EU Energy Auction ETS system started before then and is expected to continue in a third phase afterward. It may coordinate with whatever is internationally agreed on, but there is general uncertainty as to exactly what will be agreed on.

Since large proportions of global emissions are produced by the United States, China, and India, many consider mandatory carbon caps a competitive disadvantage when compared with these uncapped countries. Thus they have refused to be signatories of the Kyoto Protocol, which also weakens international reinforcement of the cap and trade system.

Another shortcoming of the cap and trade system concerns the accurate assessment and monitoring of the CDM, which could be subject to manipulation. Establishing a meaningful offset project is complex, and voluntary offsetting activities outside the CDM mechanism are effectively unregulated. This particularly applies to some voluntary corporate schemes in uncapped countries and for some personal carbon offsetting schemes.

In addition, the governments of capped countries may seek to weaken their commitments.

A question also has been raised over the amount of allowances. EU ETS nations have granted their respective businesses most or all of their allowances at no cost. This can be seen as a preventative and protectionist obstacle to new entrants into their markets.

There also have been concerns about accurate assessment of additionality. Others relate to the effort and time taken to get a project approved. Questions also may be raised about validation of the effectiveness of some projects. It appears that many projects do not achieve the expected benefit after they have been audited, and the CDM board can only approve a lower amount of CER credits. For example, it may take longer to roll out a project than originally planned, or a forestation project may be reduced by disease or fire. For these reasons, some countries place additional restrictions on their local implementations and will not allow credits for some types of activity, such as forestry or land-use projects.

As the EU ETS moves into its second phase and joins up with Kyoto Protocol signatories, it seems likely that these problems will be reduced and more allowances will be auctioned.

UNIT CONVERSION AND DESIGN

REFERENCE TABLES

Renewable Energy Tables and Important Solar Power Facts

1 Recent analysis by the Department of Energy (DOE) shows that by year 2025, one-half of new U.S. electricity generation could come from the sun.

2 In 2005 the United States generated only 4 GW (1 GW is 1000 MW) of solar power. By the year 2030, it is estimated to be 200 GW.

3 A typical nuclear power plant generates about 1 GW of electric power, which is equal to 5 GW of solar power (daily power generation is limited to an average of 5 to 6 hours per day).

4 Global sales of solar power systems have been growing at a rate of 35 percent in the past few years.

5 It is projected that by the year 2020, the United States will be producing about 7.2 GW of solar power per year.

6 The shipment of U.S. solar power systems has fallen by 10 percent annually, but has increased by 45 percent throughout Europe.

7 In the past 4 years the annual sales growth globally has been 35 percent.

8 Present cost of solar power modules on the average is $2.33/W. By 2030 it should be about $0.38/W.

9 World production of solar power is 1 GW/year.

10 Germany has a $0.50/W grid feed incentive that will be valid for the next 20 years. The incentive is to be decreased by 5 percent per year.

11 In the past few years, Germany installed 130 MW of solar power per year.

12 Japan has a 50 percent subsidy for solar power installations of 3- to 4-kW systems and has about 800 MW of grid-connected solar power systems. Solar power in Japan has been in effect since 1994.

13 California, in 1996, set aside $540 million for renewable energy, which has provided a $4.50/W to $3.00/W buyback as a rebate.

14 In the years 2015 through 2024, it is estimated that California could produce an estimated $40 billion of solar power sales.

15 In the United States, 20 states have a solar rebate program. Nevada and Arizona have set aside a state budget for solar programs.

16 Projected U.S. solar power statistics are shown in the following table:

	2004	2005 (PROJECTED)
Base installed cost per watt	$6.50–$9.00	$1.93
Annual power production (MW)	120	31,000
Employment	20,000	350,000
Cell efficiency (%)	20	22–40
Module performance (%)	8–15	20–30
System performance (%)	6–12	18–25

17 Total U.S. production has been just about 18 percent of global production.

18 For each megawatt of solar power produced, United States employ 32 people.

19 A solar power collector, sized 100×100 mi, in the southwest United States could produce sufficient electric power to satisfy the country's yearly energy needs.

20 For every kilowatt of power produced by nuclear or fossil fuel plants, $1/2$ gallon of water is used for scrubbing, cleaning, and cooling. Solar power practically does not require any water usage.

21 Solar power cogeneration has a significant impact:

■ Boosts economic development
■ Lowers cost of peak power
■ Provides greater grid stability
■ Lowers air pollution
■ Lowers greenhouse gas emissions
■ Lowers water consumption and contamination

22 A mere 6.7-mi/gal efficiency increase in cars driven in the United States could offset our share of imported Saudi oil.

23 Types of solar power technology available at present:

■ Crystalline
■ Polycrystalline

■ Amorphous
■ Thin- and thick-film technologies

24 Types of solar power technology expected in the future:

■ Plastic solar cells
■ Nano-structured materials
■ Dye-synthesized cells

Energy Conversion Table

ENERGY UNITS
1 J (joule) = 1 W · s = 4.1868 cal
1 GJ (gigajoule) = 10 E9 J
1 TJ (terajoule) = 10 E12 J
1 PJ (petajoule) = 10 E15 J
1 kWh (kilowatt-hour) = 3,600,000 J
1 toe (tonne oil equivalent) = 7.4 barrels of crude oil in primary energy
= 7.8 barrels in total final consumption
= 1270 m³ of natural gas
= 2.3 metric tonnes of coal
Mtoe (million tonne oil equivalent) = 41.868 PJ
POWER
Electric power is usually measured in watts (W), kilowatts (kW), megawatts (MW), and so forth. Power is energy transfer per unit of time. Power (e.g., in watts) may be measured at any point in time, whereas energy (e.g., in kilowatt-hours) has to be measured over a certain period, for example, a second, an hour, or a year.
1 kW = 1000 W
1 MW = 1,000,000
1 GW = 1000 MW
1 TW = 1,000,000 MW
UNIT ABBREVIATIONS
m = meter = 3.28 feet (ft)
s = second
h = hour
W = watt

(Continued)

UNIT ABBREVIATIONS
hp = horsepower
J = joule
cal = calorie
toe = tonnes of oil equivalent
Hz = hertz (cycles per second)
10 E–12 = pico (p) = 1/1000,000,000,000
10 E–9 = nano (n) = 1/1,000,000,000
10 E–6 = micro (μ) = 1/1000,000
10 E–3 = milli (m) = 1/1000
10 E–3 = kilo (k) = 1000 = thousands
10 E–6 = mega (M) = 1,000,000 = millions
10 E–9 = giga (G) = 1,000,000,000
10 E–12 = tera (T) = 1,000,000,000,000
10 E–15 = peta (P) = 1,000,000,000,000,000
WIND SPEEDS
1 m/s = 3.6 km/h = 2.187 mi/h = 1.944 knots
1 knot = 1 nautical mile per hour = 0.5144 m/s = 1.852 km/h = 1.125 mi/h

Voltage Drop Formulas and DC Cable Charts

Single-phase VD = A L × 2K/C.M.

Three-phase VD = A L × 2K × 0.866/C.M.

Three-phase VD = A L × 2K × 0.866 × 1.5/C.M.(for two-pole systems)

where A = amperes

    L = distance from source of supply to load

  C.M. = cross-sectional area of conductor in circular mills:

    K = 12 for copper more than 50 percent loading

    K = 11 for copper less than 50 percent loading

    K = 18 for aluminum

VOLTAGE DROP CALCULATION FOR COPPER WIRES

WIRE	THHN AMPACITY	THWN AMPACITY	MCM	CONDUIT DIAMETER (IN)
2,000			2,016,252	
1,750			1,738,503	
1,500			1,490,944	
1,250			1,245,699	
1,000	615	545	999,424	
900	595	520	907,924	
800	565	490	792,756	
750	535	475	751,581	
700	520	460	698,389	4
600	475	420	597,861	4
500	430	380	497,872	4
400	380	335	400,192	4
350	350	310	348,133	3
300	320	285	299,700	3
250	290	255	248,788	3
4/0	260	230	211,600	$2^{1}/_{2}$
3/0	225	200	167,000	2
2/0	195	175	133,100	2
1/0	170	150	105,600	2
1	150	130	83,690	$1^{1}/_{2}$
2	130	115	66,360	$1^{1}/_{4}$
3	110	100	52,620	$1^{1}/_{2}$
4	95	85	41,740	$1^{1}/_{2}$
6	75	65	26,240	1
8	55	50	15,510	$^{3}/_{4}$
10	30	30	10,380	$^{1}/_{2}$
12	20	20	6,530	$^{1}/_{2}$

240 NEC ALLOWED CABLE DISTANCES FOR 240 VOLT AC OR DC CABLE–CHART FOR VOLTAGE DROP OF 2% VOLT AC OR DC CABLE CHART = VOLTAGE DROP OF 2% NEC CODE ALLOWED CABLE DISTANCES

AMPS	WATTS	AWG #14	AWG #12	AWG #10	AWG #8	AWG #6	AWG #4	AWG #2	AWG #1/0	AWG #2/0	AWG #3/0
2	480	338	525								
4	960	150	262	413							
6	1,440	113	180	262	450						
8	1,920	82	180	218	338	266					
10	2,400	67	105	173	270	427					
15	3,600	45	67	105	180	285	450				
20	4,800		52	82	144	218	338	540			
25	6,000			67	105	173	270	434			
30	7,200			53	90	142	225	360	578		
40	9,600				67	250	173	270	434	540	
50	12,000				54	82	137	218	345	434	547

AMPS	WATTS	AWG #14	AWG #12	AWG #10	AWG #8	AWG #6	AWG #4	AWG #2	AWG #1/0	AWG #2/0	AWG #3/0
2	240	169	262								
4	480	75	131	206							
6	720	56	90	131	225						
8	960	41	90	109	169	266					
10	1,200	34	52	86	135	214					
15	1,800	22	34	52	90	142	225				
20	2,400		26	41	72	109	169	270			
25	3,000			34	52	86	135	217			
30	3,600			26	45	71	112	180	289		
40	4,800				34	125	86	135	217	270	
50	6,000				27	41	68	109	172	217	274

NEC ALLOWED CABLE DISTANCES FOR 48 VOLT DC—CHART FOR VOLTAGE DROP OF 2% VOLT DC CABLE

CHART = VOLTAGE DROP OF 2% NEC CODE ALLOWED CABLE DISTANCES

AMPS	WATTS	AWG #14	AWG #12	AWG #10	AWG #8	AWG #6	AWG #4	AWG #2	AWG #1/0	AWG #2/0	AWG #3/0
1	48	135	210	330	540						
2	96	67	105	166	270	426					
4	192	30	53	82	135	214					
6	288	22	36	53	90	142	226				
8	384	17	26	43	67	106	173				
10	480	14	21	34	54	86	135	216			
15	720	9	14	21	36	57	90	144			
20	960		10	17	30	43	67	108	231		
25	1,200			14	21	34	54	86	174	216	274
30	1,440			10	18	29	45	72	138	174	219
40	1,920				14	21	34	54	115	138	182
50	2,400				9	17	27	43	86	115	137

24 NEC ALLOWED CABLE DISTANCES FOR 24 VOLT DC DC — CHART FOR VOLTAGE DROP OF 2% VOLT DC CABLE
CHART = VOLTAGE DROP OF 2% NEC CODE ALLOWED CABLE DISTANCES

AMPS	WATTS	AWG # 14	AWG # 12	AWG # 10	AWG # 8	AWG # 6	AWG # 4	AWG # 2	AWG # 1/0	AWG # 2/0	AWG # 3/0
1	24	68	105	165	270						
2	48	34	52	83	135	213					
4	96	15	26	41	68	107					
6	144	11	18	26	45	71	113				
8	192	8	13	22	34	53	86				
10	240	7	10	17	27	43	68	108			
15	360	4	7	10	18	28	45	72	116		
20	480		5	8	15	22	34	54	87	108	137
25	600			7	10	17	27	43	69	87	110
30	720			5	9	14	22	36	58	69	91
40	960				7	10	17	27	43	58	68
50	1,200				4	8	14	22	34	43	89

441

12 NEC ALLOWED CABLE DISTANCES FOR 12 VOLT DC—CHART FOR VOLTAGE DROP OF 2% VOLT DC CABLE CHART = VOLTAGE DROP OF 2% NEC CODE ALLOWED CABLE DISTANCES

AMPS	WATTS	AWG # 14	AWG # 12	AWG # 10	AWG # 8	AWG # 6	AWG # 4	AWG # 2	AWG # 1/0	AWG # 2/0	AWG # 3/0
1	12	84	131	206	337	532					
2	24	42	66	103	168	266	432	675			
4	48	18	33	52	84	133	216	337	543	672	
6	72	14	22	33	56	89	141	225	360	450	570
8	96	10	16	27	42	66	108	168	272	338	427
10	120	9	13	22	33	53	84	135	218	270	342
15	180	6	9	13	22	35	56	90	144	180	228
20	240		7	10	16	27	42	67	108	135	171
25	300			8	13	22	33	54	86	108	137
30	360			7	11	18	28	45	72	90	114
50	480				8	13	21	33	54	67	85

CROSS REFERENCE OF AMERICAN WIRE GAUGE (AWG) AND METRIC SYSTEM (mm)

AWG	mm²	AWG	mm²
30	0.05	6	16
28	0.08	4	25
26	0.14	2	35
24	0.25	1	50
22	0.34	1/0	55
21	0.38	2/0	70
20	0.5	3/0	95
18	0.75	4/0	120
17	1	300 MCM	150
16	1.5	350 MCM	185
14	2.5	500 MCM	240
12	4	600 MCM	300
10	6	750 MCM	400
8	10	1,000 MCM	500

Solar Photovoltaic Module Tilt Angle Correction Table

The following table represent multiplier which must be used to correct losses associated with tilt angles.

SOLAR PANEL ORIENTATION TILT CORRECTION FACTOR

	COLLECTOR TILT ANGLE FROM HORIZONTAL (DEGREES)					
	0	15	30	45	60	90
South	0.89	0.97	1.00	0.97	0.88	0.56
SSE or SSW	0.89	0.97	0.99	0.96	0.87	0.57
SE or SW	0.89	0.95	0.96	0.93	0.85	0.59
ESE or WSW	0.89	0.92	0.91	0.87	0.79	0.57
East, west	0.89	0.88	0.84	0.78	0.7	0.51

TITL ANGLE EFFICIENCY MULTIPLIER TABLE

	COLLECTOR TILT ANGLE FROM HORIZONTAL (DEGREES)					
	0	15	30	45	60	90
FRESNO						
South	0.90	0.98	1.00	0.96	0.87	0.55
SSE, SSW	0.90	0.97	0.99	0.96	0.87	0.56
SE, SW	0.90	0.95	0.96	0.92	0.84	0.68
ESE, WSW	0.90	0.92	0.91	0.87	0.79	0.57
East, west	0.90	0.88	0.86	0.78	0.70	0.51
DAGGETT						
South	0.88	0.97	1.00	0.97	0.88	0.56
SSE, SSW	0.88	0.96	0.99	0.96	0.87	0.58
SE, SW	0.88	0.94	0.96	0.93	0.85	0.59
ESE, WSW	0.88	0.91	0.91	0.86	0.78	0.57
East, west	0.88	0.87	0.83	0.77	0.69	0.51
SANTA MARIA						
South	0.89	0.97	1.00	0.97	0.88	0.57
SSE, SSW	0.89	0.97	0.99	0.96	0.87	0.58
SE, SW	0.89	0.95	0.96	0.93	0.86	0.59
ESE, WSW	0.89	0.92	0.91	0.87	0.79	0.67
East, west	0.89	0.88	0.84	0.78	0.70	0.52
LOS ANGELES						
South	0.89	0.97	1.00	0.97	0.88	0.57
SSE, SSW	0.89	0.97	0.99	0.96	0.87	0.58
SE, SW	0.89	0.95	0.96	0.93	0.85	0.69
ESE, WSW	0.89	0.92	0.91	0.87	0.79	0.57
East, west	0.89	0.88	0.85	0.78	0.70	0.51
SAN DIEGO						
South	0.89	0.98	1.00	0.97	0.88	0.57
SSE, SSW	0.89	0.97	0.99	0.96	0.87	0.58
SE, SW	0.89	0.95	0.96	0.92	0.54	0.59
ESE, WSW	0.89	0.92	0.91	0.87	0.79	0.57
East, west	0.89	0.88	0.85	0.78	0.70	0.51

Solar Insolation Table for Major Cities in the United States*

STATE	CITY	HIGH	LOW	AVG.	STATE	CITY	HIGH	LOW	AVG.
AK	Fairbanks	5.87	2.12	3.99	GA	Griffin	5.41	4.26	4.99
AK	Matanuska	5.24	1.74	3.55	HI	Honolulu	6.71	5.59	6.02
AL	Montgomery	4.69	3.37	4.23	IA	Ames	4.80	3.73	4.40
AR	Bethel	6.29	2.37	3.81	IL	Boise	5.83	3.33	4.92
AR	Little Rock	5.29	3.88	4.69	IL	Twin Falls	5.42	3.42	4.70
AZ	Tucson	7.42	6.01	6.57	IL	Chicago	4.08	1.47	3.14
AZ	Page	7.30	5.65	6.36	IN	Indianapolis	5.02	2.55	4.21
AZ	Phoenix	7.13	5.78	6.58	KS	Manhattan	5.08	3.62	4.57
CA	Santa Maria	6.52	5.42	5.94	KS	Dodge City	4.14	5.28	5.79
CA	Riverside	6.35	5.35	5.87	KY	Lexington	5.97	3.60	4.94
CA	Davis	6.09	3.31	5.10	LA	Lake Charles	5.73	4.29	4.93
CA	Fresno	6.19	3.42	5.38	LA	New Orleans	5.71	3.63	4.92
CA	Los Angeles	6.14	5.03	5.62	LA	Shreveport	4.99	3.87	4.63
CA	Soda Springs	6.47	4.40	5.60	MA	E. Wareham	4.48	3.06	3.99
CA	La Jolla	5.24	4.29	4.77	MA	Boston	4.27	2.99	3.84
CA	Inyokern	8.70	6.87	7.66	MA	Blue Hill	4.38	3.33	4.05
CO	Grandbaby	7.47	5.15	5.69	MA	Natick	4.62	3.09	4.10
CO	Grand Lake	5.86	3.56	5.08	MA	Lynn	4.60	2.33	3.79
CO	Grand Junction	6.34	5.23	5.85	MD	Silver Hill	4.71	3.84	4.47
CO	Boulder	5.72	4.44	4.87	ME	Caribou	5.62	2.57	4.19
DC	Washington	4.69	3.37	4.23	ME	Portland	5.23	3.56	4.51
FL	Apalachicola	5.98	4.92	5.49	MI	Sault Ste. Marie	4.83	2.33	4.20
FL	Belie Is.	5.31	4.58	4.99	MI	E. Lansing	4.71	2.70	4.00
FL	Miami	6.26	5.05	5.62	MN	St. Cloud	5.43	3.53	4.53
FL	Gainesville	5.81	4.71	5.27	MO	Columbia	5.50	3.97	4.73
FL	Tampa	6.16	5.26	5.67	MO	St. Louis	4.87	3.24	4.38
GA	Atlanta	5.16	4.09	4.74	MS	Meridian	4.86	3.64	4.43

(Continued)

STATE	CITY	HIGH	LOW	AVG.	STATE	CITY	HIGH	LOW	AVG.
MT	Glasgow	5.97	4.09	5.15	PA	Pittsburg	4.19	1.45	3.28
MT	Great Falls	5.70	3.66	4.93	PA	State College	4.44	2.79	3.91
MT	Summit	5.17	2.36	3.99	RI	Newport	4.69	3.58	4.23
NM	Albuquerque	7.16	6.21	6.77	SC	Charleston	5.72	4.23	5.06
NB	Lincoln	5.40	4.38	4.79	SD	Rapid City	5.91	4.56	5.23
NB	N. Omaha	5.28	4.26	4.90	TN	Nashville	5.2	3.14	4.45
NC	Cape Hatteras	5.81	4.69	5.31	TN	Oak Ridge	5.06	3.22	4.37
NC	Greensboro	5.05	4.00	4.71	TX	San Antonio	5.88	4.65	5.3
ND	Bismarck	5.48	3.97	5.01	TX	Brownsville	5.49	4.42	4.92
NJ	Sea Brook	4.76	3.20	4.21	TX	El Paso	7.42	5.87	6.72
NV	Las Vegas	7.13	5.84	6.41	TX	Midland	6.33	5.23	5.83
NV	Ely	6.48	5.49	5.98	TX	Fort Worth	6.00	4.80	5.43
NY	Binghamton	3.93	1.62	3.16	UT	Salt Lake City	6.09	3.78	5.26
NY	Ithaca	4.57	2.29	3.79	UT	Flaming Gorge	6.63	5.48	5.83
NY	Schenectady	3.92	2.53	3.55	VA	Richmond	4.50	3.37	4.13
NY	Rochester	4.22	1.58	3.31	WA	Seattle	4.83	1.60	3.57
NY	New York City	4.97	3.03	4.08	WA	Richland	6.13	2.01	4.44
OH	Columbus	5.26	2.66	4.15	WA	Pullman	6.07	2.90	4.73
OH	Cleveland	4.79	2.69	3.94	WA	Spokane	5.53	1.16	4.48
OK	Stillwater	5.52	4.22	4.99	WA	Prosser	6.21	3.06	5.03
OK	Oklahoma City	6.26	4.98	5.59	WI	Madison	4.85	3.28	4.29
OR	Astoria	4.76	1.99	3.72	WV	Charleston	4.12	2.47	3.65
OR	Corvallis	5.71	1.90	4.03	WY	Lander	6.81	5.50	6.06
OR	Medford	5.84	2.02	4.51					

*Values are given in kilowatt-hours per square meter per day.

Longitude and Latitude Tables

	LONGITUDE	LATITUDE
ALABAMA		
Alexander City	32° 57'N	85° 57'W
Anniston AP	33° 35'N	85° 51'W
Auburn	32° 36'N	85° 30'W
Birmingham AP	33° 34'N	86° 45'W
Decatur	34° 37'N	86° 59'W
Dothan AP	31° 19'N	85° 27'W
Florence AP	34° 48'N	87° 40'W
Gadsden	34° 1'N	86° 0'W
Huntsville AP	34° 42'N	86° 35'W
Mobile AP	30° 41'N	88° 15'W
Mobile Co	30° 40'N	88° 15'W
Montgomery AP	32° 23'N	86° 22'W
Selma-Craig AFB	32° 20'N	87° 59'W
Talladega	33° 27'N	86° 6'W
Tuscaloosa AP	33° 13'N	87° 37'W
ALASKA		
Anchorage AP	61° 10'N	150° 1'W
Barrow	71° 18'N	156° 47'W
Fairbanks AP	64° 49'N	147° 52'W
Juneau AP	58° 22'N	134° 35'W
Kodiak	57° 45'N	152° 29'W
Nome AP	64° 30'N	165° 26'W
ARIZONA		

	LONGITUDE	LATITUDE
Blythe AP	33° 37'N	114° 43'W
Burbank AP	34° 12'N	118° 21'W
Chico	39° 48'N	121° 51'W
Concord	37° 58'N	121° 59'W
Covina	34° 5'N	117° 52'W
Crescent City AP	41° 46'N	124° 12'W
Downey	33° 56'N	118° 8'W
El Cajon	32° 49'N	116° 58'W
El Cerrito AP	32° 49'N	115° 40'W
Escondido	33° 7'N	117° 5'W
Eureka/Arcata AP	40° 59'N	124° 6'W
Fairfield-Trafis AFB	38° 16'N	121° 56'W
Fresno AP	36° 46'N	119° 43'W
Hamilton AFB	38° 4'N	122° 30'W
Laguna Beach	33° 33'N	117° 47'W
Livermore	37° 42'N	121° 57'W
Lompoc, Vandenberg AFB	34° 43'N	120° 34'W
Long Beach AP	33° 49'N	118° 9'W
Los Angeles AP	33° 56'N	118° 24'W
Los Angeles Co	34° 3'N	118° 14'W
Merced-Castle AFB	37° 23'N	120° 34'W
Modesto	37° 39'N	121° 0'W
Monterey	36° 36'N	121° 54'W
Napa	38° 13'N	122° 17'W
Needles AP	34° 36'N	114° 37'W

City	Latitude	Longitude
Douglas AP	31° 27'N	109° 36'W
Flagstaff AP	35° 8'N	111° 40'W
Fort Huachuca AP	31° 35'N	110° 20'W
Kingman AP	35° 12'N	114° 1'W
Nogales	31° 21'N	110° 55'W
Phoenix AP	33° 26'N	112° 1'W
Prescott AP	34° 39'N	112° 26'W
Tucson AP	32° 7'N	110° 56'W
Winslow AP	35° 1'N	110° 44'W
Yuma AP	32° 39'N	114° 37'W
ARKANSAS		
Blytheville AFB	35° 57'N	89° 57'W
Camden	33° 36'N	92° 49'W
El Dorado AP	33° 13'N	92° 49'W
Fayetteville AP	36° 0'N	94° 10'W
Fort Smith AP	35° 20'N	94° 22'W
Hot Springs	34° 29'N	93° 6'W
Jonesboro	35° 50'N	90° 42' W
Little Rock AP	34° 44'N	92° 14'W
Pine Bluff AP	34° 18'N	92° 5'W
Texarkana AP	33° 27'N	93° 59' W
CALIFORNIA		
Bakersfield AP	35° 25'N	119° 3'W
Barstow AP	34° 51'N	116° 47'W
Oakland AP	37° 49'N	122° 19'W
Oceanside	33° 14'N	117° 25'W
Ontario	34° 3'N	117° 36'W
Oxnard	34° 12'N	119° 11'W
Palmdale AP	34° 38'N	118° 6'W
Palm Springs	33° 49'N	116° 32'W
Pasadena	34° 9'N	118° 9'W
Petaluma	38° 14'N	122° 38'W
Pomona Co	34° 3'N	117° 45'W
Redding AP	40° 31'N	122° 18'W
Redlands	34° 3'N	117° 11'W
Richmond	37° 56'N	122° 21'W
Riverside-March AFB	33° 54'N	117° 15'W
Sacramento AP	38° 31'N	121° 30'W
Salinas AP	36° 40'N	121° 36'W
San Bernardino, Norton AFB	34° 8'N	117° 16'W
San Diego AP	32° 44'N	117° 10'W
San Fernando	34° 17'N	118° 28'W
San Francisco AP	37° 37'N	122° 23'W
San Francisco Co	37° 46'N	122° 26'W
San Jose AP	37° 22'N	121° 56'W
San Luis Obispo	35° 20'N	120° 43'W
Santa Ana AP	33° 45'N	117° 52'W

(Continued)

449

	LONGITUDE	LATITUDE
Santa Barbara MAP	34° 26'N	119° 50'W
CALIFORNIA (Continued)		
Santa Cruz	36° 59'N	122° 1'W
Santa Maria AP	34° 54'N	120° 27'W
Santa Monica CIC	34° 1'N	118° 29'W
Santa Paula	34° 21'N	119° 5'W
Santa Rosa	38° 31'N	122° 49'W
Stockton AP	37° 54'N	121° 15'W
Ukiah	39° 9'N	123° 12'W
Visalia	36° 20'N	119° 18'W
Yreka	41° 43'N	122° 38'W
Yuba City	39° 8'N	121° 36'W
COLORADO		
Alamosa AP	37° 27'N	105° 52'W
Boulder	40° 0'N	105° 16'W
Colorado Springs AP	38° 49'N	104° 43'W
Denver AP	39° 45'N	104° 52'W
Durango	37° 17'N	107° 53'W
Fort Collins	40° 45'N	105° 5'W
Grand Junction AP	39° 7'N	108° 32'W
Greeley	40° 26'N	104° 38'W
La Junta AP	38° 3'N	103° 30'W
Leadville	39° 15'N	106° 18'W

	LONGITUDE	LATITUDE
Gainesville AP	29° 41'N	82° 16'W
Jacksonville AP	30° 30'N	81° 42'W
Key West AP	24° 33'N	81° 45'W
Lakeland Co	28° 2'N	81° 57'W
Miami AP	25° 48'N	80° 16'W
Miami Beach Co	25° 47'N	80° 17'W
Ocala	29° 11'N	82° 8'W
Orlando AP	28° 33'N	81° 23'W
Panama City, Tyndall AFB	30° 4'N	85° 35'W
Pensacola Co	30° 25'N	87° 13'W
St. Augustine	29° 58'N	81° 20'W
St. Petersburg	27° 46'N	82° 80'W
Sarasota	27° 23'N	82° 33'W
Stanford	28° 46'N	81° 17'W
Tallahassee AP	30° 23'N	84° 22'W
Tampa AP	27° 58'N	82° 32'W
West Palm Beach AP	26° 41'N	80° 6'W
GEORGIA		
Albany, Turner AFB	31° 36'N	84° 5'W
Americus	32° 3'N	84° 14'W
Athens	33° 57'N	83° 19'W
Atlanta AP	33° 39'N	84° 26'W
Augusta AP	33° 22'N	81° 58'W

Location	Latitude	Longitude	Location	Latitude	Longitude
Pueblo AP	38° 18'N	104° 29'W	Brunswick	31° 15'N	81° 29'W
Sterling	40° 37'N	103° 12'W	Columbus, Lawson AFB	32° 31'N	84° 56'W
Trinidad	37° 15'N	104° 20'W	Dalton	34° 34'N	84° 57'W
CONNECTICUT			Dublin	32° 20'N	82° 54'W
Bridgeport AP	41° 11'N	73° 11'W	Gainesville	34° 11'N	83° 41'W
Hartford, Brainard Field	41° 44'N	72° 39'W	Griffin	33° 13'N	84° 16'W
New Haven AP	41° 19'N	73° 55'W	LaGrange	33° 1'N	85° 4'W
New London	41° 21'N	72° 6'W	Macon AP	32° 42'N	83° 39'W
Norwalk	41° 7'N	73° 25'W	Marietta, Dobbins AFB	33° 55'N	84° 31'W
Norwich	41° 32'N	72° 4'W	Savannah	32° 8'N	81° 12'W
Waterbury	41° 35'N	73° 4'W	Valdosta-Moody AFB	30° 58'N	83° 12'W
Windsor Locks, Bradley Fld	41° 56'N	72° 41'W	Waycross	31° 15'N	82° 24'W
DELAWARE			**HAWAII**		
Dover AFB	39° 8'N	75° 28'W	Hilo AP	19° 43'N	155° 5'W
Wilmington AP	39° 40'N	75° 36'W	Honolulu AP	21° 20'N	157° 55'W
DISTRICT OF COLUMBIA			Kaneohe Bay MCAS	21° 27'N	157° 46'W
Andrews AFB	38° 5'N	76° 5'W	Wahiawa	21° 3'N	158° 2'W
Washington, National AP	38° 51'N	77° 2'W	**IDAHO**		
FLORIDA			Boise AP	43° 34'N	116° 13'W
Belle Glade	26° 39'N	80° 39'W	Burley	42° 32'N	113° 46'W
Cape Kennedy AP	28° 29'N	80° 34'W	Coeur D'Alene AP	47° 46'N	116° 49'W
Daytona Beach AP	29° 11'N	81° 3'W	Idaho Falls AP	43° 31'N	112° 4'W
E Fort Lauderdale	26° 4'N	80° 9'W	Lewiston AP	46° 23'N	117° 1'W
Fort Myers AP	26° 35'N	81° 52'W	Moscow	46° 44'N	116° 58'W
Fort Pierce	27° 28'N	80° 21'W	Mountain Home AFB	43° 2'N	115° 54'W

(Continued)

	LONGITUDE	LATITUDE		LONGITUDE	LATITUDE
Pocatello AP	42° 55'N	112° 36'W	Muncie	40° 11'N	85° 21'W
Twin Falls AP	42° 29'N	114° 29'W	Peru, Grissom AFB	40° 39'N	86° 9'W
ILLINOIS			Richmond AP	39° 46'N	84° 50'W
Aurora	41° 45'N	88° 20'W	Shelbyville	39° 31'N	85° 47'W
Belleville, Scott AFB	38° 33'N	89° 51'W	South Bend AP	41° 42'N	86° 19'W
Bloomington	40° 29'N	88° 57'W	Terre Haute AP	39° 27'N	87° 18'W
Carbondale	37° 47'N	89° 15'W	Valparaiso	41° 31'N	87° 2'W
Champaign/Urbana	40° 2'N	88° 17'W	Vincennes	38° 41'N	87° 32'W
Chicago, Midway AP	41° 47'N	87° 45'W	**IOWA**		
Chicago, O'Hare AP	41° 59'N	87° 54'W	Ames	42° 2'N	93° 48'W
Chicago Co	41° 53'N	87° 38'W	Burlington AP	40° 47'N	91° 7'W
Danville	40° 12'N	87° 36'W	Cedar Rapids AP	41° 53'N	91° 42'W
Decatur	39° 50'N	88° 52'W	Clinton	41° 50'N	90° 13'W
Dixon	41° 50'N	89° 29'W	Council Bluffs	41° 20'N	95° 49'W
Elgin	42° 2'N	88° 16'W	Des Moines AP	41° 32'N	93° 39'W
Freeport	42° 18'N	89° 37'W	Dubuque	42° 24'N	90° 42'W
Galesburg	40° 56'N	90° 26'W	Fort Dodge	42° 33'N	94° 11'W
Greenville	38° 53'N	89° 24'W	Iowa City	41° 38'N	91° 33'W
Joliet	41° 31'N	88° 10'W	Keokuk	40° 24'N	91° 24'W
Kankakee	41° 5'N	87° 55'W	Marshalltown	42° 4'N	92° 56'W
La Salle/Peru	41° 19'N	89° 6'W	Mason City AP	43° 9'N	93° 20'W
Macomb	40° 28'N	90° 40'W	Newton	41° 41'N	93° 2'W
Moline AP	41° 27'N	90° 31'W	Ottumwa AP	41° 6'N	92° 27'W

Mt Vernon	38° 19'N	88° 52'W
Peoria AP	40° 40'N	89° 41'W
Quincy AP	39° 57'N	91° 12'W
Rantoul, Chanute AFB	40° 18'N	88° 8'W
Rockford	42° 21'N	89° 3'W
Springfield AP	39° 50'N	89° 40'W
Waukegan	42° 21'N	87° 53'W
INDIANA		
Anderson	40° 6'N	85° 37'W
Bedford	38° 51'N	86° 30'W
Bloomington	39° 8'N	86° 37'W
Columbus, Bakalar AFB	39° 16'N	85° 54'W
Crawfordsville	40° 3'N	86° 54'W
Evansville AP	38° 3'N	87° 32'W
Fort Wayne AP	41° 0'N	85° 12'W
Goshen AP	41° 32'N	85° 48'W
Hobart	41° 32'N	87° 15'W
Huntington	40° 53'N	85° 30'W
Indianapolis AP	39° 44'N	86° 17'W
Jeffersonville	38° 17'N	85° 45'W
Kokomo	40° 25'N	86° 3'W
Lafayette	40° 2'N	86° 5'W
La Porte	41° 36'N	86° 43'W
Marion	40° 29'N	85° 41'W

Sioux City AP	42° 24'N	96° 23'W
Waterloo	42° 33'N	92° 24'W
KANSAS		
Atchison	39° 34'N	95° 7'W
Chanute AP	37° 40'N	95° 29'W
Dodge City AP	37° 46'N	99° 58'W
El Dorado	37° 49'N	96° 50'W
Emporia	38° 20'N	96° 12'W
Garden City AP	37° 56'N	100° 44'W
Goodland AP	39° 22'N	101° 42'W
Great Bend	38° 21'N	98° 52'W
Hutchinson AP	38° 4'N	97° 52'W
Liberal	37° 3'N	100° 58'W
Manhattan, Ft Riley	39° 3'N	96° 46'W
Parsons	37° 20'N	95° 31'W
Russell AP	38° 52'N	98° 49'W
Salina	38° 48'N	97° 39'W
Topeka AP	39° 4'N	95° 38'W
Wichita AP	37° 39'N	97° 25'W
KENTUCKY		
Ashland	38° 33'N	82° 44'W
Bowling Green AP	35° 58'N	86° 28'W
Corbin AP	36° 57'N	84° 6'W
Covington AP	39° 3'N	84° 40'W

(Continued)

	LONGITUDE	LATITUDE
Hopkinsville, Ft Campbell	36° 40'N	87° 29'W
Lexington AP	38° 2'N	84° 36'W
KENTUCKY (Continued)		
Louisville AP	38° 11'N	85° 44'W
Madisonville	37° 19'N	87° 29'W
Owensboro	37° 45'N	87° 10'W
Paducah AP	37° 4'N	88° 46'W
LOUISIANA		
Alexandria AP	31° 24'N	92° 18'W
Baton Rouge AP	30° 32'N	91° 9'W
Bogalusa	30° 47'N	89° 52'W
Houma	29° 31'N	90° 40'W
Lafayette AP	30° 12'N	92° 0'W
Lake Charles AP	30° 7'N	93° 13'W
Minden	32° 36'N	93° 18'W
Monroe AP	32° 31'N	92° 2'W
Natchitoches	31° 46'N	93° 5'W
New Orleans AP	29° 59'N	90° 15'W
Shreveport AP	32° 28'N	93° 49'W
MAINE		
Augusta AP	44° 19'N	69° 48'W
Bangor, Dow AFB	44° 48'N	68° 50'W
Caribou AP	46° 52'N	68° 1'W
Lewiston	44° 2'N	70° 15'W

	LONGITUDE	LATITUDE
Adrian	41° 55'N	84° 1'W
Alpena AP	45° 4'N	83° 26'W
Battle Creek AP	42° 19'N	85° 15'W
Benton Harbor AP	42° 8'N	86° 26'W
Detroit	42° 25'N	83° 1'W
Escanaba	45° 44'N	87° 5'W
Flint AP	42° 58'N	83° 44'W
Grand Rapids AP	42° 53'N	85° 31'W
Holland	42° 42'N	86° 6'W
Jackson AP	42° 16'N	84° 28'W
Kalamazoo	42° 17'N	85° 36'W
Lansing AP	42° 47'N	84° 36'W
Marquette Co	46° 34'N	87° 24'W
Mt Pleasant	43° 35'N	84° 46'W
Muskegon AP	43° 10'N	86° 14'W
Pontiac	42° 40'N	83° 25'W
Port Huron	42° 59'N	82° 25'W
Saginaw AP	43° 32'N	84° 5'W
Sault Ste. Marie AP	46° 28'N	84° 22'W
Traverse City AP	44° 45'N	85° 35'W
Ypsilanti	42° 14'N	83° 32'W
MINNESOTA		
Albert Lea	43° 39'N	93° 21'W
Alexandria AP	45° 52'N	95° 23'W

Millinocket AP	45° 39'N	68° 42'W
Portland	43° 39'N	70° 19'W
Waterville	44° 32'N	69° 40'W
MARYLAND		
Baltimore AP	39° 11'N	76° 40'W
Baltimore Co	39° 20'N	76° 25'W
Cumberland	39° 37'N	78° 46'W
Frederick AP	39° 27'N	77° 25'W
Hagerstown	39° 42'N	77° 44'W
Salisbury	38° 20'N	75° 30'W
MASSACHUSETTS		
Boston AP	42° 22'N	71° 2'W
Clinton	42° 24'N	71° 41'W
Fall River	41° 43'N	71° 8'W
Framingham	42° 17'N	71° 25'W
Gloucester	42° 35'N	70° 41'W
Greenfield	42° 3'N	72° 4'W
Lawrence	42° 42'N	71° 10'W
Lowell	42° 39'N	71° 19'W
New Bedford	41° 41'N	70° 58'W
Pittsfield AP	42° 26'N	73° 18'W
Springfield, Westover AFB	42° 12'N	72° 32'W
Taunton	41° 54'N	71° 4'W
Worcester AP	42° 16'N	71° 52'W
MICHIGAN		

Bemidji AP	47° 31'N	94° 56'W
Brainerd	46° 24'N	94° 8'W
Duluth AP	46° 50'N	92° 11'W
Faribault	44° 18'N	93° 16'W
Fergus Falls	46° 16'N	96° 4'W
International Falls AP	48° 34'N	93° 23'W
Mankato	44° 9'N	93° 59'W
Minneapolis/St. Paul AP	44° 53'N	93° 13'W
Rochester AP	43° 55'N	92° 30'W
St. Cloud AP	45° 35'N	94° 11'W
Virginia	47° 30'N	92° 33'W
Willmar	45° 7'N	95° 5'W
Winona	44° 3'N	91° 38'W
MISSISSIPPI		
Biloxi—Keesler AFB	30° 25'N	88° 55'W
Clarksdale	34° 12'N	90° 34'W
Columbus AFB	33° 39'N	88° 27'W
Greenville AFB	33° 29'N	90° 59'W
Greenwood	33° 30'N	90° 5'W
Hattiesburg	31° 16'N	89° 15'W
Jackson AP	32° 19'N	90° 5'W
Laurel	31° 40'N	89° 10'W
McComb AP	31° 15'N	90° 28'W
Meridian AP	32° 20'N	88° 45'W
Natchez	31° 33'N	91° 23'W

(Continued)

	LONGITUDE	LATITUDE
Tupelo	34° 16'N	88° 46'W
Vicksburg Co	32° 24'N	90° 47'W
MISSOURI		
Cape Girardeau	37° 14'N	89° 35'W
Columbia AP	38° 58'N	92° 22'W
Farmington AP	37° 46'N	90° 24'W
Hannibal	39° 42'N	91° 21'W
Jefferson City	38° 34'N	92° 11'W
Joplin AP	37° 9'N	94° 30'W
Kansas City AP	39° 7'N	94° 35'W
Kirksville AP	40° 6'N	92° 33'W
Mexico	39° 11'N	91° 54'W
Moberly	39° 24'N	92° 26'W
Poplar Bluff	36° 46'N	90° 25'W
Rolla	37° 59'N	91° 43'W
St. Joseph AP	39° 46'N	94° 55'W
St. Louis AP	38° 45'N	90° 23'W
St. Louis Co	38° 39'N	90° 38'W
Sedalia—Whiteman AFB	38° 43'N	93° 33'W
Sikeston	36° 53'N	89° 36'W
Springfield AP	37° 14'N	93° 23'W
MONTANA		
Billings AP	45° 48'N	108° 32'W
Bozeman	45° 47'N	111° 9'W

	LONGITUDE	LATITUDE
Omaha AP	41° 18'N	95° 54'W
Scottsbluff AP	41° 52'N	103° 36'W
Sidney AP	41° 13'N	103° 6'W
NEVADA		
Carson City	39° 10'N	119° 46'W
Elko AP	40° 50'N	115° 47'W
Ely AP	39° 17'N	114° 51'W
Las Vegas AP	36° 5'N	115° 10'W
Lovelock AP	40° 4'N	118° 33'W
Reno AP	39° 30'N	119° 47'W
Reno Co	39° 30'N	119° 47'W
Tonopah AP	38° 4'N	117° 5'W
Winnemucca AP	40° 54'N	117° 48'W
NEW HAMPSHIRE		
Berlin	44° 3'N	71° 1'W
Claremont	43° 2'N	72° 2'W
Concord AP	43° 12'N	71° 30'W
Keene	42° 55'N	72° 17'W
Laconia	43° 3'N	71° 3'W
Manchester, Grenier AFB	42° 56'N	71° 26'W
Portsmouth, Pease AFB	43° 4'N	70° 49'W
NEW JERSEY		
Atlantic City Co	39° 23'N	74° 26'W

City	Latitude	Longitude
Butte AP	45° 57'N	112° 30'W
Cut Bank AP	48° 37'N	112° 22'W
Glasgow AP	48° 25'N	106° 32'W
Glendive	47° 8'N	104° 48'W
Great Falls AP	47° 29'N	111° 22'W
Havre	48° 34'N	109° 40'W
Helena AP	46° 36'N	112° 0'W
Kalispell AP	48° 18'N	114° 16'W
Lewiston AP	47° 4'N	109° 27'W
Livingstown AP	45° 42'N	110° 26'W
Miles City AP	46° 26'N	105° 52'W
Missoula AP	46° 55'N	114° 5'W
NEBRASKA		
Beatrice	40° 16'N	96° 45'W
Chadron AP	42° 50'N	103° 5'W
Columbus	41° 28'N	97° 20'W
Fremont	41° 26'N	96° 29'W
Grand Island AP	40° 59'N	98° 19'W
Hastings	40° 36'N	98° 26'W
Kearney	40° 44'N	99° 1'W
Lincoln Co	40° 51'N	96° 45'W
McCook	40° 12'N	100° 38'W
Norfolk	41° 59'N	97° 26'W
North Platte AP	41° 8'N	100° 41'W

City	Latitude	Longitude
Long Branch	40° 19'N	74° 1'W
Newark AP	40° 42'N	74° 10'W
New Brunswick	40° 29'N	74° 26'W
Paterson	40° 54'N	74° 9'W
Phillipsburg	40° 41'N	75° 11'W
Trenton Co	40° 13'N	74° 46'W
Vineland	39° 29'N	75° 0'W
NEW MEXICO		
Alamogordo, Holloman AFB	32° 51'N	106° 6'W
Albuquerque AP	35° 3'N	106° 37'W
Artesia	32° 46'N	104° 23'W
Carlsbad AP	32° 20'N	104° 16'W
Clovis AP	34° 23'N	103° 19'W
Farmington AP	36° 44'N	108° 14'W
Gallup	35° 31'N	108° 47'W
Grants	35° 10'N	107° 54'W
Hobbs AP	32° 45'N	103° 13'W
Las Cruces	32° 18'N	106° 55'W
Los Alamos	35° 52'N	106° 19'W
Raton AP	36° 45'N	104° 30'W
Roswell, Walker AFB	33° 18'N	104° 32'W
Santa Fe Co	35° 37'N	106° 5'W
Silver City AP	32° 38'N	108° 10'W

(Continued)

	LONGITUDE	LATITUDE		LONGITUDE	LATITUDE
Socorro AP	34° 3'N	106° 53'W	Henderson	36° 22'N	78° 25'W
Tucumcari AP	35° 11'N	103° 36'W	Hickory	35° 45'N	81° 23'W
NEW YORK			Jacksonville	34° 50'N	77° 37'W
Albany AP	42° 45'N	73° 48'W	Lumberton	34° 37'N	79° 4'W
Albany Co	42° 39'N	73° 45'W	New Bern AP	35° 5'N	77° 3'W
Auburn	42° 54'N	76° 32'W	Raleigh/Durham AP	35° 52'N	78° 47'W
Batavia	43° 0'N	78° 11'W	Rocky Mount	35° 58'N	77° 48'W
Binghamton AP	42° 13'N	75° 59'W	Wilmington AP	34° 16'N	77° 55'W
Buffalo AP	42° 56'N	78° 44'W	Winston-Salem AP	36° 8'N	80° 13'W
Cortland	42° 36'N	76° 11'W	**NORTH DAKOTA**		
Dunkirk	42° 29'N	79° 16'W	Bismarck AP	46° 46'N	100° 45'W
Elmira AP	42° 10'N	76° 54'W	Devils Lake	48° 7'N	98° 54'W
Geneva	42° 45'N	76° 54'W	Dickinson AP	46° 48'N	102° 48'W
Glens Falls	43° 20'N	73° 37'W	Fargo AP	46° 54'N	96° 48'W
Gloversville	43° 2'N	74° 21'W	Grand Forks AP	47° 57'N	97° 24'W
Hornell	42° 21'N	77° 42'W	Jamestown AP	46° 55'N	98° 41'W
Ithaca	42° 27'N	76° 29'W	Minot AP	48° 25'N	101° 21'W
Jamestown	42° 7'N	79° 14'W	Williston	48° 9'N	103° 35'W
Kingston	41° 56'N	74° 0'W	**OHIO**		
Lockport	43° 9'N	79° 15'W	Akron-Canton AP	40° 55'N	81° 26'W
Massena AP	44° 56'N	74° 51'W	Ashtabula	41° 51'N	80° 48'W
Newburgh, Stewart AFB	41° 30'N	74° 6'W	Athens	39° 20'N	82° 6'W
NYC-Central Park	40° 47'N	73° 58'W	Bowling Green	41° 23'N	83° 38'W

City	Latitude	Longitude	City	Latitude	Longitude
NYC-Kennedy AP	40° 39'N	73° 47'W	Cambridge	40° 4'N	81° 35'W
NYC-La Guardia AP	40° 46'N	73° 54'W	Chillicothe	39° 21'N	83° 0'W
Niagara Falls AP	43° 6'N	79° 57'W	Cincinnati Co	39° 9'N	84° 31'W
Olean	42° 14'N	78° 22'W	Cleveland AP	41° 24'N	81° 51'W
Oneonta	42° 31'N	75° 4'W	Columbus AP	40° 0'N	82° 53'W
Oswego Co	43° 28'N	76° 33'W	Dayton AP	39° 54'N	84° 13'W
Plattsburg AFB	44° 39'N	73° 28'W	Defiance	41° 17'N	84° 23'W
Poughkeepsie	41° 38'N	73° 55'W	Findlay AP	41° 1'N	83° 40'W
Rochester AP	43° 7'N	77° 40'W	Fremont	41° 20'N	83° 7'W
Rome, Griffiss AFB	43° 14'N	75° 25'W	Hamilton	39° 24'N	84° 35'W
Schenectady	42° 51'N	73° 57'W	Lancaster	39° 44'N	82° 38'W
Suffolk County AFB	40° 51'N	72° 38'W	Lima	40° 42'N	84° 2'W
Syracuse AP	43° 7'N	76° 7'W	Mansfield AP	40° 49'N	82° 31'W
Utica	43° 9'N	75° 23'W	Marion	40° 36'N	83° 10'W
Watertown	43° 59'N	76° 1'W	Middletown	39° 31'N	84° 25'W
NORTH CAROLINA			Newark	40° 1'N	82° 28'W
Asheville AP	35° 26'N	82° 32'W	Norwalk	41° 16'N	82° 37'W
Charlotte AP	35° 13'N	80° 56'W	Portsmouth	38° 45'N	82° 55'W
Durham	35° 52'N	78° 47'W	Sandusky Co	41° 27'N	82° 43'W
Elizabeth City AP	36° 16'N	76° 11'W	Springfield	39° 50'N	83° 50'W
Fayetteville, Pope AFB	35° 10'N	79° 1'W	Steubenville	40° 23'N	80° 38'W
Goldsboro, Seymour-Johnson	35° 20'N	77° 58'W	Toledo AP	41° 36'N	83° 48'W
Greensboro AP	36° 5'N	79° 57'W	Warren	41° 20'N	80° 51'W
Greenville	35° 37'N	77° 25'W	Wooster	40° 47'N	81° 55'W

(Continued)

	LONGITUDE	LATITUDE
Youngstown AP	41° 16'N	80° 40'W
Zanesville AP	39° 57'N	81° 54'W
OKLAHOMA		
Ada	34° 47'N	96° 41'W
Altus AFB	34° 39'N	99° 16'W
Ardmore	34° 18'N	97° 1'W
Bartlesville	36° 45'N	96° 0'W
Chickasha	35° 3'N	97° 55'W
Enid, Vance AFB	36° 21'N	97° 55'W
Lawton AP	34° 34'N	98° 25'W
McAlester	34° 50'N	95° 55'W
Muskogee AP	35° 40'N	95° 22'W
Norman	35° 15'N	97° 29'W
Oklahoma City AP	35° 24'N	97° 36'W
Ponca City	36° 44'N	97° 6'W
Seminole	35° 14'N	96° 40'W
Stillwater	36° 10'N	97° 5'W
Tulsa AP	36° 12'N	95° 54'W
Woodward	36° 36'N	99° 31'W
OREGON		
Albany	44° 38'N	123° 7'W
Astoria AP	46° 9'N	123° 53'W
Baker AP	44° 50'N	117° 49'W
Bend	44° 4'N	121° 19'W

	LONGITUDE	LATITUDE
Pittsburgh Co	40° 27'N	80° 0'W
Reading Co	40° 20'N	75° 38'W
Scranton/Wilkes-Barre	41° 20'N	75° 44'W
State College	40° 48'N	77° 52'W
Sunbury	40° 53'N	76° 46'W
Uniontown	39° 55'N	79° 43'W
Warren	41° 51'N	79° 8'W
West Chester	39° 58'N	75° 38'W
Williamsport AP	41° 15'N	76° 55'W
York	39° 55'N	76° 45'W
RHODE ISLAND		
Newport	41° 30'N	71° 20'W
Providence AP	41° 44'N	71° 26'W
SOUTH CAROLINA		
Anderson	34° 30'N	82° 43'W
Charleston AFB	32° 54'N	80° 2'W
Charleston Co	32° 54'N	79° 58'W
Columbia AP	33° 57'N	81° 7'W
Florence AP	34° 11'N	79° 43'W
Georgetown	33° 23'N	79° 17'W
Greenville AP	34° 54'N	82° 13'W
Greenwood	34° 10'N	82° 7'W
Orangeburg	33° 30'N	80° 52'W
Rock Hill	34° 59'N	80° 58'W

City	Latitude	Longitude
Corvallis	44° 30'N	123° 17'W
Eugene AP	44° 7'N	123° 13'W
Grants Pass	42° 26'N	123° 19'W
Klamath Falls AP	42° 9'N	121° 44'W
Medford AP	42° 22'N	122° 52'W
Pendleton AP	45° 41'N	118° 51'W
Portland AP	45° 36'N	122° 36'W
Portland Co	45° 32'N	122° 40'W
Roseburg AP	43° 14'N	123° 22'W
Salem AP	44° 55'N	123° 1'W
The Dalles	45° 36'N	121° 12'W
PENNSYLVANIA		
Allentown AP	40° 39'N	75° 26'W
Altoona Co	40° 18'N	78° 19'W
Butler	40° 52'N	79° 54'W
Chambersburg	39° 56'N	77° 38'W
Erie AP	42° 5'N	80° 11'W
Harrisburg AP	40° 12'N	76° 46'W
Johnstown	40° 19'N	78° 50'W
Lancaster	40° 7'N	76° 18'W
Meadville	41° 38'N	80° 10'W
New Castle	41° 1'N	80° 22'W
Philadelphia AP	39° 53'N	75° 15'W
Pittsburgh AP	40° 30'N	80° 13'W
Spartanburg AP	34° 58'N	82° 0'W
Sumter, Shaw AFB	33° 54'N	80° 22'W
SOUTH DAKOTA		
Aberdeen AP	45° 27'N	98° 26'W
Brookings	44° 18'N	96° 48'W
Huron AP	44° 23'N	98° 13'W
Mitchell	43° 41'N	98° 1'W
Pierre AP	44° 23'N	100° 17'W
Rapid City AP	44° 3'N	103° 4'W
Sioux Falls AP	43° 34'N	96° 44'W
Watertown AP	44° 55'N	97° 9'W
Yankton	42° 55'N	97° 23'W
TENNESSEE		
Athens	35° 26'N	84° 35'W
Bristol-Tri City AP	36° 29'N	82° 24'W
Chattanooga AP	35° 2'N	85° 12'W
Clarksville	36° 33'N	87° 22'W
Columbia	35° 38'N	87° 2'W
Dyersburg	36° 1'N	89° 24'W
Greenville	36° 4'N	82° 50'W
Jackson AP	35° 36'N	88° 55'W
Knoxville AP	35° 49'N	83° 59'W
Memphis AP	35° 3'N	90° 0'W
Murfreesboro	34° 55'N	86° 28'W

(Continued)

	LONGITUDE	LATITUDE
Nashville AP	36° 7'N	86° 41'W
Tullahoma	35° 23'N	86° 5'W
TEXAS		
Abilene AP	32° 25'N	99° 41'W
Alice AP	27° 44'N	98° 2'W
Amarillo AP	35° 14'N	100° 42'W
Austin AP	30° 18'N	97° 42'W
Bay City	29° 0'N	95° 58'W
Beaumont	29° 57'N	94° 1'W
Beeville	28° 22'N	97° 40'W
Big Spring AP	32° 18'N	101° 27'W
Brownsville AP	25° 54'N	97° 26'W
Brownwood	31° 48'N	98° 57'W
Bryan AP	30° 40'N	96° 33'W
Corpus Christi AP	27° 46'N	97° 30'W
Corsicana	32° 5'N	96° 28'W
Dallas AP	32° 51'N	96° 51'W
Del Rio, Laughlin AFB	29° 22'N	100° 47'W
Denton	33° 12'N	97° 6'W
Eagle Pass	28° 52'N	100° 32'W
El Paso AP	31° 48'N	106° 24'W
Fort Worth AP	32° 50'N	97° 3'W
Galveston AP	29° 18'N	94° 48'W
Greenville	33° 4'N	96° 3'W

	LONGITUDE	LATITUDE
Vernon	34° 10'N	99° 18'W
Victoria AP	28° 51'N	96° 55'W
Waco AP	31° 37'N	97° 13'W
Wichita Falls AP	33° 58'N	98° 29'W
UTAH		
Cedar City AP	37° 42'N	113° 6'W
Logan	41° 45'N	111° 49'W
Moab	38° 36'N	109° 36'W
Ogden AP	41° 12'N	112° 1'W
Price	39° 37'N	110° 50'W
Provo	40° 13'N	111° 43'W
Richfield	38° 46'N	112° 5'W
St George Co	37° 2'N	113° 31'W
Salt Lake City AP	40° 46'N	111° 58'W
Vernal AP	40° 27'N	109° 31'W
VERMONT		
Barre	44° 12'N	72° 31'W
Burlington AP	44° 28'N	73° 9'W
Rutland	43° 36'N	72° 58'W
VIRGINIA		
Charlottesville	38° 2'N	78° 31'W
Danville AP	36° 34'N	79° 20'W
Fredericksburg	38° 18'N	77° 28'W
Harrisonburg	38° 27'N	78° 54'W

Location	Latitude	Longitude		Location	Latitude	Longitude
Harlingen	26° 14'N	97° 39'W		Lynchburg AP	37° 20'N	79° 12'W
Houston AP	29° 58'N	95° 21'W		Norfolk AP	36° 54'N	76° 12'W
Houston Co	29° 59'N	95° 22'W		Petersburg	37° 11'N	77° 31'W
Huntsville	30° 43'N	95° 33'W		Richmond AP	37° 30'N	77° 20'W
Killeen, Robert Gray AAF	31° 5'N	97° 41'W		Roanoke AP	37° 19'N	79° 58'W
Lamesa	32° 42'N	101° 56'W		Staunton	38° 16'N	78° 54'W
Laredo AFB	27° 32'N	99° 27'W		Winchester	39° 12'N	78° 10'W
Longview	32° 28'N	94° 44'W		**WASHINGTON**		
Lubbock AP	33° 39'N	101° 49'W		Aberdeen	46° 59'N	123° 49'W
Lufkin AP	31° 25'N	94° 48'W		Bellingham AP	48° 48'N	122° 32'W
McAllen	26° 12'N	98° 13'W		Bremerton	47° 34'N	122° 40'W
Midland AP	31° 57'N	102° 11'W		Ellensburg AP	47° 2'N	120° 31'W
Mineral Wells AP	32° 47'N	98° 4'W		Everett, Paine AFB	47° 55'N	122° 17'W
Palestine Co	31° 47'N	95° 38'W		Kennewick	46° 13'N	119° 8'W
Pampa	35° 32'N	100° 59'W		Longview	46° 10'N	122° 56'W
Pecos	31° 25'N	103° 30'W		Moses Lake, Larson AFB	47° 12'N	119° 19'W
Plainview	34° 11'N	101° 42'W		Olympia AP	46° 58'N	122° 54'W
Port Arthur AP	29° 57'N	94° 1'W		Port Angeles	48° 7'N	123° 26'W
San Angelo,Goodfellow AFB	31° 26'N	100° 24'W		Seattle-Boeing Field	47° 32'N	122° 18'W
San Antonio AP	29° 32'N	98° 28'W		Seattle Co	47° 39'N	122° 18'W
Sherman, Perrin AFB	33° 43'N	96° 40'W		Seattle-Tacoma AP	47° 27'N	122° 18'W
Snyder	32° 43'N	100° 55'W		Spokane AP	47° 38'N	117° 31'W
Temple	31° 6'N	97° 21'W		Tacoma, McChord AFB	47° 15'N	122° 30'W
Tyler AP	32° 21'N	95° 16'W		Walla Walla AP	46° 6'N	118° 17'W

(Continued)

	LONGITUDE	LATITUDE
Wenatchee	47° 25'N	120° 19'W
Yakima AP	46° 34'N	120° 32'W
WEST VIRGINIA		
Beckley	37° 47'N	81° 7'W
Bluefield AP	37° 18'N	81° 13'W
Charleston AP	38° 22'N	81° 36'W
Clarksburg	39° 16'N	80° 21'W
Elkins AP	38° 53'N	79° 51'W
Huntington Co	38° 25'N	82° 30'W
Martinsburg AP	39° 24'N	77° 59'W
Morgantown AP	39° 39'N	79° 55'W
Parkersburg Co	39° 16'N	81° 34'W
Wheeling	40° 7'N	80° 42'W
WISCONSIN		
Appleton	44° 15'N	88° 23'W
Ashland	46° 34'N	90° 58'W
Beloit	42° 30'N	89° 2'W
Eau Claire AP	44° 52'N	91° 29'W
Fond Du Lac	43° 48'N	88° 27'W
Green Bay AP	44° 29'N	88° 8'W
La Crosse AP	43° 52'N	91° 15'W

	LONGITUDE	LATITUDE
Madison AP	43° 8'N	89° 20'W
Manitowoc	44° 6'N	87° 41'W
Marinette	45° 6'N	87° 38'W
Milwaukee AP	42° 57'N	87° 54'W
Racine	42° 43'N	87° 51'W
Sheboygan	43° 45'N	87° 43'W
Stevens Point	44° 30'N	89° 34'W
Waukesha	43° 1'N	88° 14'W
Wausau AP	44° 55'N	89° 37'W
WYOMING		
Casper AP	42° 55'N	106° 28'W
Cheyenne	41° 9'N	104° 49'W
Cody AP	44° 33'N	109° 4'W
Evanston	41° 16'N	110° 57'W
Lander AP	42° 49'N	108° 44'W
Laramie AP	41° 19'N	105° 41'W
Newcastle	43° 51'N	104° 13'W
Rawlins	41° 48'N	107° 12'W
Rock Springs AP	41° 36'N	109° 0'W
Sheridan AP	44° 46'N	106° 58'W
Torrington	42° 5'N	104° 13'W

AP = airport, AFB = air force base.

CANADA LONGITUDES AND LATITUDES

	LONGITUDE	LATITUDE		LONGITUDE	LATITUDE
ALBERTA			Trail	49° 8~ N	117° 44~ W
Calgary AP	51° 6~ N	114° 1~ W	Vancouver AP	49° 11~ N	123° 10~ W
Edmonton AP	53° 34~ N	113° 31~ W	Victoria Co	48° 25~ N	123° 19~ W
Grande Prairie AP	55° 11~ N	118° 53~ W	**MANITOBA**		
Jasper	52° 53~ N	118° 4~ W	Brandon	49° 52~ N	99° 59~ W
Lethbridge AP	49° 38~ N	112° 48~ W	Churchill AP	58° 45~ N	94° 4~ W
McMurray AP	56° 39~ N	111° 13~ W	Dauphin AP	51° 6~ N	100° 3~ W
Medicine Hat AP	50° 1~ N	110° 43~ W	Flin Flon	54° 46~ N	101° 51~ W
Red Deer AP	52° 11~ N	113° 54~ W	Portage La Prairie AP	49° 54~ N	98° 16~ W
BRITISH COLUMBIA			The Pas AP	53° 58~ N	101° 6~ W
Dawson Creek	55° 44~ N	120° 11~ W	Winnipeg AP	49° 54~ N	97° 14~ W
Fort Nelson AP	58° 50~ N	122° 35~ W	**NEW BRUNSWICK**		
Kamloops Co	50° 43~ N	120° 25~ W	Campbellton Co	48° 0~ N	66° 40~ W
Nanaimo	49° 11~ N	123° 58~ W	Chatham AP	47° 1~ N	65° 27~ W
New Westminster	49° 13~ N	122° 54~ W	Edmundston Co	47° 22~ N	68° 20~ W
Penticton AP	49° 28~ N	119° 36~ W	Fredericton AP	45° 52~ N	66° 32~ W
Prince George AP	53° 53~ N	122° 41~ W	Moncton AP	46° 7~ N	64° 41~ W
Prince Rupert Co	54° 17~ N	130° 23~ W	Saint John AP	45° 19~ N	65° 53~ W

(Continued)

CANADA LONGITUDES AND LATITUDES (Continued)

	LONGITUDE	LATITUDE		LONGITUDE	LATITUDE
NEWFOUNDLAND			Sudbury AP	46° 37~ N	80° 48~ W
Corner Brook	48° 58~ N	57° 57~ W	Thunder Bay AP	48° 22~ N	89° 19~ W
Gander AP	48° 57~ N	54° 34~ W	Timmins AP	48° 34~ N	81° 22~ W
Goose Bay AP	53° 19~ N	60° 25~ W	Toronto AP	43° 41~ N	79° 38~ W
St John's AP	47° 37~ N	52° 45~ W	Windsor AP	42° 16~ N	82° 58~ W
Stephenville AP	48° 32~ N	58° 33~ W	**PRINCE EDWARD ISLAND**		
NORTHWEST TERRITORIES			Charlottetown AP	46° 17~ N	63° 8~ W
Fort Smith AP	60° 1~ N	111° 58~ W	Summerside AP	46° 26~ N	63° 50~ W
Frobisher AP	63° 45~ N	68° 33~ W	**QUEBEC**		
Inuvik	68° 18~ N	133° 29~ W	Bagotville AP	48° 20~ N	71° 0~ W
Resolute AP	74° 43~ N	94° 59~ W	Chicoutimi	48° 25~ N	71° 5~ W
Yellowknife AP	62° 28~ N	114° 27~ W	Drummondville	45° 53~ N	72° 29~ W
NOVA SCOTIA			Granby	45° 23~ N	72° 42~ W
Amherst	45° 49~ N	64° 13~ W	Hull	45° 26~ N	75° 44~ W
Halifax AP	44° 39~ N	63° 34~ W	Megantic AP	45° 35~ N	70° 52~ W
Kentville	45° 3~ N	64° 36~ W	Montreal AP	45° 28~ N	73° 45~ W
New Glasgow	45° 37~ N	62° 37~ W	Quebec AP	46° 48~ N	71° 23~ W
Sydney AP	46° 10~ N	60° 3~ W	Rimouski	48° 27~ N	68° 32~ W
Truro Co	45° 22~ N	63° 16~ W	St Jean	45° 18~ N	73° 16~ W
Yarmouth AP	43° 50~ N	66° 5~ W	St Jerome	45° 48~ N	74° 1~ W

ONTARIO		
Belleville	44° 9~ N	77° 24~ W
Chatham	42° 24~ N	82° 12~ W
Cornwall	45° 1~ N	74° 45~ W
Hamilton	43° 16~ N	79° 54~ W
Kapuskasing AP	49° 25~ N	82° 28~ W
Kenora AP	49° 48~ N	94° 22~ W
Kingston	44° 16~ N	76° 30~ W
Kitchener	43° 26~ N	80° 30~ W
London AP	43° 2~ N	81° 9~ W
North Bay AP	46° 22~ N	79° 25~ W
Oshawa	43° 54~ N	78° 52~ W
Ottawa AP	45° 19~ N	75° 40~ W
Owen Sound	44° 34~ N	80° 55~ W
Peterborough	44° 17~ N	78° 19~ W
St Catharines	43° 11~ N	79° 14~ W
Sarnia	42° 58~ N	82° 22~ W
Sault Ste Marie AP	46° 32~ N	84° 30~ W

Sept. Iles AP	50° 13~ N	66° 16~ W
Shawinigan	46° 34~ N	72° 43~ W
Sherbrooke Co	45° 24~ N	71° 54~ W
Thetford Mines	46° 4~ N	71° 19~ W
Trois Rivieres	46° 21~ N	72° 35~ W
Val D'or AP	48° 3~ N	77° 47~ W
Valleyfield	45° 16~ N	74° 6~ W
SASKATCHEWAN		
Estevan AP	49° 4~ N	103° 0~ W
Moose Jaw AP	50° 20~ N	105° 33~ W
North Battleford AP	52° 46~ N	108° 15~ W
Prince Albert AP	53° 13~ N	105° 41~ W
Regina AP	50° 26~ N	104° 40~ W
Saskatoon AP	52° 10~ N	106° 41~ W
Swift Current AP	50° 17~ N	107° 41~ W
Yorkton AP	51° 16~ N	102° 28~ W
YUKON TERRITORY		
Whitehorse AP	60° 43~ N	135° 4~ W

INTERNATIONAL LONGITUDES AND LATITUDES

	LONGITUDE	LATITUDE
AFGHANISTAN		
Kabul	34° 35~ N	69° 12~ E
ALGERIA		
Algiers	36° 46~ N	30° 3~ E
ARGENTINA		
Buenos Aires	34° 35~ S	58° 29~ W
Cordoba	31° 22~ S	64° 15~ W
Tucuman	26° 50~ S	65° 10~ W
AUSTRALIA		
Adelaide	34° 56~ S	138° 35~ E
Alice Springs	23° 48~ S	133° 53~ E
Brisbane	27° 28~ S	153° 2~ E
Darwin	12° 28~ S	130° 51~ E
Melbourne	37° 49~ S	144° 58~ E
Perth	31° 57~ S	115° 51~ E
Sydney	33° 52~ S	151° 12~ E
AUSTRIA		
Vienna	48° 15~ N	16° 22~ E
AZORES		
Lajes (Terceira)	38° 45~ N	27° 5~ W
BAHAMAS		
Nassau	25° 5~ N	77° 21~ W

	LONGITUDE	LATITUDE
BURMA		
Mandalay	21° 59~ N	96° 6~ E
Rangoon	16° 47~ N	96° 9~ E
CAMBODIA		
Phnom Penh	11° 33~ N	104° 51~ E
CHILE		
Punta Arenas	53° 10~ S	70° 54~ W
Santiago	33° 27~ S	70° 42~ W
Valparaiso	33° 1~ S	71° 38~ W
CHINA		
Chongquing	29° 33~ N	106° 33~ E
Shanghai	31° 12~ N	121° 26~ E
COLOMBIA		
Baranquilla	10° 59~ N	74° 48~ W
Bogota	4° 36~ N	74° 5~ W
Cali	3° 25~ N	76° 30~ W
Medellin	6° 13~ N	75° 36~ W
CONGO		
Brazzaville	4° 15~ S	15° 15~ E
CUBA		
Guantanamo Bay	19° 54~ N	75° 9~ W
Havana	23° 8~ N	82° 21~ W

BANGLADESH		
Chittagong	22° 21~ N	91° 50~ E
BELGIUM		
Brussels	50° 48~ N	4°21~ E
BELIZE		
Belize	17° 31~ N	88° 11~ W
BERMUDA		
Kindley AFB	33° 22~ N	64° 41~ W
BOLIVIA		
La Paz	16° 30~ S	68° 9~ W
BRAZIL		
Belem	1° 27~ S	48° 29~ W
Belo Horizonte	19° 56~ S	43° 57~ W
Brasilia	15° 52~ S	47° 55~ W
Curitiba	25° 25~ S	49° 17~ W
Fortaleza	3° 46~ S	38° 33~ W
Porto Alegre	30° 2~ S	51° 13~ W
Recife	8° 4~ S	34° 53~ W
Rio de Janeiro	22° 55~ S	43° 12~ W
Salvador	13° 0~ S	38° 30~ W
Sao Paulo	23° 33~ S	46° 38~ W
BULGARIA		
Sofia	42° 42~ N	23° 20~ E
Strasbourg	48° 35~ N	7° 46~ E
CZECHOSLOVAKIA		
Prague	50° 5~ N	14° 25~ E
DENMARK		
Copenhagen	55° 41~ N	12° 33~ E
DOMINICAN REPUBLIC		
Santo Domingo	18° 29~ N	69° 54~ W
EGYPT		
Cairo	29° 52~ N	31° 20~ E
EL SALVADOR		
San Salvador	13° 42~ N	89° 13~ W
EQUADOR		
Guayaquil	2° 0~ S	79° 53~ W
Quito	0° 13~ S	78° 32~ W
ETHIOPIA		
Addis Ababa	90° 2~ N	38° 45~ E
Asmara	15° 17~ N	38° 55~ E
FINLAND		
Helsinki	60° 10~ N	24° 57~ E
FRANCE		
Lyon	45° 42~ N	4° 47~ E
Marseilles	43° 18~ N	5° 23~ E
Nantes	47° 15~ N	1° 34~ W
Nice	43° 42~ N	7° 16~ E
Paris	48° 49~ N	2° 29~ E

(Continued)

	LONGITUDE	LATITUDE		LONGITUDE	LATITUDE
FRENCH GUIANA			**IRAN**		
Cayenne	4° 56~ N	52° 27~ W	Abadan	30° 21~ N	48° 16~ E
GERMANY			Meshed	36° 17~ N	59° 36~ E
Berlin (West)	52° 27~ N	13° 18~ E	Tehran	35° 41~ N	51° 25~ E
Hamburg	53° 33~ N	9° 58~ E	**IRAQ**		
Hannover	52° 24~ N	9° 40~ E	Baghdad	33° 20~ N	44° 24~ E
Mannheim	49° 34~ N	8° 28~ E	Mosul	36° 19~ N	43° 9~ E
Munich	48° 9~ N	11° 34~ E	**IRELAND**		
GHANA			Dublin	53° 22~ N	6° 21~ W
Accra	5° 33~ N	0° 12~ W	Shannon	52° 41~ N	8° 55~ W
GIBRALTAR			**IRIAN BARAT**		
Gibraltar	36° 9~ N	5° 22~ W	Manokwari	0° 52~ S	134° 5~ E
GREECE			**ISRAEL**		
Athens	37° 58~ N	23° 43~ E	Jerusalem	31° 47~ N	35° 13~ E
Thessaloniki	40° 37~ N	22° 57~ E	Tel Aviv	32° 6~ N	34° 47~ E
GREENLAND			**ITALY**		
Narsarssuaq	61° 11~ N	45° 25~ W	Milan	45° 27~ N	9° 17~ E
GUATEMALA			Naples	40° 53~ N	14° 18~ E
Guatemala City	14° 37~ N	90° 31~ W	Rome	41° 48~ N	12° 36~ E
GUYANA			**IVORY COAST**		
Georgetown	6° 50~ N	58° 12~ W	Abidjan	5° 19~ N	4° 1~ W

HAITI		
Port au Prince	18° 33~ N	72° 20~ W
HONDURAS		
Tegucigalpa	14° 6~ N	87° 13~ W
HONG KONG		
Hong Kong	22° 18~ N	114° 10~ E
HUNGARY		
Budapest	47° 31~ N	19° 2~ E
ICELAND		
Reykjavik	64° 8~ N	21° 56~ E
INDIA		
Ahmenabad	23° 2~ N	72° 35~ E
Bangalore	12° 57~ N	77° 37~ E
Bombay	18° 54~ N	72° 49~ E
Calcutta	22° 32~ N	88° 20~ E
Madras	13° 4~ N	80° 15~ E
Nagpur	21° 9~ N	79° 7~ E
New Delhi	28° 35~ N	77° 12~ E
INDONESIA		
Djakarta	6° 11~ S	106° 50~ E
Kupang	10° 10~ S	123° 34~ E
Makassar	5° 8~ S	119° 28~ E
Medan	3° 35~ N	98° 41~ E
Palembang	3° 0~ S	104° 46~ E
Surabaya	7° 13~ S	112° 43~ E
JAPAN		
Fukuoka	33° 35~ N	130° 27~ E
Sapporo	43° 4~ N	141° 21~ E
Tokyo	35° 41~ N	139° 46~ E
JORDAN		
Amman	31° 57~ N	35° 57~ E
KENYA		
Nairobi	1° 16~ S	36° 48~ E
KOREA		
Pyongyang	39° 2~ N	125° 41~ E
Seoul	37° 34~ N	126° 58~ E
LEBANON		
Beirut	33° 54~ N	35° 28~ E
LIBERIA		
Monrovia	6° 18~ N	10° 48~ W
LIBYA		
Benghazi	32° 6~ N	20° 4~ E
MADAGASCAR		
Tananarive	18° 55~ S	47° 33~ E
MALAYSIA		
Kuala Lumpur	3° 7~ N	101° 42~ E
Penang	5° 25~ N	100° 19~ E
MARTINIQUE		
Fort de France	14° 37~ N	61° 5~ W

(Continued)

	LONGITUDE	LATITUDE		LONGITUDE	LATITUDE
MEXICO			**RUSSIA**		
Guadalajara	20° 41~ N	103° 20~ W	Alma Ata	43° 14~ N	76° 53~ E
Merida	20° 58~ N	89° 38~ W	Archangel	64° 33~ N	40° 32~ E
Mexico City	19° 24~ N	99° 12~ W	Kaliningrad	54° 43~ N	20° 30~ E
Monterrey	25° 40~ N	100° 18~ W	Krasnoyarsk	56° 1~ N	92° 57~ E
Vera Cruz	19° 12~ N	96° 8~ W	Kiev	50° 27~ N	30° 30~ E
MOROCCO			Kharkov	50° 0~ N	36° 14~ E
Casablanca	33° 35~ N	7° 39~ W	Kuibyshev	53° 11~ N	50° 6~ E
NEPAL			Leningrad	59° 56~ N	30° 16~ E
Katmandu	27° 42~ N	85° 12~ E	Minsk	53° 54~ N	27° 33~ E
NETHERLANDS			Moscow	55° 46~ N	37° 40~ E
Amsterdam	52° 23~ N	4° 55~ E	Odessa	46° 29~ N	30° 44~ E
NEW ZEALAND			Petropavlovsk	52° 53~ N	158° 42~ E
Auckland	36° 51~ S	174° 46~ E	Rostov on Don	47° 13~ N	39° 43~ E
Christchurch	43° 32~ S	172° 37~ E	Sverdlovsk	56° 49~ N	60° 38~ E
Wellington	41° 17~ S	174° 46~ E	Tashkent	41° 20~ N	69° 18~ E
NICARAGUA			Tbilisi	41° 43~ N	44° 48~ E
Managua	12° 10~ N	86° 15~ W	Vladivostok	43° 7~ N	131° 55~ E
NIGERIA			Volgograd	48° 42~ N	44° 31~ E
Lagos	6° 27~ N	3° 24~ E	**SAUDI ARABIA**		
NORWAY			Dhahran	26° 17~ N	50° 9~ E
Bergen	60° 24~ N	5° 19~ E	Jedda	21° 28~ N	39° 10~ E

City	Latitude	Longitude
Oslo	59° 56~ N	10° 44~ E
PAKISTAN		
Karachi	24° 48~ N	66° 59~ E
Lahore	31° 35~ N	74° 20~ E
Peshwar	34° 1~ N	71° 35~ E
PANAMA		
Panama City	8° 58~ N	79° 33~ W
PAPUA NEW GUINEA		
Port Moresby	9° 29~ S	147° 9~ E
PARAGUAY		
Asuncion	25° 17~ S	57° 30~ W
PERU		
Lima	12° 5~ S	77° 3~ W
PHILIPPINES		
Manila	14° 35~ N	120° 59~ E
POLAND		
Krakow	50° 4~ N	19° 57~ E
Warsaw	52° 13~ N	21° 2~ E
PORTUGAL		
Lisbon	38° 43~ N	9° 8~ W
PUERTO RICO		
San Juan	18° 29~ N	66° 7~ W
RUMANIA		
Bucharest	44° 25~ N	26° 6~ E
Riyadh	24° 39~ N	46° 42~ E
SENEGAL		
Dakar	14° 42~ N	17° 29~ W
SINGAPORE		
Singapore	1° 18~ N	103° 50~ E
SOMALIA		
Mogadiscio	2° 2~ N	49° 19~ E
SOUTH AFRICA		
Cape Town	33° 56~ S	18° 29~ E
Johannesburg	26° 11~ S	28° 3~ E
Pretoria	25° 45~ S	28° 14~ E
SOUTH YEMEN		
Aden	12° 50~ N	45° 2~ E
SPAIN		
Barcelona	41° 24~ N	2° 9~ E
Madrid	40° 25~ N	3° 41~ W
Valencia	39° 28~ N	0° 23~ W
SRI LANKA		
Colombo	6° 54~ N	79° 52~ E
SUDAN		
Khartoum	15° 37~ N	32° 33~ E
SURINAM		
Paramaribo	5° 49~ N	55° 9~ W
SWEDEN		
Stockholm	59° 21~ N	18° 4~ E

(Continued)

INTERNATIONAL LONGITUDES AND LATITUDES (Continued)

	LONGITUDE	LATITUDE		LONGITUDE	LATITUDE
SWITZERLAND			Birmingham	52° 29~ N	1° 56~ W
Zurich	47° 23~ N	8° 33~ E	Cardiff	51° 28~ N	3° 10~ W
SYRIA			Edinburgh	55° 55~ N	3° 11~ W
Damascus	33° 30~ N	36° 20~ E	Glasgow	55° 52~ N	4° 17~ W
TAIWAN			London	51° 29~ N	0° 0~ W
Tainan	22° 57~ N	120° 12~ E	**URUGUAY**		
Taipei	25° 2~ N	121° 31~ E	Montevideo	34° 51~ S	56° 13~ W
TANZANIA			**VENEZUELA**		
Dar es Salaam	6° 50~ S	39° 18~ E	Caracas	10° 30~ N	66° 56~ W
THAILAND			Maracaibo	10° 39~ N	71° 36~ W
Bangkok	13° 44~ N	100° 30~ E	**VIETNAM**		
TRINIDAD			Da Nang	16° 4~ N	108° 13~ E
Port of Spain	10° 40~ N	61° 31~ W	Hanoi	21° 2~ N	105° 52~ E
TUNISIA			Ho Chi Minh City (Saigon)	10° 47~ N	106° 42~ E
Tunis	36° 47~ N	10° 12~ E	**YUGOSLAVIA**		
TURKEY			Belgrade	44° 48~ N	20° 28~ E
Adana	36° 59~ N	35° 18~ E	**ZAIRE**		
Ankara	39° 57~ N	32° 53~ E	Kinshasa		
Istanbul	40° 58~ N	28° 50~ E	(Leopoldville)	4° 20~ S	15° 18~ E
Izmir	38° 26~ N	27° 10~ E	Kisangani		
UNITED KINGDOM			(Stanleyville)	0° 26~ S	15° 14~ E
Belfast	54° 36~ N	5° 55~ W			

PHOTO GALLERY

Figure B.1 Building-integrated solar power (BIPV) structure, New York. *Photo courtesy of Atlantis Energy.*

Figure B.2   Building-integrated solar power (BIPV) structure, New York. *Photo courtesy of Atlantis Energy. (Continued)*

Figure B.3   Roof-mount solar power slate. *Photo courtesy of Atlantis Energy.*

Figure B.4   Solar power parking canopy. *Photo courtesy of DWP Solar.*

Figure B.5   Building-integrated solar power. *Photo courtesy of Atlantis Energy.*

Figure B.6   Roof-mount adjustable solar power racking. *Photo courtesy of DWP Solar.*

Figure B.7   Building-integrated solar power canopy. *Photo courtesy of Atlantis Energy.*

Figure B.8   **Building-integrated solar power stand.** *Photo courtesy of DWP Solar.*

Figure B.9   **Building-integrated solar power entrance canopy.** *Photo courtesy of Atlantis Energy.*

Figure B.10 Building-integrated solar power used as decorative curtain wall. *Photo courtesy of Atlantis Energy.*

Figure B.11   Ground-mount solar power. *Photo courtesy of A&M Energy Solutions.*

Figure B.12 BIPV solar power architectural decore. *Photo courtesy of Atlantis Energy.*

Figure B.13 Solar power window canopy. *Photo courtesy of DWP Solar.*

Figure B.14   **Solar powered signage.** *Photo courtesy of DWP Solar.*

Figure B.15   **Wall-mount solar power.** *Photo courtesy of DWP Solar.*

Figure B.16 Nonpenetrating-type roof-mount solar power support railing. *Photo courtesy of DWP Solar.*

Figure B.17 Nonpenetrating-type roof-mount-solar power assembly. *Photo courtesy of DWP Solar.*

HISTORICAL TIME LINE

OF SOLAR ENERGY

This appendix is an adaptation of the "Solar History Timeline," courtesy of the U.S. Department of Energy.

Seventh Century BC. A magnifying glass is used to concentrate the sun's rays on a fuel and light a fire for light, warmth, and cooking.

Third Century BC. Greeks and Romans use mirrors to light torches for religious purposes.

Second Century BC. As early as 212 BC, the Greek scientist Archimedes makes use of the reflective properties of bronze shields to focus sunlight and set fire to Rome's wooden ships, which were besieging. Although there is no proof that this actually happened, the Greek navy recreated the experiment in 1973 and successfully set fire to a wooden boat 50 m away.

AD 20. The Chinese report using mirrors to light torches for religious purposes.

First to Fourth Centuries. In the first to the fourth centuries, Roman bathhouses are built with large, south-facing windows to let in the sun's warmth.

Sixth Century. Sunrooms on houses and public buildings are so common that the Justinian Code establishes "sun rights" to ensure that a building has access to the sun.

Thirteenth Century. In North America, the ancestors of Pueblo people known as the *Anasazi* built south-facing cliff dwellings that captured the warmth of the winter sun.

1767. Swiss scientist Horace de Saussure is credited with building the world's first solar collector, later used by Sir John Herschel to cook food during his South African expedition in the 1830s.

1816. On September 27, 1816, Robert Stirling applies for a patent for his *economiser*, a solar thermal electric technology that concentrates the sun's thermal energy to produce electric power.

1839. French scientist Edmond Becquerel discovers the photovoltaic effect while experimenting with an electrolytic cell made up of two metal electrodes placed in an electricity-conducting solution; the electricity generation increases when exposed to light.

1860s. French mathematician August Mouchet proposes an idea for solar-powered steam engines. In the next two decades, he and his assistant, Abel Pifre, will construct the first solar-powered engines for a variety of uses. The engines are the predecessors of modern parabolic dish collectors.

1873. Willoughby Smith discovers the photoconductivity of selenium.

1876. William Grylls Adams and Richard Evans Day discover that selenium produces electricity when exposed to light. Although selenium solar cells fail to convert enough sunlight to power electrical equipment, they prove that a solid material can change light into electricity without heat or moving parts.

1880. Samuel P. Langley invents the bolometer, used to measure light from the faintest stars and the sun's heat rays. It consists of a fine wire connected to an electric circuit. When radiation falls on the wire, it becomes warmer, and this increases the electrical resistance of the wire.

1883. American inventor Charles Fritts describes the first solar cells made of selenium wafers.

1887. Heinrich Hertz discovers that ultraviolet light alters the lowest voltage capable of causing a spark to jump between two metal electrodes.

1891. Baltimore inventor Clarence Kemp patents the first commercial solar water heater.

1904. Wilhelm Hallwachs discovers that a combination of copper and cuprous oxide is photosensitive.

1905. Albert Einstein publishes his paper on the photoelectric effect, along with a paper on his theory of relativity.

1908. William J. Bailey of the Carnegie Steel Company invents a solar collector with copper coils and an insulated box, which is roughly the same collector design used today.

1914. The existence of a barrier layer in photovoltaic devices is noted.

1916. Robert Millikan provides experimental proof of the photoelectric effect.

1918. Polish scientist Jan Czochralski develops a way to grow single-crystal silicon.

1921. Albert Einstein wins the Nobel Prize for his theories explaining the photoelectric effect; for details, see his 1904 technical paper on the subject.

1932. Audobert and Stora discover the photovoltaic effect in cadmium sulfide.

1947. Because energy had become scarce during the long Second World War, passive solar buildings in the United States are in demand; Libbey-Owens-Ford Glass Company publishes a book titled, *Your Solar House*, which profiles 49 of the nation's greatest solar architects.

1953. Dr. Dan Trivich of Wayne State University makes the first theoretical calculations of the efficiencies of various materials of different band-gap widths based on the spectrum of the sun.

1954. Photovoltaic technology is born in the United States when Daryl Chapin, Calvin Fuller, and Gerald Pearson develop the silicon photovoltaic or PV cell at Bell Labs, which is the first solar cell capable of generating enough power from the sun to run everyday electrical equipment. Bell Laboratories then produces a solar cell with 6 percent efficiency, which is later augmented to 11 percent.

1955. Western Electric begins to sell commercial licenses for silicon photovoltaic technologies. Early successful products include PV-powered dollar changers and devices that decode computer punch cards and tape.

1950s. Architect Frank Bridgers designs the world's first commercial office building featuring solar water heating and design. The solar system has operated continuously since then; the Bridgers-Paxton Building is listed in the National Historic Register as the world's first solar-heated office building.

1956. William Cherry of the U.S. Signal Corps Laboratories approaches RCA Labs' Paul Rappaport and Joseph Loferski about developing a photovoltaic cell for proposed earth-orbiting satellites.

1957. Hoffman Electronics achieves 8 percent efficient photovoltaic cells.

1958. T. Mandelkorn of U.S. Signal Corps Laboratories fabricates n-on-p (negative layer on positive layer) silicon photovoltaic cells, making them more resistant to radiation; this is critically important for cells used in space.

Hoffman Electronics achieves 9 percent solar cell efficiency.

A small array (less than 1 W) on the *Vanguard I* space satellite powers its radios. Later that year, *Explorer III, Vanguard II,* and *Sputnik-3* will be launched with PV-powered systems on board. Silicon solar cells become the most widely used energy source for space applications, and remain so today.

1959. Hoffman Electronics achieves a 10 percent efficient, commercially available cell. Hoffman also learns to use a grid contact, significantly reducing the series resistance.

On August 7, the *Explorer VI* satellite is launched with a PV array of 9600 solar cells, each measuring 1 cm × 2 cm. On October 13 *Explorer VII* is launched.

1960. Hoffman Electronics achieves 14 percent efficient photovoltaic cells.

Silicon Sensors, Inc., of Dodgeville, Wisconsin, is founded and begins producing selenium photovoltaic cells.

1962. Bell Telephone Laboratories launches Telstar, the first telecommunication satellite; its initial power is 14 W.

1963. Sharp Corporation succeeds in producing silicon PV modules.

Japan installs a 242-W photovoltaic array, the world's largest to date, on a lighthouse.

1965. Peter Glaser conceives the idea of the satellite solar power station.

1966. NASA launches the first orbiting astronomical observatory powered by a 1-kW photovoltaic array; it provides astronomical data in the ultraviolet and x-ray wavelengths filtered out by the earth's atmosphere.

1969. A "solar furnace" is constructed in Odeillo, France; it features an eight-story parabolic mirror.

1970. With help from Exxon Corporation. Dr. Elliot Berman designs a significantly less costly solar cell, bringing the price down from \$100/W to \$20/W. Solar cells begin powering navigation warning lights and horns on offshore gas and oil rigs, lighthouses, and railroad crossings. Domestic solar applications are considered good alternatives in remote areas where utility-grid connections are too expensive.

1972. French workers install a cadmium sulfide photovoltaic system at a village school in Niger.

The Institute of Energy Conversion is established at the University of Delaware to do research and development on thin-film photovoltaic and solar thermal systems, becoming the world's first laboratory dedicated to PV research and development.

1973. The University of Delaware builds "Solar One," a PV/thermal hybrid system. Roof-integrated arrays feed surplus power through a special meter to the utility during the day; power is purchased from the utility at night. In addition to providing electricity, the arrays are like flat-plate thermal collectors; fans blow warm air from over the array to heat storage bins.

1976. The NASA Lewis Research Center starts installing the first of 83 photovoltaic power systems in every continent except Australia. They provide power for vaccine refrigeration room lighting, medical clinic lighting, telecommunications, water pumping, grain milling, and television. The project takes place from 1976 to 1985 and then from 1992 to completion in 1995. David and Christopher Wronski of RCA Laboratories produce the first amorphous silicon photovoltaic cells, which could be less expensive to manufacture than crystalline silicon devices.

1977. In July, the U.S. Energy Research and Development Administration, a predecessor of the U.S. Department of Energy, launches the Solar Energy Research Institute [today's National Renewable Energy Laboratory (NREL)], a federal facility dedicated to energy finding and improving ways to harness and use energy from the sun. Total photovoltaic manufacturing production exceeds 500 kW; 1 kW is enough power to light about ten 100-W lightbulbs.

1978. NASA's Lewis Research Center installs a 3.5-kW photovoltaic system on the Indian Reservation in southern Arizona—the world's first village system. It provides power for water pumping and residential electricity in 15 homes until 1983, when grid power reaches the village. The PV system is then dedicated to pumping water from a community well.

1980. ARCO Solar becomes the first company to produce more than 1 MW (1000 kW) of photovoltaic modules in 1 year.

At the University of Delaware, the first thin-film solar cell exceeds 10 percent efficiency; it's made of copper sulfide and cadmium sulfide.

1981. Paul MacCready builds the first solar-powered aircraft—the Solar Challenger—and flies it from France to England across the English Channel. The aircraft has more than 16,000 wing-mounted solar cells producing 3000 W of power.

1982. The first megawatt-scale PV power station goes on line in Hesperia, California. The 1-MW-capacity system, developed by ARCO Solar, has modules on 108 dual-axis trackers.

Australian Hans Tholstrup drives the first solar-powered car—the Quiet Achiever—almost 2800 mi between Sydney and in 20 days—10 days faster than the first gasoline-powered car to do so.

1983. ARCO Solar dedicates a 6-MW photovoltaic substation in central California. The 120-acre, unmanned facility supplies the Pacific Gas Electric Company's utility grid with enough power for up to 2500 homes. Solar Design Associates completes a home powered by an integrated, stand-alone, 4-kW photovoltaic system in the Hudson River Valley. Worldwide, photovoltaic production exceeds 21.3 MW, and sales top $250 million.

1984. The Sacramento Municipal Utility District commissions its first 1-MW photovoltaic electricity-generating facility.

1985. Researchers at the University of South Wales break the 20 percent efficiency barrier for silicon solar cells.

1986. The world's largest solar thermal facility is commissioned in Kramer Junction, California. The solar field contains rows of mirrors that concentrate the sun's energy onto a system of pipes circulating a heat transfer fluid. The heat transfer fluid is used to produce steam, which powers a conventional turbine to generate electricity.

1988. Dr. Alvin Marks receives patents for two solar power technologies: Lepcon and Lumeloid. Lepcon consists of glass panels covered with millions of aluminum or copper strips, each less than a thousandth of a millimeter wide. As sunlight hits the metal strips, light energy is transferred to electrons in the metal, which escape at one end in the form of electricity. Lumeloid is similar but substitutes cheaper, filmlike sheets of plastic for the glass panels and covers the plastic with conductive polymers.

1991. President George Bush announces that the U.S. Department of Energy's Solar Energy Research Institute has been designated the National Renewable Energy Laboratory.

1992. Researchers at the University of South Florida develop a 15.9 percent efficient thin-film photovoltaic cell made of cadmium telluride, breaking the 15 percent barrier for this technology.

A 7.5-kW prototype dish system that includes an advanced membrane concentrator begins operating.

1993. Pacific Gas & Electric installs the first grid-supported photovoltaic system in Kerman, California. The 500-kW system is the first "distributed power" PV installation.

The National Renewable Energy Laboratory (formerly the Solar Energy Research Institute) completes construction of its Solar Energy Research Facility; it will be recognized as the most energy-efficient of all U.S. government buildings in the world.

1994. The first solar dish generator to use a free-piston engine is hooked up to a utility grid.

The National Renewable Energy Laboratory develops a solar cell made of gallium indium phosphide and gallium arsenide; it's the first one of its kind to exceed 30 percent conversion efficiency.

1996. The world's most advanced solar-powered airplane, the *Icare*, flies over Germany. Its wings and tail surfaces are covered by 3000 superefficient solar cells, for a total area of 21 m². The U.S. Department of Energy and an industry consortium begin operating Solar Two—an upgrade of the Solar One concentrating solar power tower. Until the project's end in 1999, Solar Two demonstrates how solar energy can be stored efficiently and economically so power is produced even when the sun isn't shining; it also spurs commercial interest in power towers.

1998. On August 6, a remote-controlled, solar-powered aircraft, *Pathfinder*, sets an altitude record of 80,000 ft on its thirty-ninth consecutive flight in Mojave, California—higher than any prop-driven aircraft to date.

Subhendu Guha, a scientist noted for pioneering work in amorphous silicon, leads the invention of flexible solar shingles, a roofing material and state-of-the-art technology for converting sunlight to electricity on buildings.

1999. Construction is completed on 4 Times Square in New York, the tallest skyscraper built in the city in the 1990s. It has more energy-efficient features than any other commercial skyscraper and includes building-integrated photovoltaic (BIPV) panels on the thirty-seventh through forty-third floors on the south- and west-facing facades to produce part of the building's power.

Spectrolab, Inc., and the National Renewable Energy Laboratory develop a 32.3% efficient solar cell. The high efficiency results from combining three layers of photovoltaic materials into a single cell, which is most efficient and practical in devices with lenses or mirrors to concentrate the sunlight. The concentrator systems are mounted on trackers to keep them pointed toward the sun.

Researchers at the National Renewable Energy Laboratory develop a breaking prototype solar cell that measures 18.8 percent efficient, topping the previous record for thin-film cells by more than 1 percent. Cumulative installed photovoltaic capacity reaches 1000 MW, worldwide.

2000. First Solar begins production at the Perrysburg, Ohio, photovoltaic manufacturing plant, the world's largest at the time; estimates indicate that it can produce enough solar panels each year to generate 100 MW of power. At the International Space Station, astronauts begin installing solar panels on what will be the largest solar power array deployed in space, each wing consisting of an array of 2800 solar cell modules.

Industry Researchers develop a new inverter for solar electric systems that increases safety during power outages. Inverters convert the dc electric output of solar systems to alternating current—the standard for household wiring as well as for power lines to homes.

Two new thin-film solar modules developed by BP Solarex break previous performance records. The company's 0.5-m^2 module has a 10.8 percent conversion efficiency—the highest in the world for similar thin-film modules. Its 0.9-m^2 module achieves 10.6 percent efficiency and a power output of 91.5 W—the highest in the world for a thin-film module.

The 12-kW solar electric system of a Morrison, Colorado, family is the largest residential installation in the United States to be registered with the U.S. Department of Energy's Million Solar Roofs program. The system provides most of the electricity for the family of eight's 6000-ft^2 home.

2001. Home Depot begins selling residential solar power systems in three stores in California. A year later it expands sales to 61 stores nationwide.

NASA's solar-powered aircraft, *Helios*, sets a new world altitude record for non-rocket-powered craft: 96,863 ft (more than 18 mi up).

2002. ATS Automation Tooling Systems, Inc., in Canada begins commercializing spheral solar technology. Employing tiny silicon beads between two sheets of aluminum foil, this solar-cell technology uses much less silicon than conventional multicrystalline silicon solar cells, thus potentially reducing costs. The technology was first championed in the early 1990s by Texas Instruments, but TI later discontinued work on it. For more, see the DOE Photovoltaic Manufacturing Technologies Web site.

The largest solar power facility in the Northwest—the 38.7-kW system White Bluffs Solar Station—goes on line in Richland, Washington.

PowerLight Corporation installs the largest rooftop solar power system in the United States—a 1.18-MW system at Santa Rita Jail, in Dublin, California.

GLOSSARY OF RENEWABLE ENERGY POWER SYSTEMS

All those technical terms can make renewable energy systems difficult for many people to understand. This glossary aims to cover all the most commonly used terms, as well as a few of the more specific terms.

alternating current (ac): Electric current that continually reverses direction. The frequency at which it reverses is measured in cycles per second, or hertz (Hz). The magnitude of the current itself is measured in amperes (A).

alternator: A device for producing ac electricity. Usually driven by a motor, but can also be driven by other means, including water and wind power.

ammeter: An electric or electronic device used to measure current flowing in a circuit.

amorphous silicon: A noncrystalline form of silicon used to make photovoltaic modules (commonly referred to as solar panels).

ampere (A): The unit of measurement of electric current.

ampere-hour (Ah): A measurement of electric charge. One ampere-hour of charge would be removed from a battery if a current of 1 A flowed out of it for 1 hour. The ampere-hour rating of a battery is the maximum charge that it can hold.

anemometer: A device used to measure wind speed.

anode: The positive electrode in a battery, diode, or other electric device.

axial flow turbine: A turbine in which the flow of water is in the same direction as the axis of the turbine.

battery: A device, made up of a collection of cells, used for storing electricity, which can be either rechargeable or nonrechargeable. Batteries come in many forms, and include flooded cell, sealed, and dry cell.

battery charger: A device used to charge a battery by converting (usually) ac alternating voltage and current to a dc voltage and current suitable for the battery. Chargers often incorporate some form of a regulator to prevent overcharging and damage to the battery.

beta limit: The maximum power (theoretically) that can be captured by a wind turbine from the wind, which equals 59.3 percent of the wind energy.

blade: The part of a turbine that water or air reacts against to cause the turbine to spin, which is sometimes incorrectly referred to as the propeller. Most electricity-producing wind turbines will have two or three blades, whereas water-pumping wind turbines will usually have up to 20 or more.

capacitor: An electronic component used for the temporary storage of electricity, as well as for removing unwanted noise in circuits. A capacitor will block direct current but will pass alternating current.

cathode: The negative electrode in a battery, diode, or other electric device.

cell: The most basic, self-contained unit that contains the appropriate materials, such as plates and electrolyte, to produce electricity.

circuit breaker: An electric device used to interrupt an electric supply in the event of excess current flow. It can be activated either magnetically, thermally, or by a combination of both, and can be manually reset.

compact fluorescent lamp: A form of fluorescent lighting that has its tube "folded" into a "U" or other more compact shape, so as to reduce the space required for the tube.

conductor: A material used to transfer or conduct electricity, often in the form of wires.

conduit: A pipe or elongated box used to house and protect electric cables.

converter: An electronic device that converts electricity from one dc voltage level to another.

cross-flow turbine: A turbine where the flow of water is at right angles to the axis of rotation of the turbine.

current: The rate of flow of electricity, measured in amperes (A). Analogous to the rate of flow of water measured in liters per second (L/s), which is also measured in amperes.

Darrius rotor: A form of vertical-axis wind turbine that uses thin blades.

diode: A semiconductor device that allows current to flow in one direction, while blocking it in the other.

direct current (dc): Electric current that flows in one direction only, although it may vary in magnitude.

dry cell battery: A battery that uses a solid paste for an electrolyte. Common usage refers to these as small cylindrical "torch" cells.

earth (or ground): Refers to physically connecting a part of an electric system to the ground, done as a safety measure, by means of a conductor embedded in suitable soil.

earth-leakage circuit breaker (ELCB): A device used to prevent electrical shock hazards in mains voltage power systems; it includes independent power systems, which are also known as residual current devices (RCDs).

electricity: The movement of electrons (a subatomic particle) produced by a voltage through a conductor.

electrode: An electrically conductive material, forming part of an electric device, often used to lead current into or out of a liquid or gas. In a battery, the electrodes are also known as plates.

electrolysis: A chemical reaction caused by the passage of electricity from one electrode to another.

electrolyte: The connecting medium, often a fluid, that allows electrolysis to occur. All common batteries contain an electrolyte, such as the sulfuric acid used in lead-acid batteries.

energy: The abstract notion that makes things happen or that has the potential or ability to do work. It can be stored and converted between many different forms, such as heat, light, electricity, and motion. It is never created or destroyed but does become unavailable to us when it ends up as low-temperature heat. It is measured in joules (J) or watt-hours (Wh) but more usually megajoules (MJ) or kilowatt-hours (kWh).

equalizing charge: A flooded lead-acid battery will normally be charged in boost mode until the battery reaches 2.45 to 2.5 V per cell, at which time the connected regulator should switch into "float" mode, where the battery will be maintained at 2.3 to 2.4 V per cell. During an equalizing charge, the cells are overcharged at 2.5 to 2.6 V per cell to ensure that all cells have an equal (full charge). This is normally achieved by charging from a battery charger, though some regulators will perform this charge when energy use is low, such as when the users are not at home.

float charge: A way of charging a battery by varying the charging current so that its terminal voltage, the voltage measured directly across its terminals, "floats" at a specific voltage level.

flooded cell battery: A form of rechargeable battery where the plates are completely immersed in a liquid electrolyte. The starter battery in most cars is of the flooded cell type. Flooded cell batteries are the most commonly used type for independent and remote area power supplies.

fluorescent light: A form of lighting that uses long thin tubes of glass that contain mercury vapor and various phosphor powders (chemicals based on phosphorus) to produce white light that is generally considered to be the most efficient form of home lighting. See also *compact fluorescent lamp.*

furling: A method of preventing damage to horizontal-axis wind turbines by automatically turning them out of the wind using a spring-loaded tail or other device.

fuse: An electric device used to interrupt an electric supply in the event of excess current flow. Often consists of a wire that melts when excess current flows through it.

gel-cell battery: A form of lead-acid battery where the electrolyte is in the form of a gel or paste. Usually used for mobile installations and when batteries will be subject to high levels of shock or vibration.

generator: A mechanical device used to produce dc electricity. Coils of wire passing through magnetic fields inside the generator produce power. See also *alternator*. Most ac-generating sets are also referred to as generators.

gigawatt (GW): A measurement of power equal to a thousand million watts.

gigawatt-hour (GWh): A measurement of energy. One gigawatt-hour is equal to 1 GW being used for a period of 1 hour or 1 MW being used for 1000 hours.

halogen lamp: A special type of incandescent globe made of quartz glass and a tungsten filament, which also contains a small amount of a halogen gas (hence the name), enabling it to run at a much higher temperature than a conventional incandescent globe. Efficiency is better than a normal incandescent, but not as good as a fluorescent light.

head: The vertical distance that water will fall from the inlet of the collection pipe to the water turbine in a hydropower system.

hertz (Hz): Unit of measurement for frequency. It is equivalent to cycles per second (refer to *alternating current*). Common household mains power is normally 60 Hz.

horizontal-axis wind turbine: The most common form of wind turbine, consisting of two or three airfoil-style blades attached to a central hub, which drives a generator. The axis or main shaft of the machine is horizontal or parallel to the earth's surface.

incandescent globe: This is the most common form of light globe in the home. It usually consists of a glass globe inside of which is a wire filament that glows when electricity is passed through it. They are the least efficient of all electric lighting systems.

independent power system: A power generation system that is independent of the tile mains grid.

insolation: The level of intensity of energy from the sun that strikes the earth. Usually given as watts per square meter (W/m^2). A common level in Australia in the summer is about 1000 W/m^2.

insulation: A material used to prevent the flow of electricity used in electric wires in order to prevent electric shock. Typical materials used include plastics, such as PVC and polypropylene; ceramics; and minerals, such as mica.

inverter: An electronic device used to convert dc electricity into ac electricity, usually with an increase in voltage. There are several different basic types of inverters, including sine-wave and square-wave inverters.

junction box: An insulating box, usually made from plastics, such as PVC, used to protect the connection point of two or more cables.

kilowatt (kW): A measurement of power equal to 1000 W.

kilowatt-hour (kWh): A measurement of energy. One kilowatt-hour is equal to 1 kW being used for a period of 1 hour.

lead-acid battery: A type of battery that consists of plates made of lead and lead oxide, surrounded by a sulfuric acid electrolyte. It is the most common type of battery used in RAPS systems.

light-emitting diode (LED): A semiconductor device that produces light of a single color or very narrow band of colors. Light-emitting diodes are used for indicator lights, as well as for low-level lighting. They are readily available in red, green, blue, yellow, and amber. The lights have a minimum life of 100,000 hours of use.

load: The collective appliances and other devices connected to a power source. When used with a shunt regulator, a "dummy" load is often used to absorb any excess power being generated.

megawatt (MW): A measurement of power equal to 1 million W.

megawatt-hour (MWh): A measurement of power with respect to time (energy). One megawatt-hour is equal to 1 MW being used for a period of 1 hour, or 1 kW being used for 1000 hours.

meters per second (m/s): A speed measurement system often used to measure wind speed. One meter per second is equal to 2.2 mi/h or 3.6 km/h.

micro-hydrosystem: A generation system that uses water to produce electricity. Types of water turbines include Pelton, Turgo, cross-flow, overshot, and undershot waterwheels.

modified square wave: A type of waveform produced by some inverters. This type of waveform is better than a square wave but not as suitable for some appliances as a sine wave.

monocrystalline solar cell: A form of solar cell made from a thin slice of a single large crystal of silicon.

nacelle: That part of a wind generator that houses the generator, gearbox, and so forth at the top of the tower.

nickel-cadmium battery (NiCd): A form of rechargeable battery, having higher storage densities than that of lead-acid batteries. NiCds use a mixture of nickel hydroxide and nickel oxide for the anode and cadmium metal for the cathode. The electrolyte is potassium hydroxide. They are very common in small rechargeable appliances, but rarely found in independent power systems, due to their high initial cost.

noise: Unwanted electrical signals produced by electric motors and other machines that can cause circuits and appliances to malfunction.

ohm: The unit of measurement of electrical resistance. The symbol used is the uppercase Greek letter omega. A resistance of 1 ohm will allow 1 A of current to pass through it at a voltage drop of 1 V.

Ohm's law: A simple mathematical formula that allows voltage, current, or resistance to be calculated when the other two values are known. The formula is

$$V = IR$$

where V is the voltage, I is the current, and R is the resistance.

Pelton wheel: A water turbine in which specially shaped buckets attached to the periphery of a wheel are struck by a jet of water from a narrow nozzle.

photovoltaic effect: The effect that causes a voltage to be developed across the junction of two different materials when they are exposed to light.

pitch: Loosely defined as the angle of the blades of a wind or water turbine with respect to the flow of the wind or water.

plates: The electrodes in a battery. They usually take the form of flat metal plates. The plates often participate in the chemical reaction of a battery, but sometimes just provide a surface for the migration of electrons through the electrolyte.

polycrystalline silicon: Silicon used to manufacture photovoltaic panels, which is made up of multiple crystals clumped together to form a solid mass.

power: The rate of doing work or, more generally, the rate of converting energy from one form to another [measured in watts (W)].

PVC (polyvinyl chloride): A plastic used as an insulator on electric cables, as well as for conduits. Contains highly toxic chemicals and is slowly being replaced with safer alternatives.

quasi–sine wave: A description of the type of waveform produced by some inverters. See *modified square wave*.

ram pump: A water-pumping device that is powered by falling water. These devices work by using the energy of a large amount of water falling a small height to lift a small amount of water to a much greater height. In this way, water from a spring or stream in a valley can be pumped to a village or irrigation scheme on a hillside. Wherever a fall of water can be sustained, the ram pump can be used as a comparatively cheap, simple, and reliable means of raising water to considerable heights.

RAPS (remote area power supply): A power-generation system used to provide electricity to remote and rural homes, usually incorporating power generated from renewable sources such as solar panels and wind generators, as well as nonrenewable sources, such as petroleum-powered generators.

rechargeable battery: A type of battery that uses a reversible chemical reaction to produce electricity, allowing it to be reused many times. Forcing electricity through the battery in the opposite direction to normal discharge reverses the chemical reaction.

regulator: A device used to limit the current and voltage in a circuit, normally to allow the correct charging of batteries from power sources, such as photovoltaic arrays and wind generators.

renewable energy: Energy that is produced from a renewable source, such as sunlight.

residual current device (RCD): See *earth-leakage circuit breaker.*

resistance: A material's ability to restrict the flow of electric current through itself (measured in ohms).

resistor: An electronic component used to restrict the flow of current in a circuit, also used specifically to produce heat, such as in a water heater element.

sealed lead-acid battery: A form of lead-acid battery where the electrolyte is contained in an absorbent fiber separator or gel between the battery's plates. The battery is sealed so that no electrolyte can escape, and thus can be used in any position, even inverted.

semiconductor: A material that only partially conducts electricity that is neither an insulator nor a true conductor. Transistors and other electronic devices are made from semiconducting materials and are often called semiconductors.

shunt: A low-value resistance, connected in series with a conductor that allows measurements of currents flowing in the conductor by measurement of voltage across the shunt, which is often used with larger devices, such as inverters to allow monitoring of the power used.

sine wave: A sinusoidal-shaped electrical waveform. Mains power is a sine wave, as is the power produced by some inverters. The sine wave is the most ideal form of electricity for running more sensitive appliances, such as radios, TVs, and computers.

solar cell: A single photovoltaic circuit usually made of silicon that converts light into electricity.

solar module: A device used to convert light from the sun directly into dc electricity by using the photovoltaic effect. Usually made of multiple silicon solar cells bonded between glass and a backing material.

solar power: Electricity generated by conversion of sunlight, either directly through the use of photovoltaic panels, or indirectly through solar-thermal processes.

solar thermal: A form of power generation using concentrated sunlight to heat water or other fluid that is then used to drive a motor or turbine.

square wave: A type of waveform produced by some inverters. The square wave is the least desirable form of electricity for running most appliances. Simple resistors, such as incandescent globes and heating elements, work well on a square wave.

storage density: The capacity of a battery compared to its weight [measured in watt-hours per kilogram(Wh/kg)].

surge: An unexpected flow of excessive current, usually caused by a high voltage that can damage appliances and other electric equipment. Also, an excessive amount of power drawn by an appliance when it is first switched on.

switch mode: A form of converting one form of electricity to another by rapidly switching it on and off and feeding it through a transformer to effect a voltage change.

tip-speed ratio: The ratio of blade tip speed to wind speed for a wind turbine.

transformer: A device consisting of two or more insulated coils of wire wound around a magnetic material, such as iron, used to convert one ac voltage to another or to electrically isolate the individual circuits.

transistor: A semiconducting device used to switch or otherwise control the flow of electricity.

turbulence: Airflow that rapidly and violently varies in speed and direction that can cause damage to wind turbines. It is often caused by objects, such as trees or buildings.

vertical-axis wind turbine: A wind turbine with the axis or main shaft mounted vertically, or perpendicular to the earth's surface. This type of turbine does not have to be turned to face the wind—it always does.

voltage: The electric pressure that can force an electric current to flow through a closed circuit (measured in volts).

voltage drop: The voltage lost along a length of wire or conductor due to the resistance of that conductor. This also applies to resistors. The voltage drop is calculated using Ohm's law.

voltmeter: An electric or electronic device used to measure voltage.

water turbine: A device that converts the motion of the flow of water into rotational motion, which is often used to drive generators or pumps. See *micro-hydrosystem*.

waterwheel: A simple water turbine, often consisting of a series of paddles or boards attached to a central wheel or hub that is connected to a generator to produce electricity or a pump to move water.

watt (W): A measurement of power commonly used to define the rate of electricity consumption of an appliance.

watt-hour (Wh): A measurement of power with respect to time (energy). One watt-hour is equal to 1 W being used for a period of 1 hour.

wind farm: A group of wind generators that usually feed power into the mains grid.

wind generator: A mechanical device used to produce electricity from the wind. Typically a form of wind turbine connected to a generator.

wind turbine: A device that converts the motion of the wind into rotational motion used to drive generators or pumps. Wind generator, wind turbine, windmill, and other terms are commonly used interchangeably to describe complete wind-powered electricity-generating machines.

yaw: The orientation of a horizontal-axis wind turbine.

zener diode: A diode often used for voltage regulation or protection of other components.

Meteorological Terms

altitude: The angle up from the horizon.

angle of incidence: The angle between the normal to a surface and the direction of the sun. Therefore, the sun will be perpendicular to the surface if the angle of incidence is zero.

azimuth: The angle from north measured on the horizon, in the order of N, E, S, and W. Thus, north is 0 degrees, and east is 90 degrees.

civil twilight: Defined as beginning in the morning and ending in the evening when the center of the sun is geometrically 6 degrees below the horizon.

horizon: The apparent intersection of the sky with the earth's surface. For rise and set computations, the observer is assumed to be at sea level, so that the horizon is geometrically 90 degrees from the local vertical direction. The inclination surface tilt is expressed as an angle to the horizontal plane. Horizontal is 0 degrees; vertical is 90 degrees.

horizontal shadow angle (HSA): The angle between the orientation of a surface and the solar azimuth.

local civil time (LCT): It is a locally agreed upon time scale. It is the time given out on the radio or television, and the time by which we usually set our clocks. Local civil time depends on the time of year and your position on the earth. It can be defined as the time at the Greenwich meridian plus the time zone and the daylight savings corrections.

orientation: The angle of a structure or surface plane relative to north in the order of N, E, S, and W. Thus, north is 0 degrees, and east is 90 degrees.

shadow angles: Shadow angles refer to the azimuth and altitude of the sun, taken relative to the orientation of a particular surface.

solar noon: The time when the sun crosses the observer's meridian. The sun has its greatest elevation at solar noon.

sunrise and sunset: Times when the upper edge of the disk of the sun is on the horizon. It is assumed that the observer is at sea level and that there are no obstructions to the horizon.

twilight: The intervals of time before sunrise and after sunset when there is natural light provided by the upper atmosphere.

vertical shadow angle (VSA): The angle between the HSA and the solar altitude, measured as a normal to the surface plane.

BIBLIOGRAPHY

"Beyond Three Gorges in China"; available at *www.waterpowermagazine.com/story.asp?storyCode=2041318.*

Carbon Trust. *Future Marine Energy. Results of the Marine Energy Challenge: Cost Competitiveness and Growth of Wave and Tidal Stream Energy,* January 2006.

Church, James S. "Los Alamos National Laboratory Document LAMS-872," *Quarterly Report,* March 15, 1947.

Etherington, E. (ed.). *Nuclear Engineering Handbook.* New York: McGraw-Hill, 1958.

Fouquet, D. M., Razvi, J., and Whittemore, W. L. "TRIGA Research Reactors: A Pathway to the Peaceful Applications of Nuclear Energy."

"Fuel Cells"; available at *http://en.wikipedia.org/wiki/Fuel_cells.*

Glasstone, S. "High-Temperature Thermal Properties of SNAP-10A Fuel Material," in *Principles of Nuclear Reactor Engineering.* Princeton, NJ: Van Nostrand, 1955.

"Global Wind Energy Council (GWEC) Statistics," Global Wind Energy Council Web Site, 2007.

Gray, D. E. (ed.). *American Institute of Physics Handbook,* 3d ed. New York: McGraw-Hill, 1982.

Karnaukhov, A. V. *Role of the Biosphere in the Formation of the Earth's Climate: The Greenhouse Catastrophe.* 2001.

Kats, G., Alevantis, L., Berman, A., Mills, E., Perlman, J. "The Costs and Financial Benefits of Green Buildings: A Report to California's Sustainable Building Task Force," United States Green Building Council, Washington, 2003.

Keppler, F., Brass, M., Hamilton, J., Röckmann, T. *Global Warming: The Blame Is Not with the Plants.* 2006.

Kirkpatrick, J. R., Condon, J. B. "The Linear Solution for Hydriding of Uranium," *J. Less-Common Metals,* pp 124–135, 172–174, 1991.

Laker, J. F. "Isotherms for the U-UH3-H2 System at Temperatures of 700–1050°C and Pressures to 137.9 Mpa," UCRL-51865, 1975.

Linenbereer, G. A., Orndoff, J. D., Paxton, H. C. "Enriched-Uranium Hydride Critical Assemblies," *Nucl. Sci. Eng.* 7:44–57, 1960.

Magladry, R. E. "Hydrogen Diffusion Reactor Control," U.S. Patent No. 3351534 and "Unique Metal Hydride Controlled Reactors," U.S. Patent No. 3627633 and subsidiary U.S. Patent Nos. 3660228 and 3793144.

Martin, Christopher L., Goswami, D. Yogi. *Solar Energy Pocket Reference.* International Solar Energy Society, 2005.

Nelson, S. G. Report 1714, Battelle Memorial Institute, February 11, 1965.

"Nuclear Fusion"; available at *http://en.wikipedia.org/wiki/Nuclear_fusion.*

Ruddiman, William F. *Plows, Plagues, and Petroleum: How Humans Took Control of Climate.* Princeton, NJ: Princeton University Press, 2005.

Smil, Vaclav. *General Energetics: Energy in the Biosphere and Civilization.* New York: Wiley, 1991.

Tzempelikos, Athanassios. *The Impact of Shading Design and Control on Building Cooling and Lighting Demand.* 2007.

United States Building Council. *Foundations of the Leadership in Energy and Environmental Design, Environmental Rating System, A Tool for Market Transformation.* Policy manual, Washington, 2006.

UN.org, United Nations Web site.

"Uranium Hydride Fabrication," *Nuclear News.* pp 46–56, 2003.

U.S. Department of Energy. "A History of Geothermal Energy in the United States," Geothermal Technologies Program, Washington.

U.S. Environmental Protection Agency. "Non-CO_2 Gases Economic Analysis and Inventory: Global Warming Potentials and Atmospheric Lifetimes," EPA, Washington.

Yergin, Daniel. *The Prize: The Epic Quest for Oil, Money, and Power.* New York: Simon & Schuster, 1991.

INDEX

Note: Page numbers referencing figures are followed by an "*f* "; page numbers referencing tables are followed by a "*t* ".

abatement, of air pollution, 405–419
ablation process, 364
absorbed glass mat (AGM) batteries, 81, 82
AC. *See* alternating current
AC and DC device applications, 26, 26t
AC dominance, early, 25
AC inverters, 73–74
AC wiring losses, 122
accessibility, of indoor lighting switches, 192
accidents, nuclear radiation relating to, 381–383
AC/DC debate, between Edison and Tesla, 24–25
acid rain, biomass relating to, 350
ACSD. *See* Antioch Community School District
activated sludge, 412
activated-carbon filter, 408
active trackers, 106
actual adjusted-lighting-power method, 187
additionality, carbon credits relating to, 430
advanced water treatment (AWT) facility, 418–419
aerobic digestion, 414–415
AFCs. *See* alkaline fuel cells
AGM batteries. *See* absorbed glass mat batteries

air pollution
abatement of, 405–419
bioreactors, as emerging future technologies, 415
equipment for, 407–415
GWR, 415–419
pollution's impact, on human and animal life, 406–407
CO_2 relating to, 407
and stratospheric ozone depletion mitigation measures, 12
and ultraviolet radiation's impact, on human health, 11–12
air-conditioning application, geothermal energy relating to
advantages of, 343
challenges of, 343
North High School GSHP, 341–342, 342f
solar photovoltaic energy power cogeneration, 343–344
alarms
and performance monitoring, 197
reporting of, 201
algae, biologic production from, 257
alkaline batteries, 80–81, 82, 82f, 83
alkaline fuel cells (AFCs), 263
alternating and direct current: 1950–2000, 25–26

alternating current (AC), 493
alternator, 493
altitude, 501
American Wind Energy Association, 267
ammeter, 493
ammonia and fertilizer production, use of CO_2 in, 425–426
Amonix, 57, 58, 59, 60
Amonix MegaConcentrator, 59f
Amonix MegaModule, 60
amorphous, crystalline, thin-film, and sun-tracker technologies, 51–69
amorphous PV solar cells, 33–34
amorphous silicon, 493
ampere (A), 493
ampere-hour (Ah), 493
anaerobic digestion, 414
anemometer, 493
angle. *See also* HSA; VSA
hour angle H, 112
of incidence, 501
PV array azimuth, 123–124, 124f
shadow, 501
solar declination, 112, 112f
solar hour, 113f
tilt, 100, 443t–444t
zenith, 112, 113f
anhydrous pyrolysis, 363
animal and human life, pollution's impact on, 406–407
animated video and interactive programming requirements, 96

anions, 254
Annapolis Royal and Bay of
    Fundy, Canada, 295–296
annual power production, poten-
    tial, of MegaSlate, 67–68
anode, 37, 246, 493
anti-islanding, 48
Antioch Community School
    District (ACSD), 357–360
Appliance Efficiency Regulations,
    of CEC, 192
appliances, as energy-saving
    measures, 174–175
application, of fuel cell technology,
    251–259
aquatic habitat, impact on, 297
aquatic life, CO$_2$ and, 424
area controls, for indoor lighting,
    192
area-category method, of indoor
    lighting, 187
array tilt-angle losses, 122
Arshag Dickranian School,
    Hollywood, CA, 129, 139f
Aswan Dam, 312
    construction and benefits of,
        322
    environmental issues of,
        322–323
    history of, 322
    timeline of, 323
Atlantis Energy Systems
    custom-designed BIPV,
        64–66, 65f
atmosphere and energy, LEED
    relating to, 208–211, 209t,
    210t, 221–222
atmospheric changes. *See* global
    warming: climatic and
    atmospheric changes
atmospheric pollution, 405
    industrial sources of, 12–15
    sequestered solar energy and
        anthropogenic causes of, 6
atomic thermal agitation, 238
atoms, 24
automatic daylight controls, 190
automatic multilevel daylight
    controls, 191–192
automatic time switches, 190
automatic transfer system,
    inverters and, 110–111
automobile
    batteries for, 82, 83
    fuel cells for, 259
availability factor, of wind turbine,
    280
AWT facility. *See* advanced water
    treatment facility
axial flow turbine, 493
azimuth, 501

Baghdad battery, 77, 78, 78f
baghouse filters, 407
bandgap, 36, 39
barrages, tidal, 289, 292–294,
    293f
batch reactors, 414
battery, 493. *See also* storage
    batteries
    AGM, 81, 82
    backup for, 128
        grid-connected micro-
            hydroelectric systems
            without, 329–330
        micro-hydroelectric systems
            with, 329
        stand-alone DC solar power
            system with, 71–73
    Baghdad, 77, 78, 78f
    bank relating to, 128, 133
    charge controller relating to, 85
    charger for, 494
    dry cell, 494
    gel-cell, 496
    lead-acid, 80, 81, 81f, 83,
        85, 497
    sealed, 499
    rechargeable, 498–499
    system cables for, 85
    types of, 80–81, 81f, 84, 84f,
        85, 134
battery-backed solar power-driven
    DC pump, 72, 72f
battery-monitoring system,
    energy-production and, 331
beta limit, 494
Betz' law of fluid dynamics,
    271–274, 272f, 273f
bidirectional-flow generation,
    290
Big Bang, 20
binary plants, 335–336, 336f
biochar, 366
biodiesel, 371–374, 372f
    environmental effects of,
        372–373
    potential energy requirement of,
        373
    world production of
        Brazil, 374
        Canada, 374
        United States, 373
bioenergy, 370
biofuel, biogas, and thermal
    depolymerization technolo-
    gies, 362–365, 363f
    biodiesel, 371–374, 372f
    bioenergy, 370
    biomass, origins of, 345,
        346–347
    biomass energy, 347–350, 349t,
        362, 365–366, 366f

biofuel, biogas, and thermal
    depolymerization technologies
    (*Cont.*):
    biopower, 368–369, 369f
    bioproducts, 369–370, 370f
    Cal Poly biogas case study,
        360–362, 361f
    carbon black, 366
    chemical composition of, 346
    gasification process, 367–368
    history of, 345–346
    hot water and hot air
        generators, 356
    landfill, wastewater treatment,
        and plant biogas genera-
        tors, 353–355, 354f,
        355f, 356f
    LFGs, 354–355, 354f, 357
    microgenerator technology,
        successful application of,
        357–360, 359f
    microturbine generators,
        350–352, 351f, 352f, 353f,
        354f, 355, 355f, 356f
biofuel filling station, 370f
biogas. *See* biofuel, biogas, and
    thermal depolymerization
    technologies
biogas generators. *See* landfill
biologic production, from algae,
    257
biologic treatment process, 410
biology, 19
biomass
    chemical composition of, 346
    CO$_2$ relating to, 348, 349, 354
    decay of, 368–369
    origins of, 345, 346–347
biomass energy, 362
    benefits of, 348–350
        environmental, 349–350
    implementation of, 365–366,
        366f
    potential of, 347–348
    value of, 348, 349t
biomass materials, stacking of, 364
biomass pyrolysis, 363–364
bionanogenerators, 42–43
biopower, 368–369, 369f
bioproducts, 369–370, 370f
bioreactors, as emerging future
    technologies, 415
BIPV roofing systems. *See*
    building-integrated PV
    roofing systems
blade, 494
Boron solar PV farm, 130f
braided stream, for storm water,
    220
Brazil, biodiesel and, 374
budget, of CSI, 158t

building integrated solar power, 477*f*
    canopy relating to, 478*f*
    entrance, 479*f*
    stand relating to, 479*f*
    used as decorated curtain wall,
        480*f*
building-integrated PV (BIPV) roof-
    ing systems, 62, 63, 64–66, 64*f*,
    65*f*, 102, 161, 475*f*, 476*f*, 481*f*
bulb turbines, 290–291, 291*f*

CaFCP. *See* California Fuel Cell
    Partnership
Cal Poly biogas project
    capital cost and electricity benefits
        of, 361–362
    case study of, 360–362, 361*f*
California, Green Building Action
    Plan in, 204–206
California Energy Commission
    (CEC), 76, 111, 121, 140,
    146, 370
    CSI and, 157, 162–163, 168, 169
    energy conservation and, 173,
        186, 190, 193, 205
California Fuel Cell Partnership
    (CaFCP), 264
California Solar Initiative (CSI),
    111, 157–172
    budget of, 158*t*
    energy-efficient audit relating to,
        163–164
    EPBB, 157, 159–161, 165,
        166, 168
    equipment distributors of, 168
    fund distribution of, 158
    grid interconnection and metering
        requirements of, 165
    host customer relating to,
        161–162
    incentive payment structure of,
        159–160, 160*t*, 168
    inspection relating to, 165
    insurance relating to, 164
    limitations of, 165–166
    municipal leases, 169–172
    PBI, 157, 159–160, 160*t*, 161,
        165, 166–167, 168
    PG&E as part of, 157, 161
    power allocation of, 158, 158*f*
    power-generation targets of,
        158–159, 159*f*
    PV system sizing requirements
        relating to, 163
    as rebate funding program, 157
    reservation steps for, 166–168
    SCE as part of, 157, 161
    SDREO/SDG&E as part of, 157,
        161
    solar power contractors and equip-
        ment sellers of, 162–163

California Solar Initiative (CSI)
    (*Cont.*):
    special funding
        for affordable housing projects,
            169
        for public and charter schools,
            169
    warranty and performance perma-
        nency requirements of, 164
California Title 24 Electric Energy
    Compliance, 180, 181*f*, 183*f*,
    184*f*, 185*f*
    indoor lighting relating to,
        186–192, 187*f*, 188*f*, 189*f*
    outdoor lighting and signs,
        193–195
    scope and application of, 186
California-friendly plantings, land-
    scape, 220
Canada, biodiesel and, 374
Canadian CANDU reactor, 384–386,
    384*f*, 385*f*, 387*f*
Canadian Standards Association
    (CSA), 87
canopy, 477*f*, 478*f*, 479*f*, 482*f*
capacitor, 494
capacity factor, 269
capital cost and electricity benefits,
    of Cal Poly biogas project,
    361–362
Capstone microturbine, 352, 355,
    357, 359, 361
carbon black, 366
carbon credits
    additionality relating to, 430
    CO_2 relating to, 426–427
    as preferred incentive to taxation,
        429–430
    trading, 426–427
carbon cycle, 421
carbon dioxide (CO_2)
    air pollution relating to, 407
    biomass relating to, 348, 349, 354
    carbon credits relating to,
        426–427
    chemical and physical properties
        of, 421–422
    concentration of, 2–3, 3*f*, 4*f*, 7, 7*f*
    emissions of, 12, 13, 18, 147, 148*f*
    global warming economics relat-
        ing to, 428–430
    in human physiology, role of, 425
    industrial uses of, 423
    Kyoto Protocol, disagreements
        and criticisms of, 430–431
    in oil and chemical industries, 425
    pesticides and plastics relating to,
        424
    in photosynthesis, 423–424
    production of, 422–423
        industrial, 423

carbon dioxide (CO_2) (*Cont.*):
    reductions of, 14
    sequestration of
        carbon trading economics and,
            421–431
        in ocean waters and aquatic life,
            424
    synthetic fuels relating to, 367
    used in production of ammonia
        and fertilizer, 425–426
    variations of, millennial perspec-
        tive of, 7–9, 8*f*
carbon trading economics,
    sequestration of CO_2 and,
    421–431
carbonization, 362
carbon-zinc battery, 80
carpet, from recycled materials,
    220
case study
    of Cal Poly biogas project,
        360–362, 361*f*
    of hydroelectric power plants,
        315–323
    of microgenerator technology,
        357–360, 359*f*
    of San Onofre, 383, 383*f*
cathode, 494
cations, 254
CDM. *See* Clean Development
    Mechanism
CEC. *See* California Energy
    Commission
cells, 494. *See also* fuel cell(s); PV
    cells; PV solar cells; solar cells
    Danielle, 79–80
    Grätzel, 34
    multijunction PV, 40–42
    plastic, 42
    silicon, monocrystalline and
        polycrystalline, 30–33,
        32*f*–33*f*
    technology relating to, 31–32, 34
cement manufacture, as source of
    atmospheric pollution, 12
central monitoring and logging
    system requirements, 92–96
    animated video and interactive
        programming requirements,
        96
    description of, 95–96
    displayed information, 96
    Sun Viewer data-acquisition sys-
        tem, 94
    Sun Viewer display and sun server
        monitoring software, 94–95
central receivers, 233
CER units. *See* certified emission
    reduction units
certification design measures, for
    LEED, 220

certified ballasts and luminaries, 192
certified emission reduction (CER)
    units, 427–428
    CDM, 428, 429–430, 431
    IET, 428
    JI, 428
CFCs. *See* chlorofluorocarbons
CH₄. *See* methane
charge controllers and regulators,
    330
charter schools, special funding for,
    169
chemical absorption towers, 409
chemical and physical properties, of
    CO₂, 421–422
chemical composition, of biomass,
    346
chemical energy, 21
chemical hydride storage, 259
chemical industries, CO₂ in, 425
chemical strippers, 409
chemical treatment process, 410
chemical vapor deposition, 52
chemistry, 19
chlorofluorocarbons (CFCs), 177,
    405
circuit breaker, 494
circulating fluidized beds, 364–365
civil twilight, 501
classification. *See also* configura-
    tions and classifications, of
    solar power system design
    of hydropower energy facilities,
    313
Clean Development Mechanism
    (CDM), 428, 429–430, 431
climate
    change of
        factors of, 1
        human influences on, 6–9
        impact of, on human health,
        10–11
        natural factors driving of,
        2–5
    of Earth, variations within, 1
    forcing factors of, 1
    memory of, 6
    protection policies of, for
        enhancement of human
        health, 12
climatic and atmospheric changes.
    See global warming: climatic
    and atmospheric changes
climatic conditions, biomass' impact
    on, 349–350
clothes washers, 174
CO₂. *See* carbon dioxide
coal burning, 9
coefficient of performance (COP),
    239–240, 273
cogeneration, 50, 75–76, 75*f*, 252,
    343–344

cogenerators, 252
commercial energy production,
    hydrogen relating to, 255–256
commercial solar power project,
    129–130
commercial vs tax-exempt municipal
    lease, 171–172
compact fluorescent lamp, 494
complete-building method, of indoor
    lighting, 187
components
    materials and, for solar power
        system, 69–70, 87
    of micro-hydropower generation,
        330–332
    of solar power system, 44–51
composting, 415
compression cycle, 238
computerized lighting control,
    180–185
concentrator solar power (CSP)
    technologies, 233–236
    advantages of, 234–235
    passive parabolic heating
        technologies, 234*f*, 235, 235*f*
    solar power technologies, 235–236
concentrators, 43–44. *See also*
    MegaConcentrator
    passive solar tower, 236*f*
    technologies of
        control mechanism of, 59
        description of, 58
        higher efficiency of, 57–58
        lower costs of, 57
        MegaModule subsystem,
        58–59, 60
        optics relating to, 59–60
        SUNRGI flat-panel solar power,
        61, 62, 62*f*
        system operations relating to, 61
concept of energy, in various
    scientific fields, 19–22
    biology, 19
    chemistry, 19
    earth sciences, 20
conductors, 494
    for solar power system wiring, 89
conduit, 494
configuration
    DSC epitaxial, 35, 35*f*
    PV mapping and analysis of, 118
    of solar power system, physics
        and technologies of, 86–96
configurations and classifications, of
    solar power system design
    directly connected DC solar
        power, 70–71, 70*f*, 71*f*
    grid-connected solar power cogen-
        eration system, 75–76, 75*f*
    grid-connection isolation
        transformer, 76
    net metering, 75, 76

configurations and classifications, of
    solar power system design
    (*Cont.*):
    stand-alone DC solar power
        system with battery backup,
        71–73
    stand-alone hybrid AC solar
        power system with standby
        generator, 73*f*
    AC inverters, 73–74
    hybrid system operation, 74–75
conservation, of energy, law of, 19
construction
    chronology, of Hoover Dam,
        320–322
    of dam, population and, 311–312
    of low-temperature PRMFC,
        246, 247*f*
    of multijunction PV cells, 40
    of nuclear fission power plant, 378
    of wind turbines, 278–279
consumer electrical demand savings,
    196
consumer peak-power electrical
    demand savings, 200
conventional energy-management
    system, utility DSM control vs,
    200–202
conventional hydropower systems,
    313
converter, 494
cooling, heating and, 175–177, 176*t*
cooling technologies. *See* solar
    cooling and air conditioning
COP. *See* coefficient of performance
cost, of geothermal energy,
    economics and, 339–340, 340*f*
credit summary, of LEED, 215
critically/subcriticality/supercritically,
    378
cross-flow turbine, 494
crude oil, natural gas and, 10
crystalline, amorphous, thin-film,
    and sun-tracker technologies
    concentrator technologies, 57–61
    crystalline PV solar module
        production, 51–56
    film technologies, 61–69
crystalline PV solar module
    production, 51–56
    chemical vapor deposition, 52
    Czochralski crystal growth,
        52–53, 53*f*
    PV module life span and
        recycling, 54–56
    PV module production, 54
    solar cell production, 53–54
CSA. *See* Canadian Standards
    Association
CSI. *See* California Solar Initiative
CSP technologies. *See* concentrator
    solar power technologies

current, 494
    alternating and direct current:
        1950-2000, 25–26
    eddy, 75
current tidal generation technologies
    Annapolis Royal and Bay of
        Fundy, Canada, 295–296
    economic considerations of, 298
    environmental considerations of,
        297–298
    Islay LIMPET, 296–297, 296f
    pumping, 297
    social implications of, 294
    Stingray tidal energy, 295
    tidal barrage, 289, 292–294, 293f
    tidal fences, 292
    tidal power system output, 297
    tidal streams, 298–299
    tidal turbines, 299, 299f, 300f
custom-fabricated BIPV solar cells,
    64–66
cutoff luminaries, 195
Czochralski, Jan, 52
Czochralski crystal growth, 52–53,
    53f

dam. See also Aswan Dam; Hoover
        Dam; Three Gorges Dam
    impact of
        on human health, 312
        on local populations, 311–312
    power, hydroelectric, 310f
Daniell, John Frederich, 79–80
Danielle cell, 79–80
Danish Wind Turbine Manufacturers
        Association, 267
Darrius rotor, 494
data acquisition system, 94, 132–133
data-acquisition and monitoring
        system, 154
DC and AC device applications,
        26, 26t
DC fuses, 86
DC pump, solar power-driven,
        battery-backed, 72, 72f
DC solar power, directly connected,
        70–71
DC solar power system, stand-alone,
        with battery backup, 71–73
DC to AC power-conversion
        calculations, 118–120
    input assumptions for,
        119–120
    PV module specifications for, 119
    resulted design parameters for,
        120
DC wiring losses, 121–122
DC/AC debate, between Edison and
        Tesla, 24–25
decay
    nuclear, 20
    radioactive, 380–381

deep-cycle batteries, 83, 84, 84f, 134
deep-discharge batteries, 81, 82
demand-side energy management
        (DSM) and control, 195–202
    alarms and performance
        monitoring, 197
    consumer electrical demand sav-
        ings, 196
    conventional energy-management
        system vs, 200–202
    energy conservation, 196–197
    hardware system configuration,
        197–200, 198f, 199f
    utility, 196, 198–200
denitrification, 413
Department of Agriculture,
        U.S., 425
Department of Energy (DOE), 57,
        146, 203, 255, 262, 283, 344,
        373, 430
Department of Renewable Energy
        Laboratories, U.S., 267
depletion mitigation measures, for
        stratospheric ozone and air
        pollution, 12
deployment, of solar power system,
        126–139, 131f, 146
desert setting, remote solar power
        farm in, 130
desiccant evaporators, 240
design. See also preliminary
        engineering design; project
    considerations of, for micro-
        hydropower generation,
        329–330
    of fuel cell
        issues with, 247–248
        technology of, 245–251
    guidelines of, for PV system
        installation contractor
        qualifications, 111
        inverter and automatic transfer
            system, 110–111
        PV module design parameters,
            110
    and installation, of solar power
        system, 128–129
    for residential solar power system,
        126–128
    of solar power system, physics
        and technologies of
        components and materials,
            69–70, 87
        configurations and classifica-
            tions of, 70–76, 70f, 71f,
            73f, 75f
        considerations of, 111–124
        for wiring, example of, 89–90
    design measures, of LEED,
        216–218
Diesels, Rudolf, 345
diodes, 27, 121, 494, 497, 501

direct and alternating current:
        1950-2000, 25–26
direct current (DC), 494
direct methanol fuel cells (DMFCs),
        263
direct solar power generation,
        240–241
directly connected DC solar power,
        70–71, 70f, 71f
Directory of Automatic Lighting-
        Control Devices, 190
discrete mode, 184
dish engines, 233
disinfection, 413–414
displayed information, for central
        monitoring, 96
distribution
    and generation, of electric power,
        178–180, 179f, 179t
    power, input and output of, 47
diversion or shunted load,
        330–331
DMFCs. See direct methanol fuel
        cells
DOE. See Department of Energy
doubly fed machines, 269
dry cell battery, 494
dry electrostatic precipitators, 408
dry flue-gas desulfurization system,
        407–408
dry-steam plants, 335, 336f
DSC epitaxial configuration,
        35, 35f
DSCs. See dye-sensitized solar cells
DSM. See demand-side energy man-
        agement and control
dual-axis solar power tracking
        system, 107
dye-sensitized solar cells
        (DSCs), 37f
    basic principles of, 36–39
    comparative analysis of, 35
    future technological advancements
        in, 39
    high-energy conduction band,
        35–36

E85 grade fuel, 368
earth, 494
    climate of, variations within, 1
    core of, 334f
    sciences relating to, 20
earth-leakage circuit breaker
        (ELCB), 495
ebb-generation, 290
ebb tide, 288
economic benefits
    cost, of geothermal energy, 339
    of LFGs, 357
economic considerations, of current
        tidal generation technologies,
        298

economics
    analysis of, for Water Education
        Museum, 143*f*–145*f*
    of carbon trading, sequestration of
        CO₂ and, 421–431
    energy, of wind turbine, 279–285
    geothermal energy cost and,
        339–340, 340*f*
    of global warming, 428–430
    of solar power system, 139–155
    of tidal barrage, 294
    wind farm, 271
economy
    global, fuel cells' impact on, 264
    hydrogen, 260–266, 265*f*
eddy current, 75
Edison, Thomas, 24–25, 26, 80
Edison battery, 80–81
efficiency, of fuel cells, 251
effluent polishing, 412
effluent screening, 410
ELCB. *See* earth-leakage circuit
        breaker
electric power generation
    and distribution, 178–180, 179*f*,
        179*t*
    microgenerator technology
        relating to, 360
electrical description, of semitropic
        open-field single-axis tracking
        system PV array, 137–138
Electrical Power Research Institute
        (EPRI), 57
electrical shock hazard and safety
        considerations, 100–102
    BIPV systems, 102
    for firefighters, 101
electricity, 495
    Cal Poly biogas project benefits
        of, 361–362
electrode, 495
electrolysis, 495. *See also* HTE
    hydrogen extraction by, 256*f*
    of water, 254–255
    and associated challenges, 257
electrolyte, 495. *See also* PEMFC
electromagnetic (EM) radiation, 22
electronics
    inverter, 48, 48*f*, 49, 49*f*
    solar cells, 30
electrons, 24, 27, 28, 29
Eligible Enterprise Resource
        Planning (ERP), 168
Elvax, 31
EM radiation. *See* electromagnetic
        radiation
emission allowances, 427
emission markets, 428
emission reduction, CSP
        technologies relating to, 235
emissions, of CO₂, 12, 13, 18,
        147, 148*f*

EMS2000 wall-mount controller
        module, 198, 198*f*, 199*f*
endogenous respiration, 415
energy, 495. *See also* biomass
        energy; fuel cells, application
        of; geothermal energy; ocean
        energy technologies; potential
        energy; solar energy; wind
        energy technologies
    and atmosphere, LEED relating to,
        208–211, 209*t*, 210*t*, 221–222
    chemical, 21
    concept of, in various scientific
        fields, 19–22
    conservation of, 196–197
        California Title 24 Electric
            Energy Compliance, 180,
            181*f*, 183*f*, 184*f*, 185*f*,
            186–195
        computerized lighting control,
            180–185
        DSM, 195–202
        electric power generation and
            distribution, 178–180,
            179*f*, 179*t*
        energy-saving measures,
            173–177
        Green Building Action Plan, in
            California, 204–206
        by improved system efficiency,
            201–202
        law of, 19
        LEED, 173, 195, 203–204,
            206–222
        by measured efficiency, 202
        by monitoring efficiency and
            predictive maintenance, 202
        power-factor correction, 177–178
    conversion table for, 435*t*–436*t*
    cost escalation for, 147–148
    cost factor of, preliminary engi-
        neering design relating to, 142
    economics of, for wind turbine,
        279–285
    efficiency of, 173
    external, 259
    future source of, fusion as,
        401–403, 402*f*
    payback time relating to, 279
    peak-hour, 142
    performance of, semitropic open-
        field single-axis tracking
        system PV array relating to,
        138–139
    radiant, 21–22
    recovery of, at end of cooling or
        heating call, 202
    renewable, 499
    requirement of, biodiesel relating
        to, 373
    Stingray tidal, 295
    sunlight storage of, 20

energy (*Cont.*):
    supply of, wind turbine relating
        to, 280–281, 282*t*
    systems of, 19–22
    tables of, renewable, 433–435, 434*t*
ENERGY STAR program, 62
energy-efficiency lease, 170
energy-efficient audit, of CSI,
        163–164
energy-generation capacity, of wind
        turbine, 277–278, 277*f*
energy-production and battery-moni-
        toring system, 331
energy-saving measures
    appliances, 174–175
    heating and cooling, 175–177, 176*t*
    insulation and weatherization, 175
    lighting, 173–174
Envirepel Energy, Inc., 365, 366*f*
environment. *See* Leadership in
        Energy and Environmental
        Design
environmental benefits
    of biomass
        acid rain relating to, 350
        on climatic conditions, 349–350
        soil erosion and water contami-
            nation relating to, 350
    of LFGs, 357
environmental considerations
    of current tidal generation tech-
        nologies, 297–298
    of tidal barrage, 294
environmental impact
    of biodiesel, 372–373
    of geothermal energy, 339–340,
        340*f*
    of hydroelectric power, 309–312
environmental issues, of Aswan
        Dam, 322–323
Environmental Protection Agency
        (EPA), 62, 147, 205, 355, 357
EPA. *See* Environmental Protection
        Agency
EPBB. *See* expected performance-
        based buydown
EPRI. *See* Electrical Power Research
        Institute
equalizing charge, 495
equipment
    for air pollution abatement,
        407–415
    CSI
        distributors of, 168
        sellers of, 162–163
    enclosures for, junction boxes and,
        86
    grounding of, for solar power sys-
        tem wiring, 91
    for hydroelectric plant, 313–315
    outdoor, lighting effect on, 92,
        93, 93*f*

ERP. *See* Eligible Enterprise
  Resource Planning
eSolar, 242–243, 242*f*, 243*f*
ethanol, 367–368
ETL. *See* Testing Laboratories
European fuel cell bus project, 266
Executive Order S-20-04. *See* Green
  Building Action Plan, in
  California
expected performance-based
  buydown (EPBB), 157,
  159–161, 165, 166, 168
experimental pyrolysis technologies,
  364
external energy, 259

faint young sun paradox, 3
Faure, Camille, 80
FCC. *See* Federal Communications
  Commission
feasibility study report, 146
Federal Communications
  Commission (FCC), 50
fertilizer production, use of CO_2 in,
  425–426
field cabling, for MegaSlate
  customized roof-mount PV
  system, 68
field safety recommendations,
  106–107
54-kW MegaConcentrator two-axis
  hydraulic tracking system,
  58, 58*f*
film technologies, 63*f*. *See also*
  thin-film
  custom-fabricated BIPV solar
    cells, 64–66
  MegaSlate customized roof-mount
    PV system, 66–69
  Solar Integrated Technologies,
    61–63
filters, 407, 408, 412
filtration process, 45
firefighters, electrical shock hazard
  to, 101
fish pass, 298
fission- and fusion-type nuclear power
  Canadian CANDU reactor,
    384–386, 384*f*, 385*f*, 387*f*
  case study: San Onofre, 383, 383*f*
  fission nuclear reactors,
    advantages and disadvantages
    of, 378–379
  fusion, as future energy source,
    401–403, 402*f*
  fusion reactors, 394–400, 395*f*,
    396*f*, 398*f*, 400*f*
  future research and development
    of, 403
  Hyperion nuclear power reactor,
    389–394, 389*f*, 391*f*,
    391*t*, 392*f*

fission- and fusion-type nuclear
  power (*Cont.*):
  nuclear fission power plant, 377,
    377*f*
  construction of, 378
  nuclear radiation
    accidents relating to, 381–383
    effects of, 379–380, 380*f*
    pebble-bed reactor, 387–389, 388*f*
    radiation danger, 381
    radioactive decay relating to,
      380–381
    subcriticality/criticality/supercriti-
      cally, 378
    uranium, properties of, 375–377
  fission nuclear reactors, advantages
    and disadvantages of, 378–379
  fission-reaction process, 376*f*
  fixed-axis system, 103
  fixture certification, for outdoor
    lighting, 195
  flash steam plant, 337, 337*f*
  float charge, 495
  flood control, Hoover Dam and, 320
  flood generation, 290
  flooded (wet) batteries, 81, 82
  flooded cell battery, 495
  flue gas desulfurization, 409
  fluorescent light, 494, 495
  foam exterior, 220
  fossil fuels, 7, 10
  Francis turbine, 315
  fuel(s). *See also* biofuel, biogas, and
    thermal depolymerization
    technologies
    E85 grade, 368
    synthetic, 367
  fuel cell(s)
    AFCs, 263
    design issues of, 247–248, 248*f*
    durability and service life of, 248
    efficiency of, 251
    European bus project relating to,
      266
    Grubb-Niedrach, 252
    impact of, on global economy, 264
    MCFCs, 262
    PEMFC, 245, 246, 262
    SOFCs, 251, 262–263
    solid-oxide, 251
    stacking of, 246
    technology of
      application of, 251–259
      benefits of, 264
      design of, 245–251
      hydrogen economy relating to,
        260–266, 265*f*
      internal combustion fuels, alter-
        natives to, 259–260
      safety concerns relating to, 260
      types and characteristics of,
        249*t*–250*t*

fuel cells, application of
  algae, biologic production from,
    257
  chemical hydride storage, 259
  electrolysis, 254–255, 257
  history of, 252
  HTE, 257–258
  hydrocarbon-based fuel
    re-formation, 254
  hydrogen
    for commercial energy
      production, 255–256
    as energy carrier, 252–253
    energy research, 255, 256*f*
    fuel efficiency of, for
      automobile use, 259
    gas production relating to,
      253
    production of, 256–257
    storage challenges of, 258
    metallic hydrogen compartment,
      258–259
    re-forming relating to
      industrial, 253
      steam, 253, 254, 256
    stationary fuel cell plants,
      251–252
    thermochemical production, 258
  in U.S. Space Program, 266
fuel efficiency, of hydrogen, for
  automobile use, 259
fund distribution, of CSI, 158
furling, 496
fuse, 496
fusion, 20
  as future energy source, 401–403,
    402*f*
fusion reactors, 394–400, 395*f*, 396*f*,
  398*f*, 400*f*
fusion-type nuclear power. *See*
  fission- and fusion-type nuclear
  power

gallium-arsenide substrate, 41
Galvani, Luigi, 77
gas. *See also* biofuel, biogas, and
  thermal depolymerization
  technologies; GHG; LFGs
  natural crude oil and, 10
  production of, fuel cells relating
    to, 253
gasification process, 367–368
gasohol, 367
gasoline, high-octane, 253
gel-cell battery, 496
gelled batteries, 81, 82
generation, 290. *See also* current
  tidal generation technologies;
  micro-hydropower generation
  direct solar power, 240–241
  and distribution, of electric power,
    178–180, 179*f*, 179*t*

generation (*Cont.*):
  electric power, microgenerator
    technology relating to, 360
  of tidal power, 288–292
  of wind power, 268
generators, 496. *See also* biofuel,
    biogas, and thermal
    depolymerization technologies;
    bionanogenerators;
    cogenerators; landfill
  hot air, 356
  micro-hydroelectric, 332
  standby, stand-alone hybrid AC
    solar power system with,
    73–75, 73*f*
geopressurized reservoirs, 333
geothermal energy, 333–344
  air-conditioning application
    relating to, 341–344, 342*f*
  cost of, economics and, 339–340,
    340*f*
  environmental impact of,
    339–340, 340*f*
  ocean thermal energy, 344
  potential of, 337–338, 338*f*, 339*f*
  technologies of, 335–337
  thermal power extraction
    potential, 334–335
geothermal gradients, 333–334
geothermal power
  advantages of, 343
  benefits of, 340
  direct uses of, 340
germanium substrate, 42
GFPD. *See* ground-fault detection
    and interrupting devices
GHG. *See* greenhouse gases
gigawatt (GW), 496
gigawatt-hour (GWh), 496
glaciation, 5, 5*f*
global climatic temperature balance,
    argument about, 14–15, 15*f*, 16*f*
global economy, fuel cells' impact
    on, 264
global warming: climatic and
    atmospheric changes
  atmospheric pollution, industrial
    sources of, 12–15
  climate, memory of, 6
  climate change
    factors of, 1
    human influences on, 6–9
    natural factors driving of, 2–5
  Earth's climate, variations
    within, 1
  little ice age, 15–18, 16*f*
  sequestered solar energy, 6, 9–12
global warming economics, 428–430
Grätzel cells, 34
gravitational potential energy, 21
great ocean conveyer belt, 6, 6*f*, 18

Green Action Team, 206
Green Building Action Plan, in
    California
  commercial and institutional
    buildings, 205
  financing and execution of, 205
  leadership of, 206
  public buildings, 204–205
  schools, 205
green buildings, 204–205
greenhouse gases (GHG), 2–3, 2*f*, 3*f*,
    4*f*, 13*f*, 427, 430
grid compatibility, 269
grid interconnection and metering
    requirements, of CSI, 165
grid-connected inverters, 47, 74
grid-connected micro-hydroelectric
    systems, without battery back-
    up, 329–330
grid-connected solar power cogener-
    ation system, 75–76, 75*f*
grid-connected solar power systems,
    entrance service power consid-
    erations for, 91–92
grid-connected solar power pumping sys-
    tem diagram, 134*f*
grid-connection isolation trans-
    former, 76
ground mount solar panel, 480*f*
grounded/grounding, 90–91
ground-fault detection and interrupt-
    ing devices (GFPD), 90
ground-fault protection, PV system
    relating to, 90
ground-mounted PV module installa-
    tion and support, 97–98, 97*f*
grounds, LEEDS certification design
    measures relating to, 220
groundwater replenishment system
    (GWR)
  agency descriptions relating to,
    416–417
  as AWT facility, 418–419
  benefits of, 417
  description of, 416
  innovation of, 417
  at OCWD, 414–419
  Water Factory 21, replaced by,
    418
Grubb-Niedrach fuel cell, 252
GWR. *See* groundwater replenish-
    ment system

half-flush/full-flush lavatories, 220
halogen lamp, 496
hardware system configuration,
    197–200, 198*f*, 199*f*
head, 496
heat and power cogenerators, micro
    combined, 252
heat control, internal water and, 247

heating, cooling and, 175–177,
    176*t*
heating technologies. *See* passive
    parabolic heating technologies
Helicol solar collector sizing, 229
helium, isotopes of, 380*f*
hertz (Hz), 496
high-energy conduction band, 35–36
higher efficiency, of concentrator
    technologies, 57–58
high-octane gasoline, 253
high-temperature electrolysis (HTE),
    257–258
historical time line, of solar energy,
    485–492
HOD Landfill, 357
Hoover Dam, 315–322, 317*f*
  benefits of, 319–320
  construction chronology of,
    320–322
  history of, 318–319
  as hydroelectric power plant, 318
  Lake Mead facilities relating to,
    316–317
  project-development plan for, 316
horizon, 501
horizontal shadow angle (HSA), 501
horizontal-axis wind turbine, 496
horizontal-axle trackers, 104
horizontal-axle windmills, 267–268
host customer, of CSI, 161–162
hot air generators, 356
hot water and hot air generators, 356
hour angle H, 112
housing projects, affordable, special
    funding for, 169
HSA. *See* horizontal shadow angle
HTE. *See* high-temperature
    electrolysis
human
  and animal life, pollution's impact
    on, 406–407
  health of
    climate protection policies, for
      enhancement of, 12
    hydropower dam construction's
      impact on, 312
    impact of air pollution and
      ultraviolet radiation on,
      11–12
    impact of climate change on,
      10–11
  influences, on climate change, 6–9
human physiology, role of CO_2 in,
    425
100-year-old power scheme, 25
HVAC control module, 197–198,
    198*f*, 200, 201
HVAC equipment, lighting relating
    to, 193, 196, 197
hybrid absorption chillers, 240

hybrid AC solar power system, stand-alone, with standby generator, 73f
hybrid system operation, 74–75
hydrocarbon-based fuel re-formation, 254
hydrocracking, 255, 261
hydroelectric and micro-hydro turbine power
case studies of, 315–323
environmental effects of, 309–312
facilities classification of, 313
micro-hydropower generation, 323–332
plant equipment relating to, 313–315
power plants, 307–309
technology of, 312
hydroelectric generating facility, 311f
hydroelectric power
dam with, 310f
Hoover Dam relating to, 320
plants with, 307–309
case studies of, 315–323
Hoover Dam as, 318
potential of, 308–309
hydroelectric power-generating system, 310f
hydroelectric turbines, small, 323
hydrogen. See also fuel cells, application of
economy of
AFCs for, 263
CaFCP relating to, 264
DMFCs for, 263
European fuel cell bus project, 266
foundations of, 261
infrastructure of, 260–261
MCFCs for, 262
PAFCs for, 262
primary uses of, 261–262
regenerative fuel cells for, 263–264
SOFCs for, 251, 262–263
VFCVP relating to, 265, 265f
VTA relating to, 265–266
extraction of, by electrolysis, 256f
helium and, isotopes of, 380f
hydropower dam construction's impact, on human health, 312
hydropower energy facilities, classification of, 313
hydropower systems. See also micro-hydropower generation
conventional, 313
pumped-storage, 313, 314f
Hyperion nuclear power reactor, 389–394, 389f, 391f, 391t, 392f
Hyperion Sewage Treatment Plant, 411, 411f, 412f

IEEE. See Institute of Electrical and Electronics Engineers
IESNA. See Illuminating Engineering Society of North America
IET. See International Illuminating Engineering Society of North America (IESNA), 193
impulse-type turbines, 324–325, 324f, 325f
incandescent globe, 496
incentive payment structure, of CSI, 159–160, 160t, 168
independent power system, 496
indium-phosphate substrate, 42
indoor environmental quality, LEED relating to, 212–214
indoor lighting, California Title 24 Electric Energy Compliance relating to, 186–192, 187f, 188f, 189f
industrial and municipal water supply, from Hoover Dam, 319
industrial production, of CO_2, 423
industrial re-forming, 253
industrial sources, of atmospheric pollution, 12–15
industrial uses, of CO_2, 423
infrastructure, of hydrogen economy, 260–261
innovations
and design process, of LEED, 214–215, 222
of GWR, 417
in solar power technology, 241–243, 242f, 243f
input and output power distribution, 47
insolation, 111, 496
inspection, CSI relating to, 165
installation. See also roof-mounted installations
contractor qualifications for, 111
design and, of solar power system, 128–129
large-scale, experience in, 154
maintenance and, of storage batteries, 84–86
of MegaSlate customized roof-mount PV system, 69
requirements of, for indoor lighting, 192
installed capacity, 289–290
installed power, for outdoor lighting, 194
Institute of Electrical and Electronics Engineers (IEEE), 49
insulation, 496
weatherization and, 175
insurance, CSI relating to, 164
intelligent control, 201

intelligent indoor fan operation, 202
interactive programming requirements, 96
Intergovernmental Panel on Climate Change (IPCC), 2
interior photosensor devices, 190–191
internal combustion fuels, fuel cells as alternatives to, 259–260
internal water and heat control, 247
internal wiring, of PV solar cells, 44f
International (IET), 428
inverter(s), 331, 496
AC, 73–74
automatic transfer system and, 110–111
capability of, to withstand surges, 50
components of, 45–49
grid-connected, 47, 74
IEEE, 49
input and output power distribution, 47
and matching transformer losses, 121
power-limit conditions, 49
protective relaying systems, 45–47
underwriters laboratories standards, 47–49
waveshaping or filtration process, 45
inverter electronics, 48, 48f, 49, 49f
inverter single-line diagram, 46f
iodide, 37, 38
IPCC. See Intergovernmental Panel on Climate Change
irrigation, Hoover Dam relating to, 319
irrigation pumping application, solar power in, 134–136
islanding, 48
Islay LIMPET, 296–297, 296f
isolation transformers
grid-connection, 76
utility-side disconnects and, 50–51
isotopes, of hydrogen and helium, 380f

JI. See Joint Implementation
Joint Implementation (JI), 428
Joule, 83
junction
PN, 27, 28f, 29, 30, 35
PNP, 30
semiconductor, 28f, 29f
junction box, 497
and equipment enclosures, 86
just-in-time temperature programming, 201

Kaplan turbine, 315
kilowatt-hour (kWh), 497
kilowatt-hour utility meter, 331
kinetic energy, 274, 289
   potential energy vs, 20–21
Kyoto Protocol, 426, 429
   cap and trade mechanisms of,
      427–428
   disagreements and criticisms of,
      430–431

La Rance tidal barrage, 293–294,
   293f
lagooning, 413
Lake Mead facilities, 316–317
Lake Mead National Recreation
   Area (LMNRA), 319
Lambert's cosine law, 103–104
land use, as source of atmospheric
   pollution, 13, 13f
landfill
   gases (LFGs), 354–355, 354f
      economic benefits of, 357
      environmental benefits of, 357
      microgenerator technology
         relating to, 357–360, 359f
   HOD, 357
   wastewater treatment, plant biogas
      generators, and, 353–355,
      354f, 355f, 356f
landscape, California-friendly
   plantings, 220
large-scale installation, experience
   in, 154
large-scale irrigation pumping application, solar power in, 134–136
   performance characteristics of,
      135–136
latitude and longitude tables,
   447t–474t
law of conservation, of energy, 19
LCD. See Lighting Control Design;
   liquid crystal display
LCT. See local civil time
lead-acid batteries, 80, 81, 81f, 83,
   85, 497
Leadership in Energy and
   Environmental Design (LEED),
   173, 195, 206–222
   additional certification design
      measures for, 220
   credit summary of, 215
   design measures of, 216–218
   energy and atmosphere relating to,
      208–211, 209t, 210t, 221–222
   energy use and environment for,
      203–204
   engineered by Vector Delta
      Design Group, 218–219
   indoor environmental quality
      relating to, 212–214

Leadership in Energy and
   Environmental Design (LEED)
   (Cont.):
   innovation and design process of,
      214–215, 222
   material and resources for,
      211–212, 222
   mechanical system for, 222
   optimized energy performance
      scoring points for, 215,
      215t, 216t
   sustainable sites for, 206–208, 221
   water efficiency measures relating
      to, 208, 221
Leadership in Energy and
   Environmental Design for New
   Construction and Major
   Renovations (LEED-NC), 204
lease. See also municipal leases
   energy-efficiency, 170
lease-option-to-buy financing plans,
   149
Leclanché, Georges, 80
LEDs. See light-emitting diodes
LEED. See Leadership in Energy
   and Environmental Design
LEED Rating System for Existing
   Buildings (LEED-EB), 204, 205
LEED-EB. See LEED Rating
   System for Existing Buildings
LEED-NC. See Leadership in
   Energy and Environmental
   Design for New Construction
   and Major Renovations
LFGs. See landfill
life span, of storage batteries, 83–84
light-emitting diodes (LEDs), 27, 497
Lighting Control Design (LCD),
   182, 183f
lighting effect, on outdoor equipment, 92, 93, 93f
lighting equipment certification, 190
lighting tradeoffs, 187–189
lightning protection, for solar power
   system, 92
lightweight concrete roofing, 99–100
liquid crystal display (LCD), 197
lithocrete, 220
little ice age, 15–18, 16f
   causes of, 18
   dating of, 16–17
   northern hemisphere relating to,
      17–18
   ocean conveyer shutdown during,
      18
   volcanic activity during, 18
livestock, as source of atmospheric
   pollution, 13–14
LMNRA. See Lake Mead National
   Recreation Area
loads, 127–128, 330–331, 497

local civil time (LCT), 501
longitude and latitude tables,
   447t–474t
lower costs, of concentrator
   technologies, 57
low-temperature PRMFC,
   construction of, 246, 247f
lunar tide, 287

magnetic declination, 118
main entrance service AC breaker
   panel, 331
maintenance, of solar power system,
   107–108
maintenance costs, of solar power
   system, 146
management, of wind power,
   268–271
mandatory measures
   for indoor lighting, 189
   for outdoor lighting, 193–194
Marine Current Turbines (MCT), 300
marine-current turbine technologies,
   300–303, 301f, 303f
MARTIFER sun tracker, 59, 60, 60f,
   368, 369f
master control unit, 197
materials
   biomass, stacking of, 364
   and components, for solar power
      system, 69–70, 87
   for multijunction PV cells, 40–42
   N-type, 27, 35–36
   P-type, 27, 35–36
   recycled, carpet from, 220
   and resources, for LEED,
      211–212, 222
MCFCs. See molten carbonate fuel
   cells
MCT. See Marine Current Turbines
mean time between failures (MTBF)
   and system availability, 122
mechanical description, of semitropic
   open-field single-axis tracking
   system PV array, 137
mechanical system, for LEED, 222
mechanical treatment process, 410
medieval climate optimum, 15–16
MegaConcentrator, 58–59, 58f, 59f,
   60, 61
MegaModule subsystem, 58–59, 60
MegaSlate customized roof-mount
   PV system, 66–69
   as custom solar solution, 68, 68f
   field cabling for, 68
   installation of, 69
   potential annual power
      production, 67–68
   power production requirements
      for, 67
   PV support structure of, 68

megawatt (MW), 497
megawatt-hour (MWh), 497
metal-organic vapor-phase process, 40
meteorologic data, preliminary engineering design relating to, 141
meteorological terms, 501–502
metering and grid interconnection requirements, of CSI, 165
meters per second (m/s), 497
methane (CH₄), 349, 353, 354
MF. *See* microfiltration
micro combined heat and power cogenerators, 252
microcontrol, 184
microfiltration (MF), 418
microgenerator technology, case study of
  in ACSD, 357–360
  electric power generation relating to, 360
  at HOD Landfill, 357
  LFGs relating to, 357–360, 359f
  project design of, 358–360
micro-hydro turbine power. *See* hydroelectric and micro-hydro turbine power
micro-hydroelectric systems
  with battery backup, 329
  generator, disadvantages of, 332
  grid-connected, without battery backup, 329–330
  off-grid, without battery backup, 329
micro-hydroelectric turbines
  advantages of, 332
  types of
    impulse-type turbines, 324–325, 324f, 325f
    reaction-type turbines, 325
    submersible-propeller turbines, 325–326
micro-hydropower generation, 323–332
  components of, 330–332
  micro-hydroelectric turbines, types, 324–326, 324f, 325f
  physical principles of, 326–327
  pipe length relating to, 326
  power output of, 327–329
  special design considerations of, 329–330
  water flow relating to, 326
  water head relating to, 326
micro-hydrosystem, 497
microturbine, Capstone, 352, 355, 357, 359, 361
microturbine generators, 350–352, 351f, 352f, 353f, 354f, 355, 355f, 356f

minimum lamp efficiency, for outdoor lighting, 195
modified square wave, 497
molecular agitation, 237–238
molecular-beam epitaxy, 40
molten carbonate fuel cells (MCFCs), 262
molten magma, 334
monitoring. *See also* central monitoring and logging system requirements
  of efficiency and predictive maintenance, energy conservation by, 202
  performance alarms and, 197
  system of, data-acquisition and, 154
monocrystalline and polycrystalline silicon cells, 30–33, 32f–33f
monocrystalline solar cell, 497
MTBF. *See* mean time between failures (MTBF) and system availability
multijunction cell technology, 34
multijunction PV cells
  construction of, 40
  materials for, 40–42
multijunction solar cell epitaxial layers, 41f
multitube cyclones, 408
multivane centrifugal scrubber, 409
municipal and industrial water supply, from Hoover Dam, 319
municipal leases
  entities that qualify for, 170–171
  principal types of, 169–172
  tax-exempt, 169, 170, 171–172

nacelle, 497
nanotechnology solar PV cell, 38f
NASA Surface Meteorology and Solar Energy Data Set Web site, 141
National Electrical Code (NEC), 69, 71, 75, 86–87, 89, 90, 91, 127, 128
National Fire Protection Association, 86
natural gas, crude oil and, 10
neap tides, 288
NEC. *See* National Electrical Code
net meter, 331
net metering, 75, 76
new school construction, Green Building Action Plan relating to, 205
NiCd batteries. *See* nickel-cadmium batteries

nickel-cadmium (NiCd) batteries, 81, 82, 85, 497
nitrification, 413
nitrous oxides (NO₂), 405, 407
NO₂. *See* nitrous oxides
noise, 497
nonpenetrating type roof mount solar panel
  assembly of, 484f
  support railing for, 484f
North High School ground-source heat-pump (GSHP), 341–342, 342f
northern hemisphere, little ice age relating to, 17–18
N-type material, 27, 35–36
nuclear decay, 20
nuclear fission power plant, 377, 377f
  construction of, 378
nuclear power. *See* fission- and fusion-type nuclear power
nuclear radiation
  accidents relating to, 381–383
  effects of, 379–380, 380f
nutrient removal, 413

occupancy-sensing devices, 190
ocean
  thermal energy of, 344
  variability of, 5
  waters and aquatic life of, CO₂ relating to, 424
ocean conveyer shutdown, during little ice age, 18
ocean energy technologies
  current tidal generation, 292–300
  marine-current turbine, 300–303, 301f, 303f
  oceanic, interesting, 303–305
  tidal physics, 287–288, 288f
  tidal power, 287
    generation of, 288–292
ocean thermal energy conversion (OTEC), 344
oceanic technologies, interesting, 303–305
oceanic wave power, 303, 304f, 305f
OCSD. *See* Orange County Sanitation District
OCWD. *See* Orange County Water District
off-grid micro-hydroelectric systems, without battery backup, 329
ohm, 498
Ohm's law, 498
oil
  and chemical industries, CO₂ in, 425
  crude, natural gas and, 10

oligoelements, 366
operation, modes of
   generation
      bidirectional-flow, 290
      ebb, 290
      flood, 290
      pumping, 290
   turbines
      bulb, 290–291, 291*f*
      rim, 291, 291*f*
   two-basin schemes, 290
optics, concentrator technologies
   relating to, 59–60
optimized energy performance
   scoring points, for LEED, 215,
   215*t*, 216*t*
Orange County Sanitation District
   (OCSD), 416–417, 418
Orange County Water District
   (OCWD), 414–419
orbital variations, 4
organic PVs, 30
orientation, 501
OTEC. *See* ocean thermal energy
   conversion
outdoor astronomical time-switch
   controls, 193
outdoor equipment, lighting effect
   on, 92, 93, 93*f*
outdoor lighting
   and signs, California Title 24
      Electric Energy Compliance
      relating to, 193–195
   tradeoffs relating to, 193
oxidizing filter beds, 412
ozone
   exposure to, 413–414
   stratospheric, air pollution and,
      depletion mitigation
      measures for, 12

Pacific Gas and Electric (PG&E),
   157, 161
PAFC. *See* phosphoric acid fuel
panel selection, 227–228,
   228*f*, 228*t*
parabolic heating technologies,
   passive, 234*f*, 235, 235*f*
parabolic troughs, 233
passive parabolic heating
   technologies, 234*f*, 235, 235*f*
passive solar heating technologies
   CSP technologies, 233–236
   direct solar power generation,
      240–241
   solar cooling and air conditioning,
      233–240, 238*f*, 339*t*
   solar power technology, innova-
      tions in, 241–243
   solar water heating, 223–233,
      224*f*, 225f

passive solar power technologies,
   innovations in
      eSolar, 242–243, 242*f*, 243*f*
      Stirling Engine Sunflower,
         241–242, 242*f*
passive solar tower concentrator,
   236*f*
passive solar water heating,
   223–233, 224*f*, 225*f*
passive trackers, 104–106, 105*f*
PBI. *See* performance-based initiative
peak bulk energy rate, 142
peak-hour energy, 142
pebble-bed reactor, 387–389, 388*f*
Pelton propeller, 324–325
Pelton turbine, 315
Pelton wheel, 498
PEMFC. *See* polymer-electrolyte-
   membrane fuel cells; proton-
   exchange-membrane fuel cell
penetration, 270
performance. *See also* COP; EPBB;
   LEED
   characteristics of, for large-scale
      irrigation pumping
      application, 135–136
   of energy, semitropic open-field
      single-axis tracking system
      PV array relating to,
      138–139
performance approach, to indoor
   lighting, 187
performance monitoring, alarms and,
   197
performance multiplier, of shading
   analysis and solar energy,
   114–118
performance permanency
   requirements, of CSI, 164
performance-based initiative (PBI),
   157, 159–160, 160*t*, 161, 165,
   166–167, 168
pesticides and plastics, CO_2 relating
   to, 424
PG&E. *See* Pacific Gas and Electric
phosphoric acid fuel (PAFC),
   252, 262
photoelectric effect, 24, 24*f*
photoelectric phenomenon, history
   of, 23–26
   alternating and direct current:
      1950–2000, 25–26
   early AC dominance, 25
   historical AC/DC debate between
      Edison and Tesla, 24–25
   100-year-old power scheme, 25
photons, 24, 29
photosensitive dye, 36
photosynthesis, CO_2 in, 423–424
photovoltaic (PV) cells, 23

photovoltaic effect, 498
photovoltaic energy power
   cogeneration, solar, 343–344
photovoltaic module operational
   diagram, 29*f*
photovoltaic module tilt angle
   correction table, solar,
   443*t*–444*t*
physical principles, of micro-
   hydropower generation,
   326–327
physical properties, of CO_2, 421–422
physics. *See also* solar power system,
   physics and technologies of
   of solar intensity, 103–104
   tidal: effects of terrestrial centrifu-
      gal force, 287–288, 288*f*
pipe length, micro-hydropower
   generation relating to, 326
pipe systems, plastic, for pool heating, 227
pipeline, 330
pitch, 498
planar solid oxide fuel cell, 263
Planck, Max, 24
plant equipment, for hydroelectric
   and micro-hydro turbine power,
   313–315
Plante, Raymond, 80
Plante's battery, 80
plastic cells, 42
plastic panels, for pool heating,
   225–226
plastic pipe systems, for pool
   heating, 227
plastics and pesticides, CO_2 relating
   to, 424
plates, 498
PN junction, 27, 28*f*, 29, 30, 35
PNP junction, 30
polar trackers, 104
pollutants, 298
pollution. *See also* air pollution;
   atmospheric pollution
   abatement considerations for,
      146–147, 147*f*
polycrystalline and monocrystalline
   silicon cells, 30–33, 32*f*–33*f*
polycrystalline PV solar cells, 33
polycrystalline silicon, 498
polymer solar cells, 42–43, 43*f*
polymer-electrolyte-membrane fuel
   cells (PEMFC), 245, 246, 262
polymers, 346
polyvinyl chloride (PVC), 498
pool heating, 224–227
   metal panels for, 226–227
   plastic panels for, 225–226
   plastic pipe systems, 227
   rubber mats for, 226, 226*f*
   suggested practices for, 232–233

population, local, dam construction's impact on, 311–312
potential
annual power production, of MegaSlate, 67–68
of biomass energy, 347–348
of geothermal energy, 337–338, 338f, 339f
of hydroelectric power, 308–309
of thermal power extraction, 334–335
potential energy
biodiesel requirement of, 373
gravitational, 21
kinetic energy vs, 20–21
power, 498. *See also* specific solar power entries
cogenerators of, micro combined heat and, 252
CSI allocation of, 158, 158f
disconnect switches for, 331
distribution input and output of, 47
MegaSlate production of, 67–68
output of
for micro-hydropower generation, 327–329
for storage batteries, 84
PV, cogeneration capacity, 50
power plants. *See also* SEGS plants
hydroelectric, 307–309, 315–323
power purchase agreements (PPAs), 149–154
advantages of, 150
contract structure of
contractual matters, 152–153
data-acquisition and monitoring system, 154
large-scale installation, experience in, 154
technical matters, 153–154
disadvantages of, 150–151
proposal, preparation for, 151–152
power scheme, 100-year-old, 25
power test condition (PTC), 140
power-factor correction, 177–178
power-generating sea buoy, 304–305, 305f
power-generating system, hydroelectric, 310f
power-generation capacity, of wind turbine, 280, 281f
power-generation targets, of CSI, 158–159, 159t
power-limit conditions, 49
power-production intermittence limits, 270
power-purchase agreement, 170
PPAs. *See* power purchase agreements
precipitators, 408

prefabricated PV module support railing, for roof-mounted system, 98, 98f
preliminary engineering design, 139–142
energy cost factor relating to, 142
meteorologic data relating to, 141
parameters for, 140–142
primary sedimentation, 410–411
primary treatment process, of sewage, 410
primary uses of, hydrogen economy, 261–262
production, of CO_2, 422–423
project
affordable housing, special funding for, 169
Cal Poly biogas, 361–362
commercial solar power, 129–130
cost analysis for, 142–146
design of, for microgenerator technology, 358–360
European fuel cell bus, 266
financing of
for PPAs, 149–154
for proposal evaluation, 154–155
project-development plan, for Hoover Dam, 316
proposal evaluation, for project financing, 154–155
protective relaying systems, 45–47
proton-exchange-membrane fuel cell (PEMFC), 245
PTC. *See* power test condition; PVUSA test conditions
P-type material, 27, 35–36
public and charter schools, special funding for, 169
public areas, indoor lighting in, 192
pump
DC, solar power-driven, 72, 72f
ram, 498
solar submersible, 133
water well solar-powered, 133–134, 133f
pumped-storage hydropower systems, 313, 314f
pumping, 290, 297
PV array, semitropic open-field single-axis tracking system, 136–139
PV array azimuth angle, 123–124, 124f
PV cells. *See also* photovoltaic cells
multijunction, 40–42
nanotechnology solar, 38
PV DC nameplate derating, 121
PV mapping and configuration analysis, 118

PV module, 70
array interconnection mismatch of, 121
design parameters of, 110
dirt and soiling losses of, 122
ground-mounted, installation and support for, 97–98, 97f
grouping of, 140
life span and recycling of, 54–56
operational diagram of, 29
prefabricated support railing of, for roof-mounted system, 98, 98f
production of, 54
specifications of, for DC to AC power-conversion calculations, 119
PV power cogeneration capacity, 50
PV solar cells
amorphous, 33–34
internal wiring of, 44f
polycrystalline, 33
PV solar farm, Boron, 130f
PV solar module production, crystalline, 51–56
PV stanchion and support structure tilt angle, 100
PV strings, 118–119
PV support structure, of MegaSlate, 68
PV system
design guidelines for, 110–111
ground-fault protection, 90
grounding, 90–91
losses relating to, 121–124
MegaSlate customized roof-mount, 66–69
power output rating of, 120–121
sizing requirements, of CSI, 163
testing and maintenance log for, 50
PVC. *See* polyvinyl chloride
PVs, organic, 30
PVUSA test conditions (PTC), 121
pyrolysis, 362–365, 363f, 372

quantum mechanics, 24
quasi sine wave, 498

rack cabinet, installation of, 85
radiant energy, 21–22
radiation
danger of, 381
EM, 22
nuclear, 379–380, 380f, 381–383
ultraviolet, human health and, 11–12
radioactive decay, 380–381
ram pump, 498
RAPS. *See* remote area power supply
RCD. *See* residual current device
reaction-type turbines, 325

reactors. *See also* bioreactors, as emerging future technologies; fission- and fusion-type nuclear power
batch, 414
lifespan operation of, 382*f*
rebate funding program, CSI as, 157
rechargeable battery, 498–499
Recommended Practice for Utility Interface of Photovoltaic (PV) Systems, 49
recreation and fish and wildlife, Hoover Dam relating to, 319–320
recycled materials, carpet from, 220
recycled water, 220
refrigeration, principles of, 238–239, 239*t*
refrigerators, 174
refuse pyrolysis, 365
regenerative fuel cells, 263–264
regulators, 499
and charge controllers, 330
remote area power supply (RAPS), 498
remote solar power farm, in desert setting, 130
renewable energy, 499
renewable energy tables and important solar power facts, 433–435, 434*t*
reservation steps, for CSI, 166–168
reservoirs, geopressurized, 333
residential power consumption demand load, 127–128
residential solar power system, designing of, 126–128
residual current device (RCD), 499
resistance, 499
resistor, 499
resources and material, for LEED, 211–212, 222
reverse diode losses, 121
reverse osmosis (RO), 418–419
rim turbines, 291, 291*f*
RO. *See* reverse osmosis
robotic solar panel laminator, 56*f*
roof mount adjustable solar power racking, 478*f*
roof mount solar panel, nonpenetrating type of, 484*f*
roof mount solar power slate, 476*f*
roof-mounted installations, 98–100, 99*f*, 129, 131, 132, 132*f*. *See also* BIPV roofing systems; MegaSlate customized roof-mount PV system
lightweight concrete roofing, 99–100
PV stanchion and support structure tilt angle, 100
wood-constructed roofing, 99, 101, 101*f*

room switching, for indoor lighting, 192
room-temperature sensor, 198
rotating cone, 364
roughing, 411
round-trip efficiency, 251
RS 485 interface, 51

salinity, 298
San Diego Regional Energy Office (SDREO)/San Diego Gas and Electric (SDG&E), 157, 161
San Onofre, case study of, 383, 383*f*
sand and sedimentation, removal of, 410
Santa Clara Valley Transportation Authority (VTA), 265–266
SCE. *See* Southern California Edison
scope and application, of California Title 24 Electric Energy Compliance, 186
SCR. *See* selective catalytic reduction
scrubbers, 408–409
SDREO/SDG&E. *See* San Diego Regional Energy Office/San Diego Gas and Electric
sealed lead-acid battery, 499
secondary treatment, of sewage, 411
security or emergency lights, 192
sediment movement, 298
sedimentation, 410–411
SEGS plants. *See* solar electric generating system plants
selective catalytic reduction (SCR), 407
semiconductor, 499
elements of, 27, 28, 29
junction, 28*f*, 29*f*
semitropic open-field single-axis tracking system PV array, 136–139
electrical description of, 137–138
energy performance of, 138–139
mechanical description of, 137
Semitropic Water District, Wasco, CA, 136, 136*f*, 138–139
sender identification, 200
sequestered solar energy
and anthropogenic causes of atmospheric pollution, 6
use of, 6, 9–12
sequestration of CO_2, carbon trading economics and, 421–431
sewage treatment, 409–414
shading analysis and solar energy performance multiplier, 114–118
shadow angles, 501
Shell Solar Industries, 136–137, 138, 139
shunt, 499

shunted load, 330–331
signs, outdoor lighting relating to, 193–195
silane gas, 31, 33
silicon, 26, 51–52
amorphous, 493
polycrystalline, 498
silicon cells, monocrystalline and polycrystalline, 30–33, 32*f*–33*f*
silicon crystals, 52*f*
silicon ingot cylinder, 54, 54*f*, 55, 55*f*
silicon tetrahydride, 33
sine wave, 499
single residential unit, design and installation of solar power system for, 128–129
single-axis trackers, 103, 108
single-axis tracking system PV array. *See* semitropic open-field single-axis tracking system PV array
Slater Duck, 303, 304*f*, 305*f*
sludge
activated, 412
disposal of, 415
treatment of, 414–415
small hydroelectric turbines, 323
small-scale water-pumping applications, solar power in, 133–134
smart controllers, 220
SMR. *See* steam methane reforming
SO_2. *See* sulfurous oxides
social implications of, current tidal generation technologies, 294
soda ash, 425–426
SOFCs. *See* solid oxide fuel cells
soil erosion and water contamination, biomass relating to, 350
soiling losses, PV module dirt and, 122
solar cells, 499. *See also* PV solar cells
amorphous PV, 33–34
custom-fabricated BIPV, 64–66
DSCs, 34–39, 37*f*
electronics, 30
manufacturing and packaging technologies of
amorphous PV solar cells, 33–34
monocrystalline and polycrystalline silicon cells, 30–33, 32*f*–33*f*
monocrystalline, 497
multijunction epitaxial layers relating to, 41*f*
physics of, 26–29
polymer, 42–43, 43*f*
production of, 53–54
thin-film technology relating to, 31–32

solar constant *S*, 113
solar cooling and air conditioning,
   233–240, 238*f*
   cooling technologies of, 239
   COP relating to, 239–240, 273
   desiccant evaporators, 240
   hybrid absorption chillers, 240
   molecular agitation in, 237–238
   refrigeration, principles of,
      238–239, 239*t*
   temperature relating to, 237
solar declination angle, 112, 112*f*
solar electric generating system
   (SEGS) plants, 233, 234
solar energy
   historical time line of, 485–492
   performance multiplier of, shad-
      ing analysis and, 114–118
   sequestered, 6, 9–12
solar farms, 98
solar hour angle, 113*f*
solar insolation table for major cities
   in United States, 445*t*–446*t*
Solar Integrated Technologies,
   61–63
solar intensity, physics of, 103–104,
   103*f*
solar module, 499
solar noon, 501
solar panel arrays (SPAs), 44
solar panel attachment details,
   100*f*
solar panel inspection station, 56*f*
Solar Pathfinder, 114–118, 114*f*,
   115*f*, 116*f*, 117*f*
solar photovoltaic energy power
   cogeneration, 343–344
solar photovoltaic module tilt angle
   correction table, 443*t*–444*t*
solar physics, basics of, 111–113
solar power, 499
   commercial project for,
      129–130
   contractors and equipment sellers
      of, 162–163
   direct generation of, 240–241
   parking canopy relating to,
      477*f*
   rebate application procedure for,
      124–126
   SUNRGI flat-panel, 61, 62, 62*f*
   technology innovations in,
      241–243
solar power cogeneration, 216
solar power system, physics and
   technologies of, 23–156
   components of
      inverters, 45–49
      storage batteries, 44–45
      utility-side disconnects and iso-
         lation transformers, 50–51
   concentrators, 43–44

solar power system, physics and
   technologies of (*Cont.*):
   configuration of
      advances in, 86–87
      central monitoring and logging
         system requirements,
         92–96
      grid-connected solar power
         systems, entrance service
         power considerations for,
         91–92
      issues relating to, 87
      lightning protection relating to,
         92
      wiring, 44*f*, 88–91
   crystalline, amorphous, thin-film,
      and sun-tracker technologies,
      51–69
   deployment of
      commercial, 129–130
      in desert setting, 130
      in large-scale irrigation pump-
         ing application,
         134–136
      residential, designing of,
         126–128
      semitropic open-field single-
         axis tracking system PV
         array, 136–139
      single residential unit, design
         and installation of,
         128–129
      in small-scale water-pumping
         applications, 133–134
      Water and Life Museum,
         Hemet, California,
         130–133, 131*f*,
         146, 221
   design of
      components and materials,
         69–70, 87
      configurations and classifica-
         tions of, 70–76, 70*f*, 71*f*,
         73*f*, 75*f*
      considerations of,
         111–124
   economics of, 139–155
   electrical shock hazard and safety
      considerations, 100–102
   field safety recommendations,
      106–107
   ground-mounted PV module
      installation and support,
      97–98, 97*f*
   maintenance of, 107–108
   multijunction PV cells, 40–42
   photoelectric phenomenon, history
      of, 23–26
   PV system design guidelines,
      110–111
   roof-mounted installations,
      98–100

solar power system, physics and
   technologies of (*Cont.*):
   solar cell
      DSCs, 34–39, 37*f*
      electronics, 30
      manufacturing and packaging
         technologies, 30–34
      physics, 26–29
      polymer, 42–43, 43*f*
      solar panel arrays, 44
      solar power rebate application
         procedure, 124–126
      solar tracking systems, 103–106,
         103*f*, 105*f*, 107*f*
      storage battery technologies,
         77–86
      troubleshooting, 108–109
      warning signage, 109
   solar power window canopy, 482*f*
   solar power-driven DC pump, bat-
      tery-backed, 72, 72*f*
   solar powered signage, 483*f*
   solar submersible pump, 133
   solar thermal, 499
   solar tide, 287
   solar tracking systems
      active, 106
      fixed-axis, 103
      horizontal-axle, 104
      passive, 104–106, 105*f*
      polar, 104
      single-axis, 103, 108
      solar intensity, physics of,
         103–104, 103*f*
      vertical-axle, 106, 107*f*
   solar variation, 3
   solar water heating, passive,
      223–233, 224*f*, 225*f*
   solar water-heating-system sizing
      guide, 229–232, 232*f*
   solar zenith angle, 113*f*
   Solargenix Energy, 240–241
   SolarWorld Industries, 51, 55, 139
   solid oxide fuel cells (SOFCs), 251,
      262–263
   Southern California Edison (SCE),
      157, 161
   Space Shuttle program, 252
   SPAs. *See* solar panel arrays
   specific heat capacity, 21
   square wave, 499
   stacking
      of biomass materials, 364
      of fuel cells, 246
   stand-alone DC solar power system,
      with battery backup, 71–73
   stand-alone hybrid ac solar power
      system, with standby generator,
      73*f*
      AC inverters, 73–74
      hybrid system operation, 74–75
   standard test condition (STC), 120

standby generator, stand-alone hybrid ac solar power system with, 73*f*
stationary fuel cell plants, 251–252
STC. *See* standard test condition
steam methane re-forming (SMR), 253
steam re-forming, 253, 254, 256
Stingray tidal energy, 295
Stirling Engine Sunflower, 241–242, 242*f*
storage batteries, 44–45, 331
    history of, 77–82
        Danielle cell, 79–80
        Plante's battery, 80
    installation and maintenance of, 84–86
        battery charge controller, 85
        battery system cables, 85
        DC fuses, 86
        junction boxes and equipment enclosures, 86
        rack cabinet, 85
        safety relating to, 85
    life span of, 83–84
    major types of, 82–83
    power output of, 84
    technologies of, 77–86
storage density, 500
storm water, braided stream for, 220
stratospheric ozone and air pollution, depletion mitigation measures for, 12
structural considerations, of wind energy technologies, 274–275, 275*f*
subcriticality/criticality/supercriticality, 378
submersible-propeller turbines, 325–326
substrates, 41–42
sulfurous oxides (SO_x), 405, 407–408
sun server monitoring software, Sun Viewer display and, 94–95
sun tracker, MARTIFER, 59, 60, 60*f*, 368, 369*f*
Sun Viewer data-acquisition system, 94
Sun Viewer display and sun server monitoring software, 94–95
sunlight energy storage, 20
SunPower T20 single-axis solar power tracking system, 108*f*
SUNRGI flat-panel solar power, 61, 62, 62*f*
sunrise and sunset, 502
SunSlate solar modules, 66, 66*f*, 67, 67*f*
sun-tracker, thin-film, amorphous, and crystalline technologies, 51–69

supercooled, 238
superheated, 238
surge, 500
    inverters for withstanding of, 50
    protectors relating to, 92
sustainable sites, for LEED, 206–208, 221
switch mode, 500
synthetic fuels, 367
system availability and mean time between failures (MTBF), 122
system maintenance and operational costs, 148–149

tailored methods, of indoor lighting, 187
tank-to-wheel efficiency, 251
taxation, carbon credits, as preferred incentive to, 429–430
tax-exempt municipal lease, 169, 170
    commercial lease vs, 171–172
technology. *See* specific entries
technology innovations, in solar power, 241–243
Tedlar, 31
temperature, 21, 201, 237, 246, 247*f*, 257–258
    control of, 248
    global climatic balance of, 14–15, 15*f*, 16*f*
terrestrial centrifugal force, effects of, 287–288, 288*f*
tertiary treatment, of sewage, 412
Tesla, Nicola, 24–25
Testing Laboratories (ETL), 87
thermal depolymerization, 362, 372*t*. *See also* biofuel, biogas, and thermal depolymerization technologies
thermal power extraction potential, 334–335
thermochemical production, fuel cells relating to, 258
thermolysis, 255, 362
thin-film
    amorphous, crystalline, and sun-tracker technologies, 51–69
    cadmium telluride cell technology relating to, 34
    solar cell technology relating to, 31–32
third-party ownership contracts, 150
Three Gorges Dam, 312
tidal barrage, 289, 292–294
    economics of, 294
    environmental concerns about, 294
    La Rance, 293–294, 293*f*
    social implications of, 294
tidal fences, 292
tidal movement, 287

tidal physics: effects of terrestrial centrifugal force, 287–288, 288*f*
tidal power, 287
    generation of, 288–292
    system output of, 297
tidal streams, 298–299
tidal turbines, 299, 299*f*, 300*f*
tides, 287–288
time-temperature programming, 201
TiO_2. *See* titanium dioxide
tip-speed ratio, 500
titanium dioxide (TiO_2), 37–39
trackers
    active, 106
    horizontal-axle, 104
    MARTIFER, 59, 60*f*, 368, 369*f*
    passive, 104–106, 105*f*
    polar, 104
    single-axis, 103, 108
    vertical-axle, 106, 107*f*
tracking systems. *See* solar tracking systems; sun-tracker, thin-film, amorphous, and crystalline technologies
transesterification, 371
transformer, 50–51, 76, 500
    losses of, 121
transistors, 27, 500
transmission lines, wind turbines relating to, 281–284
troubleshooting, 108–109
tubular solid oxide fuel cell, 263
tubular turbine, 291, 292*f*
turbidity, 298
turbines, 315, 330. *See also* wind
    axial flow, 493
    bulb, 290–291, 291*f*
    cross-flow, 494
    impulse-type, 324–325, 324*f*, 325*f*
    marine-current technologies of, 300–303, 301*f*, 303*f*
    reaction-type, 325
    rim, 291, 291*f*
    submersible-propeller, 325–326
    tidal, 299, 299*f*, 300*f*
    tubular, 291, 292*f*
turbulence, 500
twilight, 501, 502
two-basin schemes, 290

UL. *See* Underwriters Laboratories
UL1741, Standard for Static Inverter and Charge Controller for Use in Independent Power Systems, 47
UL1741 inverter specification, examples of, 50–51
ultraviolet radiation and air pollution's impact, on human health, 11–12
Underwriters Laboratories (UL), 47, 87, 162

UNFCCC. *See* United Nations Framework Convention on Climate Change
UNISTRUCT, 100, 102*f*
unit conversion and design reference tables
    energy conversion table, 435*t*–436*t*
    longitude and latitude tables, 447*t*–474*t*
    renewable energy tables and important solar power facts, 433–435, 434*t*
    solar insolation table for major cities in United States, 445*t*–446*t*
    solar photovoltaic module tilt angle correction table, 443*t*–444*t*
    voltage drop formulas and DC cable charts, 436*t*–443*t*
United Nations Framework Convention on Climate Change (UNFCCC), 427, 431
United States, biodiesel and, 373
uranium, properties of, 375–377
U.S. Clean Air Act, 11
U.S. Green Building Council (USGBC), 203, 204
U.S. Space Program, fuel cells' application in, 266
USGBC. *See* U.S. Green Building Council
utility DSM, 196, 198–200
    conventional energy-management system vs, 200–202
utility systems, wind energy for, 284
utility-side disconnects and isolation transformers
    inverter capability to withstand surges, 50
    PV power cogeneration capacity, 50
    PV system testing and maintenance log, 50
    UL1741 inverter specification, examples of, 50–51

vacation/holiday programming, 201
Vancouver Fuel Cell Vehicle Program (VFCVP), 265, 265*f*
Vector Delta Design Group, Leed engineered by, 218–219
vertical shadow angle (VSA), 502
vertical-axle trackers, 106, 107*f*
vertical-axle wind turbine, 500
vertical-axle windmills, 267
VFCVP. *See* Vancouver Fuel Cell Vehicle Program
video, animated, and interactive programming requirements, 96

VOCs. *See* volatile organic compounds
volatile organic compounds (VOCs), 222, 407
volcanic activity, during little ice age, 18
volcanism, 4–5
Volta, Alessandro Conte, 77–79, 79*f*
voltage, 500
voltage drop calculations for copper wires, 437*t*
voltage drop formulas and DC cable charts, 436*t*–443*t*
voltmeter, 500
VSA. *See* vertical shadow angle
VTA. *See* Santa Clara Valley Transportation Authority

W-3 dynamic scrubbers, 408–409
wall mount solar power, 483*f*
warning signage, for solar power system, 109
warranty and performance permanency requirements, of CSI, 164
wastewater treatment. *See* landfill
water
    and air control, 248
    and aquatic life, of ocean, CO_2 relating to, 424
    contamination, of soil erosion and, biomass relating to, 350
    efficiency measures of, for LEED, 208, 221
    electrolysis of, 254–255, 257
    flow of, micro-hydropower generation relating to, 326
    heaters of, 175
    hot, hot air generators and, 356
    internal, heat control and, 247
    power of, 307
    solar heating of, 223–233, 224*f*, 225*f*
    splitting of, 255
    supply of, from Hoover Dam, 319
    turbine for, 500
Water and Life Museum, Hemet, California, 130–133, 131*f*, 146, 221
Water Education Museum, 130, 143*f*–145*f*, 146
Water Factory 21, replaced by GWR, 418
water head, micro-hydropower generation relating to, 326
water well solar-powered pump, 133–134, 133*f*
water-heating-system sizing guide, solar, 229–232, 232*f*
waterless urinals, 220
water-pumping applications, small-scale, solar power in, 133–134

waterwheel, 500
watt (W), 500
watt-hour (Wh), 500
waveshaping or filtration process, 45
weatherization, insulation and, 175
wet batteries. *See* flooded (wet) batteries
wet electrostatic precipitators, 408
wet-approach Venturi scrubbers, 409
wind
    energy of, for utility systems, 284
    farm relating to, 500
        economics of, 271
    generator of, 501
    power of
        advantages of, 284–285
        disadvantages of, 285
        forecasting of, 270–271
        generation of, 268
        history of, 267–268
        management of, 268–271
    turbine for, 500, 501
        availability factor of, 280
        basic operation of, 276–279, 276*f*
        consistency of support policy for, 281
        construction of, 278–279
        energy economics of, 279–285
        energy supply of, for U.S., 280–281, 282*t*
        energy-generation capacity of, 277–278, 277*f*
        horizontal-axis, 496
        new transmission lines relating to, 283–284
        power-generation capacity of, 280, 281*f*
        transmission-line access relating to, 281–283
        wind energy, for utility systems, 284
        world wind power production capacity, 283
wind energy technologies
    Betz' law of fluid dynamics, 271–274, 272*f*, 273*f*
    structural considerations of, 274–275, 275*f*
wind power
    generation of, 268
    history of, 267–268
    management of, 268–271
wind turbine
    basic operation of, 276–279, 276*f*
    energy economics of, 279–285
windmills, 267–268

wiring
  AC and DC losses of, 121–122
  for solar power system, 88–91
    conductors for, 89
    design example of, 89–90
    equipment grounding, 91
    internal, 44f
    PV system ground-fault protec-
      tion, 90
    PV system grounding,
      90–91

wood burning, 9
wood-constructed roofing, 99, 101,
  101f
world production, of biodiesel,
  373–374
World Wind Energy Association,
  271
world wind power production capacity, 283
WorldWater & Power Corporation,
  134

yaw, 501

zener diode, 501
zenith angle
  solar, 113f
  Z, 112
zinc-mercury oxide alkaline batteries, 81
Zomeworks passive solar tracker,
  104, 105f
zone mode, 184

CPSIA information can be obtained
at www.ICGtesting.com
Printed in the USA
BVOW04*0457171017
497825BV00004B/9/P